A Compendium of The History of Lace Making

Lace Making in the British Midlands, France, Italy, Spain and Brussels

- Four Volumes in One -

By

Various

British Library Cataloguing-in-Publication Data
A catalogue record for this book is available from
the British Library

CONTENTS

LACE,

ANCIENT AND MODERN.

COMPRISING

A HISTORY OF ITS ORIGIN AND MANUFACTURE, WITH INSTRUCTIONS CONCERNING THE MANNER OF MAKING IT.

BY MRS. C. D. BEEBE

NEW YORK:
SHARPS PUBLISHING COMPANY.
1880.

PREFACE.

Lace and gems are to women what stock and real estate are to men, and are the crowning glory of woman's attire; but, while many are familiar with facts in regard to gems, few are wise in lace lore, for little has been published upon the subject. The student in lace, therefore, is obliged to pick up a scrap of information here and a crumb there, and usually finds both unsatisfactory.

In Europe the love of lace at one time amounted to a passion, which was only broken up by the French Revolution and other European wars. At present lace is again extremely popular, and still growing in favor on both sides of the Atlantic. A history of its origin and manufacture, therefore, will not only prove highly interesting, but will supply a long-felt want, alike to the dealer, the wearer and the student in lace.

The author has gleaned from many sources the material for the book. Many interesting facts have been obtained from the work of a deceased English author; files of the London, Paris and New York papers; reports of the International Exhibitions; from various publications deposited in the New York libraries; from Madame Carter, teacher of lace-making; and from obliging merchants of the Empire City.

INDEX.

LACE, ANCIENT AND MODERN.

CHAPTER I.

ORIGIN OF LACE.

NETTING and embroidery are of extremely ancient origin, but we have no authentic record concerning the existence of lace until about 1400. Europe has always been the centre of the lace industry, its invention being claimed by both Italy and Belgium. Without doubt, Italy produced the first point and Flanders the first pillow lace; but it is impossible to tell which was the earlier production, as the mediæval records throw but little light upon the subject. Italian reticella, which is the oldest needle-made lace, evolved from cutwork, which was an open embroidery, filled in, usually, with lace stitches; afterward reticella gradually merged into point. Pillow lace, probably, sprung from netting.

Almost from the beginning mention is made in the bible of embroidery and netting. In Exodus, Aholiab is spoken of as an embroiderer in blue; in the description of Solomon's temple nets of checker-work are mentioned; and in Isaiah occurs the passage, "They that work in fine flax and weave net-work." The ancient Egyptians used netting to border state or festival garments, and upon the bodies of mummies has been found a net-work of blue beads. Still it is probable that lace proper was not known in Oriental countries, as no record or other evidence of it exists. Even at the present day, when we have all manner of fanciful trifles, curious carving and embroidery in Japanese and Chinese work, and exquisite shawls, scarfs and hand-made carpets from India, we have nothing from these countries in the way of lace, except a drawnwork which appears on some tissues from China or Japan. Even Turkey manufactures nothing except a crochet guipure, although in the harems a silk guipure is made with the needle, which seldom appears in the market.

It was anciently the custom for women to wear veils over their faces in Christian churches, and a writer of the second century complained that these coverings ministered to vanity rather than modesty, as they were so rich in material and elaborate in design; often exposing the face to view, from the fact of their being of silk netting, interwoven with gold and silver thread.

The first records of lace belong to Italy, and come from Milan, in the shape of an ancient document usually spoken of as the Sforza Inventory, it being a complete catalogue or list of an Italian wardrobe in 1493. As a matter of course, the articles therein mentioned must have been manufactured at an earlier date. This inventory was made for the purpose of properly dividing the wardrobe it described between two sisters, Angela and Ippolita Sforza Visconti. It mentions many curious and interesting things; among others, mosquito curtains, veils of gold network, reticella and groppi, the latter being undoubtedly punto a gropo, the first knotted lace known. It also speaks of patterns for ladies' work.

Though lace-making was not practised in England at so early a date, in the wardrobe accounts of Henry VIII., a quarter of a century later, mention is made of articles ornamented with lace. In the Harleian Inventory, 1519, a pair of hose is spoken of as the property of King Henry, "edged with passamaine lace, of purple silk and gold, worked at Milan." Again, in the king's privy-purse expenses, 1530, is noted "eight pieces of yolowe lace, for the King's Grace," but where the "yolowe" lace came from does not appear.

Although no inventory or other documentary writing attests the fact of lace existing in Belgium as early as in Italy, Baron Reiffenberg, who gave some time to research upon the subject, declares that lace caps were worn in Belgium before 1400, the fact being proved by paintings bearing date of the fourteenth century. In the church of St. Gomar in Lierre, and the collegiate church of St. Peter's at Louvain, are paintings of the fifteenth century in which lace appears as an article of adornment upon the costumes displayed, or portrayed by the artist's skill. In St. Peter's at Louvain is an altar-piece by Quentin Matsys, dated 1495, in which a young girl appears making lace with bobbins upon a pillow. The inference derived from this is that pillow lace-making was generally practiced at this period, or it would scarcely have been chosen as a subject for the painting.

To Italy, however, most modern writers concede the earliest invention of lace. Its manufacture was for a long time confined exclusively to convents, and its use to the Church, hence it derived the name of "nuns' work," bearing it in some parts of Italy and Spain to this day. From Italy, Spain and Greece learned the art of lace-making, and France learned her point d'Alençon; but Flanders taught pillow-lace making to Germany, France and England—in fact, all Northern Europe.

Gold and silver lace, which, properly speaking, is not lace, but a sort of braiding and festooning of gold or silver wires, was invented at a very early date, long before lace proper, and was used to decorate royal robes and martial trappings.

CHAPTER II.

LACE IN CONVENTS AND CHURCHES.

NUNS of all ages have been accustomed to devote their leisure time to needlework. Possibly, to all but those who were exceptionally devout, the Pater Nosters, Ave Marias, and other numerous prayers which they repeated daily and hourly, as well as the fasts and vigils they kept for the good of their souls and those of their less pious friends and the faithful at large, were rather trying upon mind and body when unrelieved by anything approaching recreation, and so they were driven to their needle to vary, even in a slight degree, the monotonous routine of their lives. For themselves they had taken the vow of poverty, and could not appropriate anything in the line of fancy work to their own use, and so they derived great consolation in decorating their churches—the altars, *prie-dieus*, images of the Saviour, Virgin and saints, as well as the priestly robes, grave-clothes, and other articles connected with the service of the Church, with the most artistic needlework they could devise.

In ancient days even monks were not ashamed of being considered skillful with the needle. In some of the pattern books for embroidery, cutwork and lacis of the sixteenth century, men are represented as sitting at a lace or embroidery frame. Indeed, some of the pattern books of this period were designed by monks or priests. The St. Geneviève monastery in Paris collected a large number of these books, afterward bequeathing them to the St. Geneviève library, where they may still be seen.

Long before drawnwork, cutwork and lacis were used to any extent upon ordinary wearing apparel, nuns were celebrated for making them, and nearly all the churches were rich in the possession of the most rare and elegant articles of needlework that taste could devise or time and patience execute—work not wrought in one lifetime, but which occupied the spare moments of many lives. For when one pair of hands failed, or the eyes directing them grew dim, others, younger and stronger, took up the task, and so, in time, the work was finished, devotion to the church making it a labor of love. These articles were carefully preserved, and many of them remain almost intact, having, through great care, withstood the ravages of time in a remarkable degree. The linen, tapestry and silk used for this work, however, was almost imperishable, as the preserved specimens show.

The inventories of ancient churches still exist, and serve to give some idea of the articles most decorated. One, in Paris, of the Church of the Oratoire, in the seventeenth century, speaks of veils for the host. One of these is of white taffeta bordered with guipure lace; another is of satin, with white flowers in similar lace. In the Convent of the Visitation at Le Puy is the lace trimming of an alb twenty-eight inches long, and of superb scroll design. This is of point d'Angleterre. In the inventory of the sacristy of the Benedictine Monastery, at St. Aligre, in 1684, nearly everything mentioned is trimmed with lace, much of it, however, being gold point d'Espagne. In the inventory of Massillon's Chapel at Beauregard, 1742, albs are trimmed with point d'Aurillac, and veils with point d'Espagne. A writer in 1691, in speaking of the images of the saints in a French church, says: "St. Winnifred was in a point lace commode, and St. Dennis with a laced hat and embroidered coat and sash."

At the time of the dissolution of the Spanish monasteries in 1830, a large quantity of the most exquisite specimens of nuns' work was thrown suddenly upon the market, and found eager purchasers. Much of this lace was Spanish point, but there were many rare pieces of work not met with elsewhere. Some interesting relics of the ancient work of Spanish nuns have been found in the convent of Jesú Bambino. Here, ages ago, these sisters taught to novices their art. Some of the specimens—many of them being unfinished—were sent to Rome. We give a portion of one, the work of Sister Felice Vittoria, left unfinished at her death, the thread still hanging from the work.

NUNS' WORK.

When, in the twelfth century, St. Dunstan was disinterred, his body being removed from his coffin in the Cathedral of Durham, his grave-clothes were found to be ornamented in curious ways—the linen with embroidery and cutwork; the cloak or cope, as well as the maniple, being of the most exquisite embroidery. The latter was adorned with gold lace, of that kind of guipure which was anciently worked over parchment. The sheet thrown over the body had a deep linen fringe, woven into a border representing figures of beasts and birds, with branching trees between. These relics are in the Chapter Library of Durham.

The manner of making this ancient work was generally considered as a secret of the Church, as only the nuns were skilled in the art. Gradually, however, the knowledge of their handiwork spread abroad—at first through Italy, and thence into the other countries of Europe—until, about 1450, it came into use for ornamenting royal as well as priestly robes, household linen as well as grave-clothes, and finally was even worn by the peasantry. In the convents, instruction was given to the novices; and at last they opened schools in which children, and women also, were taught to make lace and other work. Even the daughters of kings were sent to be instructed in these womanly arts. Similar schools are kept up to the present day in many countries of Europe. In 1826 two nuns from the convent of La Providence, at Rouen, started a lace school at Dieppe which proved very successful, being patronized by the Empress Eugenie and other noble ladies of France.

Nuns and priests generally have done much toward spreading the knowledge of lace work in more modern times, and Father François Régis is held in great veneration by the people of Auvergne, who consider him the patron saint of lace-making. In 1640, when an edict against the wearing of lace by any person in the province was put in force by the Parliament of Toulouse, in order to check the lace industry, the poor lace-makers were reduced almost to starvation. Father Régis bade the sufferers put their trust in God, and then set out for Toulouse, where, by his remonstrances and eloquent statements of the case, he prevailed upon Parliament to revoke the edict. He afterwards advised the lace-makers concerning the disposition of their manufactures, which, being followed, led them to send to Spain and England the product of their labor, the result being unusual prosperity for the province. Dying soon after, the good father was canonized for this and other beneficent acts, and is held in grateful memory and adoration as St. François Régis.

The laces of the Vatican and Holy Conclave are magnificent in the extreme, defying description. Those belonging to each cardinal, however, are sold at his death, and often purchased by one newly elected. Pope Clement IX. was famed for presenting rich laces to his friends.

Many Catholic churches of Europe are in possession of rare laces, presented by reigning sovereigns and members of the nobility who are strong in the faith. At the Church of the Madre a Dios, in Lisbon, was exhibited for many years the bridal dress of Princess Barbara, sister to King Joseph of Portugal. After her marriage to Prince Ferdinand of Spain, in 1729, she repaired to the church and offered her bridal robe and jewels to the blessed Virgin. The dress was of Portuguese point lace, beautiful in fabric and design; it was put in a glass case, and exhibited to curious visitors for many years, but, at the time when the French occupied the Peninsula, the robe disappeared. It was supposed to have been appropriated by one of the imperial generals, or, to use the term applied to stealing in time of war, it was confiscated by one of them.

In the cathedral of Granada, in Spain, is a lace alb, said to have been presented by Ferdinand and Isabella, of rare beauty and great value. In the seventeenth century albs of Brussels point were worn by the clergy. Altar-cloths in French churches were trimmed with Argentan point. Albs were also ornamented with point de France, the Church following in a certain degree the prevailing fashions in lace. A point de Venise alb in old rose point is still preserved in the Musée de Cluny.

Only for the care given to ancient lace and relics of rare needlework by the Church, we should have few specimens at the present day. Two prelates of the Church purchased a set of lace which once belonged to Marie Antoinette. It was offered for sale in the time of the first Napoleon, and was bought and consecrated to the use of the Church. It consisted of squares of old point de Flandre, each different from the other, beautiful in quality and curious in design.

CHAPTER III.

ENGLISH FASHIONS IN LACE.

SINCE 1450, the period when lace ceased to be devoted to the use of the Church exclusively, it has been greatly sought after by the royal families of Europe, and been subjected to many a caprice of fashion. During the sixteenth and seventeenth centuries, and a portion of the eighteenth, it was used in the most lavish manner, appearing on nearly every article of dress or household use to which it could possibly be applied. Its manufacture at this period added more to the support of the peasantry and middle classes of Europe than any other one industry known. For half a century after the beginning of the French Revolution it was worn sparingly or cast aside almost altogether; since that time its use has been resumed for ladies' costumes, infants' wear, and many purposes of household decoration. It is still subjected to fashion's changes, the favorite of to-day being forgotten in the popular choice of to-morrow.

Though France set the fashions in the days when lace was used by men and women alike, as it does at the present time, many of England's sovereigns had wills of their own, and, though usually following the footsteps of France in the matter of dress, they sometimes introduced into their courts styles of their own choosing.

The first articles of womanly adornment partaking of the nature of lace were the caul, or net, and the veil. The latter was one of the primitive head-coverings of women, and was worn within and without the church. It has always been considered as belonging to feminine apparel exclusively, and, though men grew to wear nearly all manner of lace and lace-trimmed articles, they never usurped the veil. In ancient days, as well as in the middle ages, it was thought to be a necessary appendage to the head of a modest woman, and no lady was respected who appeared in the street without it. Before lace was in general use, network and tissue of various sorts, thin lawn and gauze, were all used to form veils.

Matilda of Scotland, queen of Henry I. of England, in her portrait taken about Christmas, 1115, while she and her royal husband were spending the festival season at the abbey of St. Albans, is represented as wearing a white gauze veil, arranged squarely over the brow, and surmounted by a gold crown. The veil flows behind her shoulders, with lappets. This portrait, which, without doubt, is authentic, is preserved in a handsome illuminated volume called the Golden Book of St. Albans, now in the British Museum.

Eleanora of Aquitaine, queen of Henry II. of England, in some of her portraits taken about the year 1154, appears with her hair braided and bound with jewels, and over all is thrown a square of fine gauze, which supplied the place of a veil.

Berengaria of Navarre, queen of Richard I. (Cœur de Lion) is represented with a veil in all her portraits. In one she wears a flowing robe of rich brocade, and a veil of what appears to be figured gauze, with a crown above it. In another she appears with her hair parted above her brow, and a transparent veil, open on each side like a Spanish mantilla. Her long hair flows free beneath it.

At this time—1191—embroidery in gold and silver, with laces and fringes of the same materials, were much worn, mingled with the royal ermine. Richard himself is described as wearing a mantle of striped silver tissue, brocaded with silver half moons, and a scarlet bonnet brocaded in gold with figures of animals.

Veils continued to be greatly worn, and at this time, as well as in the thirteenth century, the woman who walked in the street without one was liable to insult. Eleanor of Provence, queen of Henry III. of England, wore her hair gathered in a gold network, and over this was thrown a veil; this was in 1240. From this period, for three centuries following, the queens of England are represented in their portraits generally as wearing veils, the material having the appearance of white lace, but being in all probability plain or figured gauze. Among those represented with such veils are Philippa of Hainault, queen of Edward III.; Margaret of Anjou, queen of Henry VI.; Elizabeth Woodville, queen of Edward IV.; and Elizabeth of York, queen of Henry VII.

In the reign of Edward III. the government waxed wroth because the common people, and especially servant maids, wore veils that were fine in texture and extremely expensive in regard to price. Accordingly, an act was issued, in 1363, forbidding the wearing of silk veils, or those of any material that should cost more than tenpence. In the monument of Queen Philippa, in Westminster Abbey, she is represented as wearing a net, or caul of network, and this is supposed to be of similar style to the veils worn at this period; and, as a sort of crochet edging was manufactured at the time, it was undoubtedly used as a trimming to these veils, for the Duchess of Exeter, who died in 1425, is said to have worn a caul of network with a needlework edging.

Katharine of Arragon, first wife of Henry VIII., introduced the Spanish mantilla into England, though at this time it was not made of the black lace of which, later, this coquettish garment was invariably composed. Before Henry had any but the most remote prospects of ever ascending the throne, and at the time of Katharine's early marriage with his elder brother Arthur, Prince of Wales, she wore a Spanish mantilla which partly veiled her face and form. It was composed of white silk, and was bordered with gold and precious stones. She never fully abandoned wearing this article of Spanish costume, usually appearing in a black mantilla veil. This fashion, though not extensively copied by the ladies of the English court, wrought a change in the wearing of the veil, black being substituted for the white material, which, until now, had been popular for this face-covering. Jane Seymour, Henry's third, and Katharine Parr, his sixth wife, both wore veils, and are so represented in their portraits, but they are black.

From this period, about 1542, the portraits of queens, except those taken in bridal costume, are without the veil altogether, this appendage being considered unnecessary for house wear, though still adopted for the street. Queen Mary, the daughter of Henry VIII. and Katharine of Arragon, being fondly attached to her divorced mother's memory, wore in her honor, and probably to gratify her own taste, veils of black lace or network. In her New Year's gifts is mentioned "a veil of black network, flourished with flowers of silver and a small bone lace;" and after her death the inventory of her effects mentions "vales of black network."

That lace was used to ornament the hair of women even in King Henry's time is proven by a list of his plate taken in 1543, though the description is so obscure but little other information can be obtained from it. We give it intact: *Item*, oone picture of a woman made of erthe, with a carnacion Roobe knitt with a knott in the lefte shoulder, and bare hedid, with her heere rowlid up with a white lace set in a box of woode."

Queen Elizabeth, who succeeded her sister Mary in 1558, was the first sovereign of England who made any extensive use of lace, for the very good reason that during her long reign lace first became plentiful throughout Europe. She is said to have left three thousand dresses behind her, nearly all of them being ornamented with lace in a more or less lavish manner. Mention of veils is constantly made in her wardrobe accounts, and of laces wherewith to trim them. In 1584 occurs an entry for starching a veil of white cutwork, trimmed with needlework lace, the latter being in all probability reticella; for Elizabeth, unlike many English sovereigns who reigned after her, had no compunctions of conscience regarding the encouragement given to foreign manufactures by purchasing their finest laces, silks and other handsome textiles and trinkets. So great, indeed, was her love of finery, and her greed for possessing articles wherewith to adorn herself, she overhauled the wardrobe of Mary, Queen of Scots, on its way to its owner, who was in prison, and plundered it of any article of dress which pleased her fancy.

In Queen Elizabeth's New Year's gifts (1578) is mentioned "a veil of whitework, with spangles and small bone lace of silver." Veils, however, were less used in Queen Elizabeth's time than formerly, the ruff taking the most prominent place in the queen's affections, but bridal veils became a prominent feature in trousseaux.*

In the reign of Henry VII. (from 1485 to 1503) gold and thread laces were imported from Italy, though in limited quantities, and as yet it was little worn, especially thread lace, though sometimes mentioned in the royal wardrobe accounts of the times. In 1502, Elizabeth of York, queen of Henry VII. and mother of Henry VIII., pays "forty shillings for laces, rybands," etc., and other mention of lace is made from time to time, though rarely.

The first garment which was extensively ornamented with white lace was the shirt or smock. In the inventory of Sir Thomas L'Estrange, of Norfolk, is entered, in 1519, three ells of Holland cloth and one yard of lace for a shirt; and it is reasonable to suppose that shirts at this time were decorated in various ways, as a law of Henry VIII. forbids the wearing of shirts and partlets that are "garded and pynched," whatever that may have been, by any person below a knight in degree.

In 1556, Lady Jane Seymour presented Queen Mary with "a fair smock of white work, Flanders make," as a new year's gift, and more than a score of years later Sir Philip Sidney presents Queen Elizabeth with a smock of cutwork, which seems a strange gift. Queen Elizabeth, however, having been somewhat spoiled on account of her beauty and position, seems to have received this and similar gifts with evident satisfaction. Many were em-

---

* See chapter on Bridal Laces.

broidered, others trimmed with lace. One is described as wrought with black work and edged with bone lace of gold of various kinds.

Smocks are constantly mentioned, in and after the reign of Elizabeth, some wrought, some seamed through with cutwork, some seamed and trimmed with lace, at enormous cost; and these articles were trimmed with lace in the most extravagant manner up to the middle of the eighteenth century; even after the fall of Charles I. and during the period of Puritan rule, when lace-trimmed articles were preached against as vain and useless, Cromwell could not forbear to indulge his fondness for them.

Soon after the time when smocks began to be decorated with thread lace, nightcaps became very elaborate affairs, and were trimmed with cutwork and thread or bone lace in the most extravagant manner. In 1539, when Henry VIII. seized the correspondence of Lady Lisle to Sister Antoinette de Sevenges, it was found to be upon the treasonable subject of nightcaps, one half-dozen of those Lady Lisle had purchased of the good nun being too large, and not of the cutwork pattern selected.

Charles I. wore satin nightcaps, trimmed with gold and silver parchment lace, and Queen Elizabeth had similar articles of white cutwork, flourished with silver and set with spangles. It was while arrayed in one of these that the son of Lord Shrewsbury, while walking in the tilt-yard, caught a glimpse of her majesty, or, as the queen herself expressed it, he had seen her "unready and in her night stuff, whereat she was greatly ashamed."

James II. of England died, in the fashion set by Louis XIV., with a Mechlin lace nightcap on, which is still preserved as a choice relic at the museum of Dunkirk.

CHAPTER IV.

ENGLISH FASHIONS IN LACE—CONTINUED.

THE ruff was the first article of adornment worn by both men and women upon which a profusion of lace was displayed. Small ruffs were worn at first, and ruffles to match, about the wrists. As Queen Mary and her consort, Philip, are the first sovereigns of England in whose portraits ruffs appear, it follows that they were first introduced in England during Mary's reign. At this period, however, they were quite plain, being made of white cambric, and not trimmed with lace. They were called the Spanish ruff.

But when Queen Elizabeth ascended the throne she adopted ruffs most extravagant in size. To this day a standing fluted ruffle, if extra large, invariably bears the name of a "Queen Bess ruff," yet, in comparison with those worn by Queen Elizabeth herself, they appear but diminutive ruffles. For there was method in the queen's madness, or extreme fondness, for this peculiar article of adornment. With all her charms, her neck was undeniably yellow, and, to conceal it, she affected ruffs of monstrous size, wearing the largest in Europe, except those of Marguerite of Navarre, the first queen of Henri IV. of France. Besides, especially to a bright, pretty face, and where the form was inclined to be slender, the ruff was very becoming. When bordered by rich lace, fluted regularly with the poking-stick, and starched so stiffly there was no suspicion of irregularity or wilting about it, it enveloped the head like the petals of a white lily, giving a graceful, flower-like appearance to the face. Whether Queen Elizabeth understood all this or not it is impossible to say, but certain it is that she so fully appreciated the importance of the effect of her ruff that she never appeared without one.

The ladies of her court were quick to follow her example, and, though imitation is said to be the sincerest flattery, the queen was not partial to this mode which her subjects took of expressing their approbation and admiration of her taste. Ruffs were tolerated, certainly, but only those of a certain depth, much narrower than her own. To enforce this law she had certain officers stationed at various portions of the city of London to cut all ruffs which exceeded the size allowed. Upon the other hand, no lady was allowed to expose her neck, especially if it were fair, or she was sure to be visited with the lasting displeasure of the queen.

The ruff was a very expensive article. Though the most popular method of ornamentation was to edge and seam it with elegant lace, many other trimmings were adopted. The queen's ruffs were a quarter of a yard deep, and usually double. A writer of her reign, in describing this article of dress, after mentioning many of its peculiarities, says: Some are wrought with open worke donne to the midst of the ruffe, and, further, some with close worke; some with purled lace so closed and other gewgawes so pestered, as the ruffe is the leest part of itself." The ruffs of the queen were often trimmed with gold or silver lace and set with gems, the most beautiful being white with snowy lace and set with pearls. When ruffs of lawn were substituted for those of cambric, the caustic writers of the day suggested that the next step would be to make them of spider-webs.

The manner in which these ruffs were laundried was something wonderful. Fluting-irons were then never dreamed of; indeed, starching itself was in its infancy—an art known to but few—and, though practiced by the lace manufacturers of Belgium, was unknown in England until the early part of Queen Elizabeth's reign. Madam Dinghen van der Plasse was the first starcher of London, and she came from Flanders about 1570. She not only starched ruffs for gentle dames and chivalrous knights, but also taught the art of clear starching to daughters of the nobility. Many of the ruffs were wired, in addition to the starch, but the nice art of stiffening them with starch alone was the most popular method. After being put through several processes to render them exactly right in point of stiffness, they were fluted in immense waves with iron poking-sticks. These sticks were made by blacksmiths especially for fluting ruffs, were large and round, of the proper length, and long handles were attached to prevent the heat from injuring the hand. The yellow starching process was not in vogue in Queen Elizabeth's day, but during the reign of James I. a Mrs. Turner set up as a yellow starcher. This process was practiced in England only, and was supposed to give a rich effect to the lace. The yellow hue sought after in lace at the present day is not due to starch, but because the art of lace-making is in such a measure lost that the fine old specimens which remain at the present day are necessarily yellow with age. This, however, could not have been the cause of the popularity of yellow starch in the time of King James, for lace was then in its first prime, and few yellow specimens were extant, except they had become so by much bad washing and starching. Mrs. Turner was afterward hung for murder at Tyburn, in a yellow ruff of cobweb lawn, and some writers assert that this put an end to the fashion of using yellow starch, though it probably died a gradual death, unlike the woman who invented it.

The wardrobe accounts of Queen Elizabeth swarm with entries of articles used in making ruffs, for the quantity contained in a single article of the kind was positively alarming. Cambric, lawn, cutwork and all the various laces then in vogue were employed. In the wardrobe accounts of James I. are mentioned similar articles for like purposes, one being twenty-five yards of "fyne bone lace" to border a ruff. But this enormous appendage was constantly rebuked by the clergy and satirized by the poets and writers of the day.

The falling collar, or band, succeeded the ruff toward the close of the reign of King James, or about 1620, though Charles I., who succeeded him, in some of his earlier portraits appears in one. The band was at first narrow, but it speedily grew into a wide collar, which was made of linen and edged with the richest lace. In many instances this falling collar was made of lace altogether. Toward the last of the days of the ruff a sort of compromise between this and the collar was found in what was called a gorget, this being a collar of cambric and lace, without flutings usually, but standing up or flaring out in somewhat the same style as a ruff. The falling collar was adopted by men and women alike, for the dress of a gentleman of these times was quite as fanciful as that of a lady. With the fall of the ruff came the end of the lace ruffles worn in the sleeves, and in their stead were adopted, as more in keeping with the band, flat cuffs turning back from the hand, sometimes composed of a strip of linen bordered with rich lace, or of lace entirely, but usually stiffened with starch in order to lie close to the sleeve. The falling collars were tied with a small cord and tassel, as with such an elaborate dressing of the neck a tie would be superfluous; but, after a time—and the collars held their sway through the reign of Charles I., the Commonwealth and into the reign of Charles II.—they were discarded, lace cravats were worn instead, and, with these, exaggerated lace ruffles soon appeared, falling over the hands. These were worn through the reigns of William III., Queen Anne and the three Georges, until, in the time of George III., lace was discarded altogether as far as gentlemen's wearing apparel was concerned, and, indeed, used very sparingly by ladies.

Lace aprons, though of French origin, found their way into England in Queen Elizabeth's reign. They were regarded with more or less favor for more than a century, and were frequently made of point lace, though always considered by many as a plebeian appendage.

William III. of England made the most extensive purchase of laces for his royal wear, among which was six point cravats, and "cutwork" for trimming twelve pocket-handkerchiefs. His queen, resolved not to be eclipsed in the matter of laces, indulged freely in the luxury of lace aprons. When this lady died the king went into mourning for her by curtailing his laces, using his razor-cloths simply hemmed. Having ceased to indulge in grief, the use of lace-trimmed razor-cloths were resumed, and £499 10s. were expended for lace to trim twenty-four new night-shirts for his majesty.

Night-robes came in for their share of lace ornamentation soon after this fabric was used to trim other articles of underwear. Upon the marriage of Frederick, Prince of Wales, son of George II., the Princess of Wales is described as wearing the most superb night-robe of rich lace.

Gloves, handkerchiefs, fans, household linen, bathing wrappers—nearly everything that could be trimmed in this manner—was ornamented with lace. Lace lappets were worn upon the hair, often in mantilla fashion; shawls and scarfs were wrought of the finest lace. Infants' wardrobes, bridal trousseaux, even shrouds and grave-clothes, were richly bordered with the fashionable trimming.

Lace rosettes were introduced upon low shoes, and worn by gentlemen especially, in the time of James I. Lace garters were also worn at this time, and were often of fine lawn, as wide as a sash, the ends elaborate with lace. These broad garters were considered especially suitable as an accompaniment to shoes with rosettes, and were tied in a large bow just below the knee. With high top boots the canon—a flaring bit of linen bordered with lace, to cover the top—was worn, or, with very broad flaring tops, ruffles of lace were resorted to in order to fill the open space; below this was fastened the spur, in comical contrast.

The commode was an exaggerated head-dress of lace, rising in row after row of plaitings, usually a box-plait in front, over the forehead, and side-plaits on either side. The lace used was very wide, and stiffened with starch.

This commode was adopted in England in the reign of William III. and collapsed in Queen Anne's time, whereupon, according to the *Spectator*, ladies were reduced from seven feet to five. When this commode was in the height of its glory Addison also remarks that the men appeared as grasshoppers beside the women.

From the time of Queen Elizabeth lace grew more and more plentiful, and also in greater favor steadily, until the downfall of Charles I. Then it received a check, the Puritans having plainer views of dress, though many of them could not resist the fascinating power of lace. It was not so generally worn during the Commonwealth, but, after the Restoration, grew more popular than ever. Charles II. wore it upon all occasions; but the "good William and Mary" expended more money upon their laces than any other sovereigns of Europe. In 1694 the lace bill of Mary amounted to nearly $10,000 for the year, and this, we must remember, was at a time when there was but little money in circulation, and prices were, in consequence, very low. But, extravagant though Mary may have been, her husband was still more lavish in his use of lace, his private bill for this article being for a year—in 1696—over $12,000. Queen Anne was less extravagant, but lace-trimmed sacques and lace flounces of every description flourished in her day. At the beginning of the French Revolution, during the reign of George III., England copied France in the wearing of gauzes and tissues, and lace gradually declined. Gentlemen threw it aside, adopting a plainer dress, which is still in vogue. But when, years afterward, ladies again began to wear lace, the manufacture of many of the rarer kinds was found to be a lost art, and those who had valuable collections had been so careless as to preserve very little of what was the rarest and best. Queen Victoria has given encouragement to English lace-makers, however, and during her reign the manufacture has increased, and a new love of lace has sprung up among Englishwomen. Mrs. Fanny Bury Pallister collected much documentary knowledge concerning lace, and was the chief patroness of a lace exhibition at South Kensington, for which many ladies of rank loaned valuable collections. The present fashion in England is to copy after the royal family and wear Honiton upon nearly every occasion, thus encouraging home industry.

In the days of William IV., shortly before he was succeeded by Victoria, a petition was sent to his wife, Queen Adelaide, in behalf of the distressed lace-workers, whereupon she sent them, among others, an order for a dress of Honiton sprays, which were to be put on fine net as a foundation. The design was of flowers formed into wreaths, the initial letter of each flower, as it was placed in order, spelling her name. The flowers were arranged as follows: Amaranth, Daphne, Eglantine, Lilac, Auricula, Ivy, Dahlia, Eglantine.

CHAPTER V.

FRENCH FASHIONS IN LACE.

Lace was but little worn in France until the time of Henri III. It is true the fraise, as the ruff was called in France, was invented especially for Henri II., about 1540, to conceal a scar upon his neck, but this fraise was at first unornamented by lace, and was quite unpretentious. In the time of Henri III. it reached an enormous size, and a writer of his day likens the head of a man decked out in one to the head of John the Baptist on a charger. Henri III. was so much attached to his ruffs, and so particular about their appearance, that he was often known to flute them with poking-sticks himself. In the reign of Henri IV. the fraise was worn alternately with the rabat, a turn-down collar, but Marguerite of Navarre, Henri's first queen, wore ruffs of enormous size, larger even than those of Queen Elizabeth. The ruff of Queen Marguerite however, as seen in her portraits, differs from that of Queen Elizabeth, in parting in front and terminating in long pointed lace ends, exposing her throat and neck to view. Queen Marguerite was passionately fond of lace, particularly point coupé and point à l'aiguille, as her wardrobe accounts show. Henri IV. strove at one time to set an example of simplicity in dress to his subjects, discarding lace and other ornaments; but little notice was taken of this by the lace-loving nobles of his Court. Marie de Medici, second wife of Henri IV., whom she married in 1600, brought with her from Tuscany

Italian laces of gold and thread, and a love of Italian lace generally. Her fraise or collarette was stiff, and high at the back, well-wired and spreading out like a fan. When her first child, Louis XIII., was born, the Pope sent a consecrated layette of linen, trimmed with the richest point, for his use, a custom which continued at the birth of each dauphin. After the assassination of Henri, and during the regency of Marie, lace was used more lavishly than ever; but later, when her courtiers desired her to increase their pensions, which were inadequate considering the amount they were obliged to spend in lace, she issued a law to regulate superfluous habits, which forbade the wearing of laces altogether.

Flemish points next became popular at the French Court, rivaling those of Italy, and when Anne of Austria married Louis XIII., in 1615, Spanish laces were also introduced. Anne did not take kindly to the fraise or collarette, but substituted the rabat, wearing also berthes of exquisite lace, and the outside cuff, which, whether of lace or embroidery, whenever introduced by fashion (as was recently the case), still bears her name. Her hand was small, fair and beautifully shaped, and this cuff of soft lace, usually in two rows of deep points, set it off to the best advantage.

The Court of France now reveled in lace. The ladies wore the high or falling collar according to the dictates of their tastes, long, narrow, lace-trimmed aprons, and dainty caps of the same frost-like fabric. The gentlemen wore the deep rabat, almost covering their shoulders like a cape, and of the richest point, or bordered deeply with the favorite lace. With the low shoe a large rosette of lace was adopted, and the lace garter, tying in a bow below the knee, slightly inclining to the inside. The favorite manner of dressing the feet, however, was in very fine boots, with enormous tops flaring out like a huge funnel, so very bulky as to render walking an art, and walking gracefully an impossibility; these boot-tops were filled in with row upon row of Genoa point. Canons were also worn—flaring strips of linen, edged with lace and tied below the knee to cover the open tops of the boots, resembling a large collar in shape. Rheingraves were adopted for a similar purpose, being a sort of pantalette, composed of a straight strip of linen, the bottom hemmed and bordered with lace, the top gathered and tied round the knee with a draw-string.

Cinq-Mars—Louis' favorite of an hour—is said to have worn the most exquisitely-trimmed boots of any gentleman in France, and at his death he left three hundred pairs, all elaborately decorated with lace, in various styles; canons, rheingraves or plaitings of point.

Gloves, at this time, were rather long, and were pulled up on the wrists without buttons, the backs of the hands being embroidered in gold or silver thread, the tops finished with gold, silver or point lace.

Louis XIII.—morose, fickle and captious, sincere in little save animosity toward his queen, which feeling Richelieu seemed to share—alternately forbade the wearing of lace, and revoked the edict; yet his whims had little effect, especially so far as restricting the use of lace was concerned. The birth of Louis XIV., however, reconciled him to Anne in some degree, and when, in dying, he appointed her regent, she was able to indulge her love of lace and all that was luxurious and beautiful to her heart's content; though, through the influence of Mazarin, the young king is said to have been reared amid plain surroundings. The Court of Anne of Austria, however, was proverbial for its cleanliness, its rare laces, jewels and general grandeur.

Louis XIV., like his father, issued various edicts, especially prohibiting the points of Italy and Flanders; but, as yet, France was not a lace-making country. Judging from the portraits of Louis, however, he was inclined to inherit his mother's love of lace, for his canons were of the richest Genoa point, and nearly as deep as a bed-valance. After his marriage with the Infanta of Spain, point d'Espagne and other Spanish laces were worn at the French Court in her honor. The gold and silver points became more popular than the points of Italy and Flanders, until Colbert established the manufacture of point de France, and thereafter this lace was adopted by Louis and his Court almost exclusively. When the Grand Dauphin was born, he was presented to his father in a cap and wrap trimmed with deep rich point de France. Infants' robes, caps, shawls and cradle furniture were richly ornamented with lace, the poor babes being nearly smothered in it at their christenings.

The rabat, or falling collar, continued popular until early in the regency of Anne of Austria, when long perukes or wigs came into favor. These wigs were made up of a great quantity of hair, and fell in curls down the back and over the shoulders, which, together with lace, jewelry and other prettinesses, gave to man an effeminate appearance. As this wig covered the collar almost entirely except in front, it was thrown aside, and cravats and lace ties used in its stead. Louis XIV. is represented in all his portraits with this wig, its long ringlets carefully arranged; and so great a stickler for etiquette and propriety was he, it is said that no one, not even his valet, ever saw him without it.

Fontanges, commonly called commodes in England, now became popular. They originated, it is stated, in a novel way. During a hunt, in which the king took part, the hair of one of the ladies became unbound, and she hastily tied her lace pocket-handkerchief about her head with the ribbon which had fastened her refractory locks. The king was charmed with this careless yet graceful head-dress, and requested her to wear it that evening. She did so, and the style was admired and immediately copied by the other ladies of the Court. It grew, at last, into such an exaggerated form that the ladies, upon entering their carriages, were said to be obliged to go down upon their knees. This fashion, pretty in moderation, but absurd when row after row of lace made the ladies seem to be carrying steeples about upon their heads, continued in favor for many years.

The Steinkirk now became the rage. Lace cravats had been worn since the rabat was banished; and when Marshal Luxembourg and William of Orange fought against each other on the field of Steinkirk, in 1692, the French princes who participated in the action found their lace neckties had become unfastened. Hastily giving them a twist, and drawing the ends through a button-hole of the coat to keep them out of the way, they dashed into the fray, and won it, too. So, thereafter, it was for a long time the fashion for both ladies and gentlemen to wear Steinkirks in memory of the day—the gentlemen in the manner described, and the ladies with the lace cravat carelessly twisted, and the end fastened in front of the bodice at the left, with a fancy pin similar to the scarf-pins of the present time. The English wore these Steinkirks, too, not in honor of the day, but because it was the fashion.

Lace now became greatly used in France to decorate the churches and robes of officiating priests. England, being a Protestant nation since lace became plentiful, had no occasion for displaying it in this manner; but in France the Church followed in a certain degree the fashions of the Court in regard to lace. So in the time of Louis XIV. point de France became the most popular and general ornamentation for church and funeral robes. It also was greatly used in trimming household linen, table-cloths, napkins, towels, bathing wrappers, and in some cases a flounce of the lace encircled the bath-tub. This led to the custom of ladies receiving callers while taking their bath, a strange proceeding as it appears to us, yet, after all, no worse than taking a bath in the ocean in company with friends. The French ladies, therefore, when a caller was announced just as they had entered their bath, gave orders for their visitor to be shown up at once, where the hostess might be seen attired in the most tasteful of bathing robes, embroidered and lace-trimmed, with perhaps a flounce of lace about the bath-tub, and the water perfumed and rendered milky by the use of some favorite extract, as wholly at her ease as though seated in her *salon*, and arrayed in the most attractive costume.

CHAPTER VI.

FRENCH FASHIONS IN LACE—CONTINUED.

THE fashion of wearing lace ruffles in elbow sleeves, came in vogue during the latter part of the reign of Louis XIV., and continued in favor for many years. Ladies of rank wore them from choice and by rule, for there was a great deal of ceremony regarding the wearing of them. One, two or three lace ruffles, therefore, were adopted, according to age, occasion or station, and the etiquette concerning them was nearly as long as the moral law, and far more rigidly observed.

The gentleman also, early during the reign of Louis XV., wore ruffles at the wrists, called manchettes or pleureuses (weepers), which fell over the hands, half concealing them. Some writers assert that these deep ruffles were introduced for the purpose of affording an easy hiding-place for cards, when gentlemen wished to cheat at the game. This, however, is scarcely probable, for all gentlemen wore them, young and old, and those occupying the meaner stations in life as well as the noble and wealthy.

Jabots invariably accompanied these manchettes, and, between the two, the shirt was completely hidden, hence the origin of the old saw about "ruffles instead of a shirt." These appurtenances to a gentleman's toilet were considered necessary for night as well as the day, though the night jabots and ruffles were usually of a less expensive lace. Point d'Alençon was the favorite for full dress, and Valenciennes, or something similar in quality, for night. Pages, valets and the upper class of servants invariably wore lace.

The use of lace, however, in France, was carried, perhaps, to a greater extravagance in the ornamentation of bed canopies, coverlets and linen than in anything else, for in bedsteads and bed-hangings the French excel. The ivory bedstead of the Duchesse de Beaufort, in the days of Henri IV., with its rich hangings and drapery of lace, was a marvel, as was also the gold bed of Versailles. Invalids, in France, were accustomed to receive their friends in their bed-chamber, and, upon such occasions, the bed-curtains, counterpane and pillow-covers were composed of lace, sometimes lined with silk or satin, either white or colored, while the invalid wore a most elaborate lace robe, or, if it were a gentlemen, he wore a bed-gown of the finest cambric, with the usual jabots and manchettes. There was also great etiquette concerning the receiving of friends *couchée*, since it was a great breach of decorum for a person of lesser rank to recline in the presence of one of greater, who was sitting or standing. This embarrassing state of affairs was met in a novel manner upon a visit of Louis XIII. to Richelieu, during the minister's last illness. A second bed was prepared, upon which the monarch reposed during the interview. In case of the invalid being a lady, the affair was more readily managed. The beautiful Madame de Récamier, of whom it is said she could truly boast of having half the celebrated men of Europe for her admirers, without ever losing one of them for a friend, was noted for her choice entertainments as well as her beauty and rare conversational powers, being one of the society leaders in the first Empire. It was in 1802, when Paris was in the early glory of Napoleon's reign, that Madame de Récamier issued invitations for a grand ball. The evening came and the guests assembled. Madame, however, was not to be seen when they entered the *salon*. She was indisposed, suddenly confined to her bed by illness, but would receive her guests in her chamber, which, as is customary in Paris, is near one of the principal drawing-rooms. Accordingly, they were ushered into her presence, where, upon a gilded bedstead, looking as fair and graceful as a lily, she reposed.

Her bed-curtains were of rare Brussels point, as was the counterpane, and both were lined with pale rose-colored satin, the pillows of cambric, richly embroidered, and elaborately trimmed with Valenciennes. Madame wore a white robe, literally covered with point d'Angleterre, and she received her guests in such a graceful manner that she carried all hearts by storm. Napoleon himself was among the invited, and never did one of her entertainments prove more thoroughly charming, for when her guests retired, at a late hour, they could think and speak of but one thing, and that was how angelic Madame appeared, and how devoted she was to society.

Afterward, when in 1810 Napoleon married Maria Louisa, he expended fabulous sums upon the laces for her trousseau; but one of the chief articles of interest was a complete set of bed furniture of point d'Alençon, which was made expressly for the royal bed-chamber. The set was composed of a tester, or top piece, curtains encircling the bed, counterpane and pillow-cases. The imperial arms and emblems were in the centre, or formed the principal figure, while the ground was thickly dotted with imperial bees, arranged so that the rows of bees alternately faced in opposite directions. The illustration shows a portion of the ground.

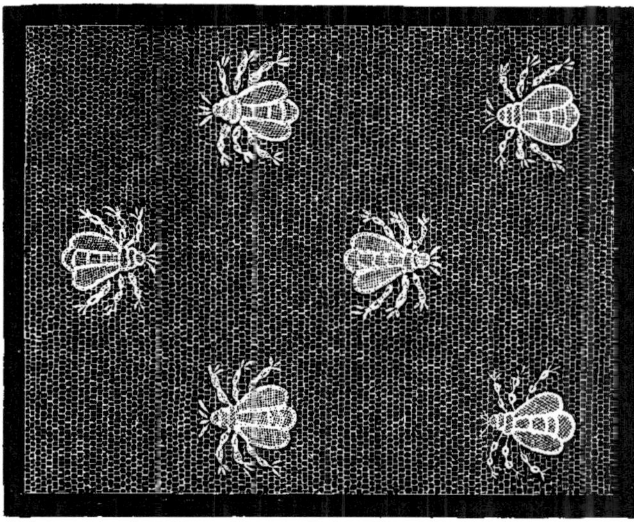

When, in the following year, the imperial prince was born, a sum was expended for his layette which almost equaled that expended at the time of the marriage; for Napoleon I. was remarkably fond of lace, probably because Josephine admired and expended almost fabulous sums upon it, and then, too, he was especially attached to point d'Alençon, being proud of it as a French production. The layette of his long-wished-for son was magnificent in the extreme, being adorned with Alençon point, as was the layette of the prince who was called the fourth Napoleon, though never Napoleon IV.

After the banishment of Napoleon I. the fashion of

using lace profusely in France declined for a time, in nearly as great a degree as it did at the period of the French Revolution. Louis XVI. and Marie Antoinette used it less freely than the previous sovereigns of France, and the revolution broke up almost entirely both the manufacture and the wearing of it.

Lace, however, was worn somewhat after the downfall of the First Empire, but not until the beginning of the Second was the fashion of wearing it revived to any great extent. In the trousseau of the Empress Eugénie lace played a conspicuous part, many single pieces being worth a small fortune; and the Court of France, when she ruled it—as she ruled the fashionable world at large—again appeared resplendent in lace. Alençon point was her favorite, and though the Brussels point á l'aiguille is a finer and more costly lace, which can only be afforded by royal or extravagantly wealthy purses, yet France, who set the fashions for the civilized world, gave the preference to her own Alençon, hence its great popularity. As Eugénie's trousseau was rich in lace, one single dress flounce of Alençon point costing over $4,000, so the layette of the little Prince Imperial was the most magnificent ever known. The robes, skirts, shirts, caps, and other similar articles prepared for the use of this wee scion of imperialism—and there were twelve dozen of each—were composed of or elaborately trimmed with Alençon point. The christening robe, cap and mantle were of this favorite lace, and the caps and aprons of his nurses were all trimmed with it. His bed-curtains, coverings and pillow-cases were also of Alençon, with their accompanying quilts of eider-down, that wrapped him lightly in the summer weather, or more closely in the cooler days and nights of winter; but what fabric has yet been invented by human hand which could shelter even a prince ever so little from the winds of adversity? When, an exile from fair France, he fell in far Zululand, pierced by relentless savage spears, how sharp and strangely bitter the contrast between this and the day when his birth was heralded by the thunder of cannon, the shouts of the multitude, and the homage paid one born to the imperial purple, when the people saw only the beginning: that an heir was born to a prosperous royal house, and no one could guess the end.

Since Eugénie is banished from France, though the display of lace is less magnificent than before, it is still in favor—still used to a great extent in the trousseaux and layettes of the rich, and also forms an important part of the garniture of fashionable costumes generally. But woven laces have, in a great degree, superseded those made by hand, and it is not probable that hand-made laces will be worn in the future to as great an extent as they have been in the past, though those who can afford them still cling to and treasure them as rare artistic productions.

Lace, in France, is now worn more or less by all classes, and as France still sets the fashions for the world, lace is used to a great extent, though the cheaper grades appear even on rich toilettes, as the imitations are many of them executed so cleverly they can hardly be detected from the hand-made by any but an expert. For a time, in white laces, cluny was used for nearly everything; then one of the cheapest laces—torchon—took the lead for more than a year. At this moment a better lace—Breton—is most in favor; and some of the bolder fashion leaders predict that Mechlin—a finer lace still—will soon take its place for select purposes; while for more ordinary uses the light and pretty French lace called point d'esprit will be greatly in demand. Valenciennes can be applied to almost any use, and on that account never loses ground.

In black laces guipure held great prominence for a time, but gave place to a lace which, in the better qualities, is a perfect imitation of the black thread lace which is manufactured in France. A black Spanish blonde, in bold designs, occasionally disputes the supremacy of this French lace, but as it cannot be applied to so many purposes, it is far less popular.

CHAPTER VII.

SPANISH FASHIONS IN LACE.

Except in the use of black and white blonde—especially the former—and gold and silver laces, the Spaniards are not a lace-wearing people. Like Italy, the laces made in Spain were for a long time consecrated to the use of the Church, and afterward exported to France and England, the two lace-wearing countries of Europe. Even in Belgium, until in later years, little lace was worn, except simple edgings to border the caps of the peasantry, and a few of the choicest points to deck the robes of royalty.

In the trousseaux of Spanish royal brides, veils and dresses of Brussels or Alençon point are in demand, and Portuguese point also in a certain degree; but while England followed the lead of France in fashions concerning laces as well as other fabrics, Spain, copying after the French in various minor things, clung tenaciously to many of the characteristics of her own national dress.

The Spanish señora having, doubtless, arrived at the conclusion that the mantilla is a becoming article of dress, besides being adapted to the climate, and giving little trouble in its arrangement, clings to it year after year, as did her mother and her great grandmother before her. She may be fickle in many things—in love, friendship, and in her likes and dislikes generally—but she is constant to her mantilla, wearing it upon all occasions.

Some writers declare that lace was worn to some extent in Spain in the time of Ferdinand and Isabella, near the close of the fifteenth century, and quote, as evidence of the fact, the lace alb presented to the Cathedral of Granada by them; yet this proves nothing further than that, as has already been stated, lace was greatly used in the churches at this period. No mention of it is made in the wardrobe accounts of the Spanish sovereigns until a much later date, and little lace was exported from Spain until the seventeenth century. There is one account of black Spanish lace being used for Queen Elizabeth's ruffs, but she was not, usually, partial to this lace. During the reign of Louis XIV. much point d'Espagne was used in France, especially after the marriage of Louis with the Infanta, but this was a heavy gold lace, often worked with silks in bright colors.

This lace was greatly used by the royal families of Spain for the adornment of the black dresses worn by the señoras, for trimming carriage curtains of the nobility, bed-curtains, and even the uniforms of army officers, while silver point d'Espagne appeared on the uniforms of an order of soldiers formed from the nobility. The celebrated Valladolid banner of the Spanish Inquisition was trimmed with point d'Espagne of the finest gold.

White lace came into use to some extent in trimming underwear and bed linen during the seventeenth century. French jabots and manchettes were introduced, but soon forbidden by law, a law which seems to have been obeyed. Spanish noblemen, however, wore ruffs of moderate size, and also falling collars.

The mantilla was worn in Spain from the close of the sixteenth century, but at the beginning it was made of silk instead of lace. A century later black lace was used in its manufacture, and soon after it was made in one piece. It is always of silk, the thread being of a very fine quality. In delicacy of design the Spanish blonde laces are inferior to the French, but there is a certain boldness in the pattern which is strikingly becoming to its dark-eyed wearers. There are three mantillas, or, rather, three separate styles of mantilla in the wardrobe of every Spanish señora who lays claim to being at all distinguished or fashionable, and the quality of the garment in question varies greatly according to her wealth or rank. For ordinary wear the mantilla is made of black silk, with a trimming of black lace or velvet, sometimes both. The second mantilla, which is used for choicer purposes, is of black blonde trimmed with a border of rich lace, or it is a black blonde of Spanish pattern, woven in some elaborate design. This mantilla is worn more than either of the other two, and answers for nearly all full-dress purposes. Upon rare State occasions, however, the third mantilla, which is supposed to be the acme of all that is grand and graceful, is displayed. This is of white blonde —too often, alas! a dirty white from long use and much wearing. It is principally worn at bull-fights, but is also considered especially suitable for birthday festivals, or the feast of Easter. Of the three, the black lace mantilla is the most becoming, and a Spanish señora or señorita who possesses even ordinary charms is especially captivating when arrayed in it, for custom and suitability unite to make it a charming addition to her dress. Even those who are old and ugly are rendered passable by this attractive wrap and head-dress combined. The reverse is true of the white mantilla. Spanish women invariably grow stout in middle age, or they become wizened, with faces like parchment. But no matter how old, or ugly, or toothless is the crone when she goes to a bull-fight, she will wear a white lace mantilla. She can afford to look the reverse of charming, but she cannot afford to commit such a flagrant breach of etiquette as to appear at a bull-fight, or on Easter Monday, in a mantilla composed of any other material than white lace.

Spanish ladies seem more attached to their mantillas than any other article of dress, and often appear in one of the finest lace, while the remainder of their costume, with the exception of a rare jewel or two, may be very simple, often, indeed, shabby in the extreme. They are partial to thin gauzy black dresses, with innumerable flounces bordered with black or gold lace; but whatever the dress may be, the mantilla must be of excellent quality. One reason, perhaps, why these señoras take such comfort in this one article of apparel is that it cannot be sold for debt, and whatever misfortune may overtake them, the law protects them against being obliged to part with their favorite mantilla.

The fan is another object of a Spanish woman's particular esteem, and a popular style is gilt or gold sticks with black or gold-colored satin, covered with black lace. Or, it may be white satin, with white or black lace trimmings; but to meet the requirements of a pretty fan, it must be ornamented with lace in some manner. The Spanish señoritas manipulate a fan with the most charming grace. They use it to accent their words, to show anger or approbation; they half screen their faces with it, knowing well their bright dark eyes, which they understand so well how to use in the most effective manner, appear brighter than ever when peeping over the edge of a handsome fan.

So the costume of a Spanish lady gains nearly all of its piquant character from the use of lace. A woman of any other country, however much lace she may add to the attractiveness of her costume, can still make a most becoming toilette without it, but the absence of lace in the dress of a Spanish lady would be like the play of "Hamlet" with that melancholy prince left out altogether. And as Spain has never secured a foothold in colder climes, but her dominions are all situated where the sun shines warmly the long year through, her daughters can wear their laces and wave their fans at all seasons, without being frightened into laying them aside at the approach of winter.

After the marriage of the Empress Eugénie there was quite an intimacy between the French and Spanish Courts, the pretty Empress clinging to her native tongue and people—to the former with such tenacity that, though she might use French in discussing Love, Art or Fashion, yet, whenever vexed and inclined to scold, she invariably took refuge in Spanish. To her lady friends in Spain she made many gifts of laces, especially the French point d'Alençon. In 1855 she gave to Queen Isabella and her mother, Queen Christina, two elegant costumes—to the latter one of rare point d'Alençon. The skirt was composed of flounces of this lace, while the bodice was trimmed with it in a most artistic manner.

CHAPTER VIII.

EDICTS CONCERNING LACE.

No other article of adornment or apparel has been the subject of so many laws, edicts or proclamations as was lace from the sixteenth to the nineteenth century. These edicts caused not only great fluctuations in the price of lace, occasioned by the varying demand, but they also led to a large amount of smuggling, which for a long time was carried on in so clever a manner it was almost impossible to detect it. Aside from this, these edicts were often the cause of great distress among the lace-makers, who were unable to sell their manufactures after some royal proclamation forbidding the wearing of lace was put forth, and, consequently, they were often reduced to the verge of starvation; while those laws forbidding the wearing of foreign laces, though advantageous to home industry, led to a vast amount of smuggling.

Edward IV. of England issued various laws concerning apparel, but these did not allude to lace. In the reign of Henry VII. gold thread and lace were imported into England from Venice, and laws were issued to prevent those dealing in them from selling at scant weight, or providing that every pound should weigh fully twelve ounces. In the "acts of apparell" of Henry VIII. a fine of $10.00 and forfeiture of the garment worn was imposed upon all men below a knight in degree who presumed to wear a laced shirt. King Henry also provided by law for the importation of various laces into England. Queen Mary issued a proclamation forbidding all below the rank of a baron to wear cutwork ruffles wrought outside of England. Queen Elizabeth issued various laws regarding the wearing of lace generally, and in regulating the size of ruffs, but she did not forbid the purchase of foreign laces by those whom she allowed to wear them, or refuse to use them herself. She was very fond of all manner of novelties in dress, and obtained all she could, both domestic and foreign; but she strove, by numerous proclamations and fines, to repress the use of lace and other articles of ornamental dress, though these laws were often disregarded.

James I. granted numerous monopolies to various favorites, among others one to the Earl of Suffolk, for the importation of gold and silver laces. The laces of Italy and Flanders were also extensively imported at this time. These monopolies had a tendency to depress the home manufacture of lace, and caused great distress in several lace-making districts of England. Through the efforts of his queen the manufacture somewhat revived, and as lace was worn in great profusion during the reign of Charles I., it continued prosperous until the time of the Commonwealth, which was a dark time for the lace-makers of England, as by laws, proclamations, a few examples and much expostulation, the making as well as the wearing of lace was frowned down as absurdly vain.

Charles I. had issued an act prohibiting the importation of bone or thread lace, and, after the Restoration, Charles II. enforced this act, though he wore all manner of foreign laces himself. Afterward he put forth a law forbidding the importation of foreign laces of nearly every soil, and all persons found importing or bringing them into the kingdom were to forfeit the lace and pay a fine of $500. This was in 1662. The lace which caused the most annoyance to English manufacturers was the Flemish pillow, or bone lace as it was then called, for the English lace, though copied after it, was far inferior to the Flemish, both in quality of the thread and workmanship, as well as design. King Charles afterward allowed the importation of foreign lace by one John Eaton, in sufficient quantity to supply his own majesty and the royal family, under pretense that this lace would serve as patterns for the English lace-workers.

But the most effective law of all concerning the importation of lace into England was passed during the reign of William III. by the English parliament in 1698. This law forbade the importation of "bone lace, loom lace, needlework point and cutwork" under a far heavier penalty than had ever been imposed before, besides forfeiture. Flanders was at this time subject to the Spanish government, and it became so incensed as to pass an act forbidding the importation of English wool into the country, which caused such general distress among the wool-growers and merchants of England as to lead to the repeal of the act prohibiting the importation of Flemish lace, England retiring from the conflict badly worsted. John Cary, a Bristol merchant, in his "Discourse on Trade," says this retaliation by Flanders "lessened our exportation of woolen manufactures by about £100,000 per annum."

Queen Anne issued a proclamation in 1711 prohibiting the importation of gold and silver lace, which at this time became in great demand. Although the law prohibiting the importation of Flemish lace had been repealed, all other foreign laces of any beauty or value were forbidden, including the points of France, Italy and Spain.

Smuggling was carried on to an unusual extent in England, and we find as early as 1627 mention made of "sundry packages" on which the custom had not been paid. Although the edict regarding Flanders lace had been revoked it was still in force so far as other favorite laces were concerned. George III. desired to protect home manufactures, but the lovers of foreign laces were resolved to wear them. Constant seizures were being made, and when the king's sister was married to the Duke of Brunswick, the Court, in defiance of the order, had their costumes adorned with foreign laces, which the officers did not scruple to confiscate and destroy. During this time lace was conveyed to England in every possible way. It was hid in dolls, in boxes with false bottoms, and even in bread and bottles. Even coffins containing dead bodies were used to hide away laces and thus evade the custom-house officers, though in time these officials came to search the corpse, usually with good result. One was found to be only a head, with hands and feet, the body being false and crammed with lace; another had its limbs wrapped in the choicest point. The utmost vigilance failed to stop smuggling in England until free trade laws were passed, when it died a natural death.

In France, edicts concerning dress, and particularly the wearing of lace, began about the middle of the sixteenth century, but did not have the best effect, for the reason that, though the French kings were excellent at sending forth such laws and proclamations, they set very bad personal examples in economy, and most especially in regard to wearing lace, for they, as well as their subjects, seemed to have gone regularly lace-mad. Henri IV. did make one weak little struggle to dress plainly, but even this sacrifice upon the good king's part had little effect in restraining his luxury-loving people from indulging in their fondness for fine apparel. Flemish laces were forbidden to be worn, or imported even; but Henri's first, and also his second, queen, as well as the nobles generally, disobeyed both these commands. Marie de Medicis, his second wife, after his death and during her regency, though very fond of lace, was at length obliged, through the necessity to retrench the expenses of her household and her courtiers, to prohibit the wearing of both lace and embroidery, which had the effect to relieve her from immediate embarrassment, though this result was but temporary.

Her son, Louis XIII., in reality cared less for pomp and fine dress than did the French sovereigns generally, though neither over-good nor wise in most matters. He issued half a score of edicts against lace, many of them being very absurd, and provoking a number of satires by the poets and writers of the day. One, the "Révolte des Passemens," is particularly amusing, and interesting and valuable from giving the names of all the laces then worn in France. This was published during the reign of Louis XIV., in 1661. It represents the different laces meeting in order to decide what is best to be done. They conclude they had better retire to their own countries, as they are nearly all foreign; but a French lace rushes in at this moment and declares for war. When they come to consider the matter they recollect that they all know something of war, as they have nearly all been in battles, as generals of the day were extensively rigged out in lace.

One had gone as a cravat, others as ruffles, etc. A council of war was held; they organized and went forth boldly to battle, to conquer and abolish Parliament altogether. At the first charge of the enemy, however, they unfortunately take refuge in flight, becoming greatly terrified in spite of their boasted valor. They are all captured and sentenced to various terrible fates. Some are to be made into tinder, others converted into paper, still others to be twisted into rope and sent to the galleys; and the poor gold and silver laces, being the instigators of the rebellion, are doomed to be burned alive. Love, however, intercedes for them, and they are all at last pardoned and restored to favor at Court. This poem was written in a peculiarly happy and sparkling style, but the author had never seen an English translation of it.

As edicts failed to banish lace, or prevent the people from wearing it, during the reign of Louis XIV., Colbert, then minister, wisely resolved to make France a lace-producing country. Accordingly he brought from Italy and Flanders the most skillful lace-workers, and established extensive manufactories under their tutorship in a dozen different cities of the kingdom. The result was as perfect a success as he could have desired. This was the beginning of the point lace industry of France.

Louis XIV. urged the wearing of point de France—as the result of Colbert's experiment was called—both by edict and example, and, in consequence, it flourished surprisingly, soon becoming the most important manufacture of the country. It continued prosperous, and in favor at Court, from 1665 to 1683, when, on account of Colbert's death, it received something of a blow; but this was slight in comparison to the effect which the revocation of the Edict of Nantes had upon it in 1685. The principal seat of the manufacture of the French points having been established at Alençon, the town gave its name to the lace, which dropped its name of point de France for that of point d'Alençon.

The revocation of the Edict of Nantes sent four thousand lace-makers away from Alençon. Many settled in Holland and founded a manufactory at Amsterdam. Frederick William, Elector of Bradenburg, issued an edict in favor of the fleeing lace-makers, which caused them to crowd into his dominions, and it was not long before Berlin alone possessed four hundred and fifty lace manufactories. Various parts of Germany were enriched by the presence of these artists, and France saw her folly when she had to buy her laces from that country.

This also led to fresh importations of Flemish lace, and as the fabric was still in favor at Court, and edicts continued to be issued concerning it, smuggling became very prevalent in France. It ceased for a time, however, when Napoleon I. endeavored to re-establish the industry, but in the early days of the Republic smuggling was very prevalent. Dogs were made use of as lace smugglers at this time, even as they are now employed to smuggle Swiss watches. In order to prepare these dogs for service they were made to undergo a siege of starvation before leaving France; and when about to leave Belgium, a large skin was stuffed with laces and drawn over their emaciated forms, which gave them the appearance of an ordinary dog. In due course of time the dog-smuggler returned to his home with a valuable cargo of precious laces. These unlawful proceedings having been discovered, an effort was made to stop them, and, during the short period of sixteen years, 40,278 of these irresponsible smugglers were put to death. Later, the edicts concerning the importation of laces having been revoked, smuggling ceased almost altogether. As the other countries of Europe wore but little foreign laces, few laws regarding them and their importation were issued, except in England and France, the only laws being necessary were a few for the protection of home industry, and, as a rule, the fewer of these promulgated, the more flourishing the manufactures.

CHAPTER IX.

PATRONS OF LACE-MAKING.

THE nuns who established schools for giving instructions in the art of making lace were its first patrons. The earliest of these schools were in Italy and Flanders, the latter being at that time a Catholic country. Much good resulted from the founding of these institutions, for lace-making soon became the means of gaining respectable livelihoods to many who had previously been in great want, the cheapness of flax enabling even the very poorest to obtain materials for their work.

The making of lace has always, in Italy, been more or less under the patronage of the Church, but in Belgium the Emperor Charles V. caused the art to be regularly taught to the young in all the schools as early as the middle of the sixteenth century. This custom has been kept up almost without intermission to the present day, and has, no doubt, been the chief cause of the almost uninterrupted prosperity of the lace manufacturers of Belgium, which, from the time that Flemish pillow laces first came into demand in France and England, has suffered few reverses and fluctuations compared with the lace industries of other countries.

In Spain and Portugal, as well as Italy, the nuns were the principal patrons of lace-making. In France, however, little lace was made until Colbert started the manufactories of point and pillow laces in 1665. In Normandy, however, the wives and daughters of fishermen made a coarse kind of guipure, Valenciennes, and also copied to some extent after the laces of Flanders from the beginning of the sixteenth century. At a still earlier period the women of the mountainous district of Vélay made a cheap lace, and a similar production was wrought in Auvergne, which was used to trim underwear and for other purposes. It was the manufacture of these laces—the centre of the district being Le Puy—which met with a reverse at the time when Father François Régis interceded with Parliament in their behalf. Except the countenance given to point de France by Louis XIV., the sovereigns of France gave little patronage to the lace industry. Colbert's masterly plan, however, was productive of greater advancement in lace-making than that of any other known person. Napoleon I. endeavored to revive point d'Alençon, giving it all the encouragement in his power; and Napoleon III. and the Empress Eugénie followed his example, so that the lace manufacturers of France are to-day in as flourishing a condition as the introduction of blondes and machine laces will allow.

Barbara Uttman, the wife of a rich mine-master in Annaberg, was almost as great a benefactor to the poorer classes in Germany as was Colbert to those of France, although the result of her labors may have been less beneficial to the country at large, for they were far less extensive, and existed at a much earlier date, when the markets were not so great nor the remuneration for the work so large. Some, indeed, accord to Barbara Uttman the invention of pillow lace; but as this lace was made in Flanders previous to 1561, the period of the beginning of her labor, it could not rightfully be accorded to her, though for her earnest interest in the work, and able management of it, she deserves the highest honor and praise. The story of her having learned lace-making from a woman of Brabant is the more probable of the two. The fact is universally acknowledged that she sent to Flanders to procure teachers of pillow lace at the time of setting up her establishment in Annaberg. Here she taught and manufactured laces of various designs, and the industry spread into the neighboring towns until thirty thousand workers were employed. Her manufactory was established under her own name, her husband, Christopher Uttman, having, it appears, enough to do with his mines; though, only for being the husband of Barbara, he would, in all possibility, have never been known to posterity. Barbara died while yet comparatively young, in 1575, but her good works and their influence lived after her. She lies in the cemetery at Annaberg in a handsome tomb, which has a long and affectionate inscription, showing the grateful memory in which she was held by her people; and in the Green Vault at Dresden is a small ivory statue, embellished with gems and enamel, representing her seated in a folding chair, her feet resting upon the lower portion of a standard which supports a pillow for lace-making. As, aside from the results which followed the introduction of the art in the country by Barbara Uttman, but little lace has ever been made there, she may certainly be regarded as almost the sole patron of lace-making in Germany. The country, more than a century later, had an impetus given to its lace industry by the workers who fled from France after the revocation of the Edict of Nantes, and similar refugees established the manufacture of lace in Switzerland.

The earlier English sovereigns gave little encouragement to the production of lace. When a number of Flemish refugee lace-makers sought a home in England, in 1572, Queen Elizabeth exercised a mistaken zeal in not only refusing to harbor them, but in having them forcibly expelled from the country, thereby nipping in the bud what might have proved of great good to England. Later sovereigns strove to make the manufacture of bone lace profitable by keeping out Flemish laces, but the early lace industry of England was not prosperous, at least, in comparison with that of most Continental countries of Europe. The foundation of what it had, however, was laid by a few of the scattering Flemish exiles, or at least they helped to strengthen somewhat a tottering foundation. James I. managed to blight it to a great extent by granting importing monopolies, but his queen, Anne of Denmark, strove to make amends for the ill-advised course pursued by her husband, by giving it what protection she could in patronizing it, and using domestic laces largely for her own wardrobe and that of her children. The making of Honiton grew somewhat prosperous, at length, though lace was never a leading manufacture of the country. Queen Adelaide, wife of the old sailor king, William IV., encouraged it to some extent, as had George II. and George III., and Queen Victoria has patronized it in a still greater degree, until it is now almost as prosperous as in the days when loom lace was unknown.

Lace-making in Denmark was introduced by fugitive monks at the time of the Reformation, and Elizabeth of Denmark, queen of Christian II., is also credited with first causing its production in the country; possibly both aided, though but one lace establishment has ever existed in Denmark, that being situated at North Schleswig. Christian IV. gave it encouragement, and in 1712 some women from Brabant settled at Tönder, making what is called Tönder lace.

St. Bridget is said to have founded lace-making in Sweden, at Wadstena, on her return from Italy, though this is also disputed. There are, however, at the Northern Museum at Stockholm, some altar cloths in rich point, said to be the work of Swedish nuns before the monasteries and convents were abolished, and it is probable, therefore, that nuns introduced the work; though whether St. Bridget or Swedish nuns is a matter of little consequence, since the lace manufactures of Sweden are not extensive or important.

The Duchess of Hamilton, afterward Duchess of Argyll, introduced lace-making in Scotland, forming a sort of home, or school, in 1752, where orphan girls learned to make a simple lace of a lozenge pattern. A few years later, children in the schools generally were taught to make lace, or "pearlin" as it was universally called; but the custom, as well as the industry itself, soon died out.

We have no account of lace being made in Ireland until the close of the seventeenth century. About 1700, the Dublin Society was formed, though not regularly incorporated until many years later, and the members strongly encouraged bone lace-making in Ireland, especially by the children. Lady Denny was the chief patroness of the industry at this time, and the Society commissioned her to offer prizes for the best specimens of lace-work. A Mrs. Armstrong, of County Kilkenny, also employed and instructed girls in making lace. Lady Bingham founded and supported a lace manufactory in County Mayo, which is still prosperous. Lady de Vere instituted the manufacture of Irish point at Curragh, using her Brussels point as patterns, and the result was such a complete success that Louise, Queen of the Belgians, happening upon a dress of this lace, was so much pleased with it that she purchased it and took it to Brussels, thereby literally "carrying coals to Newcastle." Charles Walker introduced the manufacture of Limerick lace in 1829 at Mt. Kennet, in Limerick, and a school established at Belfast by Miss Jane Clark imitated successfully Spanish and Venetian points. There is still a lace school in County Cork under the patronage of the nuns of the convent at Mallow.

The Countess of Erne has also established schools for Valenciennes in County Fermanagh. Other schools exist, but the emigration of young Irish girls to the United States has interfered greatly with the enlargement of the lace industry.

Greece, though termed the cradle of embroidery, as well as the cradle of liberty, learned her lace-making from Italy. This one naked fact history vouchsafes us, but seems to have omitted altogether any account of the patrons of the art.

Russia makes little fine lace, though Peter the Great established a manufactory of silk laces at Novogorod, which has since died out. Another, more successful, was begun in Moscow by a Russian lady. This establishment makes what is called Moscow point.

In 1872 the Princess Marie Chigi Giovanelli and the Countess Andriana Marcello established a school for lace-workers at Burano. An old lace-worker, named Cencia di Scarpariola, who had not forgotten the mode of making Venetian laces, was employed to teach the different methods and stitches. The school was placed under the charge of Anna d'Este Bellorio. Burano, a small island near Venice, had formerly been the seat of manufacture for the grounded Venetian points, which failed to compete with those of Brussels and Alençon, and the manufacture was discontinued altogether. The school established in 1872, however, has prospered and really been of great benefit to the island. The lace-making in the school has been varied, no one point, however, being manufactured, though both ancient and modern points are copied with great skill—among them the ancient Venetian, both flat and raised, the Venetian grounded, the early Brussels point or point d'Angleterre, and point d'Alençon. These reproductions nearly equal the original laces, and are very encouraging to the patrons of the school, as well as creditable to the pupils and lace-workers. The fishermen's wives on the island have also adopted the plan of employing their leisure in making lace, and, though still in its infancy, this industry may win back some faint glimmer of the ancient glory the lace-makers of Italy enjoyed.

CHAPTER X.

PATTERNS IN LACE.

The patterns or designs in lace have varied greatly during the four centuries in which the fabric has been generally known, but at all times they have been influenced in a measure by the prevailing taste or fashion of the period in which it was made—so much so that an expert in lace can fix with absolute certainty within a few years of the date of its manufacture, and, in laces of comparatively modern make, can state also the country which produced them.

The designs have, therefore, been classified into five separate styles, no two resembling each other in any remarkable degree, although the style of one period following upon another began to vary gradually until the new design was fixed in a uniform manner, and quite unlike that which preceded it. The five different styles are, first, the Mediæval, which prevailed up to 1550, at which time lace-work was confined to churches and convents. This style is quite remarkable, and is made up of curious figures often grouped together—hideous monsters, sacred emblems, birds, beasts, scroll-work, trees, wreaths and symbols of various kinds. Second on the list comes the Geometrical style, which was greatly in vogue for a period of about seventy years, or from 1550 to 1620. This style was as unlike the Mediæval as possible, being composed of triangles, diamonds, squares, fragments of circles, lozenges, wheels, and all manner of sharp angles and geometrical designs. This style came in favor when lace was first emancipated from the Church, or devoted to general purposes. The object of the lace-workers seemed to be to rid it of all sacred symbols, even at the expense of taste in design; and even the patterns which did not represent sacred subjects seemed so connected with them that a general change was adopted. There was, therefore, a stiffness and exactness about it—a certain regularity which was, in some designs, almost painful. There was also a difference, quite as marked, between Mediæval and Geometrical lace—the former was almost universally worked upon the articles it adorned, while the latter was made movable in order to trim various objects at will, as articles of personal use would scarcely ever wear so long as the trimming, which, being about the edges, did not receive much strain, and might answer for a second garment. Mediæval lace, being often worked upon, or of the threads of the material which it ornamented, could not be removed except by a laborious transferring process, which was quite unsatisfactory, and, indeed, scarcely ever necessary upon articles devoted to church use, which had little wear and were most carefully preserved. At this period, too, art, comparatively speaking, was in its infancy.

Early in the seventeenth century a new life seemed to be given to every branch of art then known and new birth to others. Painting, sculpture, mosaic and marquetry works, inlaying with metals and precious stones, artistic dress, furniture and household decoration, became the passion of the hour. As if by magic, clever artists and workmen endowed with wonderful skill sprang up in various countries of Europe, representing every department of art. This period has been called the Renaissance, and, in many respects, the works then performed have not since been surpassed. Lace at this time became a most artistic production; new, graceful patterns were substituted for the old, angular ones, and the style, workmanship and design of the lace of this period has never been equaled by later efforts.

The Renaissance style in lace is as far as possible removed from the Geometrical. It is rather flowery, being composed of sprays, flowing garlands and festoons of leaves and flowers, mingled with scroll-work. These were distributed over the lace rather closely at the beginning, but latterly at greater distances, the grounds being a variety of handsome lace stitches, and all put together in exquisite combinations. This style dates from 1620, and holds its sway for a full century by the force of its beauty alone.

But time and the people must have changes, even though they may be from better to worse, and for worse it certainly was when the styles of the Renaissance degenerated into the Rococo. Instead of artistic carvings in house decorations, the ormolu and gilding of the Rococo period are now seen, and lace-work, like other arts, seems to decline. The designs become more angular and disconnected; stiff, upright bouquets, with scarcely a drooping flower, are set closely together, uncompromising in their dignity and angularity, leaving little room for a ground of any sort. This Rococo style extends from 1720 to 1770, and, at first, some of the careless grace of arrangement which characterizes the Renaissance clings to it; but this, in time, is altogether lost.

From 1770 the fifth, or Dotted style, gradually comes in vogue, a decided improvement upon the Rococo, certainly, yet lacking the fresh and spirited grace of the Renaissance, and being rather insignificant in design than otherwise. The bouquets still appear, but they have shrunk into small proportions, are placed far apart, the ground between being powdered with open or closed dots, small flowers, rosettes, bees, etc. This style, the last distinct one invented, continued in vogue until 1810. Soon after, machine laces began to supplant those made by hand, and from this, and because the demand was far less than formerly, lace-workers could not earn a living by their skill, and so the manufacture seemed almost to die out. Yet, not quite this, for, as an old Danish woman said, "The lace trade slumbers, but it does not die;" and though the art of making many of the rarest kinds is, to all appearance, lost, and clever inventors may contrive and improve machinery until it works like some human thing, yet there will always be found lovers of art in the world to copy and improve upon the old designs in hand-made lace, and a certain market for it, too, among the wealthy and those who have a passion for procuring what is difficult to obtain. Rarity alone makes many things dear to avaricious eyes, but artistic rarities are dear to us all.

The present patterns among lace workers partake, in some degree, of all the five general styles, and some of the old designs have been copied by skillful fingers intact. As a rule, each country has peculiar patterns of its own; for instance, the Valenciennes of France and of Belgium differs in pattern, and can at once be recognized by a person learned in lace-lore. Aside from this there have been, at all times, special patterns invented for special purposes. The arms of royalty or nobility have, in many instances, been wrought in lace made to order for kings and princes; and there have been found original artists in every period who stepped aside from the old beaten track to shape rare and cunning devices of their own. All Mahommedan lace-workers—and there are but few—refrain from introducing figures of animals or any living thing in their laces, as this is forbidden by the Mahommedan law. The Moors at one time manufactured a chequered lace, upon which the representation of a single living thing never

DEFEAT OF THE SPANISH ARMADA IN POINT D'ARGENTAN.

appeared. For many years the lace-makers of Antwerp clung tenaciously to one pattern, until their products in this line were called *potten kant*, or pot lace, the design being always a vase or flower-pot. This pattern was also worked in other countries.

A family in England preserves a curious piece of lace, upon which is worked Tilbury Fort and queer old ships, said to have been made in memory of the defeat of the Spanish Armada. It is in Argentan point, but was probably the work of some skillful English lace-maker. It was once the property of Queen Charlotte, wife of George III. of England, and was labeled "Queen Elizabeth's lace." It is very doubtful, however, if Queen Elizabeth ever saw it.

We give a section of this curious lace in the cut on previous page. The design is well executed and the ground clear. Many other pieces of lace, peculiar in design, commemorative of some particular occurrence, exist, but they are seldom seen except in special collections, or as heirlooms in old families.

Pattern books for lace have abounded since 1527. The older ones contained designs for cutwork, drawnwork, darned netting, reticella, and the other laces of the day. One, by Quintelle, said to be published in Cologne in 1527, and another by P. Quinty, bears the same date. The former, in a second edition, bears the portrait of Charles V., who established a lace school in Belgium. Taglienti's pattern book, however, issued in Venice about 1530, is the most noted of these early productions, having been pirated from by all the other publishers of pattern books throughout Europe for many years after. In 1530 another was published in Paris by F. Pelegrin. Zoppino, in Venice, put forth another which bears different dates, one being 1529 and the other 1532. In 1534 one was published in Augsburg, by Schartzemberger, but this had many embroidery patterns. Indeed, nearly all had embroidery designs of some sort. Vorsterman, of Antwerp, issued one without date, but as he worked from 1514 to 1542, the book must have been published between these two dates, probably near the latter. Venice then issued several similar books, four appearing before 1550. Later, others were published in Paris, Lyons, Zurich and Frankfort-on-the-Main. The greater number, and most important ones during the sixteenth century, were from Venice, by Valvassore, Pagan, Torello, Bindoni, Foresto, Calepino, Franceschi, Vecellio, Valvassore's heirs, and others. Vinciclo's, which was published in Paris, was composed of various parts, and went through almost numberless editions, as did Vecellio's, near the close of the sixteenth century in Venice. Vinciolo's book was again published in Paris, in 1623, and dedicated to Anne of Austria. One by Mignerak, Paris, 1605, was dedicated to Marie de Medici.

CHAPTER XI.

BRIDAL LACE.

EVER since the period when lace was first used as an article of personal adornment it has been considered especially appropriate for decorating bridal robes, as well as the garments of the lady guests at marriage festivals and ceremonies. Italian reticella was the first needle-made lace known, and though its patterns were unusually geometrical, two or three of its styles were made for especial

ANCIENT BRIDAL LACE.

purposes, with corresponding designs. Chief among these was bridal lace, which was executed in the same manner as reticella, and differed from it only in being invariably made of white flax-thread, and in having its pattern woven of crests, symbols and devices of the family of the bride who wore it, or that of her husband, though often of both. It was much in vogue in Italy at the beginning of the seventeenth century, and was worn upon the wedding day and at the festivities following it.

The design on previous page is from a piece of Italian bridal lace, and is composed of the intermingled devices of the families of Delle Revere and D'Urbino.

Bridal lace of this description was put aside after marriage, being carefully laid away amid sprigs of lavender or other perfume. In many instances, and especially if the bride died young, it was brought forward and used to deck her burial robe. In the south and eastern portions of France this was the invariable custom. In Italy, however, it was often handed down as a precious heirloom, the eldest daughter wearing it upon her marriage day, particularly if a short engagement prevented her from having lace made especially for herself, as the process consumed considerable time, the lace being handmade, and requiring an adept in the art to work out original designs, and those who were especially skillful were often engaged upon previous orders.

This custom of having the bridal lace made especially for the wedding, of designs belonging to the two houses which were to be united, was easily followed in the countries of Italy and France, where the engagement was considered quite as binding as a marriage; but it would hardly find favor in the United States, where engagements are broken at the last moment to gratify a mere whim, and no one wonders at or scarcely remarks it. In this case much bridal lace would become worthless before it was worn, and prove dreadfully inconvenient to the modern young lady whose trousseau, prepared for her wedding with one lover, is often used at her marriage with a second or third, so quickly does another engagement follow the one previously broken.

Although the ancient Italian bridal lace is among the things that were, it is still the fashion, especially in the royal families of Europe, to have the lace which adorns the bridal dress, whatever its quality or style, as well as the veil itself, worked in a pattern in which the royal arms, crests or emblems are displayed. Sometimes, indeed, the whole dress is composed of rare lace worked in national designs.

The Empress Josephine of France was married in a dress trimmed with beautiful lace, her veil being a present from the city of Brussels. It was of the most exquisite point lace, for which the city presenting it is so justly famed; the groundwork was like a cobweb in texture, with a graceful pattern of delicate flowers. In each corner were wrought the imperial crown and cypher, encircled with tasteful flower wreaths. This veil was very long, extending far over the train.

Nor were the bridal laces of Napoleon's second bride less beautiful in design. They were not altogether of Brussels point, being ordered by the Emperor himself, and partly of his favorite lace, of which he was so proud as being French manufacture—point d'Alençon—costing an almost fabulous sum.

Napoleon gave generous orders, aside from this, for

Brussels point á l'Aiguille, both before and after his marriage with the Empress Maria Louisa, for her personal use, and the layette of their son, the King of Rome.

Queen Victoria, being a sovereign in her own right, had the privilege accorded her which few women enjoy—that of choosing her husband; and, as a matter of course, the selection of her own bridal laces. Being patriotic, and wishing to encourage the lace manufacture of her realm, her wedding dress and veil were of English Honiton. The lace industry of the country was at such a low ebb it was a difficult matter to collect a sufficient number of skillful workers to complete the dress within a reasonable length of time. It was made at Beer, a small fishing village, whose workers have always shown much taste and skill. The sprigs were worked separately, and when enough were completed the flowers and other designs were connected by a variety of lace stitches. The workers all wore large white aprons and mob caps, and seemed much elated at being chosen to fill the order for the royal bridal lace. The robe cost a thousand pounds, and was beautifully done, the effect being very graceful and pleasing.

One of the most elaborate trousseaux on record, however, was that of the Empress Eugénie. At the date of her marriage—January 29th, 1853—the Alençon makers were so scattered and few in number it was impossible to procure a veil of this French point. Flounces and other lace garnitures could be had in abundance, but as the veil could not be obtained in Alençon, it was of point d'Angleterre, and the bridal dress was ornamented with the same lace, in order to correspond. The majority of the dresses, however, were trimmed with Alençon.

The trousseau was composed of fifty-four dresses. Mme. Vignon made those for the morning and Mme. Palmyre those intended for evening wear. Among the morning dresses was one of fine embroidery and Valenciennes and Mechlin lace. The robe was lined with white, rose and blue silk. In the evening dresses was one of velvet with flounces of blonde lace decked with bees and crowned eagles in gold. Another was of blue velvet richly trimmed with point d'Alençon; and still another was of pearl-gray satin with nine flounces of Brussels point á l'Aiguille.

There was a civil and a religious marriage, and elaborate costumes were prepared for each. For the civil marriage, which was performed at the Tuilleries on the 29th, Madame Palmyre made two dresses, one of rose-colored satin, profusely ornamented with point d'Angleterre, the corsage and bottom of skirt being draped with bunches of white lilac. The second dress prepared for this ceremony was of white satin, covered with point d'Alençon, an exquisite pattern, and profusely ornamented with diamonds. The empress chose to wear the rose-colored satin, but at the religious ceremony, which was celebrated at the Church of Nôtre Dame on the 30th, she wore a white velvet costume, with an immense train, which was covered with rich point d'Angleterre. The corsage was with basques, heavily trimmed with lace, and sparkling with diamonds. Upon her head she wore a diadem and crown of diamonds and rare sapphires, with orange-blossoms mingled in her hair.

The trousseau of the empress was remarkable in having laces of nearly every description employed in it, there being more foreign than French laces used. Afterward the empress strove to encourage the Alençon as well as other lace industries in France, giving them all the encouragement in her power.

Queen Victoria's eldest child, the Princess Royal of England, who was the namesake and especial pet of her mother, was married in 1858 to Frederick William, then Crown Prince of Prussia only, but now Prince Imperial of Germany. The wedding of the Princess Royal was attended with much pomp, for her father, Prince Albert, was then living, and the Queen seemed to enter into the spirit of the occasion with a greater zest than she has since shown at the marriage of her other children. When the Prince of Wales and the Princess Alice were married she was in the deepest mourning, and too sad and dejected to appear in public; and though she has since laid aside the deeper habiliments of woe, she seems to take little interest in public displays of any sort.

The Princess Royal's bridal dress was of white moiré antique, the petticoat trimmed with three flounces of Honiton lace, each flounce headed with wreaths or festoons of orange-blossoms and myrtle. The bodice was ornamented with Honiton lace, myrtle and orange-blossoms, arranged in a bouquet, with trailing sprays. The train was of moiré, lined with white satin, bordered with satin ruchings, and over these a handsome flounce of Honiton headed with orange and myrtle to match the remainder of the costume. The veil was fastened with Spanish and Moorish pins, and was also of Honiton lace, the design being alternate medallions of rose, shamrock and thistle, with a rich groundwork of leaves of the three national flowers scattered carelessly here and there between the medallions. The princess wore a necklace ear-rings and brooch of diamonds. Her wedding gifts were very handsome, the Emperor William presenting her with some rare jewels, and the King of the Belgians, in accordance with his usual custom, gave her a magnificent lace gift. It was a superb dress of Brussels point *Gaze*, valued at $10,000, which was said to be a marvel of beauty.

Upon this occasion Queen Victoria wore a train of rich mauve velvet, ornamented with three rows of wide Honiton lace, the corsage being covered with lace and sparkling with diamonds. She wore the famous Kohinoor as a brooch. The petticoat was of mauve and silver moiré antique, with a deep flounce of Honiton lace. The Queen wore a royal diadem of diamonds and pearls.

The bridal laces of each of the Queen's daughters—the Princesses Alice, Helena and Louise—were also of the English Honiton, the patterns being like those of the Princess Royal, of the national flowers, the rose, shamrock and thistle. The designs were not precisely similar, yet they did not differ sufficiently to merit separate descriptions.

When the Princess Alexandra of Denmark was married to the Prince of Wales, in 1863, her laces, in deference to her husband's country, were Honiton also. The corsage and petticoat of her dress were white satin, with chatelains of orange flowers and myrtle, and also a garniture of puffs of tulle and flounces of Honiton lace. Her train was of silver moiré antique, beautifully ornamented with tulle puffs, Honiton lace and bouquets of orange and myrtle. Her veil was also of Honiton, fastened with a wreath of orange-blossoms and myrtle. The pattern of her veil and lace flounces was also of the rose, shamrock and thistle; but to these designs were added the Prince of Wales feathers, making an attractive combination. The princess wore a necklace, ear-rings, and brooch of diamonds and pearls, presented by the prince, rivere of diamonds by the corporation of London, a diamond bracelet given by the ladies of Leeds, and an opal and diamond bracelet from the ladies of Manchester.

When Prince Alfred, the Duke of Edinburgh, was married to the Princess Marie of Russia, it was in the Winter Palace, at St. Petersburgh, where the marriage dress, in accordance with the climate, was trimmed with ermine instead of lace.

But when Prince Arthur, the Duke of Connaught, wedded the Princess Louise Margaret of Prussia, March 13th, 1879, her bridal costume was ornamented with rare laces in exquisite patterns. The dress was of white satin, both dress and train being profusely trimmed with point d'Alençon, the veil, which was long and flowing, being of the same beautiful lace, and both veil and flounces in a design of orange-blossoms, roses and myrtle, the latter a favorite flower with Queen Victoria, and also the German emblem of marriage. The veil did not fall over the face, but was attached to a wreath of orange flowers. The handkerchief was of point d'Alençon also, the monogram of the princess being wrought in the lace in one corner, and in the opposite corner was the Prussian eagle. The fan was of Alençon point, attached to a pearl frame, and, like the handkerchief, had the monogram of the princess, the eagle, and also a floral design. The ornaments were elegant diamonds. Among the wedding presents of the duchess was a complete garniture of Brussels point *Gaze*, a gift from the King and Queen of the Belgians.

In the recent royal weddings no profusion of lace has appeared, except in the trousseau of Queen Mercedes of Spain. This was the gift of King Alfonso, and contained many lace and lace-trimmed costumes, fans, mantillas and smaller articles, adorned not only with Spanish laces but foreign points also. The young Queen was especially fond of lace as a garniture, and in all her portraits is represented as wearing it. At her bridal, January 23d, 1878, her dress was of white satin ornamented with lace, and she wore a white mantilla veil. Over her brow was a light crown of diamonds. Among her bridal gifts were gems of rare value as well as rich laces, from her husband and other crowned heads of Europe, the whole array of gifts and trousseau being so extensive and superb as to awaken the wonder of those who obtained the privilege of examining it as to how the fair young queen would manage to wear them all, a doubt soon set at rest by her sad and early death, following so soon upon her marriage that the bridal laces were still a theme for appreciative tongues when her burial robes were donned.

CHAPTER XII.

MATERIALS USED IN LACE.

THE most ancient laces were made of silk thread, gold or silver. Flax was used later, and for centuries it was solely employed for all laces denominated "thread," whether point or pillow-made. At the time when hand-made laces were in their glory, sought after by king and court, and the industry employed half, at least, of the women of the lower classes of Europe, the flax thread used was all spun by hand.

The flax grown in Belgium is finer and better adapted to making lace thread than that of any other country in the world. At one time, when England strove to increase her lace manufactures in order to compete with Flanders, it was found impossible, and the chief reason given was because the flax grown, no matter how carefully cultivated, was far inferior to that of Flanders. The meer at Haarlem was also considered the best place for bleaching the flax-thread in all Europe. The flax is grown at Brabant, Courtrai, Tournay and St. Nicholas, and usually steeped at Courtrai, on account of the clearness of the waters of the river Lys, another celebrated place for bleaching. In Belgium the flax is not now prepared for spinning by those who cultivate it. When the crop is gathered it is sold to factors, who subject it to the steeping, scutching, and all processes necessary to render it ready for spinning.

For many laces, and especially Brussels point, the

thread used is still a cobweb, so even it is and fine. The spinning, therefore, requires a skillful and experienced hand, and so much time and labor is expended upon it that the material itself is very valuable before it passes into the lace-maker's hands. This exceedingly fine thread was first spun in Mechlin, but it is now chiefly manufactured at Brussels, Ghent and Antwerp; also, to some extent, at Lille, Manchester, and other places; Brussels thread, however, bearing the palm in point of fineness.

Darkness and dampness are conditions most favorable to the production of the finest thread, and usually considered indispensable. The spinner, therefore, sits in an underground room, in perfect darkness save for one ray of light, usually sunlight, which is thrown upon the thread as it comes from the distaff. She spins flax of the finest quality, which has been carefully prepared, and as the thread, when drawn out, is scarcely visible to the naked eye, both sight and feeling must be keenly alert, for the touch assists the eye in detecting the slightest unevenness. So sensitive does the spinner's touch become, that every trifling variation in the size of this cobweb is quickly discovered, and the wheel is stopped and the defect remedied at once. A background of black cloth or paper is arranged for the thread where the light falls upon it, to assist the sight in rendering it as distinctly as possible.

Sitting steadily day after day in the gloom and dampness of this cheerless room, the face of the flax-spinner grows very white; her fingers are worn from the constant attrition of the thread, fine though it be; for, as the constant dropping of water will wear stone, so this ceaseless, weary spinning wears the fingers sharp and thin.

The eyes grow dim from the perpetual strain upon them; often, indeed, their sight goes altogether while their owner is yet young in years. Owing to the unhealthfulness of the work, and the extremely high prices hand-spun thread commands, the work pays better than ordinary labor, yet the industry is steadily diminishing. It is to be hoped that at no distant day machines will be improved to such an extent as to be able to produce thread as fine as that which, so far, can only be made by hand, for then this trying and unhealthy labor would be abolished at once. As yet, no machine has been manufactured "whose touch is as gentle as a woman's," the trouble being that the friction is so great as to break the delicate fibre. As the dry air also snaps it, there is no remedy against the underground rooms, for artificial wetting does not answer the same purpose. The amount of thread which these women draw from a single pound of flax is almost beyond belief. In Brussels, from one pound of the flax, thread has been produced which is worth in value from $1,000 to $3,000. What wonder, then, when the thread is so costly, that the laces into which it is wrought are almost priceless? And more especially when a few yards of the lace manufactured from it may be the constant work of one busy woman's lifetime, or, at the very least, the work of her life's prime.

Recently, however, since pillow laces have been so successfully imitated by loom-woven lace, since cotton has become so cheap and plentiful, and the machines for producing fine thread from flax or cotton are growing yearly more and more perfect in their operation, machine-made thread is fast superseding the hand-spun, and cotton is often employed instead of linen, not only in the machine-made and cheaper pillow laces, but also in many of the finer kinds. It is hard to detect the difference between cotton and flax after it is made up into lace, but adepts say the linen is slightly softer than the cotton; it is also considered more durable. As modern point and hand-made pillow laces are manufactured in less quantities than formerly, the choicest of these are still made from flax thread spun by hand.

The cotton thread used in Nottingham, bobbin-net and other machine laces, as well as that employed for the loom-made imitations of the pillow—Valenciennes, Mechlin, Cluny, Honiton, Torchon, Maltese, Russian, Breton and others—is but slightly twisted and made from the very finest material, usually of that kind called "Sea Island cotton," though the small islands where this superior cotton grows are scarcely large enough to supply material for all the thread and textiles which are stamped with their name. The thread manufactured in Scotland is considered the best. Lace-makers are partial to using cotton, as it does not break in the working so easily as flax.

Black flax and cotton threads are employed, to some extent, in the manufacture of a few laces, usually French. The black thread laces, however, are losing ground, as they do not preserve their color, or, rather, the black dye soon fades. Black cotton thread is greatly used in the cheap black netting and other loom laces, though usually the thread is white when woven and afterward dyed.

Black silk thread is used to a great extent in manufacturing French and Spanish laces. The early nuns, in both Italy and Spain, spun their own thread, whether of flax or silk, and it was for a long time called "nun's thread." The black silk used in lace-making is of the best quality that can be obtained, and has for a long time been spun altogether by machinery. There is a large spinning establishment at Barcelona, Spain, where black silk thread of a very superior quality for laces is made. This thread is extensively used for French and Spanish blondes, for Chantilly laces and the silk guipures. The silk thread for Chantilly lace is prepared without gloss, and for this reason many suppose Chantilly to be a black flax-thread lace. Sedan also spins black silk lace thread, and it is produced to some extent in other parts of France, and also in England.

White silk is prepared for blondes and white guipures, and colored silks in smaller quantity at Barcelona.

Llama thread, used to make a lace bearing the same name, is generally supposed to be manufactured from the hair of the llama, an animal common to South America, which is domesticated in Peru, and used as a beast of burthen. The hair is naturally brown and mottled, and as it is said to prove utterly useless, it is hard to discover why the worsted lace, which is generally manufactured of a wiry worsted thread, is called llama lace. Both black and white thread were used for the purpose, but it is now in little demand. The thread used for white cashmere lace is similar, but softer in texture.

Yak thread is also of wool, and used for a very coarse, cheap guipure, copying the simpler and more open patterns of the silk guipures. Mohair and alpaca threads are employed in laces of similar names; sometimes used for trimming cheap black dresses.

Aloe fibres have been prepared into a sort of thread from which the peasants of Spain, Italy, Portugal and some of the Mediterranean islands make a rude lace of little durability and value.

Gold and silver threads for lace are made in a variety of ways. The gold is of a very fine wire, drawn out until as pliable as cotton or flax, and wound so closely over a silk thread as to conceal the silk foundation altogether. This gold wire is usually in reality silver, with a very slight coating of gold, and much cheating has been done in the manufacture and sale of gold thread. The finest is altogether of gold, which varies in quality according to the purpose for which it is designed, and that with considerable alloy is said to wear better than the purer gold.

Silver thread is of silver wire wound over silk; fine twisted threads of gold or silver are also used for making lace.

CHAPTER XIII.

ANCIENT LACE.

THE mediæval laces were few in number, but extremely elaborate, though the majority of them were heavy in design. They were made entirely with the needle, except when linen or network was used for a foundation. When the latter was used, the figures were darned in ; when the former, a portion of the threads of the linen were drawn and the remainder worked with thread into fanciful patterns, or figures were cut out, button-holed and then filled in with all manner of stitches, the heavy part usually being embroidered. Later, the needle-made laces led to point, and the knotted and braided laces gave rise to the use of the pillow.

There are but six distinct varieties of ancient lace—Cutwork, Drawnwork, Darned Netting, Reticella, Knotted Lace and Plaited Lace. As being the most ancient, we give the first place to

CUTWORK.

Although this is declared by some to belong more properly to embroidery than to lace, it certainly deserves a place in a history of the latter, for cutwork seems a sort of connecting link between the two. At first, cutwork was introduced into linen embroidery in small designs, very similar to the openwork embroidery of the present day. The open spaces were small and unpretentious, only the larger being filled in with lace stitches of any sort, and these were usually very simple.

CUTWORK AND LINEN EMBROIDERY.

The above illustration shows one of these earlier designs. Gradually the open spaces grew into larger and bolder proportions, and while the smaller were often left unfilled, the larger were closed up with a variety of open-work stitches. The linen was usually cut out in some geometrical design—squares, diamonds, triangles, the Maltese cross being the most common. These lace stitches led to making an ornamentation for altar-cloths, robes and articles of wearing apparel of lace stitches alone; this was the first real lace, and was called Reticella.

Cutwork, therefore, while it sprang from embroidery, merged into the Italian reticella,* and from being mingled with embroidery, reticella came to be employed with both in ornamenting the same article; then the embroidery was dropped in connection with it, cutwork appearing with reticella only, and finally it was superseded by the latter altogether. It was, until toward the latter period of its popularity, worked upon the article it was designed to ornament, never appearing separately.

Cutwork was made in a variety of ways. The first, already mentioned, was to cut out of the linen used for the foundation the shapes desired, these being filled with lacework designs, button-holed, darned or overcast. Later, it was usually made in an altogether different manner. Threads of strong linen, fine or coarse, according to the work, were arranged in a frame, forming squares, intersected by various other designs, stars and smaller squares. When these threads had been arranged and drawn tightly in the frame after an approved design, a piece of fine open cloth, then called quintain and afterwards known as French lawn, was gummed at the back of the threads. When dry, the lines of thread were neatly and firmly overcast, and this done, the quintain between the lines was entirely cut away, which left a mere skeleton or network of the overcast threads, which was filled in with stitches or left entirely open at the pleasure of the worker.

Sometimes—and this was the most tedious and expensive kind of cutwork—the threads, after being gummed upon the quintain, were button-holed, and when the superfluous cloth was cut away the open spaces were divided up by threads and stitches, circles being ornamented with lace wheels of various sorts, and squares or diamonds with intersecting lines. Sometimes, as in the older style, the cut-out figures, when small, were left quite open.

In the earlier wardrobe accounts of Queen Elizabeth cutwork is mentioned under the name of *opus scissum;* later accounts, however, gave it the name by which it is generally known. In one instance the entry made is as follows: "A mantel of lawn cutwork wrought throughout with cutwork of pomegranates, roses, honeysuckles and cum-crowns." Again appears: "One yard of double Flanders cutwork, worked with Italian purl;" also "Three suits good lawn cutwork ruffs, edged with good bone lace."

Cutwork can be traced as far back as the twelfth century. The most ancient relics of ornamental work in existence are cutwork and embroidery. The former often appears in ancient paintings. In Hampton Court Palace is a painting of the "Last Supper," by Sabastian Ricci, in which the table-cloth is bordered with cutwork.

It was mostly worked in convents, and especially in Italy and the south of Germany. It was made with colored silks, gold and silver threads, but usually with flax thread. It was scarcely attempted in England, and though made to some extent in Flanders, the Italian was considered the finest. In Italy it was called *punto tagliato*, and in France *point coupé*.

Cutwork is but little manufactured at the present time, though it is occasionally met with in Sweden and Denmark. Collars and cuffs are made of it, decorated with stars, crosses and geometrical designs, but it always presents an ancient appearance, as though it was a relic of mediæval days.

DRAWNWORK.

This is almost, if not quite, as ancient as cutwork. It was at first rather rude and simple in design, as indeed it is at the present day; but early in the seventeenth century it became more artistic in style and execution, and many beautiful laces were successfully copied in drawnwork.

The most ancient manner of working it was to take a piece of linen, the cloth might be coarse or fine, but the threads must be even, to make the work appear well. Both warp and weft threads were then drawn out in clusters, leaving only a network ground; generally three threads of the material were left at equal distances apart, in order to give strength to the work. These threads were then overcast, or rendered firm by a single stitch at each intersection. Sometimes a design was first marked out upon the linen, and the threads to be drawn out were clipped all along the outlines of this design, care being taken to leave the three threads needed to form the groundwork intact on every side. This solid portion was then embroidered, often with colors, while the groundwork of threads was overcast or button-holed, thus appearing like regular square meshes.

This illustration of drawnwork is in the renaissance style, in which a flowing pattern is left in the solid linen, while the threads in the ground are drawn, and the remaining ones overcast in the manner just described.

DRAWNWORK—SEVENTEENTH CENTURY.

The embroidery was often in colored silks, and the threads were also overcast in colors, but linen was usually preferred for the groundwork, on account of its fineness and the strength of its wiry thread, silk being altogether too soft for the purpose.

Later, the finest linen and lawn were employed. In this

the pattern was marked out and outlined by a thread run around it, the design being delicate sprays of leaves or flowers. It was then button-holed with fine flax thread, the

MODERN DRAWNWORK.

threads of the fabric designed for the ground were clipped and drawn in regular but small spaces, the remaining threads being overcast with the finest flax, which left a ground of delicate, square meshes, like those of the finest lace. The edge was button-holed in points or scallops, or the threads were fringed and knotted in some intricate pattern. By this means delicate and beautiful work was obtained which closely imitated lace.

Drawnwork, though very ancient, was never practised to as great an extent as cutwork, darned netting or reticella; later, it could not compete with point or pillow laces, yet to a certain extent it has dragged along a poor existence, and is in some countries nearly the only kind of lace-work known. It continued in Russia, being used to decorate towels, table and bed-linen, only coarser patterns being employed for this purpose.

In the illustration entitled Modern Drawnwork is shown a specimen of that used for household linen. This work was employed almost invariably to decorate the home-manufactured linen of our grandmothers and great-grandmothers less than a century ago, in our own country. In many instances, however, the weft threads were only drawn out, and then crossed or knotted together at regular intervals with the needle and a strong thread.

In several of the countries of South America this work still exists; for, though settled by Spaniards and Portugese from countries where early lace-making was practiced, only the ruder kinds seem to have been attempted. Drawnwork, however, is quite common in Chili and Brazil. Whether it was introduced into the United States by early Spanish or Danish settlers it is impossible to say. It was little practiced in France and England at this time, though known to the Dutch settlers of New York.

In Denmark the finest specimens of drawnwork are

made at the present day, some closely resembling lace, and called "point" by courtesy. Germany also manufactures it to some extent, as well as Sweden. These appear in a limited quantity in the markets, though they do not bear a remarkably high price. They are usually known as Tönder lace, Swedish lace, and as Hamburg and Dresden point. Some of the last-mentioned kinds are of great beauty, and it is hard to believe they are made from drawn muslin.

Drawnwork was known in Italy as *punto tirato*, in France as *broderie de Nancy*. It was also anciently called *opus tiratum*, and in England it is sometimes termed Indian work.

CHAPTER XIV.

ANCIENT LACE (*continued*).

DARNED NETTING.

NETTING is of very ancient origin, and darned netting dates back as far as cutwork, though not so far as embroidery. It is impossible to give the date of its first existence, but it is generally acknowledged to have been practiced by experts in the art of needlework in the thirteenth century all over Europe; for, while cutwork, drawnwork and the ancient laces were confined to one locality, darned netting seemed more generally known.

The ancient name of darned netting was lacis; it was also called opus araneum; in Italian, it was *punta a stuora;* in Spanish, *puntas de randas;* in French, *point conté.*

It was extensively used for coverlets, for bed and window-curtains, for bed-valances and other draperies, being less employed as an article of personal adornment than other primitive laces. While used for church purposes exclusively, it was put on altar-covers, grave-clothes and the like, and often represented scriptural groups and the figures of saints, mingled with lozenge patterns, foliage or flowers. Some of these pieces were very elaborate, though they could scarcely be called true to life, since only an expert could decipher the meaning of the rather clumsy figures. Afterward Gothic monsters became popular; these appeared in a multitude of forms.

The illustration represents one of these monsters. Still later, flowers, birds, bees and foliage were taken for models, and beasts of various kinds.

ANCIENT DARNED NETTING.

The netting used was silk or linen, and the pattern was put in with the regular darning stitch, being often outlined with a heavy thread. The threads used were either linen, silk, gold or silver. Often upon a groundwork of colored silk net, the figures were darned in with a variety of other hues, usually strongly contrasting with the ground. It was often worked in squares, one square being filled with a figure, the next one being of plain net, and so they alternated throughout the work.

The early pattern books were devoted almost exclusively to darned netting, giving curious and strange designs. In one published in 1587 is given for a pattern the seven planets, together with the mythological characters of various kinds. The patterns of renaissance period are the most graceful, being composed of various flowing wreaths, flowers and scrollwork.

Spiderwork was a name given to one variety of ancient darned netting; indeed, some of the oldest specimens of it preserved bear this name. Some apply it generally to all darned netting of one period, but it is more properly given to some peculiarly delicate specimens which were darned with fine thread upon net composed of close, light meshes. The work being unusually fine and airy it was given the name from its fancied resemblance to a spider's web.

The specimens of spiderwork which have withstood the ravages of time, either from their unusual strength or from particular care, and are preserved as relics in lace collections, partake more of the geometrical than the mediæval style. Three pieces of this lace are mentioned in the Exeter "Inventory," dated 1327, and there are specimens bearing quite as old a date in the Bock collection of the South Kensington Museum, England.

The illustration we give is one of these specimens, and bears the date of the thirteenth century. It is of silk network, and the pattern has been described by a writer well versed in ancient laces as being "small embroidered shields and crosses," though to any ordinary mind the figures appear more like forget-me-nots and triangles. Another specimen of a century later, also of silk, has a a mediæval gammadion pattern, consisting of alternate small squares and a larger figure which somewhat resembles a double X, though one letter is attached to the top of its mate instead of being placed beside it, as is now the custom.

SPIDERWORK.

Darned netting, like drawnwork, lived through the age of pillow and point lacework, and still exists in the age of loom laces. It was manufactured, however, in greater quantities than drawnwork, being more easy of execution, and for a long time was almost the only thing in lacework adapted to household draperies, as other work of this character was too expensive and elaborate to be used except in small quantities. The darned netting of the present day, however, is mostly devoted to tidies and small articles of home manufacture. Lately, a darned netting of strong flax-thread, the natural color, has been revived, called antique lace or *guipure d'art*. This is made into squares, edgings and insertions, and is devoted to ornamenting curtains, cushions, counterpanes, pillow shams and similar articles; for, like the darned netting of ancient make, it seems peculiarly adapted to this class of ornamental drapery, holding a comparatively humble, though honorable, place among laces, and though unlike that of ancient date, which had no rival in this line, it is still very popular on account of its strength and beauty, though it is obliged to compete with the cheaper products of the loom.

CHAPTER XV.

ANCIENT LACE (*continued*).

RETICELLA.

THIS is the first needle-made lace of which we have any account. Like all the earlier laces it was extensively made in Italy and the Ionian isles, being called in the latter, Greek lace. This last was much coarser than the Italian, the Venetian reticella being the finest produced. It was made in nearly all the convents of Italy, and gradually spread into Spain, Germany, France, Flanders, and, lastly, England. The Italian designs were copied in Vinciolo's pattern-book of 1587, and were used all over Europe, the English patterns only having a distinctive character—they displayed more stitches than the Italian, but were, upon the whole, poorly executed; in reality, comparatively little reticella was made in England.

Reticella evolved from cutwork, as did point lace at a much later date from reticella. The first two were often confounded, although they were very unlike. Both were called nun's work, and both were invented by Italian nuns; besides, they often appeared worked side by side, and this will readily account for one being taken for the other, and especially at first, when both were comparatively little known. Alternate squares of cutwork and reticella were often worked together.

In the design given below, which is one of the sixteenth century, linen embroidery and cutwork are mingled in one square, the other is reticella.

This lace is mentioned in the Sforza inventory of 1493, and in the sixteenth century became the favorite trimming for the costumes of the nobility of Europe. As it was made entire of flax or silk thread, it was suitable both for articles of underwear, for ruffs, collars, caps, robes,

CUTWORK, LINEN EMBROIDERY AND RETICELLA.

dresses, for infant's layettes, and for ornamenting the robes of priests and bishops.

It was made by fixing threads in a linen or plaited thread-frame, these threads being in groups, or sometimes radiating from a common centre, thus forming a sort of groundwork or foundation for the figures of the pattern. The thread-frame was tacked to a piece of parchment, and over the foundation was worked in various shapes button-hole, rope and Genoa stitches. The button-hole stitch is familiar to all; the rope stitch is made by simply winding the foundation with the thread used in working; and the Genoa stitch is made by passing the needle

RETICELLA.

containing the thread over and under two or three foundation threads alternately, as in darning. When the pattern was completed, the last touches were put to the work in the way of numerous picots, or knots and dots.

Reticella changed in design, according to the period in which it was worked. The mediæval patterns were first in vogue to a small extent, then geometrical, with a partiality toward wheels and circles.

The specimen which we give on the preceding page is from Corfu, the design being somewhat Oriental. Only the coarsest productions of ancient reticella remain, as the finer have either become worn, or, under the infliction of repeated starchings, have rotted away. A few specimens may still be found in old convents and churches, but these are coarse in quality and inferior in design.

Within the past century attempts have been made to produce imitations of this lace, but usually they have been quite unsatisfactory. Mlle. Dugrenot, a French lady, however, has met with excellent success, having reproduced it in the most perfect style. She exhibited an exquisitely beautiful specimen at the International Exhibition of 1867.

Francesca Bulgaria recently instructed the Florentine schools in the art of making this lace, but her success was not remarkable. Since it is entirely produced by the needle, and evidently requires experience to render the worker expert, it is scarcely probable that it will ever again be made to any great extent, as the call for it is very limited, and only ancient specimens valued. The most interesting and really valuable pieces of reticella now in existence may be found in the convents of Milan.

Reticella was worked in almost endless designs, but the patterns were coarser than those of the laces of the present day. It may be said to belong almost exclusively to the sixteenth century, as it was little worked, if at all, previous to that date, and early in the seventeenth century it was superseded by points.

It bore few names, however, being reticella to nearly all countries; aside from this, it went by the name of Greek lace, though only the coarser productions, and in Italy it was called *punto d'aere*, and sometimes *punto a reticella.* When made in special designs, however, it went by various names, the famous bridal lace of this period being reticella, and carnival lace also.

The latter was made in the same manner as reticella, and was extremely popular in Italy toward the close of the seventeenth century. It was manufactured exclusively for carnivals and masquerades, and no lady's toilette was considered complete unless it could boast a few pieces of carnival lace.

Its peculiarity consisted in its pattern alone, which was made up of grotesque figures of various sorts—clowns, fools'-caps, and the paraphernalia of carnivals generally, or whatever would remind one most forcibly of the occasion on which it was to be worn. Many of these designs were very cleverly executed, and the lace was treasured as heirlooms in the families to which it belonged, seldom seeing the light of day, except at the carnival season. Being remarkably durable on account of the strong flax thread generally used in its making, it was almost imperishable, some pieces being retained in families long after the rage for making it had died out.

On page 108 is a specimen of this lace which was worked in the sixteenth century, being of Italian production. The piece is admirably worked, the square in the heading showing fine button-hole and rope stitches almost exclusively, the dots being small and clear. The

CARNIVAL LACE.

clown in the point is wrought in Genoa stitch, as is a portion of the surrounding work, while the edge is fine button-holing, which, being arranged in tiny scallops with occasional dots, resembles to some extent modern tatting,

ENGLISH RETICELLA, SEVENTEENTH CENTURY.

though the stitch is made with the needle instead of a shuttle.

Beetles were introduced in reticella toward the last of its popularity, their numerous legs being easy to work in the button-hole bars. The early Renaissance style rendered these latter productions rather more graceful than former ones, introducing scrollwork, marguerites and foliage, which, though imperfectly rendered, was more pleasing than the stiff, unmeaning figures and the angular designs of the geometrical period.

England manufactured reticella to a small extent during the seventeenth century; and, in fact, nearly all the attempts at point lace in England, until very recently, were of the reticella type. The patterns are rather more modern than those of the Italian or Greek reticella, and resemble to a certain extent the fine Irish crochet work, being scarcely lighter in design or finer in material and execution than the crochet, which is usually of flax thread, and worked in very pretty patterns. The reticella manufactured in England, however, was of a very limited quantity, as it was scarcely attempted until the time when that rich old lace was superseded by lighter and more modern productions.

CHAPTER XVI.

ANCIENT LACE (*continued*).

KNOTTED POINT.

THIS is an ancient lace, mention being made of it in the Sforza inventory, 1493. In Taglienti's pattern-book of 1530 are given special designs for it, by him styled "groppi." Little space, however, was given to knotted point in this or other pattern-books of the day, a proof that though known at this time it was not so popular as reticella, though it flourished, after a fashion, long after reticella was laid aside.

The manufacture of knotted lace was confined to Italy and the Ionian Isles almost exclusively. It was worked, as its name denotes, by knotting the threads together, and the style was, at best, quite heavy, almost clumsy in fact, it being impossible to carry out any effective design in this manner, and especially without the aid of the pillow. The knotted lace of this period, therefore, was primitive in pattern and rather stiff in effect. It could, in consequence, be little used, except to border table covers and window or bed drapery, though some of the finer designs were employed for trimming garments. The threads used were coarse flax or finer silk, and gold and silver tissue. The flax thread was usually in an unbleached state, and often so coarse as to be like a heavy cord.

The illustration is of Italian make. This lace was called in Italy *punto a gropo*. It flourished in the latter part of the fifteenth, and, to a certain extent, throughout the sixteenth century, but in the seventeenth it was

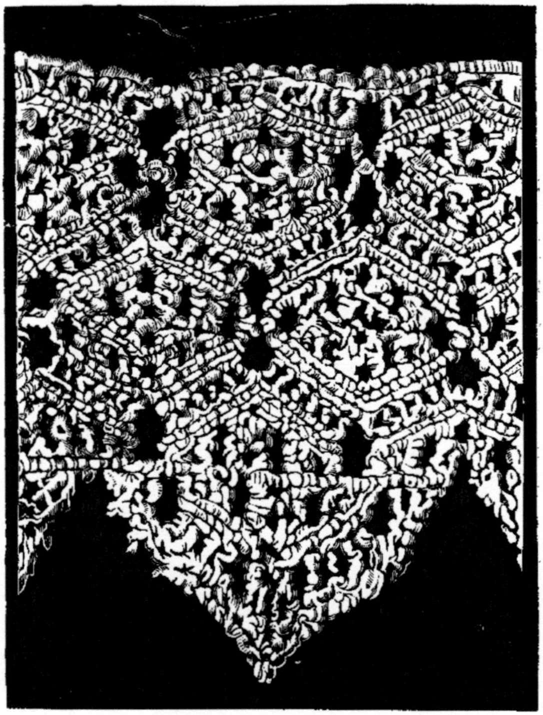

KNOTTED POINT.

eclipsed by the point and pillow laces, then in their prime. But few specimens of old knotted lace can be found at the present day, even in Italy, and it is never met with elsewhere.

In the eighteenth century it was revived under the name of macramé, which appeared in lighter and more graceful patterns, being knotted upon a pillow, though, even in macramé, coarse flax thread is often preferred, as more closely resembling the ancient lace, and also more suitable for ornamenting heavy draperies.

In the old knotted laces the only patterns consisted of clusters of knots alternating with more open spaces, the designs quite irregular or approaching the geometrical style. During the sixteenth century the pillow was adopted for knotted point, but as Italy, with the exception of Genoa, was never celebrated for pillow laces, and Flanders did not take kindly to knotted point, this scarcely rendered it more popular than before.

PLAITED LACE.

This is the most modern of what are termed mediæval or ancient laces, though gold and silver lace was braided from the beginning, and for a long time the plaiting was extremely simple in design and manner of execution, the material alone rendering the production valuable. It was called "passament," and resembled to a certain extent the simplest patterns of what we now know as passementerie Afterward, the gold-plaited laces were christened point d'Espagne, from the fact that Spain manufactured the choicest of these.

When the pillow was adopted for knotted point and other laces, it was found that plaiting was a much easier method than knotting, besides being admirably adapted to gold and silver threads. By the use of the pillow, gold lace could be plaited far more elaborately than without it, consequently the pillow was soon used altogether in the manufacture of metal laces of all sorts. Gold lace has been worn to some extent ever since the fifteenth

PLAITED LACE.

century, in simple braids at first, and only adopted by kings or warriors of high rank. Then it became a popular garniture for court dresses and trains, being greatly worn by the French Court, until at present it is but little manufactured, and only employed for military decoration, or to bedeck the liveries of servants of royalty.

At all times gold and silver laces have displayed little art in their construction, the designs being quite regular and uniform, but little ingenuity being shown in their manufacture, probably because the wire is a little stiff for being wrought in complicated designs. The pattern-books of both the sixteenth and seventeenth centuries contain many devices for plaiting gold and silver laces, but these varied little. Italy made the first gold lace, then Spain, and afterward, to some extent, France, under Colbert's administration. The latter was a copy of the Spanish production, and was called point d'Espagne, though, like most imitations, it was inferior to the original article. It is now scarcely manufactured, except at Seville, Barcelona and Valencia.

The plaited thread laces, however, exhibited much ingenuity in design and workmanship. Flax thread was used, both the natural tint and white, also silk threads of various sizes and colors. These plaited laces were the lightest of any produced at this time. Both reticella and knotted point were rather heavy, and plaited lace allowed the worker to strike out in a new path, working pointed and scalloped edges, and also making insertion. In the beginning, reticella designs were copied, but the Genoese workers at length cast these aside, adopting the lozenge pattern, and making the work much lighter in every respect. Some of these (see page 114) were so open as to suggest a certain poverty of design, but the contrast from the heavy laces previously worn was so great that this was scarcely considered a disadvantage. On account of being so light, the plaited laces were much used to border ruffs, and also used to some extent for the deep cuffs at

GENOESE COLLAR LACE.

the wrist. The illustration shows one of the lightest of the designs in plaited lace, and has the Vandyked border so popular at one time.

The plaited laces of Genoa were greatly in favor during the latter part of the sixteenth century, or until

GENOESE PLAITED LACE.

the falling collar was adopted, which was in the early portion of the seventeenth, when they were found too light to answer the purpose. Their extreme lightness, being just what was required to plait in a ruff, was quite an objection in the plain falling collar, and consequently a heavier lace was needed. Genoa plaited lace, therefore, was at once made in heavier patterns, and the Genoa stitch, used in working reticella, was mixed with the plaiting. This Genoa stitch was used for the heavier parts, and many of the outlines; the lighter portion of the design was plaited. This combined production of the pillow and needle was especially popular for collars and cuffs, and was generally denominated collar lace (see illustration on page 116).

This style of lace, of which we give an excellent representation, was worn for many years, and appears to such an extent in the portraits of the period, until its rosettes and scallops are familiar to all.

The Genoese also made a lace similar in design to this collar lace, but it was plaited upon the pillow entirely, and, consequently, somewhat cheaper in price.

The illustration on preceding page is taken from a section of a collar which has been carefully preserved for nearly two centuries. It is made of fine Lombardy thread. At present Genoa makes only silk guipures and modern macramé.

Plaited lace was imitated, from the time of its first popularity, in tape and braid, as point and pillow laces are at the present day. In the most elaborate of these ancient imitations the braid was first plaited upon the pillow, and then laid in place and connected with brides and numerous lace stitches.

The modern laces, which spring from the ancient plaited lace, are the silk and thread guipures, the Maltese and the Cluny; but these may be more properly classed among modern pillow laces.

CHAPTER XVII.

MODERN LACE.

SOME writers advance the theory that the idea of lace-making was suggested to woman by a spider's web. This idea is very reasonable, from the fact that some lace stitches—the filling up of wheels, rosette-centres and the flimsy brides that connect the heavier figures of the design when regular grounds are not employed—form an almost exact copy of a spider's web. Although the heavier ancient laces undoubtedly sprung from cutwork and embroidery, one of the lightest kinds anciently known was termed spider-work.

Again, we have writers who aver that the finest patterns of modern lacework are derived from the fantastic shapes the frost takes upon window panes; and, since frostwork and spiders' webs were in existence long before lace was dreamed of, we are unable to dispute the fact of these assertions, even if they seemed less reasonable than they now do.

For several centuries the making of lace has been one of the most popular of the art industries, and as an article of adornment it rivals jewels of gold and gems; for lace, properly worn, gives an air of delicacy and refinement to the wearer. But there is a vast difference between lace and gems, from the fact that, while gold and precious stones have an intrinsic value before the hand of the lapidary or artificer has touched them, lace, which equals in value all but a few of the rarest gems, is fabricated from the cheapest and simplest things in nature—the silk-worm's web or the fibre of the flax plant, the latter being poor, weedy-looking, with a most unassuming flower. An art industry, indeed, it may be called, since its costliness is the result of patient artistic labor alone.

During the period when lace was so extensively manufactured and worn in immoderation by the French and English Courts the writers of the day gave much attention to ridiculing or praising it. In 1651 a Flemish poet, Jacob Van Eyck, eulogied in Latin verse the making of lace. "Of many arts," he said, "one surpasses all the threads woven by the strange power of the hand, threads which the dropping spider would vainly attempt to imitate, and which Pallas would confess she had never known. For the maiden, seated at her work, plies her fingers rapidly, and flashes the smooth balls and thousand threads into the circle. Often she fastens with her hand the innumerable needles, to bring out the various figures of the pattern. Often again she unfastens them, and in this, her amusement, makes as much profit as the man earns by the sweat of his brow. The issue is a fine web, open to the air with many an aperture, which feeds the pride of the whole globe; which encircles with its fine border cloaks and tuckers, and shows grandly round the throats and hands of kings; and, what is more surprising, this web is of the lightness of a feather, which in its price is too heavy for our purses."

Lace went by the name of "passament" in both England and France throughout the sixteenth century. All braided gimps were known by this name, as well as gold and silver lace, and this is, in all probability, the reason it was bestowed upon lace. The French name, *dentelle* was not given to it until it had a toothed, or what we call a pearled, edge. In Italy lace is called by three different names—*merletto*, *trina*, and *pizzo*, the last in Genoa. In France it is *dentelle*, in Spain *encaje*, in Germany it is termed *Spitzen*, and in Holland *kanten*.

Lace is composed of two distinct parts—the ground and the pattern. The network ground, made up of round, square or hexagonal meshes, is often spoken of by its French name, *réseau*. Ancient laces did not have this ground, neither did early points, nor do guipures. In these laces the ground is made up of long or short bars of thread, which connect the figures of the pattern together in an irregular manner, and in the more elaborate laces these bars are covered with fine button-hole stitches, and edged with dots or picots.

Sometimes lace has a ground made up of large meshes surrounding one part of the principal pattern or design, and small meshes about another portion, thus producing the effect of a more elaborate pattern by simply varying the ground. When the heavier design is connected by bars, which are usually called by their French name, *brides*, the more irregularity they show the more tasteful the work. The pattern, whether it be flower, scrollwork, or other figure, is also termed the *gimp*.

Lace has two edges. One is straight, for the purpose of sewing upon the garment it is designed to decorate; this edge is called the footing. Sometimes a very narrow, straight bordering, like a fine lace braid, is made separately and sewn on the edge to strengthen it; this is also called the footing when disconnected, as well as when sewn on the broader lace. When this separate footing is not employed, a stronger thread is introduced into the extreme edge of the lace to give it body. The other edge of lace is usually scalloped or Vandyked, made firm by a thread, which is a trifle heavier than the other portion of the ground, except in cases where the heavy part of the pattern comes to the extreme border of the scallop or point. This edge is finished with a short, light, feathery fringe called the pearl or picot.

Many varieties of lace, especially the pillow, have insertions also; these insertions seem to have been first made at Genoa of the plaited lace described in the previous chapter. Insertions have the straight edge, called the footing, on both sides, and are never used for bordering, but for connecting, or, rather, dividing two portions of the garment, while lace proper is reserved for trimming the edge.

Before separate insertions were invented, garments designed for lace ornamentation through the centre had the different breadths united by what was called seaming lace. This was needle-made, of plain or elaborate pattern, wide or narrow, according to the garment decorated or the taste of the worker. If the two widths of cloth to be connected had a selvage, these selvages served as a foundation for the seaming lace, which was always connected with the cloth. If there was no selvage, the edges which were to be connected were first hemmed before the seaming lace was begun. When used upon linen, flax thread was employed; but if the article chanced to be silk, then silk was used for the seaming lace, of similar or contrasting color. The stitches used in making this seaming lace were similar to those in reticella or the earlier point laces, though usually not so fine. This lace was popular for sheets, pillow cases, cushion cloths, shirts, gowns, and many articles of outer apparel. Mention of it is often made in the wardrobe accounts of Queen Elizabeth, King James and Prince Charles, who was afterwards Charles I. It is also employed at the present day in making up household linen in Denmark, Sweden and Russia.

Insertions of the present day do not differ from lace sufficiently to need a separate description; they are almost altogether pillow-made or woven, and are manufactured usually of a pattern to match the lace to which they belong.

Modern hand-made lace is of two kinds, point and pillow, there being but few varieties of the former and many of the latter.

CHAPTER XVIII.

POINT LACE.

VENICE originated point lace, first producing it about 1620.

Point is made on a parchment pattern, and entirely with the needle. *Only one stitch* is used in making it—the button-hole stitch, worked tight or loose—and it is marvelous how many variations of it will be found in a single piece of lace.

But four different countries in Europe have ever produced point lace in any great degree. It is true that time and circumstance have occasionally scattered isolated point lace workers among other countries, but their productions almost invariably partake of the characteristics of the district where they learned the art, and if otherwise, their work appears in such extremely small quantities that it has no effect whatever upon the general market, being in most cases picked up by some lady who delights in whatever is curious in the way of lace.

The centres for manufacturing point lace are four—Italy, Spain, France and Belgium, and in these countries the manufacture is limited to almost one city each. In Italy, Venice was the chief seat; in Spain, Castile; in Belgium, Brussels; in France, Alençon and Argentan.

The real points are few in number, and half of these, being manufactured to little extent at the present day, seldom find their way to American markets, except they are procured to order for lovers of rare laces who have the means to gratify their tastes in this particular; for so elaborate is the workmanship, and so scarce have the choicest patterns become, they are worth their weight in —not gold, but diamonds.

There are but eleven different kinds of point lace known to the commercial world. The name point, however, is incorrectly applied to many of the better kinds of pillow lace, and is also given to several modern productions, which, though properly point, are simply faithful copies of the old specimens, and therefore do not merit a special name. We hear of Irish and English points, but they are only copies of old Italian and Spanish laces, or the early point de France, with a few attempts to copy Brussels point. Again, we hear on every side of point d'Angleterre, which is not an English point at all, but of Brussels manufacture. It received this name from the fact of its being smuggled into England during the latter part of the seventeenth century, when it was against the law to sell Flemish laces there, or even import them to any extent. The lace-dealers, consequently, after smuggling it into the country, rechristened it point d'Angleterre, and then disposed of it as an English production. The name was at first applied to Brussels pillow lace, and later to a lace in which Brussels point and pillow were mixed.

The eleven different point laces are as follows:

Venetian Flat Point,
Venetian Raised Point,
Venetian Grounded Point,
Spanish Flat Point,
Spanish Raised Point,
Point de France,
Point d'Alençon,

Point d'Argentan,
Brussels Point à l'Aiguille,
Brussels Point Gaze,
Brussels Point Gaze Appliqué.

The Venetian points are often termed Italian flat and raised point. The Spanish raised point is also called Spanish rose point. All the points are at times termed point à l'aiguille—aiguille being the French word for needle; hence the term means simply needle-point. It is generally, however, applied especially to the early Brussels point, for the reason that the lace usually called Brussels point is only a pillow lace. Point d'Alençon is often spoken of as French point.

Fashion writers of the day, as well as reporters generally, on both sides of the Atlantic, in describing dresses worn upon some State occasion, have a fondness for saying that Mrs. So-and-so, or the Princess Someone, wore a dress trimmed with Brussels lace. This is very definite, indeed, since Brussels manufactures two points, and no end of pillow laces, in all amounting to more than half the hand-made lace the world at present wears. The reason is, because those who write up the descriptions know little of lace, and all who were not there to see must remain in ignorance of the kind really worn. In a recent report of one of the Queen's Drawing Rooms, which was published in a London journal, a lady is described as wearing a costume trimmed with "Carrickmacross point lace." Now there is no such lace in existence—the Carrickmacross lace being a pillow guipure. In this way all, except those who are well versed in lace lore, are led to suppose the number of points almost innumerable.

In choosing laces, if one is in doubt, the points may be

readily distinguished by the button-hole stitches which compose them.

Venetian raised point, Venetian flat point, Spanish raised and flat points, and the early point de France, are never grounded—that is, the patterns are connected by brides, and have not the mesh or network ground. Some of the later Venetian flat points were grounded. There was also a lace manufactured at Brussels in the early part of the seventeenth century which was of pillow flowers put together with needle-made brides. This lace was not made to any great extent, however, and was incorrectly termed point de Venice. Though not properly belonging to point lace, it merits mention. Needle-made flowers were sometimes mingled with those of plait, but this was not usually the case.

The Venetian or Italian, the Spanish points and point de France, are manufactured only to a very limited extent at the present day. Venetian points are no longer made in Venice, and are growing very rare. Point de France is only produced by a few isolated workers, who endeavor to reproduce the old patterns. The art of making the French point d'Argentan is lost, and Brussels point à l'aiguille has given place to the more modern and popular point gaze.

So it follows that there are but three kinds of point lace which appear in the general market, the others all being classed as specialties, and rare at that. These three are point d'Alençon, Brussels point gaze, and point gaze appliqué. Of these, point gaze is the most valuable and point d'Alençon comes next.

The Venetian and Spanish raised points and early point de France are the most expensive laces known, rare specimens bringing fabulous prices. Their value varies greatly according to width, design and quality; ordinary patterns, of average workmanship and fineness, one inch wide, are valued at about $10.00 gold per yard. In wider laces the pattern is more elaborate, and the prices, as a rule, are more than double the inch-wide pieces.

The Venetian and Spanish flat points are not quite so expensive as those just quoted; the inch-wide patterns are worth about $8.00 gold per yard, wider pieces are proportionately higher in price. The Venetian grounded point is much less expensive.

Point d'Argentan comes next in value; although this lace is no longer manufactured, it was made in France extensively up to the time of the French Revolution, and, therefore, is not by any means extinct, valuable pieces being purchased and repurchased, like jewels. Aside from this, it resembles point d'Alençon too closely to be considered of remarkable value on account of its growing scarcity. Exceptionally fine pieces bring exceptional prices, but the inch-wide is valued at about $6.00 gold per yard.

Brussels point gaze ranks next, being the most beautiful and costly of modern points. The inch-wide patterns are valued at from $5.00 to $6.00 gold per yard.

Next in value are the early Brussels point à l'aiguille and the French point d'Alençon. The two laces resemble each other in a great degree. The Brussels point is not manufactured at present, except when mixed with pillow, and then it is called point d'Angleterre. These laces are worth, in inch-wide patterns, from $3.00 to $5.00 gold per yard, extra qualities and widths higher in proportion.

Lastly comes point gaze appliqué, which must not be confounded with the Brussels appliqué lace of pillow-made flowers. This lace is of needle-made flowers or other designs, worked in the manner of point gaze, and applied to fine Brussels net. The inch-wide are worth nearly the same as point d'Alençon, the price varying according to design and quality.

This list includes all the points known to the commercial world, though irresponsible dealers are addicted to the habit of giving wonderful names to laces, especially those of novel design, for the purpose of misleading the purchaser and obtaining an exorbitant price for the lace in question. Generally, the poorer the quality the longer the name, and it is invariably prefixed by the word point. It is always safest to purchase only of a responsible house, except one is an experienced judge of lace, though some choice specimens may occasionally be picked up in small hamlets of Europe, yet even these are growing fewer with each coming year.

CHAPTER XIX.

ITALIAN POINTS.

VENETIAN FLAT POINTS.

This is the oldest of the real points. About the beginning of the seventeenth century the Venetian workers of reticella began to merge this lace into point proper. The result was a number of pieces of fascinating needle-made lace, which began to take a uniform shape about 1620, under the name of *punto in aria*, or *punto de Venezia*, (flat point or Venetian point), it being termed point de Venise de France.

This lace sprang at once into popularity. The French Court was extremely partial to it, and after a time it became the subject of various edicts. It was also worn by the English Court, but to a less extent than at the French. As it originated about the beginning of the Renaissance style, the designs were of exquisite beauty. They consisted of flowing patterns of scrollwork and graceful leaves, connected by a sort of network of slender brides, the latter running one into another, a fashion in Venetian points.

These laces were exquisitely fine, being usually worked in flax thread; sometimes, however, of silk. They were wrought in nearly every household in Venice, and, as products of the needle, were certainly marvelous.

The design was first sketched upon green or white parchment, which was afterwards basted closely upon two thicknesses of coarse linen. The figures in the design were then outlined by two or three threads, which were not stitched through the parchment, but simply held in place by being sewed on with a finer thread, which was looped over the outline threads at equal distances of about an eighth of an inch. The threads, when thus fastened had the appearance of the upper thread in a lock-stitch sewing machine when the tension is so loose as to allow it to lie flat upon the upper surface of the work. It gave strength to the heavier part of the design, being afterward covered with button-hole stitches. It was called the cordonet. In Venetian flat point the outline threads put on as the foundation of the cordonet were usually confined to one or two. The fancy stitches were then wrought inside the cordonet, and the brides attached to it on the outside. When all was completed it was carefully cut from the parchment, a very sharp knife being thrust between the folds of the linen; the threads holding the lace to the parchment were thus all severed without injury to the former.

Special patterns sometimes were given especial names. Among the prettiest of these was a simple design which went by the name of "mermaid's lace," and a romantic story is still told in the Lagune Islands concerning its origin. Whether the tale be true or false, there is no doubt whatever that the pattern of this lace was copied from the coralline usually known as mermaid's lace. The story runs in this wise:

A branch of the pretty sea-weed was brought to a young Italian girl, a worker in Venetian points, by her sailor lover, upon his return from a cruise in the Southern sea. The delicate coralline attracted the girl's attention at once on account of its exquisite beauty of outline, and she seemed greatly pleased with the gift.

"You have brought me a new pattern for my lace-work," she said, "the most graceful I have known."

So, with her needle and the finest white flax-thread, she sat down to her pleasant task of imitating the coralline. The result was a more perfect success than she had anticipated, and the "mermaid's lace," as it was called, became eagerly sought for, and for a time had a regular furore of popularity.

MERMAID'S LACE.

Possibly the romantic story connected with its origin aided in making it so general a favorite, but aside from this it was very graceful in effect. The design was afterward mingled with others, each lacemaker varying it according to her will, until at last it lost its distinctive character. It was popular about the middle of the seventeenth century, and belonged to Venetian flat point.

The Venetian points continued in favor until the French edicts prohibiting their use affected them seriously; and when, in 1665, Colbert instituted the manufacture of point de France, and afterward point d'Alençon, they received their death-blow, having never rallied from it.

VENETIAN RAISED POINT.

This lace may be considered the most exquisite of the productions of the needle. It sprung from Venetian flat point, which it resembles in nearly every respect, with the exception of being raised in certain portions of the pattern. The choicest designs were reserved for this lace, it being more elaborate than the flat points. They were of the Renaissance school, in floral scrollwork, stems and leaves, with deeply-raised centres and outlines, executed in the most perfect manner, the relief being double or triple, according to quality and design of lace, or the effect required.

It was worked in the same manner as flat point, with the exception of the second and third tiers of raised work, which were wrought separately and then sewed on so perfectly as to appear worked together. Like flat point it was executed in long strips, in order to avoid unnecessary joinings.

The specimen given on page 134 is in the Renaissance style, and though the illustration is remarkably accurate, it is almost impossible to convey upon paper the rare and delicate beauty of this lace. One peculiarity of Venetian point can be readily observed by studying this specimen. The brides scarcely ever reach from one spray or flower to the other, but run together in a sort of irregular network, with two picots on each bride usually, sometimes but one, and never more than two. The designs are graceful and free, but extremely delicate also. Another fine specimen, given on page 135, is in yellow silk, a free and graceful design, carried out with extreme delicacy and exactness.

Venetian raised point for a long time found eager, almost greedy, purchasers, not only among the fashionable world at large, but also for the use of dignitaries of the Church. It was the favorite lace of Anne of Austria,

VENETIAN RAISED POINT.

and greatly worn during the regency for rabats, manchettes and canons. In a portrait of Cinq-Mars, at the National Gallery at Versailles, he is represented in a deep collar of Venetian raised point. It ornamented the garters worn at the knee, shoe-rosettes, cuffs—in short, was used with the utmost prodigality, and the prices paid for it were almost fabulous.

This point was sometimes worked in silk of various

shades, though usually of white flax-thread. The favorite colors in silk were cream, yellow and purple. It occasionally appeared shaded in different tints, yellow

VENETIAN RAISED POINT.

and cream being employed, or two shades of purple. The effect was gorgeous to a marvelous degree, and these specimens, when wrought in rarely graceful designs, commanded almost any price asked. The supply never seemed to equal the demand for raised Venetian points, as the system of manufacture was scarcely as perfect as it is in our day, when no sooner does any specialty become popular than some enterprising American opens an establishment for making it after the most approved and economical plan, and at once proceeds to flood the market with the article in question, until it becomes a drug, and, in consequence, goes out of fashion immediately. Had this system been in practice in Venice during the days when her points stood unrivaled throughout the civilized or more properly the fashionable world, her rare old laces would scarcely be valued as they are now, and, possibly, they would have been far less perfect. As it was, there were no extensive lace-works in operation; the women skilled in the art patiently plied their needles day after day in their own humble homes, one valuable piece of the lace requiring years to finish. At this time they had not even learned the art of setting several workers upon the same piece; but it was the custom for the one who began the work to finish it. The manner of selling it was also primitive. It was sought out by agents sent for the purpose by kings, queens, princes or dignitaries of the Church, and though it was the custom for cheaper laces to be sold by venders or peddlers, who went about from city to city besieging the doors of the nobility or importuning ladies of rank as they rode out in their carriages or were carried in their chairs, the fate of being hawked about never befell Venetian raised point, for it was sought after with far greater zest than diamonds. The latter could be had for the money at any time, but the rare lace then in fashion was often hard to find. It was a matter of great rivalry among ladies of the French and English Courts as to who possessed the most beautiful Venetian points; indeed, this rivalry was not confined to the ladies alone, for the gentlemen were quite as tenacious upon the subject of laces, vieing with each other in the expensive and popular lace of the time; and there was nothing that approached Venetian point in the way of elegance for collars, manchettes and canons..

At the time when this lacė reached its highest pitch of popularity all Europe seemed lace-mad. It was during the Renaissance period—the time of wonderful artists, cunning workers in metals, wood, or stone; sculptors, skilled workers in the glyptic art; indeed, for all the arts previously known to man, and others yet new and almost untried; and lace patterns and lace-making generally seemed to imbibe the poetic and artistic inspiration of the hour. The patterns were graceful and flowing, the work exquisitely fine.

Raised Venetian point is termed *punto a relievo, punto a filo grano con mezzo-relievo,* rose point, Italian raised point, and *gros point de Venise.* Like the flat point—which, however, was never as beautiful or popular as the raised—it was seriously injured by the French edicts prohibiting its use, but more especially by Colbert's establishment of point de France. Raised point, which can scarcely be distinguished from the original, has recently been produced at Burano, and was shown at the Paris Exposition of 1878.

VENETIAN GROUNDED POINT.

After the establishment of the French points by Colbert, the Italian points languished, their manufacture be-

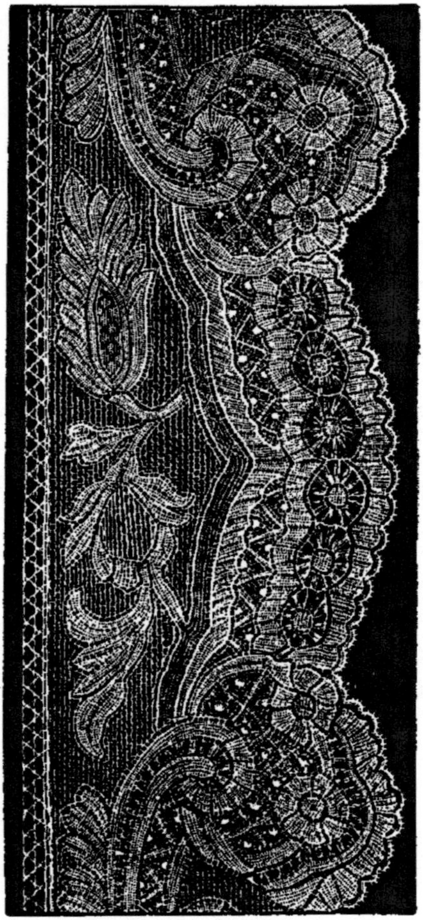

VENETIAN GROUNDED POINT.

coming almost extinct. In the beginning of the eighteenth century, however, the Venetian workers made a lace which was called *point de Venise à réseau*, or Venetian grounded point. The early Venetian flat and raised points were called Venice point guipure, in contradistinction.

This new lace, however, did not resemble the old Venetian point, as it was copied after Brussels point à l'aiguille, or, as it was sometimes termed, Brussels flat point. It was also made to compete with Brussels lace.

BURANO POINT.

It surpassed the point it copied, for its designs were very beautiful, the thread unusually fine, and the execution perfect. It differed from the Brussels point in having little raised knots or dots scattered over the design.

The illustration (page 138) shows a piece of Venetian grounded point, which has the rows of lozenge-shaped rosettes, or stars, which was a distinguishing feature of this lace. Although it excelled Brussels and Alençon points in many particulars, it failed to become a formidable rival of either; probably the industry failed from lack of organization, as well as from the fact that there was little demand for lace at this time.

The island of Burano, in the Adriatic, near Venice, made excellent specimens of point de Venise, which was also called Argentella, and sometimes Burano point. The last specimens, however, varied greatly from the first, though in minor particulars, and at length the lace industry, except so far as the manufacture of a few patternless guipures, seemed to die out in Venice and Burano.

When the school for lace-workers was established in Burano, in 1872, the manufacture of Venetian grounded points, as well as the reproduction of various other points, ancient and modern, was carried on to a certain degree. The quantity of lace produced has not been remarkable, but the quality is exquisitely fine.

We give an illustration of Venetian grounded point, as produced at Burano, and exhibited at the Paris Exposition, 1878. It resembles the original lace to a great extent, but scarcely in point of fineness. It was called, by courtesy, Burano point, though Burano has not invented a lace of its own; it only copies other point laces, both ancient and modern, and it is to be hoped this industry will meet with the patronage and encouragement it richly merits.

CHAPTER XX.

SPANISH POINTS.

Spain is said to have learned the art of making point lace from Italy, and this seems very probable, from the fact that there is a strong resemblance between the points of the two countries. Aside from this, Venice holds, undisputed, the honor of inventing point, and as the two countries were Catholic, and lying side by side, the work would be very apt to spread through the convents. Spain is also said to have taught the art of making point lace to Flanders, which country reciprocated by teaching Spain how to make pillow lace.

However this may have been, except in the manufacture of blondes, Spain has not been especially celebrated for her pillow laces, while, though Flanders and Belgium generally are famed for modern points, they do not resemble the old Spanish or Italian points except in the stitch by which they are worked. Spain has never produced a grounded point.

SPANISH FLAT POINT.

It is not quite clear whether Spanish flat or raised point was first worked in Spain. The flat, though partaking of the graceful Renaissance designs, was not quite equal to the Venetian flat point, and especially, when compared with the raised points, looks somewhat meagre or as if lacking spirit and variety, both in the pattern and in manner of execution. It appears to have been made either when point lace-work was in its infancy in

SPANISH FLAT POINT.

Spain, or upon its decline. Notwithstanding all this, it is a beautiful lace, and highly prized at the present day, though it was never as popular as Venetian flat point. Venice point was sought after by the fashionable world at large, while Spanish point, little worn by royalty, was almost altogether consumed by the Church in Spain. The working of the lace was also more confined to nunneries than the Italian, and, possibly, this accounts in a great measure for the scarcity of reliable information concerning it which is obtainable at the present day; and even the lace itself is hard to find, even small specimens being very scarce.

The distinguishing feature between the Spanish and the Venetian points is the peculiarity of the brides. It has already been observed that the brides in the Venetian points run into each other, forming a sort of network, and upon each bride are one or two picots. In the Spanish points, on the contrary (as will be seen by observing the illustration), the brides run directly from one portion of the pattern to the other, and upon each, or nearly every one, is a loop covered upon one side with picots. These are called coxcombs, and are peculiar to Spanish points, particularly the flat, when the design is rambling and rather disconnected; and only for these coxcombs scattered over the brides the lace would present an altogether too loose or open appearance. Other devices appear upon the brides in many designs, but more especially in the Spanish raised points, as will be seen later.

Flat point appeared but little in the market, the greater portion of it having been devoted to the use of the Church. It is sometimes called *Spanish point guipure à bride.*

SPANISH RAISED POINT.

This lace closely resembled the Venetian raised point, and though, like the flat point, its use was for a long time almost exclusively confined to the Church, and therefore it was not seen at the French Court, except in limited quantities, yet some declare it quite equal to Venetian raised point, for, though the brides in the Spanish raised point are fewer than in the Venetian, thus giving the appearance of less labor bestowed upon it, the patterns are bolder, quite as free and flowing, and the execution simply perfect. There is no doubt, had the manufacture of Spanish raised point been conducted upon a more extensive scale, or even had the requirements of the Church been less, it would have sharply contested with Venetian point its supremacy at the French Court.

The designs for this lace, as well as the Spanish blondes, for which that country is so famous, are said to have been first suggested by the Moorish embroideries. The Arabs who occupied Andalusia, Valencia and Murcia were celebrated for their exquisite needlework and embroideries. Later—toward the beginning of the seventeenth century—Philip II. of Spain established a school for embroidery in the convent of the Escorial, where most elaborate and beautiful patterns were wrought after designs by Tibaldi and other celebrated painters, as well as the more ancient Moorish. These patterns, being familiar to the lace-workers, were to a great extent copied in the Spanish points. The result was the production of the most admirable designs in lace. The patterns consisted of a scrollwork of acanthus and other leaves, *fleur de lis* and connecting sprays, the designer seeking after strong effects rather than extremely delicate ones, until this lace seemed to give an air that was grand and imposing to the wearer.

SPANISH RAISED POINT.

This specimen is in the Renaissance style. In it will be observed the specialties in the Spanish raised point brides—the accompanying wheels and coxcombs. In some designs the wheels resemble stars; in others, both stars and wheels occur, in which the brides cross each other at right angles.

At the dissolution of the Spanish monasteries in 1830 the most beautiful specimens of Spanish raised point now in existence were thrown upon the market. As soon as this became generally known, eager purchasers flocked to secure it. Many articles were purchased for museums, in the way of priestly robes, while lace lovers, both public and private individuals, made haste to procure specimens, well knowing that such an opportunity would never again be presented.

Spanish raised point was successfully copied in France under Colbert's administration. It was also made to some extent in Venice; but Colbert was not content to copy the points of other nations altogether, and his lace-workers found that point de France—similar, yet differing enough from the Spanish raised point to deserve a name of its own—was more popular and remunerative employment; while the Venetian lacemakers were more content to extend the manufacture of their own raised point than to copy the Spanish, which they liked less. There are also a few more modern reproductions of this point, but they are very few, many of them extremely inferior, and they fail to affect the market in even a slight degree.

On account of its resemblance to carved ivory, Spanish raised point is sometimes called bone point. Portuguese point is worked in Portugal, but is only given the name on account of the locality in which it is manufactured, as it is precisely similar to the Spanish, both flat and raised being perfect copies of these points. The Portuguese was worked at a later date than the Spanish, though never in remarkable quantity. Until the sequestration of the monasteries, however, the specimens preserved outside the Church were largely Portuguese work.

Spanish raised point was worked for a somewhat longer period than the Venetian, though never in so large a quantity. While point de France superseded Venetian point in the fashionable world, thus destroying the demand for it, and, in consequence, the manufacture also, Spanish point, being in steady demand for chausables, stoles, maniples, and other priestly vestments, flourished later on, while its manufacture was begun soon after the Venetian.

The churches in nearly all the Spanish towns are rich in the possession of rare old vestments and other articles composed of, or richly ornamented with, Spanish raised point.

CHAPTER XXI.

FRENCH POINTS.

POINT DE FRANCE.

When Colbert, who was minister of France under Louis XIV., found the people's love for lace so great that all the edicts put forth by the reigning monarch to suppress the wearing of it were not only ineffectual, but almost unregarded, he conceived the brilliant plan of making France a lace manufacturing country, and thus retaining the money within the realm which the French people persisted in spending upon lace.

He well understood the magnitude of the undertaking. To prove successful, the enterprise would require to be perfectly planned, and no small amount of skilled labor obtained to carry it into execution. The points of Spain and Italy were of such exquisite fineness, that no mean production could successfully vie with them, even though bolstered by royal edicts without number, and the pillow laces of Flanders he could not hope to surpass. Nothing daunted, however, by the prospect, he obtained his sovereign's eager consent to his plan, and fell to work with a will.

There are many conflicting reports concerning the manner in which Colbert founded the lace industry in France, and the most popular and generally accepted of these was rendered quite improbable by the published correspondence of Colbert only a few years ago. Fifty letters upon the subject of his lace project were discovered, and though they settled many things in reference to it, beyond a doubt his course, in other particulars, was not rendered quite clear.

The account given in a local French history of the town of Alençon, which was the most successful centre of the industry, says that, in 1665, Colbert sought out a lady named Madame Gilbert, born in Alençon, but who thoroughly understood the manner of working Venetian points, and gave her 50,000 crowns, aside from the use of his Château of Lonray, near Alençon, for the purpose of establishing the manufacture of point lace. He had already secured thirty Venetian lace-workers to assist her in making the lace and teaching others. The first products of their skill were brought by Madame Gilbert to Paris, and the king, accompanied by Colbert and a number of courtiers, went to inspect them. They were displayed to the best advantage, and being well-executed specimens in choice designs, the king expressed himself highly pleased. He christened the lace point de France, and announced that it was the only lace which, by royal permission, could thereafter appear at Court. His loyal subjects, glad to be able to wear lace at all with royal consent, readily purchased all that was offered, and thus, from the very beginning, the enterprise was a success.

From Colbert's correspondence it appears that, obtaining an order to establish the manufacture of both point and pillow laces in a dozen different towns in the kingdom, he formed a company, the capital of which, as early as 1668, amounted to 22,000 livres. An exclusive privilege was given for ten years (from August 5th, 1865), and a grant of 36,000 francs. Eight directors were appointed, upon a liberal salary, to superintend the manufacture. There were at first many difficulties to be

POINT DE FRANCE.

surmounted. The authorities of the several towns where the industry was conducted did little or nothing to forward it. The lace-makers, who had been obtained from Flanders as well as Venice, preferred to cling to their old patterns and styles, while it was Colbert's intention to produce specialties and laces of new and peculiar design. These laces were at first, whether pillow or point, called point de France. Soon, however, the term was limited to the point lace only, which, from being a cross between Spanish and Venetian raised point, grew gradually to have some characteristics of its own.

The term point de France is now applied exclusively to that needle-made lace which was manufactured principally at Alençon, the ground resembling in a great degree that of Spanish point, the brides stretching from one part of the pattern to another, and ornamented with coxcombs and occasional stars and crosses, but never forming a network as in Venetian raised point. Before point de France was settled upon, both Spanish and Italian raised points were copied. The designs of point de France were in many respects, however, peculiarly its own. They were scarcely as bold as the Spanish patterns, yet rather more decided than the Venetian. The workmanship was of the very best, and the lace well worthy of the patronage it received ; otherwise, even though backed by the king and prime minister, it might have failed to become popular.

It became the rage at Court, and was also affected by English nobility and royalty. In 1669 the first distribution of profits occurred ; the amount was fifty per cent. on the principal invested. The profits were again divided in 1670 and 1673, the second division amounting to much more than the first, and the third being greatly in excess of the second. In 1675, the grant expiring, the remaining profits were divided, and the capital returned to the shareholders. In all the ordinances regulating the manufacture of lace in France, and in the Colbert correspondence, no mention is made of any Madame Gilbert or of the Château of Lonray. This leads many practical people to regard Madame as a myth, though the château was the property of Colbert's son, the Marquis de Seignelay. He, however, did not come into possession of it until his marriage with Mlle. Matignon, in 1671.

A French journal, in speaking of this point, says: "We have seen some with little flowers over the large, which might be called flying flowers, being only attached in the centre." Later, it speaks of the new points as having no brides—the flowers are closer, and connected by sprays or stalks Yet in many respects did point de France so closely resemble Venetian raised point, it was called by the latter name in England and other foreign countries.

Colbert still continued to protect the industry, which at times caused him much trouble, on account of the dissentions and disputes of the lace-workers. He wore his favorite lace upon all occasions, seeming in reality to prefer it to any other point. He died in 1683, and from that hour the industry of point de France seemed to languish. Louis would undoubtedly have protected it if he had been wise enough; or, perhaps, tired of it, as a child with an old toy, he became more interested in other matters. His revocation of the Edict of Nantes in 1685 scattered many of the workers; yet, the manufacture lingered on through the long, dreary wars that filled the latter portion of his reign. It was made to some extent up to the time of his death in 1715, but soon after this period grounded points were introduced, and named for the town in which they were chiefly manufactured—Alençon.

Since then, grounded points have remained in fashion, and none of the old points with bride grounds have been revived. It is true that pillow guipures, both of silk and of thread, abound; but these bear only a ghost of resemblance to the older points, which, for artistic design and perfect execution, are not surpassed even by that queen of modern laces—point gaze; and it seems quite probable, since imitation laces—as the products of the loom are invariably called—have become so plentiful and cheap, and so pretty, too, that the prospect of reviving these ancient laces grows fainter and fainter with each year; and when we come to consider how universally even fashionable and wealthy ladies adopt these products of the loom, we are led to wonder that the manufacture of point d'Alençon—which is now half-loom made and half needle-point—is kept up in any degree, and that the points of Brussels are still so prosperous and popular.

CHAPTER XXII.

FRENCH POINTS (CONTINUED).

POINT D'ALENCON.

THIS name was given to the grounded point manufactured in Alençon, and which superseded point de France. The popularity of the older points began to wane. Brussels was manufacturing a grounded point, which was already a favorite. Venice was making a similar point to compete with that of Brussels, and the Alençon lace-workers followed the example, greatly to their profit. This was early in the eighteenth century, about 1720.

There is a dispute, however, as to whether Alençon or Brussels made the first grounded points. It is acknowledged that these points were not manufactured until the eighteenth century, and Brussels never made points with bride grounds, like Venice and Alençon. The grounded points sprang into existence during the close of the Renaissance period, and the earlier ones bore rococo designs. Those of Brussels, however, seem to have a tinge of the Renaissance in a greater degree than those of Alençon, and for this reason alone would appear to be of earlier origin.

The needle-made ground of point d'Alençon was unusually strong, wearing well, and quite unlike that of the Brussels or grounded Venetian. The mesh was often of two sizes in the same pattern, and was composed of two threads, held together by a third, thus forming a finer ground, which would not draw out of shape when wet, and therefore would bear repeated washing. Unfortunately, the manner of making this ground is lost; though many of the older specimens, still in good repair, remain, no one has been found with sufficient ingenuity to discover the way in which it was made.

The modern point d'Alençon ground is simply a fine machine net, the pattern being appliquéd on the net. The loom nets and laces are so perfect and fine that hand-made laces, except of the most exquisite pattern and fineness, cannot compete with them. Besides, labor is dearer than in the early days of the Alençon points, and only the purses of royalty can afford them, therefore the machine-made grounds are uniformly adopted.

Many attempts have been made to nurse the manufacture of Alençon lace into the popularity which the Brussels point gaze enjoys. Napoleon I. undertook the task, and the Empress Eugénie did still more—she not only used it herself, but in the using set the fashion for the world. However, she could not make the world follow altogether in this. Her superb costumes were universally copied, it is true, but those who imitated her style found, by substituting point gaze for Alençon, they could secure a far lovelier effect. Alençon was much used for lingerie and for narrow edgings of all sorts, but for bridal veils, fichus, deep flounces and large articles, it was never a favorite.

The design of point d'Alençon first partook of the rococo style, and afterward the dotted. Both were compact, and the modern designs have not improved upon either; there has always been in Alençon point a certain poverty of style, and, though the lace is fine, it has the effect of a poor, flimsy fineness. There are, it is true, some exceptions to the rule, but they are exceptions only.

This design is in the rococo style, at the period when it was fast merging into the dotted. It is pretty and delicate, but not remarkable for especial beauty.

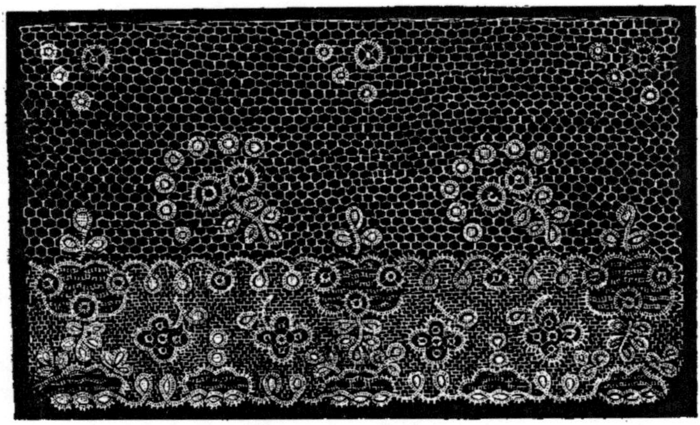

POINT D'ALENÇON.

Alençon point was formerly made by a single worker; it was composed of minute button-hole stitches, and worked upon parchment; but when Brussels conceived the plan of putting several hands at work upon the same piece of lace, Alençon followed suite, or, rather, it managed to exceed Brussels in the number of persons employed upon one pattern. The mode of procedure was as follows:

First, the design is engraved upon a copper plate, from which it is printed upon strips of green parchment, each ten inches in length, the second printed so as to take up the pattern where the first left off, the third following the second in a similar manner, and so on, each section being numbered in regular order. Green parchment is used in preference to white, as any defect in the pattern can be more readily detected upon it; aside from this, the color is said to be more restful to the eyes than any other. The parchment, as in other points, is stitched to two thicknesses of coarse linen and given into the hands of the first worker, who is called the *piqueuse*, whose duty it is to prick holes through the parchment outlining the pattern. When this is done the *traceuse* takes it and fastens the outline threads of the cordonet in place by taking two threads in her left hand, shaping them to the pattern, and fastening with a needle and fine thread at short distances, the needle being passed through the holes in the parchment. The needle is put through a hole from the wrong side, over the two outline threads, and then back through the same hole in the parchment; each stitch is made in the same manner, thus making them as smooth, even and close, as if glued to the parchment. Unlike the bride points, the ground was the first part to be put in; accordingly, the *réseleuse* and *fondeuse* next took the work, the former making the regular ground, and the latter supplying any other meshes required by the pattern. The meshes were worked backward and forward across the piece of the lace, from the straight edge where the footing was afterward added, to the scalloped edge or picot. The *remplisseuse*, when the ground was completed, put in the flat part of the pattern which is inside the cordonet, is called the *toilé*, and is made of flat button-hole stitches, after which it passed into the hands of the *brodeuse*, who button-holed the cordonet. Next, the *modeuse* put in the ornamental fillings, which are inside the cordonet, and comprise all the fillings except the toilé.

The lace had now passed through the hands of seven different workers, and was ready to be cut from the parchment. This fell to the lot of the *eboulеuse*, who passed a sharp knife between the folds of linen, and severed the threads which were put in to hold the outline threads of the cordonet in place before connected with other stitches. The *régaleuse* fastened the sections of lace, in regular order, upon a piece of doubled linen, over which green paper had been tacked, when followed the most difficult task of all, that of joining the sections without showing where they were united. This was done by the *assembleuse*, and at first seems almost impossible, but it must be borne in mind that the edges of the different sections are as strong as that to which the footing is sewn, and not composed of ragged edges of thread as is a lace which has been cut across with the scissors. The *assembleuse* connected these several divisions either by a stitch impossible to describe, and called *assemblage;* by an invisible seam which, in the parts where the pattern was divided, followed as far as possible, the outlines; or, by a third method, a stitch called *point de raccroc*, where the ground is united by a fresh row of stitches, similar to that employed in making the meshes. The *toucheuse*, *brideuse*, *boucleuse* and *gazeuse* then respectively went over the work of joining, making each part connected by the *assembleuse* as perfect as any other portions of the lace. The *mignonneuse* then sewed on the footing, or, as it is called in France, the *engrêlure*, when the *picoteuse* put the picots on the edge of the cordonet, running a horse-hair through the loops to keep them straight. The *affineuse* then went over the whole piece, rendering it as perfect as possible by adding a stitch here or a picot there, when the *affiqueuse* completed it by polishing and making perfectly smooth the toilé.

Modern Alençon manufacturers do not employ so many hands upon one piece of work, the number being reduced to nearly one-half, as more than ten or twelve are quite unnecessary. This number, however, will work to greater advantage upon a piece of Alençon point than if each is given a separate piece to work alone, as a worker is more adept when always performing the same portion of the labor than when she does the whole; and besides, nearly every one shows an aptness or preference for one particular part, and it is advisable to give her this portion.

For more than half a century Alençon point flourished, and then it declined until near the beginning of the nineteenth century. It revived in the time of Napoleon I., only to decline when he ceased to foster the manufacture. With Napoleon III. it again became important. In the year 1840 two hundred aged lace-workers were induced to aid in its manufacture; but their hands had either lost their old cunning or they clung to their own especial manner of working, and the result was a sort of mixed fabric, a rather pretty lace, but without the old Alençon ground.

The best modern Alençon point is made at Bayeux, but needle-made grounds are rarely ever made elsewhere, and here only as a specialty for some particular purpose. Bayeux sent an exquisite production to the Exposition of 1867—a dress of two flounces in shaded foliage and flowers, the design being exceedingly beautiful, and the work executed in an equally artistic manner. The dress was the admiration of all visitors, and was valued at $17,000. Forty workers had been employed upon it for seven years. The Alençon point of Bayeux is usually executed by single workers.

Point d'Alençon could never compete with either the early Brussels points or with the modern point gaze, on account of the insignificance of its designs, even though it is a more durable lace, or, rather, the old Alençon ground was more lasting; the modern has scarcely this merit, being usually of machine net. Horse-hair is sometimes introduced in the cordonet to give stiffness; it answers the purpose, but is apt to shrink with washing, more especially if very hot water is used for the purpose. The designs of Alençon point are seldom copied from Nature, flowers and foliage do not appear in it, only rather pinched sort of patterns, and, however beautiful the workmanship may have been in times past or present, lack of beauty in design has been a great drawback to its continued popularity.

In point of fashion, Alençon is not now a favorite lace, and if this continues, the manufacture will soon feel the effects more severely than ever. France stands unrivaled in many of her industries in the finer textiles, but she must accord the palm to Belgium in the production of both point and pillow laces, if we except Chantilly. The finest imitation or loom laces are made in France, and possibly this accounts for the deterioration of the hand-made productions.

CHAPTER XXIII.

FRENCH POINTS—(*continued*).

POINT D'ARGENTAN.

THIS lace has often been confounded with Alençon. Argentan was not one of the towns in which Colbert first established lace-making, though it is afterward mentioned in his correspondence. The early points of Argentan seem to have attracted but little attention, and, as Alençon took the lead in the manufacture, she also took the name of the first productions of Argentan, probably however, by accident.

The points of Argentan were superior to those of Alençon in many respects; first of all, in beauty of design. The patterns were more flowing and free, and the ground peculiar, being a compromise between a mesh and a bride. It was in reality a six-sided mesh, entirely covered with button-hole stitches. The ground as well as the pattern was printed on the parchment design, and the upper angles of each mesh pricked. Pins were put in at the angles, and the foundation laid by passing the needle and thread around these pins, after which the meshes were covered with fine, close button-hole stitches. This rendered the ground unusually strong, as well as pretty, and the lace was, in consequence, almost imperishable.

The illustration on page 162 is in the rococo style, being slightly enlarged to show the hexagonal mesh. Close examination will also discover the minute button-hole stitches of which the bride mesh is composed, there being six or seven stitches in each side of the mesh.

The pattern in point d'Argentan was worked in the same manner as point d'Alençon, on strips of parchment,

POINT D'ARGENTAN.

though the effect of the work was different. The toilé inside the cordonet was very close and flat, the cordonet and relief higher and much heavier, but this was needed with the peculiar ground, which was sometimes called *grande bride* ground. The flowers were larger and more rambling, and though Alençon was finer, Argentan was far more effective. The patterns resembled somewhat those of the early Brussels point, and the lace, though differing in the ground, was equal to the Brussels point in regard to style.

This specimen is in the rococo style also, and rather more compact than many of the patterns. Picots were

POINT D'ARGENTAN.

sometimes added to the brides composing the mesh, especially in fillings, where a small portion inside the flower-sprays was filled with the ground. The picots gave variety. Many varied and ornamental fillings were employed in this lace, especially near the border, where scarcely less than half a yard in length would be sufficient to show the different fillings. Often there was two or three times the variety in fillings there was figures in the pattern, and in this case one set would be filled with one or two kinds, the second set with others, and the third with still others; while with the fourth the fillings would begin over again in regular order. Often, again, the pattern, while being of similar sprays of leafage or flower, would be arranged differently, thus showing an almost endless but pleasing and graceful variety.

The pattern illustrated on next page is a specimen of the kind just mentioned, a page of the book being quite too small to show the whole of either the pattern or fillings. Of the latter there are four different kinds near the picot, while the sprays show two complete ones and a portion of the third, all somewhat similar, yet differing sufficiently to attract the eye at once. The sprays, too, in this pattern, as in many others in Argentan point, reach quite to the footing or engrêlure. This is often the case in the designs for Argentan; in many instances the spray is six or eight inches in length, and rambles all over the space between the picot and footing, except a very narrow border at the picot, forming irregular, long and rather flat scallops, composed in part of small stars, forget-me-nots or similar designs, alternating with minute scroll-work, among which are thrown fillings of various stitches.

Alençon made a small quantity of lace at one time with the Argentan ground, but it was inferior to the real Argentan, and the experiment failing, it was little practiced, except that it was sometimes employed to give variety to the regular Alençon ground by introducing it in some of the fillings. This was done with good effect.

Upon the other hand, Argentan essayed to make the Alençon grounds, but the result was inferior to the regular products of the Alençon workers, and the attempt

POINT D'ARGENTAN.

was discontinued. This illustrates the fact, that it is almost impossible to initiate an old lace-worker into a new manner of making lace. She rebels at once; she declares there is but one proper way of making lace, and that is the mode she was first taught; she cannot make the new, she dislikes it, and, unconsciously, mixes up with it the old stitches to which she has so long been accustomed. This caused Colbert much trouble and vexation, and it has been proved that to introduce a new lace, one must obtain beginners and teach them the art. Of course this rule does not apply to those who acquaint themselves with the different stitches and modes of making lace for the purpose of teaching or inspecting others, but only to those to whom long habit has become second nature.

Point d'Argentan can always be recognized by its ground, which, though it may be employed to a small extent in other laces, appears in none other as the regular ground, the large, six-sided mesh, covered with tiny button-hole stitches, being unmistakable even to an amateur. The lace was not, like Alençon, confined to small edgings, narrow flounces and the like, but was much employed for wedding trousseaux, for robes, deep flounces, veils, berthes, and articles in which the large and beautiful pattern showed to the best advantage.

The manufacture of Argentan point was not very large. It is said to have never included more than two thousand workers at any one time, and these were employed in three or four factories only. No mention is made of the lace in the public records until about 1800, but it appears in the wardrobe accounts of the royal family and members of the Court flourishing through the reigns of Louis XV. and Louis XVI., and declining with the Revolution.

Madame du Barry purchased a complete garniture of point d'Argentan in 1772, for which she paid more than $1,000. Only elaborate and well-paying orders were executed, and by this means inferior work was avoided.

The ground, in some specimens, had the large mesh surrounded with small picots, not only in the fillings but throughout the body of the work. This ground is usually spoken of as the *bride picotee*, and is very elaborate, though the art of making this ground is now lost.

An attempt was recently made to revive the point at Argentan, three pieces having been discovered partly completed and still attached to the parchment patterns. These three pieces had each a different ground; one, the *grande bride*, which was most common, consisting of the hexagonal mesh; another had the bride ground of point de France; and a third had the *bride picotee*, with little picots fringing the meshes. Skillful lace-workers were obtained, and with the aid of these unfinished specimens, a point was produced which resembled in some degree the grand old point imitated; however, the experiment could scarcely be called a successful one, and with the sea of loom lace which France sends out every year to contend against, it is scarcely possible to keep alive the one point now manufactured in France, and it is doubtful if the older ones will ever be resurrected, except in a ghostly sort of way. It is to be regretted, however, that point d'Argentan did not survive instead of point d'Alençon, for, as far as beauty is concerned, there is no comparison between the two, and were point d'Argentan manufactured at the present day, Brussels point gaze would have a strong rival in the field.

CHAPTER XXIV.

BRUSSELS POINTS.

Brussels made no points which resembled the ancient Venetian and Spanish brided points or guipures, though its early pillow laces, as well as those of Flanders, were the finest manufactured, and were much patronized by both the English and French. The famous lace which was called Brussels point in England, and afterward English point, being at first point de Bruxelles in France, and later, point d'Angleterre, was quite as famous in its way as the laces of Italy or Spain. This lace was not, properly speaking, a point at all, though the real point evolved from it. It was of pillow manufacture, but in the seventeenth century, point flowers were mingled with the plait in it, and in this manner the point patterns were gradually introduced until the idea seemed to occur to the manufacturers to make pure point. This was why the early Brussels needle-point was called at first by the name which the pillow lace bore, point d'Angleterre, and afterward, to distinguish it from the pillow productions, point à l'aiguille. Some authorities assert that point guipures were manufactured in Brussels to some extent, but this is rather doubtful, though the pillow flowers were sometimes connected by brides.

BRUSSELS POINT A L'AIGUILLE.

This early Brussels needle-point was first made about the time of point d'Alençon, probably a trifle earlier—

near 1700. There was a similarity between it and the grounded Venetian, as well as point d'Alençon; it was finer than point d'Argentan, especially the early productions. It was very like the Venetian grounded point in the manner in which it was worked, but the designs were more beautiful, usually consisting of sprays of leaf or flower. The Brussels point had none of the ornamental dots which distinguished the Venetian. The ground was particularly fine, which gave to the work a monotonous effect, especially where the pattern was not marked. The specimen on page 170 has the fine ground, and equally fine pattern; the latter consisting of the Flower-pot of the Annunciation, with a flower which the most learned botanist must fail to recognize. These designs were at one time quite popular, the Tree of Knowledge and the Holy Dove being among the most common. This style, however, was only in vogue for a short period.

The designs in Brussels needle-point were especially graceful, usually composed of exquisite leaves and flowers. Some of the earliest of these were in the Renaissance style, something which the Alençon points cannot claim, its patterns being of later date. A leaf and flower spray in Renaissance style is illustrated on page 171, which will be readily recognized as similar to many of the designs in Brussels points to this day, though the stitches in modern productions are more varied, while the grounds are not so thickly worked, in order to throw out the flower in greater relief.

The ground of Brussels point à l'aiguille is different from that of Alençon or Argentan. It is made of marvelously fine thread, almost like a cobweb, and consists of loose button-hole stitches, worked from left to right.

The manner of working tne grounds is shown, more clearly than a pen description can do, by the illustrations at the bottom of next page, which are enlarged to several

EARLY BRUSSELS POINT A L'AIGUILLE.

times the regular size in order to show the stitch more perfectly. If this is not borne in mind the impression

BRUSSELS POINT A L'AIGUILLE.

BRUSSELS NEEDLE-POINT GROUNDS

might be received that the Brussels needle-grounds were coarse, rather than very fine.

The pattern is worked in much the same manner as point d'Alençon, there being a number of hands employed upon the same piece; indeed, Brussels invented this plan and Alençon followed it. Brussels, however, usually employed but seven. The pattern is settled upon by the designer, who, after it is printed, cuts the parchment in pieces and gives it out to be worked. The manager settles the smaller considerations, the thread employed, the grounds—in fact, everything but the working, when each one does her part in turn.

The patterns in Brussels point à l'aiguille bore a stronger resemblance to the points of Argentan than those of Alençon, and in some respects the lace was superior to both the French points. It had the beauty of design which distinguished Argentan, it had the fineness of texture and workmanship which was the crowning beauty of Alençon, but in point of utility it was inferior to both. The ground of Alençon was fine, but durable; that of Argentan was coarser, but equally strong; while that of the Brussels needle-point was fine and frail. This defect, however, did not deter those who could afford it from buying it, and it was in great demand for bridal trousseaux, for veils, shawls, and similar large articles, often manufactured to meet remunerative orders, as was point d'Argentan. Such articles seldom required washing, and did not, usually, receive hard usage. On this account the frailty was not considered detrimental; but for articles of underwear, or anything which required hard usage, Brussels needle-point did not answer the purpose.

At the time of the French Revolution, when the manufacture of point d'Alençon and point d'Argentan was discontinued, Brussels point à l'aiguille was the only point in the market. Though there was little call for fine points during the Revolution, Brussels point à l'aiguille stood its ground, a fact which must call forth some astonishment. Napoleon patronized it until the manufacture of point d'Alençon was re-established, and to some extent afterward, as, indeed, were all who required a really handsome point obliged to do. It was Hobson's choice, and, fortunately, not a bad one; for, though the manufacture might not be quite so extensive as before, the workmanship was kept up to a high standard. In the time of Napoleon I. the dotted style was in vogue, a style eminently inferior to the Renaissance, and even the rococo.

The greatest rival to point lace, however, as well as pillow, was the loom lace which began to flood Europe about 1820. Alençon nearly succumbed to it, and the manufacture would doubtless have become extinct at the period when the Jacquard apparatus was attached to the bobbinet loom to weave pattern laces had not Napoleon III. been pleased to favor the manufacture. Brussels must have had some master hand directing her point lace manufactures, for, seeing the old Brussels needle-point did not differ from Alençon sufficiently to warrant prosperity to both, it stopped the manufacture, and substituted the most exquisite point lace which has ever been known in ancient or modern times—point gaze; and, this point being very expensive, special attention was turned to pillow laces, some of the finer kinds being mingled with a small portion of point, thereby securing a low grade in the cheaper pillow laces, a medium in the mixed point and pillow, and the highest in her unrivaled point; even the lowest of these grades being far superior to the machine-made lace.

BRUSSELS POINT A L'AIGUILLE.

The above specimen of Brussels needle-point is in the early rococo style, in which a touch of the Renaissance lingers.

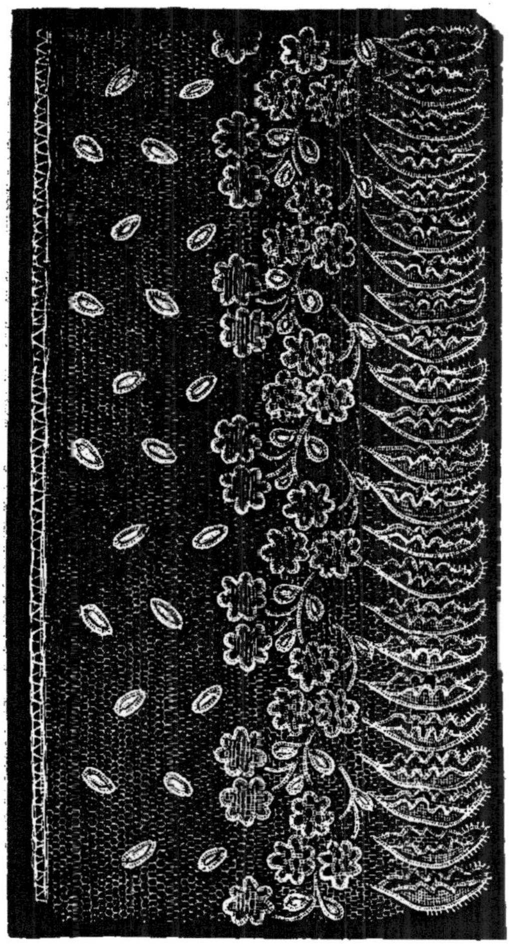

BRUSSELS POINT A L'AIGUILLE.

This illustrates the dotted style in Brussels needle-point, the patterns often being scarcely superior to those of Alençon.

CHAPTER XXV.

BRUSSELS POINTS—(*continued*).

POINT GAZE.

WHEN some special gem of prose or poetry emanates from the pen of an author, people are wont to say: "He is inspired." If the most exquisite gems of art are produced in a like manner, then the inventor or inventors of point gaze must have been blessed with inspiration of the highest order. Those who are familiar with the lace will readily assent to this; they who are unacquainted with it have only to imagine the loveliest frostwork that ever glistened upon a window pane transferred in a regular pattern in wreaths and sprays upon a spider's web for a ground, and scattered over it snow-flakes in tiny dots or star-crystals; they will then have something approaching in beauty, though approaching only, point gaze.

It has recently become the fashion for people of the nineteenth century to fall down and worship everything ancient—furniture, gems, costumes, paintings, lace; and it is quite true that there is much, especially what was produced during the Renaissance period, to admire. The old Spanish and Venetian raised points were grand in design and exquisite in workmanship; yet, surely, an unbiassed judge could never say they were superior in beauty to point gaze.

Many of the leaf-sprays in this beautiful point resemble skeleton leaves that have been bleached to a clear

BRUSSELS POINT GAZE.

white, and never was the fibre of a natural leaf more delicate or perfect than are these wonderful productions of the modern lace-worker's skill.

Point gaze receives its name from gauze; the whole lace is so gauze-like and light, the ground a mere web, and the flowers worked in millions of minute stitches, the effect being very fine. The grounds of the pure point gaze are similar to those of the early Brussels needle-point, only very light, and they are not worked before the flowers, but simultaneously with them.

The illustration on the preceding page shows the end of a point gaze scarf, and is a correct representation of the pattern, though no mere illustration can perfectly impart the beauty of the lace. The medallion in the centre of the above design is one which, with slight variation, often occurs in point gaze, while the foliage appears in nearly every pattern. Sometimes one-half the leaf will be in gauze-like relief—a perfect network of apparent fibres—while the other half will be covered with the tiny dots which appear on one side of the leaves in our illustration; they are often quite closely crowded, with just enough space between to show there is a gauzy ground beneath. This gives an effect of shading, which is beautiful in the extreme.

Point gaze is made of very fine flax thread, which is spun by hand at Ghent, and costs from $10 to $300 per pound, according to the quality, and especially the fineness. It passes, in the working, through three separate hands—the *gazeuse*, who makes the flowers and ground, working them with the same thread; the *brodeuse*, who arranges the cordonet, which, however, is not covered with button-hole stitch, but simply overcast. The *fou-*

neuse works the fancy stitches which fill in the medallion or star devices, and are called *jours.* The lace is made in small pieces and joined along the outlines of the pattern.

Many portions of point gaze are worked in what is called floating relief. For instance, a scarf with square corners will have a rose in each, which is not worked flat, but is composed of several leaves, worked in a similar manner, and placed, the smaller on the outside, the largest in the centre, and merely fastened at one edge. Other flowers and buds, particularly rosebuds, are worked in this manner, and the effect is beautiful. A fichu recently displayed in the window of a New York establishment was of this beautiful point, and through the centre, on each side, was a wreath of roses, all in floating relief. The flowers were very large, with great hearts, quite open except for the tiny dots, while the leaves were placed one over the other, like the leaves of a real rose; they almost seemed cupped, so regularly they opened one above the other, the outer ones being slightly larger than those nearer the centre. This row or garland of roses extended the whole length of the fichu, those in the front opening upward from each side when this delicate trifle was worn. Sprays of leaves were arranged on each edge; the fichu was pointed at the ends in front, each terminating in a rose in floating relief; while above, just on the breast, the beautiful cobweb was fastened together with a point gaze butterfly, the wings also in floating relief.

Simply from its own merits point gaze has been the fashionable point lace for half a century, and is still in the full tide of its popularity, bidding fair to hold its own for years to come. Probably there may in time be found a lace which will take, for a time, the fancy of the hour, but it must be a marvelous production indeed if able to supplant this wondrously beautiful lace.

At the Vienna Exhibition a beautiful garniture of point gaze was exhibited, consisting of a shawl, dress trimmings comprising seven yards of lace for flounces half a yard in depth, seven yards of narrower lace eight inches in width, and a bertha six yards in length, also an elegant barbe. Besides these, there was a handkerchief, fan and parasol cover. Twelve lace-workers were engaged three years on this set, which was valued at $8,000.

At the Centennial Exhibition were also exhibited many exquisite productions of point gaze, in the way of flouncings, garnitures and shawls. One half-shawl was so gauze-like as to lead one to wonder how human eyes could direct, or human hands fashion, anything so fine, and yet so perfect in every way. It was so light it could be readily drawn through a medium-sized gold ring. There were also many smaller articles in barbes, lappets, pompadours, etc., and single flowers—a rose, lily, or rose-bud—in floating relief.

The manufactures of point gaze in Brussels are in a very flourishing condition, the factories extending all over Belgium. The firms manufacturing this lace have agents in nearly every large city in Europe. New York purchasers seldom go to Brussels for their points, but to Paris, which is the greatest lace market in the world. Here Brussels sends her lace products, both needle and pillow; also to London, St. Petersburg, Moscow, Vienna and Milan.

POINT GAZE APPLIQUE.

This lace is very similar to point gaze, differing from it only in the ground, which is of the finest Brussels loom net, and the point gaze flowers are inserted in it. It is called *appliqué*, but the work cannot properly be classed under this head, as the net underneath the flowers and sprays, or whatever may constitute the pattern, is carefully cut away, which gives the work the same appearance as if the ground was made with the flowers. This lace is really more generally known than the point gaze proper, the former being extremely expensive, and the latter equally pretty. While pure point gaze is employed for royal trousseaux, or the use of ladies to whom money is no object, the point appliqué is within the reach of the moderately wealthy. It is seldom called by its true name, being generally spoken of as point gaze, and in ninety-nine cases out of a hundred, when a customer inquires for point gaze, even at the best mercantile establishments, she will be shown the point with machine-made ground.

The effect of this lace is precisely similar to that of the point proper, the flowers being worked in the same manner, and all needle-made; the skeleton and dotted leaves, the roses, buds and flower sprays, both flat and in floating relief. It is quite expensive, a scarf about a yard and a quarter in length and not more than six inches in width being worth a hundred dollars—often more, if the work is particularly fine—and half-shawls range from $500 to $2,000 each, even higher, if procured to order and of special fineness.

This point is also mingled with duchesse—a beautiful pillow lace of Brussels manufacture—in lappets, pompadours, barbes, scarfs and like articles. In scarfs the centre is of duchesse, while the ends will be partly or wholly of point gaze appliqué.

CHAPTER XXVI.

PILLOW LACES.

POINT and pillow lace differ not only in the making, but in many other respects also. Point is made entirely with the needle and confined to a few localities, while pillow is made to a greater or less extent all over the continent of Europe, in England, the United States, and in some of the countries of South America, and is plaited upon a cushion. The pillow laces, therefore, are legion, though many of the numerous kinds are but variations of a few standard sorts.

The best pillow lace is made in Belgium, where it is also manufactured in the largest quantity. France comes second on the list, and the lace is made in every other country in Europe except Turkey and Austria. Turkey has no lace industry, and though some of the Austrian peasant women make a coarse sort of lace for their own use, it does not appear as an article of export, and is of no commercial importance.

Pillow laces are usually named for the town in which they were first manufactured, though when more than one variety is made in one place other names are employed. For instance, the French town of Valenciennes invented a lace which is never known by any other name, though now chiefly manufactured in Belgium. Brussels makes so many laces, the city cannot give her name to all, and though they may with propriety be spoken of as Brussels lace, the term is rather ambiguous.

The manner in which pillow lace is made is rather puzzling to those unacquainted with it to understand. The pillow foundation is usually an oval board, which has a cushion on the top; this board the lace-worker takes upon her knee. The cushion or pillow has a piece of parchment fixed upon it, containing the pattern of the lace. The design is pricked through the parchment in numerous small holes, and pins are stuck through these into the pillow. The thread of which the lace is to be made is wound upon bobbins. The lace-worker fastens these threads on the pins at the beginning of her pattern, and so commences her task by twisting the bobbins round and interweaving the threads in the most complicated manner. The pattern is usually worked at the same time as the ground, though in some pillow laces it is made separately, and afterward joined together on a plain pillow or guipure ground. The pattern or gimp is generally of a thicker thread than the ground, though sometimes fine and coarse threads are worked together in the mesh. There are usually about fifty bobbins to the square inch employed in the manufacture of pillow lace. At the International Exhibition of 1874 there was shown a parasol cover in which eight thousand bobbins were used. It was manufactured at Courtrai.

The bobbins have been made of various materials since pillow lace was first invented. In Italy they were of bone, wood or lead. They are mentioned in the Sforza Inventory, 1493; these were of bone. In Flanders they are usually of wood, boxwood making the best. In England the bobbins were originally of bone—sheep and chicken bones being employed. For this reason the early English pillow lace was invariably called bone lace, though some credit this to the fact that fish bones were used to pin the lace to the cushions before metal pins were invented. The early pins were of boxwood, bone, and later, of bronze and silver, but none ever thought of making them of cheaper metal. Therefore, many lace-workers, and especially the wives and daughters of fishermen, used fish bones for their lace. These were used in Spain and Portugal also, and almost all countries possessing any larger range of coast, or where fish were abundant.

Bone bobbins are at present little used, as they are more expensive than wood. The cushions and bobbins employed by a lace-worker are often prized by her, not for their value, but from association; she learns to value her old cushion, being loth to exchange it, though faded, old and worn, for one that is bright and new. As to the bobbins, many of them are of different size and material —some of bone, ornamented with glass beads, or, if used for a great length of time, it may have a bit of silver let in; others are carved in fantastic patterns. These may have been gifts from lovers or friends. A daughter prizes the cushion and bobbins left her by her dying mother, and often these things are valued beyond almost any other worldly possession.

The laces belonging to the pillow family are legion. Some of these, but little known, often appear under wonderful names, but they are seldom of any especial importance commercially. The fashions in pillow laces change much oftener than in points, as they are in general use, while points are little patronized, except by the wealthy. It is, too, quite the fashion for manufacturers to make a run on some cheaper kind of lace as soon as it bids fair to be worn to any extent. These laces are seldom new, though almost invariably called so. Some of those recently in fashion scarcely deserve even the name of pillow lace, as so many are made almost altogether by the loom, receiving, perhaps, a slight finish in the way of hand-work, though this would entitle them to the name point rather than pillow. This is the case with the laces which have been most fashionable of late—namely, Breton and point d'esprit—though point de Medici, which is to be the next favorite, is a pillow production, one of the many Brussels laces, but almost too expensive to be used in so lavish a manner as have been Torchon, Breton and point d'esprit, unless, as is quite probable, a good imitation will, in many cases, be substituted for the real lace.

All pillow laces have been more or less successfully imitated, though there is still room for improvement in these imitations. The loom has been found to work like magic in producing not only bobbinet, but also lace with patterns that are exceedingly pretty, and if the thread used equals in quality and fineness that employed for laces made upon the pillow, and the patterns are well selected, there is no reason why the lace machines cannot be further improved until the imitations almost or quite equal the hand-made lace itself. In embroideries the Hamburg imitations have driven hand-work almost out of the market, and it is quite possible that woven laces may, at some future day not far distant, supplant the laces made by hand.

The pillow laces are too numerous to be named and described in detail, especially as many of them are unknown to the trade, and a lengthy account of how a few obscure pieces were manufactured would prove quite uninteresting. There are many standard varieties of the pillow family, however, which are more widely known than are the points.

The most important pillow laces are the following, and it is now the fashion to mingle point with a few of the most expensive kinds, in the same pattern:

Valenciennes,
Duchesse,
Point de Venice,
Point de Flandre,
Genoa Point,
Point de Medici,
Old Brussels Plait,
Plait Appliqué,
Mechlin,
Maltese,
Cluny,
Torchon,
Lille or Arras Thread,
Russian,
Honiton,
Regency Point,
Irish Point,
Baby Lace,
Trolly,
Breton,
Point d'Esprit,
Chantilly,
Grammont,
Blonde,
Guipure,
Llama,
Cashmere,
Yak.

Many of these laces are always popular, being at all times worn to some extent; others are for a season almost unknown, when suddenly they spring to light again, perhaps under a new name and modified in some slight particular.

It is almost impossible, therefore, to give a correct list of the pillow laces. A lace may be called one name where it is manufactured, and another by the merchant who imports it, and yet still a third by the retail dealer. During the war, a lady, whose husband was a great admirer of Lincoln, called at a mercantile establishment in New York, where she was slightly known. She purchased some Maltese lace of a peculiar pattern, and, not being very wise in lace lore, she asked the name. The clerk, thinking to please her, replied that it was called "Lincoln lace." The lady was delighted with her purchase, so much so that she took the whole piece.

Later, wishing to procure more of the same kind, she went into another store and inquired for Lincoln lace. No one had any idea what she required, and she was informed that they had none. Determined to procure some, she visited several stores, but could not find the lace she sought. One salesman fancied Limerick lace was the kind she desired and showed it accordingly, but was at once informed of his mistake. At length the lady, who, fortunately, had plenty of money and was determined to gratify her desire for this particular lace, went into one of the leading Broadway houses and made the same inquiry as before. She chanced to fall into the hands of an exceedingly sensible salesman, who was accustomed to hearing ladies ask for laces of nearly every known and unknown name under the sun, and therefore he replied that though they had no lace called by the name she mentioned, they had nearly every kind now manufactured; he would, therefore, show her all the varieties, adding, that special merchants gave special names, at times, to certain laces.

He began to exhibit the different kinds then in fashion, and the lady was gratified to find in Maltese the lace she sought. Though reliable houses will not mislead a customer in this manner, it is not an unusual thing to rechristen an old lace in order to give the name a more fashionable sound; therefore, many of them have no enduring title.

CHAPTER XXVII.

PILLOW LACE—(*continued*).

VALENCIENNES.

THIS deserves the first place among pillow laces, not because it is the most expensive, but because of all laces it is the most widely known. Other laces enjoy a *furore* of fashionable popularity for a few months, sometimes for a few years, and then give way to some other favorite, which is for a time applied to every decorative use possible in fashionable costumes, and then it as quietly steps aside in deference to some more recent favorite.

Not so Valenciennes. While Maltese lace enjoyed great popularity, Valenciennes, without any apparent effort, barely held its own. When Cluny came to the front at the behest of Fashion, it took the place of Maltese, but did not in the slightest degree affect Valenciennes. Afterward, duchesse became the rage; it was too expensive for all purposes, and beautiful enough to be a formidable rival to point gaze, but it did not encroach upon Valenciennes in any way whatever. The cream-colored cashmere lace was next brought forward, being popular at the same time with duchesse, as a cheaper lace was needed for ordinary purposes. Cashmere lace, therefore, was made into scarfs for a season, which were affected by rich and poor; but still Valenciennes stood its ground. Then Cashmere was thrust aside, Spanish blondes becoming the fashion, especially for scarf laces, while duchesse held its own among the most fashionable. Later, Torchon came in vogue, and was used for both outer and undergarments; then it gave way to Breton. An effort was made to introduce Mechlin afterward, but it was too expensive, considering its effectiveness; besides, at a short distance, it did not appear very unlike Breton. So point d'esprit began to be substituted for it, duchesse being still deservedly prime favorite, and Valenciennes, if possible, worn more than ever before.

One cause of the continued popularity of Valenciennes lies in the fact of its being adapted to nearly every use to which lace is applied. It is not, as a rule, manufactured in large articles, such as shawls, berthas, fichus and the like, but from narrow edgings up to deep flounces it is made in all grades. It is very strong, will wash admirably, is suitable alike for ornamenting white costumes and underclothing, while the better quality is employed for rich silks. For articles of lingerie it is admirably adapted; for handkerchiefs, collars, and what are called made-up lace goods generally, it has no rival.

Valenciennes originated in the French town whose name it bears, though the town and the province of Hainault in which it is situated were Flemish at first, and only French by conquest during the wars of Louis XIII. and XIV., being ceded to France by the treaty of Aix-la-Chapelle in 1668.

The date of the origin of this lace is unknown, but it was prior to the time Hainault became a French province. The industry was in a flourishing state under Louis XIV., and so continued for a century later, reaching its highest state of prosperity about the middle of the eighteenth century. The lace made in the city of Valenciennes was at this time far superior to that manufactured elsewhere, even in the neighboring towns, being remarkable for rare design, even texture, and skillful execution. This lace was more expensive than any other pillow manufacture at this time, as numerous bobbins were employed to make it, and the work progressed slowly. The Valenciennes lace-makers plied their task in underground rooms, the working hours being from four in the morning until

VALENCIENNES.

eight at night. Young girls usually made the lace, as firm eyesight and a delicate touch were required. No one woman could work many years at the task, as her sight failed under the pressure of long hours and the dim underground light. A piece executed by one hand was always considered superior to that upon which different workers had been employed, as there was quite a difference in the appearance of the web when manufactured by separate hands. Not more than an inch-and-a-half of narrow Valençiennes could be produced in a day, and some workers on choice pieces could not finish more than twenty-four inches in a year.

From 1750 to 1780 Valenciennes raged in France. Even the poor peasant women, who dressed plainly in other things, would save for years to purchase this favorite lace to adorn their caps, which would last them a life-

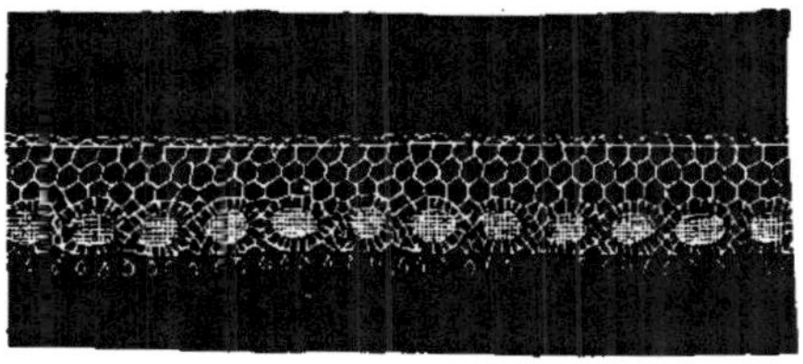

PETIT POUSSIN.

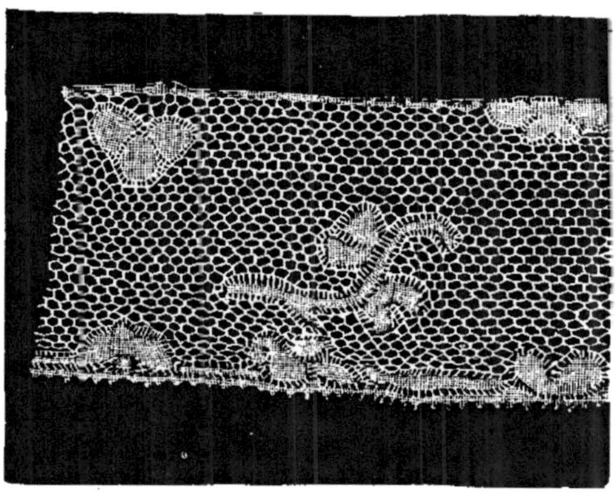

DIEPPE VALENCIENNES.

time, and, possibly, be handed down as heirlooms to their daughters. With the fall of the monarchy the manufacture of the lace in Valenciennes ceased. Napoleon strove to revive it, but in vain; the old lace-workers were either dead, or scattered in peaceful countries.

Valenciennes is made wholly upon the pillow, the ground and flower being of the same thread—the ground being firm and compact, the flower as fine and close in texture as cambric.

The lace-workers of Dieppe, Havre, Honfleur, Eu, Bolber and Fécamp all made at one time a species of Valenciennes. That of Havre was sometimes styled point du Havre, while the lace-makers of Dieppe were accustomed to give their manufactures peculiar names. Thus, a narrow trimming lace, resembling the round mesh Valenciennes, was called *petit poussin*, which, being interpreted, means little chicken.

Another style, quite as narrow, but with a square mesh, the dots in the pattern being on the extreme edge, was called Ave Maria.

The Valenciennes of Dieppe had a round mesh, and, though a very pretty lace, was not so strong or so difficult to manufacture as Valenciennes proper, being less complicated. The Dieppe ground had but three threads, while that of Valenciennes had four. Less bobbins were required, and they were not twisted so many times in making the ground.

Belgium now manufactures all the real Valenciennes in the market, Ypres, in West Flanders, producing the finest in the world. Bruges, Courtrai and Menin, also in West Flanders, and Ghent and Alos in East Flanders, produce excellent Valenciennes, that of the Courtrai being next to Ypres in quality. The Bruges Valenciennes has a round ground, and on this account is not so valuable. In this ground, like the Dieppe Valenciennes, the bobbins are twisted but twice in forming the mesh. Each town has its own peculiar mode of making the ground, though the square mesh is usually made. The Valenciennes of Ghent has the bobbins twisted in the ground two and a half times, that of Courtrai three and a half, that of Ypres and Alos four and five times.

Ypres makes the widest Valenciennes, with the exception of Courtrai which manufactures some extra widths. The Ypres Valenciennes is indeed a beautiful lace. The mesh is large, square and clear, the flower, like the finest cambric, a perfectly even tissue. M. Duhayon Brunfaut, a manufacturer of Ypres, in 1833, made a great improvement in Valenciennes. He adopted a large square mesh, exceedingly fine in texture, and a flowing pattern. Previously, the mesh had been smaller in size and thicker in substance, while the designs were contracted and scanty. This new style being exceedingly pretty, became extremely popular at once, and has so continued.

At the Exhibition of 1867 a piece of Ypres Valenciennes, a moderately wide flounce, was exhibited, for which $400 the metre was asked, a metre being three and a third inches more than a yard in length. In a week's time, working twelve hours each day, the lace-maker employed upon this piece could only produce one-third of an inch. This lace was a most exquisite production, rivaling point in beauty, as indeed does nearly all the Ypres Valenciennes. About twenty-five thousand lace-workers are engaged in the manufacture of this lace in Ypres alone, including its suburbs.

Recently, the fashion of mixing point gaze with Valenciennes has grown popular. Only the choicest specimens of Yypres Valenciennes are used in this combination. Deep flounces of this lace will have, placed here and there along the picot, medallions in point gaze, upon which the tiny dots, which lead some to call it round point, thickly occur; or, instead of these medallions, flowers of point gaze in floating relief are strewn along the edge, daisies, with many leaves placed one above the other and caught in the centre, or roses and buds, in similar relief.

Valenciennes has always been especially popular for handkerchiefs. These have the merest tiny bit of fine linen cambric for the centre, and are made almost entirely of the lace, often with a medallion of point in each corner, or a rose or daisy in floating relief. Scarfs are also made in the same manner, of the richest Valenciennes, in elaborate patterns, and point gaze flowers on either end.

As there is more real Valenciennes worn than any other lace manufactured, so the imitations are more widely scattered about the world than those of any other known lace. Some of these are of fair quality, while others scarcely deserve the name. Like Sairey Gamp's curls, which could not be called false, since they deceived nobody, from the fact that no one would have taken them for real hair, so the poorest loom productions can scarcely be called imitations of Valenciennes, for it would take an expert in lace to guess with any degree of accuracy what lace this feeble attempt was meant to imitate. The finest, as well as the cheapest, imitations of Valenciennes are made in France, though the better qualities, from the fact that good imitations were made in Italy, are usually termed Italian. These are often of linen thread, and are of good, smooth appearance, as well as soft to the touch. All the coarser imitations of Valenciennes are wiry, coarse and harsh. However, even this makes a passable trimming for cheap muslin dresses, the effect at a short distance being good. And, as the imitations are increasing in number and quality with each year, it is to be hoped that these coarser kinds will be superseded by something which will at least give some faint idea of the beauty of this really exquisite lace.

Valenciennes was at one time made to a small extent in Northampton, England.

CHAPTER XXVIII.

PILLOW LACE—(*continued*).

DUCHESSE.

This is the most beautiful of the pillow laces, and, next to Valenciennes, is the most important. It is not used for similar purposes, being unsuited to articles of underwear, as it does not bear repeated washings. For a handsome lace, however, it rivals point, showing beautifully over silks and velvets.

It is a guipure, sometimes called guipure de Bruges, but usually duchesse. It is also called point de Flandre, though incorrectly, as the laces are not the same. It is a pure white, the patterns graceful and flowing, the designs in large leafage or flowers, scrolls, etc., connected here and there by brides, though the lace, unlike Valenciennes, is nearly all pattern, with scarcely any ground. This lace is a clear white, and there is, as yet, no desire expressed on the part of the fashionable world to wear it in a yellow state.

Duchesse is particularly suited to scarfs, fichus, vests, pompadours, collars, lappets, and like articles, and is at present more freely used for these than any other lace, either point or pillow.

The engraving shows one of the collars now so fashionable in this popular lace, the design being foliage, roses and a tulip at the end of the lappet. Many of the designs are more elaborate, and so closely connected as to show but little groundwork.

Point gaze is mixed with this lace more than with any other, many of the lappets having a flower of point at the end, often a rose, daisy or bud, in floating relief.

Though duchesse lace is especially manufactured in small piece goods, like those just described, it also comes in regular lace widths, and is sold by the yard. It is a

COLLAR AND LAPPET OF DUCHESSE LACE.

very effective trimming for a rich evening dress, whatever the material or color of the costume may be. It comes in flounces, though not usually of the deepest widths, like point or Chantilly, as it is rather heavy-looking when used in this way.

Duchesse lace is made in separate sprigs upon the pillow, being afterward joined together. It is chiefly manufactured in Bruges, in West Flanders, and also in

Brussels. It is a comparatively new lace, though the plait is somewhat similar to many other plaited Brussels laces. Aside from its beauty, duchesse lace has for several years past been the most fashionable pillow lace, and therefore the manufacture is at present in an extremely flourishing condition.

POINT DE VENICE.

This lace has a plait and pattern not unlike duchesse, though it appears usually in regular lace widths, by the yard, in moderately narrow flouncings. It is a flat, broad plait, made in regular sprigs, and afterwards grounded, instead of being, like duchesse, united by brides. The mesh is the usual octagonal one, and, though the lace is very pretty, it is far less beautiful than the duchesse, and is not, just now, one of Fashion's especial favorites, though used to a certain extent by ladies who are partial to it.

Point de Venice is similar in some respects to the ancient Venetian grounded point, only it is a pillow production instead of being a needle-point. It is sometimes mingled with duchesse, and appears in scarfs and fichus. It is manufactured in Brussels and its environs.

POINT DE FLANDRE

is so similar to duchesse as to be often mistaken for it, though it is, upon the whole, a coarser production. It is not usually made up in piece goods, though it is, to a slight extent, in lappets, but these usually pass for a poor quality of duchesse. It is made in narrow widths, and, like duchesse, is never gathered when put on garments, but always laid flat.

GENOA POINT.

Though this lace bears an Italian name, from its resemblance to the ancient Genoese point, it is manufactured in Belgium chiefly. It is mingled with duchesse and point to a certain extent in small piece goods, but usually is manufactured in the regular form by the yard. It is rather a heavy lace, of the guipure order, and some of the patterns are exceedingly pretty, bearing a high price.

POINT DE MEDICI.

This is also a Brussels manufacture, and though it has not been in fashion for some years, there is an attempt being made to revive its use. It is said to have been the favorite lace of the Medici family, and specimens of it may be seen on their ancient portraits.

It resembles, in a great degree, the antique Cluny, but has a heavy cord introduced in the plait. In the cheaper qualities this cord is of cotton, but of flax in the finer productions. The lace recently appeared in the leading New York houses. Some of the merchants call it point de Medici, and others the new style of Cluny. It is not an expensive pillow case, at least not more so than Maltese and Cluny, though scarcely so cheap as Torchon. An imitation has already been produced which will probably be extensively used for ordinary purposes, and the price of the real lace, if it proves less popular than is at present expected, or after its popularity is on the wane if it does not prove a success in a fashionable way, will be much less than it is at present, as popularity greatly affects the price of lace generally, particularly the medium grades of pillow lace.

OLD BRUSSELS PLAIT.

This was for many years the most popular of laces, and, except for the early Genoa point or Genoese collar lace, it was the first popular production of the pillow; indeed, it dates as far back as the Genoese lace, though it is impossible to tell the date of its first manufacture.

There is a tradition concerning the invention of this lace, which was anciently believed by the Flemish lace-workers. A young gentleman of great wealth was in love with a poor young girl, who returned his affection; but the difference in their circumstances forbade marriage. One evening the girl was sitting alone in her cottage, weeping the night away, when a beautiful lady entered, and noiselessly approaching the girl, placed a green cloth cushion upon her knee, containing a number of bobbins filled with delicate thread. Silently seating herself beside the wondering girl, she began to teach her the art of making lace. The night wore on, and still the silent instructress pursued her task; but with the first gray dawn she flitted away, leaving the maiden perfect mistress of the art.

The girl at once began to make rare laces, and, selling them at an enormous cost, soon became rich, and was thereby enabled to wed the man of her choice. Years later, as she sat one evening in the enjoyment of peace and plenty, with her children playing about her knees, and her husband affectionately regarding them, the lady again made her appearance, not noiselessly, as before, but with regret and even anger upon her countenance.

"I helped you in your poverty," she said, "but you have not extended a helping hand to the poor about you.

OLD BRUSSELS PLAIT.

Here you enjoy wealth, while others around you are starving. The angels weep for you and turn their faces away."

Struck with remorse, the once poor girl rose early in the morning, and taking her cushion and bobbins, went about among the cottages of the poor, teaching them how to make lace. By this means they all became wealthy, and Flanders became famous for the lace which was then called Brussels point, and afterward, point d'Angleterre, but now, usually Old Brussels.

In the illustration the wrong ground is rendered, the usual round mesh being employed. In this specimen there is a mingling of point and pillow, as was often the case during the later days of the prosperity of this lace, for it continued prosperous for a longer period than any known lace, with the exception of Valenciennes. There were numerous edicts concerning this lace and the manner of weaving it, and it was copied in England and called bone lace. It was smuggled to a greater extent than any other lace known.

It is at present little manufactured, as it is not now one of Fashion's favorites, and has been obliged to give way to more modern laces.

Nearly all the early English thread laces were copies of this Brussels plait. Many of them were fairly executed, and quite attractive in pattern, but they could not compare with the real Brussels manufacture.

CHAPTER XXIX.

PILLOW LACE—(*continued*).

MECHLIN.

ALL the laces of Flanders, up to the time of Colbert's establishment of point de France, in 1665, were called Mechlin, except the old Brussels, then called Brussels point. Mechlin also went by the name of Malines lace, from the fact of its having originated there, and was sometimes called *broderie de Malines*. It was afterward manufactured at Antwerp, Turnhout and Lierre, Ypres, Bruges, Courtrai and Dunkirk.

It is made of one piece on the pillow, the same thread, which is exceedingly delicate and fine, forming the ground and flower, with the exception of one large flat thread, which is used to outline the flowers. It was this which gave it the name of embroidery, and, when the laces were both in infancy, was the only thing which distinguished it from Valenciennes. In England it was called Mechlin. It was a favorite lace in England, France and Holland. Anne of Austria was particularly fond of it for lighter uses.

It is a pretty lace, but is so delicate as to have a rather flimsy appearance. It is not suitable for putting on a garment plain, but shows best plaited or gathered. It was a favorite lace of Napoleon I., and enjoyed popularity for a long time, but was replaced by more showy laces early in the present century. Recently, however, its manufacture has been revived to a certain extent, and it is made at Malines, Turnhout and Brussels, the towns which formerly were engaged in the industry having given it up for Valenciennes.

Though not at present a very fashionable lace, Mechlin is a favorite with many ladies, who are partial to delicate laces, and therefore there is always a certain demand for

MECHLIN.

it. Though not found at all mercantile houses, nearly all the largest ones keep it in small quantities to accommodate their customers who care for it, while imitations abound. The best of these is a machine lace, of fine texture, the flowers being woven, and outlined by a flat linen thread, which is put in by the needle. This lace is usually termed "hand-run Mechlin," and is sold for a much higher price than that which is the entire product of the loom.

An attempt was recently made to substitute Mechlin for the fashionable Breton, but it was unsuccessful, as the lace is too expensive to be used in the lavish manner in which Breton and Torchon have been employed, and, as it is too delicate to bear hard usage, it is fit only for light wear.

PLAIT APPLIQUE.

This is simply a lace made of the flat Brussels pillow flowers, appliquéd to fine machine net, and sometimes further decorated by dots and fine sprays put in with the needle after the application work is completed. For this reason it is often called point appliqué. It is a very light lace, and though it gives rather indifferent service, the flowers may be applied to a new ground and thereby rendered almost like new lace. The process, however, should only be undertaken by an expert, or some one very skillful with the needle.

At present this lace is not in fashion, though it is worn, like Mechlin, to some extent by those who fancy it.

LILLE OR ARRAS THREAD.

Colbert established the manufacture of pillow lace at Arras and several other towns in France, and from a variety of laces there came at length to be only two kinds extensively manufactured in thread—Valenciennes, and the lace of Lille and Arras, which resembled Mechlin to a much greater extent than it did Valenciennes, though it was far cheaper than either. The Lille and Arras laces were quite similar; those of Lille, however, being better in quality than the productions of the Arras lace-workers. Both have plain, clear white grounds, called the Lille ground, or *fond clair*.

The Lille lace is made on a pillow, with a thick thread to form the pattern. It is of the fine Lille thread, which was bleached at Antwerp, the ground being often covered with the little square dots—point d'esprit—which characterize the present fashionable ruching lace.

Lille was a Flemish town until the peace of Aix-la-Chapelle, when it was transferred to France. It was not, therefore, one of the towns in which Colbert established

LILLE LACE.

the lace manufacture. The lace industry of Lille was of far older date. It was greatly used in France and England, being smuggled into the latter country, though to a less extent than old Brussels or Mechlin. The picot was nearly straight at one time, but, later, it followed the styles in Mechlin.

Black lace was also manufactured in Lille, which was used for trimming silks and mantles.

The Arras thread lace was almost precisely similar to that of Lille. It was not so fine, but it was strong and a clear white.

The patterns were less diversified than those of the Lille lace, and from making the same over and over again the workers grew to make it with astonishing swiftness. On this account the lace was cheap for the quality, which helped it into popularity.

The Emperor Charles V. introduced the lace industry

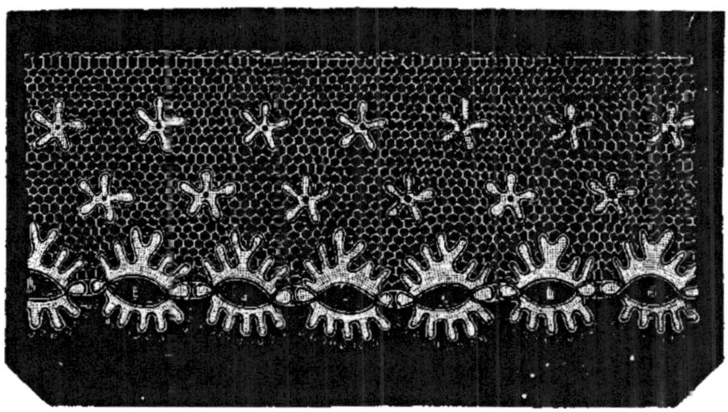

ARRAS THREAD.

in Arras, and Colbert encouraged it. The lace was sometimes called, in England, Orrice lace.

The laces of both Lille and Arras went by the name of mignonnette at a very early date. During this time they were quite narrow. They were also called *blonde de fil* and *point de tulle*. Later, nearly all the lace-making towns of France, Belgium and even Switzerland made similar lace, which was called *mignonnettes et blonde de fil*. It was made in England to a slight extent, and called by different names—run lace, Northampton point and Buckinghamshire point, the word point being used to denote clear ground, which especially distinguishes this lace.

RUSSIAN.

The pillow lace manufactures of Russia are not of an extensive or elaborate order, most of the lace being simple in design, and far from elaborate in execution. Both ground and flower are rather loosely plaited, there being little fineness about it, though, as the thread is not very fine, it wears well.

Sometimes a heavy cord is introduced in the centre of the wavy pattern, which, while adding strength, gives more character to the design. Torjok and Jetetz are the two Russian towns where the lace industry is most flourishing

Russian lace is not employed for the finer trimming purposes, except a few exceptionally fine pieces. It is used to a certain extent in ornamenting morning robes and matinées of bright-colored cashmere, also for children's dresses. The coarser kinds, and particularly the imitations, are much used for ornamenting window drapery and similar articles. The loom imitations are very good, and at a short distance are very effective. The designs are not numerous, all partaking, in a wonderful degree, of the same character, and resembling many of the patterns of modern tape and braid laces, in which the design is carried out in one braid only, and that a very simple one, the ground being filled in a loose and irregular mesh, and the wheels all precisely similar.

RUSSIAN LACE.

CHAPTER XXX.

PILLOW LACE—(*continued*).

HONITON.

THIS is the principal English lace manufactured, the only one, in fact, made to any great extent at the present day It is, in reality, the same lace as the beautiful duchesse of Bruges, but it has not the same popularity, for the reason that it is made in far less quantity. It differs from duchesse, in having two decided grades as regards quality. While duchesse is seldom made in any but effective patterns, Honiton shows some meaningless designs, which seem to be the only ones sent to this country, as at this time it is out of the question to find a piece of Honiton lace in New York City which one can really call pretty.

But the fine quality of Honiton is quite a different affair. It is so beautiful it is often called the English point, only, however, by courtesy, as it is a pillow lace. Though never mingled with point proper, like duchesse, it often has its flowers put together with the needle, instead of upon the pillow.

Honiton, in Devonshire, is the seat of the Honiton lace industry, though the work is carried on to some extent in Buckingham, Oxford, Bedford and Dorsetshire counties. It is said that lace-making was introduced in the county of Devon by Flemish refugees in 1567. The epitaph of a "bone lace seller," of Honiton, still exists upon a tombstone in the churchyard at Honiton, bearing date July, 1617.

The bone lace first manufactured in Honiton was very unlike the modern production. It was made of coarse flax thread, and was not especially noted for beauty of design. It flourished, however, even when the lace manufactures of other districts of England were on the decline. When the industry seemed to waver, a little royal patronage judiciously applied not only availed to keep it alive but imparted a healthful vitality.

Women and even children are engaged in making the lace. It is usually manufactured at their homes, and disposed of to the village merchants, who afterward sell it to city buyers. In this way the sums realized for the work is usually quite small. The lace-workers of Honiton and other English towns, however, do not usually depend upon it as the only means of obtaining a livelihood. In Bruges one can see the duchesse lace-workers busy at every cottage window or door, for lace-making is the life of the city; but the Honiton lace-workers are the wives and daughters of men who carry on some mode of gaining a livelihood, however simple it may be, and on this account they do not trouble themselves to seek higher markets for the products of their labor. If they could sell it to city merchants without the interference of middlemen a much higher profit would be realized.

The sprigs in the Honiton patterns are made separately upon the pillow, and are either joined with needle-made brides or pillow grounds. A few years since the fashion of applying them to fine machine net was introduced, but it has since fallen into disfavor.

In the Devonshire district is made what is called the Tunis lace, which is composed of the machine-made braids, the favorite one being a succession of medallions, and known to our tape and braid lace-makers as the Honiton braid. This design occurs also in the regular Honiton, in the plainer patterns. Within half a century an attempt has been made to introduce natural-looking flower sprays, instead of the stiff emblems usually employed. The result has been highly satisfactory.

RAISED BEDFORD PLAIT.

Queen Victoria has been a faithful patron of the Honiton lace industry. Not only has she ordered her own bridal laces and those of her daughters of her favorite Honiton, but she has encouraged lace schools and striven to aid the industry in every possible way. The laces produced to fill royal orders have been exquisitely beautiful, both in design and execution, and show that, with some care, Honiton lace might become a formidable rival to duchesse, not at home only, but abroad.

The lace of Bedfordshire differs considerably from the regular Honiton.

One very pretty variety is called raised plait, and is in appearance something between Honiton and Maltese. The design is slightly raised, though of pillow manufacture.

REGENCY POINT.

This is another variety of English lace, though little manufactured at present. It is one of the products of

REGENCY POINT

Northamptonshire, and consisted of a clear ground and closely plaited design, resembling in texture the Valenciennes pattern.

The illustration shows a piece of this lace, in which a most beautiful design is shown, the threads hanging from each side showing the work in an incompleted state. The threads are numerous, as will be seen in the illustration, and as each one must have a bobbin and be used in turn by the worker who plaits the lace, something of the complicated nature of the work may be imagined. This lace, called point through courtesy, was strong, durable and pretty, flower and ground being wrought with the same thread, the footing strengthened by a number of extra threads, and the flower being closely wrought to give it body.

The manufacture of this lace was never extensive, and it seldom appears in the market.

IRISH POINT.

The term Irish point is rather indefinitely applied to a number of Irish laces, among them one which has the appearance of cutwork, being a fine lawn perforated with open embroidery until only a mere skeleton remains. This is not, in the strictest sense, lace at all, but it is bought and sold under the name.

Again, the name Irish point is given to a rather pretty pillow lace, which resembles to a certain extent the old English thread laces, which were manufactured to imitate the Lille thread.

The real Irish point is made at Limerick, and is sometimes called Curragh point. It is of fair quality, but does not appear in large quantities in the market.

CARRICKMACROSS.

This is of Irish manufacture, and a very pretty thread guipure, many of the patterns resembling the Maltese lace. It is not very expensive, but it trims many articles effectively, and deserves to be a greater favorite than it really is. However, with the sharp competition which the loom laces keep up, it is not probable the Carrickmacross guipures will ever be more largely manufactured or generally used than now.

BABY LACE.

There is a pretty, delicate English lace made in Buckinghamshire, Northamptonshire and Bedfordshire, though the manufacture is not large at the present time. It is very delicate in texture and not particularly strong; but, the price being rather low, it became a favorite garniture

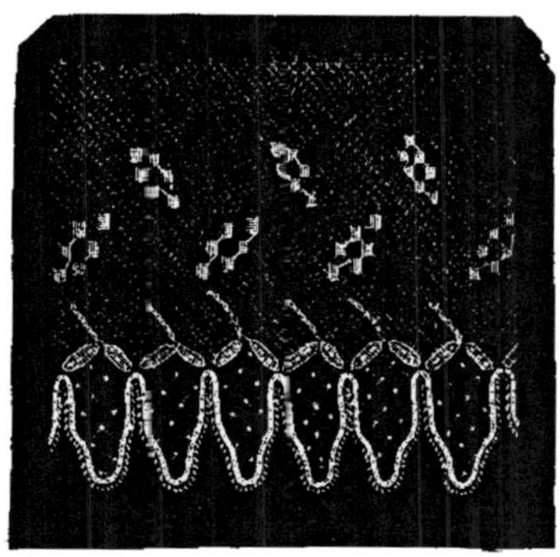

BABY LACE.

for baby linen, being extensively used for largettes, both in England and America.

Each of the districts named as the seat of its manufacture make a different pattern; but the little points d'esprit, which mark the Lille and Arras laces, are seen in nearly every design. At one time the industry was quite large, but for a few years past the lace has fallen into disuse, and the laces raging at the moment are now usually employed to trim infants' outfits. As the lace was little used for other purposes, the demand ceased, and, consequently, the manufacture also; but it is quite probable the fashion for it may spring up at no distant day, as the lace had much to recommend it, being a clear, pure white, delicate and pretty, as well as very reasonable in price.

CHAPTER XXXI.

PILLOW LACE—(*continued*).

MALTESE.

THIS lace was exceedingly popular a few years since, being the most beautiful of the pillow guipures. It is of Maltese origin, but is extensively manufactured in Germany, also to some extent in France, Belgium and England.

The patterns in Maltese lace vary but little, there being a wonderful sameness about them, which grows tiresome when the lace is generally worn. It varies greatly in quality, some pieces being very coarse and others beautifully fine. The fine designs are much handsomer than the coarse, the body of the lace being a network of pearled brides; sometimes the brides are double, the picots being on the outside of each. Often the design consists solely of this network, with a row of tiny Maltese crosses near the picot. Some of these finer patterns have tiny dots in relief upon the solid portion at the intersection of the brides, which are formed by a narrow strip being plaited by itself for a tiny space, and then joined with the other plait. This leaves a small raised dot.

The Maltese lace is quite strong, even the finer pieces wearing well. It is still in demand, and being simple in pattern, is much liked for trimming children's dresses, particularly bright-colored cashmeres for winter wear. There is a very good imitation made, the lace being so simple it is an easy matter to copy it in loom laces. It is more expensive than Torchon, but the imitations are used very freely, even for fine purposes, and these are quite cheap, many of them so perfect as to be mistaken for the real, even at a short distance.

CLUNY.

This is a cross between Maltese and Torchon, and was quite the rage a few years since, being still worn in moderation, though there is comparatively little call for it. The lace is a clearer white than Torchon, and the thread is firmer, though softer than Maltese. It is not so hard-twisted as the latter, nor yet so loose as the former; still, it partakes, in a great degree, of the characteristics of both laces, the patterns being somewhat on the guipure order, yet more flowing.

It is a French lace, though manufactured in Italy, Germany and other continental countries while it was in such extensive demand. There is a great difference in the coarse and fine productions, the coarse being inferior in pattern and general appearance, while the finer pieces were many of them beautiful.

This is also extensively imitated by the loom, and the imitations are many of them excellent, looking and wearing well. The real lace is exceedingly strong, and suited for articles of underwear, as well as for ornamenting costumes, as it washes beautifully, much better than the Maltese lace.

TORCHON.

This lace, recently so popular, was little valued in France, or indeed at any time or place until within a few years past. It is of extremely ancient origin for a pillow lace, being one of the oldest productions of the pillow in France, and in existence some time before Colbert's establishment of the lace industry, which was an era in the manufacture, as it occasioned much discussion, pro and con, upon the subject of laces, and left no doubt as to those in existence at the time. At this period Torchon was called Gueuse, and little esteemed, and being worn only by the peasantry and lower classes generally. It continued to be regarded with little favor, and was called in England beggar's lace. It was manufactured in Italy, especially at Naples, where it was hawked about the streets. The patterns in the Naples production were superior to the French.

TORCHON.

Later, the lace was manufactured in Germany and Flanders, Stavelot, near Spa, having a large establishment devoted to making Torchon. In Saxony both men and boys are employed in its manufacture, the lace made here being fine and of good quality, with rather large designs.

Torchon is also called Smyrna lace, the better qualities being usually given this term.

Torchon is in reality much better adapted to trimming underwear than outside costumes, as even the finer grades have a rather coarse appearance. There is a wide difference in the quality, some of the finer patterns being quite elaborate, though, upon the whole, the lace cannot be considered beautiful; and, only for the recent esteem in which the fashionable world has held it, would scarcely deserve mention among the many handsome pillow laces.

The thread is loose, soft, and not thoroughly bleached, being usually of a pale cream-white, which is rather an advantage, as when thoroughly bleached the lace appears coarser. Some imitations are in the market, but the lace itself is so reasonable in price, even the finer pieces being far from expensive, that the imitations are scarcely cheaper. Unlike some laces, the loom imitations do not wear so well as the lace itself, and therefore there is no advantage in purchasing them. They are usually of a coarse linen thread, which seems very brittle, breaking away with the slightest wear. The imitations are loosely woven also, in very open patterns, and they draw out of shape upon the slightest provocation, which adds to their general frailty. During the time when Torchon was so popular, it was used lavishly upon all articles of wearing apparel, even upon ball and evening costumes, for which it was eminently unfitted. At present, however, its brief day of popularity being over, it has returned to its former sphere, and, in all probability, will not soon again leave it. For underwear it is very appropriate, and it is still used to a certain extent upon this, though its popularity even for such purposes is upon the wane.

BRETON.

This is a French lace, as its name indicates, the first production being pillow-made, with small flowers plaited on a clear, delicate ground. It was not especially noted until quite recently, when it was revived and sent to the front by the fashion magnates. It is particularly adapted to light purposes, being rather too ineffective for wearing plain, and on this account it is generally plaited, though sometimes gathered. It is very pretty for light muslins, and for Swiss, organdie or other thin white dresses it is especially so, being delicate, cool and clear, and so fine it is not put to shame by the most expensive materials, though better fitted for costumes of dainty texture and soft color.

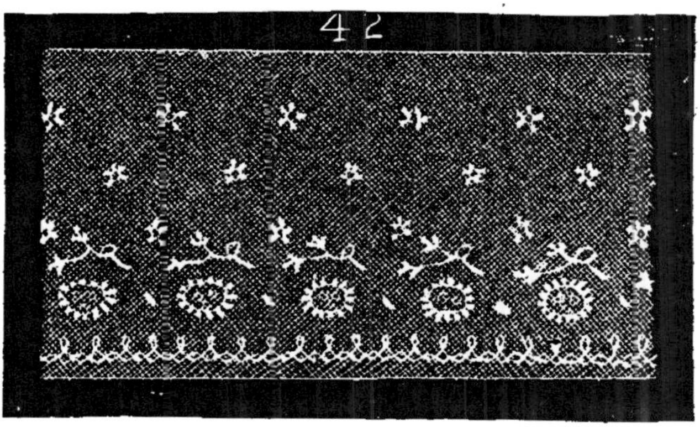

BRETON.

The modern Breton is manufactured in France, but it is not, properly speaking, a pillow lace, even what is called the real being an imitation. It is of fine Brussels net, with the pattern darned in by hand with fine linen floss. Even this, however, is a very pretty lace, extremely light and airy for making up into plaitings or ruchings, and greatly in favor for ornamenting summer and evening bonnets.

The pattern being darned upon a piece of machine net.

which is straight at both edges, and is called footing, there is neither footing nor picot to this lace, both edges being straight and precisely similar, only the pattern being darned closer to one side gives it a more finished appearance.

The illustration does not give the regular ground, but is otherwise correct. The ground is simply a net, with the ordinary round mesh.

There is, again, an imitation of this imitation, in which pattern and ground are woven together, and both are cotton. This imitation is passable at a short distance, and especially when plaited, but it has not the soft appearance which is the greatest beauty of the hand-run lace. It is, too, rather harsh to the touch, and the picot is usually finished in small points that have the appearance of being embroidered. It makes rather pretty neck-ruchings, and a neat and appropriate trimming for the plainer kinds of summer dresses.

Breton is too delicate for trimming underwear, it does not wash well, the net being tender, and the thread sometimes draws when wet. There is one quality especially which is run with white silk instead of linen, and this breaks when washed as though it had been clipped at short distances. This is not so durable as that which is run with linen, though none of the lace will endure even ordinary wear without breaking. It is, emphatically, a summer lace, and should go with soft crêpes and light gauzes, never with heavy materials.

POINT D'ESPRIT.

Like Breton, this is a French lace, the original pillow production being similar to the laces of Lille and Arras, having a clear ground with little square dots dashed over it, either singly or in clusters, which form squares or diamonds. It resembles Breton in nearly every other respect, is similarly made, what is now called the real having square or round dots put in by hand, and the imitation having the dots woven in the net.

It is adapted to the same purposes as Breton, and the present fancy is to make of it small neck coverings, which are half scarf and half collar, and more like a round-cornered handkerchief folded about the neck than either. The indications are that the popularity of this lace will be exceedingly brief, as its poverty of style unfits it for any but the very lightest purposes, it being decidedly inferior to Breton in appearance.

CHAPTER XXXII.

SILK LACES.

CHANTILLY

The name of Chantilly is applied to all the black silk French laces of pillow manufacture produced in a hundred towns and villages of which Chantilly is the centre. This lace is often called French thread, though incorrectly, as it is made of a silk that has no gloss.

The Duchesse de Longueville established the manufacture of this lace at Chantilly, which soon became prosperous, spreading to the surrounding towns. Later, the same lace was manufactured at Caen and Bayeux, always bearing the name Chantilly, however. Since then, the industry at Chantilly declined, on account of the town being situated so near to Paris that labor was dear.

The fashion for the lace fluctuated, the Chantilly alternating with blonde in favor, and as the fashion changed, so the Chantilly lace manufacture rose or fell. Shawls, fichus and all kinds of piece goods were produced in beautiful designs, the ground being like a web. The mesh is light and clear in the finer qualities, the flowers in a closer stitch, though not a very compact style, as even the pattern was worked in a variety of stitches, more or less open, their variety giving the effect of shading.

The manufacture of this lace met with a sad reverse, however, for, being expensive and worn by the nobility chiefly, it was considered a royal fabric. In consequence, at the time of the Revolution, the poor lace-makers of Chantilly perished on the scaffold with their royal patrons in 1793. The manufacture revived temporarily, however, with the first Empire, during which time all the laces of France flourished in a greater or less degree. On account of the exorbitant wages asked by the workers, the industry declined, or, rather, it removed to a greater distance from Paris, at Gisors, where beautiful shawls, flounces and scarfs are produced, but so fine are they, the price renders them obtainable by the wealthy only.

The greater portion of the Chantilly lace of the present day is made at Bayeux. Here the same system is adopted as in the Brussels and Alençon point manufacture, that of putting several workers upon the same piece. Each plaits a portion of the pattern, and when completed, they are joined by the stitch called point de raccroc, which was invented by a lace-maker of Calvados, called Cahanet. By this means orders can be filled in a comparatively short time.

Chantilly is the most beautiful of black laces, and in some of the patterns the effect of shading is carried out with wonderful skill, almost equal to that in point gaze. The lace is very successfully imitated, and the imitations are very popular at present for decorating black silk costumes and wraps of various sorts, also for trimming summer grenadines. The imitations are many of them almost equal to the poorer quality of Chantilly, which has a thicker ground, and the pattern woven in one stitch only, outlined with a heavier silk thread.

Similar laces are manufactured in various parts of Europe to a small extent, particularly in Belgium. Grammont, in East Flanders, makes a black silk lace similar to Chantilly, but the production is inferior to the French, the lace being cheaper in price and not so strong as the regular Chantilly. Piece goods only are made at Grammont.

BLONDE.

Next to Chantilly the blondes are the most important among the silk laces, and to a certain extent they are more so, for they are less expensive; in consequence, they are worn by a greater number of persons, and therefore are more widely known.

Blonde laces were first manufactured in Caen, about 1750. The first were of the natural écru tint, the silk coming from Nankin, and on account of this shade being similar to that of light hair, the production was called blonde. Afterward, white blonde was made from bleached silk of a superior quality, making a most brilliant white. This lace is harder to keep pure and white while being plaited, than the thread laces, and only particularly neat and expert workers can execute it properly. It was made in the summer only, as the least smoke of a fire affects its purity, or, if resorted to in the winter, the women worked in cow-house lofts, which were supposed to be heated by the animals themselves, although the warmth could not have been excessive. It is almost impossible for people in any country outside of France to possess so strong an imagination, though the country is not celebrated for cosey fires, even in winter.

The blonde laces of Caen are celebrated for their brilliant whiteness, and are made of two kinds of silk thread, a fine one for the ground and a thicker one for the flower.

This lace was successfully imitated at Nottingham and Calais in their loom productions, and the manufacture of the white pillow blondes has therefore been abandoned at Caen—almost, in fact, in every place where they were manufactured. The manufacture of blonde laces, however, was not affected so seriously by the machine laces as were the thread productions of the pillow. Black blonde continued to be made in considerable quantities.

At Bayeux the black blondes are extensively made in the regular Spanish patterns. Large piece goods are manu-

factured, scarfs, and especially mantillas, which are exported to Mexico, Spain, South America and Cuba. In these the ground and pattern are of the same sized silk, the design being very close, the ground open and clear.

The illustration shows a specimen of blonde in a Spanish design, but by an error of the engraver the ground is rendered in squares instead of the regular round mesh.

The regular Spanish blondes are made in Catalonia, chiefly at Barcelona. There are no large manufactories, but the lace is made by women and young girls in their own homes, when and how they like. The mantilla is the chief article produced.

There is a wide difference between the patterns of the French and the Spanish blondes. The French are smaller, the Spanish large and rather bold, but free and flowing, with a certain dash of grace. The Spanish are more popular than the French, and on this account they are copied by nearly all the French manufacturers, their own patterns being allowed to fall into disuse.

The blondes are successfully imitated by the loom laces; not only are the blondes of Caen produced in perfection, but also the Spanish mantillas of Bayeux.

GUIPURE.

The silk guipures are manufactured in France, Germany and Italy. A few years since, when the lace was in favor, it was very extensively produced, and, as there is always some demand for it, the manufacture does not die out altogether, though it has been for ten years on the decline.

This lace is so familiar to all, a description is scarcely necessary. It is manufactured in écru, white and black, but in black most extensively. It has very many of the qualities necessary to a good lace. There is no black silk lace manufactured which will give such good service. It is well adapted to trimming all manner of black dresses and wraps, and the better grades are exceedingly pretty. Added to this, it is comparatively inexpensive. These qualities render it so important that it will not remain, for any great length of time in the background, and there is every probability that it will soon be again in demand.

Guipure lace has been imitated, but not so successfully

as the Chantilly or blonde, not because the imitation is more difficult, but because, since the loom laces arrived at the greatest degree of perfection, the guipures have not been greatly in demand. The best real black silk guipures are made at Le Puy.

LLAMA.

This lace is made of worsted, and is of pillow manufacture. It was invented at a time when the lace trade was on the decline, and a cheaper material was needed in order to cheapen the manufacture. Piece goods were made of it almost exclusively, though a few edgings were also produced. It was not very long in fashion, and the production died out for a time, but was revived a few years later, and proved quite a success. The half-shawls, called llama, were at one time popular. They are rather wiry, but of a good black, and wear extremely well. They were chiefly manufactured at Le Puy, in France.

YAK.

This is only a worsted guipure, pillow-made, and the better productions make appropriate trimmings for black cashmere or other wool dresses. As a rule, however, the plainer guipure patterns were copied, and much of the Yak lace was very inferior in design. It was popular about the time the silk guipures were on the decline, and was quite successfully imitated by the loom. Like the other guipures, it is manufactured at Le Puy; in fact, it is almost altogether of French production.

CASHMERE.

A simple lace of soft wool, manufactured in patterns resembling both Chantilly and blonde, but the latter to a greater extent than the former. The ground was a clear mesh, the pattern in thicker thread. It was made in trimmings, insertions, and in scarf patterns, which resembled both, and was principally used for scarfs. It was not long in fashion, being unsuited for many purposes. It was a pale cream color, and, though soft, had considerable body. It made a most appropriate trimming for children's white cashmere or wool dresses and sacques, and for morning costumes of cream-white cashmere or bunting.

CHAPTER XXXIII.

ANCIENT LACES REVIVED.

WITHIN a few years the ancient knotted point has been revived under the name of macramé, and though scarcely worthy of the name of lace, from the fact of its being of a coarse thread, almost, in fact, a cord, and used only for trimming furniture and drapery, yet it is a very interesting work, and, being made upon a cushion, certainly is entitled to the name of pillow lace.

Darned netting, also used for window drapery, tidies and similar purposes, is another primitive lace which has been revived by lace-workers. This, however, is made by darning the pattern on net, and does not come under the head of pillow lace.

MACRAME.

Macramé is an Arabic word, signifying a fringed border, and the lace which bears the name, unlike lace proper, is usually fringed. It is not adapted to the finer uses as a trimming, but is admirable for many purposes, such as ornamenting curtains, lambrequins, chair and table covers, towels, household linen and church drapery. The better qualities, when manufactured from a fine even thread the natural color of the flax, makes a pretty and suitable trimming for linen dresses of the same écru shade. The Roman peasants wear scarfs about their heads bordered with macramé.

It is of extremely ancient origin, and the first record of

its existence was in 1494; the pattern book of Taglienti gave designs for working it half a century later, from 1530 to 1550, as *punto a gropo*. Macramé is knotted on a pillow, one kind being worked flat and rather loosely, the other is lightly knotted and raised in ridges and dots. The designs are usually geometrical, but sometimes they

MACRAMÉ.

are more elaborate, beetles, butterflies and other insects being copied, though in rather a heavy style.

The above design is geometrical, and from a piece of Italian lace. In copying it the points may be finished with a fall of fringe if desired; this is the usual style, though the ends may be clipped and worked in when preferred.

Macramé is made upon a pillow usually, though there is an American invention which has recently been patented—a sort of desk, in which pins are also used, by means of which the lace may be knotted more easily.

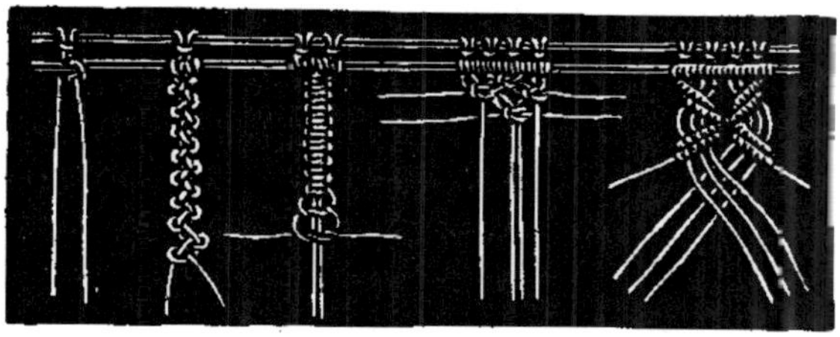

KNOTS FOR MACRAME.

In working it with the pillow a number of large pins are stuck in a row, at equal distances, across the whole length of the cushion, and to each of these pins a thread is knotted. The thread is evenly doubled before knotted to the pins, and falls with the ends toward the worker, who sits with the cushion placed upon a table before her. The length of the thread, when knotted upon the pins, should be rather more than four times the length the whole fringe is to be, as it takes up greatly in the knotting, unless the pattern is very simple.

To these threads a leader is fastened horizontally, each

strand of the threads fastened to the pins being knotted to this leader in turn.

Afterward, the threads are knotted in various fashions to form the pattern, cross threads being introduced at regular or irregular distances, according to the design. It is impossible to describe all the knots, but we give a diagram showing how the most important ones are made.

The ancient knotted point continued to be popular until 1620, when it fell into disfavor and was superseded by the plaited laces. The art of making it seemed to have died out altogether, but early in the present century was revived in Italy, which was always the principal seat of its manufacture. Some of the finest specimens come from the Albergo de Poveri at Genoa. Here the young children are employed in knotting the lace, in many instances it being the first work put into their hands. Simple patterns are executed by beginners, and more elaborate ones by experts, many inventing the pattern while they work. The ends of towels are fringed and wrought into simple and beautiful designs, and the lace is also made up separately in various widths for finer purposes. It is not extensively manufactured outside of Italy, though quite recently it has become a fashionable pastime for English and American ladies who delight to employ their leisure in this fascinating work. It is made to some extent by sailors while away at sea, for they are famous for tying knots, and invariably like the work.

When employed to decorate the ends of scarfs, towels and table linen, it is made of the raveled fringe at the end of the article decorated In this case only the cross threads are added. The popular material is unbleached flax thread, coarse or fine, according to the taste or time of the worker. It is extremely durable, will bear any amount of hard usage, and still last for generations. Unlike worsted work, it is never troubled by moth, and it will bear repeated washings.

MACRAME.

The threads used for modern macramé, which is intended for window or mantel drapery, is often dyed red or yellow, and the color is mingled with the natural écru shade, to match the curtains or furniture of the room.

The illustration on preceding page represents a piece of Italian macramé, an ancient production, in which beetles are rather vaguely represented.

Macramé may be seen in old paintings. In the "Last Supper," by Paul Veronese, the table-cloth has the borders knotted and fringed after the manner of macramé. Fine specimens of this lace were exhibited at the Paris Exhibitions of 1867 and 1878, and also at the Centennial, 1876.

GUIPURE D'ART.

This is also called guipure netting, and is known to the trade as antique lace. It comes in what are called antique squares, antique edging and antique insertion. The larger squares are used for tidies; they are quite expensive, particularly the finer grades, but being of a strong unbleached flax thread, they wear forever and a day, and therefore, in one way, are quite economical. The smaller squares are used for cushion covers, or they are put together with satin blocks or bands, to form large tidies. They are also used in the same manner for pillow shams and counterpanes, for curtains and similar articles; often the insertion is combined with the squares, and the article, when finished, is usually bordered with the lace.

The finer squares are used for lappets and tie-ends; they are really very pretty indeed, but unless exceedingly fine, are unfitted for dress decoration.

The netting is first made, and when completed in the size and shape desired, the pattern is put in with a needle and the same thread used for the netting. Sometimes two sizes of thread are employed, however, in working different portions of the design, but usually only one, as it gives the work the appearance of uniformity.

Some of the squares have straight edges, and others angular scallops, like the lower edge of lace in the

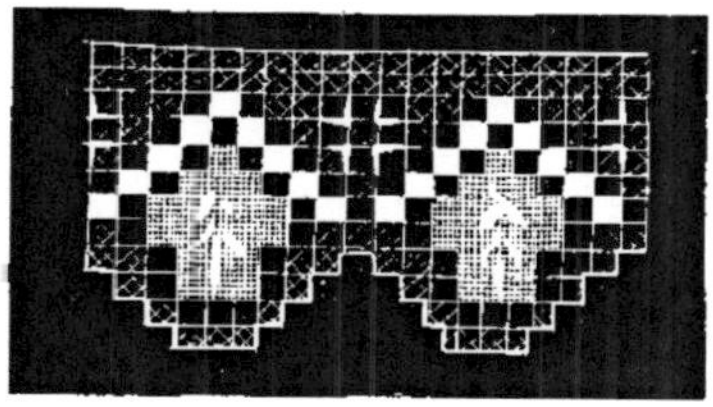

GUIPURE D'ART.

illustration. When required to be used separately, they have the scalloped border, but when joined together with satin squares, ribbon or insertion, they are perfectly square.

A number of stitches are employed in filling up the pattern on the netted foundation. The first and simplest of these is the darning stitch, or *point de reprise*, by which one or more of the netted squares are filled in with close darning, making it quite solid.

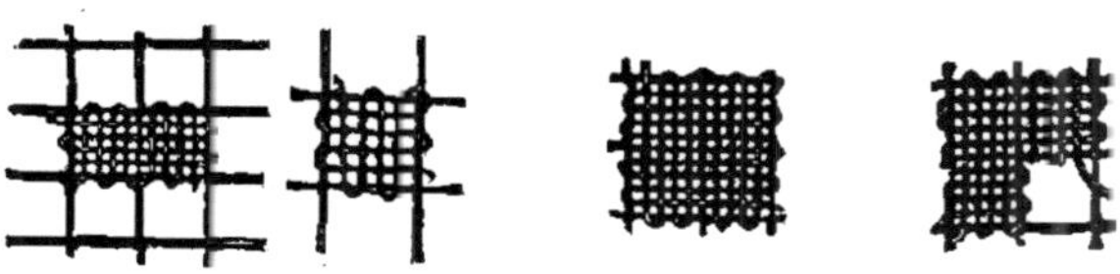

TRELLIS WORK, OR POINT DE TOILE STITCHES.

Trellis-work stitch, or *point de toile*, is similar to the darning stitch, only it is not so close, a space being left between each thread.

Point stitch, or *point crosse*, is where bars of thread are thrown diagonally across the netted square, turning it into triangles of various sizes, according to the number of stitches used.

Festoon stitch, or *point d'esprit*, is where the thread is festooned from each side of the square, and forms circles where several squares are filled in side by side in this manner.

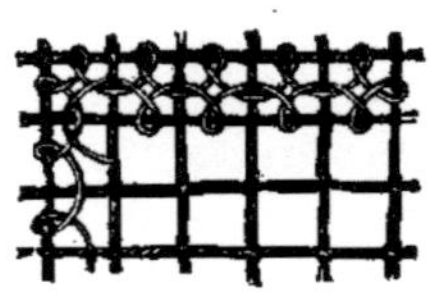

FESTOON STITCH.

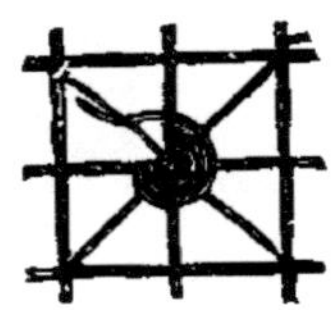

FAN STITCH.

Fan stitch is worked across several bars in the corners of squares, but does not form a complete circle, being darned backward and forward.

Guipure relief is where bars of thread are thrown across several squares to form a star, cross, stalks or leaves, and then worked over and under in darning stitch.

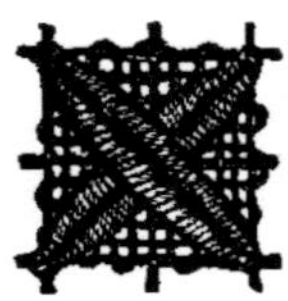

GUIPURE RELIEF.

FOUNDATION FOR RELIEF.

Besides these there are mushroom, spinning and pyramid stitches, and webs, wheels, stars, picots and various plain and tufted button-hole stitches.

The ground in the square below is in festoon stitch, the square near the corner, as well as the similar thick bars, are in trellis-work stitch. The crosses are in guipure relief, and are made by throwing two threads across for each cross-bar, and worked over and under in darning stitch. Some of the squares near the centre are filled in with cross-stitch.

ONE-FOURTH OF SQUARE IN GUIPURE D'ART.

American ladies are becoming greatly interested in the work, and there is a lady in the city of New York who gives instruction to those desiring to perfect themselves in the art. It affords a very pleasing pastime, and is certainly far preferable to employing one's time in everlasting worsted work. It is quickly learned, and the accomplishment a most satisfactory and fascinating one.

CHAPTER XXXIV.

MODERN BRAID LACES.

By the use of lace braids of various sorts, which are carefully woven in fine designs to imitate the thick portions of the patterns in ancient point and pillow laces, very fine imitations of these laces are produced. Unlike the loom imitations, they possess a certain value, from the fact of being in part wrought by the hand. Some go so far as to call the imitations of point patterns real point; but this they cannot properly be termed, since real points are produced by the work of the needle alone.

These laces, however, are many of them exceedingly beautiful. The braids are tacked on a pattern which comes for the purpose, taking care to follow it exactly and to put it on in an even manner. After this is done, the spaces will be in squares, circles, or triangles, which may be filled in with numerous wheels, rosettes and regular point lace stitches. If the braids and pattern are well-chosen, and the design worked with fine linen thread, the effect is beautiful.

The patterns come on bright-colored muslin. The braids are of different widths and designs. One is a succession of medallions and is called Honiton. Braids which are quite narrow and have a straight edge each side are called point lace braids. Then there is the narrowest of all, like a very fine feather-edge braid split in two, with a pearling on one side only; this always forms the picot. The thread is usually called the linen lace thread, and is put up in spools or balls.

After the braid is tacked upon the design, comes the filling in with point stitches, connecting bars, wheels, rosettes, and all manner of fancy stitches, the greater the variety, usually, the more effective the work. The foundation of nearly all these stitches is the point de Bruxelles, which was given in an enlarged form on page 171, and which we repeat here.

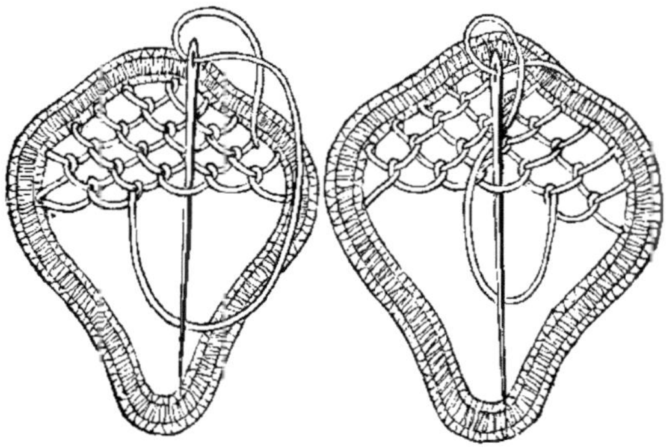

POINT DE BRUXELLES.

This shows the stitch worked backward and forward, though when made in regular rows it is usually worked from left to right. It is often more convenient to work from both sides in filling in narrow spaces.

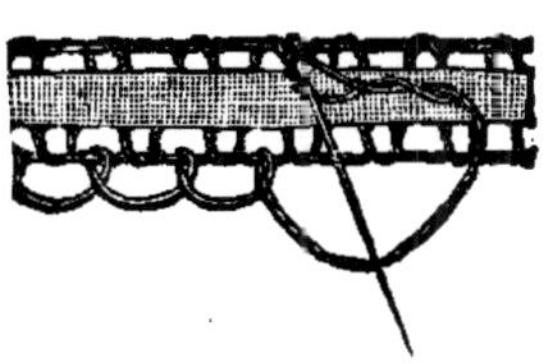

BORDER IN POINT DE BRUXELLES.

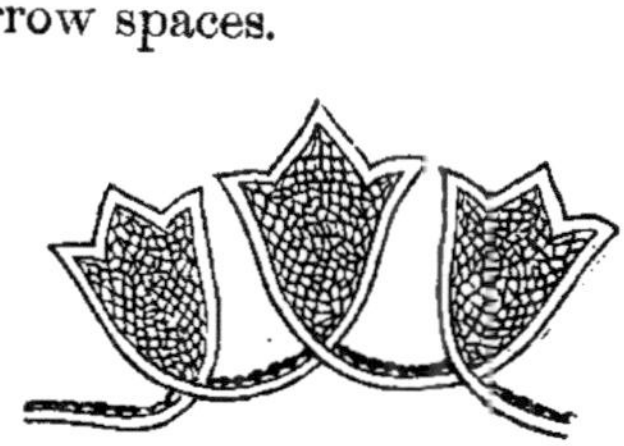

BRUSSELS NEEDLE-GROUND.

The first of these two illustrations shows a border worked in this stitch, and the second the ground in its usual size. The button-hole stitches are worked loosely, and the beauty of the ground depends upon its regularity.

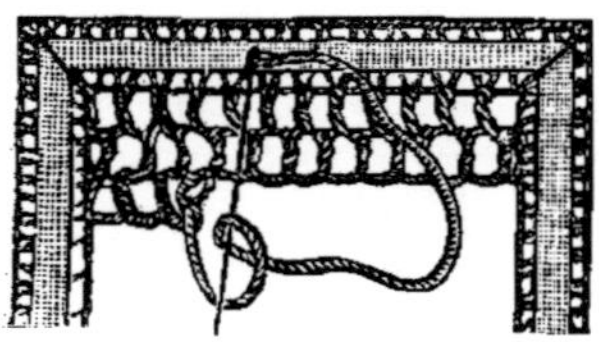

POINT D'ESPAGNE.

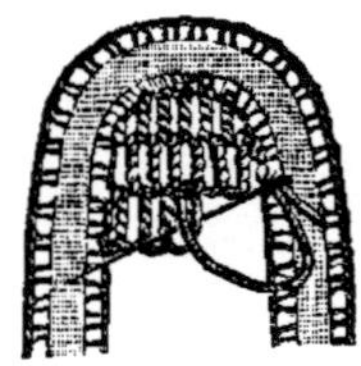

POINT D'ESPAGNE, CLOSE.

Point d'Espagne is a button-hole stitch made by twisting the thread twice about the needle, which makes it long and appear twisted.

POINT D'ESPAGNE, DOUBLE.

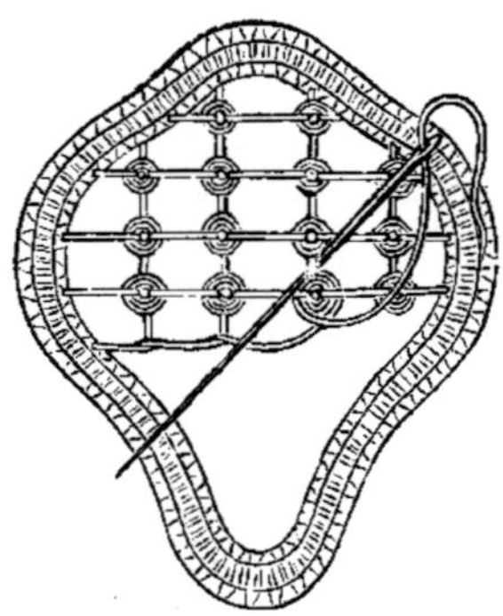

POINT D'ANGLETERRE.

Point d'Angleterre, or English stitch, or rosette stitch, is formed by drawing lines one-eighth of an inch apart, and then form similar cross-lines to intersect them. Sometimes other lines are thrown across. The rosette is formed at the intersecting angle, and is in simple *point de reprise*, or darning stitch, the needle being passed over one thread and under the next.

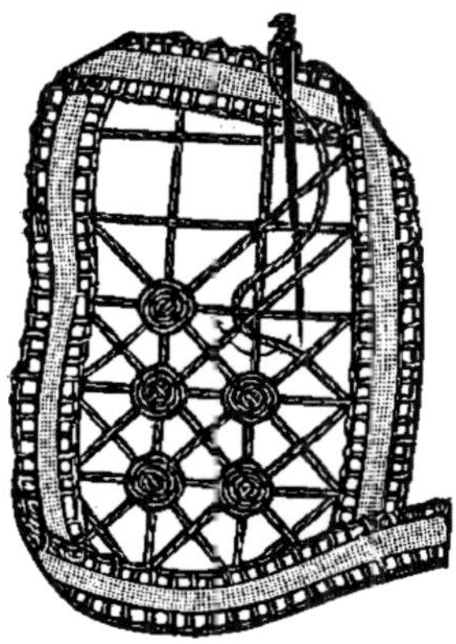

POINT D'ANGLETERRE.

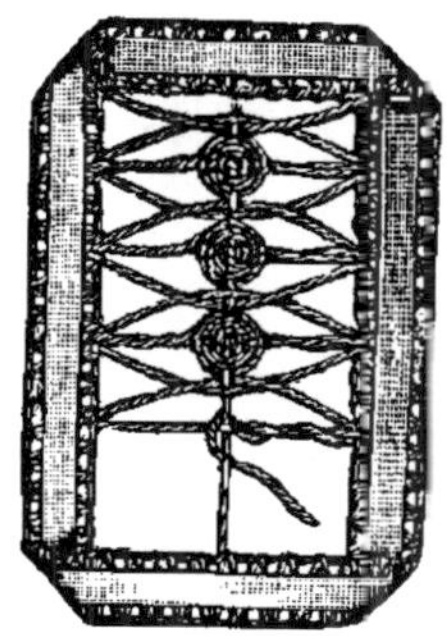

POINT D'ANGLETERRE.

The illustrations show the different styles of putting in the foundation lines for the rosettes in point d'Angleterre.

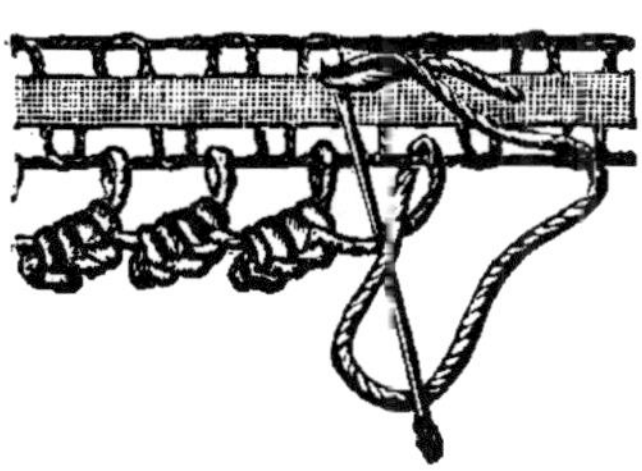

POINT DE VENISE.

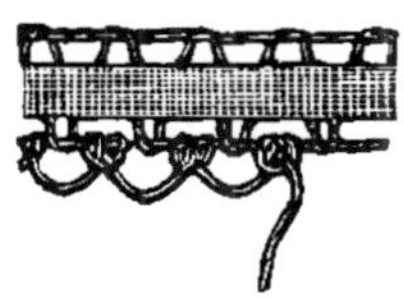

POINT DE SORRENT.

Point de Venise is a loose button-hole stitch with four tight ones worked in each. Petite point de Venise, or little Venetian point, is worked in the same manner from left to right, with one tight button-hole stitch in each large one.

Point d'Alençon stitch is used to fill in narrow spaces where a light effect is needed.

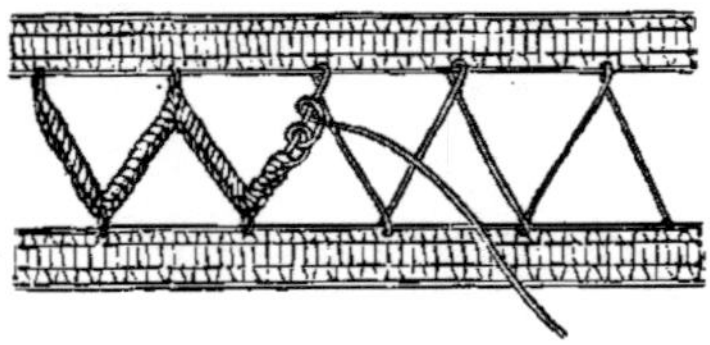

POINT D'ALENCON.

It is made by catching the thread under one side and over the other, like herring-bone stitch, and is either plain, as seen in one part of the illustration, or it may be worked twice like rope-stitch, or covered with fine button-hole stitches, as seen in the design.

Point Turque, or Turkish stitch, is also in button-hole stitch, with one straight thread drawn across between and connecting each row of stitches.

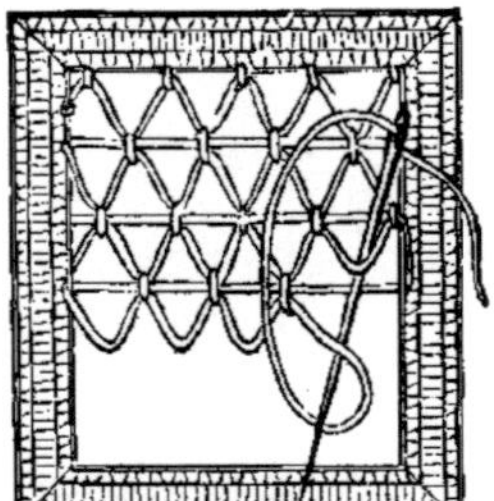

POINT TURQUE.

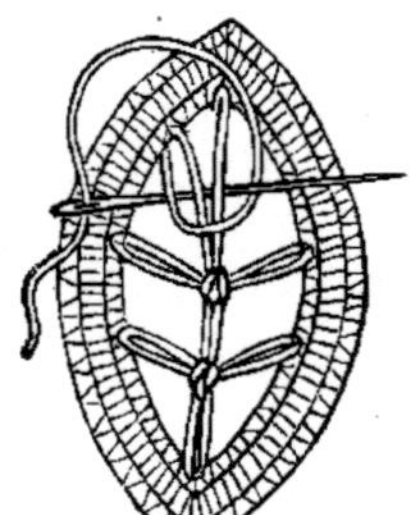

POINT GRECQUE.

Point Grecque is simple stitch which the diagram sufficiently explains.

Point de reprise is a simple darning stitch, worked over and under foundation threads.

Aside from these stitches a number of bars are used.

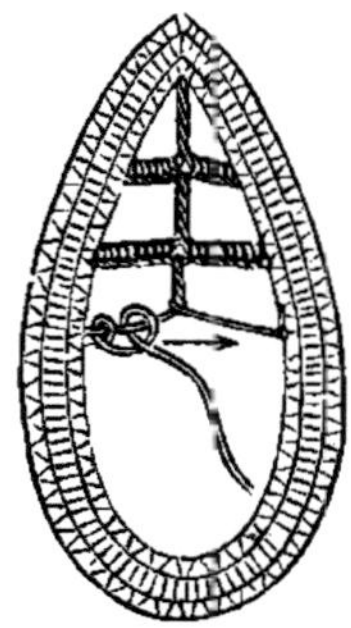

VENETIAN BARS.

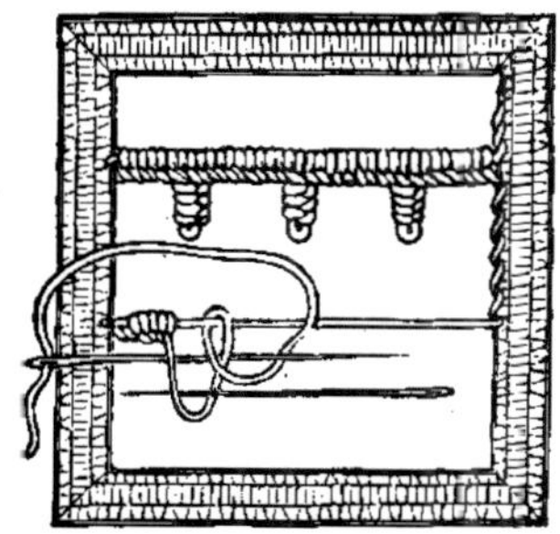

DOTTED VENETIAN BARS.

The Venetian bar is of close button-hole stitches worked over two straight threads as a foundation. They are applied to the veining of leaves, and to fill up narrow spaces.

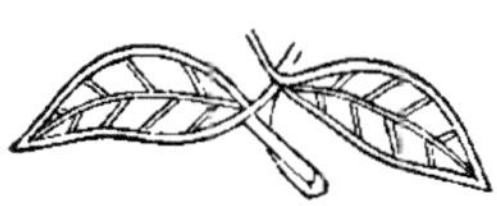

VENETIAN BARS.

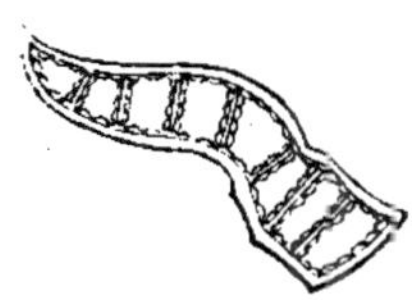

DOTTED VENETIAN BARS.

These illustrations show how the bars are applied to fill up the designs.

Sorrento bars are exceedingly simple, being a thread thrown across the space from braid to braid, and, returning, the needle is twisted over and around the first thread, forming a fine rope twist.

These illustrations show how the Sorrento bars are used; they are the simplest of all bars employed in lace-work

SORRENTO BARS.

SORRENTO BARS.

D'Alençon bars are worked upon a foundation of point de Bruxelles, and are applied to filling in the heavier part of the pattern, but not as groundwork.

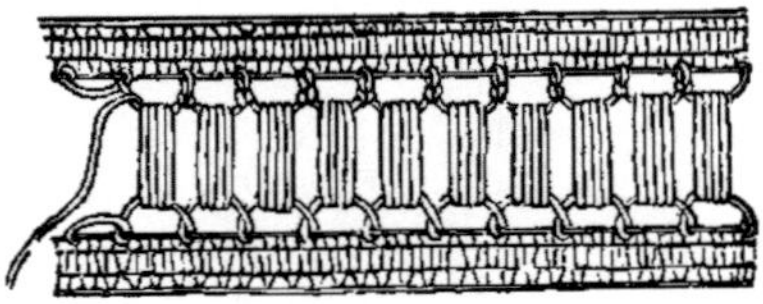

D'ALENCON BARS.

The thread is passed three times over and under the point de Bruxelles stitch, looped to tighten, and then the next bar begun.

For the sake of convenience we give, on opposite page, the various point lace stitches in one diagram.

No. 1 is point de Bruxelles, or Brussels, simple loose button-hole stitches.

No. 2 is little Venetian pcint, one Brussels stitch, and a tight button-hole stitch in the loose one.

No. 3. Point de Venise edge, with four tight button-hole stitches in each loose one.

No. 4. Sorrento point, or one long and one short button-hole stitch worked alternately.

No. 5. Venetian bars, edged with point de Bruxelles.

No. 6. Venetian bars, made by throwing threads across the space to be filled, and covering each with fine button-hole stitches.

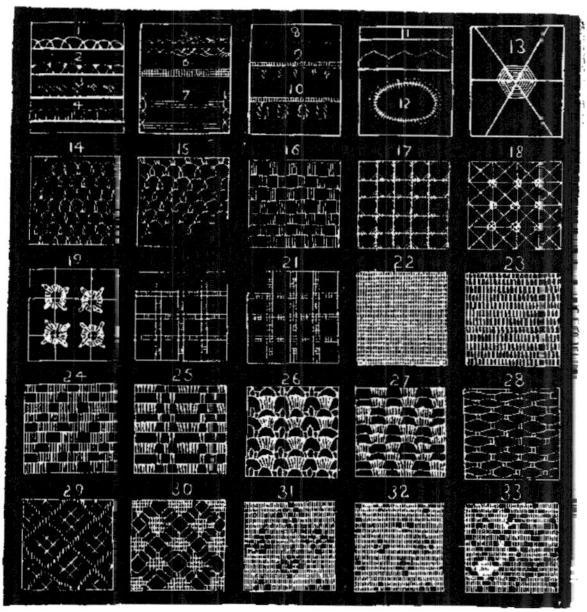

No. 7. English bars, made by passing the thread backward and forward over the space to be filled.

No. 8. Sorrento bars, are one thread thrown across and the returning thread twisted about it.

No. 9. Dotted Venetian bar, being a simple bar with dots of button-hole stitches attached.

No. 10. Raleigh bars, or Venetian bars, with dots or picots formed by making a loop of thread and twisting the needle around it several times and drawing the thread up. This makes a small twisted loop.

No. 11. D'Alençon bars, like herring-bone stitch.

No. 12. Spanish point, being close button-hole stitches over several thicknesses of thread.

No. 13. Rosette, made like a spider-web, the centre in simple darning stitch over one foundation thread and under the next.

No. 14. Brussels point ground, being loose rows of button-hole stitches.

No. 15. Venetian point ground, made like No. 2.

No. 16. Sorrento point ground, being successive rows of Sorrento stitches.

No. 17. English lace, or point d'Angleterre, is made with darning stitch, the thread being darned four times around the intersections of Sorrento bars.

No. 18. Open English lace, being similar to No. 16, only worked on four Sorrento bars.

No. 19. Mechlin lace wheels, worked in button-hole stitch on Venetian bars, with four picots on each wheel.

No. 20. Henriquez lace, in which two crossed bars are darned across at short intervals.

No. 21. Cordovan lace, like the Henriquez, but with the crossed bars in clusters of three instead of two.

No. 22. Valenciennes lace, simple darning, or *point de reprise*, which should be done with the finest thread.

No. 23. Foundation lace, being bars covered with button-hole stitches, alternating with rows of Brussels stitch.

No. 24. Escalier lace, so-called from its resemblance

to steps of stairs. Work nine button-hole stitches, miss two and repeat, making the spaces or stairs fall diagonally.

No. 25. Cadiz is similar, but the stitches and spaces alternate in each row.

No. 26. Barcelona lace. This is alternate rows of Sorrento edging, with rows in which four button-hole stitches are done in each long stitch in the Sorrento row.

No. 27. Fan lace, being six button-hole stitches and six spaces, arranged after manner of illustration.

No. 28. Spotted lace, in which two button-hole stitches are made and four missed.

No 29. Venetian spotted lace of Venetian bars crossing each other diagonally, and four spots of English lace worked in the sections.

No. 30. Open Antwerp lace, in double or long Brussels, in which the needle is twisted once in the loop. These stitches alternate with spaces, after pattern of diagram.

No. 31. Open diamond lace, like escalier, but with different spaces.

Nos. 32 and 33 are similar, and called, respectively, close diamond and Antwerp lace.

BRABANT EDGING.

Brabant edging consists of alternate rows of Brussels and Venetian stitches.

The small diagram given shows the manner of applying Brabant or any similar edge to the thicker portion of the design.

This design may be worked altogether in the stitches described, or may be carried out with the aid of point lace braids.

MODERN RAISED POINT.

CHAPTER XXXV.

MACHINE LACE.

THE first machine for making net was invented by an Englishman named Hammond, a stocking-frame knitter, who chanced one day to examine some lace in the possession of his wife, and conceived the idea of applying his machine to produce a similar fabric. He was successful, and the result was a lace made of one thread, with a ground like the Brussels. This was in 1768.

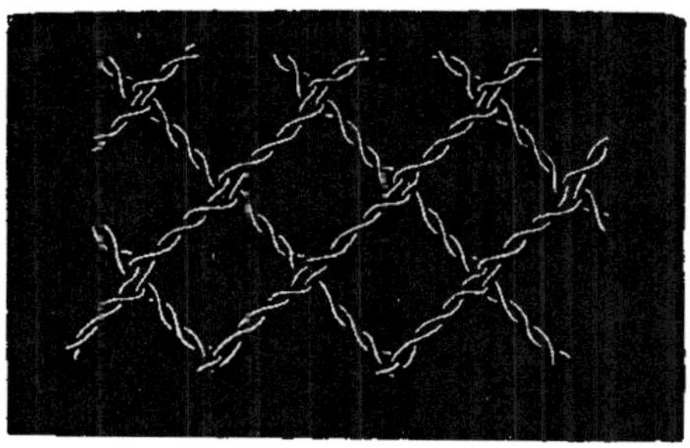

SQUARE NET.

The net produced, however, was quite frail, and if a thread broke it would all ravel out like knitting. Various inventors, therefore, went immediately to work to improve upon it. Robert Frost made a figured net in 1769, and in 1777 he obtained a patent for square net. Afterward he made a flowered and a spider net. In 1778 a Nottingham stocking-maker named Flint invented what was called a point net machine, which produced a regular six-sided mesh. The man afterward died in the work-house, before he reaped the benefit of his invention.

In 1809 John Heathcoat, son of a Leicestershire farmer, obtained a patent on the bobbinet machine, which was an improvement on Brown's fish-net machine. The patent was taken out for fourteen years in partnership with a Mr. Lacy, and was called Old Loughborough.

This machine surpasses every other invention of the human brain in the ingenuity of its machinery. A six-sided mesh is produced by the crossing and twisting of three separate sets of threads. One set works downwards in serpentine lines, a second from right to left, and a third from left to right, each in slanting directions.

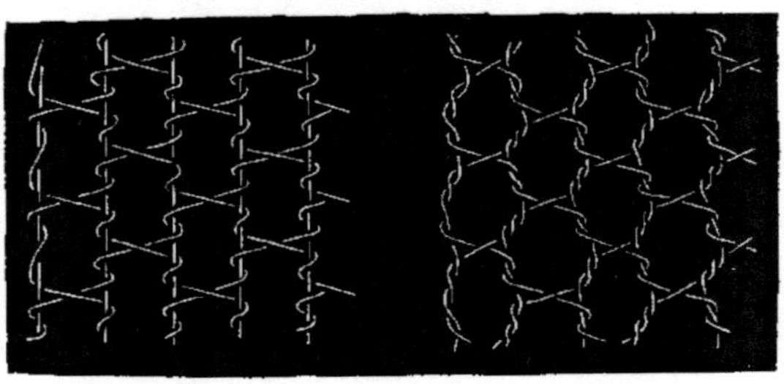

TWO-TWIST BOBBINET WHILE MAKING. TWO-TWIST BOBBINET COMPLETED.

There are six different systems of bobbinet machines —Heathcoat's patent, Brown's traverse warp, Morley's straight bolt, Morley's circular bolt, Clarke's pusher principal (single tier), and Leaver's machine (single tier).

Bobbinet is made of two cotton threads twisted into one, the sizes running from 180 to 250, and the beauty of the fabric depends greatly upon the quality and evenness of the thread, as well as the regularity of the mesh. The thread is singed to free it from fibres, and is wound upon bobbins, which must not be larger around than the mesh. There are twenty to thirty warp threads to an inch. The bobbins fit in a carriage which fastens with a spring, thus preventing them from falling out, and also from giving off the thread unless a certain amount of friction is brought to bear upon them. The bobbins contain the weft threads. The weft threads in common weaving pass over and under the warp threads alternately and at right angles with them. In the production of bobbinet there is a little twist at the time of crossing which winds the threads about each other.

In common weaving the warp threads lie horizontally, but in bobbinet vertically, ascending from a beam in the lower part of the machine to the upper part. The bobbins go backward and forward among the warp threads, like so many clock pendulums, and are guided through the spaces in the warp threads by what is called a comb. The spaces between the teeth are called gates. The bobbins go some to the right and some to the left, in a sort of counter march, during which they are contorted and twisted round the warp to form the meshes. To one who is not familiar with this weaving, the whole thing looks like a piece of legerdemain.

The width of bobbinet varies from that of half an inch, which is called footing, to three and one-half yards. A rack of the lace is a certain length of work counted perpendicularly, containing two hundred and forty-two meshes or holes. The best quality has the meshes lengthened a little in the direction of the selvages. The rack was invented to settle disputes which often rose between the workmen and their employers, on account of the elasticity of the material, which prevented exact measurement.

The best net has small, regular meshes, the hexagons being perfectly regular.

Heathcote carried on his manufactures very successfully until 1811, when an association of men, called the Luddites, entered his manufactory and destroyed twenty-seven of his machines. He then settled in Tiverton, in Devonshire. When his patent expired, all Nottingham went to work to make bobbinet.

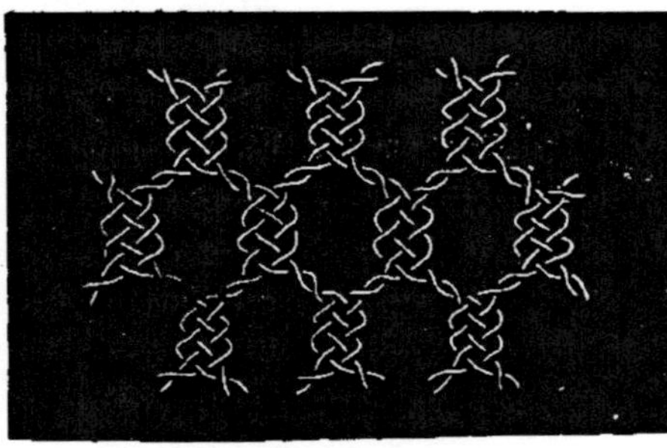

BOBBINET.

In 1837 a Mr. Ferguson, of Nottingham, conceived the plan of applying the Jacquard cards to the bobbinet machine. The Jacquard system had been used at Lyons in 1824 with the Mechlin frame, which suggested the idea to Mr. Ferguson. In 1838 he removed to France and settled at Cambrai, where, in connection with Monsieur Jourdan, he set up a large manufactory. Here he brought out a black silk-figured net, in imitation of Chantilly lace, and called it Cambrai lace. The pattern was woven, and then outlined by hand with a thread of silk.

Since then, every kind of pillow lace has been imitated by the loom, and point also, though, so far, it has not been so perfect as the pillow imitations. France manufactures these laces in immense quantities, the finest of any produced, in silk, linen, cotton and wool. The principal manufactories are at Calais, though the industry is carried on in many cities and towns. The first machine brought from England to France was in 1793, and in 1802 there were more in France than in England.

The best market for the early English machine laces was in Paris, so many manufacturers removed thither, eager to make the greatest profit upon their products. Aside from this, labor was somewhat cheaper. In 1815 a workman of Heathcoat's, named Cutts, managed to import a bobbinet machine to Valenciennes, and thence to Douay, where, in partnership with M. Thomasson, he began the manufacture of lace, and produced in 1816 the first bobbinet dress made in France. It was then embroidered and presented to the Duchesse d'Angoulême, as a sort of advertisement. In 1816 James Clark also brought, by the aid of sailors, a bobbinet machine to Calais, which he smuggled in in pieces, and afterward set it up.

The first net machine was put up in Brussels in 1801, a bobbinet followed in 1817, another was put up in Ghent in 1828, and others followed. In 1834 a Mr. Washer set up several bobbinet machines in Brussels, paying particular attention to producing a fine mesh. He soon excelled both English and French manufactures, and the net was seized upon and used as a foundation for point and pillow laces. It is called Brussels net, or Washer's machine net, and is made from very fine cotton thread.

Many varieties of net have been produced. The Mechlin was too elastic, and fell into disuse. Various styles and patterns have since been in fashion, many of them being patented by those who invented the design. One pattern is called the Grecian, another the spot or point d'esprit, and others bullet-hole, tatting, and many others.

Machine lace has been made to some extent in the United States, more especially the curtain lace known as Nottingham. Though the industry is comparatively new to this country, it bids fair to become of considerable importance at no distant day.

While machine nets and laces have almost entirely superseded the cheaper productions of the pillow, they have only added to the value of the rarer kinds of both pillow and point.

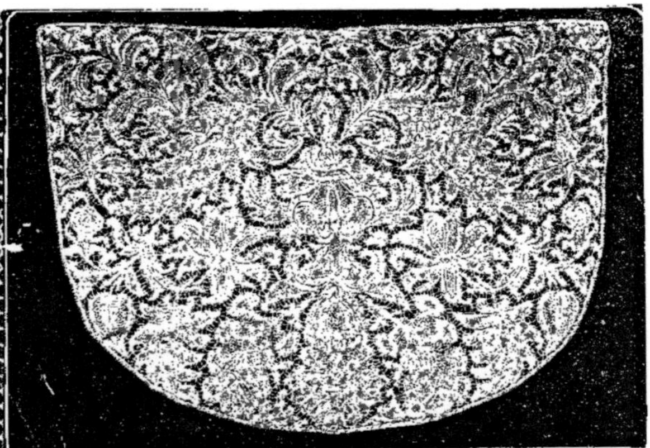

PHOTOGRAPH BY CHARLES BALLIARD

INTERESTING EXAMPLE OF ENGLISH ANTIQUE

Design in needle point of the seventeenth century. Loaned by Mrs. Astor to the Metropolitan Museum of Art, New York.

ITALIAN ANTIQUE

Loaned by Mrs. Astor to the Metropolitan Museum of Art.

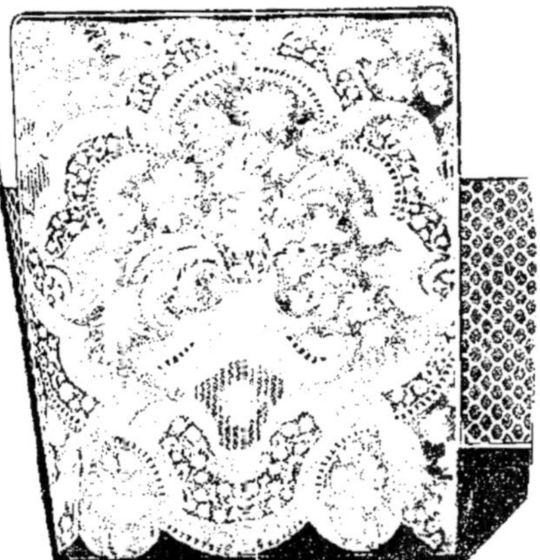

he poin

the threa

POINT D'ALENÇON, EIGHTEENTH CENTURY

This exquisite and valuable specimen of point d'Alençon was bequeathed to the Boston Museum of Fine Arts by Mr. J. W. Paige.

MODERN BRUSSELS.

BEAUTIFUL PIECE OF MODERN BRUSSELS

Nothing could be more beautiful than this piece of Brussels lace which Mrs. Astor has loaned to the Metropolitan Museum of Art, New York.

EXQUISITE HANDKERCHIEF OF BRUSSELS POINT

Valued at $1200. Presented by Mrs. George W. Childs, the widow of Philadelphia's famous editor, to the Drexel Institute, in that city.

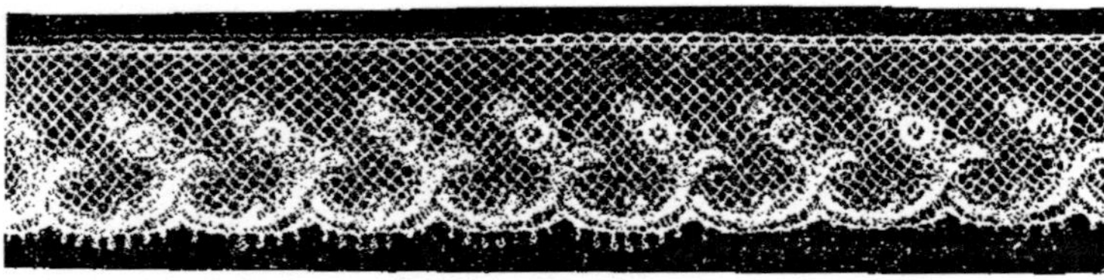

IMITATION VALENCIENNES.

IMITATION VALENCIENNES.

IMITATION VALENCIENNES.

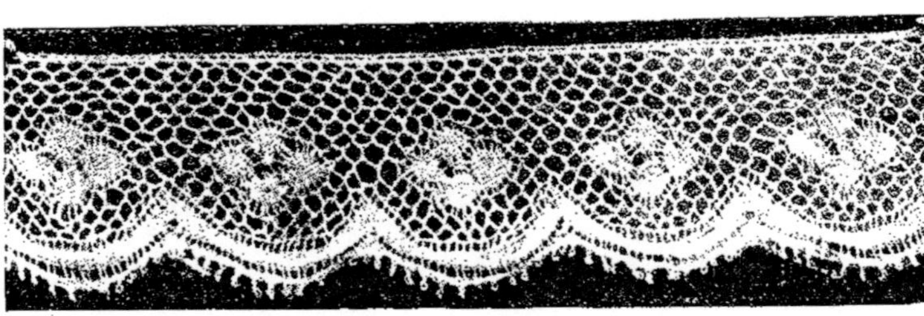

REAL VALENCIENNES.

DUCHESSE LACE.

BRUGES LACE WITH A FLANDERS POINT.

A CLUNY LACE EDGE

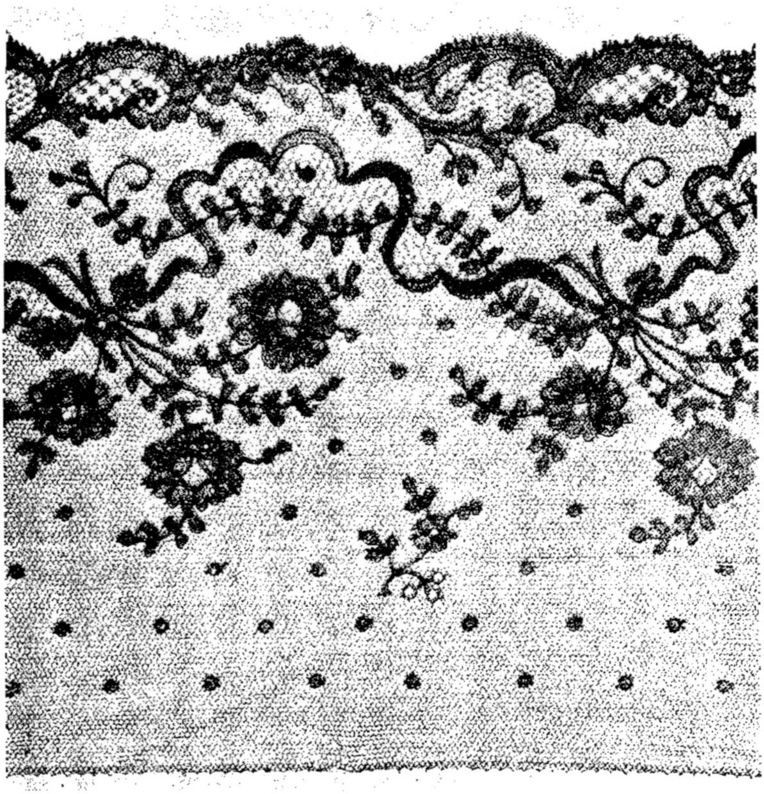

IMITATION CHANTILLY.

LACE-MAKING
IN THE MIDLANDS
PAST AND PRESENT

BY

C. C. CHANNER

AND

M. E. ROBERTS

METHUEN & CO.
36 ESSEX STREET, W.C.
LONDON
1900

DEDICATED BY PERMISSION

TO

HER ROYAL HIGHNESS THE PRINCESS LOUISE

THE DUCHESS OF ARGYLL

(President of the Ladies' Work Society)

CONTENTS

LIST OF ILLUSTRATIONS

LACE-MAKING
IN THE MIDLANDS

I

SKETCH OF THE PROGRESS OF LACE-MAKING IN EUROPE

THE history of lace-making is the history of an art. A piece of lace is an artistic composition expressed in twisted thread, just as a piece of wood-carving is the expression of the artist's idea in chiselled wood. Lace is not, like embroidery, an ornamented fabric; it is itself ornament. It is not the application of art to a craft; the whole pattern is the fabric, and the fabric is the pattern. It is this peculiarity that distinguishes lace from needlework and from woven-work.

The art is a comparatively modern one. No trace of it can be found on ancient monuments or in early records; the term "old lace" is a relative term, for before the sixteenth century nothing that we should call "lace" existed.

It was about the close of the seventeenth century that lace reached perhaps its highest point as a vehicle for the expression of artistic ideas. About the middle of the sixteenth century pattern-books began to be published, and it was the effort to carry out the ideas of the designers of patterns which perfected the craft of lace-making. In form, in line, in composition, the patterns belonging to the best periods of lace-making are among the most perfect works that artistic design can show.

Without good design lace becomes worthless rubbish, like a picture without drawing.

In seeking to discover the origin of the art we find two distinct but equally important sources. The first is the ornamentation of linen by means of drawn-thread work and cut-work; the second is the twisting of threads into narrow ornamental braids, known as lace or "purling."

Drawn-thread work, at least in its simpler forms, is familiar to most people. When very fine and elaborate it has much the same effect as a closely-worked piece of lace. Cut-work, or Greek lace as it is sometimes called, is less familiar. It is formed by cutting out in linen patterns, usually geometrical, and then closely button-holing over the threads which remain.

FIG. 1

CUT WORK OR GREEK LACE, 16TH CENTURY

Take away the linen foundation from the drawn-thread work and from the cut-work and you have a true needlepoint lace.

The second source of which I spoke is purling. Purling was a method of plaiting threads into a little looped edging, and the little loops so often to be found at the edge of lace are still called "purls." Purling is mentioned in the *Canterbury Tales*, and it was much used in the fifteenth century as an ornamental edging.

Other edgings called lace were also made. We should now call them fancy braid, but we still use the old word when we speak of "gold lace."

"Purling" and "lace" are pillow lace in embryo; but pillows, bobbins, and pins were not yet invented. These old lace-makers placed their balls of thread in a man's hand, using his fingers as pegs to assist in the plaiting and twisting. By employing two men fifteen or twenty threads could be used at once. What a laborious method of obtaining so small a result, we think, as we lightly hang our hundred or more bobbins on to the modern pin!

The early pin was large, and was made of boxwood or bone, not well adapted for lace-making. Their manufacture rapidly improved, and though they remained expensive articles of luxury they were, to a certain extent, in common use about the latter part of the sixteenth century. It was about this period that pillow lace-making commenced.

With the use of pin and pillow the early edgings became elaborated into something more like modern lace edgings, and they were probably made in England, as well as in Italy, Flanders, and other countries. A modern torchon edging is not unlike the Italian edging of the sixteenth century, as the use for such simple ornament has not passed away.

Before proceeding to describe the further progress of lace-making we must draw particular attention to this method of twisting threads into a pattern to form an *edging*, as we shall frequently need to refer to it again.

We notice that it is an outcome of the fancy braid, and that there is no distinction between pattern and ground. The pattern can easily be pricked out on lines at an angle of 45° drawn on the parchment.

The threads are kept in place by means of pins, and are continuous; that is to say, each thread can be traced zigzagging through the whole length of the lace and lace-work, across the width of the edging from side to side, just as one would plait a dozen strands of straw. I shall in future term this method "working

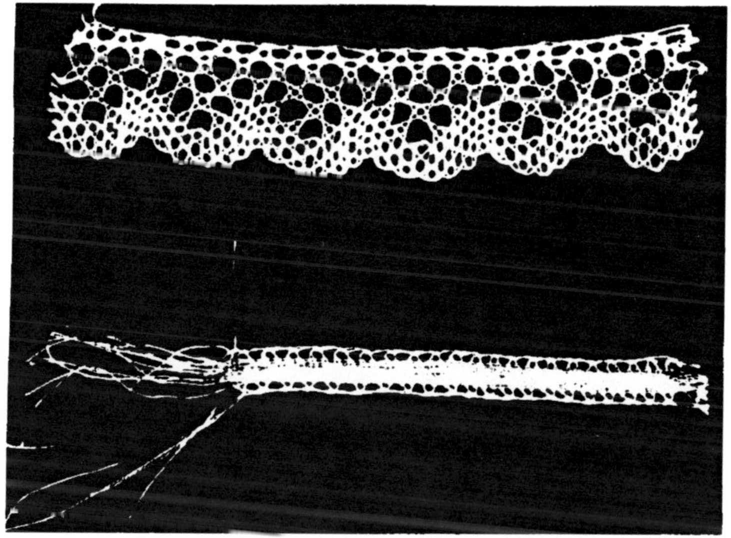

FIG. 2

TORCHON EDGING BRAID

across the pattern," in order to distinguish it from the method of following the separate lines of the pattern which we shall find in some of the elaborate pillow laces.

In describing the edgings we have wandered far from the ornamental linen-work which we mentioned as one of the sources of the art of lace-making.

Though this book deals with pillow lace, and the linen-work of Italy was more immediately the parent of needlepoint lace, it is none the less important to us. Needlepoint and pillow lace were developed side by side, first in Italy and Flanders, and afterwards in France. The same lace-making districts often produced both needlepoint and pillow work; the same patterns often serve for either. Many pillow stitches are imitations of needle stitches; without the influence of needlepoint it seems likely that purling and lace-making would never have progressed beyond the making of narrow fancy edgings.

It will be interesting to trace the evolution of the various kinds of pillow lace, the interdependent development of pattern, stitch, and method. This evolution we will regard as *being entirely independent of* the art of making the simple edgings already explained.

In the oldest Italian or Flemish lace of any

importance we find that the foundation of the fabric is a braid or tape. This braid, made with bobbins and pins on a pillow, takes the place of the button-holing which forms the solid part of needlepoint lace; it follows the curves and lines of the pattern, and the various turns and curves are connected by means of "sewings."

The sewing, as now practised by Honiton and Brussels lace-workers, is formed by catching a thread through a pinhole in an adjacent piece of braid and passing another thread through the loop thus formed. In this way a pattern worked in separate narrow lines is all joined into a homogeneous whole. Sometimes, instead of the braids being closely united, two threads are twisted, or four threads are plaited, into a little *bar* or "bride," fastened with a sewing into a part of the pattern at some distance and then carried back into the braid. These brides or connecting bars are a marked feature of some needlepoint lace, though of course here they are made in quite a different manner.

The manner in which the braid is carried round the curves is extremely ingenious, and very superior to the later methods of Honiton and Brussels workers. By working partly across the braid and then returning to the outer edge of the curve a kind of wedge can be formed, which brings the work round flat

FIG. 3

ITALIAN LACE WITH CONTINUOUS BRAID CLOSELY CONNECTED WITH SEWINGS

FIG. 4

ITALIAN PILLOW LACE, 17TH CENTURY

without any apparent thickening of the material. There are many old patterns, like the illustrations, in which the lines of the pattern are continuous, but this is not necessary. By ending a braid and beginning another in a different part of the parchment, by cutting off bobbins or adding them, in order to alter the width of the lines, any pattern published by the designers could be followed. Many fancy stitches, some taken from the edging laces, were used to vary the monotony of the plain braid, and purls like the purling of the fourteenth century could be worked along its edge.

While needlepoint lace was first confined to geometrical patterns, the braid lent itself to curves, and pillow lace may have for a time led the way in the improvement of patterns. In the seventeenth century patterns for both kinds of lace developed rapidly; from curves and scrolls we go on to stems, leaves, and flowers, and even animals and men appear—beautiful little drawings worked out in lace.

Needlepoint lace, instead of consisting only of solid work and brides, begins to show "fillings-in" or "modes"—delicate open-work stitches which form the centres of flowers, etc.

Pillow lace was not left behind. It was a simple matter to curve a braid into the form of a flower; then, by means of sewings, threads could be attached to the edge of the braid and the flower centre filled with open-work stitches to rival the modes of the needlepoint.

Perhaps it will be as well to remark, in passing, that about this time needlepoint workers sometimes used a plain pillow braid, and, sewing it on to their patterns, joined and ornamented it with their stitches, thus saving themselves the labour of working the solid part of their pattern.

This kind of work was revived in this century, and was known among lady fancy-workers as "point lace." The work was often beautifully done, and the patterns good, but it is always inferior in effect to genuine needlepoint lace or to pillow lace of the same style. The pleats and gatherings in the braid are a great blemish.

In the middle of the seventeenth century lace with a net ground appears. Hitherto, though patterns had become elaborate, and fillings were common, and the variety of stitch in pillow lace was marvellous, the *net* ground was unknown. We must also remind ourselves that there was no "working across the pattern" in real "point," or lace as we should now call it. Every line of the pattern was followed separately, the various parts of the work being connected by sewings.

Flemish lace began to be extremely fine, and

with the fine thread the necessity for the careful turning of the curves ceased, and the method was gradually forgotten. Though we see less of the absolutely continuous line, patterns remained of a continuous scrolling nature; it was the introduction of net which helped to cut patterns up till lace ceased to be a pattern and became an arrangement of separate sprigs on a net ground.

The use of braid had at first suggested continuous lines, but it was soon found possible to work a single leaf by the same method, attach it to a stem, cut off the bobbins, and begin again elsewhere with another leaf or flower.

With the introduction of lace-making into other European countries came further developments. It seems that when the art is introduced into a new home it never remains the same, but always becomes in some way characteristic of its new sphere; so that we find Italian lace, Belgian lace, French lace, English lace, all perfectly distinct from one another. Fine Flemish lace introduced into Devonshire becomes the characteristic Honiton lace, and the lace of Lille and Valenciennes, imitated in the Midlands, becomes the Buckinghamshire point.

A symmetrical arrangement of brides and the open-work fillings no doubt led to the invention of net, which appears both in needle-point and pillow lace.

The illustration shows the earliest form of pillow net. The pattern is worked first, then threads are attached to the edge of the braid and the ground is covered with net. This stitch is an extremely intricate one when compared to the modern Buckinghamshire "point ground," but it is not to be wondered at when it is understood that this net can be worked without the help of a single pin or so much as a line drawn on the parchment. The Midland lace-maker of to-day, unaccustomed to any but her own methods, is astonished and sceptical on hearing of net without pins; but in the early seventeenth century pins were not cheap, and the idea of keeping a twisted net in place by means of a forest of pins was undreamed of. Instead of twists, every side of this mesh is composed of four plaited threads; one couple is carried through from mesh to mesh to keep all firm and in place. Much must depend in such work on skill of hand and eye, and it is a slow, laborious stitch, but there is a fascination in the shaping of those hexagons which is wanting to the mechanical twisting of thread and sticking of endless pins.

As the seventeenth century proceeds, net grounds become commoner, and endless varieties

FIG. 5

CONTINUOUS BRAID PATTERN WITH FILLINGS AND PLAITED NET

appear, but the mesh is always plaited, not twisted.

By the time we reach the beginning of the eighteenth century we can associate a particular mesh with a particular lace-making district; the net is simpler, and begins to require immense numbers of pins.

Lace is now finer, and is worked in narrower widths than was the old Italian and Flemish lace. The patterns become much more detached. The lace of Mechlin and of Brussels, the ground of which is very similar, continues to be worked in pieces, the pattern first and the ground afterwards, but a very remarkable change is seen in the Valenciennes lace and in various French laces. This change is shown in a piece of lace in the South Kensington Museum marked as Dutch. It closely resembles Flemish lace with a net ground, but the ground is worked at the same time as the pattern; that is to say, threads are brought out of the pattern to form the net and carried back again into the pattern, so that the threads do not follow the lines of the pattern, but come in and out of it as convenient. In fact, the lace is worked like an edging on a large scale. Such a method requires an enormous number of pins, because every thread must be kept in place till the whole width of the pattern is worked. In the older method the twisted edge of the finished pattern was like the selvedge of a piece of woven material, and pins could quickly be moved forward to the point where the work was proceeding. By the old method it was almost as easy to work a piece of lace half a yard wide as a piece three inches wide. It was only a matter of time; the line was followed curve by curve and would never be of great width or need a very large number of bobbins.

It is easy to see how Flemish patterns led to the new plan. They are characterised by a peculiar flatness and closeness; lines are often marked in the plain work by means of little rows of twists in the working threads. It was seen that if an outline could be marked by twisted threads the same principle might be applied to the whole pattern; it might all be worked in one, the twisting of the threads outlining the design. There are some pieces of lace in the South Kensington Museum, labelled "Fausse Valenciennes," which show the progress of this method. They have the flat look of Valenciennes lace; there is very little distinction between pattern and ground—in fact, there is no true ground, the small space between the different parts of the pattern being covered with a filling-in. Valenciennes lace has to this day retained a simulation of the twisted

FIG. 6

DUTCH LACE

selvedge edge of the braid, each part of the pattern being surrounded by *simulated* pin-holes. In the lace of Lille we find the attempt to *imitate* the braid edge frankly abandoned; the pattern is kept distinct from the ground by running a thick white thread called a "gimp" round it. This gimp, which appears in Buckinghamshire lace, must not be confounded with the raised "cordonnet" which sometimes outlines the pattern in Brussels lace. The cordonnet, or "raised work," of Honiton lace is merely used to give boldness and relief, whereas the gimp is an essential part of a point-ground pattern "worked all across" the parchment.

During the eighteenth century fine pillow laces with net grounds reached their highest point of excellence, and began to be imitated by various kinds of embroidery on machine-made net known as "tambour work" and "Limerick lace."

During the nineteenth century the finest and best laces have made but little progress, but there has been a remarkable development of the torchon edgings. In almost every European country a great deal of heavy linen lace is made for the ornamentation of household linen. These laces are usually of geometrical design and are improvements on the old lace edgings, much having been learnt both in the way of workmanship and design from the true pillow points.

In the nineteenth century, then, we find a curious assimilation of the lace edging with the "point" or "passement," and we apply the same word "lace" to all ornamental fabrics of twisted and plaited thread. Let us briefly recapitulate the various steps by which this has been brought about.

Under the influence of needlepoint the ornamental braid was curved and shaped into a pattern, the various lines of the pattern being connected by sewings. The pattern became more shaped and elaborated, the brides became more ornamental and a more important part of the lace, ornamental fillings were introduced, and the work became, not a curved braid, but an arrangement of flowers and leaves —at first conventional, afterwards naturalistic. Then the net ground becomes general, and early in the eighteenth century some laces began to be worked all in one—pattern and ground as one fabric, without joins. It was now worked like a wide edging, a great many pins and a great many bobbins being employed. The only difference remaining was that the edging usually retained the geometrical pattern with the homogeneousness of pattern and ground; it still showed its character as an ornamental braid of interlaced threads. Even when a real point ground is so narrow as to be *used* as an edging its character is still obvious, and it cannot be confounded with a torchon edge.

In this short history of lace-making the aim has been not to give a history of the various lace centres, with a classification of lace by its place-name, but to show how the fabric itself grew into being and changed in nature, whether in Italy, France, or England. It is desired to show how a classification might be made, according to pattern and method of working, which would be of great use and interest to the lace-maker. Unfortunately there is a great lack of suitable technical terms for such a purpose.

The old place-names, such as Valenciennes, Brussels, or Lille, are of great value and interest, because they *do* indicate a special method and style; but for the earliest lace, which was much the same in Italy or Flanders, and probably in some other countries, and for modern lace, the system of place-names is most confusing and tiresome. Improved torchon lace is now made in Italy, Germany, Austria, Belgium, Switzerland, and England—in fact, almost all over Europe; patterns are carried from place to place, and there is little difference in the workmanship. Any lace may be made in any district—in point of fact, lace very like Brussels is made in Italy.

Something has been done of recent years to revive the manufacture of the finer and more important pillow laces. There is now a certain demand for copies of beautiful old lace, but it has not become a living, thriving industry. There can be no great sale for lace as a work of art as long as it is only an imitation.

The lace makers and designers of old were real artists, and their patrons were willing to spend great sums of money on lace. The small sums of money paid for the very best lace now make it useless for the artist to give his attention to the design, or for the lace-maker to put her best and most careful work into the execution of that wonderful web of plaited thread which some of us still love, and which unfailingly brings to its workers many happy and peaceful hours of never-wearying occupation.

II

THE PROGRESS OF LACE-MAKING IN ENGLAND, WITH SPECIAL REFERENCE TO THE MIDLAND COUNTIES

IN the preceding chapter we have roughly traced the evolution of lace-making in Europe; we must now seek to discover, in equally rough outline, the place which England holds among the lace-making nations. This place is by no means so unimportant as is sometimes represented, though the English love of French fashions has to a certain extent militated against the popularity of the purely English. Whatever difficulties in the way of good organisation of the industry we may have had to contend with, want of artistic feeling and originality cannot fairly be laid to the charge of the English lace-makers. Though often adopting French ideas from the foreign lace imported, in order to follow the foreign fashions, they have never been mere copiers. English designers, or drawers as they were called, have produced some most graceful and beautiful designs, and English workers have shown great dexterity in the adaptation of stitch and method to design. The result of an attempt to copy a foreign lace has usually been the production of a new and individual style by a natural process of development and artistic invention. This rule has been noticeable in Maltese lace, which in workmanship, texture, and design became, in English hands, a very different product from the original simple and rather coarse lace of Malta.

If artistic feeling, as is sometimes said, is shown in the workman's ornamentation of his tools, England stands pre-eminent. An intense pride in the ornamentation and arrangement of her pillow has always been a remarkable characteristic of the Midland lace-maker. More than 400 different patterns of decorated bobbins have been collected, and doubtless many more could be found.

In considering England's place as a lace-making nation we must remember that in other countries a great deal of the best lace was made in convents, and that in England it was impossible to fill the place of the cultured ladies to be found within the convent walls. The convent was like a joint-stock company; it had capital both in money and in ability; it was also a most convenient centre for the teaching

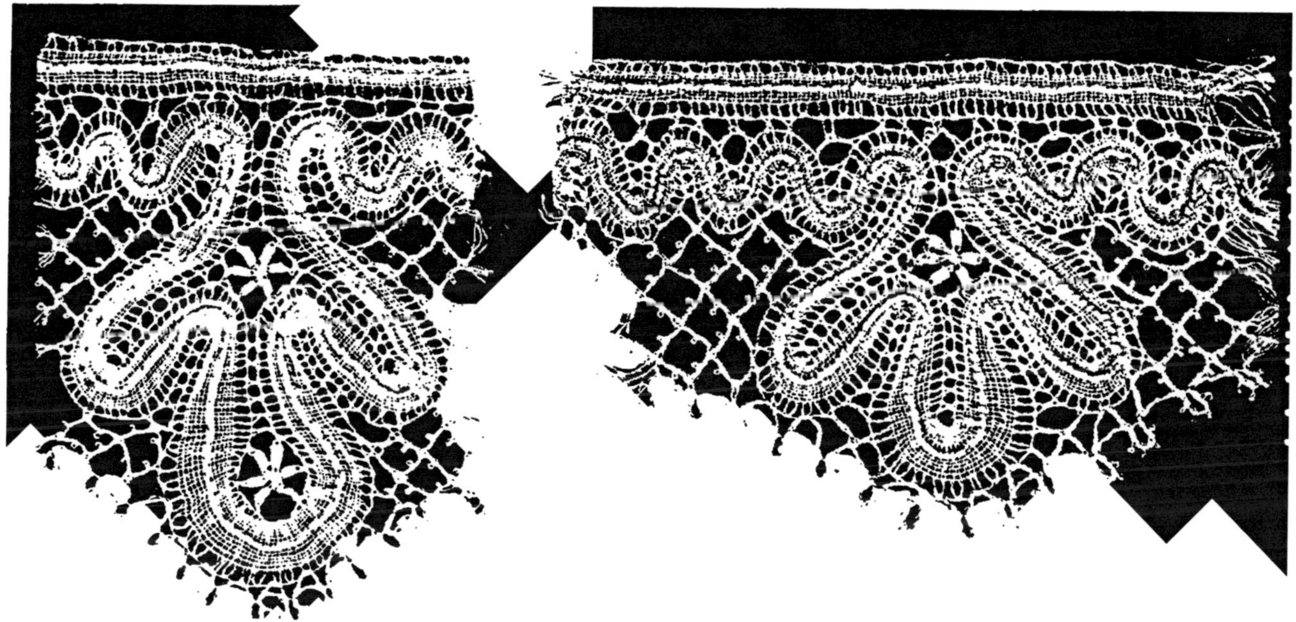

FIG. 7

CATHERINE OF ARAGON LACE

of art and craftsmanship; and it had a commanding position as a commercial house. It was manufacturer, merchant, capitalist, and instructor all at the same time. The decline of convents in England left the lace industry with but little capital and organisation; and both teaching and design generally remained in the hands of a few families who understood it and in which it was handed down from generation to generation.

Needlepoint, which requires more delicate skill of hand and eye than does pillow lace, died out entirely as an article of English manufacture, though we know that it was made in England in the sixteenth century; the making of it was doubtless taught in the convents. There is a tradition in the Midlands that Queen Catherine of Aragon worked hard to encourage it in the villages, and that she introduced new patterns. It is possible that she tried to teach pillow lace also, for there is a pattern made in Northamptonshire, very like what we should call an old Italian pattern (merely meaning that it is an early form of pillow lace), which is called Queen Catherine's pattern. There is no other Midland lace like it. It is said that she bade her ladies burn their lace that they might buy of the poor English workers. Probably want of encouragement and good technical instruction caused the industry to die out after her death. England was soon plunged into the Puritan abyss which almost killed art. We spoke in our previous chapter of the purling mentioned by Chaucer, and of the lace edgings which suggested the use of pillow and bobbins for the true "point." These edgings were extensively made in England, and were known as "bone lace." The word "lace" would not have been applied to the wide points which were the rivals of needlepoint.

In *Twelfth Night* Shakespeare shows his familiarity with the sight of lace-makers—

> "*Duke.* O fellow, come, the song we had last night :
> Mark it, Cesario, it is old and plain :
> The spinsters and the knitters in the sun,
> And the free maids that weave their thread with bones,
> Do use to chaunt it."

About 1662 Flemish workers were brought to England to teach their superior kind of lace. The industry took root in Devonshire and became the famous Honiton lace. This must have seemed to the bone-lace makers a very new and different kind of work from the weaving of their edgings. Honiton lace soon developed a style of its own, but though much beautiful Honiton work has been done the design is often poor. It is curious that Midland lace has never suffered from this poverty of design; it was not so far from the great trade routes, it is more adaptable to any form of pattern, and it requires greater technical skill to make a point-ground (Buckinghamshire) parchment. Any good design, either conventional or naturalistic, can be worked in point-ground lace, but some styles are impossible in Honiton lace. On the other hand, within certain limits, Honiton lace is a better means of expression, and it is much easier to make the parchments. This last fact tempts persons with little powers of draughtmanship to make their own parchments, whereas the point-ground design must be left in the hands of the professional.

We have seen that needlepoint spread more quickly in Europe than pillow point. Honiton lace must have been one of the earliest of the transplanted pillow points. Next in point of time must have come French pillow laces, and then Buckinghamshire point. This lace shows French influence; it is worked all in one across the pattern, like a French lace; the selvedge edge to the pattern has been replaced by a gimp; the net is not of an early character, being a twisted net dependent on pins; none of it can be earlier than the eighteenth century. Some of the parchments are very like Valenciennes parchments, though we find no trace of the Valenciennes ground or the simulated "pin-holes." The introduction of this kind of lace greatly influenced the bone-lace makers, and gave rise, especially in Northamptonshire, to the manufacture of many charming little point-ground edgings, which, while sometimes remaining geometrical in design, resembled in workmanship the wide-point grounds of Bucks.

Maltese lace, introduced in this century, is a development of an edging founded on patterns of interlacing circles instead of the more usual intersecting straight lines.

III

LACE-MAKING IN THE MIDLANDS DURING THE EIGHTEENTH AND NINETEENTH CENTURIES

"The pattern grows, the well-depicted flower,
Wrought patiently into the snowy lawn,
Unfolds its bosom: buds and leaves and sprigs,
And curling tendrils gracefully dispos'd,
Follow the nimble fingers of the fair—
A wreath that cannot fade of flowers that blow
With most success when all besides decay."

COWPER.

THE poet Cowper, living at Olney, the centre of one of the best lace-making districts, was familiar with the fine point-grounds of graceful flowery design, and his poetic muse was not neglectful of the lace-makers. The greater part of Buckinghamshire, Northamptonshire, part of Bedfordshire, and a little bit of Oxfordshire, form the lace-making district of the Midlands. These counties have always supported textile industries of one form or another, with a leaning towards dainty manufactures such as ribbons, straw-plaiting, or lace-making. Many Northamptonshire villages now given over to the unsightly shoe trade once lived by the weaving of plush and silk; other villages within living memory were occupied with darning net for window curtains, etc., the work being known as "frame-work."

The very small and dainty hands of many women in the Northamptonshire villages are often remarked upon by strangers; they are certainly an artistic race, showing it especially in their extreme fondness for flowers and appreciation of pretty scenery. From the beginning of the eighteenth century until the middle of the nineteenth, point-ground lace, generally known as Buckinghamshire point, became characteristic of the district. The best lace was made in the southern part of Northamptonshire near Towcester, and in Buckinghamshire in and round Olney. Northampton and the western part of the county were famous for the narrow edgings and cheaper laces. Bedfordshire always appears to take to work of a showy daintiness. It became the home of Maltese lace, and now makes millinery laces of horsehair and tinsel, and twists beaded wire into patterns, and works with paillettes and spangles.

The improvement in lace-making which took place in the eighteenth century was partly due to the refugees who flocked to our shores after the revocation of the Edict of Nantes. This explains the very close resemblance between French and English pillow laces.

Defoe, writing of Bedfordshire, says: "Through the whole south part of this county, the people are taken up with the manufacture of bone lace, in which they have wonderfully exercised and improved within the last few years." He also mentions Newport Pagnell and other towns in Bucks as being the centres of much trade.

During the reigns of the Georges, notwithstanding much smuggling of foreign goods, the trade steadily increased, and at the marriage of Frederick, Prince of Wales, nearly all the lace worn was of English make.

In 1750 the Society of anti-Gallicans was formed; it held quarterly meetings, and did much to encourage good work. Two years after it began, it awarded the first prize to Mr. William Marriote of Newport Pagnell for bone lace, which, according to the judges, was the best ever made in England. In 1761 the lace-makers of Bucks presented the King with a fine pair of lace ruffles. In 1763 good King George, always anxious for the welfare of his people, ordered that all stuffs and laces to be worn at his sister's wedding should be made in this country; but the nobility preferred to disobey him, and ordered, as was their habit, a quantity of foreign material. What must have been their disgust and alarm on hearing that three days before the wedding the King had sent his custom-officers to the Court milliner to carry off the prohibited goods. But a lesson had been learnt, for on His Majesty's birthday the Court appeared in garments of strictly British make.

The fluctuations in the lace industry have always been remarkable, the scale of prices rising and falling in a bewildering and astonishing manner: at one time we hear of lace-makers earning £1 a week, at another time but 3*s.* or 4*s.*

In 1780 the trade seems to have fallen into a bad condition; for Cowper, enclosing a petition to Lord Dartmouth in favour of lace-makers, declares that "Hundreds in this little town (Olney) are upon the point of starving, and the most unremitting industry is barely sufficient to keep them from it."

For many years Cowper's house was used as a lace school under the management of Mrs. Langley, the wife of a former vicar; about forty workers were employed.

In 1785 an essay was published in the *Gentleman's Magazine* dealing with the cause of deformity among the lace-makers of Bucks and Northants, and suggesting certain remedies which have long since been adopted.

FIG. 8

BUCKINGHAMSHIRE PILLOW LACE

MADE FOR THE PRINCESS ROYAL WHEN AN INFANT

As at the beginning of the eighteenth century our laces owed much to France, so in the nineteenth we received another impetus from refugees who fled from the Revolution. When war was declared and our ports were closed against French goods, energetic buyers undertook to supply the English market with lace like that made in Normandy. The "French ground" was introduced, which resembles what is now known as "Point de Paris."

At Hanslope, in Bucks, 800 out of 1,275 inhabitants made lace, and a net profit of over £800 was yearly brought into the place. Those were grand times for the lace-makers, both men and women, many of them earning as much as £1 1*s.* per week; but this state of things did not last long, for the prices dropped when peace was made.

Queen Victoria is the possessor of some lovely English lace; a small piece, made for the Princess Royal when an infant, remains in the possession of a lace-buyer at Olney, where it was worked; a photograph of it is shown on the opposite page.

The exhibition of 1851 brought about a revival of the lace industry. The wife of the lace-buyer above mentioned worked with one or two others at the exhibition. The pillows were covered for the occasion with blue velvet edged with rose colour and with rose-coloured bobbin bags. The lace worked by Mrs. Smith from the pattern shown in the illustration took the gold medal prize. The lace was exquisitely fine, twenty slip thread being used, a degree of fineness almost unknown at the present day. It took three months to make one foot of lace. Her Majesty the Queen, after watching Mrs. Smith work, asked, as so many ladies ask lace-makers, why her bobbins were of so many different patterns: "Is it in order to tell which of them should be turned over?" These bobbins used in the presence of the Queen have been carefully treasured, though Mr. Smith has given many away to those who will value them. Some are in the possession of the authors. The few words uttered by Her Majesty have been remembered and repeated with ever-increasing interest through the years that have passed, and the kindly notice given by their sovereign marked the day as a red-letter day to the Olney lace-makers.

A woman now living in Spratton remembers the time when her mother, then living at Creaton, made the lace worn by the Lady Sarah Spencer at the wedding of the Princess of Wales. She was but a child, but remembers distinctly the lady coming on horseback now and again to see how the lace was getting on.

FIG. 9

DESIGN FOR BUCKS PILLOW LACE
WORKED BEFORE THE QUEEN AT THE EXHIBITION OF 1851

She does not remember the price of it, but says that the money earned by her mother for this special piece of lace bought them a pony and trap, the first they had ever had.

About the close of the fifties Maltese lace was introduced into the Midlands, and in many places its manufacture unfortunately superseded the old points. It is more quickly made and will better bear the introduction of bad work than will the point ground. Perhaps, though much of it can have little claim to beauty, it is not altogether bad that it should have been introduced. It widened the ideas of the lace-makers, suggesting new methods and accustoming them to turn their hands to any kind of lace.

The last great outburst of prosperity was in 1870, owing to the Franco-German War, when lace-makers again earned splendid wages; but since then, until the present revival, with the exception of a short rage for "yak" lace, it had been at a very low ebb. In many villages the industry was almost entirely abandoned, and many workers had yards of beautiful lace of which they were quite unable to dispose.

IV

LACE SCHOOLS

I SHOULD be sorry to outrage the susceptibilities of my readers by suggesting that they could recall the early part of this century, but I am going to ask them if, in imagination *only*, they will be so kind as to go back through six or seven decades and visit with me one or two of the lace schools which were then scattered so thickly throughout the counties of Beds, Bucks, and Northants.

The first one that we enter strikes us as stifling, in spite of the door and the two windows being thrown open, and no wonder, for in that cottage-room are gathered thirty pupils, varying from six to sixteen years of age. The boys are dressed like the village lads of to-day, excepting that instead of knickerbockers they all wear trousers; but the girls have print frocks, low at the neck and sleeves, and very short in the skirt, from which peep white stockings and shoes, varying in neatness according to the disposition and means of the parents. Some of the children are very small, not more than six years of age.

They are sitting in rows, each little person on his or her four-legged stool, with its pillow resting against the three-legged stand in front of it. Those pillows are dressed in dark blue, and look as if they had tasted of the good things in life, so round are they, and fat, and heavy; indeed, when they carry them, the younger children's arms will hardly meet round them, and their little feet stagger under the weight.

In front of the thirty stools is a desk at which, in her majesty, is enthroned the teacher. But for the addition of spectacles and a kerchief she is dressed like the elder girls; by her side lies her sceptre, that all-powerful sceptre, her cane. Every hour she goes her rounds from pillow to pillow, and woe betide the luckless pupil whose work is badly done!

As the children turn the bobbins over and over, they sing doggerel verses called "tells," sticking pins as fast as their little fingers can plant them; at every tenth pin they call out the number, and so the room is full of counting. Now they have taken sides, and are going to "strive," or race each other, to see which can stick the greater number of pins in a given time. To escape the cane they have to put in ten pins a minute, or 600 an hour; but as the race grows in excitement many of them get in between 700 to 800, while we grow giddy at the sight, and at the sound of the ceaseless "clack, clack" of the bobbins.

It is nearly dinner-time. All but quite the little ones have been there since six o'clock; they are beginning to grow fidgety—visions of pie, cheese, and cake float over the parchments. At last comes the welcome news that "time's up." Each child covers over its pillow, turns its four-legged stool upside down, places the pillow in it, and runs off laughing and shouting, with the girls' straw or paste-board bonnets and bare necks gleaming in the sunshine.

All but a little girl of seven. She is scrupulously clean, but very small and delicate—a sweet little child, with long, fair hair hanging down her back in two tidy plaits. Her blue eyes, and very blue they are, just now are filled with tears; but the little white face is set in order to keep them from brimming over and spoiling her lace. She is faint and weak from one of those sick headaches to which poor children are so often subject. She has had nothing to eat since early morning, and, like all the others, excepting a few learners, has been working since six o'clock. As it neared the dinner-hour her spirits had revived, for had she not brought hers with her, and was it not now in the oven? Such a dinner too, gooseberry tart with sugar! Suddenly she had found herself on the floor, knocked down by the rough fist of her teacher. "I'll wake you! If you don't choose to work with the others, you'll have to stop in while they play."

At one o'clock the others troop in again and pack themselves in, row behind row, and work goes on as before, only the room grows hotter, and the "clack, clack" of the bobbins more monotonous. We wonder how the children can keep their attention. For the most part they sit very upright; for has not mother told them again and again that if they stoop over their work they will get hunchbacked?

Now and again a child falls short of pins, and goes "a-begging." Stopping before a likely giver, it sings "Mary Ann" (or whatever the name may be), "a pin for the poor; give me one, and I'll ask you no more." In this way it generally gathers for itself a nice little store.

Tea-time comes. Out run the children for half an hour; but the little figure by the window sits on, for her task is not done.

From five to six is a quiet time; you can hear a pin drop, for the children are working for dear life, many with aching backs and through a mist of tears. They know that if when "time's up" is called they should be but five pins behind they will be kept in another hour.

It is over, and the room is empty of all save three or four; but among them is the child by the window. She has had twelve hours of it; she is only seven, and suffering from want of food and a sick headache.

With a sigh we turn to watch the others, and hope that they now, after so many hours of hard work, are free to skip and play hop-scotch like their little grandchildren of to-day. But no; for many of them learning is not yet over: they are going to the night-school, where wearily they will pick up enough of reading to make in after life their leisure a blessing to them rather than a curse.

An hour later we pass a little blue-eyed child sobbing piteously. She has just been released from her work, and is holding in her arms her much-longed-for gooseberry tart; but alas! it is burnt to a cinder. She is an old woman now, but the memory of that disappointment is still fresh to her.

It is on a winter's evening that we visit our next school. As we enter we can make out some sixteen girls from the ages of seven to twenty, and we notice that they are all working by the light of one tallow candle. The little ones went home when it grew dark, and those who are left are mostly good workers.

In the centre of the room stands the four-legged candle-stool as high as an ordinary table. The top, which is called the "hole-board," is pierced by a hole in the centre and four others round it. In the middle hole is fixed a long stick with a socket for the candle at the top and peg-holes through the side, so that it can be raised and lowered at will. In the other four holes there are placed wooden cups, into each of which fits a flask made of very thin glass and filled with water. These flasks act as strong condensers or lenses. The girls sit diagonally, four to each bottle, those in the second and third circle having the better light.

The room, though stuffy, is cold, for, being so full, the fire has to be kept low. We wonder why the girls do not shiver more, for they are clad like their predecessors in print dresses, and from their low sleeves and large white collars gleam their bare necks and arms.

As usual they are singing. This time it is a "tell" that would be useful for all lace-workers to learn: "Do your stitch, stick your pin, and do your stitch about it." Indeed, it is for want of this "stitch about the pin" that so many workers' lace is faulty. Then they strike up another.

While they are singing, we will ask the teacher to tell us a little about the school, and to show us some of the lace they have made, and which is waiting to be taken to the lace-buyer, who lives in the neighbouring town.

When a little child joins the school she is usually six or seven, but sometimes one is taken who is a year or so younger. If she is sharp, she will be about three weeks learning her first little edging; during that time she pays 1*s.* a week, and afterwards 3*d.* in the summer, and 4*d.* during the winter (this varies a little in different schools, as do the hours of working). For the first six months she generally puts in only nine hours a day, but after that at least ten, with the exception of Saturday, which is a half-holiday. The winter hours are usually from eight to eight, allowing two hours for meals, but many work an hour or so longer. Every Saturday the teacher takes the lace to the buyer, and gives the girls the exact amount that they have earned, deducting only the 3*d.* or 4*d.* a week for the use of the room and lights. If they sell their work to a private customer, they are allowed to charge 1*d.* a yard more.

Then she shows us what they have made. First there is the little edging upon which the new-comers are started; it is called "the town trot." After that we see an array of the sweetest baby-laces, the narrowest being only 3*d.* a yard. Many of them are made up on the daintiest of baby-caps; for in those days babies began their lives in a staid and respectable manner, even wearing their caps under their hoods when they went out. Round the border of a cap ran one or two rows of narrow lace, plain or closely quilted in tiny box-pleats, while in the centre there is a lace "round" or "horseshoe," often exquisite in design and workmanship. Here is one set off by narrow loops of white satin ribbon. Then there are a set of cambric handkerchiefs and full-grown nightcaps, edged with the "heart" and "oak-leaf" patterns. After we have admired and wondered, she fetches a large wooden box, out of which she brings some truly lovely designs in rich lace handkerchiefs, parasol-covers, veils, etc. She tells us that the girls at her school usually earn, after deducting what they pay her, 2*s.* 3*d.* a week.

But you must not think that the teacher gives us this information all at once, for she constantly leaves us to inspect the workers. Sometimes she remarks to a girl, "I'll wake you! you've been asleep!" and wake her she does by a smart hit of her cane across the bare shoulders.

Just then a knock comes at the door—a father has come for his lass. It is a pity that there are not more like him, for the girls turned out into the darkness will find rough lads waiting round the corners for some of them, and so, hardly through their own fault, many come to sorrow.

It is St. Thomas's Day. The children are assembled; row behind row they are sitting, with their fat pillows resting against the stands before them. But by the look of repressed excitement on every face, there is evidently something about to happen. Presently the teacher leaves the room on the pretence of getting a parchment. In a minute the girl nearest the door has sprung up and bolted it; the pillows are put on one side, and an indescribable hubbub ensues. When the teacher returns she shakes the door violently, demanding to be let in; but the answer comes from thirty voices, "It's St. Thomas's Day; give us a half-holiday, and we'll let you in." For five minutes or so she stands outside grumbling and knocking, and then, finding that the children have turned the stools against her, she (not unwillingly, perhaps) gives in. The holiday is promised, the door is opened, and she walks in as the children rush out. As we watch them laughing and shouting, we think that it is a pity that custom should have fixed their holiday for one of the dullest and certainly the shortest of the days in the year.

"Are there any other days that you are turned out of your own school?" we ask the teacher.

"No; but they generally manage to work half-time on St. Andrew's Day."

"And what do they do with the other half?"

"Oh, have tea in the schoolroom," she answers grimly. "It is the young folk who are spoilt nowadays."

After that we leave her to her pillow, with the click-clack of her bobbins sounding mournfully through the now deserted room.

V

LACE-MAKERS AT HOME

"Yon cottager, who weaves at her own door,
Pillow and bobbins all her little store;
Content though mean, and cheerful if not gay,
Shuffling her thread about the livelong day—
Just earns a scanty pittance, and at night
Lies down secure, her heart and pocket light."

COWPER.

HAVING visited the lace schools, I will ask my readers if they will bear with me while I tell them a little about the workers of this century in their own homes. A child was often introduced to her pillow at three years old by her mother, and then, when she had learnt how to handle her bobbins, she was sent off to the lace school, where she would stay until she either went into service or was married; or, if she wished to save the expense of the 3*d.* or 4*d.* a week, she would work in her own home. In those days, especially in one part of the Midlands, nearly every cottager, married or single, sat at her pillow; for it was usually only farmers' or tradesmen's daughters who thought of going to service.

Whatever may be said of the "good old days," the results were most disastrous, not only to their health, but also to their morals; indeed, a lady, who is interested in a certain Midland village, tells me that although it was sad to see an old industry dying out, yet she was only too thankful when bad work and bad prices made it necessary for the girls to desert their pillows and go out into service. In this chapter we will endeavour to show how the present revival of the trade has been obtained without the slightest risk either to health or morals, and also how it is of benefit to many hundreds of families.

At the time of the Queen's accession, as has been said, the trade was very flourishing, and it was found that a man could earn more at lace-making than in the fields, where his wages would be from *7s.* to *8s.* a week, while at his pillow he could make *9s.* or *10s.* In those days, then, the workers, men and women, would sit side by side in each other's houses, in order to save firing. In the winter they had to sit very near to the windows, which did not give as much light as they do now, and it was often bitterly cold. In some parts, to keep themselves warm, they used a "dicky pot"; this was made of rough brown ware, glazed, and filled with embers begged from the bread oven of a well-to-do neighbour.

In print we often find mention of deformity and disease among lace-workers. These were greatly due, first, to the overcrowding of the schools, and secondly, to the constrained position necessarily adopted by men, women, and even babies, in order to see their work. No wonder, then, that a certain little boy in Bucks, one day growing disgusted, made away with his pillow down a well!

The patterns were usually designed and pricked either by lace-buyers, superior workers, or those brought up specially to that part of the trade, many of the designs, especially some drawn at Olney, being very lovely. (See Figs. 10 and 11.)

Here I should like to insert an account of the keeping of St. Catherine's Day, which was long held as a holiday both by lace-makers and weavers in parts of the Midlands. Its origin is probably far older than the time of Catherine of Aragon, but very possibly, being her fête-day, it has since been held in special honour by lace-makers, as tradition points to that queen as the introducer of the craft. If so, it was one certainly very different from the present pillow-work, being probably an adaptation of needlepoint.

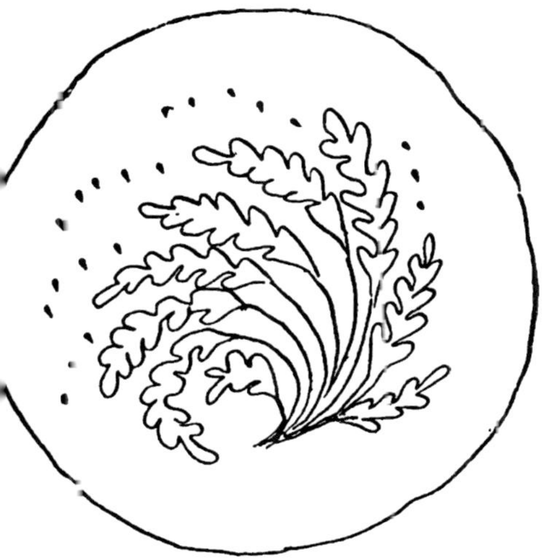

FIG. 10

DESIGN FOR CENTRE OF BADGE CAP

FIG. 11

DESIGN FOR FINE BUCKS LACE MADE AT OLNE

EARLY 19TH CENTURY

I am indebted for the following account to Mrs. Orlebar, of Hinwick House:—

"*Cattern Tea.*—In Podington and neighbouring villages the lace-makers have, within the memory of middle-aged people, 'kept Cattern' on December 6th—St. Catherine's Day (Old Style). I believe it was Catherine of Aragon who used to drink the waters of a mineral spring in Wellingborough, and who (as is supposed) introduced lace-making into Beds. The poor people know nothing of the Queen, only state that it was an old custom to keep 'Cattern.'

"The way was for the women to club together for a tea, paying 6*d.* apiece, which they could well afford when their lace brought them in 5*s.* or 6*s.* a week.

"The tea-drinking ceremony was called 'washing the candle-block,' but this was merely an expression. It really consisted in getting through a great deal of gossip, tea, and Cattern cakes—seed cakes of large size. Sugar balls went round as a matter of course. After tea they danced, just one old man whistling or fiddling for them, and '*they enjoyed theirselves like queens!*'

"The entertainment ended with the cutting of a large apple pie, which they divided for supper. Their usual bedtime was about eight o'clock.

"An old rhyme is still extant about Cattern. I cannot recover more than these lines :—

"'Rise, maids, arise !
Bake your Cattern pies !
Bake enough, and bake no waste,
So that the old bell-man may have a taste !'"

VI

THE DECLINE OF THE LACE INDUSTRY

DURING the childhood of the now middle-aged in our villages the lace industry was flourishing and well paid; ten years ago the trade was almost extinct; but one generation separates us from the time when almost every child in the village was "brought up to the pillow."

What was the cause of this sudden decline, of this astounding change in village life? Ask an old lace-maker, and the reply will be, "Machine-made lace"; inquire a little further into the subject, and the inadequacy of the answer will strike you forcibly. The question is really a most complex one; it cannot be answered without some consideration of the great social changes which were taking place all over England in the earlier part of our Queen's reign. In this short book one cannot pretend to answer it thoroughly and satisfactorily.

Let us first try to understand in what way machine-made lace did really affect the industry. It must be borne in mind that the disappearance of English pillow-made lace from the market did not coincide in time with the production of good machine work, and also that we never ceased to import pillow lace from abroad, and further that the present revival of the pillow lace industry comes at a time when imitation lace of good quality can be had at very low prices.

Until the present century lace was essentially an adjunct of the rich. It was costly, of fine and intricate workmanship, and was prized accordingly. The wealthy and the noble possessed it, the middle class had a little, the poor did not aspire to lace at all. With the introduction of machine lace the fabric became common; the imitation was eagerly bought by those to whom the real thing had been an unhoped-for luxury, and to them it seemed almost as good and as beautiful. Many could not even distinguish between the hand work and the machine work.

A rage for cheap lace set in, and with it came the introduction of Maltese, which was showy and cheap compared to the point grounds. Pillow lace tried to compete with machine lace on its own ground, that of cheapness and showy effectiveness. Until the public tired of Maltese and coarse edgings the lace-makers did not suffer—then the crash came. Machine lace

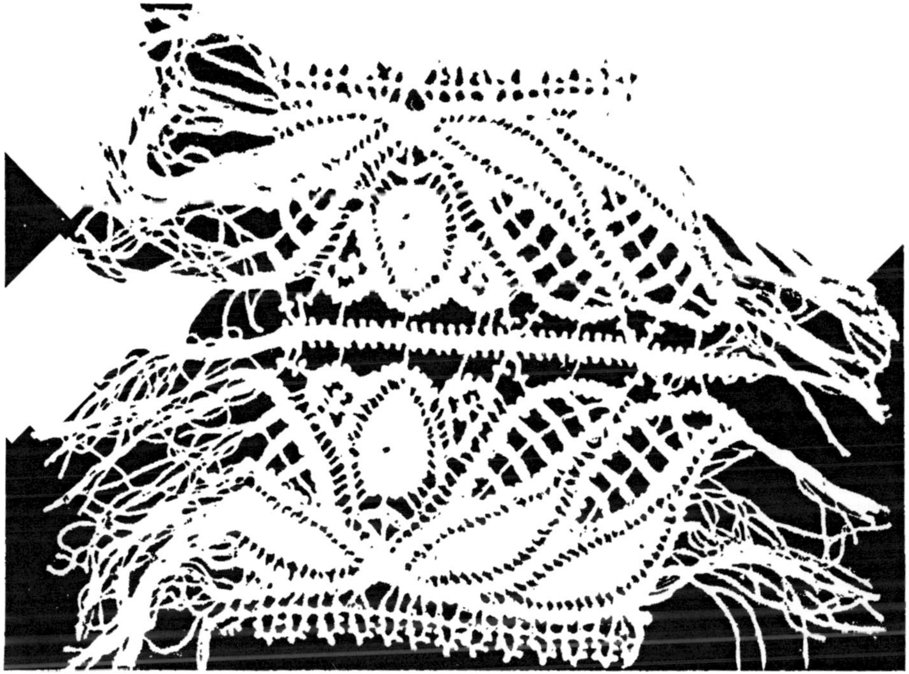

FIG. 12

MALTESE LACE

MADE IN MIDLAND COUNTIES

improved, imitations of the beautiful old laces were produced; the public had not yet learnt to distinguish the true from the false, and the pillow lace-makers had all but forgotten how to make good lace. In the race for cheapness they had begun to use cheap cotton threads, and to work in a slipshod manner. Prices fell to a deplorable level, and lace-making came to be hated as the most fearful drudgery. Only a return to the good old lace and the good old methods could save the industry; it was found impossible to turn out bad lace as cheaply and as rapidly as the machine.

Some proof of the truth of these facts may be gathered by noting the extraordinary difference of opinion which exists among former lace-makers as to the merits of the trade. An old woman of seventy or eighty, whose memory goes back to the flourishing day of the beautiful point-ground lace, or half-stitch as it is sometimes called, will say, "Ah, I always loved my pillow. I shall always love it; I will work at it as long as I can sit to it and see." "Give me a pair of spectacles as I can see with," says another, "and let me have my pillow; it's nice work." "It's nice clean work," echoes another old body; "why don't the young folk take to their pillows now? we loved our pillows." In another cottage we hear, "When I was a girl I spent all my pocket-money on my pillow; I loved to have it nice. I had some beautiful bobbins, bone ones with beads on them and names, and my pins had different-coloured heads. How we loved our pillows, and what we would spend on them!" Now talk to a buxom widow of middle age: "I *hate* it; I burnt all my bobbins; it's a bad trade." "If you go lace-making," says another, "you'll never have salt to your porridge." "It's an awful trade, lace-making," we hear from another; "you'll never make your fortune at it. I always said none of my children should be lace-makers." The explanation of the contrast is to be found in the fact that the middle-aged remember the bad times, the cheap lace and poor patterns, the fearful hurrying and ceaseless work. The older women think of the time when the work was beautiful and good and a joy to do.

We cannot leave the subject of machine-made lace without remarking the injurious effect it has upon the public taste. When it aims at imitating the work of the pillow, the spurious showiness and perfection of it—the likeness and yet unlikeness—palls when one becomes accustomed to it, and may create a distaste for the real thing, which, in contrast to the imitation, never by itself tires the eye. This difficulty is met by the manufacturers by a constant change of fashion and style, the tawdriness of the new fashion passing unnoticed. Machine lace is at its best when it does not directly imitate any pillow lace, when it takes an independent place of its own, with suitable designs made expressly for it. The distinction between the real and the imitation is now much more clearly understood than it was twenty years ago; the true place and use of each is recognised, and, though real lace cannot regain the unique position which it once held, it cannot now be said to suffer from competition with the machine.

The social change in village life had probably a far greater effect on the industry than had the imitation lace. The small, self-supporting community had become little more than a colony of agricultural labourers. The Parish Councils failed to restore the village life because the old free population had departed into the towns, the little village trades were lost or merged in the great town manufactures. The change came gradually, and as it came it threw more and more power into the hands of the landowner and tenant farmer, and it was to their interest to discourage the village industry and make the population entirely dependent upon the land. We have many proofs of what was done to bring contempt upon the lace industry. Instead of any effort being made to prevent evil in connection with the lace schools the whole system was most unjustly condemned. Farmers' wives still speak contemptuously of lace-making, and twelve or fourteen years ago few of the landowners knew or cared anything about the trade. People talk of having sometimes bought a bit of lace from some poor starving old woman, as if they had performed a great act of charity, instead of having got a fine piece of work for less than half its value.

We asked a middle-aged woman for reminiscences of the lace school.

"I never went much to a lace school, though of course I made lace. Our clergyman's wife persuaded me to leave the lace school and come to a school she had, to learn needlework."

No doubt there was much of this persuading and much demonstration of the superiority of needlework to lace, and the greater respectability of the lady's school.

No one can do too much in the cause of true education, but it was characteristic of the times that the way to improve the girls should have been the destruction of a beautiful craft. The reform of the lace school was perhaps as necessary as the reform of the factory. We know more now of the merits of fresh air and space;

but the teachers were not always tyrants, and the best of our village population—the most refined and clever and enterprising—spent their childhood at their pillows.

The rôle of the former lace-makers numbers National School teachers, shopkeepers, and the wives of the higher rank of village artisans. It can hardly be argued that the trade was the enemy of education.

The Education Act dealt the final blow at the lace industry. The school at Paulers Pury, in Northants, was continued until after the children were obliged to attend the National School; but it had to be abandoned, as the teacher (who still makes lace) found that her pupils were not able to do any good work after the day's lessons were over. They were thus left without technical training, everything being given up for the sake of learning reading, writing, and arithmetic.

At Paulers Pury the best point-ground worl had always been made—work which no machir could rival, and which was always valuab and the direct effect of the Education Act of the changing social conditions is most cl seen.

The loss of the lace schools left the ir without organisation and without capi without a fresh supply of trained

After a bad period of idling at home, the girls began to go out to service and to take the place of the tradesmen's and farmers' daughters, who were beginning to think domestic service beneath them. To go out was now considered a rise in the social scale, and so the contempt in which lace-making was held increased.

In the next chapter we shall endeavour to follow the turn of the tide which has resulted in the revival of the old trade.

VII

REVIVAL OF THE LACE INDUSTRY

IT has been felt for some time past that something must be done to prevent the utter stagnation of village life, and that to provide a good school with nothing beyond but the work on the land was to sow the seeds of discontent and the mischief that comes of dulness. We have been encouraging village entertainments and holidays, village music, and, above all, village industries. The Home Arts and Industries Association for Northamptonshire, under Miss Dryden's energetic influence, has done wonders for the lace as well as for other beautiful crafts. Other county exhibitions have encouraged lace-making competitions, and it is usually an important feature at the great annual Home Arts and Industries Exhibition at the Albert Hall.

Even before this great movement ladies were beginning to interest themselves in the beautiful but almost vanished craft of the Midland counties. Old lace-makers who remembered how to make the delicate baby-laces of a former generation were sought out and set to work. Marvellous parchments for the old wide half-stitch patterns, long thrown aside for the coarse Maltese, were discovered and wondered at. Harrowing tales were told of parchments burnt, or boiled down to make glue, and of bobbins used to light the fire. The inquiring ladies, under the spell that lace seldom fails to throw over its devotees, sought out good threads and patterns, and eagerly bought up good work.

A poor old widow, seventy-nine years of age, when visited by one of the ladies who was hunting up lace for "stock," in 1891, was found to have hoarded up in a box 15*s.* worth of lace, and was diligently working to add to her store, hoping some day to be able to sell it. When our visitor bought the boxful as it was the tears of joy came into her eyes. She is now eighty-seven years of age, and is still making lace.

In almost every village something was done. There was want of method, perhaps, and waste of force, but it was an enthusiasm; no one believed at the time that there was any great business possibility in the lace industry. An attempt to bring order into the chaos resulted in the formation of the "Midland Lace Association." A letter which appeared in the *Northampton Daily Chronicle* for January 12th, 1897, explains the genesis of this Association:—

"LACE ASSOCIATION FOR THE COUNTIES OF NORTHAMPTON, BUCKINGHAM, AND BEDFORD: A SHORT ACCOUNT OF ITS ORIGIN AND FORMATION.

"On February 3rd, 1891, an exhibition of needlework and pillow lace was held in Northampton, and was opened by H.R.H. the Duchess of Teck. There were 550 exhibits of pillow lace, all made in the above counties. A large amount of prizes was awarded to the poor lace-workers; indeed, so great was the interest exhibited, and so large the quantity of lace sold, that it seemed a pity to let the industry die out (as it was fast doing) for want of encouragement. A preliminary meeting was held in St. Giles's Vicarage, and the scheme of the Lace Association was drawn up. The Countess Spencer kindly consented to act as president, with twelve vice-presidents, and five ladies were appointed to act as a working committee. There was also a general committee of subscribers, whose subscriptions enabled the working committee to buy in a stock of lace, and to meet the expenses of postage, printing, etc.

"The objects of the Association were—

"1. To stimulate and improve the local manufacture of lace.

"2. To provide workers with greater facilities for the sale of their work at more remunerative prices.

"3. To provide instruction in lace-making.

"Wherever it was possible a lady correspondent

was appointed to act as a medium of communication between the lace-workers and the committee.

"At first the lace was sold through the agency of a depôt in Northampton, but at the end of six months the working committee took upon themselves the whole responsibility of the sales, and with so much success that the amount of lace sold has gone on steadily increasing each year, and so great now is the demand for this beautiful fabric that the committee find it difficult to keep pace with the orders that flow in.

"In consequence of the great demand for lace the work of the Association has increased to such an extent that it has been found necessary this year to appoint a special agent to buy and sell for the committee. It is hoped in time (if the demand for lace goes on increasing) that the Association will become self-supporting; but at present, owing to the increased expenses connected with its working, it is still more or less dependent upon subscriptions. I must not omit to add that in 1894 the Lace Association was honoured by an order for 360 yards of pillow lace by H.R.H. the Duchess of York. Before concluding this little sketch it is only right to mention that before the Lace Association was even thought of, ladies in Northamptonshire and the adjoining counties had endeavoured to revive the industry in their own immediate neighbourhoods. Mrs. Chettle, who is now an active member of the Lace Association, began her work in 1888, and before the Association was started had sold £200 worth of lace. Miss M. Roberts, of Spratton, in 1890, started a small subscription fund to enable her to buy the poor people's lace, which she sold for them amongst her friends.

So far back as 1880 Mrs. Harrison, of Paulers Pury, began to take an interest in it. She sold a large quantity of lace to the Ladies' Work Society in Sloane Street, and in 1883 received an order from H.R.H. the Princess Louise and the Duchess of Edinburgh. In 1883 she furnished the Princess Christian, by special request, with notes and statistics of the Bucks lace industry for an article H.R.H. was writing in *Murray's Magazine*, and this article brought the lace-makers into notice, and furnished them with fresh orders. In 1891 Mrs. Harrison joined the Lace Association, and took an active interest in the formation of County Council lace-classes for the various villages of Northamptonshire. . .

"Miss Dryden's able and interesting article in the *Pall Mall Magazine* of March last brought the lace into further notice, and has also been the means of bringing in fresh orders, amongst others one from a Russian nobleman, who sent a donation to the Association, and also asked for patterns and parchments of English-made pillow laces for his mother, who is a 'past master' in the art of Russian pillow lace-making, and who wishes to copy some of our English-made laces. In conclusion I would add that I received an 'award' from Chicago for specimens of pillow lace sent on behalf of the Midland lace-makers.

"GEORGINA M. ROBERTS.

"SPRATTON VICARAGE, NORTHAMPTON."

Mrs. Roberts, the writer of this letter, is herself a most accomplished lace-maker, familiar with the methods of the old Italian laces, of the

Honiton lace, of the heavy linen laces, as well as being a good point-ground worker. The Association beginning as it did, with far too little capital (only £15), was unable by itself to carry on a business which developed so rapidly as did the pillow-lace trade. The ladies of the working committee, therefore, dipped generously into their own pockets, and added largely to the capital without seeking for any return in the form of interest or profit. This generous spending did not appear in the accounts of the Lace Association, that business being kept separate from the further individual efforts of the ladies, though all worked harmoniously together for its good. Through stress of circumstances and from convenience, and partly on account of Mrs. Roberts's nearness to Northampton, the work of the Association proper fell mainly into her hands. She bought and sold lace and thread and parchments, superintending as no ordinary secretary could have done, carrying on for *no* pecuniary reward a business which filled the whole of the working-day with arduous labour. It must be remembered that lace teachers and prickers were almost extinct, that good thread and pins were difficult to obtain, that many of the younger lace-màkers had been trained in bad methods. Mrs. Roberts experimented with

FIG. 13

threads and patterns; there was no lace which she did not understand and could not correct. Wisely comprehending that success could not attend mere lifeless revivals of old work, she collected patterns and laces from all over Europe, and welcomed every kind of work that was good. In 1897 she was obliged to give up the work of selling and buying, and it was placed in the hands of a lady agent in Northampton, who has carried it on with untiring devotion.

Another member of the first working committee was Mrs. Chettle, who is referred to in Mrs. Roberts's letter. This lady found distress among the population about Towcester in 1865, on account of slackness in the shoe trade, and she then helped the people by disposing of £200 worth of lace amongst her friends. Afterwards she allowed her interest in lace-making to drop until the year 1888, when she began to devote herself to the task of buying and selling, and now has a large connection. Mrs. Bostock, who bought and sold in the town of Northampton, also belonged to the first committee.

At Prince's Risborough Mrs. Forrest carried on the same work, and many others laboured, following the example of the originators of the movement. Mrs. Harrison of Paulers Pury was one of the first to carry on lace-buying on a large scale, though she did not join the Association till 1891.

All these ladies took the place of the old professional lace-buyers, who had almost all given up the trade in the time of its decline. They began, generally in a small way, to buy the lace of old workers out of charity and also from the pure love of it. The rapidity with which these small beginnings became, in the hands of ladies unaccustomed to business and with no wish to make money, large affairs in which the annual expenditure amounted to hundreds of pounds, shows the real vitality of the trade; it shows that at any rate it was not dead because it was not wanted. All who entered into it were carried along, as it were, involuntarily devoting their lives and their money without any previous planning, plunging suddenly into important business transactions just because they happened to be on the spot to do the work and there was no one else to do it. There have been no great losses, neither has there been much profit, for the lace has generally been sold at very little over cost price. It has not been possible, however, to work the Association as distinct from the individual work of the ladies (though it has been only financially distinct) without expenses; it has therefore been to a small extent in debt.

VIII

THE CONDITION AND PROSPECTS OF LACE-MAKING AT THE PRESENT TIME

HAS the industry a future? is it business or is it charity? No question is more often put to the modern lady lace-buyer. There is a great demand, so great that, it must be frankly confessed, it very often cannot be met. Sometimes orders have to be refused, often orders which could be had for the asking are not asked for. Lace-buyers, both the amateur (who has by far the greater part of the business) and the genuine trader working for his own profit, constantly reiterate the cry, "I could sell if I could get the work." It is workers we want, workers by the hundred, workers who will make the *kind of lace we need.* There are some lace-makers who will offer to make you any kind of lace except the one which you happen to want at the moment. Generally you are forced to buy anything they will consent to make on account of the necessity of keeping up your stock, though it may be almost impossible to get a profit on that particular work.

This state of things very naturally suggests the question, Is the work needed, or are we so rich that we can do without such an industry? There is undoubtedly a considerable class of persons to whom it is an immense boon, to whom its disappearance would be an irreparable loss. There are hundreds of women between sixty and ninety years of age quite unfit for any other kind of work who keep themselves by it in independence; any lace-buyer can count up a large number who keep their husbands as well—husbands past work, crippled, or blind, or bedridden. The old mother living in the son's or daughter's house, past being any assistance in the housework, feels the delight of not being a burden on the hard-pressed children. She can still sit at her pillow part of the day and earn the four or five shillings a week which keeps her. Perhaps to the aged the occupation is almost as great a boon as the earnings, and this accounts for the intense pleasure with which the work is almost always spoken of. When sons and daughters are all grown up and gone away, the long days may be unspeakably dull to the old couple, but the wife can always make herself happy turning over the bobbins. We went to see a widow, over eighty years old, living all alone, and tried to buy some of her beautiful lace. "When my husband was alive," she said, "he didn't care for me working at it, so I put it on one side; but now he's dead, I couldn't do without it, I should be so dull." She could not sell us any of her work, she had orders that would keep her busy for months to come.

But it is not only the aged who are glad of the work; the mother of the family finds it a great help. When the housework is done, and the children are all away at school, she can sit down and work for a couple of hours, and the week's earnings will be a comfortable addition to her man's wages, especially when there is a large family and he a labourer on 12*s.* or 14*s.* a week. There is no other industry so convenient for the home. It is clean work and needs cleanliness, for lace must be spotlessly white if the worker is to get her full price. It creates no litter and no untidiness. The pillow stands by the window, with a cloth thrown over it and the chair ready before it. When baby is put to sleep, the mother has but to lift the cloth and begin her work: there is no getting out of material and implements, and no putting away and clearing up when the children come home to tea. Where shoe-work or stay-work is taken at home, the littered floor and whirring machine make an unpleasant contrast to the tidiness and quietness of the bobbins with their little subdued rattle so pleasant to the ear. Lace-making is not tiring, nor in any way trying; given suitable spectacles for the old women, it is not at all trying to the eyes—indeed, an expert worker on a lace she knows well, looks at it no more than a needlewoman looks at a long seam. "I could do it with my eyes shut" is a phrase one often hears of lace-making, but we take that statement for what it is worth. It is not monotonous work, for even in the simplest lace the pattern creates a variety of motion and sufficient occupation for the mind. "My mother always said that to sit down to her pillow was the best rest she could have after her work," we have been told by the daughter of a famous lace-maker.

On the advantages and pleasures of the work much more might justly be said; but there is one drawback, a drawback that in these days seems to have remarkable force: it takes, in comparison with other home industries, a long time to learn. No one loves shoe-work and stay-work, but they can be learnt with astonishingly little expenditure of time and trouble, and herein lies their superiority. An average woman working in her odd hours cannot earn more than *2s.* or *3s.* a week until she has been learning lace-making for a year; she may earn as much as that after six months; she will probably earn enough to pay for her pillow and bobbins and material after six weeks. A really first-class lace-maker needs four or five years of training. She is, of course, earning something all the time, and she is not having lessons continuously, but only when she changes from one pattern to another. During the first few weeks, before the fingers become supple and accustomed to the action, the work may seem slow and tedious, and some perseverance is necessary. Unfortunately perseverance is a rare virtue among our villagers; their faint-heartedness in every matter which does not immediately go well is very remarkable, and would be almost beyond belief.

In the old days children began very young; and a child of five or six, who has an opportunity of learning, will often think lace-making a most delightful occupation—superior to all Kindergarten games. But nowadays it cannot be taught until schooldays are over, when the girls get out of the regular school routine, and are unsettled and disinclined to steady work. Then, after a little loafing about at home, they are off to service, and we wonder where the next generation of lace-makers is to come from. If the babies could be taught to handle the bobbins in schooltime, instead of plaiting paper mats (no easier to do) and other Kindergarten occupations, and if the girls in the upper school could have an hour or two a week for lace-making instead of working thousands of sums which do not lead to any comprehension of mathematics, and are never likely to be of the smallest use to them, they would, when they leave school, be fairly efficient lace-makers. This need not in anywise prevent their going to service, but in the interval of looking out for a good place they would be useful members of society; they would have a valuable resource in a case of breakdown of health, and after their marriage they would have a pleasant and refining occupation for spare hours. If money is not greatly needed, lace can be made for baby's clothes. The first piece of lace made to trim the little daughter's pinafore has been a great source of pride and pleasure to a married lace pupil. Unless we can train young lace-makers now, the trade must pass away with the present generation. All our present workers (the exceptions are too few to be taken into account) were trained in lace schools; they paid a little for learning, and got their earnings meanwhile. The system was admirably adapted to the nature of the industry it provided; it provided an economical system of excellent technical training without the help of rates or Government grant. To commence such a period of teaching now after the girls leave school is out of the question.

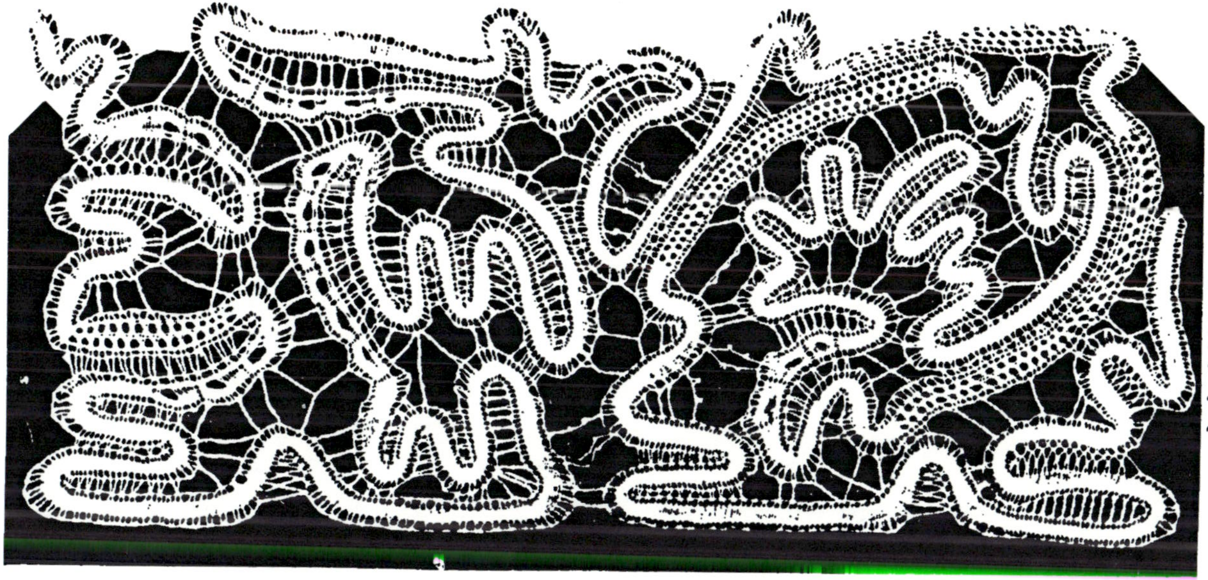

FIG. 14

MODERN PILLOW LACE

MADE AT EAST HADDON AFTER OLD ITALIAN STYLE

Even putting on one side the need of domestic servants, they could not, after thirteen years of age, be kept training for three or four years for a profession, when they should be keeping themselves. The economy of the old system lay in the fact that a girl, beginning quite young, could do very well by the time she was thirteen or fourteen. Something is, however, being done. In some villages a class is held once or twice a week after school hours, to which girls over eleven years old come. The classes generally include some who have already left school, but who are waiting to be old enough to go into good service. Unfortunately it is an expensive matter to keep such classes going for any length of time, as the girls seldom care to pay for their instruction. They expect to learn everything for nothing, because the elementary schools are free; also they do not feel sufficiently sure of being able to continue their work to care to spend money upon it. A lace school of this kind has been started by Mrs. Guthrie at East Haddon, Northamptonshire. She provides a teacher for girls twice a week in a sort of parish room in the village. Here also, on one day in the week, the writer holds a class for adults. In connection with the school is an industry for the production of fine lace-trimmed household linen. It is hoped to be able to rival the wonderfully dainty linen goods of Austria and Germany; and, indeed, there seems to be no difficulty in doing so, for the only complaint made of our towels by a Bond Street shop was that they were *too* beautiful; ladies would not buy them for the purpose for which they were intended. Yet there was no unsuitability of material; it was merely a matter of dainty needlework and perfectly harmonious design. Ladies do our drawn-thread work, and we make a point of suiting the stitch and linen to the lace. In this matter of harmony and oneness of design the beautiful foreign linen is often a failure. There is no doubt about our being able to do it, but we need more workers. East Haddon is not the only village where these classes are held. On bicycle or horseback Miss Channer goes from one to another, holding more than one class a day in villages three or four miles apart.

County Councils give but a meagre help in this great question of the technical training of the lace-maker. The Northampton County Council gives this year £15 for lace-making. One village may claim £3, which will keep a class going for about six weeks. At the end of that time, if no generous patron is ready to pay for its continuance, the girls probably give up trying, and all the time and money is wasted.

FIG. 15

MODERN PILLOW LACE IN ITALIAN STYLE

At Paulers Pury Mrs. Harrison persuades many mothers to teach their daughters. But Paulers Pury is an exceptional place; it has excellent traditions; its point-ground laces are unrivalled; there is an abundance of good patterns—in fact, patterns which do not take prizes at lace competitions are usually eliminated. Here, as many as one in three of the female population are lace-makers. In other parts of the counties a much smaller proportion of the mothers are lace-makers, and a still smaller proportion are *good* lace-makers. Many mothers cannot, and many will not take the trouble, to teach their daughters.

In Mrs. Guthrie's school linen laces, both of the German and Italian style, are taught as well as the fine point-ground edgings. At one of Miss Channer's classes held at Spratton real Valenciennes is being taught. The people are quick and ready to learn a new lace if only the teaching problem can be dealt with; this problem is successfully solved abroad and is undoubtedly the foundation of foreign lace-making. It is true that we cannot compete with foreigners in the production of cheap torchon laces. Our people will not work for so little money as the Swiss and Germans and Belgians.

After dealing with country lace-makers one wonders how, even in towns, "sweating" can be possible in England! One longs for some of the poor hard-worked Londoners to help build up our trade. When our villagers refuse to make lace as cheaply as it is imported from abroad, it must be remembered that the foreign work is generally inferior. It is surely a matter for some honest pride that most of our women would be ashamed to ask us to buy lace such as one sees in some London shop windows; they take a pride in their work, and will not often lower its quality for more gain. "Look into it and you'll see it's good work," says a woman standing out for what she considers a fair price. "I would not show it you at all if you could not say it is well made." Yet that woman was dependent on lace to keep her and her blind husband from abject poverty; her pride would not have allowed her to take a penny off the price, nor to offer anything but the best work. The public does not always distinguish between good and bad quality; it asks for something cheap. It sees in a shop window "Real Torchon, *2d.*," and it says, "How wonderfully cheap! I'll have a dozen yards." The Northamptonshire woman would have remarked, "I would not be a foreigner to make such stuff," and she would have been taunted with the reproach, "You can't do it so cheap." No, we cannot, and we do not succeed when we try to be cheap. There is a certain knack in turning out poor work of a perfectly uniform quality. The writer has deliberately tried to imitate poor Brussels lace, but she can only make it hopelessly and unevenly bad, or uniformly good and expensive. English people must triumph by the superiority of their work if they are to triumph at all, and if it is good they must be well paid for it. It is in the best and most expensive laces that we must try to make our way, leaving twopenny torchon to the foreigner. It is unfortunate that our British public has an hereditary preference for expensive foreign lace over British. Many a lady will take pleasure in spending £10 on lace in Venice when she will hesitate to spend 10*s*. on equally good lace in Northampton! It is uninteresting and unromantic to buy lace in Northampton, even if it is exactly like the Venetian and no more expensive.

Having dealt at some length with the condition of the industry as regards the worker, we must, before passing on to other aspects, show what are the earnings of a lace-maker. There are a few women who get £1 per week or more; many more could earn as much if they could be properly taught. The average among those who devote a considerable amount of time to it is perhaps 10*s*. per week. Some will only earn 5*s*., and some very old women not more than 2*s.* or 3*s.* There are hardly any women who really give up all their time to it; very few who sit at it regularly many hours a day. To earn one's shilling a day *after* the housework and cooking is done is considered a very creditable performance. These earnings ought not to be compared with those of girls working regularly in factories; for there cannot be the steady uninterrupted work at home, where four or five hours is a good measure, in addition to other duties and interruptions. How does the industry stand from the trader's point of view? This is a much-debated question.

At the time when the trade was at its lowest ebb, ten or twelve years ago, almost all the professional lace-buyers had abandoned it. Mr. Smith, at Olney, tells us that he continued merely from love of the work without hope of profit. The profits are still extremely small, but he, like everyone else, complains of having too small a staff of workers. Mr. W. Robinson, of Bedford, turned his attention to millinery laces of horsehair and fibre; they are worked on old yak and torchon parchments, but some of them resemble straw plaiting more than lace. The field then was absolutely free for the amateur; there was practically no competition with the lace-buyers. The situation was a unique one; ladies who were amateurs in the art of buying and selling found themselves masters of a rising industry, which in its former flourishing days had always been carried on from the strictly commercial point of view; nor can there have been many other trades in England so entirely in the hands of women.

It would have been surprising indeed if no mistakes had been made; it is surprising that so few were made. Time has proved that it was a mistake to begin the Lace Association with so small a capital; taking the individual lace businesses of the various ladies, those who have put the most money into it have the most flourishing industry and have suffered the least loss.

At present an attempt is being made to start the Midland Lace Association on a new basis with a solid capital, on which interest can be paid if the present conditions continue. An offshoot of this association, the North Bucks Lace Association, which remains affiliated to the parent society, has begun in a business-like way, having the advantage that always comes of beginning later and profiting by the mistakes of one's predecessors. It is excellently organised and does good work.

Another mistake was that of keeping prices too low. The women for a few years had had great difficulty in selling their lace and expected to get very little for it; they therefore accepted absurdly little remuneration for their work. The new buyers, not wishing to make any profit, sold it again for very little. This was a drawback in many ways. First of all it kept young people from wishing to learn lace-making; so little could be earned, that only old lace-makers who could do very little else, cared to take it up, and buyers were dependent upon a generation which was passing away. In the second place, no one who desired to make a profit could begin trading in lace, as they would inevitably be undersold by the ladies. The consequence, if this had continued, would have been that a very large body of workers would have been dependent upon the existence of a sufficiently large body of ladies willing to work very hard at this trade for nothing, a state of things which could not be guaranteed to last.

Another way in which low prices have been a hindrance, has been the difficulty of supplying shops, who would have been good customers. The shop could not put on its fair profit and sell the lace, when it could be had for so very much less by writing to a Northamptonshire lady, or at one of the lace sales and exhibitions. The Association, which could not sell as economically as ladies could sell among their own friends, was to a certain extent undersold. It could not make even a large enough profit to pay the expenses of keeping up an Association shop, which would undoubtedly have been an advantage to the industry. Fortunately this condition of things is now righting itself. Prices are gradually rising, though some good laces are still being sold for too little, which may soon have the effect of making them disappear from the market. Ladies in connection with the Association have agreed to add a definite percentage to the cost price of their lace. The need of a larger staff of workers has to some extent forced up the scale of remuneration to the lace-maker, though if this had happened sooner we should to-day be in a better position and able to put a larger stock into the market. With better prices, lace shops are buying, to a much larger extent than formerly, from Midland villages; but the bulk of the trade is still in the hands of the Association and those connected with it. With good management this may easily remain so, for we are more popular with the lace-makers than is the commercial traveller, and we get all the best work. When they are well served, the shops are very willing to trade, with us, and we can often send them a better selection than their own travellers can obtain. Personal experience would suggest that shop managers are the *most* satisfactory persons to deal with, for they are invariably courteous and business-like, and withal pay promptly, which cannot always be said of our lady customers. We should not be always in such need of capital if we could avoid bad debts; the necessity of paying workers immediately makes it very trying to be obliged to wait months and months for the price of lace sold, and means much drawing upon the lace banking account.

A good idea of the stock which we can show could have been gathered at the lace exhibition and sale held by kind permission of the Earl and Countess Spencer at Spencer House on July 12th of last year. The value of the lace in the room was calculated at about £800. Probably not much of what was unsold that day remained many weeks on hand. It represents pretty accurately what the Association can produce at short notice, but it does not give a correct idea of the whole output of the three counties. It did not include the work of the North Bucks Association, which held a separate and very successful sale, nor does it show the great quantity of lace made to order on which workers are continually engaged. These periodical sales are at present necessary to bring the customers into touch with the work, but it would be to the convenience of the customer and to the advantage of the trade if this stock could be shown at a permanent shop or depôt.

The existence of an industry is not entirely a question of supply and demand; opportunity and organisation are important factors. In our three lace counties we have a body of expert lace-makers capable of holding their own against any foreign manufacturers, if they are given a chance, if the trade can be organised on lines favourable to its development. We have tried to show that its life or death is very largely a question of technical education, yet all that has been done for the training of the lace-maker is owing to private generosity. The County Councils help with the merest pittance, and neutralise the little good they do by imposing oppressive regulations.

A teacher now working under the Northampton County Council is told that she cannot be paid for her work until four other villages have finished their courses of lessons. She does not know whether these villages have even begun. Besides being asked to wait for her remuneration for an indefinite period, she has to *advance money herself* for pillows, bobbins, and threads, for the same reason that no money can be paid to her until the other four villages of which she knows nothing have finished their work. Not many teachers would consent to such conditions. Such a system may answer for technical classes, like those held for teaching wood-carving, which are merely for improving amusement, but for a serious trade it is an absurdity. The supineness of the authorities of the counties concerned is extraordinary. Lace-making cannot be learnt at the Technical School in Northampton, nor is design taught with any view to its being utilised for lace-making. In spite of the number of curious relics of the past in the shape of lace-pillows, pins, winders, candle-blocks, flasks, bobbins, dicky-pots, maids, etc., which abound in the county, the Northampton museum only shows one dirty, neglected pillow and horse. There is no collection of old parchments, no collection of lace (though a collection of Northampton lace would be of supreme interest), and no collection of lace designs and draughts for the county.

Literature on the subject of lace-making is unattainable at the Northampton Public Library; we have tried in vain to hear in Northampton of one single book on the subject of lace. We have depended upon the kindness of friends having valuable books in their possession, and of Mr. Alan Cole, of the South Kensington Museum, in allowing us to make use of his splendid lecture on the art of lace-making. South Kensington is generous in allowing us to make use of photographs, and in the museum every facility is given for the study

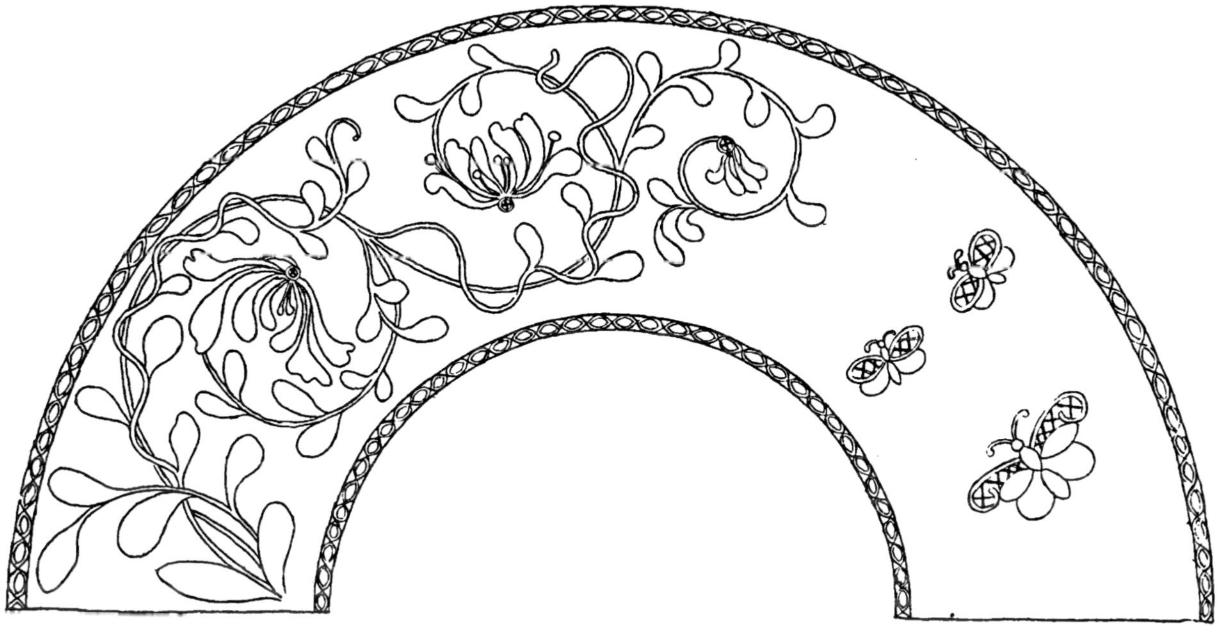

FIG. 16

DESIGN FOR LACE FAN BY MISS ROBERTS

of the splendid collection of lace, but in the counties themselves no help can be obtained by the novice in lace. We have been starved and snubbed and neglected, and then we are told the industry is not wanted because it has not been a great success! If only one little room could be found in Northampton for a good lace museum; if only a few standard books could be provided; if design, and the pricking and preparing of lace parchments could be taught in the technical school, what an improvement there would be!

The writers of this little book have turned their attention to the preparation of parchments. Miss M. Roberts, after studying the "principles of design" under Mr. Knight at the Technical School, Northampton, has tried by herself to apply her knowledge and skill to lace design, and with considerable success. She is now prepared to produce suitable patterns for all kinds of lace for any kind of purpose. Miss Channer has experimented in the pricking of parchments with a view to discovering the best method to teach others, in order that pricking may not continue to be, as it now is in England, a lost art. The so-called "prickers" who remain depend entirely upon old parchments for the pricking of a point ground; they are incapable of ruling out any pattern for themselves. The old methods can be studied in the remarkable draughts in the possession of Mr. Smith, lace-buyer, of Olney.

Surely the existence in our midst of such a beautiful art and handicraft as that of lace-making is worth an effort, worth some public attention, some public expenditure. It is natural to our people; it is absolutely at home in our three counties; it is beloved by thousands of our villagers, mixed with all the romance of their lives, a blessing to the old and the delight of the young. One notes the little girls' delight to use an old bobbin with "grandfather's name on it" as one teaches in a class of to-day, and one's mind wanders back in imagination to the days when grandmother was young and had husband's and children's names on her pillow, when the little ones were sent off day by day to the lace school, when the young man gave his sweetheart pretty beaded bone bobbins to make her pillow smart, and the old man stayed at home to make lace, and it seems as if all the romance and interest of life centred round that curious old bundle of straw, "my pillow." We must take it to heart that the words are not a mere relic of the past, but a living factor in thousands of homes to-day.

PLYMOUTH: W. BRENDON AND SON, PRINTERS.

A CATALOGUE OF BOOKS AND ANNOUNCEMENTS OF METHUEN AND COMPANY PUBLISHERS : LONDON 36 ESSEX STREET W.C.

CONTENTS

AUGUST 1900

MESSRS. METHUEN'S ANNOUNCEMENTS

Travel, Adventure and Topography

THE INDIAN BORDERLAND: Being a Personal Record of Twenty Years. By Sir T. H. HOLDICH, K.C.I.E. Illustrated. *Demy 8vo.* 15*s. net.*

This book is a personal record of the author's connection with those military and political expeditions which, during the last twenty years, have led to the consolidation of our present position in the North-West frontier of India. It is chiefly a personal history of trans-frontier surveys and boundary demarcations, commencing with Penjdeh and ending with the Pamirs, Chitral, and Tirah; but it also contains an account of some of the minor frontier expeditions which have taken us, as pioneers, into hitherto unmapped districts, and have given us an accurate topographical and ethnographical knowledge of the trans-Indus frontier from Karachi to Kafirstan.

MODERN ABYSSYNIA. By A. B. WYLDE. With a Map and a Portrait. *Demy 8vo.* 15*s. net.*

An important, comprehensive, and interesting account of Abyssinia by a traveller who knows the country intimately, and has had the privilege of the friendship of King Menelik.

THROUGH ASIA. By SVEN HEDIN. With 300 Illustrations from Photographs and Sketches by the Author, and 3 Maps. Second and cheaper Edition in 16 Fortnightly Parts at 1s. each net; or in two volumes. *Royal 8vo.* 20*s. net.*

An extract from a review of this great book, which *The Times* has called 'one of the best books of the century,' will be found on p. 18. The present form of issue places it within the reach of buyers of moderate means.

Revised by Commanding Officers.

THE HISTORY OF THE BOER WAR. By F. H. E. CUNLIFFE, Fellow of All Souls' College, Oxford. With many Illustrations, Plans, and Portraits. Vol. I. *Quarto.* 14*s.* Also in Fortnightly Parts. 1*s. each.*

The first volume of this important work is nearly ready. When complete, this book will give an elaborate and connected account of the military operations in South Africa from the declaration to the end of the present war.

Such a work, relating in a lively, accurate, and intelligible manner the events of a war which is stirring the British people as no events have stirred them since the Indian Mutiny, is certain to meet a cordial reception. It must remain for some years the standard History of the War. Messrs. Methuen have been fortunate enough to secure the co-operation of many commanding officers in the revision of the various chapters.

The History is finely illustrated.

A PRISONER OF WAR. By COLONEL A. SCHIEL. *Crown 8vo.* 6*s.*

This remarkable book contains the experiences of a well-known foreign officer of the Boer Army—from 1896 to 1900—both as a Boer officer and as a prisoner in British hands. Colonel Schiel, who was captured at Elandslaagte, was a confidential military adviser of the Transvaal Government, and his story is likely to cause some sensation.

THE SIEGE OF MAFEKING. By ANGUS HAMILTON. With many Illustrations. *Crown 8vo.* 6*s.*

This is a vivid, accurate, and humorous narrative of the great siege by the well-known Correspondent of the *Times*. Mr. Hamilton is not only an admirable writer, but an excellent fighter, and he took an active part in the defence of the town. His narrative of the siege is acknowledged to be far superior to any other account.

Poetry

WRIT' IN BARRACKS. By EDGAR WALLACE. *Cr. 8vo.* 3*s.* 6*d.*

Mr. Edgar Wallace, a member of the Royal Army Medical Corps, is a follower of Mr. Kipling, and his ballads of soldier life and sufferings are well-known in South Africa. They are spirited, pathetic, and true, and at the present time they should enjoy a considerable popularity.

History and Biography

THE LETTERS OF ROBERT LOUIS STEVENSON TO HIS FAMILY AND FRIENDS. Edited with an Introduction and Notes by SIDNEY COLVIN. Fourth Edition. *Two volumes. Crown 8vo.* 12*s.*

This is a completely new edition of the famous Letters of Robert Louis Stevenson, published in 1899.

THE LIFE AND LETTERS OF SIR JOHN EVERETT MILLAIS, President of the Royal Academy. By his son J. G. MILLAIS. With over 300 Illustrations, of which 9 are in Photogravure. Cheaper Edition, Revised. *Two volumes. Royal 8vo.* 20*s. net.*

THE WALKERS OF SOUTHGATE: Being the Chronicles of a Cricketing Family. By W. A. BETTESWORTH. Illustrated. *Demy 8vo.* 15*s.*

A HISTORY OF EGYPT, FROM THE EARLIEST TIMES TO THE PRESENT DAY. Edited by W. M. FLINDERS PETRIE, D.C.L., LL.D., Professor of Egyptology at University College. Fully Illustrated. In Six Volumes. *Crown 8vo.* 6*s. each.*

Vol. VI. EGYPT UNDER THE SARACENS. By STANLEY LANE-POOLE.

Illustrated and Gift Books

THE LIVELY CITY OF LIGG. By GELLETT BURGESS. With 53 Illustrations, 8 of which are coloured. *Small 4to.* 6*s.*

GOOP BABIES. By GELLETT BURGESS. With numerous Illustrations. *Small 4to.* 6*s.*

THE ESSAYS OF ELIA. By CHARLES LAMB. With 70 Illustrations by A. GARTH JONES, and an Introduction by E. V. LUCAS. *Demy 8vo.* 10*s.* 6*d.*

This is probably the most beautiful edition of Lamb's Essays that has ever been published. The illustrations display the most remarkable sympathy, insight, and skill, and the introduction is by a critic whose knowledge of Lamb is unrivalled.

THE EARLY POEMS OF ALFRED LORD TENNYSON. Edited, with Notes and an Introduction by J. CHURTON COLLINS, M.A. With 10 Illustrations in Photogravure by W. E. F. BRITTEN. *Demy 8vo.* 10*s.* 6*d.*

This beautiful edition contains ten charming sketches by Mr. Britten, reproduced in the highest style of Photogravure.

NURSERY RHYMES. With many Coloured Pictures by F. D. BEDFORD. *Super Royal 8vo.* 2*s.* 6*d.*

'An excellent selection of the best known rhymes, with beautifully coloured pictures exquisitely printed.'—*Pall Mall Gazette.*

Theology

THE PHILOSOPHY OF RELIGION IN ENGLAND. By ALFRED CALDECOTT, D.D. *Demy 8vo.* 10*s.* 6*d.* [*Handbooks of Theology.*

A complete history and description of the various philosophies of religion which have been formulated during the last few centuries in England and America.

ST. PAUL'S SECOND AND THIRD EPISTLES TO THE CORINTHIANS. With Introduction, Dissertations, and Notes by JAMES HOUGHTON KENNEDY, D.D., Assistant Lecturer in Divinity in the University of Dublin. *Crown 8vo.* 6*s.*

THE SOUL OF A CHRISTIAN. By F. S. GRANGER, M.A., Litt.D. *Crown 8vo.* 6*s.*

Professor Granger abandons the conventional method of psychology by which the individual is taken alone, and instead, he regards him as sharing in and contributing to the catholic tradition. Hence the book deals not only with the average religious life, but also with the less familiar experiences of the mystic, the visionary, and the symbolist. These experiences furnish a clue to poetic creation in its various kinds, and further, to the miracles which occur during times of religious enthusiasm.

REVELATIONS OF DIVINE LOVE. By the LADY JULIAN of Norwich. Edited by G. H. WARRACK. *Crown 8vo.* 6*s.*

A partially modernised version, from the MS. in the British Museum of a book which Dr. Dalgairns terms 'One of the most remarkable books of the Middle Ages.' Mr. Inge in his Bampton Lectures on Christian Mysticism calls it 'The beautiful but little known *Revelations.*'

The Library of Devotion

Pott 8vo. Cloth 2s.; leather 2s. 6d. net.

NEW VOLUMES.

A GUIDE TO ETERNITY. By CARDINAL BONA. Edited with an Introduction and Notes by J. W. STANBRIDGE, B.D., late Fellow of St. John's College, Oxford.

THE PSALMS OF DAVID. With an Introduction and Notes by B. W. RANDOLPH, D.D., Principal of the Theological College, Ely.

A devotional and practical edition of the Prayer Book version of the Psalms.

LYRA APOSTOLICA. With an Introduction by Canon SCOTT HOLLAND, and Notes by H. C. BEECHING, M.A.

Belles Lettres

The Little Guides

Pott 8vo. Cloth, 3s.; leather, 3s. 6d. net.

NEW VOLUMES.

WESTMINSTER ABBEY. By G. E. TROUTBECK. Illustrated by F. D. BEDFORD.

SUSSEX. By F. G. BRABANT, M.A. Illustrated by E. H. NEW.

Little Biographies

Fcap. 8vo. Each Volume, cloth 2s. 6d.; leather, 3s. 6d. net.

Messrs. METHUEN will publish shortly the first two volumes of a new series bearing the above title. Each book will contain the biography of a character famous in war, art, literature or science, and will be written by an acknowledged expert. The books will be charmingly produced and will be well illustrated. They will make delightful gift books.

THE LIFE OF SAVONAROLA. By E. L. HORSBURGH, M.A., With Portraits and Illustrations.

THE LIFE OF DANTE ALIGHIERI. By PAGET TOYNBEE. With 10 Illustrations.

The Works of Shakespeare

General Editor, EDWARD DOWDEN, Litt.D.

New volumes uniform with Professor Dowden's *Hamlet.*

ROMEO AND JULIET. Edited by EDWARD DOWDEN, Litt.D. *Demy 8vo.* 3s. 6d.

KING LEAR. Edited by W. J. CRAIG. *Demy 8vo.* 3s. 6d.

Methuen's Standard Library

MEMOIRS OF MY LIFE AND WRITINGS. By EDWARD GIBBON. Edited, with an Introduction and Notes by G. BIRKBECK HILL, LL.D. *Crown 8vo.* 6s.

THE LETTERS OF LORD CHESTERFIELD TO HIS SON. Edited, with an Introduction and Notes by C. STRACHEY and A. CALTHROP. *Two volumes. Crown 8vo.* 6s. *each.*

The Novels of Charles Dickens

With Introductions by GEORGE GISSING, Notes by F. G. KITTON, and Illustrations.

Crown 8vo. Each Volume, cloth 3s. net, leather 4s. 6d. net.

The first volumes are:

THE PICKWICK PAPERS. With Illustrations by E. H. NEW. *Two Volumes.* [*Ready*

NICHOLAS NICKLEBY. With Illustrations by R. J. WILLIAMS. *Two Volumes.*

BLEAK HOUSE. With Illustrations by BEATRICE ALCOCK. *Two Volumes.*

OLIVER TWIST. With Illustrations by E. H. NEW. *One Volume.*

The Little Library

With Introductions, Notes, and Photogravure Frontispieces.

Pott 8vo. Each Volume, cloth 1s. 6d. net.; leather 2s. 6d. net.

NEW VOLUMES.

THE EARLY POEMS OF ALFRED, LORD TENNYSON. Edited by J. C. COLLINS, M.A.

MAUD. By ALFRED, LORD TENNYSON. Edited by ELIZABETH WORDSWORTH.

A LITTLE BOOK OF ENGLISH LYRICS. With Notes.

PRIDE AND PREJUDICE. By JANE AUSTEN. Edited by E. V. LUCAS. *Two Volumes.*

PENDENNIS. By W. M. THACKERAY. Edited by S. GWYNN. *Three volumes.*

EOTHEN. By A. W. KINGLAKE. With an Introduction and Notes.

LAVENGRO. By GEORGE BORROW. Edited by F. HINDES GROOME. 2 Volumes.

CRANFORD. By Mrs. GASKELL. Edited by E. V. LUCAS.

THE INFERNO OF DANTE. Translated by H. F. CARY. Edited by PAGET TOYNBEE.

JOHN HALIFAX, GENTLEMAN. By Mrs. CRAIK. Edited by ANNIE MATHESON. *Two volumes.*

A LITTLE BOOK OF SCOTTISH VERSE. Arranged and Edited by T. F. HENDERSON.

General Literature

DARTMOOR: A Descriptive and Historical Sketch. By S. BARING GOULD. With Plans and Numerous Illustrations. *Crown 8vo.* 6*s.*

This book attempts to give to the visitor a descriptive history of the antiquities and natural features of this district. It is profusely illustrated from paintings and from photographs. Plans are also given of the chief antiquities. The book is uniform with the author's well-known *Book of the West.*

THE BRITISH GARDENER AND AMATEUR. By W. WILLIAMSON. Illustrated. *Demy 8vo.* 10*s.* 6*d.*

A complete handbook of horticulture by a well-known expert.

THE RUBAIYAT OF OMAR KHAYYAM. Translated by EDWARD FITZGERALD, with a Commentary by H. M. BATSON, and a Biography of Omar by E. D. ROSS, M.A. 6*s.*

This edition of the famous book, the text of which is printed by permission of Messrs. Macmillan, is the most complete in existence. It contains FitzGerald's last text, and a very full commentary on each stanza. Professor Ross, who is an admirable Persian scholar, contributes a biography, containing many new, valuable, and interesting facts.

Scientific and Educational

THE CAPTIVI OF PLAUTUS. Edited, with an Introduction, Textual Notes, and a Commentary, by W. M. LINDSAY, Fellow of Jesus College, Oxford. *Demy 8vo.* 10*s.* 6*d. net.*

For this edition all the important MSS. have been re-collated. An appendix deals with the accentual element in early Latin verse. The Commentary is very full.

THE CONSTRUCTION OF LARGE INDUCTION COILS. By A. T. HARE, M.A. With numerous Diagrams. *Demy 8vo.* 6*s.*

LACE-MAKING IN THE MIDLANDS, PAST AND PRESENT. By C. C. CHANNER and M. E. ROBERTS. With 16 full-page Illustrations. *Crown 8vo.* 2*s.* 6*d.*

AGRICULTURAL ZOOLOGY. By Dr. J. RITZEMA BOS. Translated by J. R. AINSWORTH DAVIS, M.A. With an Introduction by ELEANOR A. ORMEROD, F.E.S. With 155 Illustrations. *Crown 8vo.* 3*s.* 6*d.*

A SOUTH AFRICAN ARITHMETIC. By HENRY HILL, B.A., Assistant Master at Worcester School, Cape Colony. *Crown 8vo.* 3*s.* 6*d.*

This book has been specially written for use in South African schools.

A GERMAN COMMERCIAL READER. By S. BALLY, M.A. *Crown 8vo.* 2*s.* [*Methuen's Commercial Series.*

Fiction

THE MASTER CHRISTIAN. By MARIE CORELLI. *Crown 8vo.* 6*s.*

QUISANTE. By ANTHONY HOPE. *Crown 8vo.* 6*s.*

A MASTER OF CRAFT. By W. W. JACOBS, Author of 'Many Cargoes.' Illustrated. *Crown 8vo.* 6*s.*

THE GATELESS BARRIER. By LUCAS MALET, Author 'The Wages of Sin.' *Crown 8vo.* 6*s.*

CUNNING MURRELL. By ARTHUR MORRISON, Author of 'A Child of the Jago,' etc. *Crown 8vo.* 6*s.*

FOR BRITAIN'S SOLDIERS: Stories for the War Fund. By RUDYARD KIPLING and Others. Edited by C. J. CUTCLIFFE HYNE. *Crown 8vo.* 6*s.*

A volume of stories, the proceeds of which will be given to the War Fund. Among the contributors are:—Rudyard Kipling, Sir W. Besant, S. R. Crockett, A. E. W. Mason, Max Pemberton, H. G. Wells, C. J. C. Hyne, Mrs. Croker.

THE FOOTSTEPS OF A THRONE. By MAX PEMBERTON. Illustrated. *Crown 8vo.* 6*s.*

SONS OF THE MORNING. By EDEN PHILLPOTTS, Author of 'The Children of the Mist.' *Crown 8vo.* 6*s.*

THE SOFT SIDE. By HENRY JAMES, Author of 'What Maisie Knew.' *Crown 8vo.* 6*s.*

TONGUES OF CONSCIENCE. By R. S. HICHENS, Author of 'Flames.' *Crown 8vo.* 6*s.*

THE CONQUEST OF LONDON. By DOROTHEA GERARD, Author of 'Lady Baby.' *Crown 8vo.* 6*s.*

WOUNDS IN THE RAIN: War Stories. By STEPHEN CRANE, Author of 'The Red Badge of Courage.' *Crown 8vo.* 6*s.*

WINIFRED. By S. BARING GOULD, Author of 'Mehalah.' With 8 Illustrations. *Crown 8vo.* 6*s.*

THE STRONG ARM. By ROBERT BARR, Author of 'The Countess Tekla.' Illustrated. *Crown 8vo.* 6*s.*

THE SEEN AND THE UNSEEN. By RICHARD MARSH. Author of 'The Beetle.' *Crown 8vo.* 6*s.*

SERVANTS OF SIN. By J. BLOUNDELLE BURTON, Author 'The Clash of Arms.' *Crown 8vo.* 6*s.*

A NEW NOVEL. By STEPHEN CRANE, Author of 'The Red Badge of Courage.' *Crown 8vo.* 6*s.*

PATH AND GOAL. By ADA CAMBRIDGE. *Crown 8vo.* 6*s.*

ELMSLIE'S DRAG NET. By E. H. STRAIN. *Crown 8vo.* 6*s.*

A FOREST OFFICER. By Mrs. PENNY. *Crown 8vo.* 3*s.* 6*d.*
A story of jungle life in India.

FITZJAMES. By LILIAN STREET. *Crown 8vo.* 3*s.* 6*d.*

The Novelist

A monthly series of novels by popular authors at Sixpence. Each Number is as long as the average Six Shilling Novel. Numbers I. to XII. are now ready:—

XIII. THE POMP OF THE LAVILETTES. GILBERT PARKER. [*July*

XIV. A MAN OF MARK. ANTHONY HOPE. [*August.*

XV. THE CARISSIMA. LUCAS MALET. [*September.*

XVI. THE LADY'S WALK. MRS. OLIPHANT. [*October.*

XVII. DERRICK VAUGHAN. EDNA LYALL. [*November.*

Methuen's Sixpenny Library

A New Series of Copyright Books.

I. THE MATABELE CAMPAIGN. Maj.-General BADEN POWELL.

II. THE DOWNFALL OF PREMPEH. Do.

III. MY DANISH SWEETHEART. W. CLARK RUSSELL. [*July.*

IV. IN THE ROAR OF THE SEA. S. BARING GOULD. [*August.*

V. PEGGY OF THE BARTONS. B. M. CROKER. [*August.*

VI. IN THE MIDST OF ALARMS. ROBERT BARR. [*September.*

A CATALOGUE OF

MESSRS. METHUEN'S PUBLICATIONS

Poetry

Rudyard Kipling. BARRACK-ROOM BALLADS. By RUDYARD KIPLING. *68th Thousand. Crown 8vo.* 6*s.* *Leather*, 6*s. net.*

'Mr. Kipling's verse is strong, vivid, full of character. . . . Unmistakeable genius rings in every line.'—*Times.*

'The ballads teem with imagination, they palpitate with emotion. We read them with laughter and tears; the metres throb in our pulses, the cunningly ordered words tingle with life; and if this be not poetry, what is?'—*Pall Mall Gazette.*

Rudyard Kipling. THE SEVEN SEAS. By RUDYARD KIPLING. *57th Thousand. Cr. 8vo. Buckram, gilt top.* 6*s.* *Leather*, 6*s. net.*

'The Empire has found a singer; it is no depreciation of the songs to say that statesmen may have, one way or other, to take account of them.'—*Manchester Guardian.*

'Animated through and through with indubitable genius.'—*Daily Telegraph.*

"Q." POEMS AND BALLADS. By "Q." *Crown 8vo.* 3*s.* 6*d.*

"Q." GREEN BAYS: Verses and Parodies. By "Q." *Second Edition. Crown 8vo.* 3*s.* 6*d.*

E. Mackay. A SONG OF THE SEA. By ERIC MACKAY. *Second Edition. Fcap. 8vo.* 5*s.*

H. Ibsen. BRAND. A Drama by HENRIK IBSEN. Translated by WILLIAM WILSON. *Third Edition. Crown 8vo.* 3*s.* 6*d.*

A. D. Godley. LYRA FRIVOLA. By A. D. GODLEY, M.A., Fellow of Magdalen College, Oxford. *Third Edition. Pott 8vo.* 2*s.* 6*d.*

'Combines a pretty wit with remarkably neat versification. . . . Every one will wish there was more of it.'—*Times.*

A. D. Godley. VERSES TO ORDER. By A. D. GODLEY. *Crown 8vo.* 2*s.* 6*d. net.*

'A capital specimen of light academic poetry.'—*St. James's Gazette.*

J. G. Cordery. THE ODYSSEY OF HOMER. A Translation by J. G. CORDERY. *Crown 8vo.* 7*s.* 6*d.*

Belles Lettres, Anthologies, etc.

R. L. Stevenson. VAILIMA LETTERS. By ROBERT LOUIS STEVENSON. With an Etched Portrait by WILLIAM STRANG. *Second Edition. Crown 8vo. Buckram.* 6s.

'A fascinating book.'—*Standard.*
'Unique in Literature.'—*Daily Chronicle.*

G. Wyndham. THE POEMS OF WILLIAM SHAKESPEARE. Edited with an Introduction and Notes by GEORGE WYNDHAM, M.P. *Demy 8vo. Buckram, gilt top.* 10s. 6d.

This edition contains the 'Venus,' 'Lucrece,' and Sonnets, and is prefaced with an elaborate introduction of over 140 pp.
'We have no hesitation in describing Mr. George Wyndham's introduction as a masterly piece of criticism, and all who love our Elizabethan literature will find a very garden of delight in it.'—*Spectator.*

W. E. Henley. ENGLISH LYRICS. Selected and Edited by W. E. HENLEY. *Crown 8vo. Gilt top.* 3s. 6d.

'It is a body of choice and lovely poetry.'—*Birmingham Gazette.*

Henley and Whibley. A BOOK OF ENGLISH PROSE. Collected by W. E. HENLEY and CHARLES WHIBLEY. *Crown 8vo. Buckram, gilt top.* 6s.

H. C. Beeching. LYRA SACRA: An Anthology of Sacred Verse. Edited by H. C. BEECHING, M.A. *Crown 8vo. Buckram.* 6s.

'A charming selection, which maintains a lofty standard of excellence.'—*Times.*

"Q." THE GOLDEN POMP. A Procession of English Lyrics. Arranged by A. T. QUILLER COUCH. *Crown 8vo. Buckram.* 6s.

W. B. Yeats. AN ANTHOLOGY OF IRISH VERSE. Edited by W. B. YEATS. *Revised and Enlarged Edition. Crown 8vo.* 3s. 6d.

'An attractive and catholic selection.'—*Times.*

G. W. Steevens. MONOLOGUES OF THE DEAD. By G. W. STEEVENS. *Foolscap 8vo.* 3s. 6d.

W. M. Dixon. A PRIMER OF TENNYSON. By W. M. DIXON, M.A. *Cr. 8vo.* 2s. 6d.

'Much sound and well-expressed criticism. The bibliography is a boon.'—*Speaker.*

W. A. Craigie. A PRIMER OF BURNS. By W. A. CRAIGIE. *Crown 8vo.* 2s. 6d.

'A valuable addition to the literature of the poet.'—*Times.*

L. Magnus. A PRIMER OF WORDSWORTH. By LAURIE MAGNUS. *Crown 8vo.* 2s. 6d.

'A valuable contribution to Wordsworthian literature.'—*Literature.*

Sterne. THE LIFE AND OPINIONS OF TRISTRAM SHANDY. By LAWRENCE STERNE. With an Introduction by CHARLES WHIBLEY, and a Portrait. 2 *vols.* 7s.

Congreve. THE COMEDIES OF WILLIAM CONGREVE. With an Introduction by G. S. STREET, and a Portrait. 2 *vols.* 7s.

Morier. THE ADVENTURES OF HAJJI BABA OF ISPAHAN. By JAMES MORIER. With an Introduction by E. G. BROWNE, M.A. and a Portrait. 2 *vols.* 7s.

Walton. THE LIVES OF DONNE, WOTTON, HOOKER, HERBERT AND SANDERSON. By IZAAK WALTON. With an Introduction by VERNON BLACKBURN, and a Portrait. 3s. 6d.

Johnson. THE LIVES OF THE ENGLISH POETS. By SAMUEL JOHNSON, LL.D. With an Introduction by J. H. MILLAR, and a Portrait. 3 *vols.* 10s. 6d.

Burns. THE POEMS OF ROBERT BURNS. Edited by ANDREW LANG and W. A. CRAIGIE. With Portrait. *Second Edition. Demy 8vo, gilt top.* 6s.

'Among editions in one volume, this will take the place of authority.'—*Times.*

F. Langbridge. BALLADS OF THE BRAVE; Poems of Chivalry, Enterprise, Courage, and Constancy. Edited by Rev. F. LANGBRIDGE. *Second Edition. Cr. 8vo.* 3*s.* 6*d.* *School Edition.* 2*s.* 6*d.*

'The book is full of splendid things.'—*World.*

Methuen's Standard Library

Dante. LA COMMEDIA DI DANTE ALIGHIERI. The Italian Text edited by PAGET TOYNBEE, M.A. *Crown 8vo.* 6*s.*

'A carefully-revised text, printed with beautiful clearness.'—*Glasgow Herald.*

Gibbon. THE DECLINE AND FALL OF THE ROMAN EMPIRE. By EDWARD GIBBON. A New Edition, Edited with Notes, Appendices, and Maps, by J. B. BURY, LL.D., Fellow of Trinity College, Dublin. *In Seven Volumes. Demy 8vo. Gilt top.* 8*s.* 6*d. each. Also Cr. 8vo.* 6*s. each.*

'The time has certainly arrived for a new edition of Gibbon's great work. . . . Professor Bury is the right man to undertake this task. His learning is amazing, both in extent and accuracy. The book is issued in a handy form, and at a moderate price, and it is admirably printed.'—*Times.*

'At last there is an adequate modern edition of Gibbon. . . . The best edition the nineteenth century could produce.—*Manchester Guardian.*

'A great piece of editing.'—*Academy.*

'The greatest of English, perhaps of all, historians has never been presented to the public in a more convenient and attractive form. No higher praise can be bestowed upon Professor Bury than to say, as may be said with truth, that he is worthy of being ranked with Guizot and Milman.'—*Daily News.*

C. G. Crump. THE HISTORY OF THE LIFE OF THOMAS ELLWOOD. Edited by C. G. CRUMP, M.A. *Crown 8vo.* 6*s.*

This edition is the only one which contains the complete book as originally published. It contains a long Introduction and many Footnotes.

'"The History of Thomas Ellwood" holds a high place among the masterpieces of autobiography, and we know few books that better deserve reprinting. Moreover, Mr. C. G. Crump's new edition is accurate and convenient, and we commend it ungrudgingly to all those who love sound and vigorous English.' —*Daily Mail.*

Tennyson. THE EARLY POEMS OF ALFRED, LORD TENNYSON, Edited, with Notes and an Introduction by J. CHURTON COLLINS, M.A. *Crown 8vo.* 6*s.*

An elaborate edition of the celebrated volume which was published in its final and definitive form in 1853. This edition contains a long Introduction and copious Notes, textual and explanatory. It also contains in an Appendix all the Poems which Tennyson afterwards omitted.

'Mr. Collins is almost an ideal editor of Tennyson. His qualities as a critic are an exact and accurate scholarship, and a literary judgment, which has been trained and polished by the closest study of classics both ancient and modern. Mr. Collins' introduction is a thoroughly sound and sane appreciation of the merits and demerits of Tennyson.'—*Literature.*

The Works of Shakespeare

General Editor, EDWARD DOWDEN, Litt. D.

MESSRS. METHUEN have in preparation an Edition of Shakespeare in single Plays. Each play will be edited with a full Introduction, Textual Notes, and a Commentary at the foot of the page.

The first volume is:

HAMLET. Edited by EDWARD DOWDEN. *Demy 8vo.* 3*s.* 6*d.*

'An admirable edition. . . . A comely volume, admirably printed and produced, and containing all that a student of "Hamlet" need require.'—*Speaker.*

'Fully up to the level of recent scholarship, both English and German.—*Academy.*

The Novels of Charles Dickens

Crown 8vo. Each Volume, cloth 3s. net; leather 4s. 6d. net.

Messrs. METHUEN have in preparation an edition of those novels of Charles Dickens which have now passed out of copyright. Mr. George Gissing, whose critical study of Dickens is both sympathetic and acute, has written an Introduction to each of the books, and a very attractive feature of this edition will be the illustrations of the old houses, inns, and buildings, which Dickens described, and which have now in many instances disappeared under the touch of modern civilisation. Another valuable feature will be a series of topographical and general notes to each book by Mr. F. G. Kitton. The books will be produced with the greatest care as to printing, paper and binding.

The first volumes are:

THE PICKWICK PAPERS. With Illustrations by E. H. NEW. *Two Volumes.*

'As pleasant a copy as any one could desire. The notes add much to the value of the edition, and Mr. New's illustrations are also historical. The volumes promise well for the success of the edition.'—*Scotsman.*

The Little Library

'The volumes are compact in size, printed on thin but good paper in clear type, prettily and at the same time strongly bound, and altogether good to look upon and handle.'—*Outlook.*

Pott 8vo. Each Volume, cloth 1s. 6d. net, leather 2s. 6d. net.

Messrs. METHUEN intend to produce a series of small books under the above title, containing some of the famous books in English and other literatures, in the domains of fiction, poetry, and belles lettres. The series will also contain several volumes of selections in prose and verse.

The books will be edited with the most sympathetic and scholarly care. Each one will contain an Introduction which will give (1) a short biography of the author, (2) a critical estimate of the book. Where they are necessary, short notes will be added at the foot of the page.

Each book will have a portrait or frontispiece in photogravure, and the volumes will be produced with great care in a style uniform with that of 'The Library of Devotion.'

The first volumes are:

VANITY FAIR. By W. M. THACKERAY. With an Introduction by S. GWYNN. Illustrated by G. P. JACOMB HOOD. *Three Volumes.*

'Delightful little volumes.'—*Publishers' Circular.*

THE PRINCESS. By ALFRED, LORD TENNYSON. Edited by ELIZABETH WORDSWORTH. Illustrated by W. E. F. BRITTEN.

'Just what a pocket edition should be. Miss Wordsworth contributes an acceptable introduction, as well as notes which one is equally glad to get.'—*Guardian.*

IN MEMORIAM. By ALFRED, LORD TENNYSON. Edited, with an Introduction and Notes, by H. C. BEECHING, M.A.

'An exquisite little volume, which will be gladly welcomed.'—*Glasgow Herald.*

'The introduction, analysis, and notes by the Rev. H. C. Beeching are all of the sound literary quality that was to be expected.'—*Guardian.*

'The footnotes are scholarly, interesting, and not super-abundant.'—*Standard.*

'It is difficult to conceive a more attractive edition.'—*St. James's Gazette.*

The Little Guides

Pott 8vo, cloth 3s.; leather, 3s. 6d. net.

OXFORD AND ITS COLLEGES. By J. WELLS, M.A., Fellow and Tutor of Wadham College. Illustrated by E. H. NEW. *Third Edition.*

'An admirable and accurate little treatise, attractively illustrated.'—*World.*

'A luminous and tasteful little volume.'—*Daily Chronicle.*

CAMBRIDGE AND ITS COLLEGES. By A. HAMILTON THOMPSON. Illustrated by E. H. NEW.

'It is brightly written and learned, and is just such a book as a cultured visitor needs.'—*Scotsman.*

SHAKESPEARE'S COUNTRY. By B. C. WINDLE, F.R.S., M.A. Illustrated by E. H. NEW. *Second Edition.*

'Mr. Windle is thoroughly conversant with his subject, and the work is exceedingly well done. The drawings, by Mr. Edmund H. New, add much to the attractiveness of the volume.'—*Scotsman.*

'One of the most charming guide books. Both for the library and as a travelling companion the book is equally choice and serviceable.'—*Academy.*

'A guide book of the best kind, which takes rank as literature.'—*Guardian.*

Illustrated and Gift Books

Phil May. THE PHIL MAY ALBUM. *4to.* 6s.

'There is a laugh in each drawing.'—*Standard.*

A. H. Milne. ULYSSES; OR, DE ROUGEMONT OF TROY. Described and depicted by A. H. MILNE. *Small quarto.* 3s. 6d.

'Clever, droll, smart.'—*Guardian.*

Edmund Selous. TOMMY SMITH'S ANIMALS. By EDMUND SELOUS. Illustrated by G. W. ORD. *Fcap. 8vo.* 2s. 6d.

A little book designed to teach children respect and reverence for animals.

'A quaint, fascinating little book: a nursery classic.'—*Athenæum.*

S. Baring Gould. THE CROCK OF GOLD. Fairy Stories told by S. BARING GOULD. *Crown 8vo.* 6s.

'Twelve delightful fairy tales.'—*Punch.*

M. L. Gwynn. A BIRTHDAY BOOK. Arranged and Edited by M. L. GWYNN. *Demy 8vo.* 12s. 6d.

This is a birthday-book of exceptional dignity, and the extracts have been chosen with particular care.

John Bunyan. THE PILGRIM'S PROGRESS. By JOHN BUNYAN. Edited, with an Introduction, by C. H. FIRTH, M.A. With 39 Illustrations by R. ANNING BELL. *Crown 8vo.* 6s.

'The best "Pilgrim's Progress."'—*Educational Times.*

F. D. Bedford. NURSERY RHYMES. With many Coloured Pictures by F. D. BEDFORD. *Super Royal 8vo.* 5s.

S. Baring Gould. A BOOK OF FAIRY TALES retold by S. BARING GOULD. With numerous Illustrations and Initial Letters by ARTHUR J. GASKIN. *Second Edition. Cr. 8vo. Buckram.* 6s.

S. Baring Gould. OLD ENGLISH FAIRY TALES. Collected and edited by S. BARING GOULD. With Numerous Illustrations by F. D. BEDFORD. *Second Edition. Cr. 8vo. Buckram.* 6s.

'A charming volume.'—*Guardian.*

S. Baring Gould. A BOOK OF NURSERY SONGS AND RHYMES. Edited by S. BARING GOULD, and Illustrated by the Birmingham Art School. *Buckram, gilt top. Crown 8vo.* 6s.

H. C. Beeching. A BOOK OF CHRISTMAS VERSE. Edited by H. C. BEECHING, M.A., and Illustrated by WALTER CRANE. *Cr. 8vo, gilt top.* 3s. 6d.

History

Flinders Petrie. A HISTORY OF EGYPT, FROM THE EARLIEST TIMES TO THE PRESENT DAY. Edited by W. M. FLINDERS PETRIE, D.C.L., LL.D., Professor of Egyptology at University College. *Fully Illustrated. In Six Volumes. Cr.* 8*vo.* 6*s. each.*

VOL. I. PREHISTORIC TIMES TO XVITH DYNASTY. W. M. F. Petrie. *Fourth Edition.*

VOL. II. THE XVIITH AND XVIIITH DYNASTIES. W. M. F. Petrie. *Third Edition.*

VOL. IV. THE EGYPT OF THE PTOLEMIES. J. P. Mahaffy.

VOL. V. ROMAN EGYPT. J. G. Milne.

'A history written in the spirit of scientific precision so worthily represented by Dr. Petrie and his school cannot but promote sound and accurate study, and supply a vacant place in the English literature of Egyptology.'—*Times.*

Flinders Petrie. RELIGION AND CONSCIENCE IN ANCIENT EGYPT. By W. M. FLINDERS PETRIE, D.C.L., LL.D. Fully Illustrated. *Crown* 8*vo.* 2*s.* 6*d.*

'The lectures will afford a fund of valuable information for students of ancient ethics.'—*Manchester Guardian.*

Flinders Petrie. SYRIA AND EGYPT, FROM THE TELL EL AMARNA TABLETS. By W. M. FLINDERS PETRIE, D.C.L., LL.D. *Crown* 8*vo.* 2*s.* 6*d.*

'A marvellous record. The addition made to our knowledge is nothing short of amazing.'—*Times.*

Flinders Petrie. EGYPTIAN TALES. Edited by W. M. FLINDERS PETRIE. Illustrated by TRISTRAM ELLIS. *In Two Volumes. Cr.* 8*vo.* 3*s.* 6*d. each.*

'Invaluable as a picture of life in Palestine and Egypt.'—*Daily News.*

Flinders Petrie. EGYPTIAN DECORATIVE ART. By W. M. FLINDERS PETRIE. With 120 Illustrations. *Cr.* 8*vo.* 3*s.* 6*d.*

'In these lectures he displays rare skill in elucidating the development of decorative art in Egypt.'—*Times.*

C. W. Oman. A HISTORY OF THE ART OF WAR. Vol. II.: The Middle Ages, from the Fourth to the Fourteenth Century. By C. W. OMAN, M.A., Fellow of All Souls', Oxford. Illustrated. *Demy* 8*vo.* 21*s.*

'The whole art of war in its historic evolution has never been treated on such an ample and comprehensive scale, and we question if any recent contribution to the exact history of the world has possessed more enduring value.'—*Daily Chronicle.*

S. Baring Gould. THE TRAGEDY OF THE CÆSARS. With numerous Illustrations from Busts, Gems, Cameos, etc. By S. BARING GOULD. *Fourth Edition. Royal* 8*vo.* 15*s.*

'A most splendid and fascinating book on a subject of undying interest. The great feature of the book is the use the author has made of the existing portraits of the Caesars and the admirable critical subtlety he has exhibited in dealing with this line of research. It is brilliantly written, and the illustrations are supplied on a scale of profuse magnificence.'—*Daily Chronicle.*

F. W. Maitland. CANON LAW IN ENGLAND. By F. W. MAITLAND, LL.D., Downing Professor of the Laws of England in the University of Cambridge. *Royal* 8*vo.* 7*s.* 6*d.*

'Professor Maitland has put students of English law under a fresh debt. These essays are landmarks in the study of the history of Canon Law.'—*Times.*

H. de B. Gibbins. INDUSTRY IN ENGLAND: HISTORICAL OUTLINES. By H. DE B. GIBBINS, Litt.D., M.A. With 5 Maps. *Second Edition. Demy* 8*vo.* 10*s.* 6*d.*

H. E. Egerton. A HISTORY OF BRITISH COLONIAL POLICY. By H. E. EGERTON, M.A. *Demy* 8*vo.* 12*s.* 6*d.*

'It is a good book, distinguished by accuracy in detail, clear arrangement of facts, and a broad grasp of principles.'—*Manchester Guardian.*

Albert Sorel. THE EASTERN QUESTION IN THE EIGHTEENTH CENTURY. By ALBERT SOREL. Translated by F. C. BRAMWELL, M.A. *Cr.* 8*vo.* 3*s.* 6*d.*

C. H. Grinling. A HISTORY OF THE GREAT NORTHERN RAILWAY, 1845-95. By C. H. GRINLING. With Illustrations. *Demy* 8*vo.* 10*s.* 6*d.*

'Mr. Grinling has done for a Railway what Macaulay did for English History.'—*The Engineer.*

W. Sterry. ANNALS OF ETON COLLEGE. By W. STERRY, M.A. With numerous Illustrations. *Demy* 8*vo.* 7*s.* 6*d.*

'A treasury of quaint and interesting reading. Mr. Sterry has by his skill and vivacity given these records new life.'—*Academy.*

G. W. Fisher. ANNALS OF SHREWSBURY SCHOOL. By G. W. FISHER, M.A. With numerous Illustrations. *Demy* 8*vo.* 10*s.* 6*d.*

'This careful, erudite book.'—*Daily Chronicle.*

'A book of which Old Salopians are sure to be proud.'—*Globe.*

J. Sargeaunt. ANNALS OF WESTMINSTER SCHOOL. By J. SARGEAUNT, M.A. With numerous Illustrations. *Demy* 8*vo.* 7*s.* 6*d.*

A. Clark. THE COLLEGES OF OXFORD: Their History and their Traditions. Edited by A. CLARK, M.A., Fellow of Lincoln College. 8*vo.* 12*s.* 6*d.*

'A work which will be appealed to for many years as the standard book.'—*Athenæum.*

T. M. Taylor. A CONSTITUTIONAL AND POLITICAL HISTORY OF ROME. By T. M. TAYLOR, M.A., Fellow of Gonville and Caius College, Cambridge. *Crown* 8*vo.* 7*s.* 6*d.*

'We fully recognise the value of this carefully written work, and admire especially the fairness and sobriety of his judgment and the human interest with which he has inspired a subject which in some hands becomes a mere series of cold abstractions. It is a work that will be stimulating to the student of Roman history.'—*Athenæum.*

J. Wells. A SHORT HISTORY OF ROME. By J. WELLS, M.A., Fellow and Tutor of Wadham Coll., Oxford. *Third Edition.* With 3 Maps. *Crown* 8*vo.* 3*s.* 6*d.*

This book is intended for the Middle and Upper Forms of Public Schools and for Pass Students at the Universities. It contains copious Tables, etc.

'An original work written on an original plan, and with uncommon freshness and vigour.'—*Speaker.*

O. Browning. A SHORT HISTORY OF MEDIÆVAL ITALY, A.D. 1250-1530. By OSCAR BROWNING, Fellow and Tutor of King's College, Cambridge. *In Two Volumes. Cr.* 8*vo.* 5*s. each.*

VOL. I. 1250-1409.—Guelphs and Ghibellines.

VOL. II. 1409-1530.—The Age of the Condottieri.

O'Grady. THE STORY OF IRELAND. By STANDISH O'GRADY, Author of 'Finn and his Companions. *Crown* 8*vo.* 2*s.* 6*d.*

Byzantine Texts

Edited by J. B. BURY, M.A.

ZACHARIAH OF MITYLENE. Translated into English by F. J. HAMILTON, D.D., and E. W. BROOKS. *Demy 8vo.* 12s. 6d. net.

EVAGRIUS. Edited by Professor LÉON PARMENTIER and M. BIDEZ. *Demy 8vo.* 10s. 6d. net.

THE HISTORY OF PSELLUS. By C. SATHAS. *Demy 8vo.* 15s. net.

Biography

R. L. Stevenson. THE LETTERS OF ROBERT LOUIS STEVENSON TO HIS FAMILY AND FRIENDS. Selected and Edited, with Notes and Introductions, by SIDNEY COLVIN. *Third Edition. Demy 8vo, 2 vols.*, 25s. net.

'Irresistible in their raciness, their variety, their animation . . . of extraordinary fascination. A delightful inheritance, the truest record of a "richly compounded spirit" that the literature of our time has preserved.'—*Times.*

'There are few books so interesting, so moving, and so valuable as this collection of letters. One can only commend people to read and re-read the book. The volumes are beautiful, and Mr. Colvin's part of the work could not have been better done, his introduction is a masterpiece.'—*Spectator.*

J. G. Millais. THE LIFE AND LETTERS OF SIR JOHN EVERETT MILLAIS, President of the Royal Academy. By his Son, J. G. MILLAIS. With 319 Illustrations, of which 9 are in Photogravure. *Second Edition.* 2 vols, *Royal 8vo*, 32s. net.

'The illustrations make the book delightful to handle or to read. The eye lingers lovingly upon the beautiful pictures.'—*Standard.*

'This charming book is a gold mine of good things.'—*Daily News.*

'This splendid work.'—*World.*

'Of such absorbing interest is it, of such completeness in scope and beauty. Special tribute must be paid to the extraordinary completeness of the illustrations.'—*Graphic.*

S. Baring Gould. THE LIFE OF NAPOLEON BONAPARTE. By S. BARING GOULD. With over 450 Illustrations in the Text and 12 Photogravure Plates. *Large quarto. Gilt top.* 36s.

'The main feature of this gorgeous volume is its great wealth of beautiful photogravures and finely-executed wood engravings, constituting a complete pictorial chronicle of Napoleon I.'s personal history from the days of his early childhood at Ajaccio to the date of his second interment.'—*Daily Telegraph.*

P. H. Colomb. MEMOIRS OF ADMIRAL SIR A. COOPER KEY. By Admiral P. H. COLOMB. With a Portrait. *Demy 8vo.* 16s.

Morris Fuller. THE LIFE AND WRITINGS OF JOHN DAVENANT, D.D. (1571-1641), Bishop of Salisbury. By MORRIS FULLER, B.D. *Demy 8vo.* 10s. 6d.

J. M. Rigg. ST. ANSELM OF CANTERBURY: A CHAPTER IN THE HISTORY OF RELIGION. By J. M. RIGG. *Demy 8vo.* 7s. 6d.

F. W. Joyce. THE LIFE OF SIR FREDERICK GORE OUSELEY. By F. W. JOYCE, M.A. *7s. 6d.*

W. G. Collingwood. THE LIFE OF JOHN RUSKIN. By W. G. COLLINGWOOD, M.A. With Portraits, and 13 Drawings by Mr. Ruskin. *Second Edition. 2 vols. 8vo.* 32*s.* *Cheap Edition. Crown 8vo.* 6*s.*

C. Waldstein. JOHN RUSKIN, By CHARLES WALDSTEIN, M.A. With a Photogravure Portrait, *Post 8vo.* 5*s.*

A. M. F. Darmesteter, THE LIFE OF ERNEST RENAN. By MADAME DARMESTETER. With Portrait. *Second Edition. Cr. 8vo.* 6*s.*

W. H. Hutton. THE LIFE OF SIR THOMAS MORE. By W. H. HUTTON, M.A. With Portraits. *Second Edition. Cr. 8vo.* 5*s.*

'The book lays good claim to high rank among our biographies. It is excellently, even lovingly, written.'—*Scotsman.*

S. Baring Gould. THE VICAR OF MORWENSTOW: A Biography. By S. BARING GOULD, M.A. A new and Revised Edition. With Portrait. *Crown 8vo.* 3*s.* 6*d.*

A completely new edition of the well known biography of R. S. Hawker.

Travel, Adventure and Topography

Sven Hedin. THROUGH ASIA. By SVEN HEDIN, Gold Medallist of the Royal Geographical Society. With 300 Illustrations from Sketches and Photographs by the Author, and Maps. *2 vols. Royal 8vo.* 20*s. net.*

'One of the greatest books of the kind issued during the century. It is impossible to give an adequate idea of the richness of the contents of this book, nor of its abounding attractions as a story of travel unsurpassed in geographical and human interest. Much of it is a revelation. Altogether the work is one which in solidity, novelty, and interest must take a first rank among publications of its class.'—*Times.*

F. H. Skrine and E. D. Ross. THE HEART OF ASIA. By F. H. SKRINE and E. D. ROSS. With Maps and many Illustrations by VERESTCHAGIN. *Large Crown 8vo.* 10*s.* 6*d. net.*

'This volume will form a landmark in our knowledge of Central Asia. . . . Illuminating and convincing.'—*Times.*

R. E. Peary. NORTHWARD OVER THE GREAT ICE. By R. E. PEARY, Gold Medallist of the Royal Geographical Society. With over 800 Illustrations. *2 vols. Royal 8vo.* 32*s. net.*

'His book will take its place among the permanent literature of Arctic exploration.'—*Times.*

E. A. FitzGerald. THE HIGHEST ANDES. By E. A. FITZGERALD. With 2 Maps, 51 Illustrations, 13 of which are in Photogravure, and a Panorama. *Royal 8vo,* 30*s. net.* Also a Small Edition on Hand-made Paper, limited to 50 Copies, *4to,* £5, 5*s.*

'The record of the first ascent of the highest mountain yet conquered by mortal man. A volume which will continue to be the classic book of travel on this region of the Andes.'—*Daily Chronicle.*

W. Christian. THE CAROLINE ISLANDS. By F. W. CHRISTIAN. With many Illustrations and Maps. *Demy 8vo.* 12*s.* 6*d. net.*

A real contribution to our knowledge of the peoples and islands of Micronesia, as well as fascinating as a narrative of travels and adventure.'—*Scotsman.*

H. Johnston. BRITISH CENTRAL AFRICA. By Sir H. H. JOHNSTON, K.C.B. With nearly Two Hundred Illustrations, and Six Maps. *Second Edition. Crown 4to.* 18*s. net.*

A fascinating book, written with equal skill and charm—the work at once of a literary artist and of a man of action who is singularly wise, brave, and experienced. It abounds in admirable sketches.'—*Westminster Gazette.*

Decle. THREE YEARS IN SAVAGE AFRICA. By LIONEL DECLE. With 100 Illustrations and Maps. *Second Edition. Demy 8vo.* 10*s.* 6*d. net.*

ts bright pages give a better general survey of Africa from the Cape to the Equator than any single volume that has yet been published.'—*Times.*

Hulme Beaman. TWENTY YEARS IN THE NEAR EAST. By A. HULME BEAMAN. *Demy 8vo.* With Portrait. 10*s.* 6*d.*

nri of Orleans. FROM TONKIN TO INDIA. By PRINCE HENRI OF ORLEANS. Translated by HAMLEY BENT, M.A. With 100 Illustrations and a Map. *Cr. 4to, gilt top.* 25s.

L. Hinde. THE FALL OF THE CONGO ARABS. By S. L. HINDE. With Plans, etc. *Demy 8vo.* 12*s.* 6*d.*

St. H. Gibbons. EXPLORATION AND HUNTING IN CENTRAL AFRICA. By Major A. ST. H. GIBBONS. With full-page Illustrations by C. WHYMPER, and Maps. *Demy 8vo.* 15*s.*

Fraser. ROUND THE WORLD ON A WHEEL. By JOHN FOSTER FRASER. With 100 Illustrations. *Crown 8vo.* 6*s.*

'A classic of cycling, graphic and witty.'—*Yorkshire Post.*

R. L. Jefferson. A NEW RIDE TO KHIVA. By R. L. JEFFERSON. Illustrated. *Crown 8vo,* 6*s.*

The account of an adventurous ride on a bicycle through Russia and the deserts of Asia to Khiva.

'An exceptionally fascinating book of travel.'—*Pall Mall Gazette.*

J. K. Trotter. THE NIGER SOURCES. By Colonel J. K. TROTTER, R.A. With a Map and Illustrations. *Crown 8vo.* 5*s.*

Michael Davitt. LIFE AND PROGRESS IN AUSTRALASIA. By MICHAEL DAVITT, M.P. 500 pp. With 2 Maps. *Crown 8vo.* 6*s.*

W. J. Galloway. ADVANCED AUSTRALIA. By WILLIAM J. GALLOWAY, M.P. *Crown 8vo.* 3*s.* 6*d.*

'This is an unusally thorough and informative little work.'—*Morning Post.*

W. Crooke. THE NORTH-WESTERN PROVINCES OF INDIA: THEIR ETHNOLOGY AND ADMINISTRATION. By W. CROOKE. With Maps and Illustrations. *Demy 8vo.* 10*s.* 6*d.*

A. Boisragon. THE BENIN MASSACRE. By CAPTAIN BOISRAGON. *Second Edition. Cr. 8vo.* 3*s.* 6*d.*

'If the story had been written four hundred years ago it would be read to-day as an English classic.'—*Scotsman.*

H. S. Cowper. THE HILL OF THE GRACES: OR, THE GREAT STONE TEMPLES OF TRIPOLI. By H. S. COWPER, F.S.A. With Maps, Plans, and 75 Illustrations. *Demy 8vo.* 10*s.* 6*d.*

W. B. Worsfold. SOUTH AFRICA. By W. B. WORSFOLD, M.A. *With a Map. Second Edition. Cr. 8vo.* 6*s*.

'A monumental work compressed into a very moderate compass.'—*World.*

Katherine and Gilbert Macquoid. IN PARIS. By KATHERINE and GILBERT MACQUOID. Illustrated by THOMAS R. MACQUOID, R.I. With 2 maps. *Crown 8vo.* 1*s*.

'A useful little guide, judiciously supplied with information.'—*Athenæum.*

A. H. Keane. THE BOER STATES: A History and Description of the Transvaal and the Orange Free State. By A. H. KEANE, M.A. With Map. *Crown 8vo.* 6*s*.

'A work of clear aims and thorough execution.'—*Academy.*

'A compact and very trustworthy account of the Boers and their surroundings.' —*Morning Post.*

Naval and Military

G. S. Robertson. CHITRAL: The Story of a Minor Siege. By Sir G. S. ROBERTSON, K.C.S.I. With numerous Illustrations, Map and Plans. *Second Edition. Demy 8vo.* 10*s*. 6*d*.

'It is difficult to imagine the kind of person who could read this brilliant book without emotion. The story remains immortal—a testimony imperishable. We are face to face with a great book.'—*Illustrated London News.*

'A book which the Elizabethans would have thought wonderful. More thrilling, more piquant, and more human than any novel.'—*Newcastle Chronicle.*

'As fascinating as Sir Walter Scott's best fiction.'—*Daily Telegraph.*

R. S. S. Baden-Powell. THE DOWNFALL OF PREMPEH. A Diary of Life in Ashanti, 1895. By Maj.-Gen. BADEN-POWELL. With 21 Illustrations and a Map. *Cheaper Edition. Large Crown 8vo.* 6*s*.

R. S. S. Baden-Powell. THE MATABELE CAMPAIGN, 1896. By Maj.-Gen. BADEN-POWELL. With nearly 100 Illustrations. *Cheaper Edition. Large Crown 8vo.* 6*s*.

J. B. Atkins. THE RELIEF OF LADYSMITH. By JOHN BLACK ATKINS. With 16 Plans and Illustrations. *Second Edition. Crown 8vo.* 6*s*.

This book contains a full narrative by an eye-witness of General Buller's attempts, and of his final success. The story is of absorbing interest, and is the only complete account which has appeared.

'The mantle of Archibald Forbes and G. W. Steevens has assuredly fallen upon Mr. Atkins, who unites a singularly graphic style to an equa ly rare faculty of vision. In his pages we realise the meaning of a modern campaign with the greatest sense of actuality. His pages are written with a sustained charm of diction and ease of manner that are no less remarkable than the sincerity and vigour of the matter which they set before us.'—*World.*

'Mr. Atkins has a genius for the painting of war which entitles him already to be ranked with Forbes and Steevens, and encourages us to hope that he may one day rise to the level of Napier and Kinglake.'—*Pall Mall Gazette.*

'It is the record told with insight and sympathy of a great conflict. It is as readable as a novel, and it bears the imprint of truth.'—*Morning Leader.*

H. W. Nevinson. LADYSMITH: The Diary of a Siege. By H. W. NEVINSON. With 16 Illustrations and a Plan. *Crown 8vo.* 6*s*.

This book contains a complete diary of the Siege of Ladysmith, and is a most vivid and picturesque narrative.

'There is no exaggeration here, no straining after effect. But there is the truest realism, the impression of things as they are seen, set forth in well-chosen words and well-balanced phrases, with a mea sured self-restraint that marks the true artist. Mr. Nevinson is to be congratulated on the excellent work that he has done.'—*Daily Chronicle.*

'Of the many able and fascinating chroniclers of the sad and splendid story, Mr. Nevinson is among the ablest and most fascinating.'—*Pall Mall Gazette.*

E. H. Alderson. WITH THE MOUNTED INFANTRY AND THE MASHONALAND FIELD FORCE, 1896. By Lieut.-Colonel ALDERSON. With numerous Illustrations and Plans. *Demy 8vo.* 10*s.* 6*d.*

Seymour Vandeleur. CAMPAIGNING ON THE UPPER NILE AND NIGER. By Lieut. SEYMOUR VANDELEUR. With an Introduction by Sir G. GOLDIE, K.C.M.G. With 4 Maps, Illustrations, and Plans. *Large Crown 8vo.* 10*s.* 6*d.*

Lord Fincastle. A FRONTIER CAMPAIGN. By Viscount FINCASTLE, V.C., and Lieut. P. C. ELLIOTT-LOCKHART. With a Map and 16 Illustrations. *Second Edition. Crown 8vo.* 6*s.*

E. N. Bennett. THE DOWNFALL OF THE DERVISHES: A Sketch of the Sudan Campaign of 1898. By E. N. BENNETT, Fellow of Hertford College. With a Photogravure Portrait of Lord Kitchener. *Third Edition. Crown 8vo.* 3*s.* 6*d.*

W. Kinnaird Rose. WITH THE GREEKS IN THESSALY. By W. KINNAIRD ROSE. With Illustrations. *Crown 8vo.* 6*s.*

. W. Steevens. NAVAL POLICY: By G. W. STEEVENS. *Demy 8vo.* 6*s.*

This book is a description of the British and other more important navies of the world, with a sketch of the lines on which our naval policy might possibly be developed.

). Hannay. A SHORT HISTORY OF THE ROYAL NAVY, FROM EARLY TIMES TO THE PRESENT DAY. By DAVID HANNAY. Illustrated. 2 *Vols. Demy 8vo.* 7*s.* 6*d. each.* Vol. I., 1200-1688.

'We read it from cover to cover at a sitting, and those who go to it for a lively and brisk picture of the past, with all its faults and its grandeur, will not be disappointed. The historian is endowed with literary skill and style.'—*Standard.*

C. Cooper King. THE STORY OF THE BRITISH ARMY. By Colonel COOPER KING. Illustrated. *Demy 8vo.* 7*s.* 6*d.*

'An authoritative and accurate story of England's military progress.'—*Daily Mail.*

R. Southey. ENGLISH SEAMEN (Howard, Clifford, Hawkins, Drake, Cavendish). By ROBERT SOUTHEY. Edited, with an Introduction, by DAVID HANNAY. *Second Edition. Crown 8vo.* 6*s.*

'A brave, inspiriting book.'—*Black and White.*

W. Clark Russell. THE LIFE OF ADMIRAL LORD COLLINGWOOD. By W. CLARK RUSSELL. With Illustrations by F. BRANGWYN. *Third Edition. Crown 8vo.* 6*s.*

'A book which we should like to see in the hands of every boy in the country.'—*St. James's Gazette.*

E. L. S. Horsburgh. WATERLOO: A Narrative and Criticism. By E. L. S. HORSBURGH, B.A. With Plans. *Second Edition. Crown 8vo.* 5*s.*

'A brilliant essay—simple, sound, and thorough.'—*Daily Chronicle.*

H. B. George. BATTLES OF ENGLISH HISTORY. By H. B. GEORGE, M.A., Fellow of New College, Oxford. With numerous Plans. *Third Edition. Cr. 8vo.* 6*s.*

'Mr. George has undertaken a very useful task—that of making military affairs intelligible and instructive to non-military readers—and has executed it with a large measure of success.'—*Times.*

General Literature

S. Baring Gould. THE BOOK OF THE WEST. By S. BARING GOULD. With numerous Illustrations. *Two volumes.* Vol. I. Devon. Vol. II. Cornwall. *Crown* 8*vo.* 6*s. each.*

'They are very attractive little volumes, they have numerous very pretty and interesting pictures, the story is fresh and bracing as the air of Dartmoor, and the legend weird as twilight over Dozmare Pool, and they give us a very good idea of this enchanting and beautiful district.'—*Guardian.*

'A narrative full of picturesque incident, personal interest, and literary charm.'—*Leeds Mercury.*

S. Baring Gould. OLD COUNTRY LIFE. By S. BARING GOULD. With Sixty-seven Illustrations. *Large Cr.* 8*vo. Fifth Edition.* 6*s.*

'"Old Country Life," as healthy wholesome reading, full of breezy life and movement, full of quaint stories vigorously told, will not be excelled by any book to be published throughout the year. Sound, hearty, and English to the core.' —*World.*

S. Baring Gould. AN OLD ENGLISH HOME. By S. BARING GOULD. With numerous Plans and Illustrations. *Crown* 8*vo.* 6*s.*

'The chapters are delightfully fresh, very informing, and lightened by many a good story. A delightful fireside companion.' —*St. James's Gazette.*

S. Baring Gould. HISTORIC ODDITIES AND STRANGE EVENTS. By S. BARING GOULD. *Fourth Edition. Crown* 8*vo.* 6*s.*

S. Baring Gould. FREAKS OF FANATICISM. By S. BARING GOULD. *Third Edition. Cr.* 8*vo.* 6*s.*

S. Baring Gould. A GARLAND OF COUNTRY SONG: English Folk Songs with their Traditional Melodies. Collected and arranged by S. BARING GOULD and H. F. SHEPPARD. *Demy* 4*to.* 6*s.*

S. Baring Gould. SONGS OF THE WEST: Traditional Ballads and Songs of the West of England, with their Melodies. Collected by S. BARING GOULD, M.A., and H. F. SHEPPARD, M.A. In 4 Parts. *Parts I., II., III.,* 3*s. each. Part IV.,* 5*s. In one Vol., French morocco,* 15*s.*

'A rich collection of humour, pathos, grace, and poetic fancy.'—*Saturday Review.*

S. Baring Gould. YORKSHIRE ODDITIES AND STRANGE EVENTS. By S. BARING GOULD. *Fourth Edition. Crown* 8*vo.* 6*s.*

S. Baring Gould. STRANGE SURVIVALS AND SUPERSTITIONS. By S. BARING GOULD. *Cr.* 8*vo. Second Edition.* 6*s.*

S. Baring Gould. THE DESERTS OF SOUTHERN FRANCE. By S. BARING GOULD. 2 *vols. Demy* 8*vo.* 32*s.*

Cotton Minchin. OLD HARROW DAYS. By J. G. COTTON MINCHIN. *Cr.* 8*vo. Second Edition.* 5*s.*

W. E. Gladstone. THE SPEECHES OF THE RT. HON. W. E. GLADSTONE, M.P. Edited by A. W. HUTTON, M.A., and H. J. COHEN, M.A. With Portraits. *Demy* 8*vo. Vols. IX. and X.,* 12*s.* 6*d. each.*

J. E. Marr. THE SCIENTIFIC STUDY OF SCENERY. By J. E. MARR, F.R.S., Fellow of St. John's College, Cambridge. Illustrated. *Crown* 8*vo.* 6*s.*

An elementary treatise on geomorphology—the study of the earth's outward forms. It is for the use of students of physical geography and geology, and will also be highly interesting to the general reader.

'A fascinating book, a real fairy tale.'—*Pall Mall Gazette.*

'Mr. Marr is distinctly to be congratulated on the general result of his work. He has produced a volume, moderate in size and readable in style, which will be acceptable alike to the student of geology and geography, and to the tourist.'—*Athenæum.*

'Can be read with pleasure alike by the expert and the general reader.' —*Manchester Guardian.*

M. N. Oxford. A HANDBOOK OF NURSING. By M. N. OXFORD, of Guy's Hospital. *Crown 8vo.* 3*s.* 6*d.*

This is a complete guide to the science and art of nursing, containing copious instruction both general and particular.

'The most useful work of the kind that we have seen. A most valuable and practical manual.'—*Manchester Guardian.*

E. V. Zenker. ANARCHISM. By E. V. ZENKER. *Demy 8vo.* 7*s.* 6*d.*

'Herr Zenker has succeeded in producing a careful and critical history of the growth of Anarchist theory.

A. Silva White. THE EXPANSION OF EGYPT: A Political and Historical Survey. By A. SILVA WHITE. With four Special Maps. *Demy 8vo.* 15*s. net.*

'This is emphatically the best account of Egypt as it is under English control that has been published for many years.'—*Spectator.*

Peter Beckford. THOUGHTS ON HUNTING. By PETER BECKFORD. Edited by J. OTHO PAGET, and Illustrated by G. H. JALLAND. *Demy 8vo.* 10*s.* 6*d.*

'Beckford's "Thoughts on Hunting" has long been a classic with sportsmen, and the present edition will go far to make it a favourite with lovers of literature.'—*Speaker.*

E. B. Michell. THE ART AND PRACTICE OF HAWKING. By E. B. MICHELL. With 3 Photogravures by G. E. LODGE, and other Illustrations. *Demy 8vo.* 10*s.* 6*d.*

A complete description of the Hawks, Falcons, and Eagles used in ancient and modern times, with directions for their training and treatment. It is not only a historical account, but a complete practical guide.

'A book that will help and delight the expert.'—*Scotsman.*

'Just after the hearts of all enthusiasts.'—*Daily Telegraph.*

'No book is more full and authorative than this handsome treatise.' —*Morning Leader.*

H. G. Hutchinson. THE GOLFING PILGRIM. By HORACE G. HUTCHINSON. *Crown 8vo.* 6*s.*

'Without this book the golfer's library will be incomplete.'—*Pall Mall Gazette.*

J. Wells. OXFORD AND OXFORD LIFE. By Members of the University. Edited by J. WELLS, M.A., Fellow and Tutor of Wadham College. *Third Edition. Cr. 8vo.* 3*s.* 6*d.*

'We congratulate Mr. Wells on the production of a readable and intelligent account of Oxford as it is at the present time, written by persons who are possessed of a close acquaintance with the system and life of the University.'—*Athenæum.*

C. G. Robertson. VOCES ACADEMICÆ. By C. GRANT ROBERTSON, M.A., Fellow of All Souls', Oxford. *With a Frontispiece. Pott 8vo.* 3*s.* 6*d.*

'Decidedly clever and amusing.'—*Athenæum.*

Rosemary Cotes. DANTE'S GARDEN. By ROSEMARY COTES. With a Frontispiece. *Second Edition. Fcp. 8vo.* 2*s.* 6*d.* *Leather,* 3*s.* 6*d. net.*

'A charming collection of legends of the flowers mentioned by Dante.'—*Academy.*

Clifford Harrison. READING AND READERS. By CLIFFORD HARRISON. *Fcp. 8vo.* 2*s.* 6*d.*

'An extremely sensible little book.'—*Manchester Guardian.*

L. Whibley. GREEK OLIGARCHIES: THEIR ORGANISATION AND CHARACTER. By L. WHIBLEY, M.A., Fellow of Pembroke College, Cambridge. *Crown 8vo.* 6*s.*

L. L. Price. ECONOMIC SCIENCE AND PRACTICE. By L. L. PRICE, M.A., Fellow of Oriel College, Oxford. *Crown 8vo.* 6*s.*

J. S. Shedlock. THE PIANOFORTE SONATA: Its Origin and Development. By J. S. SHEDLOCK. *Crown 8vo.* 5*s.*

'This work should be in the possession of every musician and amateur. A concise and lucid history and a very valuable work for reference.'—*Athenæum.*

A. Hulme Beaman. PONS ASINORUM; OR, A GUIDE TO BRIDGE. By A. HULME BEAMAN. *Fcap 8vo.* 2*s.*

A practical guide, with many specimen games, to the new game of Bridge.

E. M. Bowden. THE EXAMPLE OF BUDDHA: Being Quotations from Buddhist Literature for each Day in the Year. Compiled by E. M. BOWDEN. *Third Edition.* 16*mo.* 2*s.* 6*d.*

F. Ware. EDUCATIONAL REFORM. By FABIAN WARE, M.A. *Crown 8vo.* 2*s.* 6*d.*

An attempt by an expert to forecast the action and influence of the New Secondary Education Act, with suggestions for useful developments.

'Mr. Ware's book may be warmly commended to all who have at heart the desire for the intellectual prosperity of the British race.'—*Morning Post.*

'Any one who really wants to know how education stands to-day should read it.' —*Literature.*

Philosophy

L. T. Hobhouse. THE THEORY OF KNOWLEDGE. By L. T. HOBHOUSE, Fellow of C.C.C., Oxford. *Demy 8vo.* 21*s.*

'The most important contribution to English philosophy since the publication of Mr. Bradley's "Appearance and Reality."'—*Glasgow Herald.*

W. H. Fairbrother. THE PHILOSOPHY OF T. H. GREEN. By W. H. FAIRBROTHER, M.A. *Cr. 8vo.* 3*s.* 6*d.*

'In every way an admirable book.'—*Glasgow Herald.*

F. W. Bussell. THE SCHOOL OF PLATO. By F. W. BUSSELL, D.D., Fellow of Brasenose College, Oxford. *Demy 8vo.* 10*s.* 6*d.*

F. S. Granger. THE WORSHIP OF THE ROMANS. By F. S. GRANGER, M.A., Litt.D. *Crown 8vo.* 6*s.*

Theology

W. R. Inge. CHRISTIAN MYSTICISM. The Bampton Lectures for 1899. By W. R. INGE, M.A., Fellow and Tutor of Hertford College, Oxford. *Demy 8vo.* 12*s.* 6*d.* *net.*

A complete survey of the subject from St. John and St. Paul to modern times, covering the Christian Platonists, Augustine, the Devotional Mystics, the Mediæval Mystics, and the Nature Mystics and Symbolists, including Böhme and Wordsworth.

'It is fully worthy of the best traditions connected with the Bampton Lectureship.'—*Record.*

S. R. Driver. SERMONS ON SUBJECTS CONNECTED WITH THE OLD TESTAMENT. By S. R. DRIVER, D.D., Canon of Christ Church, Regius Professor of Hebrew in the University of Oxford. *Cr. 8vo.* 6*s.*

'A welcome companion to the author's famous "Introduction."'—*Guardian.*

T. K. Cheyne. FOUNDERS OF OLD TESTAMENT CRITICISM. By T. K. CHEYNE, D.D., Oriel Professor at Oxford. *Large Crown 8vo.* 7*s.* 6*d.*

A historical sketch of O. T. Criticism.

Walter Lock. ST. PAUL, THE MASTER-BUILDER. By WALTER LOCK, D.D., Warden of Keble College. *Crown 8vo.* 3*s.* 6*d.*

'The essence of the Pauline teaching is condensed into little more than a hundred pages, yet no point of importance is overlooked. We gladly recommend the lectures to all who wish to read with understanding.'—*Guardian.*

H. Rashdall. DOCTRINE AND DEVELOPMENT. By HASTINGS RASHDALL, M.A., Fellow and Tutor of New College, Oxford. *Cr. 8vo.* 6*s.*

'A very interesting attempt to restate some of the principal doctrines of Christianity, in which Mr. Rashdall appears to us to have achieved a high measure of success. He is often learned, almost always sympathetic, and always singularly lucid.'—*Manchester Guardian.*

H. H. Henson. APOSTOLIC CHRISTIANITY: As Illustrated by the Epistles of St. Paul to the Corinthians. By H. H. HENSON, M.A., Fellow of All Souls', Oxford. *Cr. 8vo.* 6*s.*

H. H. Henson. DISCIPLINE AND LAW. By H. HENSLEY HENSON, B.D., Fellow of All Souls', Oxford. *Fcap. 8vo.* 2*s.* 6*d.*

H. H. Henson. LIGHT AND LEAVEN: HISTORICAL AND SOCIAL SERMONS. By H. H. HENSON, M.A. *Crown 8vo.* 6*s.*

Bennett and Adeney. A BIBLICAL INTRODUCTION. By W. H. BENNETT, M.A., and W. F. ADENEY, M.A. *Crown 8vo.* 7*s.* 6*d.*

'It makes available to the ordinary reader the best scholarship of the day in the field of Biblical introduction. We know of no book which comes into competition with it.'—*Manchester Guardian.*

W. H. Bennett. A PRIMER OF THE BIBLE. By W. H. BENNETT. *Second Edition. Cr. 8vo.* 2*s.* 6*d.*

'The work of an honest, fearless, and sound critic, and an excellent guide in a small compass to the books of the Bible.'—*Manchester Guardian.*

C. F. G. Masterman. TENNYSON AS A RELIGIOUS TEACHER. By C. F. G. MASTERMAN. *Crown 8vo.* 6*s.*

'A thoughtful and penetrating appreciation, full of interest and suggestion.'—*World.*

William Harrison. CLOVELLY SERMONS. By WILLIAM HARRISON, M.A., late Rector of Clovelly. With a Preface by 'LUCAS MALET.' *Cr. 8vo.* 3*s.* 6*d.*

Cecilia Robinson. THE MINISTRY OF DEACONESSES. By Deaconness CECILIA ROBINSON. With an Introduction by the Lord Bishop of Winchester. *Cr. 8vo.* 3*s.* 6*d.*

'A learned and interesting book.'—*Scotsman.*

E. B. Layard. RELIGION IN BOYHOOD. Notes on the Religious Training of Boys. By E. B. LAYARD, M.A. *18mo.* 1*s.*

T. Herbert Bindley. THE OECUMENICAL DOCUMENTS OF THE FAITH. Edited with Introductions and Notes by T. HERBERT BINDLEY, B.D., Merton College, Oxford. *Crown 8vo.* 6*s.*

A historical account of the Creeds.

'Mr. Bindley has done his work in a fashion which calls for our warmest gratitude. The introductions, though brief, are always direct and to the point; the notes are learned and full, and serve admirably to elucidate the many difficulties of the text.'—*Guardian.*

H. M. Barron. TEXTS FOR SERMONS ON VARIOUS OCCASIONS AND SUBJECTS. Compiled and Arranged by H. M. BARRON, B.A., of Wadham College, Oxford, with a Preface by Canon SCOTT HOLLAND. *Crown 8vo.* 3*s.* 6*d.*

W. Yorke Fausset. THE *DE CATECHIZANDIS RUDIBUS* OF ST. AUGUSTINE. Edited, with Introduction, Notes, etc., by W. YORKE FAUSSET, M.A. *Cr. 8vo.* 3*s.* 6*d.*

F. Weston. THE HOLY SACRIFICE. By F. WESTON, M.A., Curate of St. Matthew's, Westminster. *Pott 8vo.* 6*d. net.*

À Kempis. THE IMITATION OF CHRIST. By THOMAS À KEMPIS. With an Introduction by DEAN FARRAR. Illustrated by C. M. GERE. *Second Edition. Fcap. 8vo.* 3*s.* 6*d.* *Padded morocco,* 5*s.*

'Amongst all the innumerable English

editions of the "Imitation," there can have been few which were prettier than this one, printed in strong and handsome type, with all the glory of red initials.'—*Glasgow Herald.*

J. Keble. THE CHRISTIAN YEAR. By JOHN KEBLE. With an Introduction and Notes by W. LOCK, D.D., Warden of Keble College. Illustrated by R. ANNING BELL. *Second Edition. Fcap.* 8*vo.* 3*s.* 6*d. Padded morocco.* 5s.

'The present edition is annotated with all the care and insight to be expected from Mr. Lock.'—*Guardian.*

Oxford Commentaries

General Editor, WALTER LOCK, D.D., Warden of Keble College, Dean Ireland's Professor of Exegesis in the University of Oxford.

THE BOOK OF JOB. Edited, with Introduction and Notes, by E. C. S. GIBSON, D.D., Vicar of Leeds. *Demy* 8*vo.* 6*s.*

'The publishers are to be congratulated on the start the series has made.'—*Times.*

'It is in his patient, lucid, interest-sustaining explanations that Dr. Gibson is at his best.'—*Literature.*

'We can hardly imagine a more useful book to place in the hands of an intelligent layman, or cleric, who desires to elucidate some of the difficulties presented in the Book of Job.'—*Church Times.*

'The work is marked by clearness, lightness of touch, strong common sense, and thorough critical fairness.

'Dr. Gibson's work is worthy of a high degree of appreciation. To the busy worker and the intelligent student the commentary will be a real boon; and it will, if we are not mistaken, be much in demand. The Introduction is almost a model of concise, straightforward, prefatory remarks on the subject treated.'—*Athenæum.*

Handbooks of Theology

General Editor, A. ROBERTSON, D.D., Principal of King's College, London.

THE XXXIX. ARTICLES OF THE CHURCH OF ENGLAND. Edited with an Introduction by E. C. S. GIBSON, D.D., Vicar of Leeds, late Principal of Wells Theological College. *Second and Cheaper Edition in One Volume. Demy* 8*vo.* 12*s.* 6*d.*

'We welcome with the utmost satisfaction a new, cheaper, and more convenient edition of Dr. Gibson's book. It was greatly wanted. Dr. Gibson has given theological students just what they want, and we should like to think that it was in the hands of every candidate for orders.'—*Guardian.*

AN INTRODUCTION TO THE HISTORY OF RELIGION. By F. B. JEVONS, M.A., Litt.D., Principal of Bishop Hatfield's Hall. *Demy* 8*vo.* 10*s.* 6*d.*

'The merit of this book lies in the penetration, the singular acuteness and force of the author's judgment. He is at once critical and luminous, at once just and suggestive. A comprehensive and thorough book.'—*Birmingham Post.*

THE DOCTRINE OF THE INCARNATION. By R. L. OTTLEY, M.A., late fellow of Magdalen College, Oxon., and Principal of Pusey House. *In Two Volumes. Demy* 8*vo.* 15*s.*

'A clear and remarkably full account of the main currents of speculation. Scholarly precision . . . genuine tolerance . . . intense interest in his subject—are Mr. Ottley's merits.'—*Guardian.*

AN INTRODUCTION TO THE HISTORY OF THE CREEDS. By A. E. BURN, B.D., Examining Chaplain to the Bishop of Lichfield. *Demy* 8*vo.* 10*s.* 6*d.*

'This book may be expected to hold its place as an authority on its subject.—*Spectator.*

The Churchman's Library

General Editor, J. H. BURN, B.D., Examining Chaplain to the Bishop of Aberdeen.

THE BEGINNINGS OF ENGLISH CHRISTIANITY. By W. E. COLLINS, M.A. With Map. *Cr. 8vo.* 3s. 6d.

'An excellent example of thorough and fresh historical work.'—*Guardian.*

SOME NEW TESTAMENT PROBLEMS. By ARTHUR WRIGHT, M.A., Fellow of Queen's College, Cambridge. *Crown 8vo.* 6s.

THE KINGDOM OF HEAVEN HERE AND HEREAFTER. By CANON WINTERBOTHAM, M.A., B.Sc., LL.B. *Cr. 8vo.* 3s. 6d.

'A most able book, at once exceedingly thoughtful and richly suggestive.'—*Glasgow Herald.*

THE WORKMANSHIP OF THE PRAYER BOOK: Its Literary and Liturgical Aspects. By J. DOWDEN, D.D., Lord Bishop of Edinburgh. *Crown 8vo.* 3s. 6d.

'Scholarly and interesting.'—*Manchester Guardian.*

EVOLUTION. By F. B. JEVONS, Litt.D., Principal of Hatfield Hall, Durham. *Crown 8vo.* 3s. 6d.

'A well-written book, full of sound thinking happily expressed.'—*Manchester Guardian.*

'A singularly fresh and stimulating book.'—*Speaker.*

'We have no hesitation in saying that this is much the best general account of the philosophical consequences of the theory of Evolution that has yet appeared.'—*Guardian.*

The Churchman's Bible

General Editor, J. H. BURN, B.D.

Messrs. METHUEN are issuing a series of expositions upon most of the books of the Bible. The volumes will be practical and devotional, and the text of the authorised version is explained in sections, which will correspond as far as possible with the Church Lectionary.

THE EPISTLE OF ST. PAUL TO THE GALATIANS. Explained by A. W. ROBINSON, Vicar of All Hallows, Barking. *Fcap. 8vo.* 1s. 6d. *net.*

'The most attractive, sensible, and instructive manual for people at large, which we have ever seen.'—*Church Gazette.*

ECCLESIASTES. Explained by A. W. STREANE, D.D. *Fcap. 8vo.* 1s. 6d. *net.*

'Scholarly, suggestive, and particularly interesting.'—*Bookman.*

THE EPISTLE OF PAUL THE APOSTLE TO THE PHILIPPIANS. Explained by C. R. D. BIGGS, B.D. *Fcap. 8vo.* 1s. 6d. *net.*

'Mr. Biggs' work is very thorough, and he has managed to compress a good deal of information into a limited space.'—*Guardian.*

The Library of Devotion

Pott 8vo, cloth, 2s.; leather, 2s. 6d. net.

'This series is excellent.'—THE BISHOP OF LONDON.
'Very delightful.'—THE BISHOP OF BATH AND WELLS.
'Well worth the attention of the Clergy.'—THE BISHOP OF LICHFIELD.
'The new "Library of Devotion" is excellent.'—THE BISHOP OF PETERBOROUGH.
'Charming.'—*Record.* 'Delightful.'—*Church Bells.*

THE CONFESSIONS OF ST. AUGUSTINE. Newly Translanted, with an Introduction and Notes, by C. BIGG, D.D., late Student of Christ Church. *Second Edition.*

'The translation is an excellent piece of English, and the introduction is a masterly exposition. We augur well of a series which begins so satisfactorily.'—*Times.*

THE CHRISTIAN YEAR. By JOHN KEBLE. With Introduction and Notes by WALTER LOCK, D.D., Warden of Keble College, Ireland Professor at Oxford.

'The volume is very prettily bound and printed, and may fairly claim to be an advance on any previous editions.'—*Guardian.*

THE IMITATION OF CHRIST. A Revised Translation, with an Introduction, by C. BIGG, D.D., late Student of Christ Church. *Second Edition.*

A practically new translation of this book, which the reader has, almost for the first time, exactly in the shape in which it left the hands of the author.

'A nearer approach to the original than has yet existed in English.'—*Academy.*

A BOOK OF DEVOTIONS. By J. W. STANBRIDGE, B.D., Rector of Bainton, Canon of York, and sometime Fellow of St. John's College, Oxford.

'It is probably the best book of its kind. It deserves high commendation.'—*Church Gazette.*

LYRA INNOCENTIUM. By JOHN KEBLE. Edited, with Introduction and Notes, by WALTER LOCK, D.D., Warden of Keble College, Oxford. *Pott 8vo. 2s.; leather, 2s. 6d. net.*

'This sweet and fragrant book has never been published more attractively.'—*Academy.*

'The work is given in as dainty a form as any it has yet taken.'—*Scotsman.*

'The analysis and notes are discriminating, scholarly, and helpful.'—*Church Review.*

A SERIOUS CALL TO A DEVOUT AND HOLY LIFE. By WILLIAM LAW. Edited, with an Introduction, by C. BIGG, D.D., late Student of Christ Church.

This is a reprint, word for word and line for line, of the *Editio Princeps.*

THE TEMPLE. By GEORGE HERBERT. Edited, with an Introduction and Notes, by E. C. S. GIBSON, D.D., Vicar of Leeds.

This edition contains Walton's Life of Herbert, and the text is that of the first edition.

'As neat and desirable an edition of the work as can be found.'—*Scotsman.*

Leaders of Religion

Edited by H. C. BEECHING, M.A. *With Portraits, Crown 8vo.* 3*s.* 6*d.*

A series of short biographies of the most prominent leaders of religious life and thought of all ages and countries.

The following are ready—

CARDINAL NEWMAN. By R. H. HUTTON.

JOHN WESLEY. By J. H. OVERTON, M.A.

BISHOP WILBERFORCE. By G. W. DANIELL, M.A.

CARDINAL MANNING. By A. W. HUTTON, M.A.

CHARLES SIMEON. By H. C. G. MOULE, D.D.

JOHN KEBLE. By WALTER LOCK, D.D.

THOMAS CHALMERS. By Mrs. OLIPHANT.

LANCELOT ANDREWES. By R. L. OTTLEY, M.A.

AUGUSTINE OF CANTERBURY. By E. L. CUTTS, D.D.

WILLIAM LAUD. By W. H. HUTTON, B.D.

JOHN KNOX. By F. MACCUNN.

JOHN HOWE. By R. F. HORTON, D.D.

BISHOP KEN. By F. A. CLARKE, M.A.

GEORGE FOX, THE QUAKER. By T. HODGKIN, D.C.L.

JOHN DONNE. By AUGUSTUS JESSOPP, D.D.

THOMAS CRANMER. By. A. J. MASON.

BISHOP LATIMER. By R. M. CARLYLE and A. J. CARLYLE, M.A.

Other volumes will be announced in due course.

Fiction

SIX SHILLING NOVELS

Marie Corelli's Novels

Crown 8vo. 6s. each.

A ROMANCE OF TWO WORLDS. *Twentieth Edition.*

VENDETTA. *Fifteenth Edition.*

THELMA. *Twenty-second Edition.*

ARDATH: THE STORY OF A DEAD SELF. *Twelfth Edition.*

THE SOUL OF LILITH. *Ninth Edition.*

WORMWOOD. *Tenth Edition.*

BARABBAS: A DREAM OF THE WORLD'S TRAGEDY. *Thirty-fifth Edition.*

'The tender reverence of the treatment and the imaginative beauty of the writing have reconciled us to the daring of the conception, and the conviction is forced on us that even so exalted a subject cannot be made too familiar to us, provided it be presented in the true spirit of Christian faith. The amplifications of the Scripture narrative are often conceived with high poetic insight, and this "Dream of the World's Tragedy" is a lofty and not inadequate paraphrase of the supreme climax of the inspired narrative.'—*Dublin Review.*

THE SORROWS OF SATAN. *Forty-second Edition.*

'A very powerful piece of work. . . . The conception is magnificent, and is likely to win an abiding place within the memory of man. . . . The author has immense command of language, and a limitless audacity. . . . This interesting and remarkable romance will live long after much of the ephemeral literature of the day is forgotten. . . . A literary phenomenon . . . novel, and even sublime.'—W. T. STEAD in the *Review of Reviews.*

Anthony Hope's Novels

Crown 8vo. 6s. each.

THE GOD IN THE CAR. *Eighth Edition.*

'A very remarkable book, deserving of critical analysis impossible within our limit; brilliant, but not superficial; well considered, but not elaborated; constructed with the proverbial art that conceals, but yet allows itself to be enjoyed by readers to whom fine literary method is a keen pleasure.'—*The World.*

A CHANGE OF AIR. *Fifth Edition.*

'A graceful, vivacious comedy, true to human nature. The characters are traced with a masterly hand.'—*Times.*

A MAN OF MARK. *Fifth Edition.*

'Of all Mr. Hope's books, "A Man of Mark" is the one which best compares with "The Prisoner of Zenda."—*National Observer.*

THE CHRONICLES OF COUNT ANTONIO. *Fourth Edition.*

'It is a perfectly enchanting story of love and chivalry, and pure romance. The Count is the most constant, desperate, and modest and tender of lovers, a peerless gentleman, an intrepid fighter, a faithful friend, and a magnanimous foe.'—*Guardian.*

PHROSO. Illustrated by H. R. MILLAR. *Fourth Edition.*

'The tale is thoroughly fresh, quick with vitality, stirring the blood.'—*St. James's Gazette.*

'From cover to cover "Phroso" not only engages the attention, but carries the reader in little whirls of delight from adventure to adventure.'—*Academy.*

SIMON DALE. Illustrated. *Third Edition.*

'There is searching analysis of human nature, with a most ingeniously constructed plot. Mr. Hope has drawn the contrasts of his women with marvellous subtlety and delicacy.'—*Times.*

THE KING'S MIRROR. *Third Edition.*

'In elegance, delicacy, and tact it ranks with the best of his novels, while in the wide range of its portraiture and the subtilty of its analysis it surpasses all his earlier ventures.'—*Spectator.*

'"The King's Mirror" is a strong book, charged with close analysis and exquisite irony; a book full of pathos and moral fibre—in short, a book to be read.'—*Daily Chronicle.*

Gilbert Parker's Novels

Crown 8vo. 6s. each.

PIERRE AND HIS PEOPLE. *Fifth Edition.*

'Stories happily conceived and finely executed. There is strength and genius in Mr. Parker's style.'—*Daily Telegraph.*

MRS. FALCHION. *Fourth Edition.*

'A splendid study of character.'—*Athenæum.*

THE TRANSLATION OF A SAVAGE.

'The plot is original and one difficult to work out; but Mr. Parker has done it with great skill and delicacy.' —*Daily Chronicle.*

THE TRAIL OF THE SWORD. Illustrated. *Sixth Edition.*

'A rousing and dramatic tale. A book like this, in which swords flash, great surprises are undertaken, and daring deeds done, in which men and women live and love in the old passionate way, is a joy inexpressible.'—*Daily Chronicle.*

WHEN VALMOND CAME TO PONTIAC: The Story of a Lost Napoleon. *Fourth Edition.*

'Here we find romance—real, breathing, living romance. The character of Valmond is drawn unerringly.'—*Pall Mall Gazette.*

AN ADVENTURER OF THE NORTH: The Last Adventures of 'Pretty Pierre.' *Second Edition.*

'The present book is full of fine and moving stories of the great North, and it will add to Mr. Parker's already high reputation.'—*Glasgow Herald.*

THE SEATS OF THE MIGHTY. Illustrated. *Tenth Edition.*

'Mr. Parker has produced a really fine historical novel.'—*Athenæum.*

'A great book.'—*Black and White.*

THE POMP OF THE LAVILETTES. *Second Edition.* 3*s.* 6*d.*

'Living, breathing romance, unforced pathos, and a deeper knowledge of human nature than Mr. Parker has ever displayed before.'—*Pall Mall Gazette.*

THE BATTLE OF THE STRONG: a Romance of Two Kingdoms. Illustrated. *Fourth Edition.*

'Nothing more vigorous or more human has come from Mr. Gilbert Parker than this novel. It has all the graphic power of his last book, with truer feeling for the romance, both of human life and wild nature.'—*Literature.*

S. Baring Gould's Novels . . .

Crown 8vo. 6s. each.

'To say that a book is by the author of "Mehalah" is to imply that it contains a story cast on strong lines, containing dramatic possibilities, vivid and sympathetic descriptions of Nature, and a wealth of ingenious imagery.'—*Speaker.*

'That whatever Mr. Baring Gould writes is well worth reading, is a conclusion that may be very generally accepted. His views of life are fresh and vigorous, his language pointed and characteristic, the incidents of which he makes use are striking and original, his characters are life-like, and though somewhat exceptional people, are drawn and coloured with artistic force. Add to this that his descriptions of scenes and scenery are painted with the loving eyes and skilled hands of a master of his art, that he is always fresh and never dull, and it is no wonder that readers have gained confidence in his power of amusing and satisfying them, and that year by year his popularity widens.'—*Court Circular.*

ARMINELL. *Fourth Edition.*
URITH. *Fifth Edition.*
IN THE ROAR OF THE SEA. *Sixth Edition.*
MRS. CURGENVEN OF CURGENVEN. *Fourth Edition.*
CHEAP JACK ZITA. *Fourth Edition.*
THE QUEEN OF LOVE. *Fourth Edition.*
MARGERY OF QUETHER. *Third Edition.*
JACQUETTA. *Third Edition.*
KITTY ALONE. *Fifth Edition.*
NOÉMI. Illustrated. *Fourth Edition.*
THE BROOM-SQUIRE. Illustrated. *Fourth Edition.*
THE PENNYCOMEQUICKS. *Third Edition.*
DARTMOOR IDYLLS.
GUAVAS THE TINNER. Illustrated. *Second Edition.*
BLADYS. Illustrated. *Second Edition.*
DOMITIA. Illustrated. *Second Edition.*
PABO THE PRIEST.

Conan Doyle. ROUND THE RED LAMP. By A. CONAN DOYLE. *Sixth Edition. Crown 8vo.* 6*s.*

'The book is far and away the best view that has been vouchsafed us behind the scenes of the consulting-room.'—*Illustrated London News.*

Stanley Weyman. UNDER THE RED ROBE. By STANLEY WEYMAN, Author of 'A Gentleman of France.' With Illustrations by R. C. WOODVILLE. *Fifteenth Edition. Crown 8vo.* 6*s.*

'Every one who reads books at all must read this thrilling romance, from the first page of which to the last the breathless reader is haled along. An inspiration of manliness and courage.'—*Daily Chronicle.*

Lucas Malet. THE WAGES OF SIN. By LUCAS MALET. *Thirteenth Edition. Crown 8vo.* 6*s.*

Lucas Malet. THE CARISSIMA. By LUCAS MALET, Author of 'The Wages of Sin,' etc. *Third Edition. Crown 8vo.* 6*s.*

George Gissing. THE TOWN TRAVELLER. By GEORGE GISSING, Author of 'Demos,' 'In the Year of Jubilee,' etc. *Second Edition. Cr. 8vo.* 6*s.*

'It is a bright and witty book above all things. Polly Sparkes is a splendid bit of work.'—*Pall Mall Gazette.*
'The spirit of Dickens is in it.'—*Bookman.*

George Gissing. THE CROWN OF LIFE. By GEORGE GISSING, Author of 'Demos,' 'The Town Traveller,' etc. *Crown 8vo.* 6*s.*

'Mr. Gissing is at his best.'—*Academy.*
'A fine novel.'—*Outlook.*

S. R. Crockett. LOCHINVAR. By S. R. CROCKETT, Author of 'The Raiders,' etc. Illustrated. *Second Edition. Crown 8vo.* 6*s.*

'Full of gallantry and pathos, of the clash

of arms, and brightened by episodes of humour and love. . . .'—*Westminster Gazette.*

S. R. Crockett. THE STANDARD BEARER. By S. R. CROCKETT. *Crown 8vo.* 6*s*.

'A delightful tale.'—*Speaker.*

'Mr. Crockett at his best.'—*Literature.*

Arthur Morrison. TALES OF MEAN STREETS. By ARTHUR MORRISON. *Fifth Edition. Cr. 8vo.* 6*s*.

'Told with consummate art and extraordinary detail. In the true humanity of the book lies its justification, the permanence of its interest, and its indubitable triumph.'—*Athenæum.*

'A great book. The author's method is amazingly effective, and produces a thrilling sense of reality. The writer lays upon us a master hand. The book is simply appalling and irresistible in its interest. It is humorous also; without humour it would not make the mark it is certain to make.'—*World.*

Arthur Morrison. A CHILD OF THE JAGO. By ARTHUR MORRISON. *Third Edition. Cr. 8vo.* 6*s*.

'The book is a masterpiece.'—*Pall Mall Gazette.*

'Told with great vigour and powerful simplicity.'—*Athenæum.*

Arthur Morrison. TO LONDON TOWN. By ARTHUR MORRISON, Author of 'Tales of Mean Streets,' etc. *Second Edition. Crown 8vo.* 6*s*.

'We have idyllic pictures, woodland scenes full of tenderness and grace. . . . This is the new Mr. Arthur Morrison gracious and tender, sympathetic and human.'—*Daily Telegraph.*

'The easy swing of detail proclaims the master of his subject and the artist in rendering.'—*Pall Mall Gazette.*

M. Sutherland. ONE HOUR AND THE NEXT. By THE DUCHESS OF SUTHERLAND. *Third Edition. Crown 8vo.* 6*s*.

'Passionate, vivid, dramatic.'—*Literature.*

'It possesses marked qualities, descriptive, and imaginative.'—*Morning Post.*

Mrs. Clifford. A FLASH OF SUMMER. By Mrs. W. K. CLIFFORD, Author of 'Aunt Anne,' etc. *Second Edition. Crown 8vo.* 6*s*.

'The story is a very beautiful one, exquisitely told.'—*Speaker.*

Emily Lawless. HURRISH. By the Honble. EMILY LAWLESS, Author of 'Maelcho,' etc. *Fifth Edition. Cr. 8vo.* 6*s*.

Emily Lawless. MAELCHO: a Sixteenth Century Romance. By the Honble. EMILY LAWLESS. *Second Edition. Crown 8vo.* 6*s*.

'A really great book.'—*Spectator.*

'One of the most remarkable literary achievements of this generation.'—*Manchester Guardian.*

Emily Lawless. TRAITS AND CONFIDENCES. By the Honble. EMILY LAWLESS. *Crown 8vo.* 6*s*.

Eden Phillpotts. THE HUMAN BOY. By EDEN PHILLPOTTS, Author of 'Children of the Mist.' With a Frontispiece. *Fourth Edition. Crown 8vo.* 6*s*.

'Mr. Phillpotts knows exactly what schoolboys do, and can lay bare their inmost thoughts; likewise he shows an all-pervading sense of humour.'—*Academy.*

E. W. Hornung. THE AMATEUR CRACKSMAN. By E. W. HORNUNG. *Crown 8vo.* 6*s*.

'An audaciously entertaining volume.'—*Spectator.*

Jane Barlow. A CREEL OF IRISH STORIES. By JANE BARLOW, Author of 'Irish Idylls.' *Second Edition. Crown 8vo.* 6*s*.

'Vivid and singularly real.'—*Scotsman.*

Jane Barlow. FROM THE EAST UNTO THE WEST. By JANE BARLOW. *Crown 8vo.* 6*s*.

Mrs. Caffyn. ANNE MAULEVERER. By Mrs. CAFFYN (Iota), Author of 'The Yellow Aster.' *Second Edition. Crown 8vo.* 6*s*.

Benjamin Swift. SIREN CITY. By BENJAMIN SWIFT, Author of 'Nancy Noon.' *Crown 8vo.* 6*s.*

'"Siren City" is certainly his best book, and it is the work of a strong man. It has sobriety, not only of manner, but of spirit.'—*Academy.*

J. H. Findlater. THE GREEN GRAVES OF BALGOWRIE. By JANE H. FINDLATER. *Fourth Edition. Crown 8vo.* 6*s.*

'A powerful and vivid story.'—*Standard.*

'A beautiful story, sad and strange as truth itself.'—*Vanity Fair.*

'A very charming and pathetic tale.'—*Pall Mall Gazette.*

'A singularly original, clever, and beautiful story.'—*Guardian.*

'Reveals to us a new writer of undoubted faculty and reserve force.'—*Spectator.*

'An exquisite idyll, delicate, affecting, and beautiful.'—*Black and White.*

J. H. Findlater. A DAUGHTER OF STRIFE. By JANE HELEN FINDLATER. *Crown 8vo.* 6*s.*

J. H. Findlater. RACHEL. By JANE H. FINDLATER. *Second Edition. Crown 8vo.* 6*s.*

'A not unworthy successor to "The Green Graves of Balgowrie."'—*Critic.*

Mary Findlater. OVER THE HILLS. By MARY FINDLATER. *Second Edition. Cr. 8vo.* 6*s.*

'A strong and wise book of deep insight and unflinching truth.'—*Birmingham Post.*

Mary Findlater. BETTY MUSGRAVE. By MARY FINDLATER. *Second Edition. Crown 8vo.* 6*s.*

'Handled with dignity and delicacy. . . . A most touching story.'—*Spectator.*

Alfred Ollivant. OWD BOB, THE GREY DOG OF KENMUIR. By ALFRED OLLIVANT. *Third Edition. Cr. 8vo.* 6*s.*

'Weird, thrilling, strikingly graphic.'—*Punch.*

'We admire this book. . . . It is one to read with admiration and to praise with enthusiasm.'—*Bookman.*

'It is a fine, open-air, blood-stirring book, to be enjoyed by every man and woman to whom a dog is dear.'—*Literature.*

B. M. Croker. PEGGY OF THE BARTONS. By B. M. CROKER, Author of 'Diana Barrington.' *Fourth Edition. Crown 8vo.* 6*s.*

Mrs. Croker excels in the admirably simple, easy, and direct flow of her narrative, the briskness of her dialogue, and the geniality of her portraiture.'—*Spectator.*

Mary L. Pendered. AN ENGLISHMAN. By MARY L. PENDERED. *Crown 8vo.* 6*s.*

'Her book is most healthy in tone, and leaves a pleasant taste in the mouth.'—*Pall Mall Gazette.*

'A very noble book. It is filled with wisdom and sympathy.'—*Literary World.*

'At once sound and diverting.'—*Academy.*

Morley Roberts. THE PLUNDERERS. By MORLEY ROBERTS, Author of 'The Colossus,' etc. *Crown 8vo.* 6*s.*

'The author secures and maintains the reader's lively interest in his clever absurdities.'—*Pall Mall Gazette.*

'The whole atmosphere is one of high spirits and high comedy.'—*Globe.*

'Mr. Roberts writes of real people who do things and know things.'—*Black and White.*

Norma Lorimer. MIRRY-ANN. By NORMA LORIMER, Author of 'Josiah's Wife.' *Crown 8vo.* 6*s.*

'The heroine is rare and striking, but thorough woman and altogether lovable, and the plot is brisk and well sustained.'—*Pall Mall Gazette.*

'It is a Manx story, and a right able story. The atmosphere is excellent, the descriptive passages fine, and the story is one which will repay perusal.'—*Glasgow Herald.*

'A Manx novel which is at once sincere, poetical, and in the best sense true.'—*Academy.*

Helen Shipton. THE STRONG GOD CIRCUMSTANCE. By HELEN SHIPTON. *Crown 8vo.* 6*s.*

'A story of high merit and many attractions.'—*Scotsman.*

'An up-to-date story—and a very beautiful one—of self-sacrifice.'—*Daily Telegraph.*

'A most effective story, written with both insight and imagination.'—*Leeds Mercury.*

Violet Hunt. THE HUMAN INTEREST. By VIOLET HUNT, Author of 'A Hard Woman,' etc. *Crown 8vo.* 6*s*.

'Clever observation and unfailing wit.'—*Academy.*

'The insight is keen, the irony is delicate.'—*World.*

H. G. Wells. THE STOLEN BACILLUS, and other Stories. By H. G. WELLS. *Second Edition. Crown 8vo.* 6*s*.

'The impressions of a very striking imagination.'—*Saturday Review.*

H. G. Wells. THE PLATTNER STORY AND OTHERS. By H. G. WELLS. *Second Edition. Cr. 8vo.* 6*s*.

'Weird and mysterious; they seem to hold the reader as by a magic spell.'—*Scotsman.*

Richard Marsh. MARVELS AND MYSTERIES. By RICHARD MARSH, Author of 'The Beetle.' *Crown 8vo.* 6*s*.

'While under their immediate influence the reader is conscious of nothing but thrilling excitement and curiosity.'—*Glasgow Herald.*

'Ingeniously constructed and well told.'—*Morning Leader.*

'Admirably selected and of the very best.' —*Christian World.*

Esmé Stuart. CHRISTALLA. By ESMÉ STUART, *Crown 8vo.* 6*s*.

'The story is happily conceived, and entertaining throughout.'—*Scotsman.*

'An excellent story, pathetic, and full of humour.'—*Athenæum.*

'We wish that we came across more books like this clever and charming story.—*Leeds Mercury.*

Sara Jeannette Duncan. A VOYAGE OF CONSOLATION. By SARA JEANNETTE DUNCAN, Author of 'An American Girl in London.' Illustrated. *Third Edition. Cr. 8vo.* 6*s*.

'A most delightfully bright book.'—*Daily Telegraph.*

'The dialogue is full of wit. —*Globe.*

Sara Jeannette Duncan. THE PATH OF A STAR. By SARA JEANNETTE DUNCAN, Author of 'A Voyage of Consolation.' Illustrated. *Second Edition. Crown 8vo.* 6*s*.

'Richness and fullness of local colouring, brilliancy of style, smiting phrases, and the display of very pretty humour are graces which are here in profusion. The interest never flags.'—*Pall Mall Gazette.*

C. F. Keary. THE JOURNALIST. By C. F. KEARY. *Cr. 8vo.* 6*s*.

'It is rare indeed to find such poetical sympathy with Nature joined to close study of character and singularly truthful dialogue: but then "The Journalist" is altogether a rare book.'—*Athenæum.*

W. E. Norris. MATTHEW AUSTIN. By W. E. NORRIS, Author of 'Mademoiselle de Mersac,' etc. *Fourth Edition. Crown 8vo.* 6*s*.

'An intellectually satisfactory and morally bracing novel.'—*Daily Telegraph.*

W. E. Norris. HIS GRACE. By W. E. NORRIS. *Third Edition. Cr. 8vo.* 6*s*.

W. E. Norris. THE DESPOTIC LADY AND OTHERS. By W. E. NORRIS. *Crown 8vo.* 6*s*.

W. E. Norris. CLARISSA FURIOSA. By W. E. NORRIS. *Cr. 8vo.* 6*s*.

'As a story it is admirable, as a *jeu d'esprit* it is capital, as a lay sermon studded with gems of wit and wisdom it is a model.'—*The World.*

W. E. Norris. GILES INGILBY. By W. E. NORRIS. *Illustrated. Second Edition. Crown 8vo.* 6*s*.

'Interesting, wholesome, and charmingly written.'—*Glasgow Herald.*

W. E. Norris. AN OCTAVE. By W. E. NORRIS. *Second Edition. Crown 8vo.* 6*s*.

'A very perfect exposition of the self-restraint, the perfect knowledge of society and its ways, the delicate sense of humour, which are the main characteristics of this very accomplished author.'—*Country Life.*

Ernest Glanville. THE DESPATCH RIDER. By ERNEST GLANVILLE, Author of 'The Kloof Bride.' *Crown 8vo.* 6*s*.

A highly interesting story of the present Boer War by an author who knows the country well, and has had experience of Boer campaigning.

W. Clark Russell. MY DANISH SWEETHEART. By W. CLARK RUSSELL. *Illustrated. Fourth Edition. Crown 8vo.* 6*s.*

Robert Barr. IN THE MIDST OF ALARMS. By ROBERT BARR. *Third Edition. Cr. 8vo.* 6*s.*

'A book which has abundantly satisfied us by its capital humour.'—*Daily Chronicle.*

'Mr. Barr has achieved a triumph.'—*Pall Mall Gazette.*

Robert Barr. THE MUTABLE MANY. By ROBERT BARR. *Second Edition. Crown 8vo.* 6*s.*

'Very much the best novel that Mr. Barr has yet given us. There is much insight in it, and much excellent humour.'—*Daily Chronicle.*

Robert Barr. THE COUNTESS TEKLA. By ROBERT BARR. *Second Edition. Crown 8vo.* 6*s.*

'Of these mediæval romances, which are now gaining ground, "The Countess Tekla" is the very best we have seen. The story is written in clear English, and a picturesque, moving style.'—*Pall Mall Gazette.*

Andrew Balfour. BY STROKE OF SWORD. By A. BALFOUR. Illustrated. *Fourth Edition. Cr. 8vo.* 6*s.*

A banquet of good things.'—*Academy.*

'A recital of thrilling interest, told with unflagging vigour.'—*Globe.*

'An unusually excellent example of a semi-historic romance.'—*World.*

Andrew Balfour. TO ARMS! By ANDREW BALFOUR. Illustrated. *Second Edition. Crown 8vo.* 6*s.*

'The marvellous perils through which Allan passes are told in powerful and lively fashion.'—*Pall Mall Gazette.*

Andrew Balfour. VENGEANCE IS MINE. By ANDREW BALFOUR, Author of 'By Stroke of Sword.' *Illustrated. Crown 8vo.* 6*s.*

A vigorous piece of work, well written, and abounding in stirring incidents.'—*Glasgow Herald.*

J. Maclaren Cobban. THE KING OF ANDAMAN: A Saviour of Society. By J. MACLAREN COBBAN. *Crown 8vo.* 6*s.*

'An unquestionably interesting book. It contains one character, at least, who has in him the root of immortality.'—*Pall Mall Gazette.*

J. Maclaren Cobban. THE ANGEL OF THE COVENANT. By J. MACLAREN COBBAN. *Cr. 8vo.* 6*s.*

R. N. Stephens. AN ENEMY TO THE KING. By R. N. STEPHENS. *Second Edition. Cr. 8vo.* 6*s.*

'It is full of movement, and the movement is always buoyant.'—*Scotsman.*

'A stirring story with plenty of movement.'—*Black and White.*

R. N. Stephens. A GENTLEMAN PLAYER. By R. N. STEPHENS, Author of 'An Enemy to the King.' *Crown 8vo.* 6*s.*

'A bright and spirited romance of adventure, full of movement and changing action.'—*Scotsman.*

R. Hichens. BYEWAYS. By ROBERT HICHENS. Author of 'Flames, etc.' *Second Edition. Cr. 8vo.* 6*s.*

'The work is undeniably that of a man of striking imagination.'—*Daily News.*

J. S. Fletcher. THE PATHS OF THE PRUDENT. By J. S. FLETCHER. *Crown 8vo.* 6*s.*

J. B. Burton. IN THE DAY OF ADVERSITY. By J. BLOUNDELLE-BURTON. *Second Edition. Cr. 8vo.* 6*s.*

'Unusually interesting and full of highly dramatic situations.'—*Guardian.*

J. B. Burton. DENOUNCED. By J. BLOUNDELLE-BURTON. *Second Edition. Crown 8vo.* 6*s.*

'A fine, manly, spirited piece of work.'—*World.*

J. B. Burton. THE CLASH OF ARMS. By J. BLOUNDELLE-BURTON. *Second Edition. Cr. 8vo.* 6*s.*

'A brave story—brave in deed, brave in word, brave in thought.'—*St. James's Gazette.*

J. B. Burton. ACROSS THE SALT SEAS. By J. BLOUNDELLE-BURTON. *Second Edition. Crown 8vo.* 6*s.*

'The very essence of the true romantic spirit.'—*Truth.*

W. C. Scully. THE WHITE HECATOMB. By W. C. SCULLY, Author of 'Kafir Stories.' *Cr. 8vo.* 6*s.*

'Reveals a marvellously intimate understanding of the Kaffir mind.'—*African Critic.*

W. C. Scully. BETWEEN SUN AND SAND. By W. C. SCULLY, Author of 'The White Hecatomb.' *Cr. 8vo.* 6*s.*

'The reader passes at once into the very atmosphere of the African desert: the inexpressible space and stillness swallow him up, and there is no world for him but that immeasurable waste.'—*Athenæum.*

OTHER SIX-SHILLING NOVELS

Crown 8vo.

DANIEL WHYTE. By A. J. DAWSON.

THE CAPSINA. By E. F. BENSON.

DODO: A DETAIL OF THE DAY. By E. F. BENSON.

THE VINTAGE. By E. F. BENSON. Illustrated by G. P. JACOMB-HOOD.

ROSE À CHARLITTE. By MARSHALL SAUNDERS.

WILLOWBRAKE. By R. MURRAY GILCHRIST.

THINGS THAT HAVE HAPPENED. By DOROTHEA GERARD.

SIR ROBERT'S FORTUNE. By Mrs. OLIPHANT.

THE TWO MARYS. By Mrs. OLIPHANT.

THE LADY'S WALK. By Mrs. OLIPHANT.

LONE PINE: A ROMANCE OF MEXICAN LIFE. By R. B. TOWNSHEND.

WILT THOU HAVE THIS WOMAN? By J. MACLAREN COBBAN.

A PASSIONATE PILGRIM. By PERCY WHITE.

SECRETARY TO BAYNE, M.P. By W. PETT RIDGE.

ADRIAN ROME. By E. DAWSON and A. MOORE.

THE BUILDERS. By J. S. FLETCHER.

GALLIA. By MÉNIE MURIEL DOWIE.

THE CROOK OF THE BOUGH. By MÉNIE MURIEL DOWIE.

A BUSINESS IN GREAT WATERS. By JULIAN CORBETT.

MISS ERIN. By M. E. FRANCIS.

ANANIAS. By the Hon. Mrs. ALAN BRODRICK.

CORRAGEEN IN '98. By Mrs. ORPEN.

THE PLUNDER PIT. By J. KEIGHLEY SNOWDEN.

CROSS TRAILS. By VICTOR WAITE.

SUCCESSORS TO THE TITLE. By Mrs. WALFORD.

KIRKHAM'S FIND. By MARY GAUNT.

DEADMAN'S. By MARY GAUNT.

CAPTAIN JACOBUS: A ROMANCE OF THE ROAD. By L. COPE CORNFORD.

SONS OF ADVERSITY. By L. COPE CORNFORD.

THE KING OF ALBERIA. By LAURA DAINTREY.

THE DAUGHTER OF ALOUETTE. By MARY A. OWEN.

CHILDREN OF THIS WORLD. By ELLEN F. PINSENT.

AN ELECTRIC SPARK. By G. MANVILLE FENN.

UNDER SHADOW OF THE MISSION. By L. S. MCCHESNEY.

THE SPECULATORS. By J. F. BREWER.

THE SPIRIT OF STORM. By RONALD ROSS.

THE QUEENSBERRY CUP. By CLIVE P. WOLLEY.

A HOME IN INVERESK. By T. L. PATON.

MISS ARMSTRONG'S AND OTHER CIRCUMSTANCES. By JOHN DAVIDSON.

DR. CONGALTON'S LEGACY. By HENRY JOHNSTON.

TIME AND THE WOMAN. By RICHARD PRYCE.

THIS MAN'S DOMINION. By the Author of 'A High Little World.'

DIOGENES OF LONDON. By H. B. MARRIOTT WATSON.

THE STONE DRAGON. By MURRAY GILCHRIST.

A VICAR'S WIFE. By EVELYN DICKINSON.

ELSA. By E. M'QUEEN GRAY.

THE SINGER OF MARLY. By I. HOOPER.

THE FALL OF THE SPARROW. By M. C. BALFOUR.

A SERIOUS COMEDY. By HERBERT MORRAH.

THE FAITHFUL CITY. By HERBERT MORRAH.

IN THE GREAT DEEP. By J. A. BARRY.

BIJLI, THE DANCER. By JAMES BLYTHE PATTON.

JOSIAH'S WIFE. By NORMA LORIMER.

THE PHILANTHROPIST. By LUCY MAYNARD.

VAUSSORE. By FRANCIS BRUNE.

THREE-AND-SIXPENNY NOVELS

Crown 8vo.

DERRICK VAUGHAN, NOVELIST. *42nd thousand.* By EDNA LYALL.

A SON OF THE STATE. By W. PETT RIDGE.

CEASE FIRE! By J. MACLAREN COBBAN. *Crown 8vo.* 3*s.* 6*d.*

A stirring Story of the Boer War of 1881, including the Siege of Potchefstrom and the Defeat of Majuba.

'Brightly told and drawn with a strong and sure hand.'—*St. James's Gazette.*

'A capital novel.'—*Scotsman.*

'Fact and fiction are so deeply woven together that the book reads like a fascinating chapter of history.'—*Pall Mall Gazette.*

THE KLOOF BRIDE. By ERNEST GLANVILLE.

A VENDETTA OF THE DESERT. By W. C. SCULLY.

SUBJECT TO VANITY. By MARGARET BENSON.

THE SIGN OF THE SPIDER. By BERTRAM MITFORD.

THE MOVING FINGER. By MARY GAUNT.

JACO TRELOAR. By J. H. PEARCE.

THE DANCE OF THE HOURS. By 'VERA.'

A WOMAN OF FORTY. By ESMÉ STUART.

A CUMBERER OF THE GROUND. By CONSTANCE SMITH.

THE SIN OF ANGELS. By EVELYN DICKINSON.

AUT DIABOLUS AUT NIHIL. By X. L.

THE COMING OF CUCULAIN. By STANDISH O'GRADY.

THE GODS GIVE MY DONKEY WINGS. By ANGUS EVAN ABBOTT.

THE STAR GAZERS. By G. MANVILLE FENN.

THE POISON OF ASPS. By R. ORTON PROWSE.

THE QUIET MRS. FLEMING. By R. PRYCE.

DISENCHANTMENT. By F. MABEL ROBINSON.

THE SQUIRE OF WANDALES. By A. SHIELD.

A REVEREND GENTLEMAN. By J. M. COBBAN.

A DEPLORABLE AFFAIR. By W. E. NORRIS.

A CAVALIER'S LADYE. By Mrs. DICKER.

THE PRODIGALS. By Mrs. OLIPHANT.

THE SUPPLANTER. By P. NEUMANN.

A MAN WITH BLACK EYELASHES. By H. A. KENNEDY.

A HANDFUL OF EXOTICS. By S. GORDON.

AN ODD EXPERIMENT. By HANNAH LYNCH.

TALES OF NORTHUMBRIA. By HOWARD PEASE.

HALF-CROWN NOVELS

Crown 8vo.

HOVENDEN, V.C. By F. MABEL ROBINSON.

THE PLAN OF CAMPAIGN. By F. MABEL ROBINSON.

MR. BUTLER'S WARD. By F. MABEL ROBINSON.

ELI'S CHILDREN. By G. MANVILLE FENN.

A DOUBLE KNOT. By G. MANVILLE FENN.

DISARMED. By M. BETHAM EDWARDS.

IN TENT AND BUNGALOW. By the Author of 'Indian Idylls.'

MY STEWARDSHIP. By E. M'QUEEN GRAY.

JACK'S FATHER. By W. E. NORRIS.

A LOST ILLUSION. By LESLIE KEITH.

THE TRUE HISTORY OF JOSHUA DAVIDSON, Christian and Communist. By E. LYNN LYNTON. *Eleventh Edition. Post 8vo.* 1s.

The Novelist

MESSRS. METHUEN are making an interesting experiment which constitutes a fresh departure in publishing. They are issuing under the above general title a Monthly Series of Novels by popular authors at the price of Sixpence. Many of these Novels have never been published before. Each Number is as long as the average Six Shilling Novel. The first numbers of 'THE NOVELIST' are as follows:—

I. DEAD MEN TELL NO TALES. E. W. HORNUNG.

II. JENNIE BAXTER, JOURNALIST. ROBERT BARR.

III. THE INCA'S TREASURE. ERNEST GLANVILLE.

IV. A SON OF THE STATE. W. PETT RIDGE.

V. FURZE BLOOM. S. BARING GOULD.

VI. BUNTER'S CRUISE. C. GLEIG.

VII. THE GAY DECEIVERS. ARTHUR MOORE.

VIII. PRISONERS OF WAR. A. BOYSON WEEKES.

IX. THE ADVENTURE OF PRINCESS SYLVIA. Mrs. C. F. WILLIAMSON.

X. VELDT AND LAAGER: Tales of the Transvaal. E. S. VALENTINE.

XI. THE NIGGER KNIGHTS. F. NORREYS CONNELL.

XII. A MARRIAGE AT SEA. W. CLARK RUSSELL.

Books for Boys and Girls

A Series of Books by well-known Authors, well illustrated.

THREE-AND-SIXPENCE EACH

THE ICELANDER'S SWORD. By S. BARING GOULD.

TWO LITTLE CHILDREN AND CHING. By EDITH E. CUTHELL.

TODDLEBEN'S HERO. By M. M. BLAKE.

ONLY A GUARD-ROOM DOG. By EDITH E. CUTHELL.

THE DOCTOR OF THE JULIET. By HARRY COLLINGWOOD.

MASTER ROCKAFELLAR'S VOYAGE. By W. CLARK RUSSELL.

SYD BELTON: Or, The Boy who would not go to Sea. By G. MANVILLE FENN.

THE WALLYPUG IN LONDON. By G. E. FARROW.

ADVENTURES IN WALLYPUG LAND. By G. E. FARROW. 5*s.*

The Peacock Library

A Series of Books for Girls by well-known Authors, handsomely bound, and well illustrated.

THREE-AND-SIXPENCE EACH

THE RED GRANGE. By Mrs. MOLESWORTH.

THE SECRET OF MADAME DE MONLUC. By the Author of 'Mdle. Mori.'

OUT OF THE FASHION. By L. T. MEADE.

DUMPS. By Mrs. PARR.

A GIRL OF THE PEOPLE. By L. T. MEADE.

HEPSY GIPSY. By L. T. MEADE. 2*s.* 6*d.*

THE HONOURABLE MISS. By L. T. MEADE.

University Extension Series

A series of books on historical, literary, and scientific subjects, suitable for extension students and home-reading circles. Each volume is complete in itself, and the subjects are treated by competent writers in a broad and philosophic spirit.

Edited by J. E. SYMES, M.A.,
Principal of University College, Nottingham.
Crown 8vo. Price (with some exceptions) 2s. 6d.

The following volumes are ready:—

THE INDUSTRIAL HISTORY OF ENGLAND. By H. DE B. GIBBINS, Litt.D., M.A., late Scholar of Wadham College, Oxon., Cobden Prizeman. *Sixth Edition, Revised. With Maps and Plans.* 3*s.*

A HISTORY OF ENGLISH POLITICAL ECONOMY. By L. L. PRICE, M.A., Fellow of Oriel College, Oxon. *Third Edition.*

PROBLEMS OF POVERTY: An Inquiry into the Industrial Conditions of the Poor. By J. A. HOBSON, M.A. *Fourth Edition.*

VICTORIAN POETS. By A. SHARP.

THE FRENCH REVOLUTION. By J. E. SYMES, M.A.

PSYCHOLOGY. By F. S. GRANGER, M.A. *Second Edition.*

THE EVOLUTION OF PLANT LIFE: Lower Forms. By G. MASSEE. *With Illustrations.*

AIR AND WATER. By V. B. LEWES, M.A. *Illustrated.*

THE CHEMISTRY OF LIFE AND HEALTH. By C. W. KIMMINS, M.A. *Illustrated.*

THE MECHANICS OF DAILY LIFE. By V. P. SELLS, M.A. *Illustrated.*

ENGLISH SOCIAL REFORMERS. By H. DE B. GIBBINS, Litt. D., M.A.

ENGLISH TRADE AND FINANCE IN THE SEVENTEENTH CENTURY. By W. A. S. HEWINS, B.A.

THE CHEMISTRY OF FIRE. The Elementary Principles of Chemistry. By M. M. PATTISON MUIR, M.A. *Illustrated.*

A TEXT-BOOK OF AGRICULTURAL BOTANY. By M. C. POTTER, M.A., F.L.S. *Illustrated.* 3*s.* 6*d.*

THE VAULT OF HEAVEN. A Popular Introduction to Astronomy. By R. A. GREGORY. *With numerous Illustrations.*

METEOROLOGY. The Elements of Weather and Climate. By H. N. DICKSON, F.R.S.E., F.R. Met. Soc. *Illustrated.*

A MANUAL OF ELECTRICAL SCIENCE. By GEORGE J. BURCH, M.A. *With numerous Illustrations.* 3*s.*

THE EARTH. An Introduction to Physiography. By EVAN SMALL, M.A. *Illustrated.*

INSECT LIFE. By F. W. THEOBALD, M.A. *Illustrated.*

ENGLISH POETRY FROM BLAKE TO BROWNING. By W. M. DIXON, M.A.

ENGLISH LOCAL GOVERNMENT. By E. JENKS, M.A., Professor of Law at University College, Liverpool.

THE GREEK VIEW OF LIFE. By G. L. DICKINSON, Fellow of King's College, Cambridge. *Second Edition.*

Social Questions of To-day

Edited by H. DE B. GIBBINS, Litt. D., M.A.

Crown 8vo. 2s. 6d.

A series of volumes upon those topics of social, economic, and industrial interest that are at the present moment foremost in the public mind. Each volume of the series is written by an author who is an acknowledged authority upon the subject with which he deals.

The following Volumes of the Series are ready:—

TRADE UNIONISM—NEW AND OLD. By G. HOWELL. *Second Edition.*

THE CO-OPERATIVE MOVEMENT TO-DAY. By G. J. HOLYOAKE. *Second Edition.*

MUTUAL THRIFT. By Rev. J. FROME WILKINSON, M.A.

PROBLEMS OF POVERTY. By J. A. HOBSON, M.A. *Fourth Edition.*

THE COMMERCE OF NATIONS. By C. F. BASTABLE, M.A., Professor of Economics at Trinity College, Dublin. *Second Edition.*

THE ALIEN INVASION. By W. H. WILKINS, B.A.

THE RURAL EXODUS. By P. ANDERSON GRAHAM.

LAND NATIONALIZATION. By HAROLD COX, B.A.

A SHORTER WORKING DAY. By H. DE B. GIBBINS, D.Litt., M.A., and R. A. HADFIELD, of the Hecla Works, Sheffield.

BACK TO THE LAND: An Inquiry into the Cure for Rural Depopulation. By H. E. MOORE.

TRUSTS, POOLS AND CORNERS. By J. STEPHEN JEANS.

THE FACTORY SYSTEM. By R. W. COOKE-TAYLOR.

THE STATE AND ITS CHILDREN. By GERTRUDE TUCKWELL.

WOMEN'S WORK. By LADY DILKE, Miss BULLEY, and Miss WHITLEY.

SOCIALISM AND MODERN THOUGHT. By M. KAUFMANN.

THE HOUSING OF THE WORKING CLASSES. By E. BOWMAKER.

MODERN CIVILIZATION IN SOME OF ITS ECONOMIC ASPECTS. By W. CUNNINGHAM, D.D., Fellow of Trinity College, Cambridge.

THE PROBLEM OF THE UNEMPLOYED. By J. A. HOBSON, B.A.

LIFE IN WEST LONDON. By ARTHUR SHERWELL, M.A. *Second Edition.*

RAILWAY NATIONALIZATION. By CLEMENT EDWARDS.

WORKHOUSES AND PAUPERISM. By LOUISA TWINING.

UNIVERSITY AND SOCIAL SETTLEMENTS. By W. REASON, M.A.

Classical Translations

Edited by H. F. FOX, M.A., Fellow and Tutor of Brasenose College, Oxford.

ÆSCHYLUS — Agamemnon, Chöephoroe, Eumenides. Translated by LEWIS CAMPBELL, LL.D., late Professor of Greek at St. Andrews. 5*s.*

CICERO—De Oratore I. Translated by E. N. P. MOOR, M.A. 3*s.* 6*d.*

CICERO—Select Orations (Pro Milone, Pro Murena, Philippic II., In Catilinam). Translated by H. E. D. BLAKISTON, M.A., Fellow and Tutor of Trinity College, Oxford. 5*s.*

CICERO—De Natura Deorum. Translated by F. BROOKS, M.A., late Scholar of Balliol College, Oxford. 3*s.* 6*d.*

CICERO DE OFFICIIS. Translated by G. B. GARDENIR, M.A. *Crown 8vo.* 2*s.* 6*d.*

HORACE: THE ODES AND EPODES. Translated by A. GODLEY, M.A., Fellow of Magdalen College, Oxford. 2*s.*

LUCIAN—Six Dialogues (Nigrinus, Icaro-Menippus, The Cock, The Ship, The Parasite, The Lover of Falsehood). Translated by S. T. IRWIN, M.A., Assistant Master at Clifton; late Scholar of Exeter College, Oxford. 3*s.* 6*d.*

SOPHOCLES — Electra and Ajax. Translated by E. D. A. MORSHEAD, M.A., Assistant Master at Winchester. 2*s.* 6*d.*

TACITUS—Agricola and Germania. Translated by R. B. TOWNSHEND, late Scholar of Trinity College, Cambridge. 2*s.* 6*d.*

Oxford Classical Texts.

Crown 8vo.

Messrs. METHUEN are about to publish in conjunction with the Clarendon Press a series of classical texts edited by competent scholars from the best MSS. The first volumes are:—

THUCYDIDIS HISTORIAE, LIBRI I.-IV. By H. STUART JONES. *Paper Covers*, 3s. *Limp Cloth*, 3s. 6d.

PLATONIS OPERA, TOM. I. (TETRALOGIAE I.-II.) By J. BURNET. *Paper Covers*, 5s. *Limp Cloth*, 6s.

LVCRETI CARI DE RERVM NATVRA. By C. BAILEY. *Paper Covers*, 2s. 6d. *Limp Cloth*, 3s.

CORNELII TACITI OPERA MINORA. By H. FURNEAUX. *Paper Covers*, 1s. 6d. *Limp Cloth*, 2s.

AESCHYLI TRAGOEDIAE CUM FRAGMENTIS. By A. SIDGWICK. *Paper Covers*, 3s. *Limp Cloth*, 3s. 6d.

Educational Books

CLASSICAL

THE NICOMACHEAN ETHICS OF ARISTOTLE. Edited with an Introduction and Notes by JOHN BURNET, M.A., Professor of Greek at St. Andrews. *Demy 8vo.* 15s. *net.*

This edition contains parallel passages from the Eudemian Ethics, printed under the text, and there is a full commentary, the main object of which is to interpret difficulties in the light of Aristotle's own rules.

'An edition which reflects every credit upon its author's learning and critical acumen, and which cannot but prove heartily welcome to all classes of Greek scholars.' —*Scotsman.*

'It forms a valuable addition to the existing literature on the subject.' —*Glasgow Herald.*

'We must content ourselves with saying, in conclusion, that we have seldom, if ever, seen an edition of any classical author in which what is held in common with other commentators is so clearly and shortly put, and what is original is (with equal brevity) of such value and interest.' —*Pilot.*

PLAUTI BACCHIDES. Edited with Introduction, Commentary, and Critical Notes by J. M'COSH, M.A. *Fcap. 4to.* 12s. 6d.

A GREEK ANTHOLOGY. Selected by E. C. MARCHANT, M.A., Fellow of Peterhouse, Cambridge, and Assistant Master at St. Paul's School. *Crown 8vo.* 3s. 6d.

PASSAGES FOR UNSEEN TRANSLATION. By E. C. MARCHANT, M.A., Fellow of Peterhouse, Cambridge; and A. M. COOK, M.A., late Scholar of Wadham College, Oxford; Assistant Masters at St. Paul's School. *Crown 8vo.* 3s. 6d.

'We know no book of this class better fitted for use in the higher forms of schools.'—*Guardian.*

TACITI AGRICOLA. With Introduction, Notes, Map, etc. By R. F. DAVIS, M.A., Assistant Master at Weymouth College. *Crown 8vo.* 2s.

TACITI GERMANIA. By the same Editor. *Crown 8vo.* 2*s.*

HERODOTUS: ' EASY ' SELECTIONS. With Vocabulary. By A. C. LIDDELL, M.A. *Fcap. 8vo.* 1*s.* 6*d.*

SELECTIONS FROM THE ODYSSEY. By E. D. STONE, M.A., late Assistant Master at Eton. *Fcap. 8vo.* 1*s.* 6*d.*

PLAUTUS: THE CAPTIVI. Adapted for Lower Forms by J. H. FREESE, M.A., late Fellow of St. John's, Cambridge. 1*s.* 6*d.*

DEMOSTHENES AGAINST CONON AND CALLICLES. Edited with Notes and Vocabulary, by F. DARWIN SWIFT, M.A. *Fcap. 8vo.* 2*s.*

EXERCISES IN LATIN ACCIDENCE. By S. E. WINBOLT, Assistant Master in Christ's Hospital. *Crown 8vo.* 1*s.* 6*d.*

An elementary book adapted for Lower Forms to accompany the shorter Latin primer.

NOTES ON GREEK AND LATIN SYNTAX. By G. BUCKLAND GREEN, M.A., Assistant Master at Edinburgh Academy, late Fellow of St. John's College, Oxon. *Crown 8vo.* 3*s.* 6*d.*

Notes and explanations on the chief difficulties of Greek and Latin Syntax, with numerous passages for exercise.

NEW TESTAMENT GREEK. A Course for Beginners. By G. RODWELL, B.A. With a Preface by WALTER LOCK, D.D., Warden of Keble College. *Fcap. 8vo.* 3*s.* 6*d.*

THE FROGS OF ARISTOPHANES. Translated by E. W. HUNTINGFORD, M.A., Professor of Classics in Trinity College, Toronto. *Cr. 8vo.* 2*s.* 6*d.*

GERMAN

A COMPANION GERMAN GRAMMAR. By H. DE B. GIBBINS, D. Litt., M.A., Assistant Master at Nottingham High School. *Crown 8vo.* 1*s.* 6*d.*

GERMAN PASSAGES FOR UNSEEN TRANSLATION. By E. M'QUEEN GRAY. *Crown 8vo.* 2*s.* 6*d.*

SCIENCE

DAIRY BACTERIOLOGY. A Short Manual for the Use of Students. By DR. ED. VON FREUDENREICH. Translated by J. R. AINSWORTH DAVIS, M.A. *Second Edition, Revised. Crown 8vo.* 2*s.* 6*d.*

OUTLINES OF BIOLOGY. By P. CHALMERS MITCHELL, M.A. *Illustrated. Cr. 8vo.* 6*s.*

A text-book designed to cover the new Schedule issued by the Royal College of Physicians and Surgeons.

A MONOGRAPH OF THE MYXOGASTRES. By GEORGE MASSEE. With 12 Coloured Plates. *Royal 8vo.* 18*s. net.*

'A work much in advance of any book in the language treating of this group of organisms. Indispensable to every student of the Myxogastres.'—*Nature.*

ORNAMENTAL DESIGN FOR WOVEN FABRICS. By C. STEPHENSON, of The Technical College, Bradford, and F. SUDDARDS, of The Yorkshire College, Leeds. With 65 full-page plates. *Demy* 8*vo.* 7*s.* 6*d.*

'The book is very ably done, displaying an intimate knowledge of principles, good taste, and the faculty of clear exposition.'—*Yorkshire Post.*

GENERAL ELEMENTARY SCIENCE. By J. T. DUNN, D.Sc., and V. A. MUNDELLA. With many Illustrations. *Crown* 8*vo.* 3*s.* 6*d.*
[*Methuen's Science Primers.*

THE WORLD OF SCIENCE. Including Chemistry, Heat, Light, Sound, Magnetism, Electricity, Botany, Zoology, Physiology, Astronomy, and Geology. By R. ELLIOTT STEEL, M.A., F.C.S. 147 Illustrations. *Second Edition. Cr.* 8*vo.* 2*s.* 6*d.*

ELEMENTARY LIGHT. By R. E. STEEL. With numerous Illustrations. *Crown* 8*vo.* 4*s.* 6*d.*

VOLUMETRIC ANALYSIS. By J. B. RUSSELL, B.Sc., Science Master at Burnley Grammar School. *Cr.* 8*vo.* 1*s.* 6*d.*

'A collection of useful, well-arranged notes.' —*School Guardian.*

Textbooks of Technology

Edited by PROFESSORS GARNETT and WERTHEIMER.

HOW TO MAKE A DRESS. By J. A. E. WOOD. *Illustrated. Cr.* 8*vo.* 1*s.* 6*d.*

'Though primarily intended for students, Miss Wood's dainty little manual may be consulted with advantage by any girls who want to make their own frocks. The directions are simple and clear, and the diagrams very helpful.'—*Literature.*

CARPENTRY AND JOINERY. By F. C. WEBBER. With many Illustrations. *Cr.* 8*vo.* 3*s.* 6*d.*

'An admirable elementary text-book on the subject.'—*Builder.*

PRACTICAL MECHANICS. By SIDNEY H. WELLS. With 75 Illustrations and Diagrams. *Cr.* 8*vo.* 3*s.* 6*d.*

PRACTICAL PHYSICS. By H. STROUD, D.Sc., M.A., Professor of Physics in the Durham College of Science, Newcastle-on-Tyne. Fully illustrated. *Crown* 8*vo.* 3*s.* 6*d.*

MILLINERY, THEORETICAL, AND PRACTICAL. By Miss HILL, Registered Teacher to the City and Guilds of London Institute. With numerous Diagrams. *Crown* 8*vo.* 2*s.* 6*d.*

PRACTICAL CHEMISTRY. By W. FRENCH, M.A. Part I. With numerous diagrams. *Crown* 8*vo.* 1*s.* 6*d.*

'An excellent and eminently practical little book.'—*Schoolmaster.*

ENGLISH

ENGLISH RECORDS. A Companion to the History of England. By H. E. MALDEN, M.A. *Crown* 8*vo.* 3*s.* 6*d.*

THE ENGLISH CITIZEN: HIS RIGHTS AND DUTIES. By H. E. MALDEN, M.A. 1*s.* 6*d.*

A DIGEST OF DEDUCTIVE LOGIC. By JOHNSON BARKER, B.A. *Crown 8vo.* 2*s.* 6*d.*

A CLASS-BOOK OF DICTATION PASSAGES. By W. WILLIAMSON, M.A. *Second Edition, Cr. 8vo.* 1*s.* 6*d.*

A SHORT STORY OF ENGLISH LITERATURE. By EMMA S. MELLOWS. *Crown 8vo.* 3*s.* 6*d.*

The history of English literature told in a simple style for young students. It is particularly rich in biographical detail, and contains a considerable number of illustrative extracts.

'A lucid and well-arranged account of the growth of English literature.'—*Pall Mall Gazette.*

TEST CARDS IN EUCLID AND ALGEBRA. By D. S. CALDERWOOD, Headmaster of the Normal School, Edinburgh. In three packets of 40, with Answers. 1*s.* Or in three Books, price 2*d.*, 2*d.*, and 3*d.*

THE METRIC SYSTEM. By LEON DELBOS. *Crown 8vo.* 2*s.*

A theoretical and practical guide, for use in elementary schools and by the general reader.

METHUEN'S COMMERCIAL SERIES

Edited by H. DE B. GIBBINS, Litt.D., M.A.

BRITISH COMMERCE AND COLONIES FROM ELIZABETH TO VICTORIA. By H. DE B. GIBBINS, Litt.D., M.A. *Third Edition.* 2*s.*

COMMERCIAL EXAMINATION PAPERS. By H. DE B. GIBBINS, Litt.D., M.A. 1*s.* 6*d.*

THE ECONOMICS OF COMMERCE. By H. DE B. GIBBINS, Litt.D., M.A. 1*s.* 6*d.*

FRENCH COMMERCIAL CORRESPONDENCE. By S. E. BALLY, Master at the Manchester Grammar School. *Second Edition.* 2*s.*

GERMAN COMMERCIAL CORRESPONDENCE. By S. E. BALLY. 2*s.* 6*d.*

A FRENCH COMMERCIAL READER. By S. E. BALLY. *Second Edition.* 2*s.*

COMMERCIAL GEOGRAPHY, with special reference to the British Empire. By L. W. LYDE, M.A. *Second Edition.* 2*s.*

A PRIMER OF BUSINESS. By S. JACKSON, M.A. *Third Ed.* 1*s.* 6*d.*

COMMERCIAL ARITHMETIC. By F. G. TAYLOR, M.A. *Third Edition.* 1*s.* 6*d.*

PRÉCIS WRITING AND OFFICE CORRESPONDENCE. By E. E. WHITFIELD, M.A. 2*s.*

A GUIDE TO PROFESSIONS AND BUSINESS. By H. JONES. 1*s.* 6*d.*

THE PRINCIPLES OF BOOK-KEEPING BY DOUBLE ENTRY. By J. E. B. M'ALLEN, M.A. *Cr. 8vo.* 2*s.*

COMMERCIAL LAW. By W. DOUGLAS EDWARDS. 2*s.*

WORKS BY A. M. M. STEDMAN, M.A.

INITIA LATINA: Easy Lessons on Elementary Accidence. *Fourth Edition. Fcap. 8vo.* 1*s.*

FIRST LATIN LESSONS. *Fifth Edition. Crown 8vo.* 2*s.*

FIRST LATIN READER. With Notes adapted to the Shorter Latin Primer and Vocabulary. *Fourth Edition revised.* 18*mo.* 1*s.* 6*d.*

EASY SELECTIONS FROM CÆSAR. Part I. The Helvetian War. *Second Edition.* 18*mo.* 1*s.*

EASY SELECTIONS FROM LIVY. Part I. The Kings of Rome. 18*mo.* 1*s.* 6*d.*

EASY LATIN PASSAGES FOR UNSEEN TRANSLATION. *Sixth Edition. Fcap.* 8*vo.* 1*s.* 6*d.*

EXEMPLA LATINA. First Lessons in Latin Accidence. With Vocabulary. *Crown* 8*vo.* 1*s.*

EASY LATIN EXERCISES ON THE SYNTAX OF THE SHORTER AND REVISED LATIN PRIMER. With Vocabulary. *Eighth and cheaper Edition, re-written. Crown* 8*vo.* 1*s.* 6*d.* Issued with the consent of Dr. Kennedy.

THE LATIN COMPOUND SENTENCE: Rules and Exercises. *Second Edition. Cr.* 8*vo.* 1*s.* 6*d.* With Vocabulary. 2*s.*

NOTANDA QUAEDAM: Miscellaneous Latin Exercises on Common Rules and Idioms. *Fourth Edition. Fcap.* 8*vo.* 1*s.* 6*d.* With Vocabulary. 2*s.*

LATIN VOCABULARIES FOR REPETITION: Arranged according to Subjects. *Eighth Edition. Fcap.* 8*vo.* 1*s.* 6*d.*

A VOCABULARY OF LATIN IDIOMS. 18*mo. Second Edition.* 1*s.*

STEPS TO GREEK. 18*mo.* 1*s.*

A SHORTER GREEK PRIMER. *Crown* 8*vo.* 1*s.* 6*d.*

EASY GREEK PASSAGES FOR UNSEEN TRANSLATION. *Third Edition Revised. Fcap.* 8*vo.* 1*s.* 6*d.*

GREEK VOCABULARIES FOR REPETITION. Arranged according to Subjects. *Second Edition. Fcap.* 8*vo.* 1*s.* 6*d.*

GREEK TESTAMENT SELECTIONS. For the use of Schools. *Third Edition.* With Introduction, Notes, and Vocabulary. *Fcap.* 8*vo.* 2*s.* 6*d.*

STEPS TO FRENCH. *Fifth Edition.* 18*mo.* 8*d.*

FIRST FRENCH LESSONS. *Fourth Edition Revised. Crown* 8*vo.* 1*s.*

EASY FRENCH PASSAGES FOR UNSEEN TRANSLATION. *Third Edition revised. Fcap.* 8*vo.* 1*s.* 6*d.*

EASY FRENCH EXERCISES ON ELEMENTARY SYNTAX. With Vocabulary. *Second Edition. Crown* 8*vo.* 2*s.* 6*d.* KEY 3*s. net.*

FRENCH VOCABULARIES FOR REPETITION: Arranged according to Subjects. *Eighth Edition. Fcap.* 8*vo.* 1*s.*

SCHOOL EXAMINATION SERIES

EDITED BY A. M. M. STEDMAN, M.A. *Crown* 8*vo.* 2*s.* 6*d.*

FRENCH EXAMINATION PAPERS IN MISCELLANEOUS GRAMMAR AND IDIOMS. By A. M. M. STEDMAN, M.A. *Tenth Edition.*

A KEY, issued to Tutors and Private Students only, to be had on application to the Publishers. *Fourth Edition. Crown* 8*vo.* 6*s. net.*

LATIN EXAMINATION PAPERS IN MISCELLANEOUS GRAMMAR AND IDIOMS. By A. M. M. STEDMAN, M.A. *Tenth Edition.*

KEY (*Fourth Edition*) issued as above. *6s. net.*

GREEK EXAMINATION PAPERS IN MISCELLANEOUS GRAMMAR AND IDIOMS. By A. M. M. STEDMAN, M.A. *Sixth Edition.*

KEY (*Second Edition*) issued as above. *6s. net.*

GERMAN EXAMINATION. PAPERS IN MISCELLANEOUS GRAMMAR AND IDIOMS. By R. J. MORICH, Manchester. *Fifth Edition.*

KEY (*Second Edition*) issued as above. *6s. net.*

HISTORY AND GEOGRAPHY EXAMINATION PAPERS. By C. H. SPENCE, M.A., Clifton College. *Second Edition.*

SCIENCE EXAMINATION PAPERS. By R. E. STEEL, M.A., F.C.S. *In two vols.*

Part I. Chemistry; Part II. Physics.

GENERAL KNOWLEDGE EXAMINATION PAPERS. By A. M. M. STEDMAN, M.A. *Third Edition.*

KEY (*Second Edition*) issued as above. *7s. net.*

EXAMINATION PAPERS IN ENGLISH HISTORY. By J. TAIT WARDLAW, B.A., King's College, Cambridge. *Crown 8vo. 2s. 6d.*

LACE MAKING
AND
COLLECTING

AN ELEMENTARY HANDBOOK

BY

A. PENDEREL MOODY

CASSELL AND COMPANY, LTD.
LONDON, NEW YORK, TORONTO AND MELBOURNE
MCMIX

PLATE I.

TIE END OF BRUGES LACE.

Frontispiece

PREFACE

" But when I bought it they told me it was Brussels —Swiss Brussels," she said plaintively.

"That explains everything," the lace expert replied. "You bought it in Switzerland and paid five guineas for it. The price was iniquitous, of course, but that is the name they have given it, and by the name you were misled."

"And it is really not worth the quarter of that sum ? "

"See," said the expert. "Here is a piece of genuine applied Brussels. Do you see how the weaving threads cross and return, each time leaving a firm edge behind ? Compare it with your own. The designs are much alike, for the Swiss work has taken the Brussels for its model, but look at the edges of the pattern. The texture is just ordinary lawn attached by chain stitch to the machine made net foundation. The edges are raw where the material has been cut away, and are ready to fray out and in time drop away altogether."

"I see now, but I wonder that I never noticed it before," rejoined the would-be collector, and then she looked up thoroughly puzzled : "Now that I know my lace is only an applied material, how am I to tell that it is not Carrickmacross ? "

"Capital!" exclaimed the other. "It was quick of you to think of that. The rules relating to the classification of laces are full of exceptions and tiny differences, so that unless one works by comparison, noting every divergence of detail, it is impossible not to make mistakes. You have recognised that Swiss Brussels and Carrickmacross are akin, the truth being that the first may be called the parent of the Irish lace. The better quality of Swiss Brussels is finished off with a firmer edge—oversewn by the needle in place of the tambour stitch—and the Carrickmacross of early days so faithfully reproduced this edge that the lace could be handed down from mother to daughter, none the worse for wear."

"The new pupil has just come," interrupted a small embryo lace maker in a blue pinafore.

"I wish you had a class for lace collectors," said the stranger, as she wrapped up the unlucky purchase. "If you would explain all the little differences——"

The expert laughed, and so the sentence was unfinished.

"It would be time and money wasted," she declared, "when you think of all the many books there are to learn from."

"I have books—some of the very best, I am told," was the reply; "but they confuse me by the great variety of laces shown, as well as by the technical expressions. I feel I want to know the subject better before I can really understand them. In the last ten minutes I seem to have learnt more than

I should have found out for myself in a week's reading!"

The expert knew exactly how she felt, having passed through much the same experience herself, but in earlier days when the books relating to lace might have been counted on the fingers of one hand.

"There are no short cuts to the art of lace collecting," she affirmed, "but there is one road which I believe to be the most direct."

"And that is?"

"A practical knowledge—no matter how elementary—of lace making itself."

The blue pinafore again appeared at the door: "Will you please come down? for the new lady wants to ask you what lace she wants to learn."

Then ensued another conversation, for questions had to be answered which called for many details about the various laces. Which was the easiest? Which the quickest to learn? The kind most suitable for a class of village girls?

"We could have had everything ready for you, had we only known which lace you would decide upon," apologised the expert when at last the pupil was ready to settle down to her lesson.

"But how could I find out these things for myself?" asked the newcomer. "If only there was a book to tell one all the little things!"

The expert went back to her interrupted task of answering the morning's letters.

She put on one side a note containing queries very similar to those just brought forward by the new pupil. She puzzled over the unrecognisable description of an unnamed lace of which she was requested to quote the value, and finally came to a standstill over an Australian correspondent :

"I leave the choice of selection to you," the letter ran, "for I have no means of finding out which lace is most suitable for eyes not over young."

The expert put down the letter and considered.

"I will write a little book," she decided ; "something quite cheap, so as to be within the reach of all. It shall teach the first steps in some of the well known laces. There cannot be an exhaustive treatment of any one kind, but it must set the reader so far on her road that she may be able to see clearly what lies before her and the greater things that wait to be attained."

The expert smiled as she recalled the downcast looks of her last visitor. "There must be hints on how to distinguish between the real, the false, and—most difficult of all—the faked lace ; also the little book must show that the results of centuries of hard work can no more be grasped in a few lessons than they can be summed up in one volume."

LACE MAKING AND COLLECTING

PART I

CHAPTER I

In dealing with a subject so full of historical interest as real lace, there is always a great temptation to hark back to those early events which were instrumental in spreading its development.

From Italy, the cradle of the Arts, we are able to follow the exodus of a small band of refugees, who, fleeing from religious persecution in their native land, found new homes in districts round Geneva, while others striking westward settled in Lyons or Puy de Dôme. The intercourse between the Netherlands and Switzerland, drawn ever closer by the Puritans, naturally led to the lace made by these early emigrants quickly finding its way into Flanders.

There is plenty of research work waiting for the lace historian who would give up the time to tracing the course of these early laces. That Honiton, Brussels and Point de Flandres all owe their origin to the influence of north Italian workers is clearly traced, not only by existing records but also by the very similar methods of working. How does it come then that, to this day, the lace makers of central France make use of the methods employed by the Neapolitans, but have never adopted the easy flowing designs of Milan and Genoa? Evidently there was a second migration of lace makers from further south, who either left at a different period or kept apart from their fellow-craftsmen of Lombardy. It is certain that years elapsed before the two distinct classes of lace came to be made side by side in Flanders.

There is a great difference even in the manner of working this second lace; the bobbins are held differently and the pillows are not shaped alike. It is only of late years that an attempt has been made to unite the separate styles and out of them to form a new departure. The experiment may be seen in some of the Russian and German bobbin laces, but so far has not become really distinctive.

It is more difficult to trace the origin of the Needle Point laces, because in one style or another they seem to have been something of a natural growth throughout Europe. Legend has it that the work originated in the Far East and spread northwards passing through Greece and Rome.

In those remote days it is certain that a kind of lace was made which was the forerunner of Filet Brodé, specimens of which netted lace have been found in the tombs of Egypt, together with pieces of drawn thread work. In some of these early laces such as the Drawn Thread, it is difficult to determine whether it should not rather be classed under the heading of embroidery.

At times the threads are entirely absorbed into a foundation and covered over with needle stitches until no vestige of them is to be seen, but Venetian lace is minus even this slight groundwork, so that when *it* is under discussion no doubt can remain, it is *lace* pure and simple, at once most beautiful and most costly. The entire fabric is built up of needle stitches and its value is increased by raised ornamentations covering the original groundwork. There are two kinds, of which one is very fine and delicate, called Rose Point from the little star-like rings which join the brides together for the ground (bride is a term commonly used for a bar, and should be given the French pronunciation); while the other, Gros Point de Venise, is, as its name implies, a lace made on a heavier scale. Some of the best coarse crochet designs have been taken from it. This lace was in great request for rich Church vestments, and the bold design allowed scope for a great deal of what in carving would be called "relief" work, and was effective even at a considerable distance. The leading features of this Gros Point have much in common with not only relief carving, but also sculpture, and follow in design the classical Italian forms. The value has always been very great, and naturally such ornate work would be beyond the means of any but the most wealthy. A cheaper lace was produced on similar lines, but composed of the groundwork only. This was known as Flat Point, and was not confined to Venice, but was made in Italy and Spain, also at a later date in France, from whence it has reached Belgium, and latterly Ireland, where, under the name of Youghal Point, a well-made lace is shown of modern design. Although the Flat Point was so much less costly, it must still have been beyond the reach of the middle classes, and quite out of the question for ordinary use in the churches. A cheaper lace being needed, hand-woven tape was then made to serve instead of the needle-ground. The open spaces of the design were filled in by the same fancy stitches as were used for the better lace, and by raising the edges of the tape by a cord, a very clever effect of the original model was attained at much less cost. This tape lace was the forerunner of the "Braid" or "Needle Point Lace" of the last reign.

The reader may have noticed that in introducing the Needle laces the expression *Needle Point* is used.

The term *Point* has been found confusing by many people, although no difficulty arises abroad where the double application of the term is clearly understood.

In England, perhaps because the expression has become so closely associated with one particular Needle lace, it is supposed by some to exclude Bobbin lace altogether.

Reference to any good lace book will, however, bring to light numbers of instances where it is used in application to either method. Two well-known laces of either kind should at once settle this vexed question :

Bobbin Laces	Point de Flandres.
	Point de Milan (Punto di Milano).
Needle Point	Point de Venise.
	Youghal, or Irish Point.

In the English Midlands village workers always speak of the true Buckinghamshire lace as Point lace, but although in error they will often call the Bedfordshire Maltese, *Buckingham*—much of it being made in that county—no one would dream of speaking of the latter as Maltese Point.

We have already noticed that the lace of those two bands of early Italian refugees was dissimilar, and this is a further argument in favour of that hypothesis, the Pillow Point laces following the Lombardy methods, while the Bedfordshire Maltese taken from South Italy to Malta and thence to England claims close connection with the laces of Puy de Dôme, and might easily be mistaken for some of that work.

Let us look up the word "Point" in the French dictionary. Among its several meanings are "a stitch" and "a hole." According to the dictionary there is no reason why the word should not be equally applicable for either lace. The lace maker abroad, however, distinguishes between the two different meanings, in the case of Bobbin lace using the word to denote a *réseau* of net or holes, for Needle lace to explain its foundation of separate stitches.

Although the word "Point" is not used in conjunction with the name of a complete Peasant lace, it comes into the description of particular stitches employed. Point de Mariage, the Torchon stitch, is one of many instances.

In those provinces where both Needle and Pillow laces bear the same name it is usual to put the prefix Bobbin or Needle before the word Point, and so save confusion. Only a want of knowledge would cause mistakes in other cases, and an examination of the lace would quickly show the difference.

Up to now we have been speaking of laces as being divided into two classes. These will again be divided and subdivided almost without end, but with the space at our disposal it will be impossible to deal with more than some half-dozen classes. From the selection chosen the student should have no difficulty in continuing her studies from the more advanced books upon the subject, and best of all, by careful examination of all the lace she handles.

The laces that have been chosen for discussion all

belong to well-known types; the Pillow laces in particular touch lightly upon the foundations of three distinct methods, comprising the key to all other varieties. The student must not, however, imagine for a moment that by learning the fundamental principles of one type she becomes proficient in all its sister designs, for each lace carries its own individuality, and has hard and fast rules relating to its construction. It is easy enough to make a simple braid, to turn corners and put in a grounding, but quite another matter to make a piece of fine Bruges lace bear its stamp so clearly that no one would mistake it for Brussels or Devon. The pattern might in special instances be identical, but small differences of treatment would be employed to give a different touch, something almost intangible at times, and which, like some of the minute differences between certain kinds of old china, are to be *felt* more easily than described.

It is of course much to the student's advantage that the framework of certain laces is so exactly similar that the same preliminary instructions can be used. For this reason, and to save repetition, all such stitches are taught separately in our instructions, while individual treatment of each lace is taken first broadly to help the collector, and afterwards individually, noting the special intricacies of each pattern, for the service of the lace maker.

Perhaps some may find pleasure in trying several different kinds of lace, a valuable assistance if there is any idea of taking up the work professionally, useful for the teacher and also for the work of renovating. It is different, however, if the lace maker wishes to earn a living at her pillow, for then she should take one lace and keep to it.

It is a common error to say that Torchon is the easiest, and therefore the best lace to start upon. It requires a particular touch, a rather heavy handling that will ruin anyone for better work if kept at it too long. Each lace has its own peculiarities, and a perfect knowledge will take time to acquire, but with practice will come the increase of speed upon which the profits depend so largely.

A vital question for the would-be professional lace maker is, "Does lace making pay?" and that leads to another question in return, "What do you require as your living wage?"

In the present day plenty of work is to be had for the girls of the ordinary working classes. Wages for house servants rise steadily and the demand is generally greater than the supply. In the large towns, factories, shops and dressmakers employ large numbers of women workers, and although wages differ largely in different localities we ought to be well on the safe side in striking an average of 12s. the week for the earnings of this class.

It needs a very skilful lace maker to make as much, keeping the same number of hours and disposing of her work in the same way. Even if the girl had a private connection and was able to obtain full retail price for her lace, she would be unlikely to exceed that sum.

This then is the reason why lace makers are only to be found in villages or small country towns where there are few such openings. It must be remembered, however, that the girl who earns six or eight shillings a week in the country is often more comfortably off than her sister in the large town.

Cottages are still to be had in the lace districts for

two and three shillings a week, and the cost of living eked out by supplies from the garden can be wonderfully small. Another great advantage is that it is home work and can be done at odd times. The married women, without neglecting the home, can add considerably to the husband's wage in their spare time, also the old people keep their work going, often up to the very last.

Lace, then, is work for the country woman rather than for the town dweller.

Let us turn next to the workers of another class for whom there are, unfortunately, fewer chances of employment.

The well-educated gentlewoman must take the various openings that are possible, and find for herself the average wage they yield. She must not forget to debit that wage with the cost of the special training required for the teaching, secretarial, or artistic professions. Would it be an exaggeration to suggest 25s. the week as the average? About double the wage of the workgirl, with something like double the cost of living, and withal an appearance to be kept up.

In such a case this would seem a very decided reply in the negative to the question, "Does lace making pay as a profession for the more highly educated classes?"

Perhaps it is a happy thing after all that lace making should be unprofitable for the educated worker. It is needed by the villagers of many a poor agricultural district; it is splendid work for a cripple girl, or one too delicate for service, and all these need the co-operation of the more highly trained woman if their work is to succeed.

The higher class worker must earn her wage by skill

in such departments as *designing*, which the village girl is quite incapable of. It will need her quick wits and her good taste to keep the workers employed on up-to-date patterns, and she should be able to find a better market for the goods than they could possibly do for themselves. As a teacher, the village worker is generally a failure. We all know that teaching has at last come to be recognised as something of a science, and even in the very heart of a lace district pupils will quickly discover that many sixpences will have to be paid away to picturesque old Betty at the cottage, before as much knowledge is painfully extracted from her as the trained teacher would give in a couple of lessons.

"I larned her," said an old body in Bedfordshire, "I larned her best part every day for a month, but bless you, she didn't larn nothing." That was the old lady who told her pupil that she could not work slowly because "it scat her brains" if she had to think what she was doing!

With the growth of village industries, influenced perhaps a little by the "back to the land" movement, and also by the attention this craft is at last receiving from the educational authorities, the prospects of the trained teacher are becoming brighter.

In choosing a profession it is necessary to look beyond the present to gauge whether the work is likely to be of a lasting character, and whether it may possibly increase in value.

At present a great number are taking lessons just while lace making happens to be a popular fashion, but the lace teacher has to look beyond these lessons in order to see what regular work the future may have in store. Both at home and also in the colonies, lace making is at last being taken seriously, and who shall tell what the next few years may bring forth!

The more highly educated worker has a wide choice before her when she decides upon making it her career.

What we may call "Mechanical" lace making she will leave to others—if she is going in for industry work she will train thoroughly in the one particular lace required; if she is to go to the colonies a wider knowledge, including several kinds, may be more useful. For a teacher in a large town a general knowledge will enable her to continue the lessons of pupils who wish to carry on instructions already commenced in Italy or Venice.

It is practically impossible for one person to be proficient in every branch, and even if she confines herself entirely to the study of one of the following classes she will find infinite variety as well as much research work without going beyond it.

BOBBIN-MADE PEASANT LACES

These include the patterns of many counties, some of which have died out entirely, and are well worth reviving. This is a study very little touched upon at present, and gives a wide field for investigation. None of the Peasant laces are very expensive, therefore the work is admirably adapted for a colonial industry. Fine laces very like the needle-point Reticella are to be found in pictures of the sixteenth and seventeenth centuries, but these are exceptional nowadays when the work is usually strong and rather heavy, suitable for trimming all kinds of linen articles.

PLATE II

1
2
3
4
5
6

1. TROU-TROU.
2. TORCHON EDGING.
3. CLUNY INSERTION.
4. CLUNY EDGING.
5. BUCKS PEA PATTERN.
6. BUCKS FAN PATTERN.

To face page 10.

ENGLISH TROLLY LACES

are now confined almost entirely to the fine net laces, though the antique varieties were most elaborate. The revival of the old is well-nigh impossible, since the fine thread is no longer obtainable. Also the lace would not fetch the very heavy price that would be required for it. The modern worker would have to confine her efforts to the Midland laces principally, which with the more difficult pricking of patterns would leave her very little spare time. A homely old name for this class is "thread" lace—a term one may still hear used.

In connection with Trolly, the best openings would seem to rest with the management of a local industry, or engagement as a teacher.

The Trolly lace industries are at present so very much in the hands of charitable societies, that it is impossible to predict whether the work would once again become prosperous, if put upon a purely business footing. One thing seems clearly shown, which is that an unequal competition exists between the philanthropic societies and the trade, which, for the present, prevents the sale of this lace becoming general.

It is a pity for the country that such should be the case, but it is an *impasse* that has been brought about solely by the success that has deservedly crowned the efforts of those who freely gave their money to revive what was practically a dying industry.

Influential patronesses lent their houses for lace sales, and brought their friends to buy. Most of the management was honorary, and with the added help of donations it was possible to sell the lace at a price that allowed no margin for the ordinary expenses of the tradesman.

There is hardly a draper's shop in London where one may not find a good assortment of Valenciennes, Cluny and Torchon, but a whole day may be wasted in the search for a single specimen of Buckingham.

The London tradesman is obliged to push the sale of those laces which allow of his making a reasonable profit, without subjecting his prices to unfair criticism.

Time alone can prove whether the lace industries of the Midlands are of a forced growth which will fall away again as interest and subscriptions slacken. Meanwhile it is wisest for the professional worker to watch carefully before risking capital in this direction.

BRAID AND SPRIG LACES

There could hardly be a better choice for the teacher. This class includes inexpensive as well as the very best Pillow laces, and gives scope for much artistic skill in the arrangement of stitches or designs. Of the English varieties, Devon or Honiton is the only Sprig lace, and it stands high above the Trolly laces. The subject has been treated so fully in another book* devoted solely to the one lace that only a few general notes need be given here. During the Victorian era the trade fell away very greatly, crushed, first, by the introduction of machine net, and later by the want of interest shown to the lace trade in general.

Successful efforts have been made to bring about a revival, and at the same time to improve upon the badly constructed patterns which have been general for more than half a century. A few years ago not more than five

* "Devon Pillow Lace: Its History and How to Make It." A. Penderel Moody.

fancy fillings were in common use, but with the help of County Council classes beautiful old stitches have been re-taught, of which the following are specially charming: Pearl, Blossom, Double Point, and Toad-in-the-Hole. Of these, all but Blossom may be found in Antique Point d'Angleterre.

NEEDLE POINT LACES

Ireland is much ahead of England for these, and its lace includes Needle-run Limerick, also Tambour (made sometimes with needle fillings and again with the Tambour hook), Youghal, or Irish Rose Point, which is the best lace produced but too expensive to be very generally known. Irish Crochet is, if anything, too well known, and has been much copied abroad. Carrickmacross is made in two varieties, Guipure and Appliqué. The last generally introduces fillings of Limerick Needle Point.

There is a good demand for lessons in any of these laces, but one would not be prepared to advise on taking up the actual making as a profession. Many poor Irish ladies certainly support themselves by such work, but there always appears to be an element of charity in the way their lace is disposed of. From time to time one hears of a good opening for a manageress, but naturally those applicants in the neighbourhood have the best chance of securing the post.

If these notes on the possibility of finding work appear to be somewhat vague, the excuse must be offered that the lace revival, although it has come in with great force, is still young. As yet it is difficult to prophesy how far it may extend. Those who are now taking up the profession are doing something akin to pioneer work. They can look back a few years and see what serious obstacles have been overcome, and they can look forward hopefully to the future. What they cannot do is to point to large incomes realised, for one reason that there has not been sufficient time, for another because the competition with foreign goods has been and is a serious disadvantage.

The lace expert who combines the sale of antique and foreign laces with those of her own country, always finds that the profit on the first is double or treble that realised by the home work. Here again we may stand at the commencement of a new era, for tariff reform applied to the importation of foreign lace would make an extraordinary difference to the lives of many English workers.

The opening offered to women by the restoration of old laces is dealt with in a separate chapter.

CHAPTER II

PEASANT LACES

The word Torchon is used in France for a loose knitted dish-cloth, and applies really to anything that can be quickly squeezed dry in the hand. Probably the name was first given to the lace on account of its needing no more than ordinary care in washing, and with no idea of suggesting its secondary value.

For years many beautiful Torchons have been made in Italy, France and Belgium. More recently Germany, Russia and Bavaria have increased their output of the same lace, and coming down to our own time we find it being made in China, Ceylon, India, Madagascar, Rhodesia, Zululand, and even in the little island of St. Helena. The lace made in our own colonies mostly finds its market on the spot, but the work from China and parts of India is a serious menace to the European trade. We hear of women working twelve hours a day for twopence in the East; in some parts of Russia the pay is almost as small, and the underselling falls hard upon the peasant workers nearer home, whose pay decreases in proportion with the competition. There is always a good sale for the lace, and to comply with the demand for a cheap article, much of the thread used by the women is of the very poorest description. If some of the very cheapest Torchon is weighed, and then balanced against the weight of a really durable flax, it will be found that the cost of the good thread is almost equal to that of the cheap lace, including the making.

It has been frequently stated by experts dealing with the question of sweated trades that shoddy materials invariably mean underpayment; with the lace trade this is certainly the case.

At a recent exhibition a small cloth edged with Torchon and made in St. Helena was shown side by side with a very similar lace marked at nearly half the price.

It was rather interesting to note how many people examined first one and then the other, one even returning to ask if the good lace had not been made with silk, so different was the texture in appearance. Slowly, very slowly, and greatly through the efforts of such societies as "The Home Arts and Industries," the public are beginning to show more interest in the making of the goods they buy. To a certain class "cheapness" must and will always be the first attraction; to the thinking public the durability of the work, and the conditions under which it has been made.

In one or two of the Midland counties a little Torchon lace is made, and this is also the case in scattered districts of Scotland and Ireland, but the output is too small to be of serious consideration.

It may be advisable to consider whether the lace is really worth making before starting upon it, rather than upon one more costly and less common.

If it is needed for some village industry, not to be the sole support of the worker, but an employment for odd hours in the summer, or for the long winter evenings, then one could hardly choose better.

The lace is made of repeats following closely upon each

other, and the patterns allow of very little variation. Once the worker knows how to do one repeat, she may go on and make yards of it without any further instruction. Any teacher will understand what a great advantage this is, if there are many pupils and little time for teaching.

The pay is small, and the durable lace has the disadvantage of being easily compared with patterns advertised in sale catalogues, some of which work out as low as two shillings and ninepence for about forty-eight hours' work, thread provided by the worker.

Against this one must remember that the thoughtful buyers are every day becoming more numerous, that the knowledge of lace making is spreading among the upper classes, and where there is already knowledge, appreciation of good work and good materials must result in producing the proper wage.

The utility of Torchon is very great. There is no stronger lace for trimming children's frocks and pinafores. It is strong enough even worked in fine thread to wear as long as most lingerie. The heavier makes are invaluable for tea-cloths, pillow-covers, and all kinds of household linen. No other variety exactly takes its place unless we include the less well-known Peasant laces which will be equally useful for house linen, though hardly fine enough for personal wear.

Cluny is very similar to Torchon, and rather more decorative. The name has been adopted for this special lace quite recently, and has no real relationship to the particular patterns, many of which are quite old. During a recent revival it is said that some lace experts chose to copy certain Peasant laces from the Cluny Museum, and so first spoke of the revived lace as "Cluny" lace.

Modern Cluny has included the characteristics of most Peasant laces, and, like Torchon, owes its origin to the early Bone laces which for six centuries, at least, have been in use in Italy and many other countries. The oldest of these were the Plaited laces, so like the valuable Needle Point "Punto-in-Aria" in design that at a distance it is difficult to tell them apart.

In many antique Venetian and Italian coverlets these two laces are to be found together. The Bobbin lace was the more quickly made, and helped no doubt in bringing a large piece of work to a quicker termination.

In nearly all this early lace the pattern consisted very much of plaited bars which called for only a small expenditure in pins. We hear of thorns and fish bones being used to take their place—a substitute which could not have been very satisfactory, as we may guess from the many dodges in construction by means of which the worker managed to evade the difficulty.

It is only comparatively recently that net grounds employed pins to separate the stitches, and even to-day most of the foreign *réseaux* are made without.

To the collector these old Bone laces are full of interest. They are found upon much of the old embroidery, with drawn thread work and as a finish to Filet Brodé.

Taken as a whole, they are not yet properly appreciated, and so the collector, if not first in the field, has still a very good chance of getting together an interesting collection with a very small expenditure.

Plate II. shows some very simple patterns of Torchon and Cluny, which receive further attention among the instructions. Plate III. shows the development of these simple laces into something more elaborate. The example

PLATE III.

1

2

3

PEASANT LACES.

1. TYPICAL CLUNY.
2. PLAITED LACE.
3. REVIVAL OF AN ITALIAN STYLE.

at the top is a simple Cluny which may be seen at almost any large draper's. The middle lace shows a great advance, or we might rather call it a throw-back, for the design is very old and shows off the early style of "Plaited" lace to perfection. Designs very similar to this, and also the third lace, were in general use during the reign of Queen Elizabeth.

Of late years there has been an English revival in the making of gold and silver laces. The industry is a very old one, older on the Continent than in England.

Some of the most beautiful specimens are in the Cluny Museum. In this country we have a few old pieces to show, but it is interesting to examine the specimen which edges Queen Victoria's coronation train, shown in Kensington Palace. The pattern of this gold lace is almost identical with the Torchon on Plate II. Gold and silver lace has generally been made on Torchon lines and of no great depth as a rule. Sometimes it has been heavily jewelled, and often sequins or gold beads have been introduced. It seems odd to include such lace under the heading of Peasant laces, but all belong to the same style of design which with small local differences are to be found in nearly every country where lace is made at all. The term "Peasant" lace is most generally given to rather coarse work, which, being made in closely recurring repeats like the Torchon, can be produced in great quantities by peasant workers who would be unequal to making lace which required the exercise of artistic judgment.

Peasant laces all belong to the *Trolly* class, a name of Flemish origin, which is descriptive of work done all round the pillow, and without any break, quite different from Honiton, Brussels and Italian laces made in sprays or short repeats and afterwards joined together. Trolly lace is always worked with the background and pattern in one, and includes Lille, Buckingham, Valenciennes and Bedfordshire, many of the Flemish laces, and some of the Italian.

With the exception of such fine work as Mechlin, Lille and some Buckingham, it is always a cheap kind of lace, partly because it is easily picked up by workers who might fail with more varied patterns, but mainly because the designs are so easily copied by machine that detection is a matter of real difficulty to most people. In England the only true Peasant lace is the Bedfordshire Maltese, which, started on the Maltese lines, has run into the Torchon, and also encroached upon the Buckinghamshire. Very little attention has been paid to this English lace, and the work, never very good, was at a low ebb during the latter half of the nineteenth century. At last there are signs that it is reviving, and the most hopeful sign of all is that it is receiving the encouragement of the trade. Left to themselves the village workers use inaccurate patterns, or introduce stitches out of character with the lace, which degrades it to what we may call "mongrel."

The illustration, Plate IV., shows the great advance that has been made through the interest shown in this branch of the lace trade by Messrs. Rose of Bedford.

The collar is in every detail true to the characteristics of good Bedfordshire. The border may be seen in many patterns, but this particular design stands out from most of its fellows on account of the infinitely better arrangement of the central decoration.

It is somewhat rare to find so much drawing in a piece

PLATE IV.

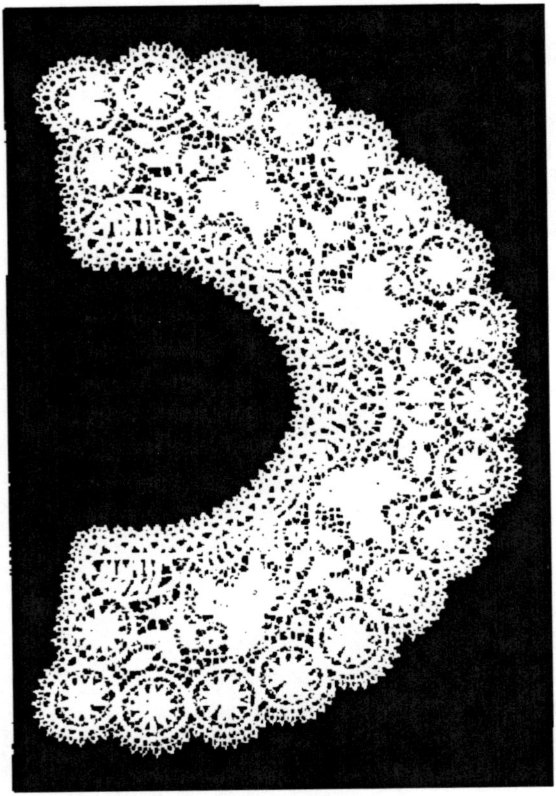

BEDFORDSHIRE MALTESE COLLAR.
The property of Messrs. Rose, Bedford.

To face page 20.

of Bedfordshire lace, and the collar example may be greeted as a decided advance. A very little time ago Bedfordshire lace was practically not worn by the upper classes; the use of a better thread and improved designs has already done much to alter this. What is needed now is to find some means of making the better lace more widely known, and so to remove the prejudice that certainly existed against the poorer work. Honiton lace is fighting the same battle, but is more severely handicapped by the larger price of the artistic work. Bedfordshire lace, on the other hand, is very little more expensive when made well, and very charming little edgings may be bought at little more than the cost of good Torchon.

FINE TROLLY LACES

At one time a very great deal of Trolly lace was made not only in England but also in Wales and Scotland. The Midlands were especially famous for it, but Suffolk, Dorset and Wiltshire produced equally dainty little edgings, each county showing a certain individuality in treatment. At one time the name Trolly was applied as often to the wider and more costly laces as to the narrow ones bought by pedlars (who carried it far afield in their baskets), and therefore the distinguishing name "Baby" lace was given to those of less importance and value. It is astonishing to hear of the long journeys made by some of these pedlars. An old lady in Penzance remembered how in her young days a man used to call at the house twice a year with a basket full of Buckinghamshire Trolly. Good profits were to be made then, when two guineas' worth would be used for a baby's cap alone.

The Trolly lace of Devon and Suffolk was very similar,

in both cases keeping closely to the same Flemish origin. The decoration consisted of rings outlined with a heavy gimp thread, and the lace took its name from the number of rings or holes.

Thirteen-hole Trolly was made near Exmouth within the memory of old lace makers, still alive, but has since died out entirely.

In Dorset and Wiltshire simple but very pretty little edgings were made, which were an adaptation of Valenciennes with Torchon.

The Scotch lace was also in the Torchon style, and is still made in Pitsligo and a few other districts.

The Midland counties, Buckinghamshire, Northamptonshire, Oxford and Bedford, have, from very early days, been the great centre of the Trolly industry, and lace may still be found there which has the same *réseau* as genuine Flemish Trolle Kant. For some years several societies have been at work in Buckinghamshire reviving the industry, which had fallen away during the past sixty years. This special county seems to have received the most attention, and with pardonable zeal the ladies engaged in this interesting work appear to have gathered together Trolly patterns from far and near, renaming all that attracted their fancy by the one title of "Buckingham."

It was rather a case of being first in the field, but so thoroughly have the patterns been absorbed that already it would be a matter of some difficulty to extricate them, even if any purpose could be served by doing so. The only real disadvantage lies with the collector, who is put to much trouble in tracing the origin of many specimens. The last two examples of Plate II. are typical "Baby"

PLATE V.

1

2

1. BUCKINGHAMSHIRE POINT.
2. OLD NORTHAMPTONSHIRE.

To face page 23

edgings, and may be found in any of the Midland counties. The pattern at the foot of illustration V. is pure Northamptonshire, and a very fine old specimen. It differs from true antique Bucks by having a rather prim, close design. The solid diamond forms, made in cloth-stitch, also belong to this county, as do the little ornamental dots called leadworks.

Northamptonshire lace is often to be found spotted with these leadworks, sometimes singly, but more often in sets of four together. This piece of lace was shown to a lace expert in Belgium, who felt convinced that it must be French work, though he was at a loss to say where it could have been made. A similar style of lace in coarser thread, and without the fine net, has been made in the lace districts of Puy de Dôme and also in the Pyrenees.

Much of the Northamptonshire lace has a French touch about it, no doubt resulting from the influence of Huguenot workers. Another French characteristic lies in the angle of the net, which is identical with that used for Valenciennes.

The lace immediately above this piece of Northamptonshire bears a certain resemblance to it, and is also French in its style of design. The small sprigs on the net are very misshapen, but nevertheless we can decipher a stem and three leaves, probably a retrograde development of the fleur de lys.

The lace this design most closely resembles is the Lille, to which it is closely allied.

Now opens up a new field of research by which we can discover for ourselves how lace found its way from Bruges to Lille, and also to England, was gradually adapted to French design in Lille and introduced again in its altered form to the Midlands. This will account, therefore, for two styles of what is now called Buckingham lace, the French and a light floral pattern not quite unlike the Appliqué Brussels of the early nineteenth century.

The one style of Buckinghamshire lace which can never be disputed is this last, but the piece under discussion may be classified as also belonging to this county.

A special feature of this specimen is the finer mesh of the net in the lower part of the pattern. It is rather rare to find this in England, and abroad it is more frequently found among such of the Needle laces as Alençon and Burano.

In the Midlands the wider Trolly laces are still spoken of as "Point Lace" by the old workers, and in some districts very heavy bobbins, weighted with leaden rings, are known by them as "French bobbins," a further instance of foreign influence in the county. Oxfordshire lace has little pattern, and is rapidly becoming extinct. Bedfordshire does not come under the heading of a Trolly lace, and so is treated of elsewhere.

A hundred years ago wedding veils and deep capes were made of Buckinghamshire lace, the pattern worked like Chantilly in narrow lengths, and joined invisibly by the needle. Such large pieces of work have been given up of recent years, and a flounce of eight or nine inches is as elaborate as anything that is made. As a rule it is difficult to buy ready-made Bucks lace deeper than three or four inches, and the wider laces are not altogether popular, a complaint being that for evening wear the new lace is not sufficiently decorative. This is perhaps true, though it is a fault that time will mend; on the other

PLATE VI.

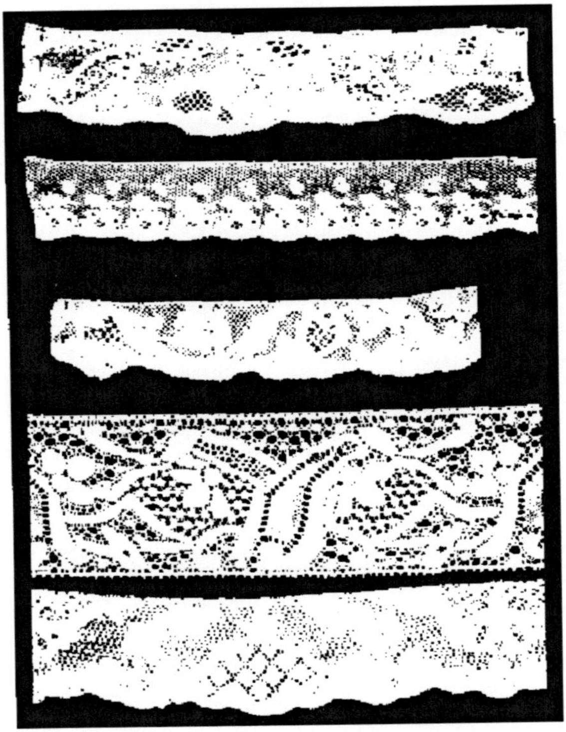

1. ANTIQUE BRUSSELS.
2 MECHLIN.
3. BINCHE.
4. DENTELLE DE LA SORCIÈRE.
5. ANTIQUE MECHLIN.

To face page 25.

hand, the infinite variety of the narrow laces, together with their strength, which will resist even the ravages of the modern laundry, make it a good investment. For handkerchiefs and fine lingerie it is charming, and in price the edgings are much the same as Valenciennes.

Plate VI. shows a set of laces which, although made in the Trolly style, are too elaborate to be actually classed as such, unless we except the simple little Mechlin, second on the plate. A good deal of Mechlin has been made in England, and is sold as such. There is always, however, one point of difference, which lies in the making of the net.

True Mechlin has a Brussels *réseau*, the threads forming the net being joined by a double stitch, while the English-made lace always has the Bucks ground. This particular pattern has the true net, and dates from the latter part of the eighteenth century. The fifth sample of lace is also Mechlin, but of an early date, and a style that has ceased to exist, though the modern lace No. 4 may have been influenced by it.

The local name for this new piece is *Dentelle de la Sorcière*. It is a revival in a new form of several very old Flemish stitches, one of which is Point de Neige, but it differs from Binche, Mechlin, and several other old laces by having no gimp or outlining thread.

The third example is Binche, of which we have just spoken. This is one of the many beautiful narrow laces that may still be found on old linen cravats. A fine old Valenciennes of the same period is sometimes confounded with it, but excepting in design the two are not really alike. Binche has always the outlining thread, which is absent in the other, also the ground is less elaborate, often less covered with detail, and therefore the design shows out more boldly.

Some of the very fine antique Valenciennes are so close both in design and weaving, that the decorative appearance is lost by excess of labour.

The last piece of lace to be mentioned is the first on the page, and is early eighteenth century Brussels. It has been included in the set as being worked on Trolly lines, and so has resulted in a very different lace from the Antique Brussels, Plate VII., which was made in sections, with the net added after completion of the sprays.

CHAPTER III

BRUSSELS LACE

It has always been a mystery to me why so much trouble should have been taken by the geography books to anglicise the names of foreign countries and towns, until the poor traveller is obliged to learn everything afresh unless he is to lose his way. With the same cheerful indifference to the nomenclature preferred by the native, we have our own British ideas as to the naming of many foreign laces, and it seems to be a part of the rule that any one that may be left over, should titles run short, must be called Brussels. Just now and again a piece that puzzles one may be put aside as Italian, a nice capacious name that will safely envelop a great many varieties, though for general utility as well as for popularity it cannot hold a candle to "Brussels."

The Parisians show equal originality, and so it happens that a Belgian dealer may have to study two sets of names given to his laces, beyond those by which they are known in their respective provinces.

Our own laces are treated much in the same way abroad. Irish Crochet is very generally known, and by its correct name; Dentelle Angleterre, however, is the name given to a cheap Braid lace most probably made in Austria. A little Honiton is to be found in the large Paris shops, where it is not unfrequently sold as Brussels, but Midland laces, Limerick and Irish Needle Point are practically unknown to the general public, and by the dealers are classed as Lille, Needle-run, etc. While the French people err in summing up all English laces as belonging to one class (and that a very poor one), in England the tendency is to fall into the opposite error, and call several distinct kinds of lace all by the one name of Brussels, without any prefix that would assist in recognition.

A great many different laces have from very early days been made in Belgium. We have already seen how some of these laces came indirectly from Italy, being introduced by refugees *via* Switzerland and France. Later on the work was much encouraged by the Government, and teachers were introduced direct from Italy. Colbert of France founded a school of Needle Point, working on Venetian lines, and from that first beginning there were many side issues. Finer Needle Point laces were made, and, the centre of the industry being situated in northern France, outstripped the boundary and reached Brussels, a town which has for long been recognised as a centre for the lace trade of Belgium.

The Needle Point and the Pillow lace were made side by side, and Plate VII. shows a fine example of true Antique Brussels lace of the latter kind.

The style of design, especially in the edge, shows a strong French influence, and many patterns of Point d'Alençon will be found closely resembling it. The *réseau* is a very fine Brussels net, hand made, and with a thread that is said to have cost as much as £80 the pound.

This fine net was not always made by the worker who was responsible for the more solid work. Sometimes the sprays would be handed over to the net maker and she would work in the net, joining the bobbins to the edge of the lace by a process known as sewing, but entirely innocent of any assistance from the needle. By this method the lace and net became actually one. It was the oldest way, and was the means most generally employed in Italy. Another way was introduced later, no doubt to carry out the orders more quickly, and the net was made separately in long strips, the lace being afterwards applied by the needle. It was probably much more convenient for the dealer to have the net at hand ready to be applied in a few hours when the sprays came home.

So fine was the thread, and so long did it take to make, that it was a very costly production. An equally fine net was made in Devonshire, and old workers still hand down tales of the times when their mothers and grandmothers earned for their work as many shillings as would cover the strip.

An immense number of bobbins were required, four to each tiny hole, and so, as it was not possible to work a very broad piece, the narrow lengths were joined invisibly by the needle before the sprays were sewn on. This joining is much used in the wide flounces of Chantilly lace. The breaking of the single thread will often cause what looks like a long rent in the lace, but the owner is generally quite as much surprised as relieved to find how small a matter it is to repair such a place. Chantilly is one of the laces often denied its proper name and called Brussels, a title to which it has no right whatever.

We have spoken of the very expensive thread that was used to make the fine Brussels net, this same thread was also used for the applying of the sprigs. To have economised by using a coarser thread would have run the risk of breaking the delicate net, and perhaps the expense as well as some difficulty in getting it may have paved the way to deception. Fine lace found its way on to the market *gummed* to its foundation but innocent of any more lasting attachment. Such a piece of work may easily land the amateur collector into a bad bargain, and not only the amateur! I remember a veil, closely dotted all over with tiny sprays, some of which were curling on one side, while others had dropped off entirely. It seemed as though the applying thread had broken, and so only a trifling sum was mentioned for re-sewing the broken places.

The lace was very limp and had been pulled out of shape, therefore a warm iron was used to smooth it out before the sewing began. The effect of the iron may be imagined!

Almost a bare piece of net was lifted off the ironing sheet, while the pattern remained behind.

After that one could have a fellow-feeling for an unlucky lace collector who, after washing her new purchase, brought in a separate wrapper the pieces she has skimmed off the top of the water during the operation.

It is only here and there that one is likely to meet with such a mishap when buying good antique lace, but there will always be unscrupulous persons ready to take in the unwary, and gummed lace still finds its way upon the market, though it would be rejected by all reliable dealers.

The test would naturally be to look at the back of the lace for the connecting stitches, needle or bobbin as the case might be. If the work was very fine and any doubt remained the expert would choose a tiny sprig and curl it tightly round the finger. If gum had been used, the natural warmth of the hand, together with the slight strain, would quickly release the lighter tendrils.

With the introduction of machine-made net a lighter style of design came into vogue. It was possible to put out wide flounces at a very small expenditure as regards the foundation, and slender trails of flowers were at once elegant and in keeping. Plate XV. shows two repeats of Brussels lace waiting to be applied. The edge, with its open spaces enclosed by floral forms is not unlike the lappet, and shows a common origin. The centre spray springing stiffly upright is distinctly French.

Both the lappet and these two sprays have raised work: the raised line which in the former encircles the more important leaves and can be seen both in the edge of the modern lace, and also decorating the larger leaves growing from the centre stalk.

There are no stitches in this Brussels lace which are not used in making fine Honiton, for of late years there has been such a revival of old stitches, thanks mainly to the excellent lace classes arranged by the Devon County Council, that many which had been entirely forgotten have been introduced afresh.

The original Devonshire lace having in the first instance been introduced by lace workers from Belgium, is still very like the pillow-made Brussels. The Antique lace, Point d'Angleterre, is so nearly identical to the specimen shown of the lappet, that even experts still argue as to whether all the lace of this kind was not really made in Brussels. It would perhaps be impossible for anyone to say absolutely that a piece of this lace belonged to the one special country, but certain stitches, the "snow filling" for example, are

PLATE VII.

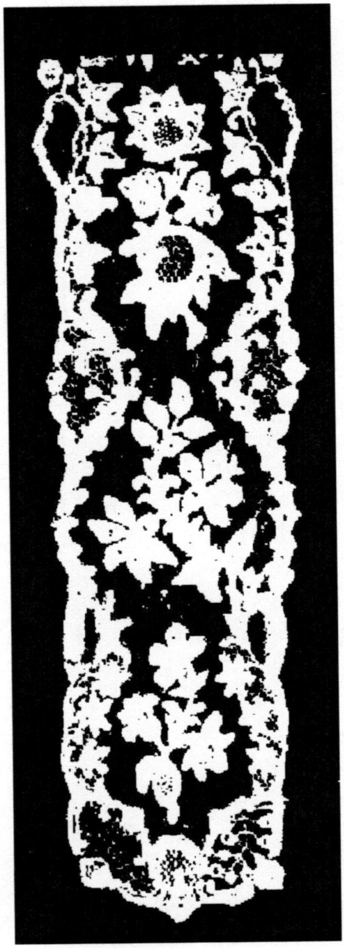

ANTIQUE BRUSSELS LAPPET.

To face page 81.

rarely to be found in the true English lace. It is not such a difficult matter to distinguish between the modern lace of the two countries. Honiton lace is more compact, more heavy in design than Brussels, which is made with delicate spiral forms, light and graceful, specially well suited for application to net. Only the applied Bobbin lace is generally known as Brussels, and when a heavier style of design is used, the sprays being joined together by bars, the lace is called Bruges. That, at least, is what it is most frequently called both in France and England, though the name is a constant source of surprise to the dentellières of that quaint old-world town.

Plate I. shows a tie end of what we will persist in calling Bruges lace. The sample is a very perfect one of its kind. The leaves show the rolled raised work as well as what is called the stem stitch. An idea of light and shade is given by the use of a more open stitch for those points which require being thrown into relief. The three leaves at the foot are typical Bruges forms, and the upper leaf, resting upon a ground of half-stitch, is seldom to be found in the laces of other countries.

If the collector is not quite so well up in design as to be able to distinguish this lace from Honiton, there is still another and a convincing proof.

Both laces have a heavy thread outlining their braid. In Honiton lace this is a bright flax thread, called by the villagers "Shiny Thread." The Belgian-made lace has a coarser thread, more like a loosely twisted cord. This thick thread is very plainly seen in the little flowers.

Bruges lace has not a very good name at present, owing to the large output of a very poor quality, made to attract cheap custom. The same trouble applies to

Honiton lace, and is a misfortune in both cases, since it robs the really fine work of its prestige. Lately efforts have been made to change the name of the finer lace to Duchesse, but rightly this name describes a fine Bruges lace with small inserted medallions of Needle Point Brussels. So far, then, we have three modern laces, all of which are frequently called Brussels, *i.e.*

Applied Brussels Bobbin Lace.
Bruges.
Duchesse.

These three, all derived from a common source, have every right to the title Brussels, but require some additional distinction if confusion is to be avoided. Brussels Appliqué, Brussels Guipure (for Bruges), Brussels Duchesse, would be the recognised names in Belgium.

Two other laces must also be mentioned, both being Needle Point. There is a great similarity of design between applied Brussels Needle Point and the Bobbin lace; the same loose floral stands are employed to spread lightly over the surface of the net, the conventional style is greatly used, and especially for the foot of the design.

The Needle Point Appliqué will usually be the more expensive of the two kinds, and is generally found upon a really fine machine net.

This style of lace is comparatively modern, for it was not until 1830 that machine-made nets came into general use.

From the date of invention fully fifty years elapsed before they were much used, and even a very secondary quality would cost as much as eight shillings for the square foot. At Kensington Palace, among the few but very interesting exhibits that are open to the public is the wedding bonnet of Queen Victoria. It is a quaint white silk poke "Granny" with no trimming beyond a veil and a wreath of orange blossoms. The veil will naturally be of special interest to us. It is of applied Brussels Needle Point, well made, but not particularly fine. What will at once strike the lace lover is the unsuitable quality of the net. This is much too coarse for the lace and would never be used in the present day. It opens up a rather interesting subject.

Either the development in net making must have gone forward very rapidly within a few years of this date, or else there may have been a special reason for the coarse net.

Many Brussels laces which belong to close upon the same date may be found with machine net so fine that a piece equal to two yards in width may be passed through a small finger ring with plenty of space to spare.

May we not presume that net, a great deal finer than that chosen by Queen Victoria, was being made in France and Belgium at the time of her wedding? And if so—why was it not used?

Just about this time a little Needle Point lace was being made in Devonshire from copies of Venetian and other laces. Those well-known experts, Mrs. Palliser and Mrs. Treadwin, were both interested in promoting the industry, and it seems quite possible the wedding veil may have been made in Devonshire from a Brussels model. It would have been like the Queen to have valued the less perfect lace as being the work of her own people, and if this supposition is correct it would also explain the use of a poorer quality of net.

The English net manufacturers were for some years behind the French, and so if the veil were entirely of home production the net would not compare favourably with the foreign article.

Point de Gaze is the next lace on our list, and as its name implies it has a very fine transparent net ground, entirely needle-made. The pattern is generally rather closely packed and the net is well covered. Some of the more elaborate flowers, such as roses, will have a double set of petals, made apart and afterwards attached. This gives them more importance and makes them stand out in the design. The idea is not original, but has probably been copied from the Gros Point de Venise.

We have already mentioned that Duchesse is a combination of the Needle and Pillow laces. The latter style always preponderates in the design, the needlework motifs only filling in spaces left for them at regular intervals.

The fillings or "jours," as they are called abroad, in Brussels Pillow lace are frequently filled in with the needle, as well as the tiny centres of the flowers.

Of late years the needle and bobbins have been used very much in conjunction with each other, the needle often being used for making the *réseau*. An example of this will be seen in Plate XI., which is described in detail under "Flemish Laces." It may be a little difficult for the novice to at first distinguish clearly between the pillow-made Brussels lace and the Devonshire. They are alike in that there is a Honiton Guipure and also an Appliqué lace, but in other respects the differences are clearly marked. Honiton is more compact, and sometimes it must be confessed very heavy in design, angular rather than flowing. Brussels, if fine, is generally made without any outlining thread, and cotton is used if at all. Honiton is nearly always outlined with a silky flax thread.

Brussels lace has Needle Point fillings more often than not; these are never used in legitimate Honiton.

As a rule the Honiton lace is more closely packed, to use a technical term, carries a larger number of bobbins, and so is firmer than the other, though this good point is sometimes carried too far, to the detriment of the lacey appearance which gives way to that of a woven material.

Having touched lightly upon those laces which have a genuine right to the name of Brussels, the lace maker will find that the instructions for making that Pillow lace are practically identical with those required for Honiton. For the Needle Point lace we have no space available in the present volume, but most of the stitches will be found in any reliable book of instructions in Point lace.

One last warning for the collector! There is some magic spell in the name of "Brussels" which is specially attractive to the novice, and sometimes rather fatal. Remember that plenty of trash is sold under this name, and do not buy for the name alone.

Another warning! The delicate designs typical of Applied Brussels are widely copied in other laces, some Needle-run, some Tambour, some deliberately faked. Quite often the vendor may misname the laces out of ignorance, misled by the design, but all are much inferior to the real, and few will stand re-applying after the original net is too badly gone for mending.

A clever imitation is got by placing a very small round hole machine net over a square net and working the design with tambour needle, or even with chain stitch done by machine.

The outlining of the pattern joins the two nets together, and the upper one with the round mesh is then cut away all round the pattern, any special stitches being put in by the needle.

When finished the effect is remarkably good, but the top net quickly pulls away from the edge, and once broken is not worth the mending.

CHAPTER IV

PART I.—BRAID AND TAPE LACES

OF the two examples given on Plates VIII. and IX. the narrower lace is of Flemish make, while the broader more probably hails from Genoa.

"How is it possible to distinguish when the two laces are so alike ?" someone may well ask, and the Belgian expert has a way of throwing out his hands with a shrug of the shoulders, by which you are to understand that an explanation is impossible, but notwithstanding, a tangible difference does exist.

Naturally where a piece of Italian lace has been faithfully reproduced in Belgium it remains Italian always, but as a rule the workers of that country have a trick of introducing certain favourite stitches which are not to be found in Italy, though some have made their way into English lace.

The first example shows the Brussels net used as a jours or filling. There is also the delicate Pearl stitch, so often to be found in Point d'Angleterre, and one of the latest stitches to be revived in Devon.

By such tiny points as these the expert can ascertain the birthplace of a certain piece, but he may well shrug his shoulders when asked to define so slight a difference which would, however, be easily apparent to a lace maker. Flemish patterns are often more broken, not in design but in the working, than the true Italian, a very

PLATE VIII.

FLEMISH-ITALIAN LACE.
From the Lace Collection at the Victoria and Albert Museum, S. Kensington.

To face page 38.

large repeat of which will often be covered without a break in the braid. This cannot, however, be taken as a rule, for certain Genoese and Milanese laces are made in many pieces, though certainly with a very different style of design.

When people speak rather vaguely of "Italian" lace it is generally the type shown in our illustration to which they refer. Perhaps there are more laces of different varieties made in Italy than even in Belgium, but the Braid or Tape style belongs especially to Genoa and Milan.

Often only a very small difference will distinguish between them—some small change that even at the last moment may convert the one into the other. The narrower of the two patterns shown would be called Genoese, but if a special *réseau* were employed in place of the bars it would then become Milanese.

"But," the reader may ask, "has it not been decided that the first of the two laces is Flemish?" Of Flemish workmanship, yes, but Italian in every other respect.

It is always a mistake to think that lace must of necessity be called after the place where it is made—Brussels lace may be made in Devonshire—but that does not in any way alter its name or value. The same thing applies to Italian lace exactly reproduced by Belgian workers—and Belgium has a little habit of cleverly reproducing very many laces and labelling them all anew!

When the transplanting results in recognised differences it is right and proper that the lace should bear a distinctive name—Buckinghamshire Point, for instance, which, springing from a common origin, has struck out a new style for itself, and can no longer be confounded with Trolle Kant or Lille.

The Flemish-made Milanese or Genoese laces should retain their original names unless, therefore, some definite distinction is to be found. Sometimes, but not always, the patterns will have been made in several sections to one repeat, and when in addition those stitches are employed which belong especially to Flanders, then the lace has every right to be called after that country.

All who are familiar with the lace will recognise how strictly our example follows upon the Italian methods, and the particular photograph was chosen for illustration because the original lace, being at the Victoria and Albert Museum, is well worth a visit.

The lace maker who takes up one variety of Tape lace will as easily copy others, and the stitches that may be employed are quite innumerable.

In the first piece of lace the special stitches which show its birthplace are the pearl filling—little rings ornamented with picots—the Brussels net, and another which is often found in Binche.

There is no rule telling which stitches are to be used, or how many—all is left to the taste of the worker, and naturally the artistic value of the lace will depend upon her knowledge and discretion.

Too much decoration will detract from the beauty of the whole even more than too little, and the proportion of plain work must act as a foil to the more elaborate.

Before passing on, mention must be made of the Russian lace, generally of very conventional design like the key pattern, but sometimes a direct copy of the Italian. The lace has little or no relief by way of fancy stitches

PLATE X.

GENOESE TAPE LACE.

From the Lace Collection at the Victoria and Albert Museum, S. Kensington.

To face page 40.

and is not very interesting. None of the patterns show striking originality of treatment, but the industry is growing, and perhaps a higher development lies in the future.

Akin to these Braid laces is the true Point de Flandres, a lace of bolder design than Brussels, more delicate and varied than the lace commonly known as Bruges.

The designs are invariably beautiful, and the introduction of open brides contrasting with a closer ground, gives a touch of light elegance to what otherwise might be a rather overweighted style. The lace was greatly in request for deep flounces, for which the large floral sprays were eminently suitable; many of the conventional shapes common to Brussels lace were employed, but the lighter spiral forms were put aside as unsuitable.

Point de Flandres was chosen by Napoleon the Great for the christening robe of the little king of Rome, and there are many portraits of Court beauties with deep flounces of it upon their skirts.

Point de Flandres was entirely made with the bobbins, but several innovations have come to pass within the last hundred years, and now the same name is applied to a lace very similar in style but with a needle *réseau*. This last is of the lesser value, but is very beautiful apart from the original. Do away with the needle ground and some of the finer stitches, and then the lace, with the aid of joining bars, which necessarily rather cramp the pattern, becomes the modern Bruges.

More than an elementary knowledge of lace making would be required before a piece of Vieux Point de Flandres could be attempted, but a study of Devon lace is of great assistance, for the two are akin in construction.

None of the fancy stitches used in either Italian or

Flemish Braid lace are ever made with the needle, but mention has already been made of the hand-woven tape of Italy and Spain.

Tape lace is the name usually given to this kind. The tape was woven on a small hand-loom, the same that would be used for making narrow ribbons. The thread was of course hand-spun in those old days, and by the time the open spaces had been filled in with delicate and varied stitches, the work became almost as valuable as the pillow lace. A heavy Cordonnet, or outlining thread, was sewn last of all to the edge, which added a rich effect. In Italy a flat Needle Point lace was made, and sometimes the Tape lace followed these designs as well. In looking over antique laces, one may at times find a piece of this Tape lace added on to the real, no doubt to lengthen it without going to the full cost. Looking closely, the difference cannot fail to be noticed, but the lace could be worn without anyone being the wiser at a short distance.

There is very little doubt that English Point lace owes its origin to the Spanish Tape lace. It was a favourite lace which had a long run from the " 'sixties " down to the commencement of the new century. It vied with crewel work as a fashionable employment, and only fell away when every shop window became full of it and it could be bought for a mere song.

Much of the lace was really well made, but it has little or no value as real lace if made with a machine braid. The specimen of lace shown was made at Branscombe near Sidmouth, a little village where some of the best Pillow lace is made as well. Ten years ago the Braid lace industry was doing extremely well down there, but gradually it has fallen away until at last there are few

PLATE X.

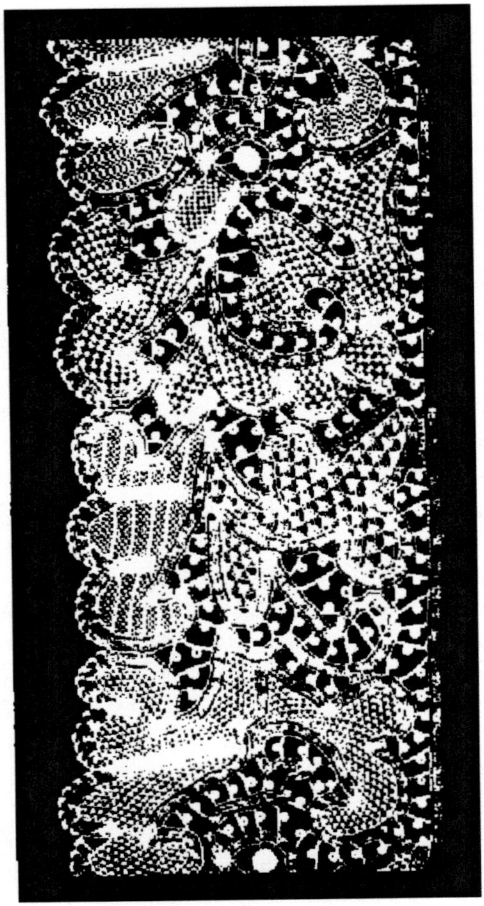

BRANSCOMBE POINT LACE.
Made under the direction of Mrs. Allen.

To face page 43.

purchasers beyond the tourists who pass that way in the summer. Perhaps a return to the old Tape lace would set the Branscombe workers on their feet again, for their Point lace stitches are too good to be lost.

Still more recently variations of the Braid lace have been introduced under such attractive names as Luxuille and Princess Point. These, however, have no legitimate foundation, and rank only as fancy work, the fashion of to-day, which will be utterly forgotten in a few years.

A Needle Point worker may very reasonably ask whether it is worth her while to take up one of these laces. The reply would in most cases have to be in the negative. Perhaps one worker may be able to work up a small connection by the aid of friends and dressmakers, but another may devote hours to work which proves unsaleable at any price that would repay her labours.

As people in general understand the value of lace better, they will grudge paying for what is not wholly real. The Point lace worker must go forward with the times and improve upon her materials, either making her own braid upon the pillow or weaving her own tape. The last method is likely to bring the more remunerative results since no machine-made tape can at present compare with one that is hand-made, while machine-made braids so closely copy the real that the amateur can rarely tell which is which.

PART II.—DEVONSHIRE LACE

For some years the name of Honiton has been used indifferently both for the Bobbin and the Braid Point laces of Devon. Because of the harm it has certainly done the Bobbin lace to be confounded with one that is only partially real, efforts have been made to revive a name by which it was equally well known in the past.

The name is now given specially to those laces of improved design which are frequently to be seen at exhibitions, though progress is slow, and the better work seldom reaches the public market. Like Brussels, there are several varieties of Devon lace:

> *Guipure.*—The sprays being joined by picot brides.
> *Point.*—The same lace joined by a *réseau* of Needle Point.
> *Appliqué.*—Upon machine-made net.

The illustration given is taken from "Devon Pillow Lace," and shows an old village design which has been re-drawn and weeded of such extraneous adjuncts as a number of little cart-wheels, which took the place of the larger leaves, together with other adjuncts which were weird rather than decorative!

For very many years the Devon lace workers have received little help or overlooking. Left to themselves they introduced all kinds of odd devices into their patterns, until the Pillow lace trade had sunk in 1890 to the lowest depths of degradation from an artistic point of view.

In 1907, when "Devon Pillow Lace" was written, there were many hopeful signs of better things.

The County Council were raising the standard of the work by giving excellent instruction to the villagers, free of charge.

The increased beauty of the lace and the improved quality were openly recognised, yet still only the old Honiton—a patchwork of ill-assorted sprigs—finds its way upon the general market.

The work begun will never arrive at thoroughly satisfactory results until the co-operation of the trained artist with the village worker is the rule and not the exception. After the teaching the women slip back again into the old patterns, and, worse still, they piece in bits of one new design with scraps from another. The old meaningless forms could be joined in upside down or sideways—with no drawing in them to start with, it mattered little what liberties were taken—but with a good design, truly the last state of the lace may be worse than the first!

The best lace in Devonshire is to be found in Beer, Branscombe, Honiton, and Sidbury—but it is spreading over the county, and has even reached Lynton in the north.

The very fine raised work is troublesome if the sight is not good, but the plainer work is quickly learnt and most effective.

As a rule, Devonshire lace is better and more firmly made than Brussels, and if work of good design is chosen it is a capital investment. The newer lace is enriched by many recently revived stitches, which, introduced first from Flanders, may be found in old Point d'Angleterre. Seventeen of these fancy stitches were included in the instructions of "Devon Pillow Lace" two years ago, and already there are others that could be added to the list.

When one remembers that ten years ago not more than five of these stitches were even known by sight to the majority of the lace workers, it will be seen that the lace revival in Devonshire has achieved something.

CHAPTER V

ON THE CARE OF OLD LACE

ALTHOUGH quite a small library of lace literature has been produced of recent years, it strikes one as being a little strange that the restoration of old lace should be either ignored altogether or very lightly touched upon by the various writers.

Possibly the reason for this apparent neglect of a very important subject may arise from so little being known —outside the trade—of the delicate and expert work that must be employed in dealing with antiques of all kinds, and of this class in particular.

Not only must the lace expert understand the principles upon which each piece is made, but she must also be able accurately to gauge its value in order to decide which particular form of restoration must be employed if its value is to be preserved undiminished. Again, it will rest with her to reject such lace as will not repay the expenditure of much time and trouble, or perhaps to advise only a secondary mending being employed upon lace of little value.

Should a tattered length of Honiton Appliqué be under inspection, she will first notice whether the original net is real or at least so fine that it is worth many hours of careful mending. She may decide to give it a new ground, and then follows a careful scrutiny of each spray lest some should not be strong enough to reapply. When all is settled comes the final decision, the choice of the net. This will vary in price from a few shillings to a pound or more, and the estimated value of the lace must decide which will be the most suitable.

Plate I. shows an old-fashioned tie end of Bruges lace, stripped of the old net and waiting to be reapplied. Although the lace is about fifty years old it was thoroughly well made at the start, and has still many years of active service before it. Just one or two places have broken away at the edge of the braid, always the weakest point. The worst is one of the three small leaves which hang down on the right, inside the open centre space. The tiny leaf is in a prominent position and will show any mending; it will be best, therefore, as well as least noticeable, to remake it upon the pillow. Such a tiny piece of work would be completed in a few minutes if the mender has her lace pillow at hand; but if much of the pattern needed remaking it might be quicker to first trace and then prick out the lost parts, handing that part of the renovation over to the lace maker. For small repairs it will be seen at once that a great saving of time and trouble will be effected by the mender being able to carry the entire work through by herself. A complete knowledge of every detail in connection with the work is very necessary, even if some of the repairing is to be done by a village worker, who, although expert in the actual making, will very often require minute instructions, even down to the choice of thread. The lace expert has no easy task before her, indeed everything that has to do with lace repairing tends to keep the unskilled worker out of the market.

Lace mending sounds attractive, and in very truth it is so, which is perhaps the reason why many gentlewomen come forward offering to undertake such orders without any knowledge beyond a certain skill in fine needlework. That this is dangerous alike for employer and worker may easily be guessed. To speak only of one instance, we will suppose some novice is ready to undertake a similar piece of work that has already been described. She is nonplussed at the start, not knowing whether the original ground is real net or merely machine-made; if she ruthlessly cuts it away she lays herself open to the risk of having to make good the depreciation in value, while, on the other hand, if she retains it and mends each tiny hole, the worn-out net may be in pieces again before the year is out, and the owner rightly grudges the expenditure. Even if she decides to remount the lace, the matching of the net is a matter that requires experience, while to avoid a join she may need to buy some yards, having immediate use only for the narrow strip required. Sooner or later discouragement and loss are almost inevitable, and if she really needs to earn her living, it is perhaps best that disillusion should come quickly before some serious mistake involves her in a heavy loss.

If one thinks how very much ground the subject covers, it seems almost incredible that many people should imagine that only a fine needle and thread are required before making a professional start.

After a very little experience the novice, if she is an artist, discovers that lace mending is not a gift that comes by nature, but a real profession reaching out into so many branches that long practice and experience are a *sine qua non* if she is to become proficient.

The lace maker and the lace mender both travel on the same road, but the mender will find her line the more profitable, although it will mean a wider study and will call for all her ingenuity.

One so frequently hears of valuable old lace having been thrown away as useless, that a few hints on what is worth keeping may tend to avoid some unnecessary loss. We have already spoken of the new life that may be restored to a good Appliqué lace. The money spent upon such work may be considered in the light of an investment as it brings the lace back to very nearly its original value. Where the investment idea fails is when the owner is unwilling to pay for such fine materials as the quality of the lace demands. To apply really fine lace on a cheap net is practically throwing money away—the value of the lace is at once decreased, which is the first loss, and then the worker's charge for her time is the same whether the materials used are good or bad.

Some laces will break away more readily than others, and of these Point de Gaze, one of the most charming, is a principal offender. The special daintiness of the lace lies in the contrast between the firmly made needlework sprays and the filmy net background. The net is made by a succession of loops, the lower line of meshes being caught by a single twist into the loops above, only a single thread is used and not the extra twisting or the strengthening threads which make the *réseau* of Burano and Alençon so much more serviceable.

It must be confessed that Point de Gaze does fall into holes very readily, but there is one consolation, that the new net can be replaced as quickly. It is one of the easiest needle grounds to make, and not at all trying to the sight.

Another point in favour of this lace is, that if the

owner loses patience with the constant breaking of the net, it may be applied to a machine net without suffering real loss, though after the alteration it has no longer the right to the name of Point de Gaze, but assumes the character of Brussels Needle Point Appliqué.

The lace collector will make a little note of this, for the same treatment applied to another lace might have quite a reverse effect—Argentan, Alençon, Burano, are all laces with needle grounds, which must be kept together as long as they will hold. To apply any one of the three would be to destroy its character. So long as mending is possible it should be done, and only when the lace is at its last gasp should it be given the new foundation. After that it may be useful and pretty as dress garniture, but it is no longer a real lace in the true sense of the word.

Where the lace has broken away from either the brides or the *réseau* of a Pillow lace, these should be replaced by the bobbins if the pattern is equal to the strain. The laces that most generally require this class of mending are the heavier Italian, Spanish and Flemish designs. Often the pattern breaks away because it is too heavy for the connecting groundwork. The brides can be mended very quickly, but the net is slow work which may require the winding and hanging up of a great number of bobbins, so that the piece must be really good to be worth the expenditure. A very fair imitation of the *réseau* can be made with the needle, quick work, effective, and very useful in mending, but the collector must remember that lace mended in this way is reduced in value and cannot be classed among the perfect specimens.

In buying this kind of lace from an unknown dealer abroad, it is always well to examine it very carefully.

A short deep flounce, not long enough to be saleable, will often be found cut into long narrow strips, joined together, and the raw edges concealed by new topping and edge, but ready to fray out after a little use. Unless the design is complete and the *réseau* or brides perfect, it is fairly safe to say that the lace is likely to prove a bad bargain.

The finer laces have, as a rule, to be mended with a needle, and the net can be reproduced so exactly as to be practically invisible. All such laces—Mechlin, Alençon, Burano, take a long time to do, and the worker is wise if she always keeps a second piece of less troublesome mending going at the same time, so that she need not strain her eyes by working too long at a stretch. To turn to the making of Pillow lace brides or a piece of applying will be a complete change and rest.

An experienced lace mender will rarely be out of employment for long, and the work has the great advantage of being easily done at home. It is always better if two friends can arrange to work together, so that one may specialise in the bobbin mending and the other with the needle. The work is really too varied to allow of one person being thoroughly *au fait* with the treatment of each different class, and also if the two are working together the orders can be got through in half the time—a great advantage, especially if working for the trade, when expedition in carrying through the order is all important.

Lace renovating is one of the few professions open to women that are not overcrowded at present, and the growing demand for real lace should ensure steady work for many years ahead. For at least five centuries lace has been a popular, almost a necessary, dress garniture, and at no time did the fashion fall out so completely as during the middle of the nineteenth century. It is possible that we have seen and passed through the lowest depths to which the industry can sink.

During that curiously inartistic period, old embroideries and laces were thrown aside as useless—with many people even a knowledge of the difference between the real and the machine article was lost, and so even valuable laces found their way into the rag-bag or were given away with old garments.

This ignorance may be said to have assisted another branch of the lace trade by which the skilled renovator may reap a very plentiful harvest from the mistakes of the past. Plenty of old lace still finds its way into the rag and small antique shops, where much of it may be bought for a few shillings if out of repair or antiquated in shape. The purchaser must understand *how* to buy, for the small dealer as a rule knows nothing whatever of real lace, and is not infrequently taken in himself. A piece of imitation Chantilly may be offered at a large price, while a length of fine old Bucks may be thrown among the oddments. Abroad the purchasing of torn and seemingly useless old lace is quite a little trade in itself, and one, moreover, in which good taste and clever fingers can take the place of invested capital. The outlay of a few shillings will, in the hands of a clever worker, often realise several pounds, but everything will depend upon her knowing first *how* to buy and secondly how to use her purchase to the best advantage.

The two illustrations on Plate XI. will show how some of the alterations may be effected.

PLATE XI.

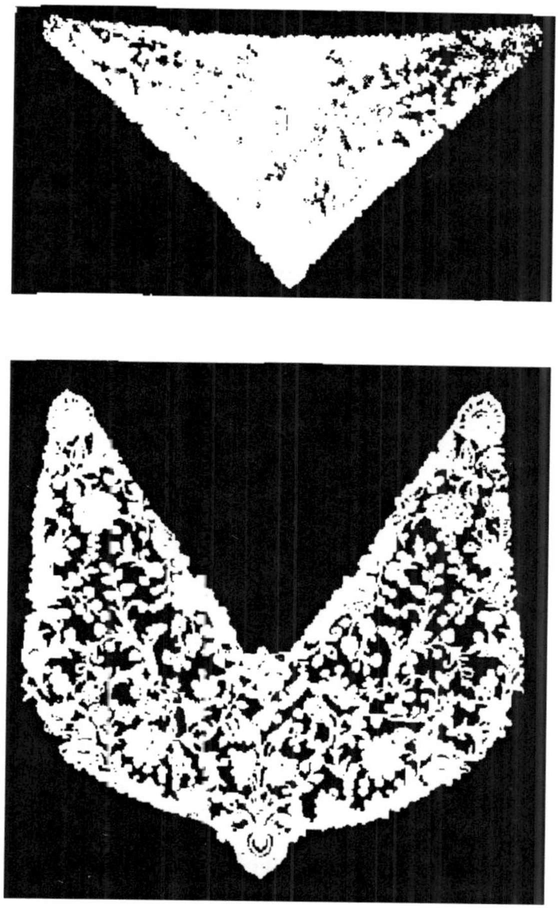

FLEMISH LACE SHAWL REPRODUCED AS A COLLAR.

To face page 53

The old-fashioned little shawl and the deep collar are the same piece of lace. The sprays were in the first instance all united by a needle ground, they were first taken apart, unpicked from the old ground, then rearranged to suit the new style, the same needle-stitch being used to join all together. Although the shape was entirely altered the lace would not be classed as mended, for the condition remains unaltered, and the more up-to-date style raises its selling value.

Often a real lace parasol cover, made for one of the tiny shades so popular in the 'sixties, may be picked up very much below its value. These often constitute a real "find" either for the collector or the lace renovator. If the lace lends itself readily to adaptation, a deep collar, a yoke, and a straight collar-band may all be evolved from the one piece, a lace set that would quickly find its market. The whole value of the completed work will depend upon the alterations being so absolutely in keeping with the lace that the transition is completely hidden; work that would probably mean a certain amount of matching and remaking in the finishing off.

It is a little difficult at times to draw a distinction between a "faked" lace and one that has been remodelled or much altered in process of restoration.

A useful rule is to think of a "faked" lace as pretending to be other than it really is. For instance, the Point de Gaze lace remounted on machine net becomes a real lace of another class—Alençon treated in the same way would be open to question if sold as real lace, and would belong to the former. Italian flounces with the Milanese *réseau* replaced by a needle ground come under the heading of faked laces, as do the scraps of patterns all joined together with crochet or needle bars, which so often pass muster as *Flemish*.

The lace repairer may often be called upon to fake up old lace into something that is quite artistic and wearable, but it should be her aim never to do so if the lace is open to any better treatment.

Not many years ago a fashion was started in Paris of making up lace collars and blouses which were little more than an ingenious patchwork of incongruous oddments. Irish crochet, fine Valenciennes, antique Brussels, old embroidery were all pieced in together quite irrespective of age or style. To the connoisseur such work appears to be the height of vandalism, though a distinctly beautiful and interesting effect can be given to a piece of work in which the laces are in keeping with each other.

Much might be written upon the harmonious setting of real lace, when certain laces may be worn, and with what accessories, but here the lace lover may fall foul of fashion which has before now decreed the use of heavy crochet for a ball dress, while delicate Brussels is relegated to adorn a sable coat.

One last word before leaving the subject of lace mending. It may be taken as a general rule that the more valuable the lace, the more costly must be the mending. Really good lace should leave the worker's hands *renewed*, not mended, for that term is a misnomer in cases where the identical stitches have been replaced.

This chapter would be very incomplete unless some few words were given to the very delicate subject of cleaning. A *delicate* subject because it is one that is hedged around with closely guarded trade secrets!

The dear old ladies of "Cranford" were in favour of first washing their lace and then steeping it in milk, "just enough to stiffen it, my dear, and give it that nice creamy colour." A very innocent receipt, and not one to be scoffed at, although in Mrs. Forrester's case a greedy cat came within an ace of being the living tomb of her old Mechlin.

The starch in the milk would be quite enough to stiffen the lace, though the creamy colour spoken of seems only to have existed in the old lady's imagination. What Mrs. Forrester forgot to add was that her lace would be nourished and strengthened by its bath.

Since "Cranford" days old traditions have been improved upon by science until even the cleaning of lace has become a separate study. Old traditions have been improved upon! Ought those words to be allowed to stand, or would it not be more honest to acknowledge that science having "improved away" the pure home-made soaps and washes, has since had to invent new means of rectifying the havoc wrought by the substitutes provided in their place?

Fine lawn baby robes will not stand the laundry now as they did a hundred years ago, even the heavy house linen has a much shorter life, so it is no wonder that the washing of lace has come to be regarded as equally injurious.

There are cases, however, where old lace must be washed at home, and then the "Cranford" receipt is as good a one to follow as any.

The purest soap possible should be procured, cut into shavings, and enclosed in a little muslin bag. The lace itself should be wrapped tightly round a smooth piece of wood so that it may float on the top of the water and be cleansed by the friction of the bubbles.

This last is a cottage receipt from Devonshire, and really a good one, though the old woman who gave it found a different reason for the use of the wood.

"If 'ee doan't do summat like thiccy, the lace it do get so mussed up with the shirtises" (shirts), she explained, and then went on to tell of a time when she neglected this precaution, and after wringing out the household wash drew the plug out of the boiler and consigned her customer's treasure to oblivion down the village drain.

Truly it is well that we do not always know what narrow escapes our fondest treasures may have sometimes!

To return to home lace cleaning—the lace thoroughly cleaned in the suds will be rinsed in clear warm water and then steeped in the milk bath.

Many delicate laces would not stand this treatment, however, and these should be entrusted only to the expert.

For instance, when the thread has become harsh and brittle it must be brought back to health, also old stains must be chemically removed before they eat their way in too deeply and become permanent.

Some will need specially prepared powders, while others will be more effectually cleaned by the use of spirits, and this last method reminds us of the latest evil threatening old lace: the home use of petrol.

The advent of the motor has brought this within easy reach of most people, but if anyone should wish to test how far this spirit is unsuitable as a cleanser for her fine lace, she has only to steep her hand in it and then notice the dry crackling sensation it leaves upon the skin.

All good thread has a certain amount of fat in it, and

it becomes less durable as that is lost. Flax bleached on the open fields will be as durable again as that which is whitened by chemicals which rob it of this element.

It is as well to bear this in mind when purchasing new lace, for the additional cost of good thread is very trifling and pays for the difference over and over again.

The subject of lace cleaning seems fated to be elusive, and once more we must apologise for a digression, and go back to the lace left steeping in the milk.

To dry, press it between a soft cloth and pin out on to a blanket. If the lace is fine put several folds of muslin over it before ironing.

Some laces will not stand the ordinary ironing, but they are among those which should never be attempted by the amateur.

A question many people ask is whether cleaning is bad for the lace, and should be done very seldom. This cannot be answered quite directly, for some lace will benefit greatly if carefully treated, while others would be best left alone as long as possible.

A badly made lace, or one made with poor thread, will never repay the cleaner's trouble. The finer Needle laces, Alençon, Venetian, Rose Point, and Burano, are best without too much cleaning, and need very special attention when their time comes.

Although the mending and cleaning are the all important subjects connected with the care of lace, apart from them there are still several other things have to be thought of. In hot climates lace will suffer from the ravages of white ant and other insects, also rust has to be contended with, and is especially destructive in the Tropics.

A glass bottle with metal screw top is an excellent receptacle for the lace under these conditions, and to prevent loss of colour it should be wrapped in dark blue tissue paper.

Rust comes from various causes, and one very easy way of saving the lace from it is to take it out of its wrappings and give it a sun bath every now and again. It comes to lace that has been packed away for some time, and is always found more frequently on French and Belgian laces than those of other countries. This is partly due to a chemical employed in these countries to brighten those places which have been soiled in the making, a remedy, the effects of which pass away in a few years, leaving the brown stain behind.

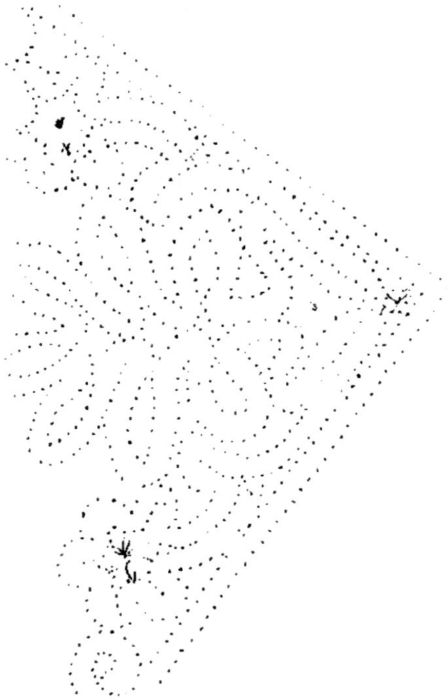

PART II

MATERIALS AND OUTFIT

Materials and Outfit for Pillow Lace Making, with Instructions in Winding and Coupling the Bobbins:

- **Whole Stitch**
- **Straight Edge**
- **Torchon Edge**
- **Half Stitch**
- **Sewing**
- **The Leadwork**
- **Picot Brides**
- **Pearl Pin**
- **Blind Pin**
- **Turning Stitch**
- **Plain Hole**
- **Fancy Hole: the Cross**
- **Fancy Hole: the Ring**
- **Twisted Bars**
- **Snatch Pin Bars**
- **Double Point Filling**
- **Diamond Filling**
- **Raised Work**
- **Stem Stitch**
- **Spider Filling**
- **Ending off the Bobbins**

PART II

MATERIALS AND OUTFIT

PILLOWS

For *Torchon* and *Trolly* laces either the French revolving pillow or the bolster shape can be used. As a rule the bolster shape is preferred for the finer laces, and is used by all old workers in the Midlands.

For Bruges and Devon laces nothing takes the place of a mushroom shaped pillow, round and almost flat. The village pillows are extremely heavy, but a lighter make may be had, generally called a "ring" pillow, which is quite flat underneath, and packs into a small space.

Italian laces may be made on a mushroom or bolster pillow, but the former is the more comfortable.

PATTERNS

The lace worker will, no doubt, make and design her own pattern, but at the start it is best to begin upon one that has been pricked by an expert, and can be relied upon as correct.

The patterns picked up in the cottages are very seldom accurate, and cause endless trouble to a beginner.

BOBBINS

For heavy laces a Torchon bobbin is most suitable, as the long neck allows for plenty of thread being wound. These may be had in white wood, also in bone stained in very delicate colours.

For all fine sprig laces Honiton bobbins may be used. The genuine Devon ones are made of spindle wood, and are capable of taking a very high polish with use. Every country, indeed, almost every lace, has its own special make, but unless the lace worker wishes to be very particular three kinds will answer every purpose, the two already mentioned, and the prettily turned Bucks bobbins, weighted with jingles, or bead rings. In the Midlands a heavier make of bobbins is used frequently for the same lace. These are thick, often rather deeply carved, and sometimes ornamented with pewter.

THREAD

Three kinds of thread are used, gassed thread, linen thread, and gimp, and unluckily each variety uses a different numbering.

Gassed thread is coarse at No. 8, moderately fine for No. 10, good average for No. 12, and above No. 14 is only used for specially fine work.

Different makes of linen thread also vary in sizes, especially French and German, the numbers of which are quite different from the English. To avoid confusion, and also because this thread is absolutely to be relied upon, we have throughout the instructions quoted Knox's linen thread numberings. The thread is pure linen, is pleasant to work with, and the numbers come out very much as follows :—

For heavy Torchon or Cluny laces . .	10— 25
For average Torchon of medium weight .	50— 70
For heavy Bruges or Italian . . .	100—140
For Buckingham	180—200
For fine Brussels	250—300

This is two-cord lace thread, and should be quoted as

such, lest the order should be confounded with "gimp," also Knox's make. *The gimp* is a soft shiny thread which is used for outlining; the silky appearance sometimes tempts people to use it by itself for Torchon and other laces, but it is of a less durable make than two-cord, and is best left to carry out the purpose for which it is made.

Lace threads may be had white or tinted, but as the dyed shades vary slightly sometimes, it is well to buy enough at the commencement to complete a special piece of work. A very trifling difference in the colour of the skein, one that will only be noticed by a practised eye, will often be quite plainly visible when worked in with the lace already made.

PINS

Special lace makers' pins are supplied in different sizes, and are longer and finer than the ordinary. The use of cheap brass pins is forbidden in all the best lace centres, and those that are glass headed are equally unsatisfactory, for unless in daily use they rust into the pillow, and are apt to tear the pattern when withdrawn.

PARCHMENT OR PRICKING CARD

Real parchment is expensive, and used mostly for fine Bucks or Bedford prickings; for other laces there are various special cards, some of which can only be bought in certain centres. A brown board is much used in England, and also a soft green card, linen backed.

WINDING AND COUPLING THE BOBBINS

To wind the bobbins twist the thread two or three times over the neck of the bobbins towards you, then wind away in the reverse direction, holding the thread in the left hand. Wind it evenly, and as tightly as possible, for this will prevent the bobbins running down during the working. To secure the thread when the neck is filled, make a loop with the left hand, bring the bobbin over it, and pass it through from underneath, drawing the thread close round the neck.

The thread can be lengthened during working by pulling against the loop.

For all Trolly and Peasant laces, the bobbins may be knotted together in a bunch, and the loose ends trimmed off after some of the lace has been made. The more valuable laces should, however, be both commenced and finished off invisibly. To do this the bobbins must be joined in couples, the threads knotted, and the ends cut off. Then some thread should be unwound from one bobbin and wound on to its fellow until the knot is hidden away. Some of the knots should be wound further back than others, so that in working out they may be disposed of by degrees.

TO MAKE WHOLE STITCH AND THE STRAIGHT EDGE

No matter what lace is going to be made ultimately, it is always quickest to learn upon a plain braid, such as that which outlines the Russian corner-piece in Plate XII.

Hang up eight couples of bobbins, round a centre-piece, and twist each couple once. The outside pair on the right are called the workers, and will pass from side to side weaving the stitch. The bobbins which hang down the centre of the braid are called "passives," and the outer couple on either side "the edge couple."

Start working on the right. Place the nearest passive in between the two workers, bring the two workers over on either side of the further passive, and then lift that bobbin

PLATE XII.

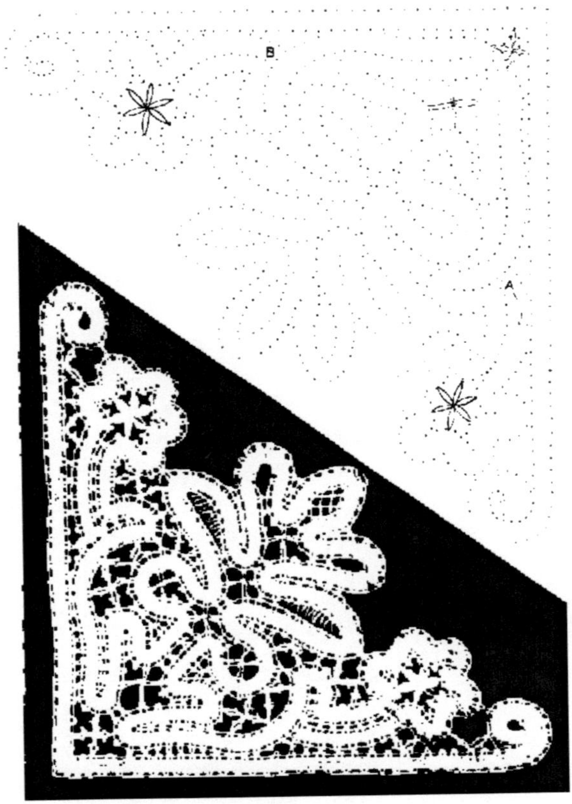

RUSSIAN LACE CORNER, SHOWING WHOLE STITCH AND THE STRAIGHT EDGE.

To face page 64.

and place it next its fellow ; this will leave the two workers together, and the two passives immediately behind them on the right. Work through all the passives in this way until the edge couple is reached. Twist the workers and put in a pin. Work them with the outside couple as previously ; twist each couple, and you are ready to work across again.

The edge couple will this time have become workers. In working back from left to right the stitch is reversed, and the first movement is made by the workers. Place the right-hand worker between the two nearest passives, lift the two passives over the worker, on the left, then place the left worker beside its fellow on the right. Work the next edge as before.

With a fine thread it may be necessary to twist three or more times to give a firm edge, while with a very coarse thread a single twist will do. There are different rules for different laces—the Brussels, Bruges, and Honiton all requiring from three to five twists, while Torchon, Russian, Cluny, and Italian need only one or two. Reference to the different laces given will show two kinds of edge—the one given above is illustrated in the Russian lace, Plate X., but this same lace and also many Torchon patterns employ another method as well, *i.e.*

THE TORCHON EDGE

The workers are brought through the passives, and twisted as usual, but the edge couples are worked *before* the pin is put in, after which the workers are again twisted, and the pin put up. They are brought round the pin and again worked through the edge couple, both pairs being twisted. With this method the workers do not change places with the edge couple, and when the pin is removed, the edge shows a series of little half loops where the threads have passed round the pin.

HALF STITCH

This is a much lighter stitch, having something of the appearance of net. The movements are exactly the same as for whole stitch, excepting that the last is omitted. Place the nearer worker between the two passives—and the two passives on either side of the remaining worker—then the stitch is complete.

It will be noticed that the same two workers do not keep together, and also that all the bobbins are left twisted.

This stitch is much used in Honiton, Bruges, and Torchon, in a less degree when making Brussels, and quite rarely for Italian.

TAKING A SEWING

In certain places bars will be used to join the pattern together, and often certain parts will have to be united so closely as to make a complete whole. The joining is done by a process known as "sewing." Perhaps a leaf is being worked, and as the pricking gives only a single row of holes up the centre, by the time it is only half finished all the inner pin-holes have been used. The joining of the second half is then done by sewing.

The workers are brought through the inside edge couple and twisted once. The pin is removed, and with a needle pin or fine crochet hook a loop of thread belonging to one of the workers is drawn through the hole left by the pin in the lace edge. The fellow worker is passed through this loop, after which both bobbins are pulled into place and worked back again.

When a bar is to be joined the same thing is done,

but if it is composed of four bobbins either two sewings may be taken into the same hole or the first pair, after sewing, may be knotted once round the remaining couple and then all worked together again.

THE LEADWORK

The daisy-like ornament in the Russian lace (Plate X.) is one of the many ways in which the leadwork may be used. It is shown alone in the Torchon lace (Plate II.). Two couples of bobbins are required for each leadwork.

One bobbin will need a longer thread than the others, as it does all the work. Let this be an outside one, and begin to weave, passing it over and under the three remaining bobbins alternately.

After making several passes, draw the outside bobbins apart, which will force the weaving threads more closely together, and also help to regulate the width. Continue the stitch until the leadwork has grown to the required size, then twist each couple and work on as the instructions for the particular pattern may direct.

PICOT BRIDES, SOMETIMES CALLED PEARL BARS

The brides are made by repeating whole stitch and a twist, whole stitch and a twist, as frequently as may be required to fill the particular space.

Brides or bars may be found without picots and also with the picot made with a single or a double thread. The single thread is used when the thread is too coarse to allow of much twisting. The bride will be plaited down to the picot pin-hole. Take the couple nearest to the hole and twist the pin round the thread of the inner bobbin, so as to make a loop, put it into the hole, twist the two bobbins once tightly, and then plait as before.

For the double picot (a stitch always used for such fine lace as Devonshire), use three extra couples, but on reaching the picot, twist the couple nearest to the hole as often as the size of the thread seems to demand, then take the outside bobbin in the left hand and bring the pin under and round the thread, making the loop and putting it into its hole. Next take the inside bobbin and twist it round the pin from the outside, then twist both bobbins together once, and plait as before.

For fine Honiton lace twist seven times before making the picot, and be guided in using other threads by the size; a coarse thread over-twisted will look "stringy" and rough.

PEARL PIN

The directions for this stitch are very similar to those given for the double picot.

Pearl pin is the name given to a series of little loops that may be found edging many fine laces, including Bucks, Mechlin, Brussels and Devonshire.

On reaching the outer edge of the lace twist the workers three times before working through the outside couple, and then twist seven times. Make the picot as already described, and after the second bobbin has been used, twist both together once and work whole stitch through the edge couple. Continue working as before.

BLIND PIN

When turning a corner it will often happen that there are more pin-holes on the outer than the inner edge. In order to get round, the same pin-hole must be used more than once.

On reaching the narrowing inside edge, the workers are only given a simple twist, after which they are put up behind the new pin and taken back, leaving the inside edge couple unworked.

Next time, when the workers return, the pin, now called a blind pin, will be taken out and replaced again in the same hole, only with the workers behind it. The same blind pin may be used several times, but the edge couples are not used until the pin is put in for the last time.

TURNING STITCH

Instead of making a blind pin, or alternately with it, the lace maker may, on reaching the inner edge, drop her workers as they reach the pin, and changing them for the nearest pair of passives, take those across instead. Returning to the edge, the new workers pass through the old and either use a new pin or put up behind a blind pin.

PLAIN HOLE

Leaving the workers at the edge, divide the bobbins equally, and work the two centre couples together in half stitch.

Bring the workers through the nearest centre couple, twist once and take them back to the edge, putting up the pin in the usual way.

Now take the second pair of centre passives, through which the workers did not pass, and work them to the outside edge on that side, put up the pin, and return.

If the hole is to be a large one, the two pairs of workers may again be taken to their respective sides and back, a second pin being used. The completion of the hole is the same in either case. The original centre couples are again united in half stitch, after which the workers are brought out from the edge and pass through them in the usual way.

FANCY HOLE: THE CROSS

Four holes will be pricked in the shape of a diamond, in the centre of the braid. On reaching the top hole leave the workers at one edge, divide the passives equally, work half stitch with the two centre couples, put in the top pin and close it with whole stitch.

Bring the workers out from the edge, but before touching the nearer centre couple twist them once and return to the edge. Put up a pin in the usual way, and working again to the middle twist once, work through the nearer centre couple, put in a pin, close it with whole stitch, twist each couple once, and again take the workers to the edge.

Make a new pair of workers for the other side, bringing out the couple nearest the pin, twisting when next to the centre couple and returning to the edge. Just as the original workers did, bring these again to the centre, and the second time pass through the centre couple, pin up and return to the edge again, putting in a pin.

Work the two centre couples again in whole stitch, put in the bottom pin, and close in half stitch. The workers on either side repeat the movements already given, and stop in their original position. The new pair of workers fall into place as passives while the old ones weave across as before.

RING HOLE

The bobbins are divided as for the previous hole, and the centre couples united in whole stitch. No pins are used, and the workers are left to one side, while new ones are chosen in their place.

Start with the centre couples, and after working them in whole stitch, twist each pair once.

Work the nearest couples on either side in half stitch, then twist each twice. Work each couple in turn through the nearest centre couple and twist both pairs again. Take each centre couple to the edge, put in a pin and return. Twist twice before passing through the two pairs now occupying the centre, and then twist both again. Unite the two centre couples again in whole stitch, and leave. Work the twisted pair hanging from either side once again in half stitch, through the nearest passive couples, and the stitch is complete.

The original pair of workers are brought in again, and weave across as before.

TWISTED BARS

Very often the braid of a pattern will suddenly widen for a short distance, and it would not be convenient to add more bobbins to keep up the appearance of equality. Different fancy stitches may be used to spread over such a space, and very often one of the fancy holes already described will answer the purpose admirably.

Twisted bars are at once very easy and quite effective. They will be found in the Flemish bird, where they have been used to fill the widening below the neck.

Bring the workers through to the centre, and twist them once, passing on to the edge. Returning, twist twice in the same space, and continue to do so until the space is well filled. The bars will look poor and thin if too long, so, should the braid widen very much, it will be well to make two divisions of the bobbins, and even to introduce a hole into the centre space, which has been done with the little bird.

SNATCH PIN BARS

"Snatch pin" is an old English expression, and is used when the workers after passing all the bobbins are put round a pin and worked back without making an edge. Snatch pin bars are seen in the Flemish-Italian lace, Plate VIII., and are used in some of the revived Devonshire fillings.

DOUBLE POINT FILLING

is used in many Flemish laces, also in Italian, and recently in some of the Devonshire laces. Although very like an elaborate net, it is only used as a filling. The pattern is pricked in little squares of four holes, close together. Eight couples are required to each square. The couples are sewn in to the edge of the space to be filled, in sets of four. These are twisted, worked together, and brought down to the top holes right and left respectively. A pin is put in at each of the top holes and divides the couples, leaving in the centre one pair from the right side and one from the left. These centre couples are worked together in whole stitch and a twist. The outside couples on right and left are then each worked with the nearer inside couple in whole stitch, and by so doing close the top pins. As the stitch is finished they are once more divided by the two lower pins. The centre couples are united again in whole stitch, and afterwards the two bottom pins are closed by the couples on the right and left working together again.

They finish as they began in whole stitch and a twist, and this constitutes the first start for the next squares. If there are two to be made in the next row then two more couples must be brought out from either side of the edge to meet those already there.

DIAMOND FILLING

This is a very favourite old Devonshire filling, and looks like a little cross with a centre of five holes, which is really Double Point.

Make the cut works as already described, but let them be longer and more slender than for Torchon. When each is finished divide its two couples by a pin.

The pricking is in sets of four holes just as for Double Point, but a little farther apart. When the two leadworks are made and both top pins put in, follow the instructions for Double Point, uniting first the centre couples, then closing the two pins by working to either side, filling the lower pin-holes, uniting in the centre again, and next making the new leadworks which go down to the row of holes below.

RAISED WORK

There are two kinds of raised work, and the easier of the two is called "Rolled raised work." Examples of this are shown in the Flemish bird and also in the Devonshire lace and the Brussels.

Any lace that contains raised work will be more expensive than one that is quite flat, for it takes much longer to do, and the best work is only undertaken by really advanced lace makers.

Raised work is used to prevent the continual ending off and restarting of certain parts of the lace. Take for an example one of the star-like flowers with six petals. Without the use of raised work, the only means of working the petals would be to hang on at the point of one, work to the centre, turn and work down to the point of the next. After that all the bobbins would have to be cut off and rejoined before working the next two petals—making three endings before the flower was completed. With the use of raised work, the bobbins would be hung on at the point of one petal, and worked to the centre, then all the bobbins would be twisted into the roll and taken up the one side to the point of the next petal, from which they would be worked down again, sewing into the roll at intervals to keep it in place.

On reaching the foot of the petal bring the workers through all but the last three couples on the outer side, and leave them.

Make new workers of the pair nearest to the old ones, and cross these over and under the remaining couples, twisting them as though they were to be cut off. Sew the new workers into the bottom hole and tie firmly. Roll again, using the same couples, and turning the pillow right round continue to roll them inside the workers, sewing into every third hole of the petal already made until the new holes are reached.

When the roll has reached the highest point put in the pin and work back across the petal. Tie the last pair of bobbins into a knot to keep the workers firmly against the roll. The knotted couple are taken for the next workers. Returning again to the roll a top sewing must be taken, Instead of the worker being looped through the outer edge it must be drawn through sideways, inside the edge couple, pulling against the twisted side bar. Continue sewing in this way until the foot of the roll is reached, and repeat as before.

The second way of making raised work is by taking the bobbins to their place not in a roll but as a very narrow one edged braid. This is called stem stitch—or, sometimes, gimp.

STEM STITCH

As a rule only five or six couples will be used, and according to their position on the pattern they will either be hung up over a pin, or sewn into a braid.

The workers may be taken from the last pair on the right, and should be worked across to the edge couple, twisted, the pin put in, and the edge made as usual. On reaching the last couple whole stitch is repeated a second time and the inner couple of bobbins lying second from the edge are then taken into use and work back to the pin without any of the usual twisting.

ITALIAN SPIDER FILLING

This is shown in the flower of Plate VIII., and is enclosed by a circle of stem stitch. Begin by sewing two couples into the same hole at the top of the space to be filled. Sew another couple in on either side about one pin-hole away. Work whole stitch twice over with the two centre couples, then twist the new couple hanging from the right twice and work it in whole stitch through the centre couples and the unused couple on the right, which must first be twisted twice.

Next bring the couple last used, the one sewn in on the extreme left, through the remaining two couples and leave.

A new couple must now be sewn in at the right edge, which is twice twisted, worked in whole stitch through the four spider couples, again twisted and sewn in to the edge on the left. This makes the straight line across the filling.

Return to the spider and take the couple on the right across to the left and leave it hanging with two twists. Return with the left couple it has just passed through, and twist that one twice as it reaches the right side. The two centre couples are then worked in whole stitch and that spider is complete. All the couples should be hanging from it, each twisted twice, and these are called its "legs." They will now be divided and will help to make the two spiders of the row beneath.

Start the second row from the left side and use the couple sewn in on completion of the straight line—for the top left leg of the left spider. This will be twisted twice and worked in whole stitch with the nearest leg from the completed spider.

The second left leg of the old spider will work through the centre couples, and also a new pair sewn in and twisted from the left edge.

The spider on the right must be made down to the same point, two new couples being sewn in for the right legs; then a third new couple is needed for the straight line which twists before and after passing through each half made spider, and finally is sewn into the left side. The two spiders are then finished, and for the third row the four centre couples would again come together, and new couples brought in to make the spiders on either side of the centre one.

ENDING OFF

For all Trolly and Peasant laces, the bobbins are simply cut off, and the lace neatly trimmed with a pair of scissors. For Braid and Sprig laces, which would be damaged by cutting, another way is always used. The gimps are thrown out and the workers are tied firmly round all the remaining bobbins. Knot the passives together in pairs to prevent them slipping; tie again with the workers, and cut off. If the lace is to be attached to some part already made, the bobbins will have to be sewn into that edge in two or more places before being knotted.

PART III

NOTES ON WORKING

Torchon Trou-trou
Torchon Edging
Cluny Insertion
Cluny Edging
Bucks Pea Pattern
Russian Lace
Flemish Bird
Italian-Flemish Braid Lace
Brussels Appliqué
Devon or Honiton

PART III

NOTES ON WORKING

TORCHON AND CLUNY LACES

Pattern No. 1

THIS little insertion is much used in fine lingerie, and can be subjected to various alterations without disturbing the pattern. A much finer thread may be used, and two or more couples of bobbins added to the edge to make a narrow braid, while a silky gimp thread outlines the path bobbins on either side. Again, it makes an effective dress trimming worked in fine grey or black silk, the path bobbins and one pair for either edge being wound with untarnishable aluminium thread.

To work the pattern exactly as it is given, Knox's No. 100 two-cord linen thread is used. The winding of the bobbins is given on page 63, and when this has been done all the loose ends will be tied together in a knot and secured by a large pin, an inch or so beyond the starting of the pattern. Start by putting a pin into the nearest of the holes which come at regular intervals exactly down the centre of the pricking. Divide the bobbins equally, so that there are ten on either side of the pin. The eight centre bobbins, four on either side of the pin, are needed for the "path," the Italian name for the ribbon work which joins and rejoins down the centre.

Take the left couple nearest to the pin, and work whole

stitch (page 64) through the two couples on the right. Drop the bobbins and start afresh, this time taking the unworked left-hand couple across in the same way through two couples, leaving it besides its fellow. This will have united the paths, the bobbins from the right having changed places with those on the left.

Leave the path and turn to the right edge. Put the edge pin into the hole immediately in a line with the centre pin, and arrange the bobbins to have two pairs inside and one outside.

Make a whole stitch between the couples on either side of the pin and twist each twice. The outer pair is called the " edge " couple, and the inner the " workers." Leave the edge couple and work whole stitch with the workers, and the unused pair that lie between them and the path. Twist each couple once after making the stitch, then work whole stitch (without twisting) through the two path couples nearest to you, twist the workers once, put in the inside pin and return. Twist once after passing through the path, work whole stitch through the couple next the pin, twist that couple once, work whole stitch through the couple next the pin, twist that couple once before dropping it and twist the workers twice. Put in the next edge pin and work with the edge couple. Repeat this exactly, passing again through the path and back to the edge, then stop. Make the edge on the left in the same way, bringing the workers through the left path couples twice to fill up the two remaining inside pin-holes on the left, then work back to edge and stop.

The two sides of the pattern should now be exactly alike, and waiting for the paths to be crossed before they can proceed. Take the left path couple nearest to the pin,

PLATE XIII.

1
2
3
4
5

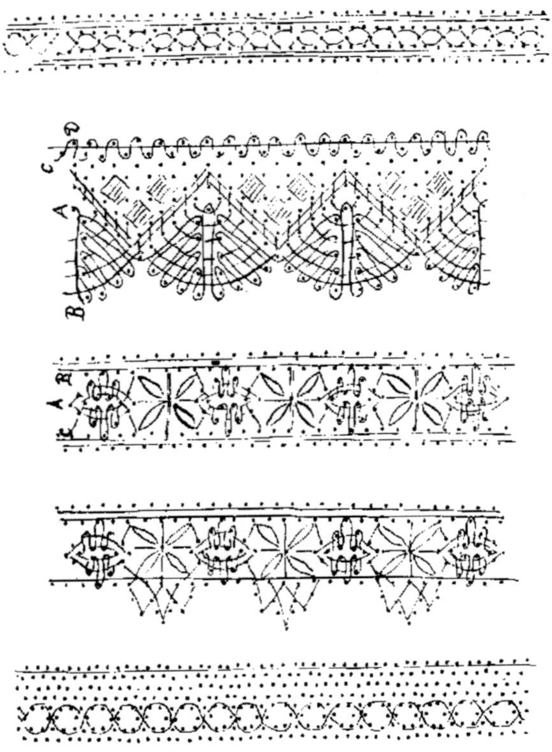

1. TROU-TROU PRICKING.
2. TORCHON EDGING.
3. CLUNY INSERTION.
4. CLUNY EDGING.
5. BUCKS PEA PATTERN.

To face page 80

and work it as before through the two couples on the right. Put a pin in the centre hole to equally divide the bobbins.

Take the unused pair of left-hand bobbins and bring them through the two pairs which were on the right. All have crossed now, and so the pattern will repeat as before.

The only difference in joining the path this time has been the putting the pin into the middle; in the opening directions it was easier for the worker to put in the pin before starting the join.

The particular name of this design is the Trou-trou—literally, Hole-hole.

Pattern No. 2

This second pattern, although more elaborate than the Trou-trou, can be used with it, and the top edge being made in the same way, makes the start so much the easier.

There is a difference of opinion among lace makers of different countries whether the scallop edge of the pattern should be worked on the worker's right or on the left. In some districts of France and in the north of Ireland the scallop would be worked on the right hand, but in other places a good sound argument is brought forward against this plan. The top of all lace should be tighter than the edge, which in very fine laces falls almost imperceptibly fluted. One may readily see the reason, and the workers, wishing to obtain this effect, make the right hand responsible for the top—that hand being the stronger unconsciously draws the lace tighter than the left.

Twenty-eight bobbins are required, and coarse or fine linen thread according to the pricking. Knox's No. 50 two-cord is a good medium size.

The pattern is made in three sections—the mitre or scallop, the ribbon, and the *réseau.*

Fasten all the bobbins together, and secure to a large pin stuck in beyond the head of the pattern.

Begin by dividing the bobbins equally, put in a pin at hole A and close it with whole stitch, working with the couple on either side of the pin. From each of the five holes which run from A to B hang one pair of bobbins, then take the couple hanging from the left side of the pin at A and work them down the line—they are your workers. Twist the workers twice between each whole stitch, the passive couples only once. When all five couples have been worked put in the pin B, twist the workers once, close the pin by working again through the last passive couple, then twist the workers twice and the passive pair once. Work through the next couple in the same way, and put in the second pin of the line, counting from the scallop. Return to the edge, reversing what you did before, put in the second scallop pin, work again back to the straight line, taking in one new couple and putting in the third pin. The workers pass backwards and forwards each time in the same way, only taking in one new pair of bobbins each time a pin is put into the straight line. When the last hanging couple has been worked and the bobbins have returned to the narrowest point of the scallop, put in the pin but do not work round it. This section is completed for the present.

There will be fourteen bobbins beyond the starting point A. Three pairs will always remain at the foot, so draw them apart from the others. Put in a pin at C, placing the three edge pairs beyond it. Close the pin with a couple taken from either side of the pin, twist each pair once, bring the workers through to the foot as in Trou-trou, put in pin D, close it and leave.

Of the eight ribbon bobbins only one pair has yet been worked and hangs from pin C. Take the farthest couple and bring it through its fellows in half stitch until it reaches the pair hanging twisted from C. Work these together in half stitch (page 66), put in the pin which is at the extreme point of the ribbon, close in with half stitch and work back to the left side. Here the couple hanging from the point of the mitre are taken in, the pin closed, and the workers brought back to the right, but *not* working through the couple hanging from the last pin. The same number of bobbins must always be kept in the ribbon (twenty for this section); as each new couple is taken in on the left, so *one* has to be thrown out on the right. When the point is reached—the narrowest part of the scallop with two bobbins already hanging from the bottom pin—the ribbon couple is joined by whole stitch to the nearer pair, the pin is closed by the two already in possession, and the ribbon bobbins are left for the time being.

You will notice now that each of the ribbon pins on the right has a twisted pair of bobbins hanging from it and these, slanting to the right, seem to fall quite naturally towards the line of holes immediately beside them.

The edge workers are hanging from the pin at D. Work them through the pair of foot passives and join with the ribbon pair from the point. Put in the inside foot pin, return to foot, put in a pin and stop.

Work the ribbon couple falling from the second ribbon hole with its fellows just attached to the inner foot pin. The net is made by half stitch, pin and half stitch. That fills the first pin-hole of the *réseau*. Work the left couple in the same way through the next pair from the ribbon and put in a pin. Now you have reached the first leadwork: directions for making this are given on page 67. Commence by using one of the ribbon bobbins as the weaver. When the leadwork is deep enough, make the net stitch with the fifth ribbon couple and make the lower leadwork. Put in the ribbon pin to keep it secure, but do not fasten it. Return to the foot, work down the second line all in net stitch, and continue till the last and shortest line is at the point of the ribbon.

For a beginner it is easiest at the end of each line to pin into the ribbon holes, but when working quickly the work will not unravel if the pins stop at the line above.

Go back to the narrow point of the scallop where the ribbon bobbins were joined to the edge couple, and start again with the former. Work them in half stitch as before to the foot of the lower leadwork, remove the pin, work through the leadwork left-hand couple, put in the pin, close and return, but do not work through the last ribbon couple on the left. That is thrown out for the mitre.

Put in the pin, close it and return, taking in the couple that ended the second row of *réseau*. Repeat again, missing the outer couple on the left, and continue in the same way until the point of the ribbon is reached.

Now only the half of the mitre remains to be made. The workers are the inside pair hanging from the pin where the last section ended. Work them as before, two twists then whole stitch, through the four nearest pairs hanging ready twisted from the ribbon. Put up a pin at the top hole of the straight line of five holes which is nearest. Work back to the first hole in the scallop edge. Next time repeat the same stitch but only work through three couples, and the time after only through two couples. When the last couple has been worked and the workers are again at the edge, see that all the mitre bobbins are hanging from their pins ready and twisted once, bring your workers through them all, twisting twice between each till the hole which corresponds to point A is reached. Work through the last pair hanging from the ribbon, put in the pin and return to the pin-hole at the foot which starts the second half of the pattern.

From this point the lace repeats as before.

CLUNY LACES

The next examples on our list of Peasant lace are Nos. 3 and 4 of the illustration. These have been purposely chosen to show the gradual development of Torchon into a lace of more decorative character. The upper edge of both examples is identical with the lace described in the previous lesson; the leadwork is also the same, though, being elongated instead of square, it gives a different effect.

At first sight the working of the insertion would seem to be the same as for the edging, but there are several small differences, and therefore it will be best to treat each separately, only not repeating in the second lesson what has already been shown in the first.

Insertion.—Twenty-four bobbins will be required, and No. 100 linen thread. Start at the point marked A, which is the commencement of the lozenge. Divide the bobbins equally, and plait the two middle couples together several times.

Plaiting is whole stitch and a twist to each couple, repeated as often as is required to make the bar long and firm.

Put in the first pin at A, close it with whole stitch and twist each couple. Plait four bobbins on either side just enough to keep them firm ; then join the outer pair from the right-hand plait to the nearest couple belonging to the right edge. Work together in whole stitch, put in a pin at B, close it and take the edge worker through two pairs of twisted passives, put in the edge or *foot* pin, twist the workers, return to put in the inner edge pin, return again to the outside, pin up and leave. Do exactly the same on the left side. Both sides now being equal, return to the two sets of bobbins hanging from the pins at B and C. Plait each set, repeating whole stitch and twist three times for each bar, then work the inside right couple with the adjoining couple belonging to the centre plait, twist and leave. Do the same on the left side and then unite the two middle couples. Twist and leave them, for now they will hang down to become the inner passives for either side of the lozenge. The couples on the extreme right and left which have not yet been used will be the workers. Bring each in turn through its two pairs of passives, unite them at the top pin in the centre, twist, take each pair in turn to the outside of the lozenge, return, put up the inside pins, next time join the workers with the edge workers, closing the inner edge pin and returning. The sides will each have to be worked down in their turn to be ready to unite with the centre of the pattern at their fourth pin.

The lozenge workers continue until they unite at the inside centre hole, when they close it, return to the outside and remain hanging. The centre passives join in whole stitch without using a pin, work through the outer passives and join the old workers, putting in the last lozenge pin and closing it.

Each bar is plaited three times, and then joined to the edge workers, the pin is put in, closed, and left.

The centre plait will take five stitches to make it nice and firm, and will be left hanging. The leadworks will then be made on either side, using the pairs that respectively made the side bars. When both are done, bring the leadwork couples from the left, through the centre couples and the right leadwork couples, just as the path was crossed in the Trou-trou, only because there are more bobbins pick up two together, so that only one whole stitch is made by eight bobbins instead of four. This takes up less time and space, and is very useful when a thick thread is being employed.

Now divide the twelve centre bobbins. Twist once and make workers of the two middle pairs, bring the left one through the two couples on the left, then twist three times and work whole stitch with the edge workers, putting in and covering the inside pin. Again twist three times and bring the same couple back again to the centre. Repeat this on the right side and then rejoin all the couples as before. The two centre pairs make the straight plait, and on either side the leadworks use the remaining bobbins. The leadworks will be worked in with the edge workers on completion, and the repeat is then ready to start again.

EDGING

Pattern No. 4

There is no need to repeat again the instructions for the foot or the lozenge. There is, however, a distinct difference in joining in the leadworks, and although the lace is more elaborate than the insertion, only twenty-two bobbins are needed. Start at the lozenge and follow the instructions already given, but only having the plait made of four bobbins, for the lower edge. The plait will take three stitches between each pin-hole excepting where it passes inside the scallop and the outgoing point—here two stitches will be enough. The picot is made by twisting the outer pair of bobbins twice when the pin-hole is reached. The inner thread is then looped once round the pin, which is put in, the two bobbins are again twisted twice and then the plaiting is resumed.

Finish the lozenge section so that the sides are equal with the centre. Make the long middle plait, the right-hand plait also the same length, but only plait the left bar twice.

Join in to the edge on the right and then make the leadwork. When it is long enough work its two couples through the middle plait and weave again. Next time connect the leadwork with the short bar on the left, plait the leadwork bobbins twice, pass them through the edge plait and work on till you have filled the three picot pin-holes that begin the scallop. After the third pin, plait again and leave the bobbins hanging. The original edge bar and also the partly made bar beside it will each be plaited twice, joined *double* as already described, one whole stitch being made with the four couples, and both are worked again. The left bar passes through the bar now making the first scallop, and to make the middle scallop the second bar works to the straight bar where it connects the whole pattern by sending a pair of twisted workers to pass through the half-made star, to connect with the edge and return.

The straight bar continues to the nearest pin, the first scallop bobbins plait, work through the middle scallop bobbins, complete the last point and return to the straight line. The other bars will have been prepared so that these, the original leadwork couples, pass through them; weave the left-hand leadwork, pass through the four centre couples, weave again, and fasten at the edge on the right.

Pattern I.—Plate III

The foregoing instructions should make this lace quite clear. The diamond may look a little alarming at first, but it is made like the ribbon. The third couple from the left begin it and pass through the two couples nearest to them (recently leadwork couples), through the two centre bar couples and the two couples from the bar on the right. The diamond is worked in half stitch, and, like the ribbon, new bobbins are taken in and thrown out as the shape of the work requires. Refer to Torchon edging.

TROLLY OR THREAD LACE

THE NARROW BUCKINGHAMSHIRE PEA PATTERN

It would be difficult to find an easier little edging to start upon, and it is a favourite pattern for edging handkerchiefs. Twenty-two bobbins are needed, of which twenty should be wound with Knox's two-cord thread No. 180, and two with "Gimp" No. 24.

Knot the ends together and hang the bobbins round a large pin, arranging them so that the two gimps fall on the left, where pearl pins finish off the edge. The opposite side, the straight braid at the top of the lace, is always called the "foot" by the Buckinghamshire women, in distinction to the "edge."

The little rings which have given the lace its name occur in many patterns, and are known for all alike as "buds."

Start by examining the net, which is made in slanting lines, running from the foot to the buds. The longest line of net containing five holes, and ending where the buds join, is a good place for a start. Begin at the foot of this five-hole line. The fourth couple from the foot must be the workers. Bring them in whole stitch through the next two couples on the right, which help to make the narrow braid, and make the outside edge in the usual way, twisting three times, putting in the foot pin, working with the outside couple, twisting both three times, and bringing the new workers through the two braid couples. (The edge is fully described on page 68.)

As the workers pass the braid, twist them twice, and put them up behind a pin in the second hole, just where they come out. Make the net stitch with the workers, and the couple next to them on the left. Buckinghamshire net is made by one half stitch and two extra twists to each couple. Continue working the net stitch with the sixth couple, putting up the pin in the third hole, counting down the slanting line. Do the same with the seventh couple, and put up the pin in the fifth hole. At this point the work will stop and be recommenced at the foot, making first the braid and then the second line of net which, this time, has only four holes. When the bottom net pin has been put in, return to the foot and work the first three holes of the third line. The last hole must not be made until the bud has been started. The bud is made in honeycomb stitch.

On a level with the place where the gimps have crossed, but a little nearer the edge, there is one solitary pin-hole, and this must be worked in honeycomb stitch by the eighth and ninth couples.

The stitch is made by half stitch and an extra twist, then the pin is put in and closed with the same stitch.

The couple nearest the left-hand gimp is next passed through it and left. The second couple from the honeycomb stitch is worked out to the edge, through the remaining couple, and used to make the pearl pin for the nearest edge hole.

The pearl pin is described on page 68, so it is only necessary to say that five twists must be given before the pin is put in, and the usual single twist afterwards. After making the pearl pin, work the same couple through the next passives and pass it through the gimp into the bud.

The couples from the last two holes of the last rows of net must also be passed through the right-hand gimp, which will make four couples inside the gimps. Twist all twice.

Begin with the two centre couples and work the top hole with honeycomb. The centre couples are then worked with the pairs on either side, using the same stitch, and filling the first hole on either side. The two inner couples remain in the bud, but the couple on the right is next passed through the gimp to make the last net hole in the third line, while the couple next the left gimp passes through it and makes the next pearl pin in the edge. Both couples are worked back into the bud, and the second hole is worked on each side. The two centre couples are used for the remaining bottom hole, and then all are passed outside the gimps which are crossed again ready for the next bud.

At the edge the first couple passed out from the bud work out and make the pearl edge, then return through the intervening bobbins and join the couple next the gimp in working the odd hole in honeycomb as before.

The two couples passed out on the foot side lie ready to make the next long line.

From this point the pattern repeats.

The next pattern, which is also the last of the set, is the Buckinghamshire Fan. It makes an excellent second step for the beginner, and is one of the laces fully taught in Weldon's Lace Making Series, No. 229. This same book also gives instructions for the Daisy, a rather more difficult pattern, after which the pupil should be able to work out for herself one of the more ambitious laces, such as No. 1, Plate V.

RUSSIAN LACE

CORNER FOR A TABLE-CENTRE

This very easy little pattern has been chosen especially for a beginner's first attempt at lace making. To avoid wearisome repetition, the instructions for the various stitches are all given by themselves in Part II., therefore it will only be necessary to look out those which are needed for each lace before making a start.

Although this class of lace is commonly known as Russian, it is made by the elementary workers of most lace countries. It is the foundation for the Italian and Flemish Braid laces, for Bruges, Brussels, and for Devon, but it is the foundation only. Each of the laces enumerated will stand the study of many years, and each needs a volume to itself. It is not the object of this little book to attempt anything beyond those first steps which in nine cases out of ten have the power of so fascinating the worker that she is obliged to go on to more elaborate and interesting designs.

Russian lace includes many of the Peasant varieties, some Needle Point after the Greek style, and a great deal of bobbin-made Braid lace, most of which is made without the introduction of the fancy stitches which add so much to the artistic value of the Italian (*see* Plates VIII. and IX). The wider of the two Italian specimens with a very slight adaptation of design, no more than crowding the pattern together so closely that the open spaces now joined by brides would be done away with, would stand for the Russian lace known as Point d'Eglise. There would be no fancy stitches and rather fewer bobbins. The fine closely-made varieties of such lace fetch a high price, but it is very monotonous work to do—continual repetition of the same stitch.

Any pillow with a good broad surface will do for the lace—the mushroom or the Bruges pillows are the best; a broad Trolly pillow can be used, though a little awkward in turning corners, but a Torchon revolving pillow is quite impossible.

The corner is worked in two parts, consisting of the centre decoration and the outer braid. The latter had better be taken last, as it starts with a rather sharp curve, which the novice would find troublesome at first. Hang up the bobbins at the point marked A on the pricking, using seven couples, of which three should fall from the centre pin and two from the pins on either side. The following instructions will be needed :—

To make	whole stitch .	page	64
„	the edge . .	„	65
„	the blind pin .	„	68
„	a turning stitch	„	69
„	a sewing . .	„	66
„	picot brides or bars	„	71

These are all the instructions needed until the flower with its stalk and leaf have been made, and the centre part of the pattern has been well started. Then it will be necessary to look up the instructions on the brides, or bars, and last of all how to make the leadworks, the daisy-like ornament inside the flowers.

Commencing at A, the braid is worked in whole stitch, and if a moderately heavy thread is used two twists at the edge will be enough both for the workers and outside couples. Different makers of threads use different numberings for their goods, which is often very misleading, and so, to avoid possible confusion, in all instructions on laces made with linen thread the numbers quoted will be those used for Knox's linen lace thread.

This is a Scotch thread of excellent quality which works remarkably smoothly. Lace makers think a great deal of a thread which "lays" well, by which they mean that it must appear even and flat. Some threads always give the appearance of being round, no matter how careful the work, but a good lace thread should be flat and smooth, with a silky sheen that is only permanent when good flax has been used.

Torchon bobbins will be needed, as the long necks

will take a greater length of thread. These bobbins may be bought in two sizes, the larger ones being intended for a coarse thread. The thread suggested for this pattern, if it is to be used as a table-centre, is Knox's No. 100, when the completed lace would be about three and a quarter inches each side. The same pattern enlarged to seven inches is very suitable for a tablecloth, and should then be worked in Knox's No. 25.

The stem will be worked down to the flower without the need of any turning stitch, but if there should be more pin-holes on the outer side it will be necessary to put up twice behind the same pin, which is called making a blind pin. It will be noticed that the edge is straight on one side, like an Italian braid, but the workers pass through the outside couple, twist, put in the pin, and return, leaving a series of little loops which show when the pin has been removed. This is done in many of the Peasant laces, and is often introduced into patterns that need frequent sewings, as to join into the loop is prettier than going into the edge and less liable to pull the braid out of place.

In turning the corners made by the shape of the flower care must be taken to keep the threads evenly in the direction required. At the commencement it will be necessary to put up twice behind the first outside pin but when the middle of the first petal is reached there will be four outside pins to only one on the inside. For the first time work to the inside pin and close as usual, returning the second time, make a blind pin, and return. The third time make the turning stitch, pass to the outer edge, put in the fourth pin, return to the inside, work through the pair left out in making the turning stitch, work through the outside couple which has not been used for four turns, and take them back as workers. This will have taken the bobbins completely round the outside, and the same process must be reversed almost immediately after, when the inside curve has as many holes against the one on the outside. If the pillow is continually turned so that the threads always lie in the direction they should go, it will be easy to keep the lace even, without continually counting the number of holes, which, however, is a help at first.

The outline of the flower being finished, the second half of the stem will be made, and the decoration will not be put in until the very last.

Sewing will be needed when the two braids join, and as the stitch is completed the pin taken during that process will be replaced. When the pins begin to get in the way of the bobbins, press them into the pillow right up to the heads. When the lace grows, remove every second or third pin, and as the pattern becomes covered, pin a cover-cloth or a folded handkerchief across the made lace, so that the threads are not caught by the old pins.

The pattern is all plain braid, sewing, and an occasional blind pin or turning stitch, until the first curve of the centre leaves a diamond-shaped open space which will later be enclosed by the outer braid. When the centre of this sharp turn is reached, pass the workers through the outside edge and leave them. Return to the inside hole, and without altering the pin bring a new pair of workers across and work them also through the outside edge, putting in but not closing the edge pin. Plait the two couples together, and make one long bride reaching across the open space to the inner edge of the unmade outer braid. Put in a pin here, close it and return, pass each pair of workers back into the pattern, thus closing the pin and making the edge with the second couple in the usual way. The remaining half of the cross will not be made until the braid has completed the centre and come down to the corresponding part of the pattern. The sewings that unite the closer parts of the pattern are done when the second part is made. There is another open space above the one already attended to, but this appears to be of less importance. There is a single pin-hole in the centre, and when the braid workers are on a level with it, they are passed through the edge, twisted several times, passed round this centre pin, and again taken back to the braid. When the time has come for the second half bar to be made the same process is repeated, but it is not until the corresponding part of the pattern has been worked that the third bar is sewn through the loop of the first, while the last is connected with the second.

This same plan is used to fill the three smaller centre spaces as well as the two which are formed by the sides.

The double brides are all made on the same principle as the one already described. The one on the left side of the pattern is started from the point of the first outward curve belonging to the centre. The two couples are thrown out as before, and are carried across and sewn into the opposite braid. From there they work to the edge of the second central curve, are held in place by a pin, and return opposite to the braid. The bars are brought back in the same way, and only the cross brides have to be completed when the braid has worked round to reach them. The crossing brides must be sewn into the others in passing and returning. It will be understood that all "sewing" alluded to in Bobbin lace making means the method given under that name in the instructions and has nothing whatever to do with the needle. When the braid reaches a point where a bride is left alone at the edge, the pin is removed, the workers sew through the brides, and the pin is again put in and closed. The bars and net which fill in other open places are like the leadworks, put in when all the rest has been completed.

After the centre ornament is finished, and when the work has reached the foot of the pattern, a second bride must be thrown out to complete the cross bar at the foot. It is re-done in the way already shown and sewn in the centre to the bar already made.

The rest of the centre part is the reversed repeat of what has been done already. The bobbins will be sewn in, tied, and cut off at B, the reverse point to where the pattern was started.

The bottom braid may be started from either end; and begins at once with alternate blind pins and turning stitches. It is best to count round the outer and the inner holes so as to know exactly how many times each inside pin must be used. As the braid passes along the section already worked there will be constant sewings, both to connect the brides and also the lace itself.

The leadworks are fully described on page 67, and it is only necessary to say that three sets of bobbins are hung on to make the upper ones. When these meet in the centre they must be joined. Six pairs of bobbins will be hanging down. Cross the second and third pairs, so that they change places, also the fourth and fifth.

Work the two centre couples together, put in the pin and work each to its respective edge. Pass the inside pair

PLATE XIV.

THE FLEMISH BIRD.

To face page 99.

on each side over the nearest centre couple, then work as before.

The centre space at the top of the ornament is very simple net. Hang a pair of bobbins from the edge of either side, twist each pair once and join in whole stitch. Twist each again and leave. Sew in one more couple on either side, work whole stitch through the hanging couples respectively, twist each pair, leave the centre pairs hanging, but sew the side pairs into their respective sides, knot and cut off. Work whole stitch with the centre couples, twist, sew into the sides, bring them out again for one more stitch, then again to the sides, and tie off.

The long narrow spaces are filled by a twisted bar, just one pair of bobbins, which, sewn in at the top, is brought twisted from side to side, sewn in at regular intervals.

THE FLEMISH BIRD

Birds, beasts and figures are to be found in antique laces of many countries. Much church lace was made with figures of saints and martyrs; the story of the Crucifixion may be seen illustrated by lace in the Cluny Museum, and the handkerchief of St. Veronica with the Saviour's face upon it, copied many hundred years ago, is in the Groote Haus of Bruges. Lacis or Filet Brodé was the special lace that was at first almost entirely devoted to representation of living forms. Old cut work cloths had beasts and figures inlet into them, and sometimes made in Pillow lace as well. Near Frankfort, a Needle lace, very much after the style of Reticella, introduced hunting subjects, stags, riders on horseback and dogs, and the bobbins followed suit, so that Dentelle de la Chasse as it was called might be had in either make.

With the revival of Lacis, the Bobbin lace workers, not to be outrivalled, have begun again to make both birds and beasts. This time, however, their destination is to be the motifs let into cloths and cushion covers, rather than a part of any particular lace. The little bird illustrated is one of these latest revivals and a capital study for the lace maker who has mastered the easier work of the Russian corner-piece and is now ambitious to try something more difficult. It is always well to begin upon something that is not too large, for the first attempt may not always compare so favourably with the next that the same pieces can be placed side by side.

Practice upon the Flemish Bird will pave the way for those Bruges, Brussels and Devon stitches for which the Russian lace was the first step.

To work :—Use a round mushroom or Bruges pillow, and wind the bobbins with Knox's two-cord linen thread No. 140. Hang on eleven couples from the top feather in the tail at point 1.

Commence by following the directions for making whole stitch and the edge, but stop making the outside edge on the left after the top holes for the second feather are reached. From this point the workers will pass through the last couple on the left, twist once, put up a pin and return.

Work down to the last of the inside holes.

Before pinning this last hole, count and see how many holes remain to be used in the outside curve before the corner is completed. There would probably be seven holes against the one hole remaining on the inside.

Before putting in the last pin use a turning stitch (page 69). Next time work as usual and put in the pin but throw out the last inside couple until the whole corner is completed. Returning from the third outside pin, use the centre pin again (page 68), work the fourth pin, and, on returning, make the turning stitch again. After the fifth outside pin is covered, work back and pass through the left-hand edge couple which were thrown out, and put up again behind the centre pin. Next time in returning from the sixth hole you will not alter the pin but will exchange the workers with the outside couple.

As you turn the corner the pillow will need to be turned as well, so that the bobbins are always in front of you, and also hang in the direction they will go. The pillow is turned completely round in working to point 2.

Sometimes the braid will narrow suddenly, and bobbins may need to be thrown out. At the narrowest part of the second feather this might have been done, but the full number of bobbins would so quickly be needed again that it is best to keep them in and treat them as an outlining thread.

Two couples will be thrown out from the narrowest point and lightly twisted to keep them together. Each time the workers pass to sew with the inside edge they will pass under the two couples, treating them as though they were one thread, passing over them on the return journey. As the feather becomes wider first one couple and then both will be taken into the braid again.

Taking a sewing is described on page 66, so that it will be enough to say that each of the centre pins will be taken out in turn, and the workers from the lower feather sewn through the loop belonging to the upper one.

Arrived at point 2, instead of cutting off the bobbins, plait them all very loosely together, and sew two of them into the edge of the second feather at 3. The two sewn bobbins will be knotted over all their fellows, which are then spread into position for working the third feather.

This is also attached to the second feather by sewing, but a little differently in order to gain a more open space.

The workers pass through the edge couple, twist, sew through the edge of the upper feather, return, twisting again, pass through the edge couple, put in and close the pin.

On the lower side of this feather there will only be the twisted loop for edge.

Arrived at the bottom of the feather, put in the last pin and make a twisted roll (*see* Raised Work, page 73), to reach to the top of the fourth feather. Keep it in place by frequent sewings into the old feather.

The fifth and sixth feathers are worked in the same way, care being taken to unite the braid work of the two feathers above the raised roll, which is completely hidden as the foot is reached. At the bottom of the sixth feather plait all the bobbins together and put in a pin at 4.

Turn the pillow round and work to the opposite pin-hole—the top hole on the right belonging to the leg. After one or two crossings twist the workers once each time they reach the centre of the bobbins. This will give the little line of open holes down the middle.

The inside bend of the leg makes an abrupt corner, but this is not so complicated as it appears at first sight. Put in the pin at 5, and leave both outside couples and workers hanging but not enclosing it. Take the nearest pair of passives back as workers, put in the outside pin on the left, return to the inside pin-hole, and then leave the new workers hanging from the far side of that pin, while the next pair of passives are used in place of them.

The next time the workers return there is no pin for them, but they exchange with a new couple.

By this time four pairs will have been left out, all of which should be hanging with a single twist. The new workers on their return from putting up the pin on the right will now pass through these original workers as well, twisting once between each stitch.

When the pin on the left is put in, the original edge couple will be used, and then the work continues as before.

As the leg becomes narrower some bobbins must be thrown out, always two at a time, but chosen apart from each other, lest two thrown out together should make an ugly gap.

By the time the narrowest part is reached only five couples will be wanted, and these must be plaited at point 6, carried across to the middle toe and finished off (page 76) at the extreme point of the third.

Now start on a wing at 7. The sides of each feather are worked separately, the open centres being the result of sewing through loops both made with a single twist round the pin, and no outside edge couple. Seven feathers are worked in this way, and then at point 8 the bobbins are brought into the body and complete the upper part, ending off at 9.

Next the head must be started. Eighteen bobbins will be hung for the upper part of the beak.

Fourteen bobbins will do for the lower, and both sets of bobbins must be worked down until they are on a level, when the workers from the lower side must be brought right across to the point 10, and worked through two new couples hung from the top pin, to start the new edge, and return. The head will all be worked in one from this point, until the eye is reached. To make the little round hole divide the bobbins equally and make a single whole stitch with the two middle couples. Bring the workers through one of these middle couples, give a single twist, and work them back again to the edge they have just left. Use the second pair of centre passives as workers, and pass them to the opposite side and back to the centre. Twist and unite the two centre couples again in whole stitch and leave them hanging. The old workers will be brought across again from the edge and the hole is completed.

Where the crest divides it must be worked separately, and the extreme point finished before returning again to the commencement of the neck. About seven couples will be quite all that are needed to finish the crest, and when the last pin has been put in, this set of bobbins must be plaited lightly together and long enough to reach back to the pin which marks the division.

Take out the pin and put it again into the same hole with all the bobbins on the left side, excepting two pairs. With these make the outside edge and carry the workers through all, including those recently neglected, and put up the pin on the left.

The open stitch down the centre of the neck has been given already, but the holes which seem to divide the lace into sections are new.

Each passive couple across the line should be given a twist, then whole stitch is worked once with each set of two passive couples. Each pair is twisted before it is left, and when all have been treated in this way the workers are brought across again as usual. From point 9, where the neck of the bird joins the body, the same sewings are made that have already been described for the third feather in the tail. More elaboration is needed as the body becomes wider, and so an extra line of twisted bars is introduced, later on divided by the plain hole used already for the eye. When so many bobbins are used it would be rather awkward to finish all off in one bunch, and so they may be divided into six groups.

The bobbins of each group will be fastened into the edge belonging to the left leg, after which they will be tightly plaited. One-third will be needed for the wing at 11, and the remainder will be sewn into position so as to work down and finish the right leg.

When that is done cut them off and recouple them, sewing them in again at point 12, at the far side of the bobbins already there. For the first feather all the bobbins will be worked together, but when the pattern narrows at 12, divide and lift half the bobbins to make the long outside line of the wing, while the others work each in turn of the five feathers mounting one above the other.

The feathers will need the raised work already employed in the tail, excepting the top one, which is fastened off at 7.

Arrange the bobbins by sewings into the feather made some time back, so that three sets, each of two couples, hang from the centre. The first of the four spaces made for fancy stitches has now to be filled. Commence each set by working a simple whole stitch.

Bring the workers from the edge, through each of the three sets and also through one spare couple on the left. Sew the workers into the edge.

Prepare the passives again in groups, but start your first group by using the spare couple and the one nearest to it.

This stitch always requires one odd couple, since the same pairs must not be worked together twice consecutively. The workers pass through only after the passives are prepared in this way.

When the empty pin-holes are reached an edge couple must be provided.

Sew in at the foot, and turning the pillow, start filling up the next space from the reverse end.

To begin the net only two couples are required. Twist each pair once, work half stitch and give an extra twist, put in the top net pin, close in half stitch and twist twice to the pin-holes on either side.

A new couple will be taken in both from left and right, the centre couples divide, each to work with a new one, and filling the next two pin-holes. For the third line the centre couples work together again, while the sides sew into their respective edges and return to make the fourth line.

These few bobbins are not worth saving for the next filling, so they may be cut off, and hung on afresh.

The next spaces repeat as before, and are finished off.

Return to the bobbins left hanging from point 12. Work them in whole stitch, not forgetting the hole at short intervals until they reach the extreme point, then tie together, passing the outside bobbins once over and under the rest and knotting. Spread them out again and work the remaining feathers.

The bird is completed when the three net spaces are each filled. The effect of a heavy cord outlining each space is got by plaiting two surplus couples and joining them into the edge in the same way the extra bobbins in some of the tail feathers were disposed of.

To Work the Flemish-Italian Lace

This is the narrower lace, Plate VIII. There are a great many Italian designs which are quite as effective as this one, but easier to work. The principal difficulty of the pattern lies in the very deep turns, which involve a good deal of sewing which could, by a very slight alteration in pricking, have been avoided. An easier pattern might have been given, but this special lace being in the Kensington Museum is at hand for any lace worker to examine, and she is free to work out all the different stitches on a pricking that runs more smoothly if she wishes.

The same forms are to be found in other patterns, and so we will start by describing the flower which grows from a stem on the right-hand border.

It has five petals of which the two lower are filled in with Double Point, the two middle ones with Snatch Pin bars, the top one with Double Point again. The ring enclosing the centre is filled in with the Italian spider stitch.

Two different fancy holes are formed in the clothing, the Cross and the Ring.

Start by working a narrow stem-stick ring for the centre (*see* instructions, page 75) hanging on the bobbins at the foot of the circle. On working round, join the bobbins to the braid where it commenced, then add eight more couples and start making the lower petal on the right. If Knox's No. 140 two-cord thread is used the bobbins will be increased in number as the braid widens up to twenty-four couples, and the finer the thread the more bobbins will be needed. Until the corner is turned all is unrelieved whole stitch, then comes a plain hole (*see* page 69). A few more lines of whole stitch, and then the passives are all twisted in couples *twice* until the centre is reached, and *once* for the remaining pairs. Whole stitch is continued as before and the result is a row of open holes graduating in size towards the inside. This will be repeated lower down and has the effect of enclosing a special space to be filled with some particular stitch. This time it will be the fancy hole, the cross (*see* page 70).

For the upper part of the next petal this division will be used before and after the ring hole (*see* page 71). The top petal, being the most prominent, is decorated on both sides by a new stitch, not unlike but more elaborate than half stitch. For this there must always be an unequal number of passive couples.

The passives have to be prepared before the workers pass through. Starting from the side which has just received the last pin, divide them in sets of two couples, joining each in half stitch and a twist. The odd couple will be twisted twice. The workers are brought through, working in whole stitch, and make the edge on the far side. Again the passives are arranged in sets of four, but the first two couples to be joined are the last which have been worked, and so include the odd couple. This arrangement of bobbins with half stitch and twist is done every time before the workers pass through, and each new line finds the odd couple on the opposite side. The stitch is very pretty, but must not be too crowded with bobbins if it is to be open, therefore is specially useful where the braid suddenly widens.

The bottom petal has a rather difficult turn into the stem, and for this the directions for the leg of the Flemish

Bird should be followed. The pattern will be less difficult for the beginner if the bird has been practised first. For the fillings it will be best to start at the top petal and work down towards the centre. Four couples will be hung on, two at either side of the extreme point, and must be worked in whole stitch and twist, before starting the square (*see* page 72), after which each set will again be worked together in whole stitch and a twist, and sewn into the sides. After the second little square has been completed two more couples will be brought out from one side to join in making the third square. When the circle is reached the bobbins will be attached to it and left hanging.

Now hang four couples on one side at the top of the second petal on the left. Work these in cloth stitch across the open space, but instead of making any edge give the workers a single twist, put in a pin and work them back. It will be necessary to prick a very narrow braid across, about three holes on either side to each little bar. A bar or braid made in this way is called "snatch pin." Bring the couples down to the centre ring and sew in. Work the corresponding petal to the same point. Now return to the bobbins hanging from the top petal and start the spider filling with them.

This filling is given on page 75. It will need more bobbins as it widens, and for the second row these must be added on either side. When the third row is reached the bobbins hanging from the petals on right and left will come in usefully, any that are not required being knotted and cut off. As the centre decreases and throws out its surplus bobbins these will fall into place for the fillings of the two remaining petals.

To Work the Brussels Lace.—Plate XV.

The beginner should practise upon the Russian corner before attempting this pattern, and if she tries the Flemish Bird next, she will have little difficulty in working out this design.

The open rings which are so very typical of Brussels lace are made in stem stitch. The bobbins will work alternately on either side of the ring, turning round at the end and sewing once into each place which they cross on the way back.

All the turning stitches, sewings and leadworks have been fully explained in the previous instructions, and the star flower, which is the most difficult part of the lace, is treated by itself in the notes on raised work.

The lace when finished would be applied on a fine net.

DEVONSHIRE LACE

The Applied Rose is an illustration taken from "Devon Pillow Lace," and the leaves, which are the principal difficulty, are fully described in the book.

Those which have an openwork centre are begun by the narrow stem stitch, filling up all the middle pins.

Each of the raised leaves is composed of several small sections or indentations which the lace makers call "taps." The leaf will be started at the highest point, worked down and sewn into the stem stitch, then raised work is employed to bring all the bobbins up again to the point of the next tap.

To make Devonshire lace—as we have already advised for Brussels—the worker should practise first on the simpler patterns, such as the corner for table-centre. If, however,

PLATE XV.

BRUSSELS LACE.

To face page 110.

she wishes to begin at once upon the Devonshire, quite simple patterns may be had without any raised work, but which are at the same time just as artistic.

It is not the purpose of this little book to deal thoroughly with the making of any one particular variety, neither would it be possible to do so, owing to the restricted space.

An idea of the attention that even one lace requires may be gathered from the fact that when the Devon Lace book was written seventeen " fillings " were included as having been made in Devon, more or less recently. Now, after only two years, there are already more revived stitches that should be added to their number. If it has needed a book of 160 pages to deal with the lace of a single county, how many apologies should be offered for disposing of the work of an entire *country* in a single chapter ?

The Needle laces have had to be treated very badly, and really demand a separate book to themselves. Our excuse for not including any of them in the instructions must be that there are many more books dealing with Needle Point than with Bobbin lace. As put forward in the preface, the aim of this little book is not to give an exhaustive treatment of lace making, but to act as a stepping-stone to a fuller knowledge, to be a means of interesting the amateur in a subject that is comparatively little understood.

If the book can show that lace making is, after all, not such a very difficult accomplishment, and that lace collecting does not necessarily mean a very long purse, it will have accomplished a good deal.

PLATE XVI

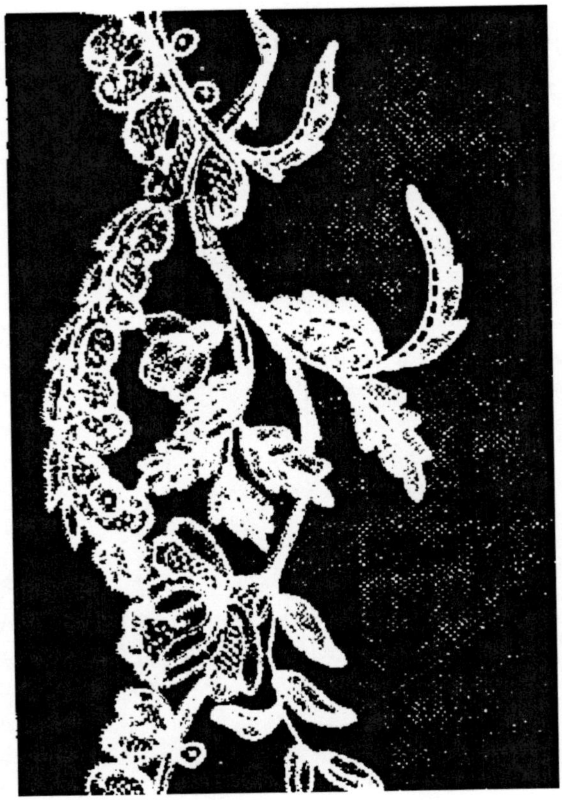

DEVON ROSE SPRAY.

To face page 111.

LACE MAKING

THE HOME CRAFT OF ALL AGES

BY

ELEANOR PAGE

PREFACE

No other fabric invented by man's ingenuity has been accorded so much admiration as lace. The desire to possess it is found in all classes. As a handicraft it is one of the most fascinating; it requires no expensive apparatus, is cleanly, makes no untidy litter, and is equally suited to the lady in her castle, the cottager, to relieve the invalid's tedious hours, and for the training of youthful hand and eye in schools.

In this twentieth century lace is used exclusively by women (with the exception of Church Dignitaries), though, when first made, lace was much worn by men; and in the "Golden Age" of lace making there was not a single article of attire from hat to shoes that was not decorated with it, and hardly a garment worn from the cradle to the grave that was not lavishly trimmed with it. No other article of attire has been so much hedged about by edicts, laws, orders, and restrictions; but neither edicts nor laws could prevent its becoming the most cosmopolitan of all art fabrics. A piece of lace that could be brought home in the pocket was easily carried from country to country and copied by adaptable fingers.

Two distinct classes of hand-made lace have survived all changes. The first is lace woven with bobbins on a pillow or cushion over stiff parchment having small holes to mark the pattern, the threads wound upon the bobbins being twisted round pins stuck in the perforations; it is known as bobbin lace and also pillow lace. The other is lace worked with a needle over a linen or thin parchment, and called needle-point lace. The two classes are often combined in making a particular kind of lace.

Laces not included in those classes are filet, which is worked on a small square-meshed net, and is a survival of darning on netting; another example of this class is needle running on fine machine-made net. There is crochet, which is executed entirely with a hook, and knit lace, which is made with two long pins. Laces which achieved a one-time popularity are: Tambourine lace, which was executed with a special hook on fine machine-made net stretched over a tambourine-shaped frame—hence its name; Tatting, executed entirely with a shuttle-shaped implement; Macramé lace, a heavy fringed lace worked with coloured twine cords. Lace has been executed in thread of every description; gold and silver metal threads, black, white, and coloured silk threads, worsted, human hair, and the hair of goats, and of angora rabbits. Yak lace is a coarse bobbin lace made from the wool of the yak. Perhaps the strangest of all lace is that woven from the pith of the aloe tree.

In this small work it is impossible to give all the kinds of lace. It is proposed to give a practical working knowledge of the principal stitches in the following: bobbin, needle-point, filet, and net-darning; and also to show the new artificial or Rayon threads executed on coloured modern machine-made nets. Readers whom we have thus far initiated into the intricacies of lace making will be able to continue their studies by consulting larger books.

Machinery has brought lace within the reach of all by producing fabrics at very low prices. And in these days of Robot human figures, and the artistic imitation by machinery capable of fabricating every kind of lace, it is not easy to distinguish the machine-made article from the handwork; but the work of the hand craftswoman still retains a place in the world's markets, and is appreciated by every one desiring artistic work of good finish in original, individual, distinctive designs; no two pieces of hand-made lace are exactly similar. Whatever changes fashion may bring, there are two occasions on which the finer, daintier handwork is supreme: to trim the dainty garments which comprise the new baby's trousseau, and the wedding garments and veil that adorns the bride.

I have to acknowledge valuable assistance from Mr. D. H. Rudd, curator of prints, Kelvingrove Art Galleries, Glasgow; Miss C. C. Channer, the Lace School, Northampton; and Miss J. M. Sweet, the School of Stitchery and Lace, Leicester.

ELEANOR PAGE.

CONTENTS

ILLUSTRATIONS

LACE MAKING

CHAPTER I

INTRODUCTORY AND HISTORICAL

THIS book is not intended to be a history of lace; but the would-be lace maker will find much to encourage her in overcoming difficulties, and in understanding the very wide field this art-craft covers, by tracing the art through its progressive stages until it reached the alluring gossamer fabric that has charmed men and women for centuries.

EGYPT. Herodotus, the "Father of History," records that Amasis, king of Egypt, sent to Athene of Lindus a corslet having figures interwoven with gold and cotton; and examples of elaborate netting, fringes drawn thread, and cut work, found on mummy wrappings in Egyptian tombs, are evidence that the earliest fabric deserving the name of lace was evolved in Egypt ten centuries before the Christian era.

In the authorized English Bible lace is frequently mentioned. In Exodus xxviii, 28 and 37, we read of how a blue lace was to be used for the adornment of the high priest Aaron; and again in chapter xxxix, 31. The knotting together of gold, silver, and coloured threads was man's first attempt to gratify the desire for beauty in attire latent in the most primitive; then followed the drawing of threads, to be succeeded by "cut" work involving the cutting out of portions of the material and the filling of the open spaces with stitchery.

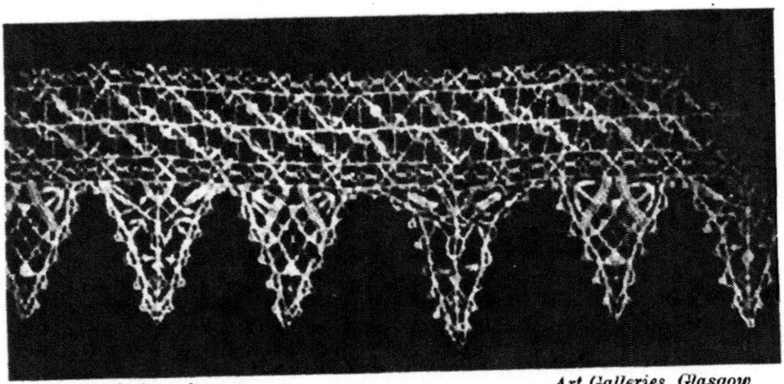

By permission of *Art Galleries, Glasgow*

RETICELLA—AFTER DESIGN IN VINCIOLO'S BOOK, 1590

By permission of *Art Galleries, Glasgow*

TAPE GUIPURE
Sixteenth Century

By permission of *Art Galleries, Glasgow*

KNOTTED PUNTO A GROPPO
Seventeenth Century

PLATE II

GREECE. The Greeks are responsible for the earliest needle-made lace called Reticella. This is entirely geometrical in design with an open-work ground.

ITALY. Lace, as we know it, originated in Italy. Venice, Milan, and Genoa each gave its name to a distinctive kind of lace. The Venetians produced what still remains one of the most beautiful of laces, Venetian Point or Point de Venise; and every modern lace owes something to the Raised Point, Flat Point, and Ground Point created by the Venetians of the sixteenth and seventeenth centuries. Milanese and Genoese laces were made with coarser thread. The designs were geometrical, and the edges vandyked or scalloped. These still remain the distinguishing features of lace so named.

In those early days patterns were difficult to obtain. Original designs were handed down from father or mother to son and daughter, and kept a family secret. The first book of patterns to be given to the world was by a Venetian, Frederick Vinciolo, in 1587. So great was the demand for it that it was reprinted in several editions throughout Europe and in England. Italian laces became the coveted possessions of all the Courts of Europe.

FRANCE. In the middle of the sixteenth century Henry III engaged Vinciolo to be "Pattern-maker for Needlework and Laces" to his Court; and under the influence of Henry III and of Louis XIV the hand lace industry was firmly established in France. Lace schools were opened at Alençon, Argentan, Quesnoy, Arras, and various other French towns. The most beautiful laces produced by the French are Mechlin, Point d'Alençon, Point de Argentan. Mechlin is a trimming lace of exquisite softness, daintily patterned with

By permission of *Art Galleries, Glasgow*

FLOUNCE OF POINT DE ARGENTAN

Eighteenth Century

PLATE III

flower sprays outlined with a brighter thread. Point d'Alençon is distinguishable in having small spots all over the net, the design being usually ribbon knots connecting flower sprays. The design of Point de Argentan is similar to that of Alençon, but the ground consists of a large six-sided mesh, each side of the hexagon being worked over with fine button-hole stitches. France also produced a point ground known as Point de Paris, used in the making of Valenciennes lace, a popular trimming extensively made at La Puy and Mirecourt in pre-war days.

SPAIN. The art spread from Italy to Spain. Barcelona was the chief lace centre, and in the early days much metal lace of gold and silver thread was made for trimming velvet. The Spanish lady's gala dress, the Mantilla of Point d'Espagne, is made of silk thread in a heavy pattern on a fine net ground; much lace is also made of white cotton thread.

BELGIUM. The Spaniards, overrunning Flanders and the low countries, carried the art with them and taught the Flemings. Able to grow flax to produce the finest quality of thread, the Flemings eventually became the world's lace makers. Brussels lace is still considered to be the aristocrat of modern laces, and is almost exclusively used for bridal veils and Court trains. It consists of three classes, Point, Appliqué, and Duchesse. Brussels Point de Gaze is distinguishable by a very fine net ground into which is worked delicate sprays of flowers. Brussels Appliqué differs from Point in that the flowers and sprays are made separately on the pillow, then applied to fine net by invisible stitchery. Brussels Duchesse is entirely a bobbin lace made on the pillow, the main portions of the design being connected by bars, *brides*, and various fillings.

Another Belgian production is Bruges lace, a bobbin lace often confused with Duchesse because of similarity in design; but in the making of Bruges lace a coarser thread is used for harder wear. Belgium also produced extensively the harder wearing quality laces: Valenciennes, Cluny, Malines, Torchon.

MALTA. In the small island of Malta lace making has been carried on extensively from the earliest days of the industry, chiefly in the convents. Maltese lace is a fine guipure lace made in white silk and in cotton thread on the pillow. A distinctive feature of the design is the Maltese cross made of four small ovals. Maltese lace has achieved a world-wide popularity.

GERMANY. Saxony claims to have originated bobbin lace in the sixteenth century—a claim disputed by several authorities—but lace making has been carried on in different parts of that country for centuries, and in the Saxony region by generations of lace-making families. In the eighteenth and nineteenth centuries Hungarian bobbin lace and Dresden lace ruffles had a wide market.

HOLLAND. Lace making in Holland dates from the Edict of Nantes, 1685, when many French refugees fled to the Netherlands. The Dutch became famed for their Haarlem thread, a fine, soft, silky flax bleached on the meers of Haarlem and Yarranton. The lace was made to a distinctive, individual scroll design composed of scrolls and ovals of irregular outline closely connected on the pillow. Dutch lace was thick, strong, and serviceable; and at one time, the people tied up their door knockers with lace to announce the birth of a baby—surely one of the strangest uses to which lace has been put.

Denmark and Sweden made lace in the sixteenth and eighteenth centuries; but both countries only supplied their own wants. The Tonder lace of the former, and the Swedish Point were generally worked into collars. Peter the Great is stated to have introduced lace into Russia, and the late Czarina opened a school at Moscow and a depot in London for the sale of Point de Moscou lace.

ENGLAND. The religious persecutions of 1568 drove many Flemings to England, and groups of lace-makers settled down in London and in the valleys of Devonshire; and a later contingent travelled farther north and settled in the Midlands. These fugitive Flemings set to work to produce the laces which are the direct ancestors of the modern Honiton, Northampton, and Bucks laces.

The so-called Point de Angleterre was not originated in England, but came to the country in the following manner. The English Parliament becoming alarmed at the huge sums being spent on foreign lace passed an edict prohibiting its import; and English merchants, in order to procure supplies of the much desired finest Brussels Point, unproduceable from the coarser English grown flax thread, resorted to the ruse of buying up the choicest pieces in Belgium, and smuggling them into England to be sold as Point de Angleterre.

Lace making soon became the favourite recreation of England's fashionable ladies of leisure. Reigning kings and queens were its patrons, and noblemen paid high fees to have their daughters instructed in the art. The English lace industry reached its zenith in William and Mary's reign. Queen Mary herself was an enthusiastic lace maker; her custom of carrying lace threads wherever she went, and working in her coach caused a Court wit to dub her Majesty the "Royal Knotter." Specimens of Queen Mary's lace are still to be seen at Windsor Castle.

Honiton has always been considered to be England's representative lace. It was the favourite lace of three English Queens. Queen Adelaide had a dress made of it, the skirt of which was encircled with a wreath of Honiton flower sprays; in each spray was worked an initial to compose her Majesty's name. Queen Victoria's wedding dress was made entirely of Honiton sprays connected on the pillow with various fillings. The dress cost £1,000 to make, and a reproduction was made impossible by the destruction of the pattern on the completion of the dress. Queen Alexandra's bridal robe had a design composed of Prince of Wales's feathers intermixed with ferns. Modern Honiton is entirely a bobbin lace, and was exclusive to Devon and the southern counties. The Midland counties of Northampton, Bedfordshire, and Leicester early became known for the production of dainty laces for the trimming of baby garments and edgings for lingerie. Tradition associates Queen Katherine of Aragon with a certain type of Midlands lace which Her Majesty is stated to have taught the cottagers whilst staying in Bedfordshire. The lace productions of the three counties are practically similar. Modern Bucks Point is distinguishable for its beautiful clear net which composes the ground; and the pattern is outlined with a thick thread.

Scotland. Lace making became known to the Scots at an early date through intercourse with France, Holland, and Flanders. Although lace was an unsuitable trimming for the Scots homespun, the Highlander, in full dress, appreciated lace ruffles of fine Flanders lace. One of the ablest exponents of the art was Queen Mary Stuart. During her captivity she solaced herself with her needle, and is credited with making lace to numerous patterns of her own designing. These included distinctive designs of fifty-two flowers, sixteen four-footed animals, and one hundred and twenty-four birds. Scotland has no representative lace. In the seventeenth and eighteenth centuries, a needle-made lace of exquisite fineness worked on delicate muslin and called Ayrshire Point Lace was made in that county; and in the middle of the seventeenth century, under the influence of the Duke and Duchess of Hamilton, lace schools were opened at Edinburgh and at Hamilton in which instruction was given in the making of lace of a coarse, durable quality.

IRELAND. A variety of laces have been produced in Ireland. The earliest, known as Innishmacsaint, was a rose point needle lace in a heavy design. Carrick-ma-cross Appliqué was extensively made in the seventeenth and eighteenth centuries. In the making the pattern was cut out on fine linen or cambric, the portions of the design not required were cut away, and the open spaces filled in with needlepoint stitchery; or, in the case of appliqué, the cambric pattern was invisibly sewn on to a machine-made net. Limerick lace was first embroidered on the tambour frame on fine machine-made net, and later worked with a needle in close running stitchery. Youghal lace, made at a convent in Cork, was a reproduction of Venetian rose and flat points. A collar of Youghal lace was presented to Princess Maud as a wedding gift. The design had the Princess's monogram and a coronet. The lace made in Ireland to-day is almost exclusively crocheted.

Lace making and needlework has ever been the daily employment in the convents of Roman Catholic communities. In the fourteenth century lace was known as "Nun's Work." To-day, the Christian missionary in eastern countries combines those crafts with evangelistic work among native women, and the crafts provide employment for outcast converts. Until the middle of the nineteenth century almost the only schools in the lace-making counties of England were lace schools, in which pupils were taught lace making in conjunction with reading. To-day, apart from private schools, where individual instruction is invariably given, the class teaching of lace is carried on in Schools of Art and in Technical Colleges by means of grants from the State-aided Education Authorities or County Council Technical Education Committees.

It has been customary for the beginner at lace making to commence with torchon, cluny, and the coarser laces until flexibility of touch in handling the bobbins and exactness of vision are acquired. But a long established lace instructress advises would-be lace students to commence straight away with the kind of lace she admires and wishes to make, whether it be Honiton or fine Brussels, or the effective coarser edgings. Lace making can be learned from books; but the student would benefit greatly in the initial stages by a few lessons from a teacher.

It is something for the lace craft worker to remember that the beautiful creations of her industrious fingers will increase in value as time goes on. Real lace has the great advantage over the machine-made fabric in that, with proper care and usage, it will last for centuries. And like jewellery, should one desire to sell it, one may expect to obtain a good price for it. Since the destruction of churches and chateaux in the Great War very little real lace has come into the market, but the following prices of real laces auctioned at Christie's just before the war will give readers some idea of lace values. For a flounce of Point de Argenton, 4 yd. long and 24 in. deep, the sum of £460 was given; for a length of Point de Venise 84 in. by 24 in., £360; while 4 yds. of finest old Italian flat Rose Point 11½ in. deep was sold for £450; and an Alençon panel for a dress front 44 in. deep, £43.

Quite apart from the pecuniary value of lace in the rush and hustle of modern life when mental and physical overstrain is the common lot, lace making provides the quiet engrossing occupation necessary for the recuperation of powers; and those suffering from nerve overstrain find in it a certain cure, just as queens and lesser women from the days of Helen to Queen Mary found in it a solace in tribulation. To quote Ruskin—

"The whole value of lace as a possession depends on the fact of its having a beauty which has been the reward of industry. . . . That it proves by the look of it the ability of the maker; that it proves by the rarity the dignity of the wearer."

CHAPTER II

BOBBIN LACE

THE OUTFIT. For the making of bobbin lace a large variety of pillows, cushions, and bobbins are procurable. A beginner's outfit may be as expensive and decorative as she wishes; or, when economy must be practised, all the apparatus to commence can be made at home. The pillow or cushion can be made of velvet, silk, or chintz, and stuffed with horsehair; or at a nominal cost by using linen or calico and stuffing with straw, hay, sawdust, or the cork dust used in packing grapes. Bobbins are obtainable in bone and ivory inlaid or carved, and in wood machine-turned.

The apparatus consists of: (1) A pillow or cushion on which the pattern is affixed, and a stand to support and steady the pillow; (2) patterns which have perforations or a tracing to show the places for the pins that support the lace in the working; (3) bobbins on which the thread is wound; (4) thread to make the lace; (5) pins. Accessories are: A bobbin winder; a pricker; a hooked needle; a pin-cushion; a carrying case for pillow; a case for holding spare bobbins; two cotton squares.

The outfit and all the materials can be bought at the depots in any of the lace-making centres in England, and there is a lace studio in most large cities.

Pillows are made in various shapes: bolster, mushroom, square, and circular.

The bolster is the most suitable for working long

lengths of edgings and insertions, as it revolves; and it is a simple matter to make a pattern long enough to circle the pillow and thus save the necessity of removing the work when one length is finished.

Mushroom shape is best for working piece lace such

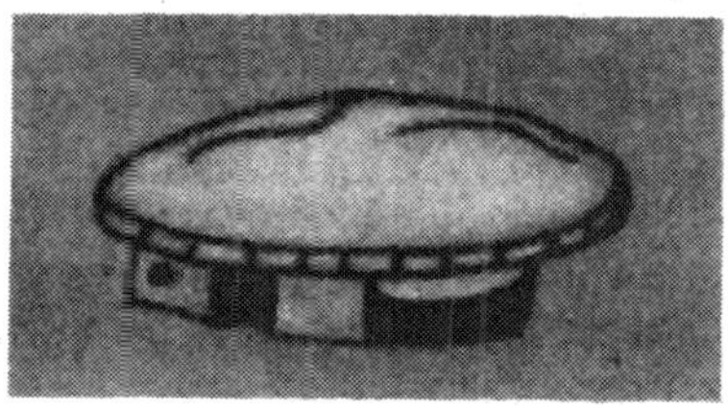

MUSHROOM CUSHION

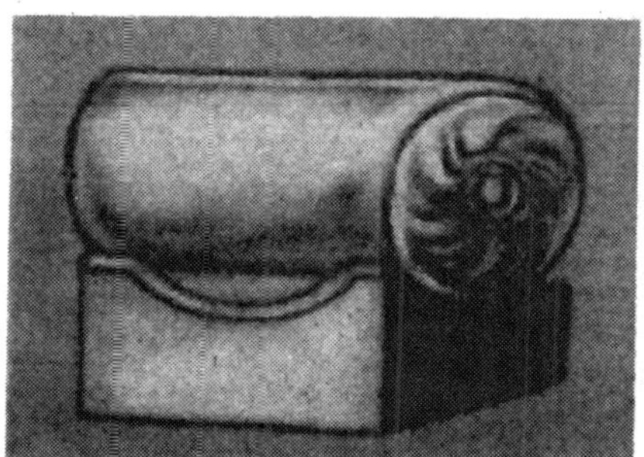

BOLSTER PILLOW ON BOX STAND

PLATE IV

as Brussels and Honiton, as the pillow must be turned in all directions, so that the bobbins hang over every part of it; on a bolster they are apt to roll, instead of hanging in their order. The square and circle cushions are preferred by many English lace makers.

To make a bolster pillow at home; cut a strip of

hessian, or similar stout material, measuring 14 in. wide and 30 in. long. With this make a case. Seam up the two short ends. Turn in a half-inch lay at both open ends, and run a cord through; draw up one end very tightly and begin to stuff the pillow. The best stuffing for lace pillows is straw or hay cut into 6 in. lengths. Wool and fluffy stuffs do not make a firm enough pillow. Put the straw in in handfuls so that it lies flat, pressing it in very firmly, and when the case is full take a mallet or wood roller and beat it, filling up the case with more straw until the pillow is very firm and hard; but there must be no lumps, or the fine pins used for delicate laces will be spoilt. Draw up the cord and tie securely. Make an outer cover of brown holland, blue linen, or a pretty cretonne. Cut it slightly larger than the case, and tie long draw cords so that the cover may be removed for washing.

To make a mushroom cushion a disc of wood about 1 in. thick and 16 in. in diameter is required for the foundation. Cut a circle of hessian 2 in. larger than the disc all round. Tack, with small nails, three-quarters of it round the edge of the disc, leaving an opening; now stuff the cut straw in as firmly as possible, shaping it like a large mushroom, high at the middle and sloping at the edges; beat with a mallet and stuff with more straw until the cushion is hard and springy. Tack down the opening, and cover with a pretty material, using brass studs or a braid to make a nice finish. Bought mushroom cushions are fitted with a small drawer to hold bobbins.

For a square cushion take a square of stout material measuring 3 ft. Fold it like an envelope with the points of the four corners meeting, and oversew three seams, leaving one open. To keep the cushion in good shape insert a square of cardboard or thin wood in the bottom, then proceed to fill up with cut straw until the cushion is firm. Sew up the opening.

The above measurements are for medium size pillows easy to carry to and from a studio. The worker may make the pillow as large as she wishes; a smaller size is useful to take when travelling to work on a steamer.

A bolster pillow requires a stand to support and keep it steady. Three types of stand are common. A very simple one can be made out of a box 6 in. deep and large enough to stand the pillow inside. It can be held on the knees or rested on a table. The box is made to look nice with a coat of art paint, or a cretonne covering both outside and inside. Also there is the tripod shape with a half-hoop that fits over the worker's knees; and a folding one like a camp stool without the seat. A carpenter will make either of the latter two types for a small sum.

In addition to the above there is the French roll pillow. This is in the form of a small cylinder with an axis fitted into grooves cut into the side of a box which is higher at the back than at the front. The lace can be worked in a continuous length by turning the cylinder, and as it is worked off it falls into the box.

A good protective cover is made with American cloth. It should be cut large enough to allow the pillow to slip in easily, and with 4 in. to flap over at the opening. The seams may be joined with a contrasting piping of leather, or bound with braid.

The type of bobbin in common use to-day is a slim, straight bobbin having a head to hold the hitched thread, and a ring of beads to weight the shaft. Wood bobbins costing 6d. to 1s. per doz. are made in various sizes and thicknesses. Torchon and other coarse laces made with thick thread require large bobbins; while fine Duchesse lace can only be made with small, light bobbins, or the work would look puckered and dragged.

Bobbins can be made with a sharp penknife and some odd pieces of wood; boxwood is best as it is smooth, light, and polishes. A large size bobbin for thick thread should measure 5 in. in length, 1½ in. round the thickest part. Half an inch from one end a head is shaped to prevent the thread from slipping off, and just below the head 1½ in. is grooved to a slim stem; on this neck the thread is wound. Bobbins for the finest lace should not measure more than 3½ in. long, and ½ in. all round; the head merely a dot ⅛ in. Two holes are bored at the end, through which a wire is passed with coloured beads. Some lace makers only use the bead ringed bobbins for the weaver pairs to help distinguish them from the warp bobbins.

Threads. When possible, linen thread should be used for lace. It adds to the beauty and value of the lace, and lace made with it keeps its shape when washed. Some ladies object to the glossiness of linen. For them a special lace thread with a dull surface called "gassed" is recommended. When cost must be considered, and a cheaper thread used, a cotton thread with a smooth finish should be chosen. For outlining flowers and leaves in Brussels and other laces a thick linen thread called a "gimp" is used.

Patterns. A special parchment skin is sold for lace patterns. On this perforations are made with a pricker for the pins that support the lace in the working. A good substitute is a thin flexible cardboard of a tough make. Some lace workers paint a wash of art green over the pattern, which shows up the lace, and is a comfort to weak eyes.

Pins. Pins for lace should be gilt or silver-plated, and must be suitable in size for the lace being worked. Pins with glass heads are used for Torchon and other laces, to help the worker to distinguish headings and footings, and the ornamental from the ground part.

A pricker is a long steel point fixed in a wood handle. To make one at home remove 1 in. of lead from a pencil and push in a fine darner or a long sewing needle.

A fine crochet hook is necessary for making the "sewings" in piece lace. A wig-maker's needle with a curved hook is the best instrument for this purpose.

A pin-cushion about 4 in. square is a necessity. It is pinned to the pillow by a small loop at one corner.

A large square of white calico or two or more handkerchiefs are required to dress the pillow so that the lace will be kept clean while it is being worked.

A bobbin winder is a time saver, but is not an essential.

A case for holding spare bobbins is useful. It may be made of chintz or linen. Cut a strip about a yard long and a foot wide. Hem all round; then, along one side turn in 4 in. to form a pocket; divide this pocket into compartments large enough to hold a pair of bobbins. The flap is folded over and the case rolled up and fastened with a tape or press stud.

The pillow, bobbins, and pins constitute a loom on a small scale, on which the worker may weave beautiful and durable laces to embellish household or personal linen, or the more fascinating, dainty laces of gossamer fineness.

Dressing the Cushion. Before beginning to make lace the student must learn how to prepare or dress the cushion or pillow. Be careful that there are no

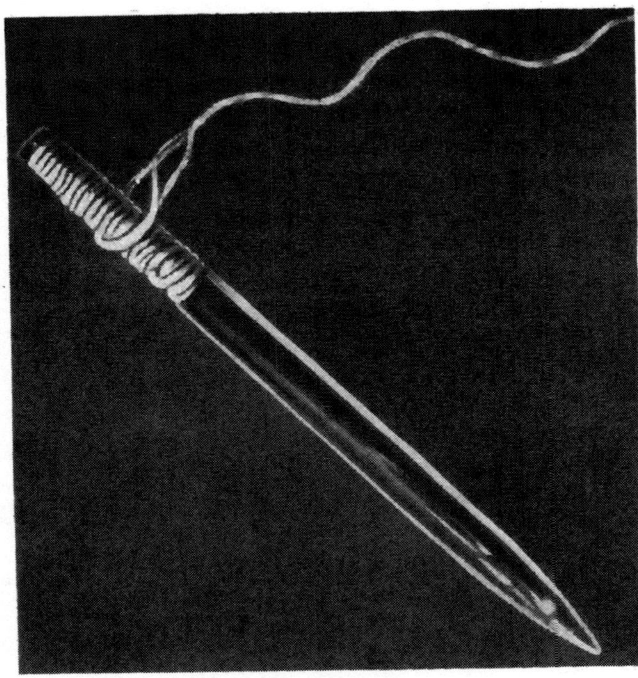

Threaded Bobbin

PLATE V

lumps or thick joins in the material, as fine pins would be bent instead of penetrating it.

To dress a flat cushion have a square of white calico or blue linen larger than the cushion. Cut a hole in the middle 3 in. across, and hem all round. Lace is always worked as near the centre of the cushion as possible. Pin the pattern on the cushion with strong pins through each corner, pushing the pins well in so that only the heads are visible. Place the cover over the pattern so that the part of the lace to be worked is exposed at the hole. As the work progresses the cover is drawn along with the hole always at the working part, whilst the rest of the lace is kept covered. If the cushion has not a detachable washing cover it is advisable to pin a square (without a hole) under the pattern. The pin-cushion, well filled with pins, is pinned on securely a few inches from the bobbins.

For dressing a bolster pillow two large-size handkerchiefs can be used. Fold them double, lay one across the pillow over the pattern, then place the other so that the part to be worked is exposed; pin both handkerchiefs securely over the ends of the pillow. When the work is not in use the ends of the cover are folded over the bobbins to keep all clean.

Winding the Bobbins. To fill the bobbins without a winder cut the thread in yard lengths, hold the bobbin in the left hand, lay an end of the thread on the neck of the bobbin, and with the thread held between the thumb and forefinger of the right hand, wind it with the thread coming from underneath towards you, and over the top of the bobbin; wind evenly, and keep a firm, regular tension, revolving the bobbin with the left hand. Leave about 6 in. of thread, and to keep the thread from unwinding make a slip loop, pass it over the head of the bobbin, and give an extra twist. If it is twisted too much the thread will not run.

Bobbins are always worked in pairs, and bobbins wound in this way require to be knotted at the ends.

To wind without knotting, use a longer length of thread. Wind one half of it on one bobbin as described above, and secure it with a slip loop; then lay the other end of the thread on the neck of the second bobbin and wind it as above; leave about 9 in. of thread between the two bobbins, and secure the second bobbin with a slip loop also. Hang each pair when wound on a pin in the cushion.

CHAPTER III

BOBBIN LACE—THE FOUNDATION STITCHES

THE two foundation stitches in bobbin lace making are called " whole-stitch " or " cloth-stitch," and " half-stitch " or " gauze-stitch." The method of making these stitches is shown in Figs. 1, 2, 3, 4, 5 (Plate VI). Use a thread of medium thickness for practice lessons.

HALF- OR GAUZE-STITCH. Wind four bobbins and knot in pairs at the ends, and hang them side by side on a pin pushed half-way into the cushion (Fig. 1). Hold a pair in the palm of each hand. Cross both pairs by giving them a twist in the hand, the right bobbin over the left one, in both hands (Fig. 2); next cross the two middle bobbins, but this time the left bobbin is crossed over the right one (Fig. 3); again cross the right bobbin over the left one (Fig. 4). The two last movements make the half-stitch. The twisting of the threads in Fig. 2 is only required at the commencement.

WHOLE- OR CLOTH-STITCH. To make a whole-stitch hang two pairs side by side as in Fig. 1. Cross the two middle bobbins, left bobbin over right one as in Fig 3; next cross each pair in both hands, right bobbin over left one (Fig. 4); again cross the two middle bobbins, left bobbin over right one, and complete the stitch by drawing the threads close together (Fig. 5). To do this pull well apart the pair held in each hand. Push a pin in between the two pairs of bobbins and commence another stitch, drawing the threads well up so that the pin is enclosed. The worker should practise this stitch until she can do it mechanically. The threads themselves should not be touched. All the movements must be made by turning the bobbins; but the worker must learn to look at the threads, and not at the bobbins in her hands.

There are four principal stitches in bobbin lace making. These are: (1) whole-stitch or cloth-stitch, which gives a similar effect to weaving; (2) half-stitch or gauze-stitch, which is more open and lacy, and is often called lace-stitch; (3) plait-stitch, which is used to join sections in a design and for bars; (4) leaf-stitch as its name implies takes the form of a leaf (see Fillings);

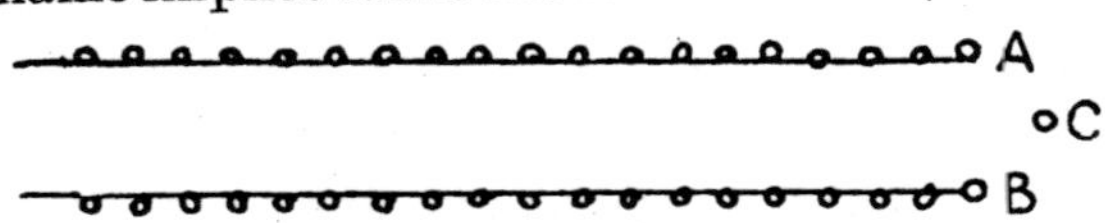

FIG. 1. DIAGRAM FOR THE MAKING OF BRAIDS

it is much used in the making of guipure laces such as Cluny and Maltese. All the other stitches used in laces made with bobbins are a variation of these four stitches.

In the following lesson on the making of braids, four examples of braids are shown, and the method of turning a curve neatly. A large variety of braids can be evolved by working cloth and gauze-stitches in alternate sections and outlining both edges with gimp to form a small square or oval; by working a small leaf across the braid; by twisting the weavers and also the warp threads a number of times between each stitch. Only one picot edge is given; this edge can be varied by working three or more picots in each edge loop; another variety of open edge is made by merely twisting the threads to form a loop of ½ in. to 1 in.

The Making of Braids. The beginner should practise the stitches by making braids, and learn to

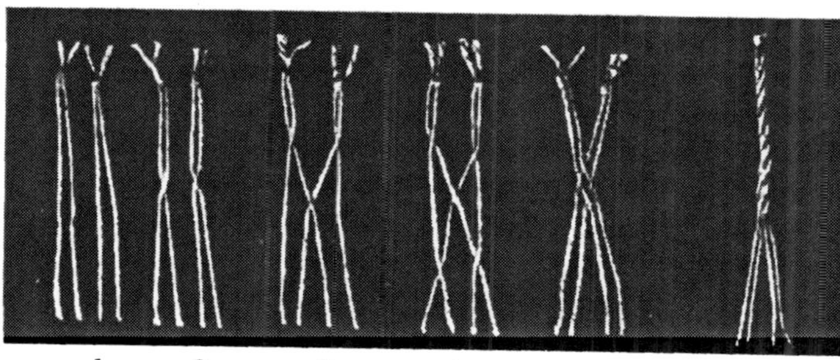

1 2 3 4 5
Foundation Stitches Plait

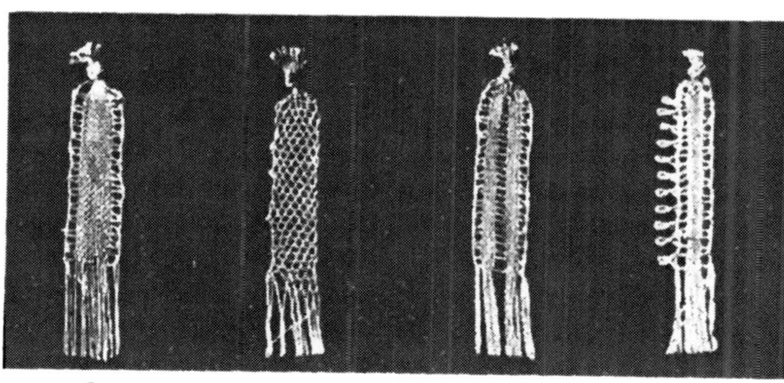

6 7 8 9

Braids

Cloth Gauze Open-centre Gimp and Picot Edge

PLATE VI

handle the bobbins with ease and dexterity before attempting even a simple lace sampler.

Ordinary Braid (Fig. 6). To make a pattern for

braids, draw two vertical lines ⅜ in. apart on a piece of paper. Mark dots for pinholes ¼ in. apart down both lines; mark the top dots *A*, *B*; make a dot in the middle of top; mark *C*. Paste the paper on flexible cardboard, fix on the cushion with a pin through each end, and prick through each dot.

In working a braid it will be noticed that some bobbins have their threads hanging straight down, and always keep that position; these are called the "warps" and form the warp of the material. Others called "weavers," travel backwards and forwards to form the woof.

A beginner will find it easier to distinguish the weavers, and to follow the movements of the threads, if three colours are used for the weavers and white for the warps in the making of a first braid.

To make braid (Fig. 6) wind six pairs of bobbins with white, one pair each with red, blue, and tan. Do not use too fine a thread for practice lessons. No. 20 is easier to work with. Tie all the white bobbins in a knot at the ends, pass a pin through the knot, and fix firmly in the cushion at *C*. These are the warps, and the threads must not be crossed, but should hang straight down (see Fig. 1). Knot two colours—blue and tan—hang on a pin at *A*, and one pair, red, at *B*.

Begin at the left and work across to the right. Stick or set a pin in the hole below *A*, between the blue and the first white pair next it. Blue are the weaver pairs. There will be two coloured pairs—blue and tan—outside the pin. Twist each pair three times (twists are always made right bobbin over left, see Fig. 2), make a whole-stitch with them, and lay the tan aside on the cushion at the left. Take up blue (weavers) in the left hand and the first white pair in the right hand, make a whole-stitch with them, and enclose the pin by pulling each pair well apart so that the stitch is drawn against the pin. Lay down the white pair, and with blue (weavers) make a whole-stitch with the second white pair and then with each succeeding pair until the weavers have passed through the last of the warps. There will now be the blue and red pairs outside *B*: twist each pair three times, make a whole-stitch, set a pin in the hole below *B*, and lay the blue pairs aside on the cushion at the right. Use the red as weavers this time and work across to the left. Take red (weavers) in the right hand and the first white pair lying next to it in the left hand, make a whole-stitch, enclose the pin by drawing the stitch against it; lay down the white pair and make a whole-stitch with red (weavers) and the second white pair.

Repeat until all the warps are worked through. Twist red three times and tan three times, and make a whole-stitch with them. Set a pin in the next hole; lay aside red, use tan as weavers, and work across to the right. Continue the braid. It will be noticed that the twisted threads form the firm edge. Remember always to twist the weavers after they have passed through the warps, and to twist them again before crossing to the opposite side. One outside pair must be left at each side at every crossing. Some lace makers always use the same pair as weavers, but that method does not make so firm an edge.

Pull the warp threads well down to prevent the braid from rucking up or looking puckered. At each crossing set a pin in the next pinhole at the side the weavers arrive at. Push the pins well into the cushion, but with the heads slanting slightly outwards, so that the braid is held taut.

Gauze Braid (Fig. 7). This is made with half-stitch. It is quite easy to make, but a mistake not only shows plainly, but will put the whole row wrong. Only one weaver is carried across the pattern, and as one of each pair becomes a weaver in turn, winding three colours is of little use; but it is a good plan to wind all the pairs with different colours.

Knot seven pairs of bobbins at the ends, and fix firmly in the cushion at *C*. Cross each pair once, right bobbin over left (Fig. 2). Begin at the left and work across to the right. Twist the 1st and 2nd pairs three times (to make an edge), make a whole-stitch, set a pin in *A*, and lay aside the 1st pair. Take the 2nd pair in the left hand and the 3rd pair in the right hand, and make a half-stitch (Figs. 3 and 4). Work half-stitch through the 4th, 5th, and 6th pairs; twist the weaver pair three times and the 7th pair three times, make a whole-stitch, set a pin in *B*, and lay aside the outside pair. The 6th pair now becomes the 2nd in that row; take it in the right hand and the pair lying next to it in the left hand, work half-stitch across to *A*, twist the weaver and outside pairs three times as before, make a whole-stitch, set a pin in the hole below *A*, and lay aside the outside pair and work across to *B*.

Braid with Open Centre (Fig. 8). Ornamental clothwork is made by twisting the threads in a variety of ways. Of these, open-centre braid is one (Fig. 8). Knot nine pairs of bobbins at the ends and pin in the cushion at *C*. Begin at the left and work across to the right. Work the first row as in braid (Fig. 6), make the edge at *B*.

In the return row make whole-stitch with pairs 7, 6, 5, twist the weavers three times, then continue whole-stitch with pairs 4, 3, 2. Make edge at left side with weavers and pair 1, and set a pin in the hole below *A*. In the third row twist the weavers three times between pairs 4 and 5. It is the twisting of the weavers that makes the open centre, and the twists must be made between the same pairs in each row.

This open centre is often used for the veining of leaves. A great variety of ornamental cloth-work can be made by the twisting of both the weavers and the warps in different parts of the work. A fine braid with an oblong open centre makes a pretty ribbon beading.

Braid with Gimp and Picot Edge (Fig. 9). Picots give a dainty finish to the edge of lace. They are made in several ways, and used at the edge of length laces to edge flowers, leaves, scrolls; in centres, and as "bar fillings."

Gimp is the thick linen thread used to outline flowers, leaves, scrolls, to vein leaves and give a roll edge to braid.

Wind seven pairs of bobbins with No. 20 thread, and one bobbin only with the gimp. Knot all together at the ends and fix in the cushion at *C*. Twist the 1st and 2nd pairs thrice, make a whole-stitch, set a pin in *A*, lay aside the 1st pair, work whole-stitch with pairs 3, 4, 5, 6, pass the gimp through the weaver pair, twist the weavers and the 7th pair thrice, and set a pin in *B*.

In the return row pass the gimp through the weaver pair, work whole-stitch with pairs 5, 4, 3, 2, twist the weavers and the 1st pair thrice, make a whole-stitch, but do not set a pin; twist the weavers six times, take a pin and make a small loop in the weavers by giving a twist round the pin, then set the pin in the pattern ¼ in. outside the hole. Twist the weavers six times and the 1st pair of warps thrice, make a whole-stitch, and repeat across to *B*. The picot may be shortened or lengthened as desired.

Continue the braid. Always pass the gimp through the weaver pair at the right, keeping the gimp well to the edge. Make a picot at the left of each return row by twisting the weavers six times outside the edge, and insert the pin in a half loop of the weavers before pushing it in the pattern.

Curved Braid. A braid having a curve can seldom be worked in the usual way. The pinholes are very unequal in number, there being more on the outside than on the inside curve. Sometimes it is possible to re-arrange the holes, and put the outside ones farther apart and the inside ones closer together, and work the braid in the usual way.

In re-arranging the holes it must be remembered that if the outside ones are too far apart the warp threads will look bare, and if the inside ones are too close the gimp and the woven threads will look overcrowded.

Each loop in the inside curve should show distinctly, and the weavers should lie in a straight line to the outside curve. Twisting the edge pairs once instead of thrice will prevent the inner curve from looking clumsy at the edge.

Count the pinholes from where the curve begins, and see if it is possible to work the braid in the usual way by using the holes in the inner curve twice; to do so is called "gaining on a pin."

Work from the outside curve in the usual way, at the inner curve twist the weavers once, but do not use the edge pair; work across to the outside and back. Take out the last pin, work the weavers and edge pair, put the pin back in the same hole and pass the weavers round it. Work across to outside curve as usual. Put a pencil mark at the holes it will be necessary to use twice.

Another method is called "turning a stitch." Work from the outside as usual; at the inner curve, instead of twisting the weavers, lay them aside. Take up the last warp pair, twist once (right bobbin over left), use that pair as weavers and work across to outside. On the return journey work weavers and edge pair as usual, set a pin in the next hole, and cross to outside.

When the curve is a very sharp one, another method is advisable. When a pinhole has to be used more than once "false pinholes" are made at the inner curve, about one-quarter the width of braid, but just above the usual pinholes. The weavers are worked from the outside until the "false pinhole" is reached, the pin is set in that hole, the weavers passed round it, and worked to the outside. On the return journey the pin is taken out and the warps pulled to tighten the loop made by it; the weavers are worked to the inner curve, the edge made, and the pin set in its proper hole.

Throwing Out and Adding Bobbins. When making leaves, curves, and the petals of flowers which narrow in parts, it is often necessary to throw out one or two pairs of bobbins to prevent the work from looking clumsy. The bobbins thrown out should always be warps, and care must be taken in selecting them so that the stopped threads will not show in the finished work. Lay the pair back on the cushion so that it hangs in a straight line with the warps in use, but do not cut off. Continue the braid until that part is completed, pulling the warps closely, and when finished cut off the thrown out pairs.

Sometimes it is necessary to add more bobbins. Wind a pair without knotting and hang over a pin in the work at a part where the fresh bobbins will hang straight with the warps. Work several rows, remove the pin holding the fresh pair, and pull down the loop made by it.

Another method is to hang a pair on the thread of a warp by a half-loop stitch, and support it with a pin until several rows are worked, which will keep it from dragging down. Extra pairs are best hung in the middle of the work and worked through the warps. If hung on a weaver, an edge, or a gimp, the fresh pair is apt to drag these out of place. In working a sharp curve, the outside edge may need more threads. Hang the fresh pair on a pin outside the curve, work it with the weavers, and do several rows before removing the pin and pulling down the loop.

Fastening Off. To fasten off the threads, if a broad lace is being worked, tie each pair separately, knotting them two or three times; tie the outside pairs with the nearest warps and fasten along the edge for an inch or so by "sewing"; cut off close to the knots.

To fasten off at a narrow braid or the stem of a leaf, tie each pair first; then open out a pair, and pass them round the bobbins held in a bunch, crossing the threads to keep them firm; tie the pair used for binding several times, then sew to the edge, and cut off.

Expert lace makers have a special way of cutting

off bobbins which leaves them tied in pairs. There is a knack in doing this, and a beginner should practise it with a pair of loose bobbins before attempting it with lace. Place the blades of the scissors under the threads with the points of the scissors towards you. Now give the scissors a twist so that the threads will be across them, turn their points over the bobbins, then under the threads from which they hang, and with the points of the scissors catch the threads above and draw them through the loop. Cut the threads of the loop and draw away the loose ones. The fastened-off threads should be knotted, and quite close to the lace.

BROKEN THREADS AND KNOTS. A knot must never be worked into the lace. Always tie with a weaver's knot. If a warp thread breaks, tie the threads, then loop the knot over a pin in the work some distance above the break, continue the work, and do not cut off the knotted ends until a good piece of the work has been done. If the break occurs in the weaver, tie the threads and try if it will work to the edge without taking in the knot; if not, unwork to the starting edge, "sew" the broken thread at a pinhole, then twist it with the other weaver.

CHAPTER IV

BOBBIN LACE—" SEWINGS " AND " BARS "

" Sewing " in lace making is quite unlike needlework. It is used when two braids or parts of lace are to be joined, for adding a pair of bobbins invisibly, and at fastening off. The " sewing " is made with a needle-pin or a fine crochet hook; a wig-maker's needle is most convenient for certain parts of lace.

Remove the pin from the hole at the part to be joined, insert the hook through the edge at the hole, draw through a loop of the weaver, and pass the other weaver through the loop, pull tight, and continue the work. In joining two parts the " sewing " should always be done with the weaver pair. When bobbins are added by " sewing " the pair must be wound without knotting.

Bars. " Bars " or " brides " as they are often called are used to connect the flowers, leaves, etc., in certain kinds of lace. It is the simplest and quickest method of making the groundwork in lace and for filling in open spaces. The bobbins for " bars " are wound without knotting and " sewn " at a pinhole in the edge. They must be spaced very evenly and regularly, and care must be taken that the points of leaves and flower petals are not pulled out of shape.

A simple " bar " is made with one pair of bobbins twisted and a thicker one with two pairs plaited. Picots are introduced to vary them, and in some laces the " bars " are placed in a double or oblong form.

A SCROLL WITH FESTOONED EDGING. Festooning is much used to ornament scrolls, the outside edge of leaves and flower petals.

Make a pattern from the diagram Fig. 3. The sampler scroll is made with fine Duchesse thread, and is suitable for appliqué work on Brussels net.

Wind seven pairs of bobbins with fine thread, and one bobbin only with gimp. Hang on a pin at *A*. Work whole-stitch with a small veined edge at each side, keeping the gimp at the outer curve. Count the holes in the curve and mark the ones to be used twice, and places where a "turning-stitch" is required. When *B* is reached do not cut off the bobbins, but continue round the festooning.

The gimp is used to outline the edge and the divisions of the petals. Make a small picot at the outside edge by twisting the weavers thrice, pass the gimp through the weavers, work across to the braid, "sew" the weaver in a pinhole. Work to the outside, make a picot, work back to the braid, "sew" the weaver to the edge, repeat. Always replace the pin removed for "sewing" in order to keep the scroll a good shape.

In working this kind of lace the cushion must be turned in all directions, the part being worked always towards you. The pins must be pushed well into the pillow with only the heads visible, as threads are apt to catch on them and break.

At the division of the petals pass the gimp through each pair of warps, "sew" to the edge of braid, and pass again through each pair of warps on the return to the outer edge. Count the holes and mark the ones it is necessary to "sew" into twice.

Repeat. Always "sew" the weaver pair to the

braid at each crossing, and make a small picot at the outside edge each time.

Work each petal alternately in whole-stitch and gauze-stitch.

A Duchesse Spray. The spray consists of one large flower and three small ones, three leaves worked in

Fig. 2. Duchesse Spray

halves, and a scroll stem filled in with "bars"; open festooning ornaments one of the leaves and two of the small flowers. The spray is suitable for appliqué on Brussels net.

Make a pattern from the diagram. Wind the fine thread bobbins in pairs, but use only one gimp bobbin.

To make the large flower begin at the centre ring. Hang five pairs fine bobbins and one gimp at *A*. Make a small open edge at the outer curve, and keep the gimp at that edge. The inner curve has no pinholes; instead of a pin a turning-stitch is used, and the shaping done by the hand.

Work from the outer curve, pass the gimp through the weavers, work whole-stitch with warp pairs 3 and 4, make a "turning-stitch" with the weavers and the 5th pair, and work back to outer curve.

Repeat. Add more bobbins as the ring broadens, and keep the inner curve neatly shaped. When *A* is reached "sew" the weavers to the hole without removing the pin; do not cut off the bobbins but continue to work round the petals.

It will be necessary to make several "turning-stitches" as well as to "sew" into each ring hole twice. Make an edge with the outside pairs and set a pin in the first hole, pass the gimp through weavers, work whole-stitch with warp pairs 3 and 4, make a "turning-stitch" with weavers and 5th pair, work back to the outside and set a pin in the next hole.

Repeat. Make a "turning-stitch" with weavers and the 6th pair, and work back to the outside.

Repeat. Make a "turning-stitch" with the 7th pair and work back to the outside. Work across and "sew" the weavers to the first ring hole.

If more bobbins are needed to fill the petal neatly hang the extra pairs on the 3rd and 4th warp pairs. Always keep the gimp to the outside, and at the division of the petals pass it through each warp pair, "sew" to a ring hole, pass through each warp pair again on the return to the outside. Work all the petals in whole-stitch, and fasten off the bobbins at the pinholes at the first petal.

For the short stem hang five pairs and one gimp in

three holes at the petal edge. Work whole-stitch all the way, keeping the gimp to the outside. Fasten off by tying the bobbins in a bunch, binding securely with one pair before cutting the threads.

The Scroll. Hang five pairs and one gimp on a pin at *A*. Count the pinholes and mark the ones it will be necessary to use twice in the inner curve. Work whole-stitch all the way, keep the gimp to the outside,

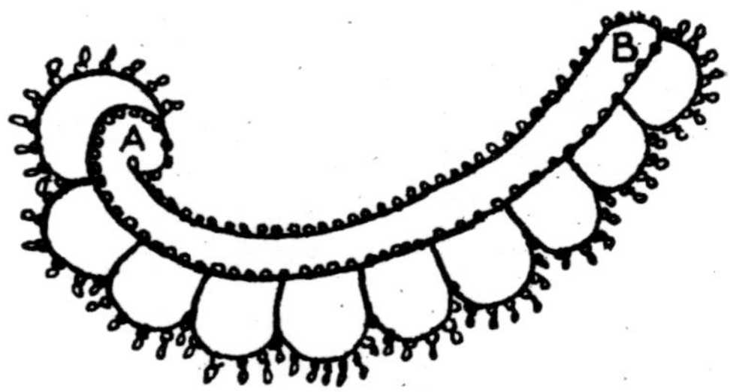

Fig. 3. Festooned Scroll

bind the threads at fastening off and "sew" to pinholes on the short stem.

In the trefoil the two plain leaves are made first. "Sew" five pairs and one gimp at a pinhole in the short stem. Work whole-stitch to *A*, and continue working up the outside half of left leaf. At each crossing set a pin in the hole in the centre of leaf, pass the weavers round the pin, but do not twist them. Keep the gimp to the outside edge. At the point of the leaf make a "turning stitch" at each side of the top hole, which use twice or oftener if required to make a neat turning. Work down the left of the leaf. At each crossing remove one of the centre pins, "sew" the weavers to the hole and replace the pin.

Continue the work up the outside half of the second

leaf without cutting off. At each crossing pass the weavers round the pin in the centre hole, without twisting, and in working down the leaf make a "sewing" at each hole. Fasten off the bobbins by binding and "sewing" two pairs at the edge.

Begin the third leaf by "sewing" the bobbins at

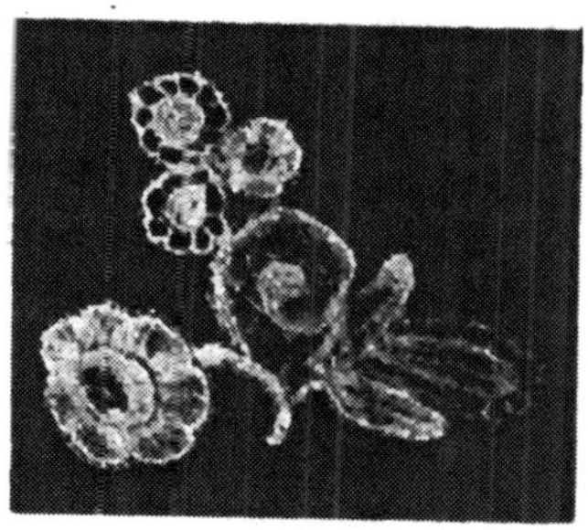

DUCHESSE SPRAY

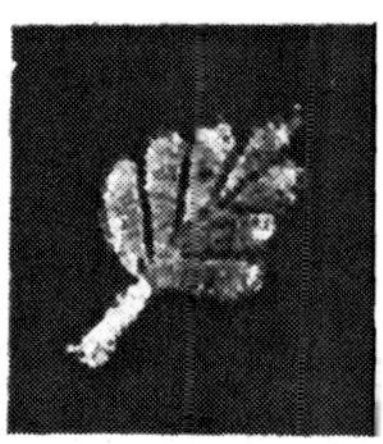

RAISED LEAF

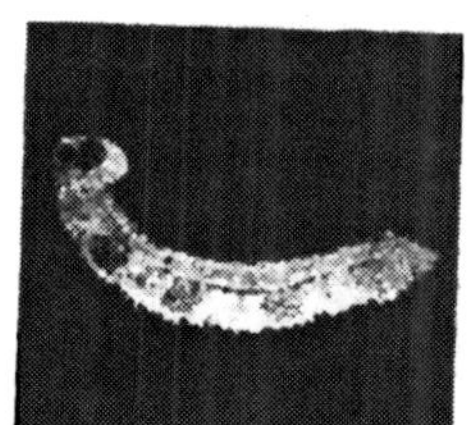

FESTOONED SCROLL

PLATE VII

the junction of the double leaves. Work it in the same way and fasten off by binding the threads and "sewing" two pairs at the starting place.

To make the festooning "sew" four pairs at the starting place of the leaf, work whole-stitch and at the curve "sew" into two pinholes at the leaf edge.

Continue in the same way all round the leaf, and fasten off by " sewing " into two or three holes at the end.

The small flower with the five petals is made in the same way as the large one. The tiny ring in the centre will only require three pairs of bobbins; continue these round the first petal, and add more when needed. Miniature " bars " fill the centre of both large and small flowers.

Four pairs of fine bobbins and one gimp are used to work the centres of the other two. Hang on a pin in the centre and work in a neat circle by means of " turning stitches " and " sewing " to the pin. Keep the gimp at the outside and cut it off before beginning to work the festooning. Two of the flowers are attached to the scroll by " sewing " the edges.

The small " bars " which fill in the scroll are made with two fine pairs plaited. " Sew " them to a hole in the edge of the leaf, plait three times, make a small picot by twisting a pin in one of the outside threads, plait three times, cross to the stem and " sew " in a pinhole in the edge.

Repeat. Mark the holes in each side of the scroll for " sewings," placing them at regular intervals. Cross the " bar " from one side to the other until the centre is reached, and knot threads very securely before cutting off.

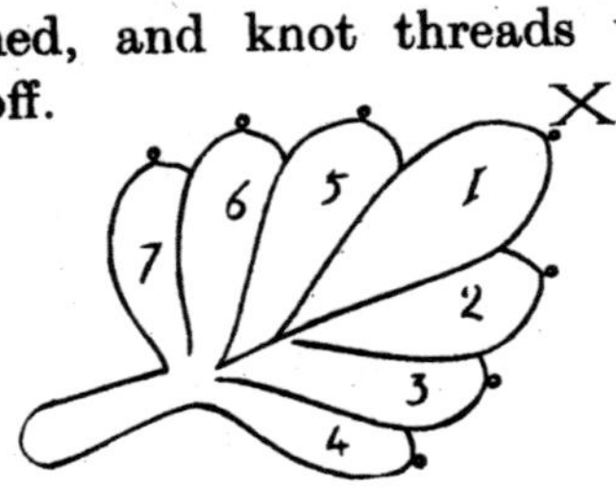

THE SAMPLER LEAF

CHAPTER V

BOBBIN LACE—"RAISED WORK"; "MESHES"

"RAISED" work is a method of outlining flowers and stems and veining leaves. It is much used in Brussels and Honiton, and adds greatly to the value of the lace.

The student must have become expert with "sewings" and the use of the crochet hook before she attempts raised work. A broken thread in "sewing" is difficult to replace, and if the hook catches in a worked part much damage may be done to fine lace, whilst careless raised work is unsightly and detracts from the beauty of the lace.

Stem stitch used for thin stems and tendrils is a simple compound of whole-stitch and half-stitch made with two pairs of bobbins—the weaver and outside pairs—passed round the warps.

"Rope sewing" is more intricate, but it is the quickest way of getting from one point to another without cutting the threads and having to make a new start. The oftener fastening off can be avoided in lace making the greater will be the strength and beauty of the lace.

The sampler leaf opposite is a good example of "rope sewing" in Duchesse thread. To make it, wind fourteen pairs and hang at *X* at top of leaf. Work with the stem towards you.

Work whole-stitch, with open edge each side, to base of a leaf section. Gather all the warps together, knot the weavers round them, and pass the bunch round the pin, turning the cushion so that the points of the leaves are towards you. Twist the warps several times to make a rope and bind it with the weavers, crossing them in a contrary direction until the rope reaches the top of leaf section 2. Now separate the bobbins, turn the cushion back again and work whole-stitch to the base of the section with an open edge at the outside, and at the vein " sew " the weavers over the rope into a hole in opposite leaf section, and lower down the rib pass the weavers round the pins without twisting.

The underside is the right side of the lace always; therefore the raised roll will show on that side, while the fastening off and cut ends will be on the surface.

When the base of leaf section 2 is reached, gather the warps into a rope, pass it round the pin and bind the rope with weavers until the top of leaf section 3 is reached. Separate the bobbins and work whole-stitch to the base of the section, " sewing " the weavers into the edge holes of leaf section 2 and passing them round the pins set in the rib lower down. The cushion must be turned always so that the strands hang straight in front of worker.

Make section 4 in the same manner as 3 and 2 sections. When the base is reached gather the warps into a rope, pass it round the pin, and bind it the length of the mid-rib to base of section 1.

" Sew " it to holes at intervals to keep it in position and continue the rope to the top of leaf section 5. Separate the bobbins and work half-stitch to the base of the section, in the same manner as the sections in the opposite side of the leaf. Work sections 6 and 7 in half-stitch also. At the narrow part in section 7 throw off bobbins in each row until only sufficient to work the short stem is left. At the stem hang a gimp at each side, and work in whole-stitch with the gimp well to the edge. Fasten off by knotting the weavers round

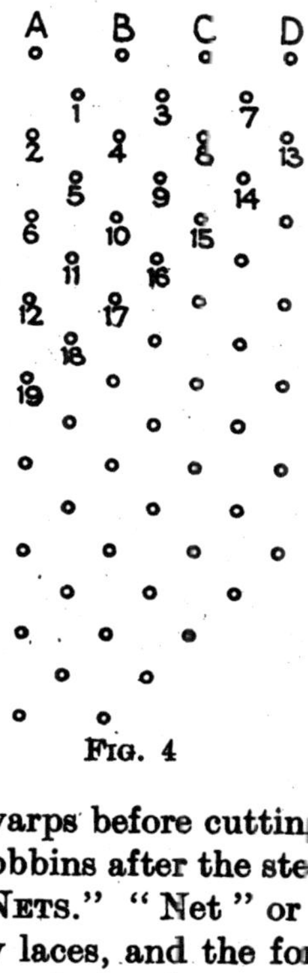

FIG. 4

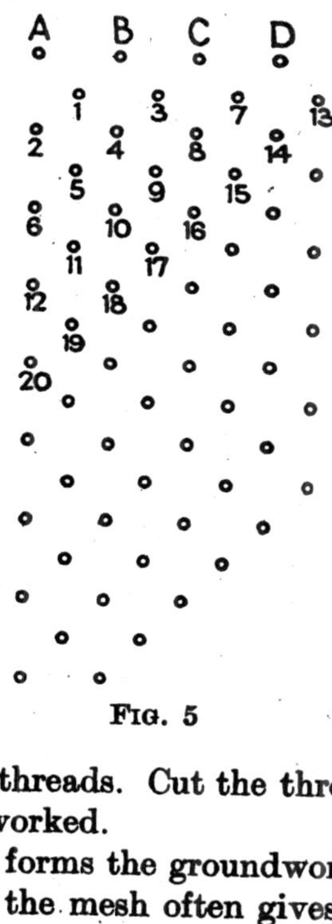

FIG. 5

the warps before cutting the threads. Cut the thrown-off bobbins after the stem is worked.

"NETS." "Net" or mesh forms the groundwork of many laces, and the form of the mesh often gives the name of the lace. There are six distinct meshes: Torchon, Lille, Valenciennes, Point de Paris, Filet, and Brussels, and the great variety of nets in use to-day are an adaptation of one of these.

In many kinds of lace the meshes are formed at the same time as the pattern, threads are brought out of the pattern to form the mesh and carried back into the pattern again. While in other laces the design is worked first and mesh put in afterwards to fill spaces and to connect the solid parts of the design.

Four diagrams are given. On Fig. 4 both Torchon and Brussels can be worked, Fig. 5 is for Valenciennes, Fig. 6 for Point de Paris, and on Fig. 7 can be worked Lille and many Flemish laces.

Five sampler patterns of nets are given: Torchon, Valenciennes, Point de Paris, Brussels, and Point de Mariage. When the student has mastered these she will be able to make the ground of almost every variety of lace by studying a sampler copy of it.

In the instructions for working the nets the following abbreviations are used: t. = twist; c. = cross; p. = plait; c.t. = cross and twist; t.c. = twist and cross; c.t.c. = cross, twist and cross.

Torchon. Torchon is a simple mesh in half-stitch. Wind eight pairs of bobbins, knot two pairs together, and hang on pins at *A*, *B*, *C*. *D*.

t.c. 2nd and 3rd pairs, pin 1 (set a pin in hole at numeral given and enclose each pin); t.c. 1st and 2nd pairs, pin 2, c.t.; t.c. 4th and 5th pairs, pin 3, c.t.; c. 3rd and 4th pairs, pin 4, c.t.; c. 2nd and 3rd pairs, pin 5, c.t.; c. 1st and 2nd pairs, pin 6. c.t.; t.c. 6th and 7th pairs, pin 7, c.t.; c. 5th and 6th pairs, pin 8, c.t.; c. 4th and 5th pairs, pin 9, c.t.; c. 3rd and 4th pairs, pin 10, c.t.; c. 2nd and 3rd pairs, pin 11, c.t.; c. 1st and 2nd pairs, pin 12, c.t.; t.c. 7th and 8th pairs, pin 13, c.t.; repeat, and work the pairs to pin 19 as in previous rows.

Valenciennes. Valenciennes mesh is entirely plaited, and two pairs are used in each plait. Very fine thread is used in making it, and there are two varieties of mesh—a round one and a square one as sampler. The ground of Cluny lace is made with a similar mesh.

Wind fourteen pairs of bobbins. Knot two pairs together and hang at *A*, knot four pairs together and hang at *B*, *C*, *D*.

p. five times 1st and 2nd, 3rd and 4th pairs; c. 2nd and 3rd pin 1, c.t.; c. 1st and 2nd, pin 2, c.t.; p. five times 1st and 2nd, 3rd and 4th, 5th and 6th, 7th and 8th pairs; c. 6th and 7th pairs, pin 3, c.t.; p. 5th and 6th pairs five times; c. 4th and 5th pairs, pin 4, c.t.; p. 3rd and 4th pairs five times; c. 2nd and 3rd pairs, pin 5, c.t.; p. 2nd pair five times; c. 1st and 2nd pairs, pin 6, c.t.; p. five times each 1st and 2nd, 3rd and 4th, 5th and 6th, 7th and 8th, 9th and 10th, 11th and 12th.

c. 10th and 11th pairs, pin 7, c.t.; p. 9th and 10th five times; c. 8th and 9th pairs, pin 8, c.t.; p. 7th and 8th five times; c. 6th and 7th pairs, pin 9, c.t.; p. 5th and 6th pairs five times; c. 4th and 5th pairs, pin 10, c.t.; p. 3rd and 4th pairs five times; c. 2nd and 3rd pairs, pin 11, c.t.; p. 2nd pair five times; c. 1st and 2nd pairs, pin 12; p. five times each from the 1st and 2nd to 13th and 14th pairs; c. 13th and 14th pairs, pin 13, c.t. and work to pin 20 as in previous rows.

Point de Paris. This is a mesh with a striped effect. Point Binche, and several Flemish laces, Milanese, and some laces made in the Midlands, are variations of this mesh. In England it is known as "wire ground."

Wind thirteen pairs of bobbins. Knot four pairs together, hang at *A* and *B*, and five pairs at *C*.

Begin at the right. Take up 1st and 2nd pairs, pin 1,

c.t.; lay down 1st pair, take up 2nd pair and work w.s. with 3rd pair with 4th and 5th pairs, pin 2, c.t.; work w.s. with 5th, 6th, 7th pairs, pin 3, c.t.; work w.s. with 7th, 8th, 9th pairs, pin 4, c.t.; work w.s. with 9th, 10th, 11th pairs, pin 5, c.t.; work w.s. with 11th, 12th, 13th pairs, pin 6, c.t.; c.t. 12th and 11th, 10th and 9th, 8th and 7th, 6th and 5th, 4th and 3rd pairs.

Take up 3rd pair, w.s. with 2nd and 1st pairs, pin 7, c.t.; w.s. 2nd with 3rd, 4th, and 5th pairs, pin 8, c.t.; w.s. 5th, 6th, 7th pairs, pin 9, c.t.; w.s. 7th, 8th, 9th pairs, pin 10, c.t.; w.s. 9th, 10th, 11th, pin 11, c.t.; w.s. 11th, 12th, 13th, pin 12; c.t. 12 and 11th, 10th and 9th, 8th and 7th, 6th and 5th, 4th and 3rd, and repeat from 7.

Brussels. Brussels and Mechlin are two of the most popular grounds for the finest Duchesse thread. The sampler is made with coarse thread to better show the working.

Brussels mesh has two threads twisted twice and four threads plaited three times. Wind eight pairs of bobbins. Knot two pairs together and hang at *A*, *B*, *C*, *D*.

t. twice 2nd and 3rd pairs, c.t., pin 1, c.t. twice.

t. twice 1st and 2nd pairs, c.t.c., pin 2, c.t. twice; t. twice 4th and 5th pairs, c.t.c., pin 3, c.t. twice; t. twice 3rd and 4th pairs, pin 4, c.t. twice; t. twice 2nd and 3rd pairs, pin 5, c.t. twice; t. twice 1st and 2nd pairs, pin 6, c.t. twice.

t. twice 6th and 7th pairs, pin 7, c.t. twice; t. twice 5th and 6th pairs, pin 8, c.t. twice; t. twice 4th and 5th pairs, pin 9, c.t. twice; t. twice 3rd and 4th pairs, pin 10, c.t. twice; t. twice 2nd and 3rd pairs, pin 11, c.t. twice; t. twice 1st and 2nd pairs, pin 12, c.t. twice.

t. twice 7th and 8th pairs, pin 13, c.t. twice, and repeat as in previous rows.

Point de Mariage. Wedding mesh is also known as honeycomb ground. It is an elaborate variation of Lille mesh; but in Lille the whole mesh is twisted,

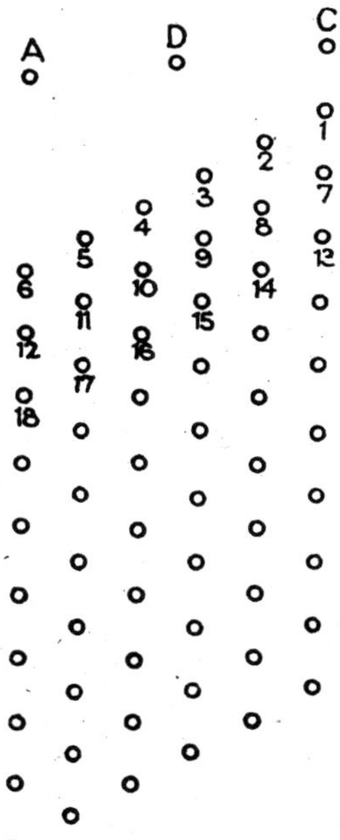

FIG. 6

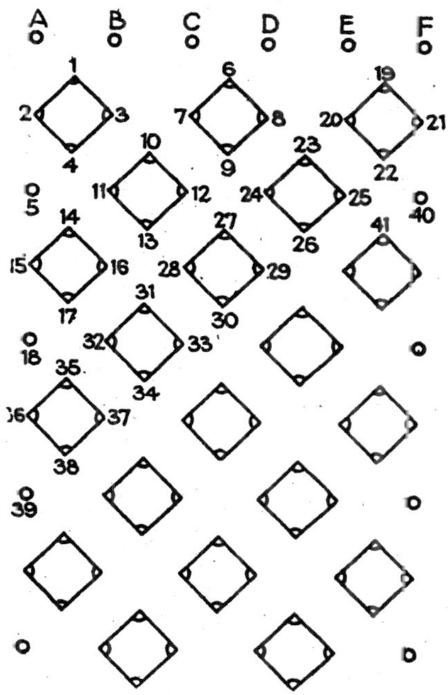

FIG. 7

while honeycomb is worked in half- and whole-stitches. Wind twelve pairs of bobbins. Knot two pairs and pin at *A*, *B*, *C*, *D*, *E*, *F*. The mesh is a diamond one.

Take up 2nd and 3rd pairs, t.c., pin 1, c.t.; take up 1st and 2nd pairs, t.c., pin 2, c.t.; take up 3rd and 4th pairs, t.c., pin 3, c.t.; t.c. 2nd and 3rd pairs, pin 4; p. 2nd and 3rd, 4th and 5th pairs.

Take up 1st and 2nd pairs, t.c., pin 5, c.t.; t.c. 6th and 7th pairs, pin 6, c.t.; t.c. 5th and 6th pairs, pin 7,

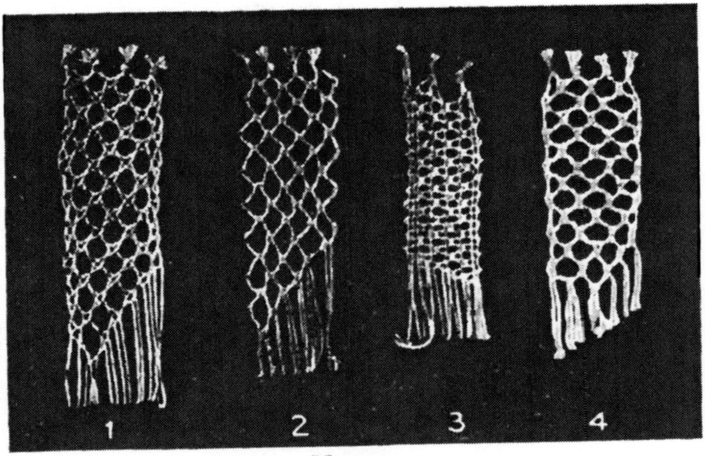

MESHES

Torchon Valenciennes Point de Paris Brussels

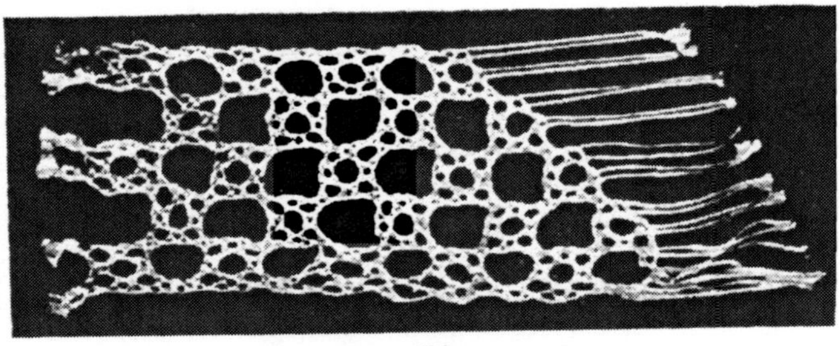

POINT DE MARIAGE

PLATE VIII

c.t.; t.c. 7th and 8th pairs, pin 8, c.t.; t.c. 7th and 8th pairs, pin 9, c.t.; p. 7th and 9th, 9th and 8th; t.c. 3rd and 7th pairs, pin 10, c.t.; t.c. 10th and 9th pairs, pin

12, c.t.; t.c. 4th and 10th pairs, pin 11, c.t.; t.c. 11th and 12th pairs, pin 13, c.t.; t.c. 4th and 11th pairs, pin 14, c.t.; t.c. 5th and 14th pairs, pin 15, c.t.; t.c. 14th and 15th pairs, pin 16, c.t.; t.c. 15th and 16th pairs, pin 17, c.t.; p. 15th and 17th, 17th and 16th; t.c. 15th and 17th pairs, pin 18, c.t.

Take up 10th and 11th pairs, pin 19, c.t.; t.c. 9th and 10th pairs, pin 20, c.t.; t.c. 19th and 12th pairs, pin 21, c.t.; t.c. 20th and 21st pairs, pin 22, c.t.; p. 20th and 22nd, 22nd and 21st; t.c. 8th and 20th pairs, pin 23, c.t.; and continue as in previous row, plaiting the two connecting pairs as each diamond is completed.

Begin at the right always. t.c. 21st and 22nd pairs, pin 40, c.t.; t.c. 25th and 40th pairs, pin 41, c.t.; t.c. 40th and 41st, and continue as in previous row.

Sectional square-ruled paper is used for drawing lace patterns. A mesh pattern is quite simple to draw even by those who have no gift for designing. Honeycomb mesh can be drawn on paper having 30 squares to the linear inch. Eight holes are allowed to each diamond, but four of each belong to a neighbouring diamond. A dot is marked at the point of each diamond and pricked after the paper is pasted on to thin cardboard.

An attempt at making narrow Bucks Point mesh or ground on sectional paper might be made by a beginner. Use paper with 20 squares to the inch. Make a dot in each alternate square for the first row, pass over the second row of squares. In the third row make a dot in every alternate square, each dot under the square that separates from the first row. Leave a row of squares unused between each two rows of dots.

Bucks Point. Narrow Bucks point ground is formed of half-stitches; each stitch is followed by two twists and it is worked diagonally downwards either from right to left or from left to right. A pin is stuck between the two couples after every half-stitch. Wider Buckingham ground mesh is made with a variety of fillings.

POINT D'ESPRIT. Point d'esprit mesh, so popular with Bedfordshire lace makers, can be worked on the Brussels pattern. But the mesh is made like Lille with twisted threads, and at every hole a small square is made (see fillings) instead of the usual half-stitch. No pins are used in working it, but the student will probably find pins necessary at first.

Having thoroughly mastered the making of grounds, the student will find the making of edgings and insertions easy work.

CHAPTER VI

BOBBIN LACE—" FILLINGS " (PLATE IX)

A " FILLING " is used to cover a small vacant space such as the centre of a flower in Brussels and Honiton. In Torchon, Cluny, etc., the " filling " is generally in the centre of a medallion, and is worked as part of the design.

Practise with a medium thread the sampler " fillings " shown in Plate IX.

The leaf and the cobweb are very popular " fillings," and other " fillings " are variations of those two.

To make a leaf (Fig. 1) hang two pairs of bobbins on a pin in the cushion. Use the first bobbin, the one at the right hand as weaver; it is worked in and out of the strands of thread.

In the first row pass the weaver over the 2nd strand, under the 3rd, over, then under the 4th. In the second row pass the weaver over the 3rd or middle strand, under, then over the 2nd strand. Repeat those two rows alternately; do not lay down the weaver until the leaf is finished. Pull down the warp or straight strands, and shape the leaf by pulling the outside bobbins wide in the middle, and drawing them in at the point. Take the weaver to the right and knot it with the 3rd bobbin. Make a whole-stitch. Four of those joined together make a pretty flower.

The " beehive " (Fig. 2) is, like the first, worked from two pairs hung on a pin. Work six rows or more if a large " filling " is required, shaping it by holding the outer bobbins apart and pulling down the centre strand. Take the weaver to the right and knot with the 2nd strand, then twist the two strands, also twist the 3rd and 4th strands.

The "hourglass" (Fig. 3). Set two pins in the cushion ½ in. apart, and hang one pair of bobbins on each. Begin at the right and work to a point; make a whole-stitch and continue the second part. Work the same number of rows, finish at the right, and twist each pair six or seven times.

The "square leaf" (Fig. 4) hang one pair bobbins on two pins placed ⅝ in. apart. Work four rows, or until the leaf is a nice square. Finish at the right and twist each pair.

The "square leaf" cross with open centre (Fig. 5). Set the pins for each leaf with an inch space between them. When the leaves are made twist the strands six times. Plait the two middle pairs once, and set a pin in the centre to keep it in position. Twist three times, and plait the middle pair with the outside pair at left hand. Twist both pairs of left leaf three times, twist the outside pair of left leaf six times, plait once with the middle pair, set a pin to keep it in position, twist three times, plait once with outside pair of left leaf, set a pin. Twist each pair six times and make the third and fourth leaves. Take each weaver to the right and fasten off. Twist each pair six times.

Drawing the shape of the leaves in pencil, and using pins at the corners, help in making a good shape until the eye is accustomed to shaping the leaves. In all the leaves it is necessary to hold the weaver bobbin all the time, and to pull the middle warp down fairly tightly.

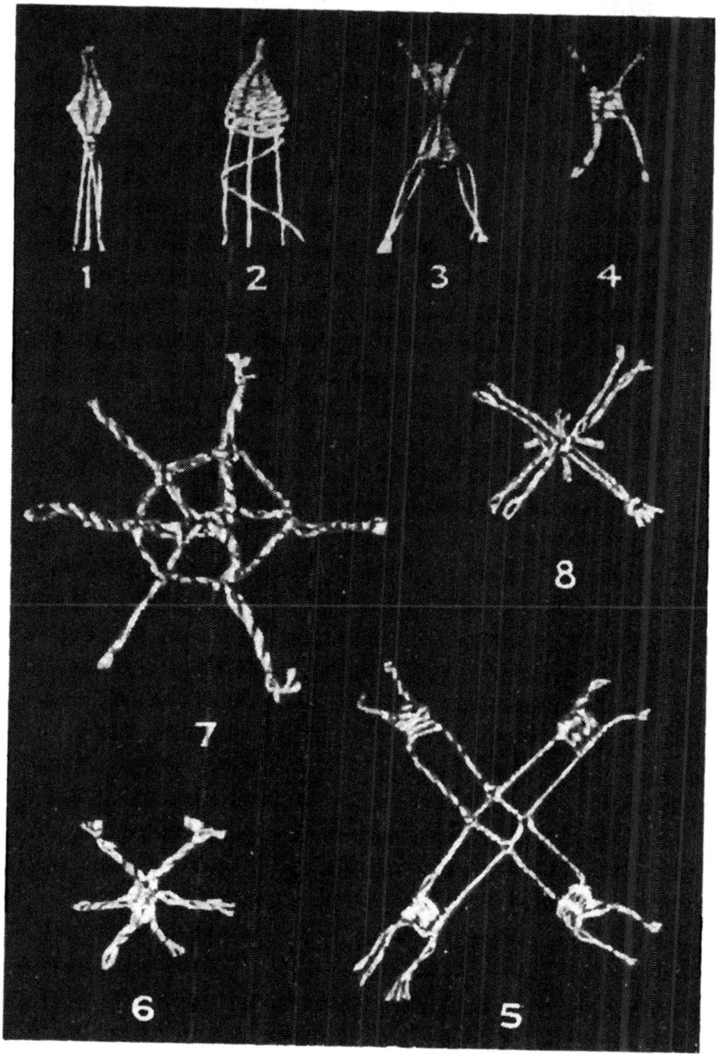

1. Leaf
2. Beehive
3. Hourglass
4. Square Leaf
5. Squares with Open Centre
6. and 7. Cobwebs
8. Picoted Strands

PLATE IX

"Cobweb" (Fig. 6). Mark six pinholes at equal distances apart in the space to be filled. "Sew" one pair in three holes and work the cobweb with the bobbins facing you. Twist each pair well, make a half-stitch with the middle and the left pairs, then with the middle and right pairs, again with the middle and left pairs, set a pin in the exact centre of space, with three bobbins on each side of it; work half-stitch with the middle and right pairs, then with the left, and again with the right pair, twist each pair well, and "sew" each to a hole directly opposite each strand.

When the space to be filled is very large eight strands may be required to fill it; in that case "sew" four pairs.

"Cobweb" (Fig. 7) has a cross strand midway. Mark six holes equally spaced. "Sew" a pair in three holes. Make one half of cobweb, set a pin in the centre and make the other half. Twist one strand and secure it with a pin midway in the space to be filled, twist well, then "sew" the other two strands to holes directly opposite. Take up the loose strand, twist well and "sew" it to the next strand midway, then to the 3rd and 4th strands, twisting well between each. When the starting place is reached "sew" to the pin-hole, twist and "sew" to a hole in the edge.

Fig. 8 is a simple "filling" of crossed strands with picots. It may be square or round. Mark four places at equal distances. Four pairs of bobbins are used. "Sew" two pairs in two holes side by side, at two of the spaces. Twist each pair well, make a whole-stitch with two pairs, set a pin to secure them now take up the right pair, twist well and make a picot, which secure with a pin; make a whole-stitch. Do the same with the other two pairs; make a picot at the right. Plait the four pairs once, set a pin in the centre, enclose it by plaiting the four pairs again. In plaiting them plait the first with the second, then within the third and the fourth, next divide the four pairs by plaiting the first and second together and the third and fourth together. Make picots with the left pair of each, plait with its neighbour, twist each strand well and "sew" to holes in the edge directly opposite the first strands.

CHAPTER VII

BOBBIN LACE TORCHONS—ROSE POINT LACE—CLUNY LACE—GENOESE LACE

As in all laces with the ground or mesh worked at the same time as the design Torchon needs a large number of bobbins. For Edging (Fig. 8) wind twelve pairs bobbins with linen or lace thread No. 50. The following abbreviations are used: c. = cross; c.t. = cross and twist; t. = twist; p. = plait; w.s. = whole-stitch; h.s. = half-stitch. Pin means push a pin into the pricked hole at the number or letter given.

Knot eight pairs, hang at 1; knot four pairs, hang at 2: c.t. 4th–3rd pairs; p. 3rd–2nd pairs, pin 3, c.t.; t. 1st pair thrice, p. 1st–2nd pairs.

p. 3rd–4th pairs, pin *B*, c.t.; p. 3rd–2nd pairs, pin 4, c.t.; t. twist 1st pair thrice, p. 1st–2nd pairs.

p. 5th–4th pairs, pin *D*, w.s. to *A*, taking in all the pairs, pin *A*, pass round pin to enclose it, leave one pair at *D*; w.s. *A–I* pass round pin and leave one pair; w.s. to *C* pass round pin to enclose it; w.s. to *G* pass round pin, leave one pair; w.s. to *F* pass round pin to enclose it; w.s. to *M*, pass round pin, leave one pair; w.s. to *H*, pass round pin to enclose it; w.s. to *N*, pass round pin, leave one pair; w.s. to *L*, pass round pin to enclose it, leave four pairs.

c.t. *D*–3rd pairs; p. 3rd–2nd pairs, pin 3, c.t.; t. 1st pair thrice; p. 1st–2nd pairs.

c.t. *I*–4th pairs; c.t. 4th–3rd pairs; p. 3rd–2nd pairs pin *K*, c.t.; t. 1st pair thrice, p. 1st–2nd pairs.

p. *I*–4th pair, pin *J*, c.t.; p. 4th–*I*–*G*; p. *G*–*I*–*J*–3rd pairs, leave 3rd pair; p. *J–I–G–M*; p. *M–G–I–J*; p. two middle pairs, pin *O*, *C*; c.t. 4th–3rd pairs; p. 3rd–2nd pairs, pin *P*, c.t.; t. twist 1st pair thrice, p. 1st–2nd pairs.

p. 7th–6th–5th–4th pairs; p. 4th–5th–6th–7th pairs; p. 5th–6th pairs; p. 5th–4th pairs, pin *Q*, c.t.; c.t.

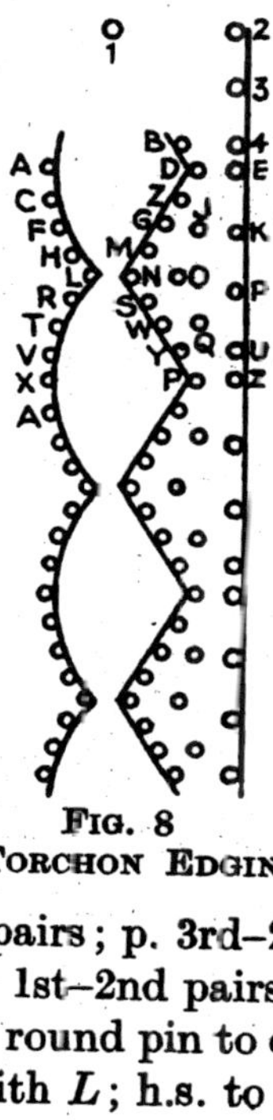

FIG. 8
TORCHON EDGING

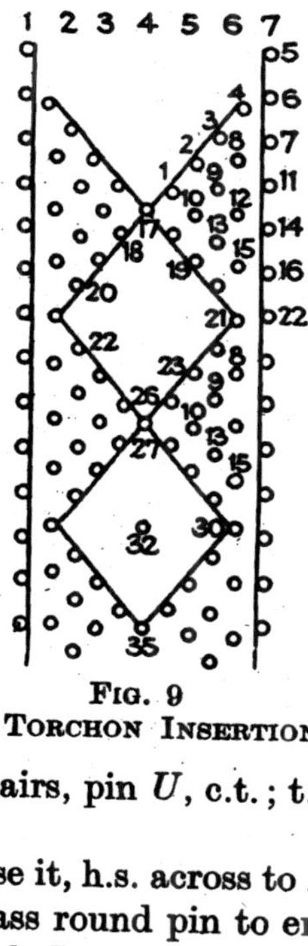

FIG. 9
TORCHON INSERTION

4th–3rd pairs; p. 3rd–2nd pairs, pin *U*, c.t.; t. 1st pair thrice, p. 1st–2nd pairs.

Pass *L* round pin to enclose it, h.s. across to *N*, t. 7th pair *P* with *L*; h.s. to *R*, pass round pin to enclose it, h.s. across; t. 6th pair *P* with *R*, pin *S*, h.s. to *T*, pass round pin to enclose it, h.s. across; t. 5th pair *P* with *T*, pin *W*, h.s. to *V*, pass round pin to enclose it, h.s. across; t. 4th pair *P* with *V*, pin *Y*, h.s. to *X*, pass round pin to enclose it, h.s. across.

c.t. 4th–3rd pairs; p. 3rd–2nd pairs, pin *Z*, c.t.; t. 1st pair thrice, p. 1st–2nd pairs; t. 3rd pair *P* with *Y*, pin

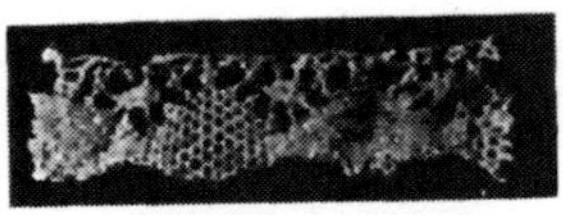

TORCHON EDGING

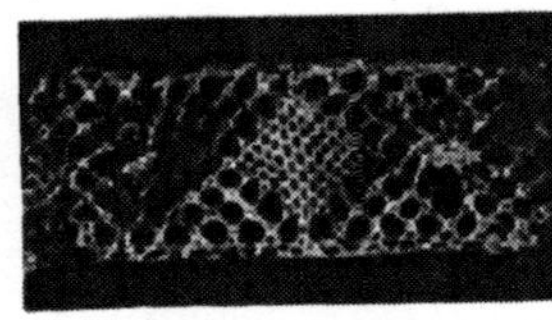

TORCHON INSERTION

ROSE POINT DE MARIAGE EDGING

PLATE X

D, h.s. across. Repeat from *A*, *D*, *E*. Make alternate sections in whole-stitch and half-stitch.

TORCHON INSERTION. Materials: Linen or lace thread No. 50. Sixteen pairs of bobbins. Abbreviations: c. = cross; t. = twist; p. = plait; c.t. = cross and twist.

Knot and hang two pairs at 1, 2, 3, 4, 5, 6, 7. Have eight pairs hanging at each side.

c. two middle pairs, pin 1, leave both pairs at pin; c. 7th–6th pairs, pin 2, c.t.; leave left pair; c. 6th–5th pairs, pin 3, c.t., leave left pair; c. 5th–4th pairs, pin 4, c.t., leave one pair; c.t. 4th–3rd pairs; p. 3rd–2nd pairs, pin 6, c.t., t. 1st pair thrice, p. 1st–2nd pairs.

c.t. 4th–3rd pairs, p. 3rd–2nd pairs, pin 5, c.t.; t. 1st pair thrice, p. 1st–2nd pairs. Repeat left of diamond.

c. 4th–5th pairs, pin 8, c.t., leave right pair; c. 5th–6th pairs, pin 9, c.t., leave right pair; c. 6th–7th pairs, pin 10, c.t., leave two pairs; p. 3rd–2nd pairs, pin 11, c.t., t. 1st pair thrice, p. 1st–2nd pairs.

c. 4th–5th pairs, pin 12, c.t., leave right pair; c. 6th–7th pairs, pin 13, c.t., leave two pairs; c.t., 4th–3rd pairs; p. 3rd–2nd pairs, pin 14, c.t., t. 1st pair thrice, p. 1st–2nd pairs.

c. 4th–5th pairs, pin 15, c.t. leave two pairs; c.t. 4th–3rd pairs; p. 3rd–2nd pairs, pin 16, c.t., t. 1st pair thrice, p. 1st–2nd pairs. Repeat at left of diamond.

Gauze Diamond : There are two pairs at 17, take up the right pair, c. with 10, pin 18, c.t.; h.s. across to left, c. with 10, pin 18, c.t.; h.s. across to right, c. with 13, pin 19, c.t.; continue until pins 21 are filled. Now leave one pair at each crossing from 21 to 26. There should again be eight pairs at each side, repeat from 4, 7. Both sides of diamond.

Cobweb Centre : c. two pairs at 10, pin 18, c.t.; c. two pairs at 13, pin 19, c.t.; c. two pairs at 15, pin 20, c.t.; c.t. 4th–3rd pairs; p. 3rd–2nd pairs, pin 22, c.t., t. 1st pair thrice, p. 1st–2nd pairs.

Now begin the cobweb. Directions for making it is given in "Fillings." Take up the two pairs at 26 and

P, taking in one pair at each crossing, at right and left, until 32 is reached, pin 32; then in making the second half of cobweb leave one pair at each hole from 31 to 35.

Rose Lace. This has a rose design worked into a

Cluny Mat

PLATE XI

honeycomb mesh ground and a fan edging. To make it use linen or lace thread No. 20, twenty-two pairs of bobbins, and strong pins.

Follow the directions for working Point de Mariage mesh. Begin at the right-hand corner of ground and work diagonally towards the rose, pass two pairs from each diamond to make one petal, work four petals, join them by plaiting, then work four more petals, pass into the ground again, and from thence to the fan edge.

The fan edge is worked entirely in plait-stitch. Two straight lines form double ribs down the centre, and are intersected by semicircular ribs; each plaited

ITALIAN MAT

PLATE XII

pair passes through them to the centre rib, then is carried back to the outer edge.

CLUNY MAT (Plate XI). This dainty mat is worked in leaf-stitch, plait, and whole-stitch.

Each daisy has 18 petals, and two pairs of bobbins are used to work each petal. A pattern can be drawn on sectional paper. Each daisy measures 1¼ in. in diameter, and is surrounded by a double wheel spaced

¼ in. apart; four small semicircles are drawn to the outer edge of each daisy.

Begin at the centre by working a small ring with two pairs. Hang 30 pairs round the ring, making 32 pairs on the ring. Two pairs are required for the wheel encircling it. Each completed petal is passed through the wheel pairs to make the daisy at the edge, and thence to the outer edge, which is made with open edge (see Braid 9).

ITALIAN MAT (Plate XII). This Italian mat is a beautiful example of Genoese lace, and shows how braid can be varied. The braid is worked continuous throughout the pattern, changing from cloth to gauze, and at intervals other stitches are introduced to give an open or a lacy effect. Two meshes are worked in large open spaces, and the bars are double plaited ones enriched with pearl picots. The pattern can be enlarged; worked in fine flax thread the design makes a fine set of graded mats for the dinner or luncheon table.

CHAPTER VIII

BOBBIN LACE—MOTIFS

Motifs are favourite ornaments. In fine lace or silk threads they are used for dresses, etc., and in flax thread for tablecloths, bedspreads, curtains, etc.

Leaf Motif. A leaf motif is simple and is quickly made. Draw a pattern of a skeleton leaf. Begin at the stem and work whole-stitch with five pairs of bobbins all round the outline. The bars are picoted plaited ones. Sew a pair at three pinholes near the stem, and others as the leaf broadens; when the rose centre is reached there should be two pairs for each petal. Work three petals in leaf-stitch, plait all three together, then work three more petals and divide to make the bars towards the tip of leaf.

Basket Motif. Draw a skeleton basket pattern. Use six pairs of bobbins to work whole-stitch round the basket and the handle. The flowers are worked in half-stitch with one gimp bobbin at the outer edge. The ground of the basket is a plaited square mesh with two small pieces in cloth stitch. The mesh is worked with bobbins sewn at the foot and sides.

Owl Motif. Draw a skeleton bird pattern outlining wings, tail, and head. The body, head, and tail are worked in whole-stitch; the wings and a small triangle at the base in half-stitch. The open spaces on the body and separating it from the wings are made with a pair from the body, twisted, then worked to the edge of wing, and back into the body. Small holes are left open for eyes, and the beak is a loose leaf.

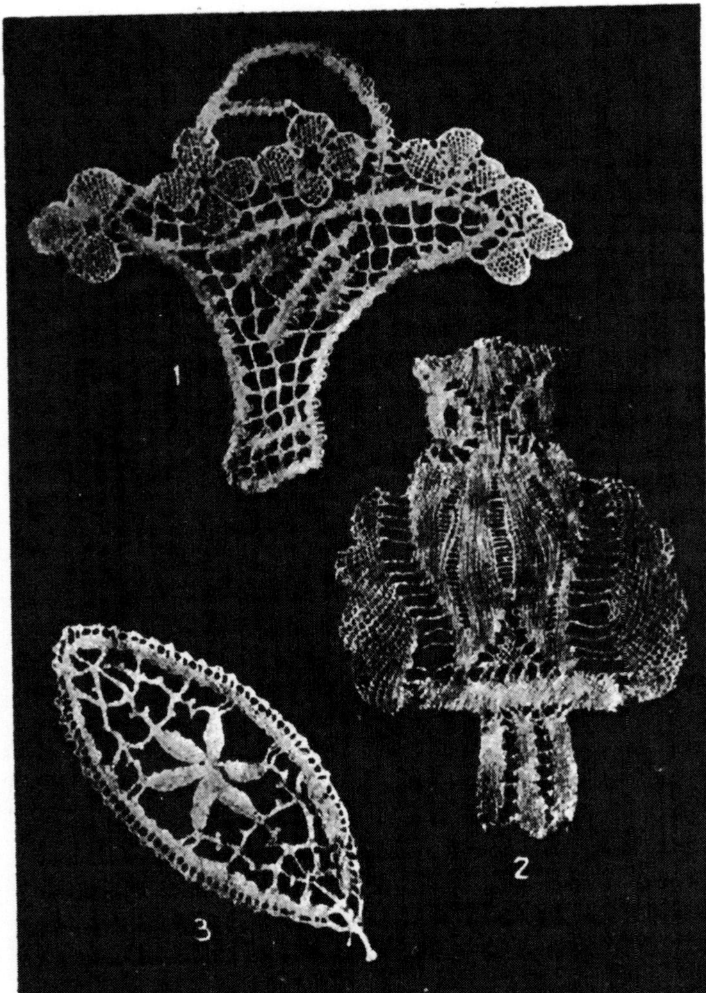

1. Basket Motif. 2. Owl Motif 3. Leaf Motif

PLATE XIII

CHAPTER IX

ECCLESIASTICAL LACE

In great cathedrals there are stored priceless lace albs, altar cloths, and chalice cup cloths, the work of a succession of patient women. Since lace was first made all kinds have been used for church purposes; and in the early days of the industry, high Church Dignitaries had first choice of the most exquisite pieces of lace made in convents, where time was no object, where only the beauty of the fabric was studied, and its enrichment—because nothing could be too beautiful for the service of God.

In the twelfth century a robe worn by Pope Bonifice was composed of fine linen profusely enriched with needle-point cut-work lace.

When the Venetian lace industry was at its height, the doge—the chief magistrate in charge of civil, military, and ecclesiastical affairs in Venice—forbade the sale of any lace until it had first been submitted to him. If he decided that the lace was required for the robes of a Prelate or the dresses of a saint or a Madonna, or to adorn an altar he would buy it, or appropriate it. In this connection a pretty story is told of the doge's annual visit to the convent Delle Virgini. On each occasion the youngest novice would present him with a bouquet of flowers grown in the convent garden. The bouquet had a holder of pure gold, and it was surrounded by the finest lace Venice could produce. This is believed to have originated the custom of

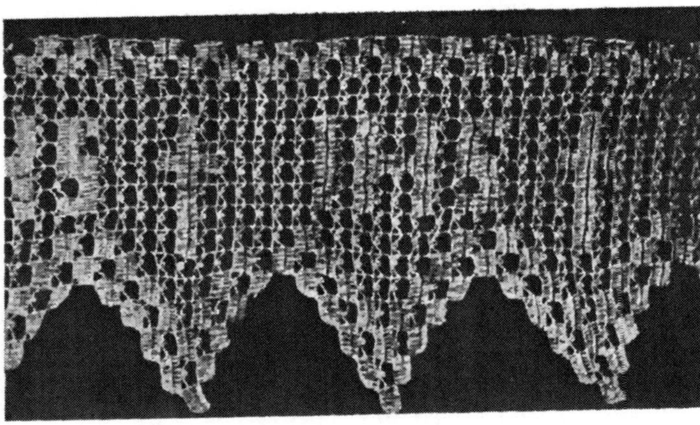

By permission of *School of Lace, Leicester*

LACE WITH THE SACRED MONOGRAM AND CROSS

PLATE XIV

surrounding presentation bouquets with silver or white lace paper.

A seventeenth century book on church ceremonies gives an instruction for the working of a cross in "blew thread" to denote the spot where the altar cloth was to be kissed. "Blew" thread was a special product of the town of Coventry at that date.

The earliest types of lace were known as "Hollie (Holy) Points" because the pattern was formed of subjects taken from Scripture, or contained some sacred emblems. A favourite design contained the Sacred Monogram surrounded by rays of glory, and having the instruments of the Passion: the dice, the crown of thorns, the cock, the ladder, hammer, and pincers in solid needle-point on a reaseau made with needle or bobbins.

On Vestment lace a scene taken from the Old Testament would compose the pattern: the Creation, Jacob's Heavenly Dream, or perhaps the Beasts of the Apocalypse. For palls, deaths-heads, cross bones, and the sacramental cup were considered the most suitable. But historical pieces of lace stored in great cathedrals are seldom used nowadays, and are only exhibited at the great festivals of the Church.

By permission of *Church of Scotland, Women's Foreign Missions*

GIRLS' LACE SCHOOL, MADRAS, INDIA

PLATE XV

CHAPTER X

FILET LACE

FILET lace ranks among the earliest type of laces; it has enjoyed a greater or lesser vogue since the fifteenth century, and is one of the laces that have never fallen completely out of use.

In its earliest form it was known as Lacis, and was made from a loose woven linen. Portions of the linen were left solid to make a pattern of geometrical symbols, and human and animal figures. The making of the square-holed ground was known as "pulled" work; the threads were not drawn out but were pulled together in groups of three both ways and oversewn.

Its second form was the making of an opener and clearer ground by working a mesh in the manner of fishing netting, and the pattern was worked on the netting with a needle and softer thread, either in plain flat darning stitch, or with an outline made with a thicker thread in rope stitch. Filet lace makers became very expert in originating new patterns, and picture scenes which included trees, flowers, birds, animals, and human figures were worked into the netting. Filet lace has also been a favourite lace for Church use.

Both classes are still worked to-day, and, in addition, a very fine, square-holed machine-made net can be purchased for the making of hand-worked filet lace. Filet lace can also be made with bobbins. The lace edging used to finish filet work is generally bobbin made. Filet lace for window curtains is often finished with a fringe made with the same thread as is used in the darning.

Filet lace can be made with linen flax, soft darning cotton, mercerized cotton, silk, and rayon twisted thread. The purpose for which the lace is intended to

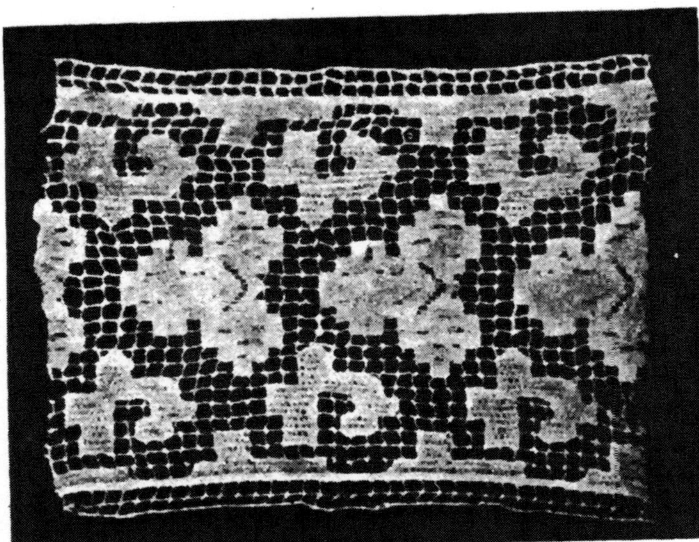

FILET INSERTION

PLATE XVI

ornament should decide the kind of thread chosen. A blunt-pointed needle is used. The mesh instructions in Figs. 3 and 4 in Needle Point chapters can be followed by the student who wishes to make her own net. A design can be drawn on sectional square-holed paper, and the paper pasted on; or the design may be transferred to calico when a machine-made net is used or for bobbins.

Filet lace is very easily copied from a lace sampler,

FILET MAT

OVAL FILET MAT

PLATE XVII

as the pattern is worked into the net by the counting of squares. The needle is inserted over one, and under the next thread, backwards and forwards the length of the design, until each square is neatly and evenly filled.

FILET INSERTION. The subject of Plate XVI was worked in mercerized cotton thread No. 30; the net is $\frac{3}{8}$ in. square. The design is a simple geometrical symbol. The edge line and symbols are worked in ordinary darning stitch, but the centre pattern of conventional flowers is worked in padded satin stitch, with the centre portions of the flowers worked in darning stitch.

FILET MATS. The oblong mat and the round mat are examples of the finest filet lace. Both are worked in simple darning stitch. The outline details in the piping cherubs, the vase, and the flowers are made by leaving a line of hole squares unfilled. The same method is used in the outline details of the roses, leaves, and the three-cornered pieces in the round mat.

BOBBIN FILET. The square mat is made with bobbins from a pattern affixed to a cushion by pinning securely. A pattern can be drawn on sectional square-holed paper. A square space covering six holes is inked black for the rose, and three squares at each side for the small leaf squares. Fine linen flax thread was used to work it, with six pairs of bobbins to work the border all round the square in cloth-stitch with open outer edge. The square-holed mesh is made by sewing one pair to each pinhole in one side, twisting each pair, and plaiting it with a pair carried across from the side. In the third line of the pattern, three squares are covered with leaf-stitch, and the mesh is continued for two more squares, when two pairs of bobbins are plaited to make four petals in leaf-stitch, the four petals are joined in the centre by plaiting, four more petals are made, then the bobbins are separated for the mesh, which is worked in the same manner as the first half of the mat. The mesh can also be worked by

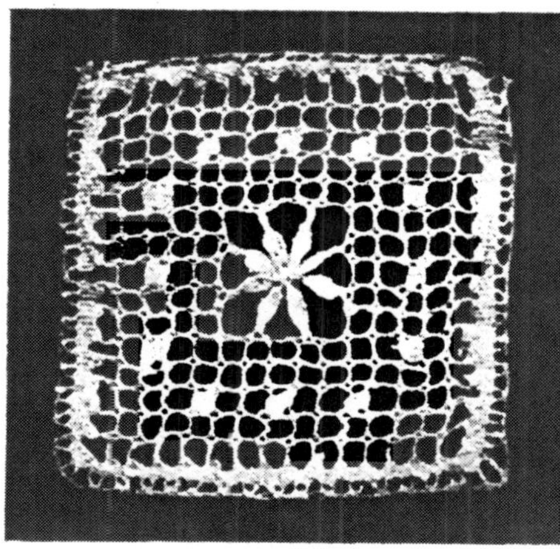

BOBBIN FILET SQUARE

PLATE XVIII

starting at a corner. Pins are not used in making the mesh, but a beginner will find that it is an advantage to insert pins at each line crossing.

Motifs of filet lace, oblong, round, or square-shaped are much used to ornament tea-cloths, table-cloths, and cosies. Filet squares are used with embroidered linen squares in alternate sections to make bedspreads. Filet lace edgings are used on modesty vests, on tea and table-cloths, and bedspreads. Some tea-cloths are entirely composed of filet lace; and a favourite window shade screen is the straight panel in filet work. A scenic pattern is darned in the centre of the panel, a border down the sides, and along the foot; and the foot, straight or scalloped, is finished with a loose or knotted fringe made with the thread used for darning.

CHAPTER XI

NEEDLE-POINT LACE

NEEDLE-POINT lace is made chiefly by button-hole stitchery and the twisting and interlacing of threads. Button-hole stitch, familiar to every one of elementary school education standard, is the basis of the solid portions in a pattern of lace made with needle and thread. A great variety of button-hole stitchery is used according to whether a close solid fabric is desired, or an open lacy one. Small stitches worked close together make a solid fabric, while lengthening the loops and increasing the distance between them makes open fabric; and a button-hole mesh can be enriched by working picots, small squares, and roses at intervals.

A large variety of threads is procurable for making lace with a needle. Linen and cotton threads are the best for most needle-point laces. Lace-craft workers will find a wide range of suitable threads and silks at most fancy-work shops and departmental stores. Ordinary sewing needles of a size suited to the thread are used. A small piece of lace can be worked on the wooden hoops used for embroidery, though for a large piece an embroidery frame is advisable. *Toile cirée*, procurable from needlework repositories or depots, is the name of the material upon which needle-point lace is worked. Bobbin-made and also machine-made braids are employed in making certain kinds of needle lace.

By permission of *Art Galleries. Glasgow*

RETICELLA PUNTO IN ARIA

PLATE XIX

The earliest type of needle-point lace was worked over a foundation of fine linen or the finest cambric. Portions of the foundation material were cut away and the open spaces filled in with various stitchery. This lace was known as "cut work." Examples of sixteenth century cut-work lace are shown in Plate XIX. Carrickmacross lace is the modern prototype. This lace was made in flat point and in raised point by the introduction of outlined threads called a cordonnet, which were closely oversewn and gave the lace the appearance of embossed ivory.

The next step in lace evolution was to do without the foundation material. The scrolls and other solid parts in the pattern were outlined with a thread or cord, oversewn, and connected with bars. The early designs were geometrical. Reticella lace is an example of it. The name given to it, Punto in Aria, means worked in the air, that is, without a foundation.

Lace made with a narrow tape was much used in the seventeenth century, and was the forerunner of lace made with braids on the pillow or by machinery. Patterns for this type of lace have the scrolls and solid parts drawn in parallel instead of in single lines, and a braid is chosen to correspond in width with the parallel lines on the pattern. The open spaces are filled in with bobbin or needle-point fillings.

Before attempting a lace sampler the worker should practise making the various fillings, bars, and edgings given here, and from them originate others. A thick thread tacked on to a piece of calico placed between wooden hoops is quite suitable for practice. A coloured calico which will show up the stitches is better than a white. Stranded cotton threads in penny skeins may be used; the strands can be separated for fine work.

Button-hole Fillings. Plate XX, Fig. 1 shows button-hole stitches worked close together to make a cloth-like filling. Horizontal lines across the open space aid in keeping the work even, but the work can be done without the lines. Commence at the left and work a row of small stitches into the outlining thread; at the right oversew two stitches down and make a line across to the left. In the second row the needle is inserted behind each loop in the upper row and connects the two rows.

Fig. 2 of Plate XX shows the loops of the button-hole stitches enlarged and worked in groups of three stitches. Make a horizontal line across from the left to the right of the outlining thread; make three button-hole stitches into the top thread, oversew three on the line thread, make three more button-hole stitches, and continue to the left. In the second row work the three buttonhole stitches into the spaces between the groups to connect the rows. This filling can be varied by making single loose button-hole stitches evenly spaced, or by merely twisting the thread and knotting each twisted stitch to the horizontal lines.

Knotted Meshes. In working Fig. 3 (XX) the equal length of each loop is important; a pin holding down each loop as it is made is a help. The stitch can be worked with or without the strengthening horizontal lines, and either diagonally or in straight lines. To work diagonally, begin at the left, make the first loop, overcast a few stitches along the top, make the second loop securing it with a knot stitch, overcast a few more stitches and continue making loops to fill the space; at

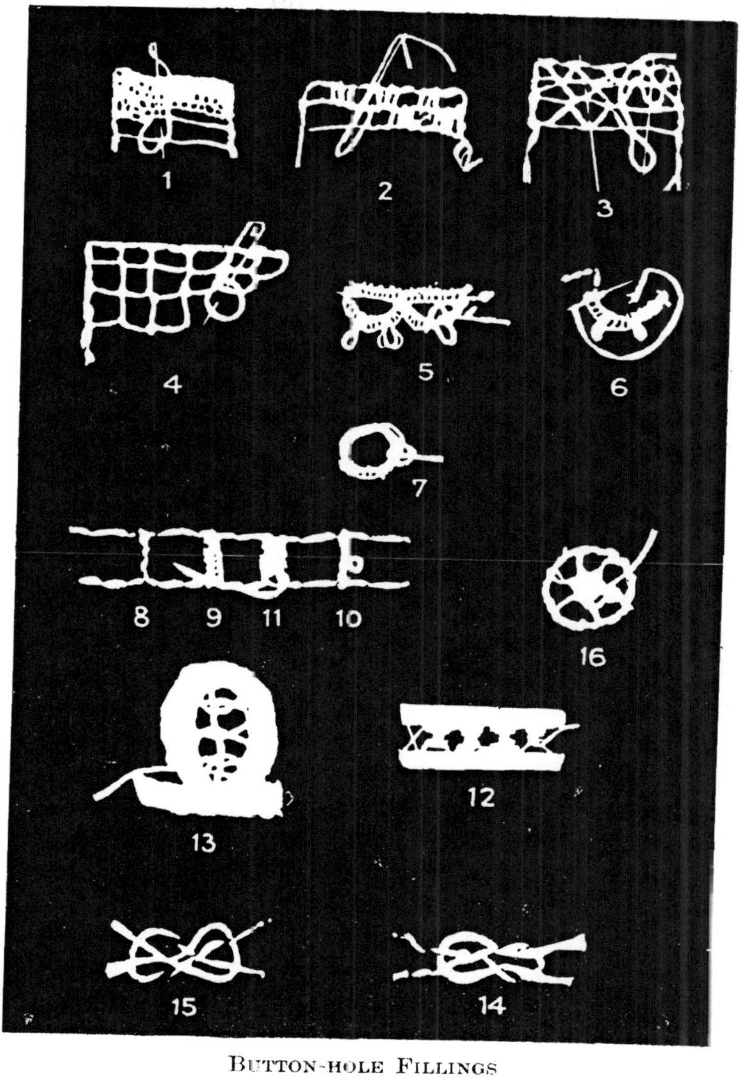

BUTTON-HOLE FILLINGS

PLATE XX

the right, overcast a few stitches down, make a line across to the left, overcast a few stitches down the left. In working the second row insert the needle behind the loop of the upper row and the thread stretching to it, then twist the working thread over and under the needle and draw up to make a knot stitch.

Fig. 4 is worked in the same knotted stitch, but the loops are formed square to make a filet mesh. It is commenced across a corner and worked backwards and forwards; the rows are connected by working a knot stitch into each loop of the previous row.

Button-hole stitch is also used in making dainty edgings. A straight line is button-holed, and button-holed loops formed along it at ½ in. intervals are made more ornamental with small loops; and button-hole stitched loops are further enriched by working picots in bullion stitch at intervals. Figs. 5 and 6 in Plate XX are examples.

Button-hole stitched rings are much used in certain kinds of needle-made lace. They are arranged in groups and joined with a few stitches. A ring stick enables one to make rings in graduated sizes, but it is possible to practise making them by winding a few strands of thread round a finger, working a button-hole stitch into them before removing from the finger, then working button-hole stitches together until the ring is completely covered. (See Fig. 7, Plate XX.)

Bars. As in bobbin lace, bars are used in needle-point to connect the solid parts in a pattern.

Plate XX, Fig. 8 is a simple twisted bar made by carrying a thread across an open space, and on returning; sewing round it and fastening off at the starting point.

Plate XX, Fig. 9 is managed in the same way; but, instead of twisting, the returning thread is worked in button-hole stitch.

Plate XX, Fig. 10 is also a button-hole stitched bar, and is further ornamented with a small picot worked in bullion stitch.

Plate XX. Fig. 11 is a stouter bar and is worked in reprise or basket-stitch. To make it, fasten two strands across an open space and work by passing the needle over one and under the other until the bar is completely filled with stitches.

Reprise can also be used with braids. Plate XX, Fig. 12 shows two lengths of braid joined by it. A double row of faggoting stitch is the foundation upon which the basket-stitch is worked. Begin at the edge of the braid so that the stitches will meet in a point in the centre of the cone, work to the opposite braid edge, pass the needle into the next cone leaving an open space between each cone. To ensure that the cones are equal in size count the stitches.

Plate XX, Fig. 16 is a cobweb to fill a round space. Six threads are crossed at equal distances apart; then the centre is filled in by basket-stitch.

Plate XX, Fig. 13 shows how a braid leaf or oval is simply and quickly filled in. The centre thread is fastened first, forming a rib, and the loops are worked across it by passing the needle under and over the rib from edge to edge.

Knotting. Ordinary knots are used in lace making at the start and finish of threads, but it is sometimes necessary to join a new thread directly on to the old one with a smooth non-slipping knot. Plate XX, Fig. 14 is a knot used by weavers for joining the warp threads;

it consists of two loops interlaced. Take the end of the new thread and form it into a loop with the threads crossed, the short end under, and the long thread above and pointing to the right. Hold the loop upright between the finger and thumb of the left hand, take the end of

NEEDLE POINT MOTIF

PLATE XXI

the working thread in the right hand and, putting it from under and through the loop, pass it round between the thumb and the first finger, under the short end of the new thread and over the long one and down into the upright loop again; draw tight.

Plate XX, Fig. 15 is a knot used by sailors and is known as the Carrick Bend. It is used with cords and narrow braids. A number of them connected by a few stitches, end to end, make an ornamental filling in a lace border. To make it, form one piece of braid into a loop, cross the ends with the under and shorter

By permission of *Art Galleries, Glasgow*

ROSE POINT DE VENISE

PLATE XXII

towards the worker, take the second piece of braid in the right hand and pass it under the loop in a diagonal direction over the long and under the short end, then into the loop, and pass it under the diagonal thread and out over the loop.

The knot can be drawn tight to make a firm join, or left loose for an ornamental knot. A very decorative

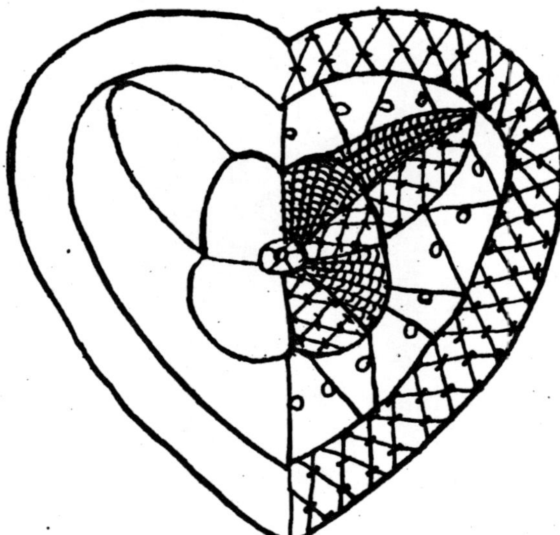

Fig. 10. Motif Diagram

knot is the Chinese. It consists of two hearts reversed and interlaced with a loop at the sides.

Rose Point de Venise. The Rose Point de Venise (p. 81) is a specimen of the richest class of Venetian seventeenth century raised needle-point lace. A thick cordonnet outlines the flowers, all the petals, leaves, and stems. The close toile inside portions are varied with different open-work stitchery. The bars are enriched with small wheel-shaped picots, and the edging with pearl loops.

This lace is much too intricate for a beginner to accomplish; the heart-shaped modern motif is within the scope of the student who has mastered the needlework stitches in the foregoing chapter.

The diagram can be copied by placing a carbon paper under it. One-half shows the outline and the other half the working details. To work it, tack an outlining thread on the calico pattern; work button-hole stitch over all the outlining thread. The centre of the braid is worked in a diagonal knotted mesh, and the knotted mesh covers one-half of each flower and leaf; the other half is filled with close button-hole stitch. The picoted bars are strands of thread covered with button-hole stitch. A small cobweb fills the centre of the flower. Cut the tacking thread at the back and remove the motif. Use couching stitch to tack outlining thread on the pattern.

CHAPTER XII

NEEDLE-RUN LACE

The use of lace for personal and house adornment is said to be one of the distinguishing marks of civilization and of refined taste. The need for airy and lighter hangings probably became felt when plastered walls and better fitting windows made protection from cold draughts by heavy hangings unnecessary. Hand-darned netting draperies supplied the demand for such until the invention of machinery capable of imitating all kinds of continental laces made machine embroidered lace curtains cheap and within reach of all classes.

To-day the long machine-embroidered lace curtains have lost the popular favour; the pendulum has swung backwards and netting draperies are the favoured vogue. Machinery has been so perfected that nets of the finest gossamer texture are produced for personal wear, and stouter meshes for house adornment. The ornamentation and enrichment of machine-made nets provide limitless scope for the imaginative, original hand-craft worker. It is proposed in this chapter to initiate the lace maker into a few of the methods of enriching plain machine-made netting.

Nets can be purchased in bleached and in coloured threads of many artistic shades. And threads can be purchased in every conceivable colour and fineness or thickness. Modern metal threads made without a wire core are practically untarnishable; they are much used both for the entire covering of net and for outlining thread patterns. Coloured beads, pearls, and semi-precious stones are lavishly sewn upon net, and spangles or sequins are never out of favour.

A frame is required for a large piece of work. A lap

By permission of *School of Lace, Leicester*

NEEDLE-RUN TABLE SCARF

PLATE XXIII

frame can easily be made at home with four laths of wood screwed or nailed together at the corners, and a large size to stand upon two stools or trestles. Bought frames have two rollers with webbing attached, on to which the work is sewn, and two side pieces that slip through holes in each end of the rollers, to keep the frame taut. A linen pattern with the design traced on it is sewn or affixed with drawing pins to the frame, and the netting is placed over the pattern; the tracing on the design should show distinctly through the net. Blunt-pointed embroidery needles of a size suited to the thread used are best for needle-running work.

Plate XXIII shows an example of exquisite needle-run

NEEDLE-RUN LACE

PLATE XXIV

stitchery. It is one-half of a runner for a dressing table, to be placed under a glass top. The design, carried out in fine white cotton net and worked in mercerized cotton thread, is a very artistic piece of lace. When a border pattern is to be worked a firmer edge is given to the net by working button-hole in small and fairly close stitches all round the cut edge. A thick outlining thread can be used for any parts in the pattern that should stand out distinctly. The working is simple. The part to be covered must be crossed in each direction by lines of darning to fill it

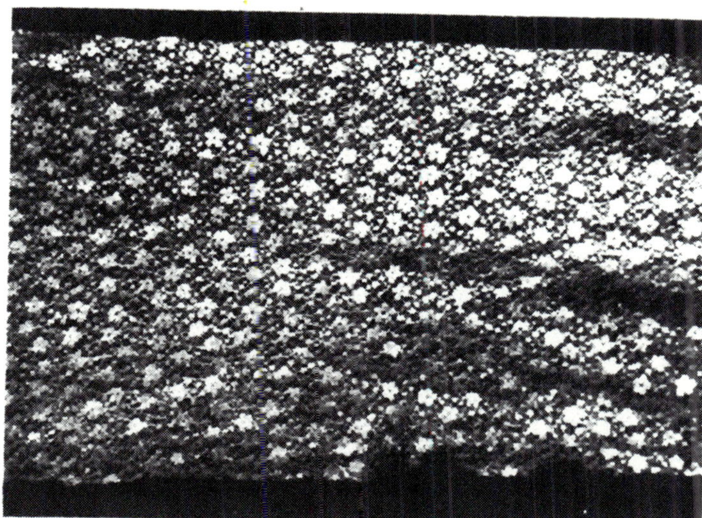

FABRIC LACE

PLATE XXV

up. The various lines are run in and out of the net as continuously as possible, each succeeding line taking up the thread passed over in the previous line. The work should appear alike on both sides. When a new thread is to be joined a smooth non-slipping weaver's knot is best. Varied effects for centre fillings can be achieved by working lines in trellis fashion, a twill effect by diagonal lines, and fishbone effect by wave lines.

Plate XXIV shows an all-over design well within the

scope of the beginner. A large flower with six petals and a long stem with leaves on both sides are the only parts of the design requiring to be drawn on the linen pattern. Two colours were used to work it—blue and white. Worked on fine silk net with silk floss or rayon twist threads it makes a beautiful soft lace for ladies' dresses; worked in stouter cotton or silk net and threads, it makes an effective lace for window curtains. The net is very quickly covered with the needle-running-stitch.

The flower petals, leaves, and both sides of the stem were, first of all, outlined with the white thread. The centres of them were then filled with blue thread. The closest running-stitch is made by taking up every alternate thread and passing over one; a longer stitch is made by passing over two threads and taking up two. The running can be worked in any direction straight across from edge to edge of a petal, up and down it, or diagonally. The all-over scroll ground is worked with white thread in a continuous single line which is carried into the stem after forming each group of skeleton loops. A corolla of skeleton loops is worked in white thread in the centre of the flower, and also three single lines. The lace should appear alike on both sides; joining of new threads should be made with weaver's knot.

Plate XXV illustrates one of the newest lace fabrics for ladies' dresses. The design of daisies would also make dainty dresses for young children. This lace was made entirely in green silk thread upon an open six-sided mesh of green silk net. No pattern is required to work it; but the net can be tacked upon a linen foundation to prevent the stretching of the delicate threads while working. The thread for working the design should be as near as possible in texture to that composing the net. The daisies and the square spots scattered over the ground are worked by counting the holes in the net. They can be worked in running-stitch or in

BEADED LACE

PLATE XXVI

reprise-stitch with the needle, or with bobbins in cloth-stitch; the bobbins are "sewn" into the net at the tip of a petal, and down the sides of it. The spots are worked in leaf-stitch. Worked on a pale green net with the daisies in their natural white with yellow spot centres, a very effective and beautiful lace can be produced at a small outlay of money and time.

Plate XXVI shows a pattern worked on net with

beads and sequins. The net is white silk of fairly strong texture; the colour scheme, black and white with gold outline. A pattern is necessary to work it. A transferable paper pattern of any large flower design can be bought and stamped with a hot iron on to a linen foundation. The net is tacked upon the foundation pattern and worked on a frame. The working can only be done with needle and thread. The flowers, leaves, stem, and scroll are first of all outlined with a running thread of stranded gold metal thread. To give a broad outline effect to flowers, leaves, and scroll, black bugle beads were sewn in close formation inside the gold running thread. Another gold running thread was worked inside the beaded line which made a guide for a line of tiny oblong-shaped silver sequins; a small black bead was sewn between each sequin. The centres of the flowers are made to stand out effectively by drawing three threads together and forming another type of mesh. For instance: two white silk threads run in straight lines across a space produces Point de Paris mesh; drawing the threads into a six-sided hole makes the hexagonal mesh of Alençon fame; reprise-stitch produces small squares to fill an open space more effectively, and to work straight lines at edges; small round silver and black sequins were used to vary the line effects in the curves of the petals and scrolls. There are two methods of sewing sequins on net. One method is to sew a small bead into the heart of each sequin and make the sewing thread invisible from the right side of the lace. The other method is worked with a fine silk thread either to match the colour of the sequin, or with a contrasting thread. Knot the end of the thread, insert the needle from under the sequin, lay the second sequin just over the edge of the first, put the needle through sequin two from under, then through sequin one from upper, lay sequin three in position, put the needle through the hole from under, then insert it through sequin two from the upper side. Sewn in this way there is small chance of the sequins dropping off. When sewing rows of pearls or small beads a good method of securing each bead firmly is to make a French knot between each bead. When silk thread is used the knots have a decorative effect.

Beaded lace can be worked all over a net to make an entire dress; a long panel can be worked on a dress composed of net, or the ornamentation may take the form of a straight or a scalloped border, a yoke, collar, and cuffs.

With numerous beautiful threads and the traditional designs of generations of lace makers at her command, the hand-lace worker of to-day has the privilege of assisting in the preservation of what we believe to be most precious in our National life. For crafts have always been bound up in the local history and tradition of the people. And it is not to the giant automatically moving machine capable of production on mass scale, but to the individual ideas and thoughts, and the diminutive tools of the hand-craft worker that we look for maintaining that high standard of beauty and workmanship that can only originate in the creative human brain quickened by the joy of doing.

CHAPTER XIII

MARKETING LACE

THE lace maker who wishes to earn a livelihood at this craft is confronted with the problem of disposing of her work.

The usual way, if she has sufficient capital, is to open a small studio in a large town, give exhibitions of her finished lace, take orders for similar work, or make lace to order. If she has teaching ability she can take pupils to help pay studio expenses. And she can extend her clientèle by holding periodical exhibitions in other large towns. A hall is often taken by a number of crafts-women specializing in different art-crafts, and this is not an expensive venture. A small advertisement inserted in ladies' magazines and papers is helpful in working up a private connection. Nowadays there are many Women's Institutes and Associations, and the private worker who becomes a member of a Rural Women's Institute, or the National Federation of Women's Institutes, or one of the Applied Arts Associations has the privilege of submitting specimens of her work at yearly exhibitions held by the organization. Gold and silver medals and other prizes are often awarded at these exhibitions for exhibits showing distinctive design, or merit in workmanship.

An alternative to a studio is a shop in a coast town or on a motoring route. To make a success of a studio or shop needs a certain business ability combined with a knowledge of the particular public, their tastes, and their purchasing powers. The lace must be of professional standard, not amateurish; attractive to the eye as well as being in the vogue of the moment—it is useless making and trying to sell sailor collars and wrist ruffles when such are not worn! The lace maker who can show a distinctive style in her work or in the display of it has a better chance of success than one who merely imitates other people. And while the lace should compare favourably with the machine-made fabric in price, it should show a superiority over the machine goods.

The lace maker without capital must try to dispose of her work to the large stores and those shops which stock handiwork. Or she may become a worker to a lace-buying firm when she will be supplied with parchments and materials, and will be paid for the finished lace. The Lace School, Northampton, the School of Stitchery and Lace, Leicester, and the Cottage Workers' School at Olney, are a few of the principal lace-buying firms. Those firms are conducted on strictly business lines, and besides being sold locally, it is sold by Mail Order throughout the British Isles, and to all parts of the world.

Some years ago Lace Associations were organized throughout England with the object of reviving the industry. The Midlands Lace Association had a depot at Northampton, and Miss C. C. Channer, whose connection with the English Lace Industry is of long standing, acted as secretary for a period. But Miss Channer informs me that the old Lace Associations are now extinct. The private home worker can only obtain work through the lace-buying firms; as I am authoritively informed that private lace buyers often have difficulty in getting the lace they need, it is evident that there is a market for the real laces of the home hand-craft worker.

The Rural Industries Bureau, whose London headquarters is 27 Bedford Square, W.C.1, gives information and advice to craftswomen by post or otherwise. The Bureau works in close touch with the National Federation of Women's Institutes, the National Council of Social Service, and Government departments in the Labour and Co-operation Movements. The Bureau keeps for the use of buyers a list of the names of craftswomen whose work is of a high standard.

Lightning Source UK Ltd.
Milton Keynes UK
UKOW052037130112

185336UK00001B/86/P

9 781447 413189

Flow-Based Programming

A New Approach to Application Development

Flow-Based Programming

A New Approach to Application Development

J. Paul Morrison

VAN NOSTRAND REINHOLD
An International Thomson Publishing Company

New York • London • Bonn • Boston • Detroit • Madrid • Melbourne • Mexico City
Paris • Singapore • Tokyo • Toronto • Albany NY • Belmont CA • Cincinnati OH

Library of Congress Catalog Card Number 94-1822
ISBN 0-442-1771-5

ITP Van Nostrand Reinhold is an International Thomson Publishing company. ITP logo is a trademark under license.

Printed in the United States of America.

Van Nostrand Reinhold
115 Fifth Avenue
New York, New York 10003

International Thomson Publishing
Berkshire House
168-173 High Holborn
London WC1V 7AA
England

Thomas Nelson Australia
102 Dodds Street
South Melbourne, Victoria 3205
Australia

Nelson Canada
1120 Birchmount Road
Scarborough, Ontario
M1K 5G4, Canada

International Thomson Publishing GmbH
Königswinterer Strasse 418
53227 Bonn
Germany

International Thomson Publishing Asia
221 Henderson Road
#05-10 Henderson Building
Singapore 0315

International Thomson Publishing Japan
Hirakawacho Kyowa Building, 3F
2-2-1 Hirakawa-cho, Chiyoda-ku
Tokyo 102
Japan

ARCFF 16 15 14 13 12 11 10 9 8 7 6 5 4 3 2 1

Library of Congress Cataloging-in-Publication Data

Morrison, John Paul.
Flow based programming : a new approach to application development / John Paul Morrison.
p. cm.
Includes bibliographical references and index.
ISBN 0-442-01771-5
1. Application software. 2. Computer software—Development.
3. Electronic digital computers—Programming. I. Title.
QA76.76.A65M675 1994
005.1′1—dc20 94-1822
CIP

Contents

Preface

This book describes a highly productive approach to application development, based on a new and significantly different programming paradigm, referred to as "Flow-Based Programming" (FBP). Although at least one sizable application built using software based on these concepts has been in continuous use for about 20 years, it is not well known to the programming community, so it will be novel to most of the readers of this book. Over the 20 years it has been under development and in use, it has been found to significantly enhance both the productivity of the programmers who use it and the reliability and maintainability of applications built with it.

The material described here has practical application to many of the problems that beset today's information technology industry. At the same time it has solid theoretical underpinnings and also strong affinities with a lot of other theoretical work going forward in universities and research institutions worldwide. A number of articles on this concept have appeared over the years in different publications, but they have been widely scattered and I feel that no single article has been able to do justice to the whole set of concepts. Therefore, it seems timely to assemble this material into a single book, thus allowing it to be presented as a coherent whole.

Flow-based programming provides a view of data processing that is consistent from the largest scale (e.g., organizations talking to other organizations) all the way down to the programming level, without the sudden changes of viewpoint characteristic of conventional programming. It can be used from early in the design stage all the way through to implementation in a seamless manner. It is a good match with design techniques such as Structured Analysis, and with a number of implementation approaches, such as prototyping and incremental development. It is a natural reuse tool and strongly supports good programming disciplines. It has many non-procedural aspects, which give it many of the advantages of this type of code. It should not be surprising, therefore, that it has caught the interest of some of the most experienced people in our business. I feel strongly and hope to prove in this book that these concepts have the potential to save computer-using organizations significant amounts of money and, perhaps more importantly, to lay the foundations of a true software marketplace and programming discipline in the broadest sense.

This book is aimed at systems architects, software and hardware engineers, application developers and analysts, researchers—in fact, everyone who is involved in computing or even just interested in this field. Educators should find that this book places a number of the advanced concepts of computing science into context in a natural way and perhaps will find this book of assistance in passing them on to their students.

This book is not intended to be a manual for any one piece of software, but as a fairly general introduction to a new and powerful set of concepts. Like object-oriented programming, FBP does involve a new programming paradigm, which profoundly changes the way programmers look at the process of constructing applications. Although a number of its concepts seem very different from conventional programming, there are many real-world analogies that help the reader make the transition to this new way of thinking about building systems. Also, once the basics have been mastered, most of the remaining material will follow naturally. It is interesting to note that, in the long run, FBP appears to be on a convergent path with the more advanced work in object-oriented programming. I also hope that this book might contribute somewhat towards bridging the present divide in the area of computer programming between business and academia.

For anyone wishing to get hands-on experience with some of these concepts, a PC-based system called THREADS, which embodies a number of the concepts of flow-based programming, is available from:

HOMEDATA (Rochester) Inc.
77 Loch Revan Heights
Rochester NY 14617-3301
USA
Compuserve I.D.: 74363, 2621

THREADS is written in C and runs on Intel-based machines. It has been tested on the 286, 386, and 486 processors. THREADS is used from time to time in the course of this book to illustrate FBP concepts, and its API is shown in the appendix.

Acknowledgments

To my wife Brenda, for her loving support, encouragement, and sound common sense and for having helped to make the time available that I needed to finish this process. I have always thought that a programmer's wife has to be a bit of a saint—and now I'm convinced of it!

To the late Wayne Stevens, my friend and mentor, who died much too young, for his creativity and sense of fun, his openness to new ideas, his wide-ranging knowledge and experience, and his perennial optimism and enthusiasm. This book is intended to be in a small way a tribute to his memory.

To Nate Edwards, Skip Folden, Harrison Tellier, Bob Kendall, Perry Crawford, Bob Ballow, and many of the "old guard," who understood intuitively the ideas I talk about in this book, but retired before they could get anyone to listen. I always enjoy your anecdotes, your optimism, and your down-to-earth attitudes. There are also others who have encouraged me over the years who are too many to mention—you know who you are! Thank you all!

To my son, Joseph Morrison—who, thanks to his education in computer science at the University of Waterloo and at MIT, is at ease in esoteric areas that I can hardly guess at—for his useful and always constructive input and comments. Also to the rest of my family, for their support and encouragement!

To the various teams I have worked with over the years at IBM, several of whose personnel are mentioned in this book. In particular, the last team I worked with at IBM—one of the best I have ever worked with, and a number of whom have become personal friends. It was a pleasure and an essential part of my education working with you all! Also to Robbie Kemeny, who very early on helped me to develop some of the key ideas during after-work bus rides up the side of the mountain in Montréal, and to our director, Doug Croth, who was excited about the concept and promoted it strongly within our organization.

Also to the team in Japan who succeeded in putting out the only FBP product that has made it into the marketplace so far. Although it was definitely a team effort, I would like to make special mention of my friend Kenji Terao, who saw the potential years before most other people and was key to getting the concept accepted by IBM Japan.

I must also mention the people at the company that decided to use an untried technology to help build one of the biggest business systems ever built in Canada, and the people from IBM Canada, particularly John Jensen, and from the IBM Federal Systems Division, particularly Kim Seward, who helped me to first sell and then implement it.

Next I would like to thank IBM Canada for supporting this work over the last 20 years and for their kind permission for me to talk about my experiences during this time. Of course, it should be made clear to the reader that the views expressed in this book are not necessarily those of the company. As I look back over my years with IBM in three different countries, I realize that I have been more fortunate than most to have been able to work on so many exciting things for a very large part of that time.

Last, but not least, I would like to thank the publisher, my editors at Van Nostrand Reinhold and Northeastern Graphic Services, and the various reviewers, both the ones known to me and the anonymous ones, who together have helped to turn this book from a dream into a reality.

Disclaimers

1. I may at times inadvertently use the pronoun "he" to refer to individuals in general. If I do, I wish to state that this is not to be taken as implying any particular gender. Unfortunately, English lacks a good pronoun meaning "he or she."
2. Occasionally in the literature, one finds the word "data" being treated as a plural, presumably that of the slightly archaic word "datum." It is high time we put this affectation to rest. For at least the last 20 years in North America, "data" has been a collective noun, taking singular verbs and adjectives, just like "information," which means approximately the same thing. I remember protesting against this particular piece of pedantry 15 years ago, but apparently the rulebook was never updated! In today's programming parlance, "data" is no longer experienced as the plural of "datum" (most programmers wouldn't recognize a datum if it bit them on the leg), so "data are" should be relegated to treatises on the history of programming, where it belongs. Interestingly, in the Indo-European languages there is an ancient affinity between the neuter plural and the singular number—Ancient Greek *required* the use of a singular verb with the neuter plural, such as in *Panta rheei* (Everything flows). If you still have any lingering doubts, ask yourself which sounds better: "a few data" or "a little data," "many data" or "much data."

Prologue

Before we get started with the subject matter of this book, let me introduce myself, as a way of providing some background to what you are going to read about. I was born in London, England, just before the start of World War II, received what is sometimes referred to as a classical education, learned to speak several languages (including the usual dead ones), and studied Archaeology and Anthropology at King's College, Cambridge. I have since discovered that Alan Turing had attended my college, but while I was there I was learning to recognize Neanderthal skulls and hearing Edmund Leach lecture about the Kachin, so I regret that I cannot claim to have programmed EDSAC, the machine being developed at Cambridge, although I later took an aptitude test for another marvelous machine, the Lyons LEO (Lyons Electronic Office), whose design was based on EDSAC's. But maybe computing was in the air at King's!

In 1959 I joined IBM (UK) as an Electronic Data Processing Machines Representative. I had come into computers by a circuitous route. Around the age of 12, I was bitten by the symbolic logic bug. This so intrigued me that all during my school and university years I read up on it, played with the concepts for myself, and looked forward to the time when all the world's problems would be solved by the judicious rearrangement of little mathematical symbols. Having also been fascinated by the diversity of human languages since childhood, the idea of really getting to the root of what things meant was very exciting. It wasn't until later in life that I realized that many great minds had tried this route without much success and that, while it is certainly a beguiling concept, and there have been many such attempts in earlier centuries, the universe of human experience is too complex and dynamic, with too many interacting factors, to be encoded in such a simple way. This does not mean that attempts to convey knowledge to a computer will not work—just that there seem to be certain built-in limitations. The human functions that we tend to think of as being simple, almost trivial, such as vision, speech comprehension, or the ability to make one's way along a busy street, are often the hardest to explain to a computer. What we call common sense turns out to be quite uncommon.

While symbolic logic has not delivered on its original promise of making the world's important decisions simpler, it *is* perfectly adapted to the design of computers, and I became fascinated by the idea of machines that could perform logical operations. This fascination has stayed with me during my 33 years with the IBM Corporation in three different countries (most of the systems I will be mentioning will be IBM systems). However, I've always been struck by the apparent mismatch between the power of these machines and the difficulty of getting them to do what we want. Gradually I've come to concentrate on one basic problem: Why should the process of developing applications on computers be so difficult, when they can obviously do anything we can figure out the rules for?

There is definitely an advantage to having cut my proverbial teeth in this field at a time when very few people had even heard of computers; over the intervening years I have had time to digest new concepts and see which of them succeeded and which failed. Over the course of three-plus decades, many concepts, techniques, and fads have sprung up with great attendant fanfare, and have either faded out or just become part of the regular curriculum. Ideas that took a decade or two to evolve are now familiar to kids fresh out of the university. Of the many new ideas and wonders—a list too long to include here, and perhaps only of interest to historians—some have fallen by the wayside; but many of them are still around—some good and some not-so-good! We who have been working in the field also contributed our fair share of techniques and fads, some good and some not-so-good!

I think my first enthusiasm was compiler compilers. I first worked with a system called BABEL (appropriately named) that was going to make it far easier to write compilers. (I still use some of its ideas today.) We shall see later in this book that there are interesting parallels between compiler theory and the subject matter of this book, and there seems to be an important role for what are sometimes called "mini-languages" (more about them in chapter 17). Certainly compiler compilers comprise a piece of the answer, but they did not result in the productivity improvement that we were looking for.

I have also always been taken with interpreters. I believe my first exposure to these was BLIS (the Bell Laboratories Interpretive System), which made the 650 look like a sequential machine. Probably the characteristic of interpreters that really appeals to people is the ability to debug without having to change languages. Of course, some of the recent debugging tools are starting to bring this capability to the world of higher-level-languages (HLLs), but the ability merely to slot in a TYPE or "say" command and rerun a test is so impressive that all the languages that became popular have always been interpreters, no matter how awkward the syntax! A survey of machine cycle usage, done a few years ago at IBM's Research Center at Yorktown Heights, found that the vast majority of cycles were being used by CMS EXEC statements—strings of CMS commands and simple logic and looping statements glued together to do specific jobs of work.

Another important concept for productivity improvement is that of a reusable subroutine library. (I also believe strongly that reuse is another key piece of the solution, but not exactly in the form in which we visualized it in those days.) In company after company, I have seen people start up shared subroutine libraries with a fine flurry of enthusiasm, only to find the action slowing to a standstill after some 30 or 40 subroutines have been developed and made available. Some companies are claiming much higher numbers, but I suspect these are shops that measure progress, and reward their people, based on how many subroutines are created and added to the library, rather than on whether they are actually used. Although organizational and economic changes are also required to really capitalize on any form of reuse, I believe there is a more fundamental reason why these libraries never really take off, and that is the philosophy of the von Neumann machine. I will be going into this in more detail in chapter 1, but I found I was able to predict which subroutines would end up in these libraries, and it was always "one moment in time" functions, e.g. , binary search, date routines, various kinds of conversions. I tried to build an easy-to-use, general purpose update and I just couldn't do it (except for supporting a tiny subset of all the possible variations)! This experience got me thinking about a radically different approach to producing reusable code. I hope that, as you read this book, you will agree that there *is* another approach, and that it is completely complementary to the old one.

Rapid prototyping and the related idea of iterative development were (and still are) another enthusiasm of mine. Rapid prototyping is a process of reducing the uncertainties in the development process by trying things out. I believe that *anything* you are uncertain about should be prototyped: complex algorithms, unfamiliar hardware, database structures, human interfaces (especially), etc. This technique will become even more important in the next few decades as we move into ever more complex environments. Here again, we will have to modify or even abandon the old methodologies. (Dave Olson's 1993 book, *Exploiting Chaos: Cashing in on the Realities of Software Development,* describes a number of approaches to combining iterative development with milestones to get the best of both worlds, plus some fascinating digressions into the new concepts of chaos and "strange attractors." (There are some very strange attractors in our business.) I have also believed for some time that most prototypes should not just be thrown away once they have served their purpose. Prototypes should be able to be "grown," step by step, into a full-fledged system. Since the importance of prototypes is that they reduce uncertainty, rewriting applications in a different language is liable to bring a lot of it back!

The pattern of all these innovations is always the same—from the subroutine to object-oriented programming: someone finds a piece of the answer and we get a small increment in productivity, but not the big breakthrough we have been looking for, and eventually this technique makes its way into the general bag of tricks that every experienced programmer carries in his or her back pocket.

By the way, I should state at the outset that my focus is not on mathematical applications, but on business applications. Mathematical applications are a different ballgame, and one happily played by academics all over the world. Business applications are different, and much of my work has been to try to determine exactly why they should be so different, and what we can do to solve the problem of building and maintaining them. These kinds of applications often have a direct effect on the competitiveness of the companies that use them, and being able to build and maintain this type of application more effectively will be a win-win situation for those of us in the industry and for those who use our services.

Before discussing a set of concepts that, based on my experience of the last 20 years, really does provide a quantum jump in improving application development productivity, I would like to mention something that arises directly out of my personal background. Coming from an artistic background, I tend to think about things in visual terms. One of the influences in the work described in this book was a feeling that one should be able to express applications in a graphical notation that takes advantage of people's visualization abilities. This feeling may have been helped along by exposure to a system called GPSS (General Purpose Simulation System). This system can be highly graphical, and it (along with other simulation systems) has another very interesting characteristic, namely that its constructs tend to match objects in the real world. It is not surprising that Simula (another language originally designed for simulation) is viewed as one of the forerunners of many of today's advanced programming languages.

Another effect of my personal orientation is a desire, almost a preoccupation, with beauty in programming. While I will stress many times that programming should not be the production of unique pieces of cabinetry, this does not mean that programs cannot exhibit beauty. There are places and times in the world's history where people have invested great creativity in useful objects such as spoons or drinking cups. Conversely, the needs of primitive mass-production, supported by a naive view of value, resulted in factories turning out vast numbers of identical, artistically crude objects (although obviously there were some exceptions), which are thought by some to have led to a deadening of the sensibilities of a whole culture. I believe that modern technology can do more than just make our lives more comfortable—it can actually help to bring the aesthetic back into its proper place in our life experience.

One more comment about my personal biases (of which I have many, so I'm told): It has always seemed to me that application design and building is predominantly a *creative* activity, and creativity is a uniquely human ability—one that (I believe) computers and robots will never exhibit. On the other hand, any activity which bores people *should* be done by computers, and will probably be done better by them. So the trick is to split work appropriately between humans and machines—it is the partnership between the two that can lead to the most satisfying and productive era the world has ever known. One of the points often missed by the purveyors of methodologies is that each stage of refinement of a design is not simply an expansion of information already in existence, but a creative act. We should absolutely avoid reentering the same information over and over again—that's boring!—but, on the other hand, we should never imagine that any stage of refinement of a design can somehow magically be done without human input. Robots are great at remembering and following rules—only humans *create*.

Corollary I: Do not use humans for jobs computers can do better—this is a waste of human energy and creativity, the only real resource on this planet, and devalues the human spirit.

Corollary II: Do not expect computers to provide that creative spark that only humans can provide. If computers do become creative, they won't be computers anymore—they will be people!

The other personal slant I bring to this quest is the result of a unique educational system that inculcated in its victims (sorry, students) the idea that there is really no area of human endeavor that one should be afraid to tackle, and that indeed we all can realistically expect to contribute to any field of knowledge we address. This perhaps outdated view may have led me to rush in where angels fear to tread. However, this pursuit has at the least kept me entertained and given my professional life a certain direction for several decades.

In past centuries, the dilettante or amateur has contributed a great deal to the world's store of knowledge and beauty. (Remember, most big paradigm shifts were instigated by outsiders!) The word "amateur" comes from the idea of loving. One should be proud to be called a computing amateur! "Dilettante" is another fine word with a similar flavor, coming from an Italian word meaning "to delight in." I therefore propose another theorem: If an activity isn't fun, humans probably shouldn't be doing it. People should use the feeling of fun as a touchstone to see if they are on the right track. Here is a quote from my colleague, P.R. Ewing, which also agrees with my own experience: "The guys who turn out the most code are the ones who are having fun!" Too many experts are deadly serious. Play is not something we have to put away when we reach the state of adulthood—it is a very important way for humans to expand their understanding of the universe and all the delightful beings who occupy it. This feeling, that the subject matter of this book is *fun,* is one of the most common reactions we have encountered and one that makes my collaborators and myself believe that we have stumbled onto something important. In what follows I hope to convey some of this feeling. Please forgive me if some whimsy sneaks in now and then!

Trademarks

The following are trademarks or registered trademarks of International Business Machines, Inc.:

- BMS
- CICS, CICS/ESA
- CMS
- CMS Pipelines
- CP/CMS
- DB2
- DFDM
- DL/I
- GDDM
- GPSS
- IBM
- IMS, IMS/ESA, IMS TM
- ISPF
- MFS
- MQSeries
- MVS, MVS/ESA
- OS/2
- PDF
- PGF
- PL/I
- REXX
- System/370
- VM/XA
- VS/COBOL II
- VTAM

The following are products of their respective suppliers:

- C++
- Linda
- Objective-C
- Smalltalk V/PM
- UNIX

1

Introduction

Imagine that you have a large and complex application running in your shop and you discover that you need what look like fairly complex changes made to it in a hurry. You consult your programmers, and they tell you that the changes will probably take several months, but they will take a look. A meeting is called of all the people involved—not just programmers and analysts, but users and operations personnel as well. The essential logic of the program is put up on the wall, and the program designers walk through the program structure with the group. During the ensuing discussion, they realize that two new modules have to be written and some other ones have to change places. Total time to make the changes: a week!

Quite a few parts of this scenario sound unlikely, don't they? Users, operations people, and programmers all talking the same language—unbelievable! But it actually did happen just that way. The factor that made this experience so different from most programmers' everyday experience is the truly revolutionary technology I have described in this book.

While this technology has been used for productive work for the last 20 years, it has also been waiting in the wings, so to speak, for the right time to come on stage. Perhaps because there is a "paradigm shift" involved, to use Kuhn's phrase (Kuhn 1970), it has not been widely known up to now, but I believe the time is now here to open it up to a wider public.

This technology provides a consistent application view from high-level design all the way down to implementation. It requires applications to be built using reusable "black boxes" and encourages developers to construct such black boxes, which can then improve the productivity of other developers. It forces developers to focus on data and its transformations, rather than starting with procedural code. It encourages rapid prototyping and results in more reliable, more maintainable systems. It is compatible with distributed systems and appears to be on a convergent path with object-oriented programming. In this book, I will describe the concepts underlying this technology and give examples of experience gained using it. Does it sound too good to be true? You be the judge! In the following pages, I will describe what I believe is a genuine revolution in the process of creating application programs to support the data processing requirements of companies around the world.

Today, in the early 1990s, the bulk of all business programming is done using techniques that have not changed much in 30 years. Most of it is done using what are often called higher-level languages (HLLs), by far the most popular of which is COBOL, the COmmon Business-Oriented Language. A distant second is probably PL/I, not as widespread in terms of number of customers, but in use at some of the biggest organizations in North America. C appears to be gaining steadily in popularity, especially as it is often the first programming language students encounter at college. It appears to be especially convenient for writing system software, due to its powerful and concise pointer manipulation facilities, but by the same token it may be not as well adapted for writing business applications. Some languages are used by particular sectors of the programming community or for certain specialized purposes. There are also the "fourth generation languages," which are higher level than the HLLs but usually more specialized.

There are plenty of design methodologies and plenty of front-end tools to do them with, but most of these do not really affect the mechanics of creating programs. After the design has been done, the programmer still has the job of converting his or her elegant design into strings of commands in the chosen programming language. Although generators have had some success, by and large most of today's programmers painstakingly create their programs by hand, like skilled artisans handcrafting individual pieces of cabinetry. One of the "grand old men" of the computing fraternity, Nat Rochester, said a number of years ago that programming probably absorbs more creativity than any other professional pursuit, and most of it invisible to the outside world. Things really haven't changed all that much since those days.

There are also what might be called procedural or organizational approaches to improving the application development process (e.g., structured walk-throughs, the buddy system, chief programmer teams, third-party testing). My experience is that the approaches of this type that have been successful will still be valid whatever tool we eventually use for producing applications. However, if all you do is take the existing handcrafting technology and add a massive bureaucracy to cross-check every chisel stroke and hammer blow, you will only get minor improvements in your process, at a considerable cost in productivity and morale. What is needed instead is a fundamental change in the way we do things, after which we will be able to see which procedures and organizations fit naturally into the new world.

It is obvious that most businesses in the Western world would stop functioning if it were not for the efforts of tens of thousands, if not hundreds of thousands, of application programmers. These people are practicing a craft that most of the population does not understand and would not be willing to do if it did understand it. The archetypal programmer is viewed as a brilliant but impractical individual who has a better rapport with computers than with people, slaving long hours at a terminal, which is at the very least damaging to his or her eyesight. In fact, of course, the programmer is the key interface between his or her clients, who speak the language of business, and the computer and its systems, which speak the language of electrons. The more effectively and reliably the programmer can bridge between these worlds, the better will be the applications that he or she builds, but this requires an unusual combination of talents. If you have any of these paragons in your organization, guard them like the treasures they are! In what follows, one of the recurring themes will be that the problems with today's programming technology arise almost entirely from the continuing mismatch between the problem area the programmer works in and the tools he or she has to work with. Only if we can narrow the gap between the world of users and that of application developers, can we produce applications that fit the needs of users and do it in a timely and cost-effective manner.

The significant fact I have come to realize over the last 20 years is that application programming in its present form really *is* hard and in fact has not progressed all that much since the days of the first computers. This lack of progress is certainly not due to any shortage of advocates of this or that shiny new tool, but very few of these wonder products have delivered what was promised. When I started in the business in 1959, we already had higher-level languages, interpreters, and subroutine calls—these are still the basic tools of today's programming professionals. The kind of programming most of us do has its roots in the procedural programming that arose during the 1940s and 1950s. This new invention called a computer filled a growing need for repetitive, mainly mathematical calculations, such as tide tables, ballistics, and census calculations. In these areas, computers were wildly successful. However, even then, some of the experts in this new world of computing were starting to question whether procedural application programming was really appropriate for building business applications. The combination of more and more complex systems, the sheer difficulty of the medium that programmers work in, and the need for businesses to reduce overhead is resulting in more and more pressure on today's programming professionals.

In addition, as programmers build new systems, these add to the amount of resources being expended on maintaining them, to the point where the ability of many companies to develop new applications is being seriously impacted by the burden of maintaining old systems. This in turn adversely affects their ability to compete in the new competitive global marketplace. Many writers have talked about the programming backlog—the backlog of programming work that data processing departments are planning to do but can't get to because of lack of resources. I have also heard people use the phrase "hidden backlog"—this is programming work that users would like to get done but know there's no point in even talking to their DP department about, so it tends not to show up in the statistics! This is at least partly why non-DP departments have been buying up PCs in recent years—they feel that having their own machines will make them independent of the DP department, but of course this only means they face the same old programming problems on their own machines!

At one time it was predicted that more telephone switchboard operators would be needed than the total number of available people in the workforce. Of course, this problem was solved by the development of automatic telephone switching systems. Similarly, many people believe the present situation in computing can only be solved by a quantum jump in technology, and of course each new software technology claims to be the long-awaited solution. I and a number of other people believe that the concepts described in what follows really do have the potential to solve this problem, and I hope that, as you read this book, you will come to agree with us. However, they represent a true paradigm shift that fundamentally changes the way we look at the programming process. Like many important discoveries, this new paradigm is basically quite simple but far-reaching in its implications.

Mention of a new paradigm makes one immediately think of another new paradigm that is growing steadily in popularity, namely object-oriented programming (usually abbreviated to OOP). What I am about to describe is not OOP, but bears certain similarities to it and especially to the more advanced OOP concepts, specifically that of "active objects." In the long run, these two paradigms appear to be on a converging path, and, as I will describe in a later chapter, I believe that it may well be possible to fuse the two sets of concepts to achieve the best of both worlds. In most of this book, however, I will present our concepts and experience as they evolved historically, using our own terminology.

After a few years in the computer business, I found myself puzzling over why application programming should be so hard. Its complexity is certainly not the complexity of complex algorithms or logic. From an arithmetic point of view, one seldom encounters multiplication or division in business programming, let alone anything as arcane as a square root. The vast majority of business applications do such things as transforming data from one format to another, accumulating totals or looking up information in one file and incorporating it into another file or a report. Given what seems like a fairly simple problem space, I wondered why application development should be so arduous and why, once built, a program should be so hard to maintain. Over the last few years, I and a number of other workers in the field have come to believe that the main cause of the problem is in fact the same thing that powered the computer revolution itself, namely the von Neumann computer model.

This model is the traditional one that has been so productive over the last few decades, designed around a single instruction counter that walks sequentially through strings of codes, deciding what to do at each step. These codes can be treated both as data (e.g., by compilers) and as commands. This design is usually, but not necessarily, combined with a uniform array of memory cells from which the instructions take data and into which they return it. As described in a recent article by Valiant (1990), the power of this model derives from the fact that it has acted as a bridge between the twin "diverse and chaotic" worlds (as Valiant calls them) of hardware and software, while allowing them to evolve separately. But, by the same token, its very success convinced its practitioners that the problems we are facing cannot possibly be due to any fundamental problems with this set of concepts. Programmers are not bright enough, they don't have good enough tools, they don't have enough mathematical education, or they don't work hard enough—I'm sure you've run into all of these explanations. I don't believe any of these are valid. I believe there is a far more fundamental problem, namely that at a basic level the medium is simply inappropriate for the task at hand. In fact, when you look at them objectively, the symptoms the programming business is experiencing now are quite characteristic of what one would expect when people try to do a complicated job using the wrong tools. Take a second and try to imagine building a functioning automobile out of clay! It's highly malleable when wet, so you should be able to make anything, but after it has been fired it is very hard but very brittle! In fact that's quite a good analogy for the "feel" of most of our applications today!

The time is now ripe for a new paradigm to replace the von Neumann model as the bridging model between hardware and software. The one we will describe is similar to the one Valiant proposes (I'll go into more detail about his in chapter 27) and in fact seems to be one of a family of related concepts that have appeared over the last few years in the literature. The common concept underlying much of this work is basically that to solve these problems we have to relax the tight sequential programming style characteristic of the von Neumann machine, and structure programs as collections of communicating, asynchronous processes. If you look at applications larger than a single program or go down inside the machine, you will find many processes going on in parallel. It is only within a single program (job step or transaction) that you still find strict traditional, sequential logic. People have tended to believe that the tight control of execution sequence imposed by this approach is the only way to get predictable code and that therefore it was necessary for reliable systems. It turns out that machines (and people) work more efficiently if you retain only the constraints that matter and relax the ones that don't, and you can do this without any loss of reliability. The intent of this book is to try to describe a body of experience that has been built up using a particular set of implementations of this concept over the years, so I will not go into more detail at this point. In this chapter, we will talk more about the history of this concept than about specific implementations or experience gained using them.

Another factor that suggests it is timely for this technology to be made public is that we are facing a growing crisis in application development. At the same time as new requirements are appearing, the underlying technology is changing faster and faster. The set of concepts that I will describe seems to fit well with current directions for both software and hardware. Not only can it support in a natural manner the requirements of distributed, heterogeneous applications, but it also seems an appropriate programming technology for the new multiprocessor machines being worked on by universities and leading-edge computer manufacturers all over the world. As the late Wayne Stevens, the noted writer on the subject of application design methodologies, has pointed out in several of his articles (e.g., Stevens 1985), the paradigm that we will describe provides a consistent, natural way to view applications, from the workings of whole companies all the way down to the smallest component. Since you can also describe manual applications with data flow diagrams, the connection between manual and system procedures can be shown seamlessly.

In what follows, I will use the term "flow-based programming" (or FBP for short) to describe this new set of concepts and the software needed to support it. We have in the past used the term "data flow," as it conveys a number of the more important aspects of this technology; however, there is a sizable body of published work on what is called "data flow architectures" in computer design and their associated software (for instance the very exciting work coming out of MIT), so the term data flow may cause confusion in some academic circles. Also, when control flow is needed explicitly, FBP can provide it by the use of such mechanisms as triggers, so the term flow-based programming avoids the connotation that we cannot do control flow when necessary. This is not to say that the two types of data flow do not have many concepts in common—data flow computer architectures arise also from the perception that the von Neumann machine design that has been so successful in the past must be generalized if we are to move forward, whether we are trying to perform truly huge amounts of computation, such as weather calculations, or simply to produce applications that are easier to build and maintain.

One significant difference between the two schools, at least at this time, is that most of the other data flow work has been mathematically oriented, so it tends to work with numbers and arrays of numbers. Although my early data flow work during the late 1960s also involved simple numeric values traveling through a network of function blocks, my experience with simulation systems made me realize that it would be more productive in business applications to have the things that flow be structured objects, which I called "entities." This name reflected the idea that these structured objects tended to represent entities in the outside world. (In the later work of our group, we realized that the name "entity" might cause confusion with the idea of entities in data modeling, although there are points of resemblance, so we decided to use a different word.) Such a system is also, not coincidentally, a natural design for *simulating* applications, so the distinction between applications and their simulations becomes much less significant than in conventional programming. You can think of an entity as being like a record in storage, but active (in that it triggers events) rather than passive (just being read or written). Entities flow through a network of processes, like cars in a city or boats in a river system. They differ from the mathematical tokens of data flow computers or from my early work chiefly in that they have *structure:* Each entity represents an object with attributes—for example, an employee will have attributes such as salary, date of hire, or manager. As you read this book, it should become clear why there has to be at least one layer of the application where the entities move as individual units, although it may very well be possible to integrate the various data flow approaches at lower levels.

At this point I will describe FBP briefly, to give the reader something to visualize, but first a caveat. The brief description that follows will probably not be enough to let you picture what FBP is and how it does it. If we don't do this at this point, however, experience shows that readers find it hard to relate what is being described to their own knowledge. The reverse risk is that they may jump to conclusions that may prevent them from seeing what is truly new about the concepts I will be describing later. I call this the "It's just . . ." syndrome.

In conventional programming, when you sit down to write a program, you write code down the page—a linear string of statements describing the series of actions you want the computer to execute. Since we are of course all writing structured code now, we start with a main line containing mostly subroutine calls, which can then be given "meaning" later by coding up the named subroutines. A number of people have speculated about the possibility of instead building a program by just plugging prewritten pieces of logic together. This has sometimes been called "Legoland programming" (R. Jones 1988). Even though that is essentially what we do when we use utilities, there has always been some doubt whether this approach has the power to construct large-scale applications and, if it has, whether such applications would perform. I now have the pleasure to announce that the answer is "Yes" to both these questions!

The "glue" that FBP uses to connect the pieces together is an example of what Yale's Gelernter and Carriero (1992) have called a "coordination language." I feel the distinction between coordination languages and procedural languages is a useful one and helps to clarify what is different about FBP. Conventional programming languages instruct the machine what logic to execute; coordination languages tell the machine how to coordinate multiple modules written in one or several programming languages. There is quite a bit of published material on various approaches to coordination, but much of that work involves the use of special-purpose languages, which reduces the applicability of these concepts to traditional languages and environments. As Gelernter and Carriero have said, a better approach is to have a language-independent coordination notation, which can coordinate modules written in a variety of different procedural languages. The individual modules have to have a common application programming interface to let them talk to the coordination software, but this can be relatively simple.

Coordination and modularity are two sides of the same coin, and several years ago Nate Edwards of IBM coined the term "configurable modularity" to denote an ability to reuse independent components just by changing their interconnections, which in his view characterizes all successful reuse systems and indeed all systems that can be described as "engineered." Although I am not sure when Nate first brought the two words "configurable" and "modularity" together, the report on a planning session in Palo Alto in 1976 uses the term, and Nate's 1977 paper (Edwards 1977) contains both the terms "configurable architecture" and "controlled modularity." While Nate's work is fairly nontechnical and pragmatic, his background is mainly in hardware rather than software, which may be why his work has not received the attention it deserves. One of the important characteristics of a system exhibiting configurable modularity, such as most modern hardware or flow-based programming, is that you can build systems out of "black box" reusable modules, much like the chips that are used to build logic in hardware. Of course, you also have to have something to connect them together, but they do not have to be modified in any way to make this happen. In fact, this is characteristic of just about anything that is attached to other things in real life—everywhere but in conventional programming. In FBP, these black boxes are the basic building blocks that a developer uses to build an application. New black boxes can be written as needed, but a developer tries to use what is available first, before creating new components. In FBP, the emphasis shifts from building everything new to connecting preexisting pieces and only building new when building a new component is cost-justified. Nate Edwards played a key role in getting the hardware people to follow this same principle, and now, of course, like all great discoveries, it seems that we have always known this! We have to help software developers to move through the same paradigm shift. If you look at the literature of programming from this standpoint, it is amazing how few writers write from the basis of *reuse*—in fact, the very term seems to suggest an element of surprise, as if reuse were a fortuitous occurrence that happens seldom and usually by accident! In real life, we *use* a knife or fork—we don't *re*use it!

Similarities between FBP and other related pieces of software will be described in later chapters, but perhaps it would be useful at this point to use DOS pipes to draw a simple analogy. If you have used DOS, you will know that you can take separate programs and combine them using a vertical bar (|), as follows:

```
A | B
```

This is a very simple form of what I have been calling coordination of separate programs. It tells the system to feed the output of A into the input of B, but neither A nor B have to be modified to make this happen. A and B have to have connection points ("plugs" and "sockets") that the system can use, and, of course, there has to be some software that understands the vertical bar notation and knows what to do with it. FBP broadens this concept in a number of directions that vastly increase its power. It turns out that this generalization results in a very different approach to building applications, which results in systems that are both more reliable and more maintainable. In the following pages I hope to be able to prove this to your satisfaction!

The FBP systems that have been built over the last 20 years have therefore basically all had the following components:

- A number of precoded, pretested functions, provided in object code form, not source code form ("black boxes")—this set is open ended and (hopefully) constantly growing.
- A "driver"—a piece of software that coordinates the precoded functions and implements the API (application programming interface), which is used by the components to communicate with the driver.
- A notation for specifying how the components are connected together into one or more networks (an FBP application designer starts with pictures and then converts them into specifications to be executed by the driver). This notation can then be put into a file for execution by the driver software. In the most successful implementation of FBP so far (DFDM—described in the next section of this chapter), the network could either be compiled and linkedited to produce an executable program, or it could be interpreted directly (with of course greater

initialization overhead). In the interpreted mode, the components are loaded in dynamically, so you can make changes and see the results many times in a few minutes. Our users found this mode extremely productive. Later, when debugging is finished, the interpretable form can be converted to the compilable form to provide better performance for the production version.

- Procedures to convert, compile, and package individual modules and partial networks.
- Documentation (reference and tutorial) for all of the above.

In the above list I have not included education, but of course this is probably the most important item of all. To get the user started, there is a need for formal education—this may only take a few days or weeks, and I hope that this book will get the reader started on understanding many of the basic concepts. However, education also includes the practical experience that comes from working with many different applications over a number of months or years. In this area especially, we have found that FBP feels very different from conventional programming. Unlike most other professions, the programming establishment tends to underestimate the value of experience, which may in fact be due to the nature of the present-day medium. In other professions we would never think of giving a new practitioner a pile of books and then telling him or her to go out and do brain surgery, build a bridge, mine gold, or sail across the Atlantic. Instead it is expected that there will be a series of progressive steps from student or apprentice to master. Application development using FBP feels much more like an engineering-style discipline: We are mostly assembling structures out of preexisting components with well-defined specifications, rather than building things from scratch using basic raw materials. In such a medium, experience is key. It takes time to learn what components are available, how they fit together, and what trade-offs can be made. However, unlike bridge builders, application developers using FBP *can* also get simple applications working very fast, so they can have the satisfaction of seeing quite simple programs do nontrivial things very early. Education in FBP is a hands-on affair, and it is really a pleasure seeing people's reactions when they get something working without having to write a line of code!

Now that graphics hardware and software have become available at reasonable cost and performance, it seems very desirable to have graphical front ends for our FBP systems. Since FBP is a highly visual notation, we believe that a graphical front end will make it even more usable. Some prototype work has already been done along these lines and seems to bear this idea out. Many potential users of FBP systems will already have one or more graphical design tools, and, as we shall see, there is an especially good match between Structured Analysis and FBP, so that it seems feasible and desirable to base FBP graphical tools on existing graphical tools for doing Structured Analysis, with the appropriate information added for creating running FBP programs.

Now I feel it would be useful to give a bit of historical background on FBP. I built the first implementation of this concept in 1969 and 1970 in Montréal, Québec. This proved very productive, so much so that it was taken into a major Canadian company, where it was used for all the batch programming of a major on-line system. This system was called the Advanced Modular Processing System (AMPS). This system and the experience gained from it are described in a fair amount of detail in an article I wrote a few years later for the *IBM Systems Journal* (Morrison 1978), which still provides a good introduction to the concepts, although the implementation details have changed over the intervening years.

Although the concepts are not yet well known, they have actually been in the public domain for many years. The reason for this is as follows: in late 1970 or early 1971 I approached IBM Canada's Intellectual Property department to see if we could take out a patent on the basic idea. Their recommendation, which I feel was quite prescient, was that this concept seemed to them more like a law of nature, which is not patentable. They did recommend, however, that I write up a Technical Disclosure Bulletin (TDB), which was duly published and distributed to patent offices worldwide (Morrison 1971). A TDB is a sort of inverse patent. While a patent protects a concept but requires the inventor to try to predict all possible variations on that concept, a TDB puts the concept into the public domain and thereby protects the registering body from being restricted or impeded in the future in any use they may wish to make of it. In the case of a TDB, it places the onus on other people who might be trying to patent something based on your concept to prove that their variation was not obvious to someone "skilled in the art."

Towards the end of the 1980s, Wayne Stevens and I jointly developed a new version of this software, called the Data Flow Development Manager (DFDM). It is described in Appendix A of Wayne Stevens' latest book (Stevens 1991) (which, by the way, contains a lot of good material on application design techniques in general). What I usually refer to in what follows as "processes" were called "coroutines" in DFDM, after Conway (1963), who described an early form of this concept in a paper back in the 1960s and foresaw even then some of its potential. "Coroutine" is formed from the word "routine" together with the Latin prefix meaning "with," as compared with "subroutine," which is formed with the prefix meaning "under." (Think of "*co*operative" vs. "*sub*ordinate.")

DFDM was used for a number of projects (between 40 and 50) of various sizes within IBM Canada. A few years later, Kenji Terao got a project started within IBM Japan to support us in developing an improved version for the Japanese market. This version is, at the time of this writing, the only dialect of FBP that has been made available in the marketplace, and enormous credit is due to Kenji and all the dedicated and forward-looking people in IBM Japan who helped to make this happen. While this version of DFDM was in many ways more robust or "industrial strength" than the one that we had been using at IBM Canada, much of the experience that I will describe in the following pages is based on what we learned using the IBM Canada internal version of DFDM or on the still earlier AMPS system. Perhaps someone will write a sequel to this book describing the Japanese experience with DFDM.

Last, but I hope not least, there is a PC-based system currently under development by HOMEDATA (Rochester) Inc., of Rochester, New York, written in C, that attempts to embody many of the best ideas of its ancestors. It has been available since the summer of 1993, running on Intel-based machines. It has been tested on

286-, 386-, and 486-based machines. Since it is written in C, we hope that it will also be possible to port it later to other versions of C, although there is a small amount of environment-dependent code that will have to be modified by hand. This software is called THREADS—THREads-based Application Development System (I love self-referential names!). Like DFDM, it also has interpreted and compiled versions, so applications can be developed iteratively and then compiled to produce a single EXE file, which eliminates the network decoding phase.

The terminology used in this book is not exactly the same as that used by AMPS and DFDM, as a number of these terms turned out to cause confusion. For instance, the data chunks that travel between the asynchronous processes were called "entities" in AMPS and DFDM, but, as I said above, this caused confusion for people experienced in data modeling. "Objects" would present other problems, and we were not comfortable with the idea of creating totally new words (although some writers have used them effectively). The "tuples" of Carriero and Gelernter's Linda (1989) are very close, but this name also presents a slightly different image from the FBP concept. We therefore decided to use the rather neutral term "information packet" (or "IP" for short) for this concept. This term was coined as part of work that we did following the development of DFDM, in which we also tied FBP concepts in with other work appearing in the literature or being developed in other parts of IBM. Some of the extensions to the basic AMPS and DFDM substructure that I will talk about later were also articulated during this period. When referring to ideas drawn from this work, I will use the name FPE (for Flow-based Programming Environment), although that is not the acronym used by that project. THREADS follows this revised terminology and includes a number of ideas from FPE.

As I stated in the prologue, for most of my 33 years in the computer business I have been almost exclusively involved with business applications. Although business applications are often more complex than scientific applications, or complex in different ways, the academic community generally has not shown much interest in this area until now. This is a "catch-22" situation, as business would benefit from the work done in academia, yet academia (with some noteworthy exceptions) tends not to regard business programming as an interesting area to work in. My hope is that FBP can act as a bridge between these two worlds, and in later chapters I will be attempting to tie FBP to other related theoretical work that working programmers probably wouldn't normally encounter. My reading in the field suggests that FBP has sound theoretical foundations, and yet it can perform well enough that you can run a company on it, and it is accessible to trainee programmers (sometimes more easily than for experienced ones!). AMPS has been in use for 20 years, supporting one of the biggest companies in North America, and as recently as 1992, one of their senior people told me, "AMPS has served us well, and we expect it will continue to do so for a long time to come." Business systems have to evolve over time as the market requirements change, so clearly their system has been able to grow and adapt over the years as the need arose—this is a living system, not some outdated curiosity that has become obsolete with the advance of technology.

And now I would like to conclude this chapter with an unsolicited testimonial from a DFDM user, which we received a few years ago:

> I have a requirement to merge 23 . . . reports into one. . . . As all reports are of different length and block size this is more difficult in a conventional PLI environment. It would have required 1 day of work to write the program and 1 day to test it. Such a program would use repetitive code. While drinking coffee 1 morning I wrote a DFDM network to do this. *It was complete before the coffee went cold* [italics added]. Due to the length of time from training to programming it took 1 day to compile the code. Had it not been for the learning curve it could have been done in 5 minutes. During testing a small error was found which took 10 minutes to correct. As 3 off-the-shelf co-routines were used, PLI was not required. 2 co-routines were used once, and 1 was used 23 times. Had it not been for DFDM, I would have told the user that his requirement was not cost justified. It took more time to write this note than the DFDM network.

Notice that in his note Rej (short for Réjean) (who is a visually impaired application developer with many years of experience in business applications) mentioned all the points that were significant to him as a developer. He zeroed right in on the amount of reuse he was getting, because functions he could get right off the shelf were ones he didn't have to write, test, and eventually maintain! In DFDM, coroutines are the basic building blocks that programmers can hook together to build applications. They are either already available ("on the shelf") or the programmer can write new ones, in which case he or she will naturally try to reuse them as often as possible—to get the most bang for the proverbial buck. Although it is not very hard to write new PL/I coroutines, the majority of application developers don't want to write new code—they just want to get their applications working for the client, preferably using as little programming effort as will suffice to get a quality job done. Of course, there are always programmers who love the process of programming and, as we shall see in the following pages, there is an important role for them also in this new world that is evolving.

Rej's note was especially satisfying because he uses special equipment that converts whatever is on his screen into spoken words. Since FBP has always seemed to me a highly visual technique, I had worried about whether visually impaired programmers would have any trouble using it, and it was very reassuring to find that Rej was able to make such productive use of this technology. In later discussions with him, he has stressed the need to keep application structures simple. In FBP, you can use hierarchic decomposition to create multiple layers, each containing a simple structure, rather than being required to create a single, flat, highly complex structure. In fact, structures that are so complex that he would have trouble with them are difficult for everyone. He also points out that tools that he would find useful, such as something that can turn network diagrams into lists of connections, would also significantly assist normally sighted people as they work with these structures.

Rej's point about the advantages of keeping the structures simple is also borne out by the fact that another application of DFDM resulted in a structure of about 200 processes, but the programmer involved (another very bright individual) never drew a single picture! He built it up gradually using hierarchical decomposition, and it has since had one of the lowest error rates of any application in the shop. I hope that, as you read on, you will be able to figure out some of the reasons for this high level of reliability for yourself.

In what follows, I will describe the main features of FBP and what we have learned from developing and using its various implementations. Information on some of these has appeared in a number of places, and I feel it is time to try to pull together some of the results of 20 years of experience with these concepts into a single place so that the ideas can be seen in context. A vast number of papers have appeared over the years, written by different writers in different fields of computing, which I believe are all various facets of a single gem, and I hope that, by pulling a lot of connected ideas together in one place, the reader will start to get a glimpse of the total picture. Perhaps there is someone out there who is waiting for these ideas and will be inspired to carry them further, either in research or in the marketplace!

2

Languages, 4GLs, and CASE

In the prologue I alluded to the concept of compiler compilers. At the time that I was most interested in them (the mid-60s), the accepted wisdom was that more sophisticated compilers were the answer to the productivity problem. It was clear to everyone that an expression like

```
W = (X + Y) / (Z + 3)
```

was infinitely superior to the machine language equivalent, which might look something like the following:

```
LOAD  Z
ADD   3
STORE TEMP
LOAD  X
ADD   Y
DIV   TEMP
STORE W
```

This is a made-up machine with a single accumulator, but you get the general idea. One of the reasons that the syntax shown on the first line could effectively act as a bridge between humans and computers was that it was syntactically clean, and based on a solid, well-understood, mathematical foundation, namely arithmetic, with the exception of a rather strange use of the equals sign!

During this period it was not unreasonable to expect that this expressive power could be extended into other functions that machines needed to perform. This seemed to be supported by the fact that, although I/O was getting more complex to program at the machine language level, operating systems were coming on stream that still allowed the programmer to essentially write one statement to execute a simple I/O operation. On the IBM 1401, a Read Card command consisted of one instruction and also one character! MVS's GET, on the other hand, might cause several hundreds or thousands of machine language instructions to be executed, but the programmer still basically wrote *one* statement.

On this foundation, we started getting one programming language after another: COBOL was going to be the language that enabled the person in the street to do, or at least understand, programming! Algol became a program-level documentation standard for algorithms. IBM developed PL/I (I worked on one rather short-lived version of that); people developed compilers in their basements; graduate students wrote compilers for their theses at universities (they still do). There was always the feeling that one of these languages was going to be the key to unlocking the productivity that we all felt was innate in programmers. While it is true that the science of compiler writing advanced by leaps and bounds, by and large programmer productivity (at least in business application development) did not go up, or, if it did, it soon plateaued at a new level.

COBOL and PL/I were general-purpose compilers. There were also many languages specialized for certain jobs: simulation languages, pattern-matching languages, report generation languages. And don't forget APL. APL is an extremely powerful language, and it also opened up arcane areas of mathematics like matrix handling for those of us who had never quite understood it in school. Being able to do a matrix multiply in five keystrokes ($A+.\times B$) is still a level of expressiveness that I think few programming languages will ever be able to match! Its combination of sheer power in the mathematical area and the fact that there is no compile-time typing allowed one to get interesting programs up and running extremely fast. I once read a comment in a mathematical paper that the author didn't think the work would have been possible without APL—and I believe him. Although it was used a certain amount in business for calculation-oriented programming, especially in banking and insurance, and also as a base for some of the early query-type languages, APL did little for most commercial programming, which is still plodding along using COBOL and, more recently, PL/I, PASCAL, and BASIC.

APL also illustrates in a different way the importance of minimizing the "gap" between an idea and its expression. Along with all of the most popular programming languages, it is an interpreter, which means that you can enter the program and then immediately run it, without having to go through a compile and/or link step. Granted, this is more perception than actual fact (as one can build compile steps that are so fast they don't take much of the user's time), but the fact remains that some very awkward languages have become immensely popular because they did not require a compile step. A lot of the CPU cycles used in the industry on IBM machines are being used to run CMS EXECs or TSO CLISTs. Both of these are simple languages that let you stitch commands together into runnable "programs." Both are yielding nowadays to REXX, which occupies the same niche, but also provides a vastly more powerful set of language constructs, to the point where one can build pretty complex programs with it. REXX is also interpretive, so it allows one to change a program and see the results of that change very quickly.

Why didn't languages (even the interpretive ones) improve productivity more than they did? I will be exploring this more in the next chapter, but one thing that I noticed fairly early on was that they didn't do much for logic (IF, THEN, ELSE, DO WHILE, etc.). For many kinds of business programming, what pushes up the development time is the logic—there actually may not be much in the way of straight calculations. A logical choice can be thought of as a certain amount of mental work, whether you write it like this:

```
if x > 2
then
  result = 1
else
  result = 2
endif
```

or like this:

```
result = (x>2) ? 1 : 2;
```

or even draw it as a Nassi-Shneiderman or Chapin chart. One can argue that, because both of the above phrasings involve one binary decision, they involve approximately the same amount of mental work. The more complex the logic, the more difficult the coding. In fact, there is a complexity measure used quite widely in the industry called McCabe's Cyclomatic complexity measure, which is based very directly on the number of binary decisions in a program. However, in our work we have discovered that the amount of logic in conventional programming *is* reducible, because much of the logic in conventional programming has to do with the synchronization of data rather than with business logic. Since FBP eliminates the need for a lot of this synchronization logic, this means that FBP actually does reduce the amount of logic in programs.

A number of writers have made the point that productivity is only improved if you can reduce the "gap" between the language of business and the language of computers, i.e., reduce the number of statements needed to represent an idea. What is the lower limit on the number of bits or keystrokes to represent an idea, though? If a condition and its branches comprise one "idea," then there is a lower limit to how compactly it can be represented. If it is part of a greater "idea," then there is a hope of representing it more compactly. Information theory tells us that the number of bits needed to represent something is the log of the number of alternatives you have to choose between. If something is always true, there is no choice, so it doesn't need any bits to represent it. If you have eight choices, then it takes 3 (= log of 8 to the base 2) bits to represent it. In programming terms, if you only allow an individual two marital states, you only need 1 bit (log of 2 to the base 2). If you want to support a wider "universe," where people may be single, married, divorced, widowed, or common law spouses, that is five alternatives, so you need 3 bits (2 bits are not enough as they only allow four choices). And if they're not mutually exclusive you could need even more bits!

This in turn leads to the idea that one way to reduce the information requirements of a program is to pick options from a more limited universe. However, the user has to be willing to live within this more circumscribed universe. I remember an accounting package that was developed in Western Canada, which defined very tightly the universe in which its customers were supposed to operate. Within that universe, it provided quite a lot of function. I believe that its main file records were always 139 bytes long (or a similar figure) and you couldn't change them. If you asked them about it, the developers' reaction would be: why would anyone want to? Somewhat predictably, it didn't catch on because many customers felt it was *too* restrictive. The example that sticks in my memory was that of one customer who wanted to change a report title and had to be told that it couldn't be done. Again, why would anyone feel that was so important? Well, it seems that customers, especially big ones, tend to feel that report headers should look the way *they* want rather than the way the package says they are going to look. Our experience was that smaller customers might be willing to adapt their business to the program, especially if you could convince them that you understood it better than they did, but bigger customers expected the program to adapt to their business. And it was really quite a powerful package for the price! I learned a lot from that, the main thing being that a vendor can provide standard components, but the customer has to be able to write custom components as well. Even if it costs more to do the latter, it is the customer's choice, not the vendor's. And that of course means that the customer must be able to visualize what the tool is doing. This is also related to the principle of open architectures: no matter how impressive a tool is, if it can't talk to other tools, it isn't going to survive over the long haul (paraphrased from Wayne Stevens).

The above information-theoretic concept is at the root of what are now called 4GLs (4th-Generation Language). These provide more productivity by taking advantage of frequently appearing application patterns (e.g., interactive applications). If you are writing applications to run in an interactive system, you know that you are going to keep running into patterns like:

- read a key entered by the user onto a screen
- get the correct record, or generate a message if the record does not exist
- display selected fields from that record on the screen

Another one (very often the next one) might be:

- display the fields of a record
- allow the user to change one or more of them
- determine which ones were changed
- check for incorrect formats, values, etc.

- if everything is OK,
  - write the updated record back
- else
  - display the appropriate error message(s)

Another very common pattern (especially in what is called "decision support" or "decision assist" type applications) occurs when a list is presented on the screen and the user can select one of the items or scroll up or down through the list (the list may not all fit on one screen). Some systems allow more than one item to be selected, which are then processed in sequence.

These recurrent patterns occur so frequently that it makes a lot of sense to provide skeletons for these different scenarios and declarative (non-procedural) ways of having the programmer fill in the information required to flesh them out.

The attractiveness of 4GLs has also been enhanced by the unattractiveness of IBM's standard screen definition facilities! The screen definition languages for both IMS (called MFS) and CICS (BMS) are coded up using S/370 Assembler macros (high-level statements that generate the constants that define all the parts of a screen). This technique allows them to provide a lot of useful capabilities, but screen definitions written this way are hard to write and even harder to maintain! Say you want to make a field on a screen longer and move it down a few lines; you find yourself changing a large number of different values that all have to be kept consistent (the values are often not even the same, but have to be kept consistent according to some formula). I once wrote a prototyping tool that allowed screens to be specified in WYSIWYG (What You See Is What You Get) format and could then be used to generate both the screen definition macros and also all the HLL declares that had to correspond to it. It was quite widely used internally within IBM, and, in fact, one project, which needed to change some MFS, started out by converting the old MFS into the prototyper specifications, so that they could make their changes and then generate everything automatically. This way, they could be sure that everything stayed consistent. When such a screen definition tool is integrated with a 4GL, you get a very attractive combination. It's even better when the prototyping tool is built using FBP, as it can then be "grown" into a full interactive application by incrementally expanding the network. This ability to grow an application from a prototype seems very desirable and is one of the things that make FBP attractive for developing interactive applications.

The problem, of course, with the conventional 4GL comes in when the customer, like our customer who wanted to change a report title, wants something that the 4GL does not provide. Usually, this kind of thing is handled by means of exits. A system that started out simple eventually becomes studded with exits, which require complex parametrization and whose function cannot be understood without understanding the internals of the product—the *flow* of the product. Since part of the effectiveness of a 4GL comes from its being relatively opaque and "black boxy," exits undermine its very reason for being.

An example of this in the small is IBM's MVS Sort utility (or other Sorts that are compatible with it)—as long as one can work with the standard parameters for the Sort as a whole, it's pretty clear what it is doing and how to talk to it. Now you decide you want to do some processing on each input record before it goes into the Sort. You now have to start working with the E15 exit. This requires that you form a concept of how Sort works *on the inside*—a very different matter. E15 and E35 (the output exit routine) have to be independent load modules that must be named E15 and E35, so this puts constraints on the ways in which applications can use load module libraries, and so on. Luckily, Sort also has a LINKable interface, so DFDM used this, turned E15 and E35 inside-out, and converted the whole thing into a well-behaved reusable component—much easier to use and you get improved performance as well due to the reduction in I/O! In a similar way, FBP can also capitalize on the same regularities as 4GLs do by providing reusable components (composite or elementary) as well as standard network shapes. Instead of programmers having to understand the internal logic of a 4GL, they can be provided with a network and specifications of the data requirements of the various components. Instead of having to change mental models to understand and use exits, the programmer has a single model based on data and its transformations and is free to rearrange the network, replace components by custom ones, or make other desired changes.

I should point out also that the regularities referred to above have also provided a fertile breeding ground for various source code reuse schemes. My feeling about source code reuse is that it suffers from a fundamental flaw: even if building a new program can be made relatively fast, once you have built it, it must be added to the ever-growing list of programs you have to maintain. It is even worse if, as is often required, the reusable source code components have to be modified before your program can work, because then you have lost the trail connecting the original pieces of code to your final program if one of them has to be enhanced (e.g., to fix a bug). Even if no modification takes place, the new program has to be added to the list of program assets your installation owns. In some shops, maintenance is already taking 80% of the programming resource, so each additional application adds to this burden. In FBP, ideally all that is added to the asset base is a network—the components are all black boxes, and so a new application costs a lot less to maintain.

A related type of tool are program generators—this is also source-level reuse with a slightly different emphasis. As mentioned earlier, an important question is whether you can modify the generated code. If you can't, you are limited to the choices built into the generator; if you can, your original source material becomes useless from a maintenance point of view and can only be regarded as a high-level (and perhaps even misleading) specification. Like out of date documentation, it might almost be safer to throw it away.

I don't want to leave this general area without talking about CASE (computer-aided software engineering) tools. The popularity of these tools arises from several very valid concepts. First, people should not have to enter the same information multiple times, especially when the different forms of this data are clearly related, but you have to be a computer to figure out how! We saw this in the case of the prototyping tool mentioned earlier. If you view the development process as a process of expressing creativity in progressive stages within the context of application knowledge, then you want to capture this in a machine—not just as text, but in a form that captures meaning—so that it can be converted to the various formats required by other software, added to, presented in a variety of display formats, and so on.

There are a number of such tools out in the marketplace today, addressing different parts of the development process, and I see these as the forerunners of the more sophisticated tools that will become available in the next few years. Graphical tools are now becoming economical, and I believe that graphical techniques are the right direction, as they take advantage of human visualization skills. I happen to believe that HIPOs (remember them? Hierarchical Input, Process, Output) had part of the right answer, but adequate graphical tools were not available in those days and maintaining them with pencil, eraser, and a template was a pain! However, when someone went through all that trouble and produced a finished HIPO diagram, the results were beautiful and easy to understand. Unfortunately, systems don't stand still, and they were very hard to maintain, given the technology of those days!

Our experience is that Structured Analysis is a very natural first stage for FBP development, so CASE tools that support Structured Analysis diagrams and that have open architectures are natural partners for FBP. In fact, FBP is the only approach that lets you carry this kind of design all the way to execution. With conventional programming, you cannot convert the design into an executable program structure. There is a chasm, which nobody has been able to bridge in practice, although there are some theoretical approaches, such as the Jackson Inversion, which have been partially successful. In FBP, you can just keep adding information to a design that uses the Structured Analysis approach until you have a working program. In what follows, you will see that FBP diagrams do not really require much information at the network level to create a running program that is not already captured by the Structured Analysis design. Probably the most important point is that one has to distinguish between code components and processes (occurrences of components), and some of these tools do not make a clear distinction between these two concepts. As you will see in the following chapter, an FBP network consists of multiple communicating processes, but a tool that is viewed as primarily being for diagramming may be forgiven for assuming that all the blocks in a diagram are unique, different programs. The need to *execute* a picture imposes a discipline on the design process and the designer, which means that these confusions have to be resolved. Our team actually developed some PC code , which was used successfully on several projects, to convert a diagram on one of the popular CASE tools into a DFDM network specification.

FBP's orientation towards reuse also forces one to distinguish between a particular use of a component and its general definition. This may seem obvious in hindsight, but, even when documenting conventional programs, you would be amazed how often programmers give a fine generalized description of, say, a date routine, but forget to tell the reader which of its functions is being used in a particular situation. Even in a block diagram, I find that programmers often write in the general description of the routine and omit its specific use (you need both). This is probably due to the fact that, in conventional programming, the developer of a routine is usually its only user as well, so he or she forgets to "change hats."

When the developer and user are different people, it is easier for the user to stay in character.

To summarize, HLLs, 4GLs, and CASE are all steps in the direction we want to go in, and all have lessons to teach us, and capabilities that are definitely part of the answer. What is so exciting about FBP is that it allows us to take the best qualities of all the approaches that went before and combine them into a whole that is greater than the sum of its parts.

3

Basic Concepts of Flow-Based Programming

In the middle years of this century, it was expected that eventually computers would be able to do anything that humans could explain to them. But even then some people wondered how easy this would turn out to be. A book first published in the 1950s, *Faster than Thought* (Bowden 1963), contains the following remark: "It always outrages pure mathematicians when they encounter commercial work for the first time to find how difficult it is" (p. 258), and further on: " . . . it is so hard in practice to get any program right that several mathematicians may be needed to look after a big machine in an office. . . . It seems, in fact, that experienced programmers will always be in demand" (p. 259). However, in those days, the main barrier was thought to be the difficulty of ascertaining the exact rules for running a business. This did turn out to be as hard as people expected, but for rather different reasons. Today we see that the problem is actually built right into the fundamental design principles of the basic computing engine—the so-called von Neumann machine alluded to in chapter 1.

The von Neumann machine is perfectly adapted to the kind of mathematical or algorithmic needs for which it was developed (tide tables, ballistics calculations, etc.), but business applications are rather different in nature. As one example of these differences, the basic building block of programming is the subroutine and has been since it was first described by Ada, Countess Lovelace, Lord Byron's daughter, in the last century (quite an achievement, since computers did not exist yet!). This concept was solidly founded on the mathematical idea of a function, and any programmer today knows about a number of standard subroutines and can usually come up with new ones as needed. Examples might include "square root," "binary search," "sine," "display a currency value in human-readable format," and so on. What are the basic building blocks of business applications? It is easy to list functions such as "merge," "sort," "paginate a report," and so forth, but none of these seem to lend themselves to being encapsulated as subroutines. They are of a different nature—rather than being functions that operate at a single moment in time, they all have the characteristic of operating over a period of time, across a number (sometimes a very large number) of input and output items.

You can now begin to get some inkling of what this difference might consist of. Business programming works with data and concentrates on how this data is transformed, combined, and separated, to produce the desired outputs and modify stored data according to business requirements. Broadly speaking, whereas the conventional approaches to programming (referred to as "control flow") start with process and view data as secondary, business applications are usually designed starting with data and viewing process as secondary—processes are just the way data is created, manipulated, and destroyed. This approach is often called "data flow," and it is a key concept of many design methodologies. It is when we try to convert this view into procedural code that we start to run into problems.

It will help to approach this difference from a different angle—by comparing a pure algorithmic problem with a superficially similar business-related one. We will start with a simple numeric algorithm: calculating a number raised to the *n*th power, where *n* is a positive, integer exponent. This should be very familiar to all our readers, and, although not the best way to do this calculation, it will suffice to make my point. In pseudocode, we can express this as follows:

```
/* Calculate a to the power b  */
    x = b
    y = 1
    do while x > 0
         y = y * a
         x = x - 1
    enddo
    return y
```

This is a very simple algorithm—easy to understand, easy to verify, easy to modify, and based on well-understood mathematical concepts. Now look at what is superficially a similar piece of logic, but this time involving files of records rather than integers. It has the same kind of structure as the preceding algorithm, but works with streams of records. The problem is to create a file OUT which is a subset of another one IN, where the records to be output are those that satisfy a given criterion c. Records that do not satisfy c are to be omitted from the output file. This is a common requirement and is usually coded using some form of the following logic:

```
    read into a from IN
    do while read has not reached end of file
```

```
          if c is true
               write from a to OUT
          endif
          read into a from IN
     enddo
```

What action is applied to those records that do not satisfy our criterion? Well, they disappear rather mysteriously due to the fact that they are not written to OUT before being destroyed by the next `read`. Most programmers reading this probably won't see anything strange in this code, but, if you think about it, doesn't it seem rather odd that it should be possible to drop important things like records from an output file by means of what is really a quirk of timing?

Part of the reason for this is that most of today's computers have a uniform array of pigeonholes for storage, and this storage behaves very differently from the way storage systems behave in real life. In real life, paper put into a drawer remains there until deliberately removed. It also takes up space, so that the drawer will eventually fill up, preventing more paper from being added. Compare this with the computer concept of storage—you can reach into a storage slot any number of times and get the same data each time (without being told that you have done it already), or you can put a piece of data in on top of a previous one and the earlier one just disappears. Although destructive storage is not integral to the von Neumann machine, it is assumed in many functions of the machine, and this is the kind of storage that is provided on most modern computers. Since the storage of these machines is so sensitive to timing and because the sequencing of *every* instruction has to be predefined (and humans make mistakes!), it is incredibly difficult to get a program above a certain complexity to work properly. And of course this storage paradigm has been enshrined in most higher-level languages in the concept of a "variable." In a celebrated article, John Backus (1978) actually apologized for inventing FORTRAN! That's what I meant earlier about the strange use of the equals sign in higher-level languages. To a logician the statement `J = J + 1` is a contradiction (unless `J` is infinity?), yet programmers no longer notice anything strange about it!

Suppose we decide instead that a record should be treated as a real thing, like a memo or a letter, which, once created, exists for a definite period of time and must be *explicitly* destroyed before it can leave the system. We could expand our pseudolanguage very easily to include this concept by adding a `discard` statement (of course, the record has to be identified somehow). The program might now read as follows:

```
read record a from IN
do while read has not reached end of file
     if c is true
          write a to OUT
     else
          discard a
     endif
     read record a from IN
enddo
```

Now we can reinterpret `a`: Rather than thinking of it as an area of storage, think of `a` as a "handle" that designates a particular "thing"—it is a way of locating a thing rather than the storage area containing the thing. In fact, these data things should not be thought of as being *in* storage—they are "somewhere else." (After all, it does not matter where *read* puts them, so long as the information they contain becomes available to the program.) These things really have more attributes than just their images in storage. The storage image can be thought of as rather like the projection of a solid object onto a plane—manipulating the image does not affect the real thing behind the image. Now a consequence of this is that, if we reuse a handle, we will lose access to the thing it is the handle of. This therefore means that we have a responsibility to properly dispose of things before we can reuse their handles.

Notice the difficulty we have in finding a good word for "thing." The problem is that this is really a concept that is "atomic," in the sense that it cannot be decomposed into yet more fundamental objects. It has had a number of names in the various dialects of FBP and has some affinities with the concept of "object" in object-oriented programming, but I feel it is better to give it its own unique name. In what follows, I will use the term "information packet" (or "IP"). IPs may vary in length from 0 bytes to 2 billion—the advantage of working with "handles" is that IPs are managed the same way and cost the same to send and receive, independent of their size.

So far, we have really only added one concept—that of IPs—to the conceptual model we are building. The above pseudocode was a mainline program, running alone. Since this main line can call subroutines, which in turn can call other subroutines, the structure is essentially the same as in a conventional program, with one main line and subroutines hung off it, and so on. Now, instead of just making a single program more complex, as is done in conventional programming, let us head off in a rather different direction. Visualize an application built up of *many* such mainline programs running concurrently, passing IPs around between them. This is very like a factory with many machines all running at the same time, connected by conveyor belts. Things being worked on (cars, ingots, radios, bottles) travel over the conveyor belts from one machine to another. In fact, there are many analogies that might be used: cafeterias, offices with memos flowing between them, people at a cocktail party, and so forth. After I had been working with these concepts for several years, I took my children to look at a soft drink bottling plant. We saw machines for filling the bottles, machines for putting caps on them, and machines for sticking on labels, but what really struck me was the realization that it is the connectivity and the *flow* between these various machines that ensures that what you buy in the store is filled with the right stuff and hasn't all leaked out before you purchase it!

An FBP application may thus be thought of as a "data factory." The purpose of any application is to take data and process it, much as an ingot is transformed into a finished metal part. In the old days, we thought that it would be possible to design software factories, but now we see that this was the wrong image. We don't want to mass-produce code—we want less code rather than more. In hindsight it is obvious—it is the *data* that has to be converted into useful information in a factory, not the programs.

Now think of the differences between the characteristics of such a factory and those of a conventional, single mainline program. In any factory, many processes are going on at the same time, and synchronization is only necessary at the level of an individual work item. In conventional programming, we have to know exactly when events take place; otherwise things are not going to work right. This is largely because of the way the storage of today's computers works. If data is not processed in exactly the right sequence, it will produce the wrong results, and it may not even be obvious that it has happened! There is no flexibility or adaptability. In the factory image, on the other hand, it doesn't matter if one machine runs before or after another, *as long as processes are applied to a given work item in the right order*. For instance, a bottle must be filled before it is capped, but this does not mean that all the bottles must be filled before any of them can be capped. It turns out that conventional programs are full of this kind of unnecessary synchronization, which reduces productivity, puts unnecessary strains on the programmers, and generally makes application maintenance somewhere between difficult and impossible. In a real factory, unnecessary constraints of this sort would mean that some machines would not be utilized efficiently. In programming, it means that code steps have to be forced into a single sequence, which is extremely difficult for humans to visualize correctly, because of a mistaken belief that the machine requires it. It doesn't!

An application can alternatively be expressed as a network of simple programs, with data traveling between them, and we have found that this takes advantage of developers' visual or "spatial" imagination. It is also a good match with the design methodologies generally referred to under the umbrella of Structured Analysis. The so-called "Jackson Inversion model" (M. Jackson 1975) designs applications in this form, but then proposes that all the processes except one (the mainline) be "inverted" into subroutines. *This is no longer necessary!* Interestingly, Jackson starts off his discussion of program inversion with a description of a simple multiprogramming scheme, using a connection with a capacity of one (in our terminology). He then goes on to say, "Multi-programming is expensive. Unless we have an unusually favorable environment we will not wish to use the sledgehammer of multi-programming to crack the nut of a small structure clash." In FBP there is that "unusually favorable environment," and I and a number of other people believe he wrote off multiprogramming much too fast!

How is it possible to get multiple "machines" to share a real machine? That's something programmers have known how to do for years—just give the machines slices of time whenever they have something to do. In other words, let them "time-share." In conventional programming, time-sharing was mostly used to utilize the hardware efficiently, but it turns out that it can also be applied to convert the "multiple mainline" model into a working application. There are a great many possible time-sharing techniques, but in FBP we have found one of the simplest works fine: we simply let one of our "machines" (called "processes") run until an FBP service request cannot be satisfied. When this happens, the process is suspended and some other ready process gets control. Eventually, the suspended process can proceed (because the blocking condition has been relieved) and will get control when time becomes available. Dijkstra called such processes "sequential processes" and explains that the trick is that they do not know that they have been suspended. Their logic is unchanged—they are just "stretched" in time.

Now you may have guessed that the FBP service requests referred to earlier have to do with communication between processes. Processes are connected by means of FIFO (first-in, first-out) queues or connections that can hold up to some maximum number of IPs (called a queue's "capacity"). For a given queue, this capacity may run from one to quite large numbers. Connections use slightly different verbs from files, so we will convert the pseudocode in the previous example, replacing:

- `read` with `receive`.
- `write` with `send`.
- `discard` with `drop`.
- `end of file` with `end of data`.

A `receive` service may get blocked because there is no data currently in the connection, and a `send` may be blocked because the connection is full and cannot accept any more data for a while. Think of a conveyor belt with room for just so many bottles, televisions, or whatever. It can be empty, full, or some state in between. All these situations are normally just temporary, of course, and will change over time. We have to give connections a maximum capacity, not only so that our applications will fit into available storage, but also so that all data will eventually be processed (otherwise data could just accumulate in connections and never get processed).

Now processes cannot name connections directly—they refer to them by naming "ports," the points where processes and connections meet. More about ports later.

The previous pseudocode now looks like this:

```
receive from IN using a
do while receive has not reached end of data
     if c is true
          send a to OUT
     else
          drop a
     endif
     receive from IN using a
enddo
```

I deliberately used the word `using` on the `receive` to stress the nature of `a` as a handle, but `send a` seems more natural than `send using a`. Note the differences between our file processing program and our FBP component:

- Differences in the verbs (already mentioned).
- IPs "out there," rather than records in storage.
- IPs must be positively disposed of.
- Port names instead of file names.

As said earlier, IPs are *things* that have to be explicitly destroyed. In our multiprocess implementation, we require that all IPs be accounted for. Any process that receives an IP has its "number of owned IPs" incremented and must reduce this number back to zero before it exits. It can do this in essentially the same ways we dispose of a memo: destroy it, pass it on, or file it. Of course, you can't dispose of an IP (or even access it) if you don't have its handle (or if its handle has been reused to designate another IP). Just like a memo, an IP cannot be reaccessed by a process once it has been disposed of. (Most FBP implementations zero out the handle after disposing of the IP to prevent exactly that from happening).

To get philosophical for a moment, proponents of "garbage collection" tend to feel that IPs should disappear when nobody is looking at them (no handles reference them), but the majority of the developers of FBP implementations felt that that was exactly what was wrong with conventional programming—things could disappear much too easily. So we insisted that a process get rid of all of its IPs, *explicitly,* one way or another, before it gives up control. If you inject an IP in at one end of the network, you *know* it is going to get processed unless or until some process explicitly destroys it! Conversely, if you build a table IP, and forget to drop it when you are finished, many people might argue that it would be nice to have the system dispose of it. On the other hand, such an error (if it is an error) may be a sign of something more fundamentally wrong with the design or the code. And anyway, all recent FBP implementations detect this error and list the IPs not disposed of, so it is easy to figure out what went wrong. So, why not let garbage collection be automatic? Well, our team took a vote, and strict accounting won by a solid majority! It might have lost if the group had had a different composition. Eventually, it might be a good idea to make this both an environmental decision and an attribute of each component, so we could detect if a "loose" component was being run in a "tight" shop.

Now what are `IN` and `OUT`, which our pseudocode receives IPs from and sends them to? They are not the names of connections, as this would tie a component's code to one place in the network, but are things called "ports." "Portae" means "gates" in Latin, and ports (like seaports) can be thought of as specific places in a wall or boundary where things or people go in or out. Weinberg (1975) describes a port as ". . . a special place on the boundary through which input and output flow . . . Only within the location of the port can the dangerous processes of input and output take place, and by so localizing these processes, special mechanisms may be brought to bear on the special problems of input and output." Now doors have an "inside" aspect and an "outside" aspect—the name of the inside aspect might be used by people inside the house to refer to doors (e.g., "let the cat out the side door"), while the outside aspect is related to what the door opens onto, and will be of interest to city planners or visitors. Ports in FBP have the same sort of dual function—they allow an FBP component to refer to them without needing to be aware of what they open onto. Port names establish a relationship between the receives and sends *inside* the program and program structure information defined *outside* the component. This somewhat resembles subroutine parameters, where the inside (parameters) and the outside (arguments) have to correspond, even though they are compiled separately. In the case of parameters, this correspondence is established by means of position (sequence number). In fact, in AMPS and DFDM ports were identified by numbers rather than by name. While this convention gives improved performance by allowing ports to be located faster, our experience is that users generally find names easier to relate to than numbers, just as we say "back door" and "front door" rather than "door 1," "door 3," and so on. For this reason, THREADS uses port names, not numbers.

Some ports can be defined to be arrays, so that they are referenced by an index as well as a name. Thus, instead of sending to a single OUT port, some components can have a variable number of OUT ports, and can therefore say "send this IP to the first (or *n*th) OUT port." This can be very useful for components that, for example, make multiple copies of a given set of information. The individual slots of an array-type port are called "port elements." Naturally, you can also have array-type ports as input ports, which might for instance be used in components that do various kinds of merge operations. Finally, a method is provided for the component to find out how many elements of an array-type port are connected and which ones. In DFDM we did not need array-type ports, as ports were numbered, so you could define, say, ports 3 to 20 as acting as a single array.

Now let's draw a picture of the component we built above. It's called a "filter" and looks like the diagram in figure 3-1.

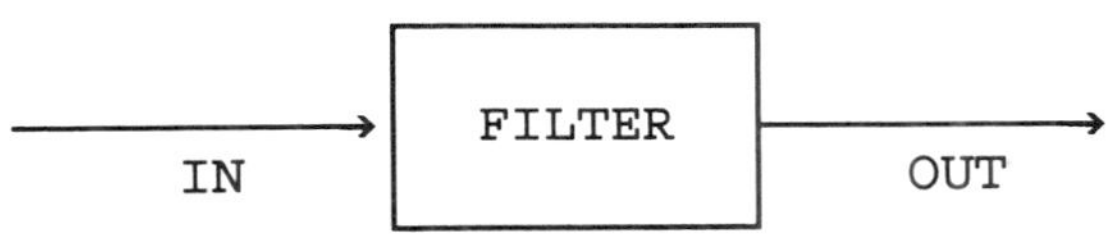

Figure 3-1.

This component type has a characteristic "shape" that we will encounter frequently in what follows. FBP is a graphical style of programming, and its usability is much enhanced by (although it does not require) a good picture-drawing tool. Pictures are an international language, and we have found that FBP provides an excellent medium of communication between application designers and developers and the other people in an organization who need to be involved in the development process.

Now we will draw a different shape of component, called a "selector." Its function is to apply some criterion `C` to all incoming IPs (they are received at port IN), and send out the ones that match the specified criterion to one output port (ACC), while sending the rejected ones to the other output port (REJ). The corresponding picture is shown in figure 3-2.

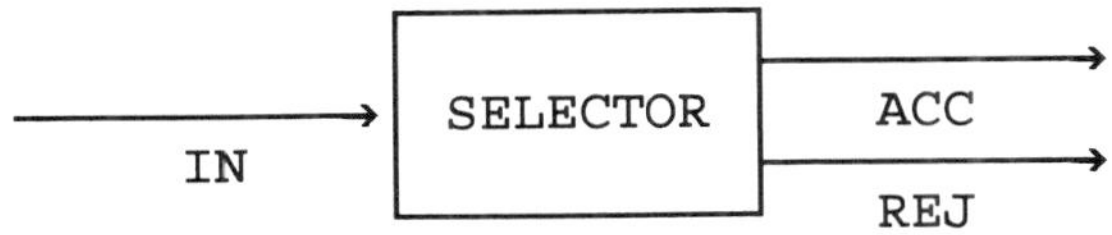

Figure 3-2.

You probably have figured out the logic for this component yourself. In any case, here it is:

```
receive from IN using a
do while receive has not reached end of data
     if c is true
          send a to ACC
     else
          send a to REJ
     endif
     receive from IN using a
enddo
```

Writing components is very much like writing simple mainline programs. Things really get interesting when we decide to put them together. Suppose we want to apply the filter to some data and then apply the selector to the output of the filter. All we need to record is that, *for this application,* OUT of FILTER is connected to IN of SELECTOR. You will notice that IN is used as a port name by both FILTER and SELECTOR, but this is not a problem, as port names only have to be unique within a given component, not across an entire application. Figure 3-3 shows this drawn schematically.

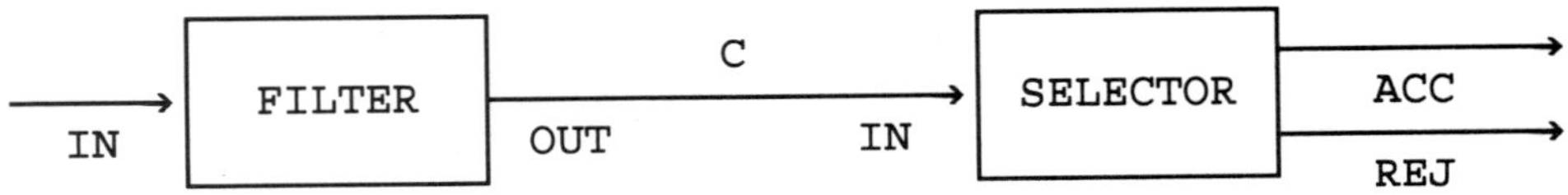

Figure 3-3.

We have just drawn our first (partial) FBP structure! FBP software can execute this kind of diagram *directly* (without our having to convert it to procedural code), and in fact you can reconfigure it in any way you like—add components, remove them, rearrange them, etc., endlessly. This is the famous "Legoland programming" that we have all been waiting for!

Now what is the line marked "C" in the diagram? It is the connection across which IPs will travel when passing from FILTER to SELECTOR. It may be thought of as a pipe that can hold up to some maximum number of IPs (its "capacity"). So to define this structure we have to record the fact that OUT of FILTER is connected to IN of SELECTOR by means of a connection with capacity of *n*.

Now how do we prove to our satisfaction that this connection is processing our data correctly? Well, there are two constraints that apply to IPs passing between any two processes. Using the names in the above example, then:

- Every IP must arrive at SELECTOR *after* it leaves FILTER.
- Any pair of IPs leaving FILTER in a given sequence must arrive at SELECTOR *in the same sequence.*

The first constraint is called the "flow" constraint, while the second is called the "order-preserving" constraint. If you think about it using a factory analogy, this is all you need to ensure correct processing. Suppose two processes A and B respectively generate and consume two IPs, X and Y. A will send X, then send Y; B will receive X, then receive Y (order-preserving constraint). Also, B must receive X after A sends it and similarly for Y (flow constraint). This does not mean that B cannot issue its `receives` earlier—it will just be suspended until the data arrives. It also does not matter whether A sends Y out before or after B receives X. The system is perfectly free to do whatever results in the best performance. This is shown schematically in figure 3-4. Clearly the second diagonal line can slide forward or back in time without affecting the final result.

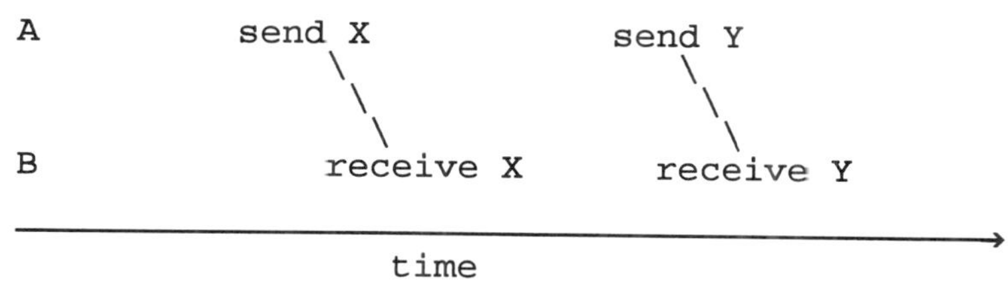

Figure 3-4.

Connections may have more than one *input* end, but they may only have one *output*. IPs from multiple sources will merge on a connection, arriving at the other end in first-come, first-served sequence. It can be argued that, by allowing this, we lose the predictability of the relationship between output and input, but it is easy enough to put a code in the IPs if you ever want to separate them again.

Up to now, we have been ignoring where IPs come from originally. We have talked about receiving them, sending them, and dropping them, but presumably they must have originally come into existence at some point in time. This very essential function is called "create" and is the responsibility of whichever component first decides that an IP is needed. The "lifetime" of an IP is the interval between the time it is created and the time it is destroyed. From one point of view, it is obvious that something needs to be created before it can be used, but how does this apply to a business application? Well, a lot of the IPs in an application are created from file records. Generally, file records are turned into IPs at file reading time, and the IPs are turned back into file records (and then destroyed) at file writing time. There are two standard components to do these functions (Read Sequential and Write Sequential), which will be covered in succeeding chapters. However, it often happens that a programmer decides to create for a particular purpose a brand new IP that may never appear on a file. One example of these are "control IPs," which will be described in a later chapter. Another example might be a counting component that counts the IPs it receives, using a "count" IP. This IP is created when the component starts up, is used to maintain the count and is finally sent to the output port when the counter terminates. Such a component will *receive* the IPs being counted, but, before it starts counting, it has to *create* a count IP in which the count is to be maintained.

Following is the typical logic of a counter component (by the way, this kind of component normally tries to send incoming IPs to an output port and drops them if this port is not connected):

```
create count IP using c
zero out count field in count IP
receive from IN using a
do while receive has not reached end of data
     increment count in count IP
     send a to OUT
     if send wasn't successful,
          drop a
     endif
     receive from IN using a
enddo
send c to COUNT port
```

To discover whether OUT is connected, we simply try to send to this port. If the send works, the IP is disposed of; if not, we still have it, so we dispose of it by dropping it. What if COUNT is not connected? Since the whole point of this component is to calculate a count, if COUNT is not connected there's not much point in even running this component, so it would be even better to test this right up front, and terminate the component in this case.

As we said above, all IPs must eventually be disposed of, and this will be done by some function that knows that the IP in question is no longer needed. This will often be Writer components, but not necessarily. For example, the selector example above should really be enhanced as follows:

```
receive from IN using a
do while receive has not reached end of data
     if c is true
          send a to ACC
     else
          send a to REJ
     endif
     if the send wasn't successful,
          drop a
     endif
     receive from IN using a
enddo
```

At the beginning of this chapter, I talked about data as being primary. In FBP it is not file records that are primary, but rather the IPs passing through the application's processes and connections. Our experience is that this is almost the first thing an FBP designer must think about. Once you start by designing your IPs first, you realize that file records are only one of the ways a particular process may decide to store IPs. The other thing file records are used for is to act as interfaces with other systems, but even here they still have to be converted to IPs before another process can handle them.

Let's think about the IPs passing across any given connection—what is their layout? Clearly it must be something that the upstream process can output and the downstream process can handle. The FBP methodology requires the designer to lay out the IPs first and then define the transforms that apply to them. If two connected components have different requirements for their data, it is simple to insert a "transform" component between them. The general rule is that two neighbors must either agree on the format of data they share or agree on data descriptions that encode the data format in some way. Suppose, for instance, that process B can handle two formats of IP. If the application designer knows that process A is always going to generate the first format, he or she may parametrize B so that it knows what to expect. If A is going to generate an unpredictable mix of the two formats, it will have to indicate to B for each IP what format it is in (e.g., by an agreed-upon code in a field, by IP length, by a preceding IP, or whatever). An interesting variant of this is to use free-form data. There may be situations where you don't want to tie the format of IPs down too tightly (e.g., when communicating between subsystems that are both undergoing change). To separate the various fields or sections, delimiters can be embedded into the data. This will cost more in CPU time, but may well be worth it if it reduces maintenance costs. This is why, for instance, communication formats between PCs and hosts often use free-form ASCII separated by delimiters (binary fields present unique problems when uploading and downloading data). Lastly, the more complete FBP implementations provide mechanisms for attaching standard descriptions to IPs, called descriptors, allowing them to be used and reused in more and more applications. Descriptors allow individual fields in IPs to be retrieved or replaced by name—these are described in more detail in a later chapter.

The next concept I want to describe is the ability to group components into packages that can be used as if they were components in their own right. This kind of component is called a "composite component." It is built up out of lower-level components, but *on the outside* it looks just like any other component. Components that are not built up of lower-level components are called "elementary" and are usually written in some higher-level language (DFDM supports both PL/I and VS COBOL II), while THREADS supports C. DFDM as distributed also includes a small set of "starter set" components written in a low-level programming language for performance reasons, but it is not expected that the majority of users will need to code at this level.

To make a composite component look like other components from the outside, obviously it must have ports of its own. We will therefore take the previous partial network, and show how we can package it into a composite. We will call the result COMPA—it is shown in figure 3-5.

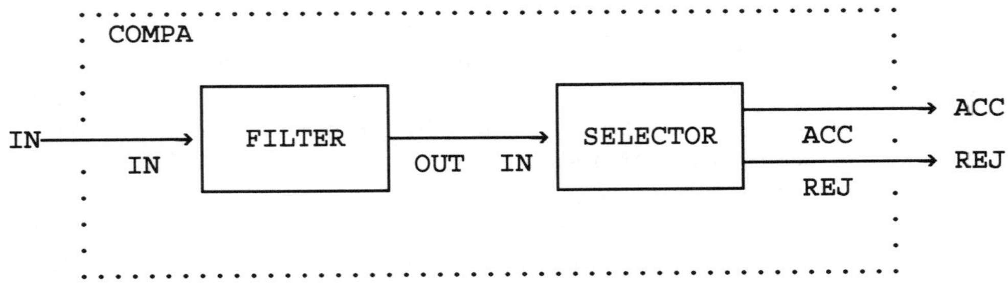

Figure 3-5.

Once this is done, COMPA can be used by anyone who knows what formats of data may be presented at port IN of COMPA and what formats will be sent out of its ACC and REJ ports. Notice that it is quite acceptable for our composite to have the same port names as its internal components. You might also decide to connect the ACC port inside to the REJ port outside, and vice versa—what you would then have is a Rejector composite process, rather than an Acceptor. Of course, COMPA is not a very informative name, and in fact it's probably not worth the bother to make this function a composite unless we plan to reuse it in the future.

Notice also that the figure shows the insides of COMPA. From the outside it looks like a regular component with one input port and two output ports, as shown in figure 3-6.

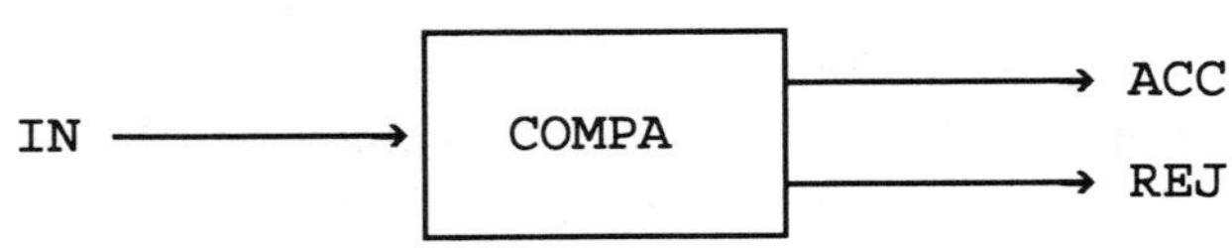

Figure 3-6.

Now, clearly, any external port on a composite must have corresponding ports "on the inside." However, the inverse is not required (i.e., not all ports on the inside have to be connected on the outside). If an inside component tries to send to an unconnected composite port, it will get a return of "unconnected" or "closed," depending on the implementation.

I have now introduced informally the ideas of "port," "connection," "elementary component," "composite component," and "information packet."

At this point, the question should be asked: Just what are the things we are connecting together? I have spoken as though they were components themselves, but actually they are *uses* or *occurrences* of components. There is no reason why the same component cannot be used many times in the same structure. Take the above structure and reverse it. This gives the layout shown in figure 3-7.

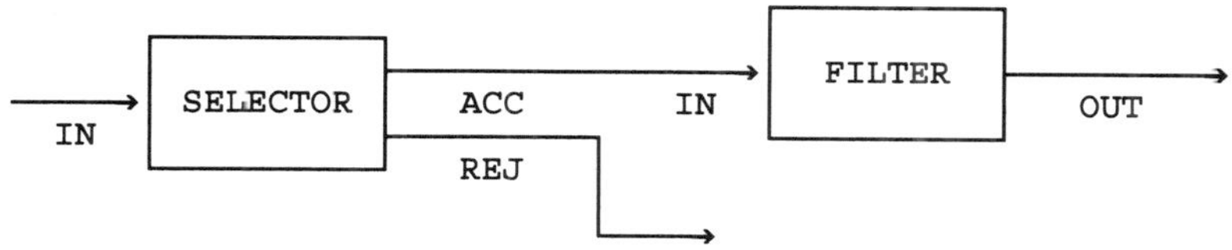

Figure 3-7.

Attach *another* FILTER to the REJ port of SELECTOR, and the picture now looks like that in figure 3-8.

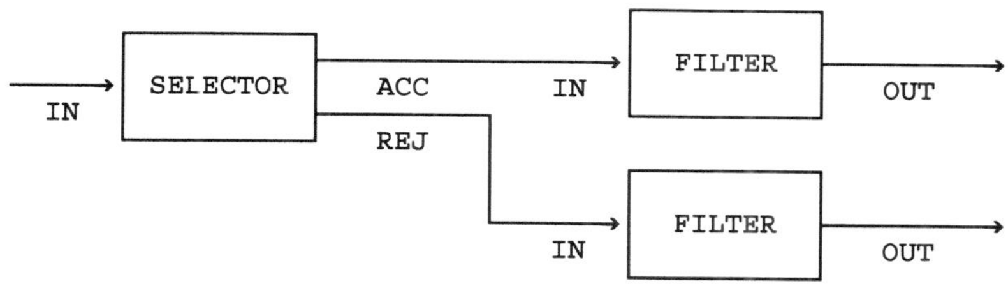

Figure 3-8.

Here are two occurrences of the FILTER component running concurrently—one "filtering" the *accepted* IPs from SELECTOR, the other filtering the *rejected* ones. This is no different from having two copiers in the same office. If we have only one copier, we don't have to identify it further, but if we have more than one, we have to identify which one we mean by describing them or labeling them—they could be called "the big copier" and "the little copier" or "copier A" and "copier B." In DFDM we took the function name and qualified it—in THREADS we make what might be called the "in context" function the name, and qualify it to indicate which component we are using. These component occurrences are called *processes*, and it is time to explain this concept in more depth.

In conventional programming, a program is said to "perform some function," but actually it is the machine that does the function—the program just encodes the rules that the machine is to follow. In conventional programming, this is not a problem much of the time, but in FBP (as also in operating system design and a number of other specialized areas of computing) you have to look a little more closely at this idea. In FBP, the different components are executed by the CPU in an interleaved manner, where the CPU gives time to each component in turn. Since there can be multiple occurrences of the same component, with each occurrence being given its own series of time slots and its own working storage, a term is needed for the thing that the CPU is allocating time slices to—this is called a "process." The process is what the CPU "multithreads" (some systems distinguish between processes and threads, but this book will only use the term "process"). Since multiple processes may execute the same code, there may be situations where the first process using the code gets suspended, the code is again entered at the top by another process, which then gets suspended, and then the first process resumes at the point where it left off. Obviously, the program cannot modify its own code (unless it restores the code before it can be used by another process); otherwise, strange things may happen! In programming terms, the code has to be "read-only." In IBM's MVS, this kind of program is called "reentrant," which is not quite as stringent as read-only, but read-only implies reentrancy, and making code read-only is a good programming discipline, as it makes a clear distinction between variable data, on the one hand, and program code together with constants, on the other. Although this may sound arcane, it is not really that far removed from everyday life. Imagine two people reading a poster at the same time—neither of them needs to be aware of the point in the text the other one has reached. Either one of the readers can go away for a while and come back later and resume at the point where he or she left off, without interfering in the least with the other reader. This works because the poster does not change during the reading process. If, on the other hand, one person changes the poster while the other is trying to read it, they would have to be synchronized in some way, to prevent utter confusion on the part of the reader, at least.

An important distinction can now be made: Composite components contain patterns of *processes,* not components. This becomes obvious in the case of a structure like the previous one—the definition has three nodes, but two of them are implemented by the same component, so they must be different processes. Of course, they don't become "real" processes until they actually run, but the nodes correspond one-to-one with processes, so they can be referred to as processes without causing confusion. Figure 3-9 shows this diagram as a composite.

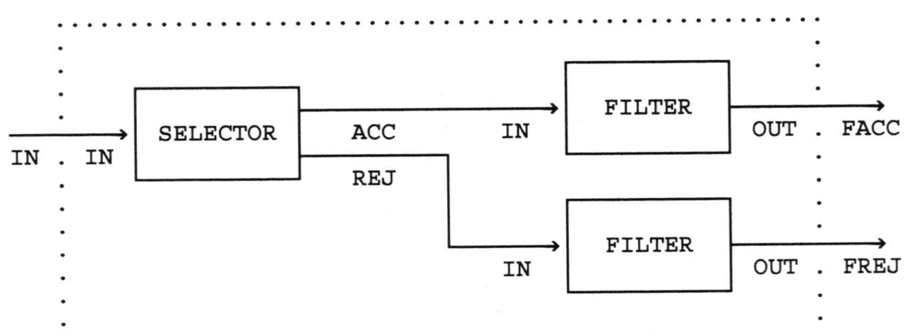

Figure 3-9.

When this composite runs, there will be three processes running in it, executing the code in two components.

Lastly, I would like to introduce the concepts of data streams and brackets. A "stream" is the entire series of IPs passing across a particular connection. Normally, a stream does not exist all at the same time. The stream is continually being generated by one process and consumed by another, so only those IPs that can fit into the connection capacity could possibly exist at the same time (and perhaps not even that many). Think of a train track with tunnels at various points. Now imagine a train long enough that the front is in one tunnel while the end is still in the previous tunnel. All you can see is the part of the train on the track between the tunnels, which is a kind of window showing you an ever-changing section of the train. The IP stream as a whole is a well-defined entity (rather like the train) with a defined length, but all that exists at any point in time is the part traversing the connection. This concept is key to what follows, as it is the only technique that allows a very long stream of data to be processed using a reasonable amount of resources.

Just as an FBP application can be thought of as a structure of processes linked by connections, an application can also be thought of as a system of streams linked by processes. Up to now, figuratively speaking, we have sat on a process and watched the data as it is consumed or generated. Another highly productive way of looking at an application is to sit on an IP and watch as it travels from process to process through the network, from its birth (creation) to its death (destruction). As it arrives at each process, it triggers an activity, much like the electrical signal that causes a phone to ring. Electrical signals are often shown in the textbooks like the diagram in figure 3-10.

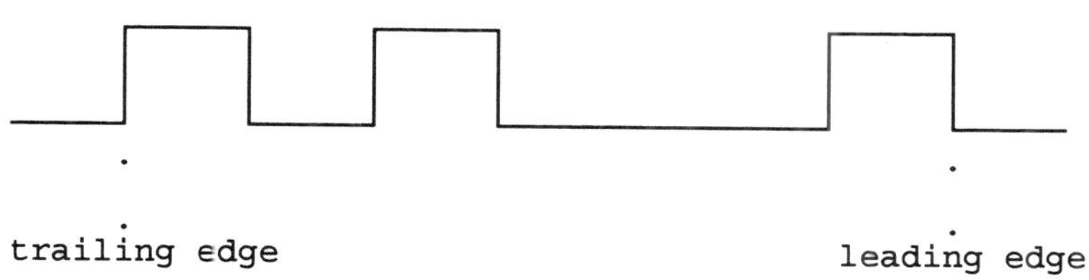

Figure 3-10.

The moment when the leading edge reaches something that can respond to it is an *event*. In the same way, every IP has both a *data* aspect and a *control* aspect. Not only is an IP a carrier of data, but its moment of arrival at a process is a distinct event. Some data streams consist of totally independent IPs, but most streams are patterns of IPs (often nested—i.e., smaller patterns within larger patterns) over time. As you design your application, you should decide what the various data streams are, and then you will find the processes falling out very naturally. The data streams that tend to drive all the others are the ones that humans will see (e.g., reports), so you design these first. Then design the processes that generate these, then the processes that generate their input, and so on. This approach to design might be called "output backwards."

Clearly, a stream can vary in size all the way from a single IP to many millions, and in fact it is unusual for all the IPs in the stream to be of the same type. It is much more common for the stream to consist of repeating patterns (e.g., the stream might contain multiple occurrences of the following pattern: a master record followed by 0 or more detail records). The patterns may in turn be nested, e.g.

```
'm' patterns of:
   city record, each one followed by
   'n' patterns of:
       customer record, each one followed by
       'p' sales detail records for each customer
```

Notice that this is in fact a standard hierarchical structure. The stream is in fact a "linearized" hierarchy, so it can map very easily onto (say) an IMS database.

To simplify the processing of these stream structures, FBP uses a special kind of IP called a "bracket." These enable an upstream process to insert grouping information into the stream so that downstream processes do not have to constantly compare key fields to determine where one group finishes and the next one starts. As you might expect, brackets are of two types: "open brackets" and "close brackets." A group of IPs surrounded by a pair of brackets is called a "substream." In THREADS, IPs with "type" of "(" and ")" are used to represent open and close brackets, respectively.

We have one more decision to make before we can show how we might use brackets in the above example. We have two cases where a single IP of one type is followed by a variable number of IPs of a different type (or substreams). The question is whether the open bracket should go before the single IP or after it. In the former case, we might see the following (I'll use brackets to represent bracket IPs):

```
( city1
   ( cust11 det1111 det1112...)
   ( cust12 det1111 det1112...))
( city2
   ( cust21 det1211 det1122...)
   ( cust22 det1221 det1222...))
etc.
```

In the latter case, we would see:

```
city1 (
   cust11 ( det1111 det1112...)
   cust12 ( det1111 det1112...))
city2 (
   cust21 ( det1211 det1122...)
   cust22 ( det1221 det1222...))
etc.
```

From the point of view of processing, these two conventions are probably equivalent, but I tend to prefer the first one as it includes each customer IP in the same substream as its detail records, and similarly includes each city in the same substream as the customers that belong to that city. At the time of writing, there is no strongly preferred convention, but make sure that all specifications for components that use substreams state which convention is being used. By the way, a very useful technique when processing substreams is the use of "control" IPs to "represent" a stream or substream. Both AMPS and THREADS and some of the versions of DFDM have the concept of a process-related *stack,* which is used to hold IPs in a LIFO sequence. In chapter 9, I will describe how these concepts can be combined.

The following concepts have now been introduced:

- Process
- Component (composite and elementary)
- Information packet (IP)
- Connection
- Port and port element
- Stream
- Substream
- Bracket

Normally at this stage in a conventional programming manual we would leave you to start writing programs on your own. However, this is as unreasonable as expecting an engineer to start building bridges based on textbook information about girders and rivets. FBP is an engineering-style discipline, and there is a body of accumulated experience based on the above concepts, which you can and should take advantage of. Of course, you will develop your own innovations, which you will want to disseminate into the community of FBP users, but this will be built on top of the existing body of knowledge. You may even decide that some of what has gone before is wrong, and that is standard in an engineering-type discipline also. Isaac Newton said: "If I have seen further than other men, it is because I have stood on the shoulders of giants." Someone else said about (conventional, not FBP) programming: "We do not stand on their shoulders; we stand on their toes!" Programmers can now stop wearing steel-toed shoes!

Before learning how to put these concepts together to do real work, two related ideas remain to be discussed: the design of reusable components and parametrization of such components. These will be covered in the next two chapters.

4

Reuse of Components

> Reuse in DFDM is natural. DFDM's technology is unsurpassed in its promotion of reuse as compared to other reuse technologies currently being promoted. (from an evaluation of DFDM performed by an IBM I/S site in the United States in 1988)

So far, I have spoken as though components are created "out of thin air" for a specific problem. You may well have suspected that I selected my components to illustrate certain concepts, without worrying about whether they would be useful in a real application. Well, the good news is that the kinds of components we have run into are in fact the ones that experience shows are very useful for building real applications. The bad(?) news is that it requires a large amount of experience in programming and a certain creative flair to come up with useful components. This should not be so surprising when you think about tools that are useful in real life. Where and when was the first hammer invented? Imagine a whole series of "proto-hammers" (reindeer antlers, rocks attached to sticks, etc.) gradually evolving into today's standard builder's hammer, with a claw on one side and balanced just so. Perhaps this should be qualified by saying "in the West." Different cultures will come up with different tools or different forms of the same tool. I seem to remember from my anthropology classes that the Australian aboriginals have a wonderful tool that is a combination of all the things they find most useful in their everyday life and yet is highly portable. It is a combination spear-thrower, shield, dish, and fire-starter. These kinds of tools are not invented overnight—they take time and experience, requiring progressive refinement by many creative people. The best tools will always evolve in this way. Tools may also pass out of use as the need for them diminishes or they are replaced by something more effective. Buggy whips are the classical example, but usually it happens without our even noticing! When did they stop putting running boards on cars? No, you don't need to phone right away! Clearly culture and the tools used are closely intertwined—within a given culture, we have strong ideas about what is the right tool for a given job, but another culture may in fact have a different definition of what that job is. In the West we consider using a knife and fork the "proper" way to eat food. A few centuries ago, we were spearing it with the point of a dagger. Knives and forks in turn mean that an acceptable Western meal might include some very large chunks of meat or even half a bird. In the Orient, on the other hand, people have been using chopsticks for a very long time, which requires that the food be served in bite-size pieces. Notice that the choice of tools also helps to determine what part of the serving is performed by the diner and what part by the cook behind the scenes.

One other thing we should consider is the need to be able to use the tool in unforeseen situations. A useful tool should not be too restrictive in the ways it can be used—people will always think of more ways to use a tool than its original designer ever imagined. Wayne Stevens (1991) tells a story about an airline attendant using a hearing set (that little plastic stethoscope you plug into the arm of your chair) to tie back some curtains. Elegant? No. Effective? Yes. It becomes counterproductive to make a hammer so intelligent that it can only be used on nails. Another example: Why do some UNIX functions have nonobvious names? There are well-known cases where a tool was originally designed for one job, but people found that it was even more useful for some function the original designer did not foresee. This is in fact a testimony to the robustness of these tools. There are many examples of this kind of thing in FBP.

Just as there are the two roles of cook and diner in the preparation and consumption of food, in FBP application development there are two distinct roles: the component builder and the component user or application designer. The component builder decides the specification of a component, which must also include constraints on the format of incoming data IPs (including option IPs) and the format of output IPs. The specification should not describe the internal logic of the component, although attributes sometimes "leak" from internal to external (restrictions on use are usually of this type). The application designer builds applications using already existing components, or, where satisfactory ones do not exist, he or she will specify a new component and then see about getting it built.

Component designers and users may of course be the same people, but there are two very different types of skill involved. This is somewhat like the designer of a recent popular game, who admitted he was not particularly fast at solving it—his skill was in *designing* games, not in *playing* them. The separation between makers and users is so widespread in real life that we don't pay any attention to it unless it breaks down. In industry, as Wayne Stevens points out, it is taken for granted that airplane builders do not build their own chairs—they subcontract them to chair manufacturers, who in turn subcontract the cloth to textile manufacturers and so on. In contrast, the world of conventional programming is as if every builder designed his or her own nails, lumber, and drywall from scratch. Talk about "reinventing the wheel"—in conventional application development we routinely reinvent the rubber, the nuts and bolts, and even the shape of the wheel!

I'd like to talk a little bit about how useful components are developed. They are unlikely to emerge from a pure "top-down" approach or from a pure "bottom-up" approach. In the first case, you do not discover drywall by progressively breaking down an architect's drawing of a house. In the second case, people who dream up useful components have to be willing to subject them to rigorous testing in real-life situations. Even after this has been done, they still may not sell. Nobody in industry would bet the business on some untried tool that has never been evaluated in the field (well, usually not), and yet this is done frequently in application development. Another of Wayne Stevens' recommendations is not to build a generalized tool until you have found yourself doing the same thing three or four times. Otherwise, you may find yourself investing a lot of time and effort in features that nobody will ever use, and you may find yourself unable to respond to customer requests for features they really do want.

In FBP a lot of the basic components have analogs in an area that is no longer well known, but has been very productive of generalized components over a number of years—namely, unit record machines. In those days there were specialized machines, such as sorters, tabulators, collators, and so on, and people learned to wire (parametrize) them and link them together into applications very effectively. And you didn't need a college degree to get applications working. In fact, I once figured how to solve a problem with a tabulating machine plug-board, over the phone, dripping wet out of the bath, without even notes or a schematic to look at!

Just as unit record machines worked with streams of punched cards, the corresponding FBP components work with streams of IPs. Let's call these "stream-based" components. Examples of such components are:

- Sort
- Collate
- Split
- Replicate
- Count
- Concatenate
- Compare

These all have the characteristic that they process data streams and that they require very little information about the format of their incoming data streams. They typically have well-defined application-independent functions.

The list could be expanded with some general-purpose components that get down to the data field level, but that still do not "understand" business processing. One such component might be a generalized transform component. Such a component, properly parametrized, could in fact do a lot of the processing in a given business application. Nan Shu of IBM in Los Angeles has written extensively about a language that she calls FORMAL (Shu 1985). Its function is to take descriptions of files and the transformations between them and use them to do the transforming automatically. She has found that a large amount of business processing consists of moving data around, changing its coding, and doing table look-ups (e.g., one application might use a number for each U.S. state, while another might use a two-character abbreviation). This suggests that another type of function in this same class is a generalized table look-up function, and in fact we have built several for DFDM.

There is another general class of components known as "technology-dependent." These components usually require specialized knowledge to build, but, once created, can be used by people who are not as technically skilled. They thus encapsulate specialized knowledge. They will usually be written in a lower-level language. We had an interesting example of this some years ago. We had a person who was an expert on paper tape. Paper tape is (was?) a medium with its own quirks. It has special codes for various purposes and in particular has a convention for correcting data (you punch all holes across the offending character, which is then treated as though there was no character there at all). This individual was able to write some components that generated regular IPs, so that no other component in the application needed to know that the input was paper tape. An application could be built and debugged using regular I/O, and then, after it was working, the reader module could be unplugged and replaced with the paper tape reader. This meant in turn that testing could be done without the tester having to monopolize a scarce (and slow) piece of equipment.

The two most widely used technology-dependent components are Read Sequential and Write Sequential. As might be expected from the names, these convert file records into IPs and IPs into file records, respectively. A matching Read/Write pair of components can be used to encode and decode any file format desired. For instance, the medium you are using may be so expensive that you want to compress the data as it is stored and expand it as you retrieve it. Another useful function pair might be encryption/decryption. In fact, any Read/Write component pair can be thought of as embodying a data organization. Generalizing this thought, a sequential Read/Write component pair provides a conversion between a format suitable for processing and a linear format on some medium. For instance, we built a Read/Write pair that was specialized for constructing tree structures from a linear medium and then "relinearizing" them later.

You may have noticed by now that components very often come in matched pairs (e.g., split/merge, read/write, compress/expand, encrypt/decrypt). This is characteristic of many FBP components—what one component does, another one *un*does. In fact, the combination of a component and its inverse should ideally result in a stream identical to the original input stream, just as in mathematics multiplying a number by its reciprocal results in unity, or composing a function with its inverse results in the Identity function.

Using separate Read and Write processes not only gives that separation between logic and I/O that is recommended by the majority of application development methodologies, but actually reduces elapsed time. The reason for this surprising result is that in FBP an I/O process that has to wait on I/O suspends only itself—other processes can proceed. This means that FBP applications tend to use as much CPU time as they are allowed to by the operating system. I will talk more about performance later on.

Another interesting group of components deriving originally from Unit Record are those connected with report generation. These include such functions as pagination and generation of page headings and footings, as well as totaling and subtotaling, cross-footing, and other report generation functions. Reports are very often the main vehicle of communication between an application and the humans who use it, and the importance of these facilities to the average business is borne out by the remarkable longevity of IBM's RPG, which, while often regarded as old-fashioned, is still fulfilling a real need in the marketplace. Later in this book, I will describe a report generation component that was used extensively in our shop.

A good guideline for the functionality of a component is that its specification should not exceed about a page. Some FBP experts have gone so far as to say that the summary of a component's function should not exceed one paragraph and should not have the word "and" in it. Another guideline we have found useful is that generalized components should not have more than four ports (array ports only count as one port). Of course, these guidelines are not mutually exclusive, and they are only guidelines—some components bring so much function together that their parameters are essentially mini-languages, but their usefulness may outweigh any awkwardness in parametrization.

The last category of component is that of "business components." These embody business rules and should hopefully be relatively simple, especially if the other categories of component have been used as far as possible. We can imagine business components for different business areas—banking, oil and gas, and so on. Some will be more mathematical, others less so. In all cases they represent the knowledge of some business expert.

After functionality, one of the major considerations in connection with designing business components is the likelihood of change. There are some types of business logic that hardly ever change and others that are changed every time they are run. An example of the latter might be the logic to generate an employee's taxable income statement at the end of the year. It is changed every year and run once a year. It would be very nice if our governments could send out a single reusable component every year that companies could then just plug into their own payroll programs. This also gets back to the question of roles: Who installs the new module? Application development or operations staff? If the former, there will be an ongoing need for application developers indefinitely; if the latter, can you be sure that the new component will be adequately tested? On the other hand, given the backlog of work that application development usually faces, something that can just be loaded up and run by operational staff is certainly attractive.

It would help if such a component does as much validation of its input data as possible to make sure it is being used in the right context. Ideally, a component should never crash. In practice, of course, it is almost impossible to prevent one component from destroying another's data, but it is certainly possible to add validation logic to protect against (say) data format errors. The reusable module could also require that incoming data be tagged with a particular descriptor. Then, if the required data format changes, the descriptor name just needs to be changed. Descriptor names are typically part of the specification of a reusable component, so this fits quite nicely. This discussion is really another form of the old compile-time versus run-time debate. In FBP, compile-time comes in two flavors: component level and network level. Actually, parameters can be specified inside a composite component and still be outside the elementary component that they control! Eventually a lot of business logic will be embodied in rules held in rules databases. Such rules, written in a suitable language, can then be modified by people outside the normal application development group. These rules may not even be expressed in what a programmer would recognize as a programming language. A forerunner of this is the IBM Patient Care System, in which a surprising amount of the system logic (including screen layouts) was held in the form of tables, designed to be updated by senior clerical or nursing staff. This was very effective, as these were usually the people who had to use the system and had the most operational experience with it. Again we see the separate roles of application developer and application user. If it bothers you to put so much control in the hands of end users, either implement authorization systems to make sure that only the right people can modify key data or specify the rules as tables hard-coded in the application definition, but outside the components that refer to them. This way control remains in the application development group, but systems become much easier to modify and debug. However, companies really should be moving away from requiring the DP department to do all systems maintenance.

If I am right that we will eventually see more and more business logic being either embedded in reusable components or captured as explicit rules on disk, then the role of the current higher-level languages in the future should diminish. We found in our experience that, given a powerful set of reusable components, people would go to enormous lengths to avoid writing HLL code. Much of the time, the resulting poorer performance does not matter. The Kendall Report (1977) contrasted the running time of the average program with the person-months required to develop it. Programs that took 6 person-months to develop often ran for just a few minutes over their entire lifetimes. So, most of the time, minor increases in the amount of CPU time really make no difference. Only in the case of long-running jobs run regularly is it worthwhile to do performance tuning, and, as we shall see in a later chapter, it is much better to instrument an FBP application to find out where the real bottlenecks are than to try to guess ahead of time and waste time optimizing code that doesn't affect your system's performance much. There are in fact a number of ways to do performance tuning in the FBP environments, once we know where the real leverage is.

Far more important than CPU time is human time, and the fundamental question is really what is the best way to spend valuable human time. When deciding to develop a new component, one must take into account the expected return on investment ("ROI" for short). Every new component must be documented, tested, supported, advertised, and incorporated into educational material (well, ideally—sometimes not all of these happen!). Small wonder, then, that our experience with FBP shows that application developers using FBP avoid writing new code—being responsible people, they are aware of the burden they take on the moment they start coding a new component. However, this realization isn't enough: we have to change the economics of the situation. Code is a cost item, as Dijkstra and others have pointed out, and someone who adds to the total amount of code when it is not justified is costing your company money, now and into the future. I have started suggesting, only half in jest, that programmers should be "penalized" for each line of code they write! In fact, some program improvements involve removing code. Is this negative productivity? It has been pointed out many times that people will modify their behavior according to how you measure them—and companies that still measure productivity in Kloc (thousands of lines of code) get what they deserve. Conversely, someone who produces a useful reusable component improves the productivity of all of its users, and deserves to be rewarded. Some companies have already started trying that—the key word, of course, being "useful." N.P. Edwards, mentioned in an earlier chapter, was a key player in getting IBM to move to reusable parts in the hardware area, and he has said that the key breakthrough for them also was in changing the economics of hardware development.

Someone who has talked and written extensively about the importance of reuse is T. Capers Jones (e.g., T. Jones 1992). He has also been aware of my work for some years and has been supportive of it. He has been active in promoting the use of code-independent metrics, such as Allan Albrecht's now well-known Function Points, for measuring productivity, and has done a lot of work on the potential of reuse for reducing the costs of application development.

How do we know whether a tool is useful? The only way is to measure its use. Will people use it? They will if it fits the hand and if support and education for it is supplied. This in turn means that the infrastructure must be in place to allow people to take advantage of this new technology, as well as measurements and incentives to get people moving in the right direction.

There is also the opposite question: What if the tool is "less than perfect"? Just as with real tools, there is no perfect tool. There are only tools that fit your hand more or less conveniently. Like many programmers who tend to be perfectionists, you may be tempted to postpone putting something on the market because you feel it isn't finished yet. The question should be: Is it useful as it is? You can always enhance it as time goes on, provided you keep the interfaces stable (or provide "expansion ports" while maintaining upward compatibility). In fact, after a tool has been in use for a while, you may find that the extensions people really want are not at all what you expected. Since your reusable component will hopefully be in widespread use by this time, it is important to allow extension while maintaining upward compatibility. In FBP, the fact that ports are named helps do this. Also, parameters (described in the next chapter) should be designed to be extendible. Parameters can be in string format, with delimiters, or, if fixed form, it is a good idea to insert a few zero bits. These can always be changed to ones to indicate that there is an extension portion.

Another kind of modification that will happen to modules occasionally is error correction. It is certainly a pleasurable feeling to have improved a component that many people are or will be using, and you might think that the users will welcome the change with open arms. Unfortunately some of the users may have adjusted to the error and will need to be convinced that you know what is right for them. The other thing users do is take advantage of undocumented features. I talked about a tool fitting the hand—it may fit the hand, even with an error in it. One team found an error in one of the DFDM components, but, instead of telling us about it, they carefully compensated for it. When we fixed it, their programs stopped working! I think they were quite indignant for a while until everybody realized what had happened. We had to spend some time explaining that everyone would be much better off if we fixed the bug rather than leaving it the way it was! There is a very important rule that you should impress on your users: *If it isn't documented, don't trust it.* IBM learned the value of this one by bitter experience and has accepted its wisdom since the day some bright user discovered an undocumented *instruction* on one of the 900-series machines.

The next question is: How will people find out about these components? There is a common misconception that reusable componentry doesn't work unless there is an elaborate catalogue that people can interrogate to find the tool they want. On the other hand, Wayne Stevens has pointed out that most examples of reuse in everyday life are done very naturally without any catalogue. People know by heart most of the things they commonly use. Say you go into a hardware store because you want to attach a wood base onto a ceramic pot. You will be familiar with half a dozen types of fastener: glue, nails, screws, rivets, and so on. Most of the time you will know exactly what kind of glue to use. In this case, say you are not quite sure what is best. You still don't have to scan the entire store—most of the time, you can go right to the shelf and start reading labels. What do you do if you are not sure where in the store to go? You ask a store clerk, who may in turn pass you on to someone who is an expert in a particular area. If your requirements are really unusual, the clerk may have to consult a catalogue, but this is likely to be a rare case. The point is that effective reuse doesn't require catalogues, although they can certainly help.

In order to measure the productivity gains we were getting from DFDM within IBM Canada, we kept statistics on the amount of reuse taking place over a number of projects. The figures for three projects are shown in table 4-1 (the numbers relate to components).

In this chart, "project" means components coded specifically for the project in question, while "general purpose" means components that are *off the shelf* (already available and officially supported). "Unique" means separate components (separate pieces of code), while "occurrences" means total number of processes (component occurrences or network nodes). Thus, project A used 154 distinct components, of which 21 came off the shelf, but accounted for 305 of the 489 processes (about 3/5). GP/T means General Purpose as a fraction of Total, and it is interesting to compare the GP/T for unique components against the GP/T for component occurrences.

The "figure of merit" (FM), to use Bob Kendall's phrase (Kendall 1983), is calculated as follows: number of project-coded *components* divided by the total number of *processes.* Since the first figure represents the amount of work a *programmer* has to do (apart from hooking together the network), while the second figure represents the amount of work the *program* is doing, we felt that the figure of merit was quite a good measure of the amount of real reuse going on. DFDM had been in use about 2 to 3 years in that shop, and we had about 40 off-the-shelf

TABLE 4-1. Sample Reuse Statistics

Project		Unique	Occurrences	Reuse Factor	FM[1]
A	Project	133	184	1.4	0.27
	Gen Purpose	21	305	14.5	
	Total	154	489	3.2	
	GP/T	0.14	0.62		
B	Project	46	48	1.0	0.13
	Gen Purpose	17	306	18.0	
	Total	63	354	5.6	
	GP/T	0.27	0.86		
C	Project	2	54	27.0	0.01
	Gen Purpose	8	216	27.0	
	Total	10	270	27.0	
	GP/T	0.80	0.80		

[1]Figure of Merit.

components available, so quite a lot of the common tasks could be done without having to code up any new components. However, when the programmer did have to code up components, quite often this code could also be reused, giving reuse factors greater than 1 (Project C had a factor of 27.0). In the third example in the above chart (Project C), the programmer only had to write two components, although there were 270 separate processes in his program. (You can probably figure out that this project involved running 27 different files through essentially the same 10 processes—so it did a lot of work, with very little investment of programmer effort!)

Although we thought at first that this last case was just a quirk, we turned up quite a few applications that were not that different from this one (e.g., Rej's letter quoted in chapter 1).

Here are some figures from an evaluation of DFDM quoted from at the beginning of this chapter:

> All of the function in the DFDM pilot application is performed by 30 unique coroutines (this is the number of coroutines that an individual would need to be familiar with in order to understand the function of the application).
>
> A total of 95 occurrences of these 30 coroutines make up the application . . . providing a 3:1 reuse ratio.
>
> These 95 coroutines are leveraged through the use of subnets and CNS [Compiled Network Specification] networks to perform the equivalent work of 225 unleveraged coroutines.

Some companies have tried to encourage people to write generalized code by offering them money or kudos. One counsel I would give them is to monitor not how many components someone has written, but *how often it is used*. An appropriate analogy is the system of royalties in the publishing industry. Every time a module is used, the author should get some kind of token, be it money or recognition. This will ensure that your company will not accumulate a collection of wonderful, Rube Goldbergish gadgets sitting on the proverbial shelf, gathering dust.

Say that you are all convinced that reusable code is the way to go—how do you get it adopted in your particular shop? You will find (unless all your people are super-altruists) that the biggest enemy of reuse is not technology—it is human psychology. While many people will accept the new ideas enthusiastically, others will resist them and for several different reasons. People who have become good at delivering applications under time pressure very often feel that they must at all costs maintain control of everything they use, and in fact all their experience has taught them that this approach works. Components developed by others will be on their critical path, and they will be pulled between the desire to reduce their own effort by using pretested components and the fear that the components they are relying on will not be ready in time, will break, or will not be maintained as the environment changes. They have to become convinced that someone will support these components, if necessary on a 24-hour basis. This may not be necessary technically, but may be very necessary psychologically.

Another source of resistance is simply that some programmers love the bits and bytes and don't want to become mere combiners of precoded components. There is a role for these people, writing the components to specs. As said earlier, two different roles seem to be emerging: component builders and component users. The latter need skills very similar to those required by analysts. They need to be able to talk to users, gather requirements, and even build systems or prototypes of systems. For the more complex parts or parts that have to perform better, they can subcontract parts to the component builders. This is the domain where the programmer's programmers ("Merlins," as a friend of mine calls them) can shine. In some senses, a component becomes an encapsulation of their particular skill or knowledge. I have found that it makes sense to get "tighter" about the external specs and "looser" about how the code is built internally. This lets programmers express their creativity, while still serving the needs of the organization as a whole. Of course, it must not be so poorly written that it doesn't perform well. And it absolutely *must* deliver the function according to the specs. Once those are assured, then the only concern is maintainability. Generalized code should be maintainable, but you probably don't have to control the format of every internal label.

A programmer once said to me, "I don't like DFDM because I don't get dumps!" At the time I took this to mean that, because programs built using FBP tend not to crash, programmers don't get to look under the covers, so it is hard for them to get a feel of how the programs work. Does not knowing how your car's engine works make you nervous? It probably does affect some people that way, but most don't care. Later I realized that it also brings up the very fundamental question of trust. If the users of a package don't trust the package or its vendor (same thing, really), they are not going to be happy. And trust is fragile: hard to build up and easy to damage. Suppose that your company has become convinced that developers should not keep "reinventing the wheel," but that, like most companies, you have only reached the stage of maintaining a library of shared subroutines. How do you get formalized sharing of components in place? Suppose I find out that Julia is working on a module that is pretty close to what I want but it needs some tweaking to fit my needs. In most shops, they don't even know what to call it. Companies that have just started to grapple with naming standards often think it's neat for module names to start with the project code. For instance, if someone is managing project ABC, then he or she can name all the modules ABC-something. This way there's no worry about module names conflicting with those of other projects. Even the library names will often have ABC built into them! So, even to be able to find the code usually requires some kind of enterprise-wide naming convention. Next question: who does the modification of the code and who pays for it? What if Julia's schedule slips and starts to impact Jim's schedules? Even if everything goes really well, who will maintain it, document it, and support it?

Many writers about reuse agree that the only solution is to set up an independent department to write and maintain components. This department must have enough resources to do the job properly, which also involves publicizing and selling their product. One tendency that must be resisted is that such departments often get tied up producing complex, generalized tools for a few users or even for none. They just figure that the component would be neat, and they'll worry about selling it afterwards. Remember the principle of ROI: The company as a whole will get more bang for the buck out of a lot of simple tools (especially if they communicate well with each other) rather than from a few very complex ones. Since good tools will often start as special-purpose modules that some other group has found useful, there must be a path for promoting such ad hoc components to a place where other people can find them *and rely on them.* Centralized software support departments must have ways to beat the bushes for new and interesting components and must then have ways to evaluate whether potential customers are interested (otherwise, why go to all that trouble?). It must also avoid getting sucked into writing or upgrading complex tools that have only a small market. It is a service organization, so it must be service quality oriented, not just a group of self-styled experts who know what is best for everyone else. It must become entrepreneurial, but not exclusively bottom-line oriented. In short, it must follow good financial and engineering practices. If this takes a major shake-up in the way your organization is structured, then get started as soon as possible!

Unless companies start to bring engineering-type disciplines to application development, not only will they fail to take full advantage of the potential of computers, but they will become more and more swamped with the burden of maintaining old systems. Not a lot can be done about old systems—I know, I've seen lots of them—but new systems can be built in such a way that they *are* maintainable. It should also be possible to gradually convert old programs over to the FBP technology piecemeal rather than "big bang." A director I once worked for called this "converting an iceberg into ice cubes"!

All true disciplines follow a sort of cycle through time, which may be represented as shown in figure 4-1.

Innovation can only be founded on a base of solid knowledge of what went before—otherwise we are doomed to keep rediscovering the same old stale concepts. On the other hand, tradition without innovation cannot result in progress,

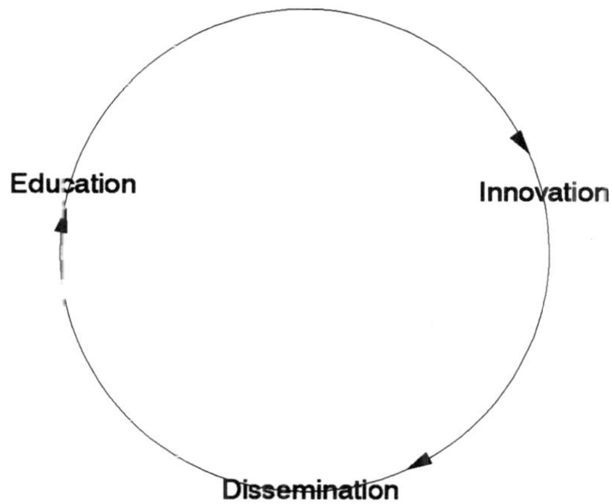

Figure 4-1.

and innovation is useless unless the word is gotten out to people who can make use of it. As I pointed out earlier, business application development has not really changed significantly since I started in the business in 1959. Now, at long last, we can start to see the promise of application development becoming a true engineering-style discipline.

5

Parametrization of Reusable Components

I will now describe the way that generalized FBP components are made reusable, using one additional, very powerful FBP mechanism, the "initial information packet" or "IIP." IIPs were developed by E. Lawton of my old department at IBM in response to some of the problems we ran into using DFDM's parameter facility.

Say you have built a component like one of the ones described in the previous chapters. Let's call it "Select." It should be clear from the foregoing that this component can be used in a variety of contexts, as long as it is sent data in the format it expects. Because a component communicates with the outside world only through data being sent to or received from its ports, it can be held in object form *and never modified.* Such reuse is often called "black box" reuse, to suggest the idea that the user cannot see the insides of the component. In addition, since the "black box" never needs to be modified, once its developer gets it working it can be relied on to work correctly *in any context.* This is the converse of "white box" or "clear box" (source level) reuse, which is what most so-called reuse tools provide today. The latter type of reuse is easy to provide, but in my view doesn't buy its users much. It may reduce the cost of developing new code, but the amount of net new code that has to be maintained still increases. Furthermore, if a bug is found in the reused code, there is no easy way to tell whether it is safe to fix all instances of it—if you can even find them (with some reuse tools, you can't even do that).

You will of course have to tell the black box Select component which fields to select on, since, otherwise, it will only be able to select on whichever fields were hardwired into it. Suppose you want to tell it that it is to do its selecting on the contents of a 6-byte field starting at offset 23 in each incoming IP and also want to give it a list of acceptable field values. In classical programming, this kind of thing is done by having the calling program specify *parameters*. In FBP you do something similar, but there is no user-written calling program in which to specify the parameters. Instead, there is a way for the application designer to specify this information right in the application structure definition. This mechanism is the IIP. You also need an additional port on the component (call it OPTIONS—it can have any name you want). An IIP can be generated as part of the structure and associated with the chosen port.

Once the process is started, an IIP is turned into an ordinary IP by the component issuing a "receive" service call against the port the IIP is connected to. This has the added advantage that the OPTIONS port can also be fed by an upstream process instead of an IIP, so component options can either be decided at structure-building time or deferred until execution time, without any modification of the component being required. What the component sees when it does its receive from the OPTIONS port is an ordinary IP. In what follows, this is sometimes referred to as an "options IP." Options IPs may start out life as IIPs or may be generated by upstream processes, but their function is primarily to control execution rather than to carry data (obviously this is not a hard and fast distinction, and you may find a need for IPs that combine both functions).

One last point about options IPs—a major decision for the component designer is whether to make them free-form or give them a fixed layout. The former will generally be easier to specify, but is going to cost more processing time to scan for delimiters, convert numeric values, and so forth. However, since this processing is usually done just once, at the beginning of the run, it may not be significant in the context of total processing time. THREADS opted for free-form IIPs for its "off-the-shelf" components because of the ease-of-use factor. One other thing you should consider if you choose to use free-form IIPs is that you will need to decide on delimiter conventions (e.g., you might opt for commas or blanks, and you might decide to use brackets to group together sets of option values). This in turn means that some convention will be needed for specifying character strings that might contain delimiter characters as valid values (the old "quotes within quoted strings" problem).

Fixed-form options, on the other hand, will take less machine processing time and avoid the above-mentioned problems of delimiter conventions. Conversely, they are more likely to result in alignment errors and are harder to make open-ended. There are other options, however, within the fixed-form category:

- Use some front-end tool to generate the fixed-form IIP, or
- Use a descriptor (see chapter 11, "Data Descriptions and Descriptors") to access the fields in the options IP.

Say you want to write a generalized selector where the column number, field length, and permissible values are received from an OPTIONS port at execution time. Using a dashed line to represent an IIP connection (by the way, IIPs and regular processes can't be attached to the same connection), you might represent your selector with its options IIP as shown in figure 5-1. The field being selected on starts at offset 23, for a length of 1 byte. IPs with a value of A at that position

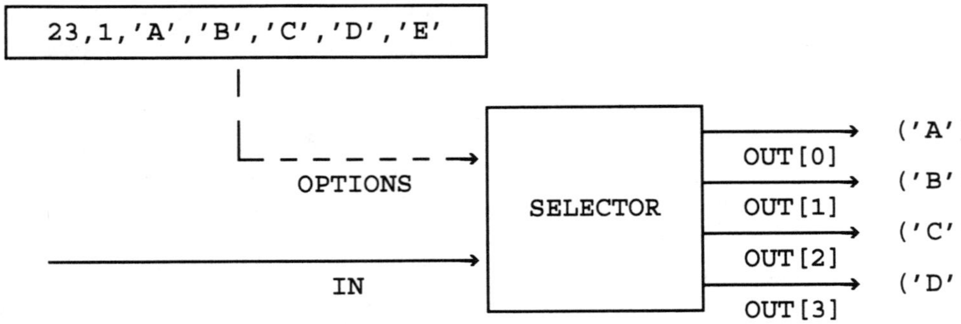

Figure 5-1.

will be sent to the *zero*th element of port OUT, IPs containing a B go to the number 1 element, and so on.

In a structure diagram, it is often useful to be able to show parameter values right in the picture. Note that this example shows a free-form IIP.

To convert this diagram to use a connection instead of an IIP, change the line feeding OPTIONS to a solid line and attach the upstream end of it to a process block (call it GENOPT), as shown in figure 5-2.

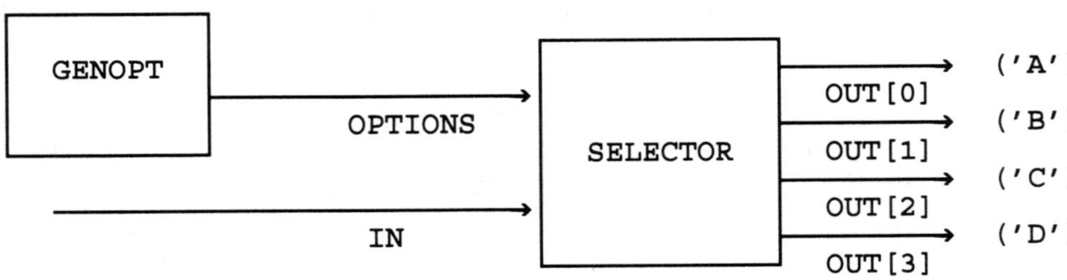

Figure 5-2.

By way of comparison, in DFDM, processes were parametrized by means of a variable-length character string (2-byte binary length followed by a character string) passed to the component at activation time (analogous to the way a parameter string is passed to a job step in IBM's MVS). This meant that parameters specified in the network and parameters coming from an upstream process could not be handled in a uniform manner.

There is a general problem of passing parameters from the "outside world" into networks. In DFDM's approach to parametrization, external parameters were only passed to the outermost structure, and there was a system of "inheritance" that allowed lower-level structures or components access to parameters at the next higher level. Although we haven't tackled this problem in THREADS yet, the IIP technique should make this whole area much simpler, as special components can be written to obtain external parameters and pass them into the network like any other IP.

At a more general level, parametrization of components may be thought of as a spectrum, running from low to high. Low parametrization (few or no parameters) occurs when a component has no variability, either because it is custom coded for a particular application or because it is so simple that it always does the same work in the same way. For instance, there is a very useful component in all existing FBP systems that simply accepts and outputs all the IPs from its first input port element, followed by all the IPs from its second input port element, and so on, until all the input port elements have been exhausted. In DFDM it was called the "sequencizer" (some of my friends like to play fast and loose with the English language). This component is often used to force a sequence on data that is being generated randomly from a variety of sources. One example might be control totals being generated by different processes that you want printed out in a fixed order on a report. You know the sequence you want them displayed in, but you do not know the time at which they are going to be created. We now use the more traditional term "concatenate." This is shown schematically in figure 5-3.

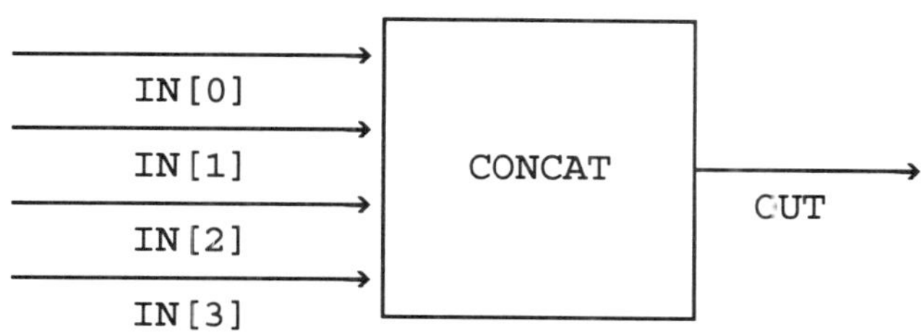

Figure 5-3.

Its function is so simple that it doesn't need an options port. Now you may be asking, "Why not simply take all the incoming data streams and merge them into a single input port?" The answer is that this is indeed an option, but the effect is somewhat different. What happens in that case is that the incoming IPs are merged in a first-come, first-served sequence, which is not what you wanted. However, there is a downside to the concatenate function: Because the data from input port element 1 is held up until Concatenate knows that port element 0 has been closed, and so on for the remaining ports, there is the potential for deadlock. Deadlocks are not as bad as they sound, and there are well-established ways of detecting places where they might occur and of preventing them before they can occur. In FBP, deadlocks are viewed as a design-time problem. We will talk about the cause and prevention of deadlocks in chapter 16.

The Select component has a median level of parametrization, and most of the components mentioned in this book are similar, but there are occasional components that have so many parameters that they can almost be thought of as mini-languages. If parameters are replaced by, say, rules held on a data set or even a large IIP, then you really do have a mini-language. A later chapter (chapter 17) goes into more detail about this whole area. Also, in chapter 18 I will describe an approach to a generalized component of this type that should be able to handle a considerable part of the logic of a business application.

6

First Applications Using Precoded Components

One of the things I like about AMPS is that there are so many more ways to do a job than with conventional programming. (a programmer at a large Canadian company)

This chapter starts with the simplest network imaginable—well, actually, a network with one process only is the simplest, but this is equivalent to a conventional program. The simplest network with at least one connection might be a Reader feeding a Writer, as seen in figure 6-1.

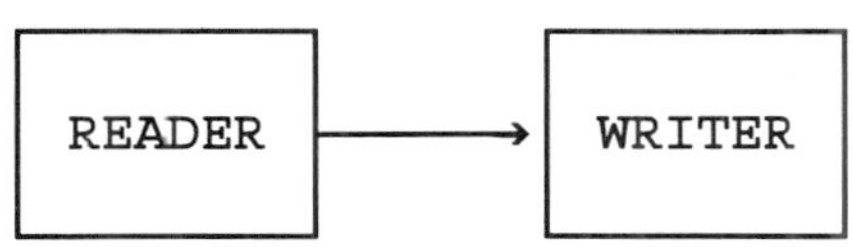

Figure 6-1.

This network just copies one file to another, so it is equivalent to the kind of "copy" utility that is provided by just about every operating system. The difference is that with FBP it's possible to combine these utilities into more and more complex functions. Utilities provide a number of functions, but one always wants something a little different. The functions that are coded into them are often not the ones one needs. This is quite understandable, given the difficulty of predicting what people are going to find useful. One alternative would be to combine a bunch of utilities by writing intermediate files out to disk. FBP effectively allows you to combine multiple utility functions without requiring any disk space, nor the I/O to read and write from and to disk (so you also use less CPU time, and more importantly, less elapsed time).

Suppose you want to combine a "copier" function with a selector and then sort the result before writing it to disk. Just string the functions you want together, as shown in figure 6-2.

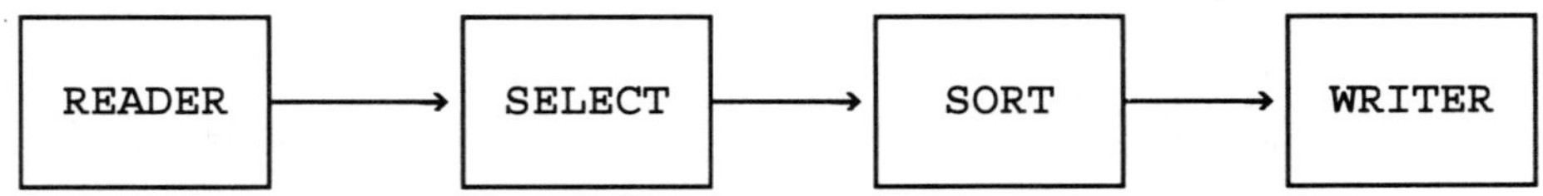

Figure 6-2.

Actually, the network doesn't even have to be fully connected. For instance, the design shown in figure 6-3 is perfectly valid and may even be useful!

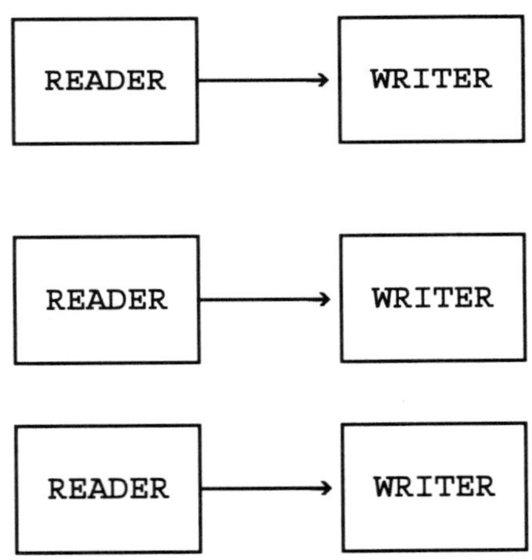

Figure 6-3.

There was a time when being able to write a program that would simultaneously read cards and write them to tape, read a tape and punch out the records, and do some printing was considered the height of a programmer's ingenuity! With FBP, all you have to do is specify the connections between six processes, as we have just seen!

Now, if you think about this diagram as a way to get something done, not to control when it happens, you will realize that the three pairs of processes shown above *do not have to run concurrently*. The point is that they *can* if there are adequate resources available, but they don't have to—it doesn't affect their correct functioning. Think of this network as three train tracks, with a train running on each one. All that matters is that each train gets to its destination, not when exactly, nor how fast. In business applications it is correct functioning that is important—not usually the exact timing of events. In the MVS implementations of FBP, the three "tracks" probably will run concurrently because I/O can be overlapped. In THREADS, which has no I/O overlap yet, they may run sequentially. In none of these cases is the order defined. I think the bottom one will run first, but I'm not sure. Naturally, this makes old-guard programmers very nervous, accustomed as they are to controlling every last detail of when things have to happen. I will keep coming back to this point, since it is so important: Application development should be concerned with function, not timing control, unless, of course, timing is part of the function, as in some real-time applications. You have to decide what is worth the programmer's attention and what can safely be left to the machine. Not knowing exactly when things are going to happen turns out to be liberating rather than disorienting (for most people). But, yes, some programmers will find the transition rather hard.

By the way, when comparing 4GLs and FBP, I have been struck by the fact that you really can do anything in FBP! FBP's power does not come from restricting what programmers can do, but from encapsulating common tasks in reusable components or designs. Since a conventional program is in fact an FBP network consisting of a single process, the programmer is free to ignore all FBP facilities, if he or she wishes, and the result is a conventional program. This may sound glib, but it says that we are not taking anything away—we are adding a whole new dimension to the programming process. While some programmers do feel a sense of restriction with FBP, it comes from having to express everything as black boxes, with well-defined interfaces between them, not from any loss of function.

In the rest of the chapter, we will put together some simple examples using reusable components, but first here is a catalogue of some of the types of components that an FBP shop will probably have in its collection, a number of which have already been covered. The types that haven't been mentioned above are fairly obvious extensions of what went before. Some of the items in this list should be understood as representing types of component rather than specific pieces of code. For example, a shop might have two or three Sort modules, with different characteristics.

- Sort
- Collate
- Split
- Assign
- Replicate
- Count
- Concatenate
- Compare
- Generate reports
- Read

- Write
- Transform
- Manipulate text (this might be a large group)
- Discard

There are also some components that have proven useful during development and debugging: a "dumper" (which displays hex and character formats) and a line-by-line printer component.

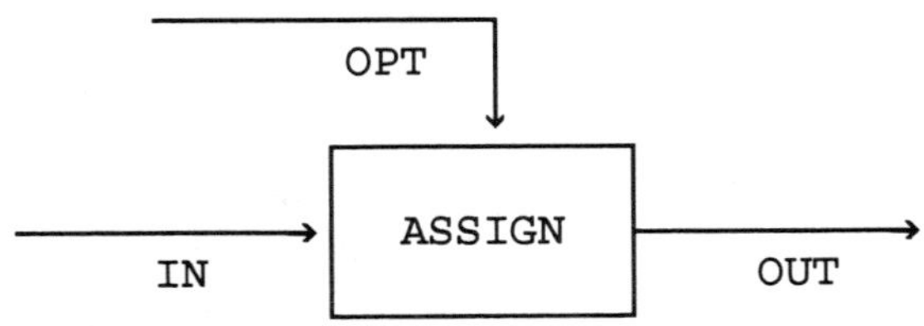

Figure 6-4.

I haven't mentioned Assign before. This is going to be used for some examples, so I will go into a little more detail on this type of component. This component (or component type) simply plugs a value into a specified position in each incoming IP and outputs the modified IPs. It has the same shape as a "filter" and can be drawn as shown in figure 6-4. In this diagram, OPT receives the specification of where in the incoming IPs the modification is to take place and what value is to be put there. For instance, we might design an Assign component that takes option IPs looking like this:

```
3,5,ABCDE
```

This might specify that `ABCDE` is to be inserted in the five characters beginning at offset 3 from the start of each IP. This may seem to be overly simple, but it can be combined with other usable components to provide a broad range of function.

By the way, this component illustrates the usefulness of IIPs: if `3,5,ABCDE` is specified in an IIP, you have essentially defined a constant assign with the value defined outside the Assign process, but fixed in the network as a whole. Now, instead, connect the OPT port of Assign to an upstream process, and you now have a variable assign, where the values can be anything you want and can be changed any time.

Now let's use Assign to mark IPs coming from different sources. Suppose you want to merge three files and do the same processing on all of them, but you also want to be able to separate them again later. You could use Assign to set a "source code" in the IPs from each file and use a splitter to separate them later.

In an earlier chapter I used the idea of a two-way selector, looking like that in figure 6-5.

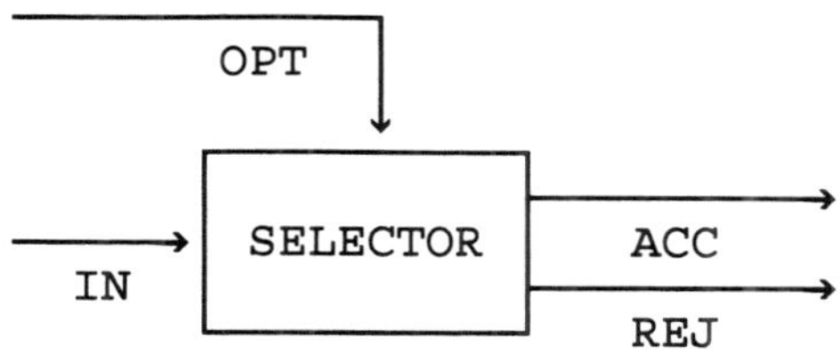

Figure 6-5.

Now this can be generalized to an n-way splitter, where, instead of two ports with specific names, there is an an array port, which uses the combination of a port name and a number to designate the actual output connection. This is shown in figure 6-6 (using the THREADS numbering convention).

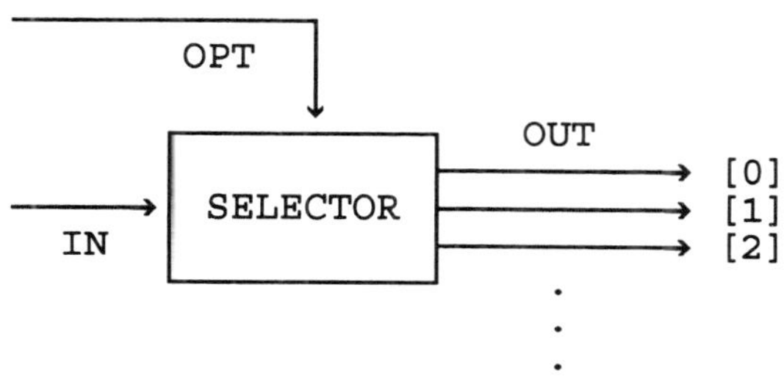

Figure 6-6.

Combining the Assign components and a splitter, we could implement the above example of merging three files as shown in figure 6-7.

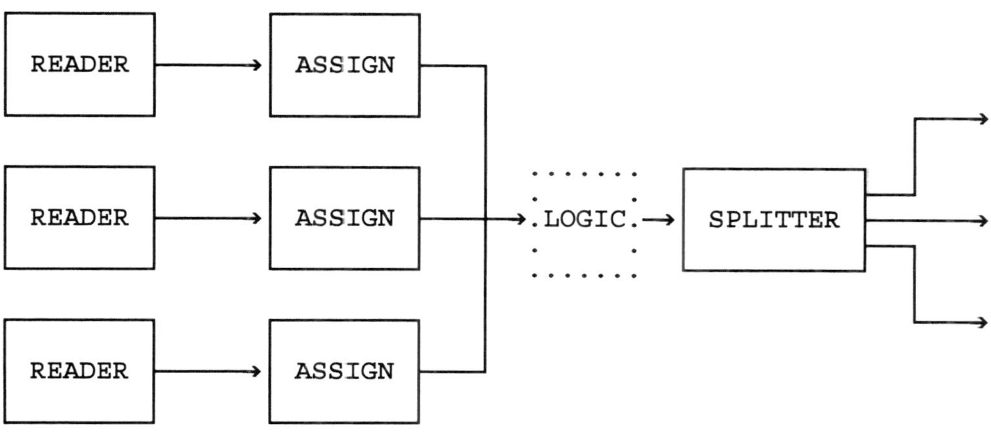

Figure 6-7.

Splitters have to be parametrized by specifying a field length and offset and a series of possible values. The above splitter might therefore be parametrized as follows:

```
54,1,'A','B','C'
```

assuming the codes A, B, and C were inserted into the IPs coming from the three readers, respectively, at offset 54.

A more complex example can be constructed based on the provinces of Canada. Say you have a file of records with province codes in them. You want to arrange them by time zone, so that you can print them out and have a courier deliver them in time for start of business. The easternmost point in Canada is 4½ hours ahead of the westernmost point, so most big Canadian companies have to wrestle with time zone problems.

Use a splitter here to split the stream of IPs by province. Once the "province" streams have been split out, you can use Assign to insert appropriate codes into the different IP. This splitter might have an option IP looking like this:

```
6,2,'ON','QU','MA','AL',...
```

This will be read as follows: Check the two characters starting at offset 6 within the incoming IP; if it is ON, route the IP to OUT[0]; if QU, to OUT[1]; if MA, to OUT[2]; and so on. Of course, in both of the above cases, it would be much more friendly to be able to use field names rather than offsets and lengths. This idea will be discussed in chapter 11.

One other question that has to be answered is: What does the selector do if the incoming IP does not match any of the specified patterns? In DFDM, the standard splitter simply sent unmatched IPs to array element $n+1$, where n equals the number of possible values given (DFDM used 1-based indexing). Another possibility might be to send unmatched IPs to a separate named port.

The application might therefore look like figure 6-8. (I'll just show two Assign processes and assume that all IPs find a match.)

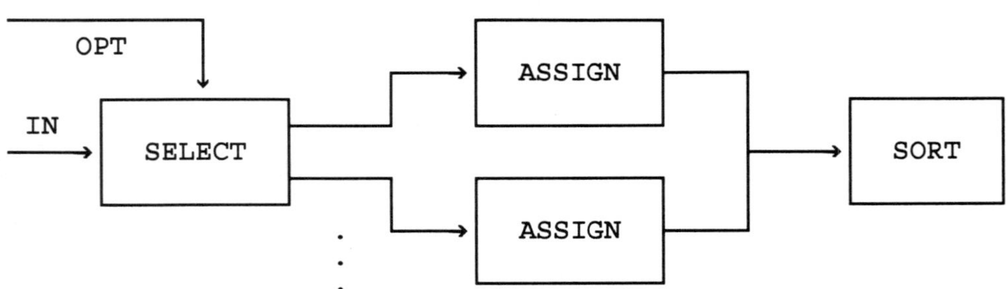

Figure 6-8.

The Assigns can insert a code that ascends as one goes from east to west. Because Sort is going to rearrange all the data, you can feed all the modified records into one port on the Sort process. This also avoids the possibility of deadlock (I'll be talking more about why this should be so in a later chapter).

I didn't show the option ports on the Assigns, but you will need to use them to specify what codes should be inserted and where.

Now add the logic to handle unmatched IPs. Since they should probably be reported to a human, we will add a printer component and use the named port technique, as shown in figure 6-9.

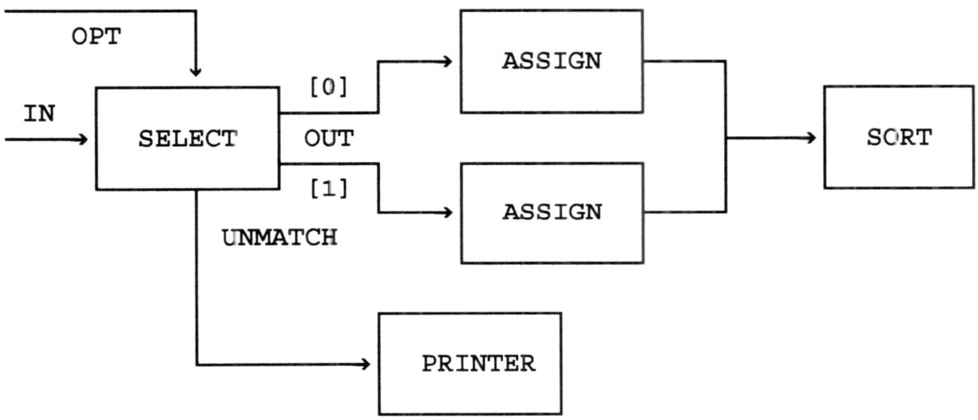

Figure 6-9.

At this point you will simply have a list of unmatched IPs streaming out onto a print file. You will probably want to put out an explanatory title and do some formatting. You will see later how to do this. Figure 6-10 shows PRINTER replaced by the kind of functions you will probably use.

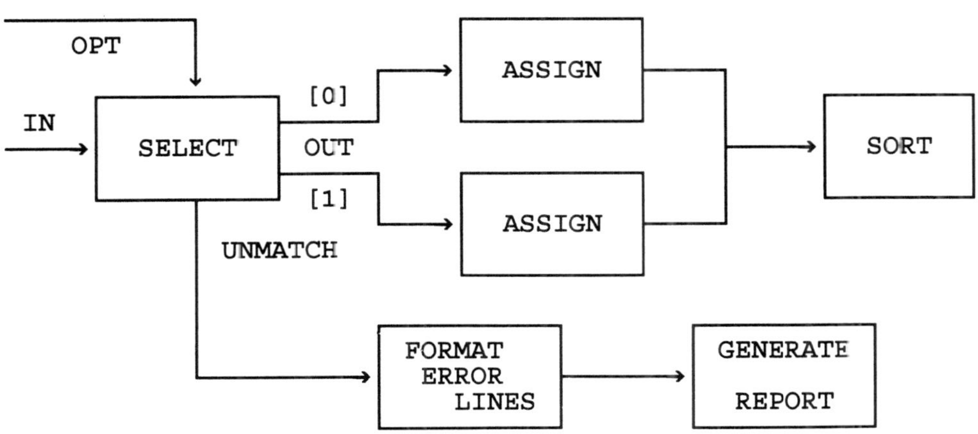

Figure 6-10.

Suppose the network is now working and doing what it is supposed to do. The question is whether this network is "industrial strength." There is a definite temptation, once something is working, to feel the job is finished. In fact, it is quite acceptable to use a program like the one shown above for a once-off utility type of application or for a temporary bridge between two applications. But there is a fundamental question that the designer must answer, and that is (in this application) how long are there going to be exactly 12 provinces in Canada? No, you did not suddenly jump into a book on Canadian politics! We have made the program structure reflect a part of the structure of the outside world, and we have to decide how comfortable we feel with this dependency. Yes, there will always be programmers, and you can always change this program, provided you can find it! Nobody can make the decision for you, but if this program may have to survive more than a few years, you might want to consider structuring your code to use a separately compiled table or database, which can pull together all the attributes of provinces of interest to your application. If you generalize SELECT to mean "determine which province it is" and ASSIGN to mean "insert the time zone code for each province," your application might then look like that in figure 6-11.

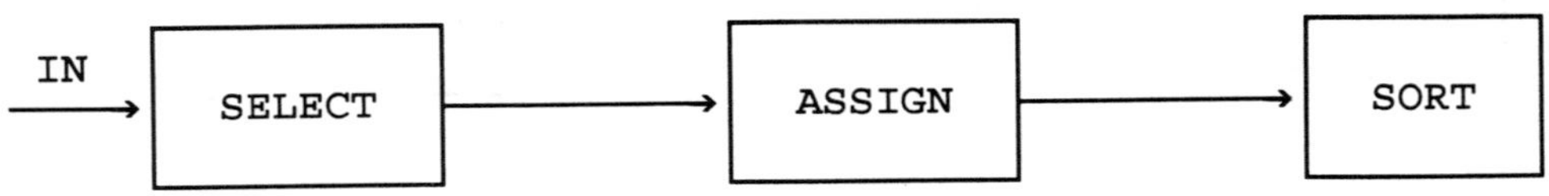

Figure 6-11.

Note that this diagram has become simpler and the components more complex. It has the same general structure as the preceding diagram, but the shape does not reflect a (possibly changeable) political structure. Another approach might be to amalgamate the SELECT and ASSIGN components shown above, using either special-purpose code or a generalized transformer module.

A better generalization, however, might be to keep the parallelism, but not tie it to individual provinces at network specification time. Assuming there will never be more than, say, 24 provinces, you can extend the earlier diagram to have 24 ASSIGN processes. SELECT will have 24 port elements on its output port, connected to the ASSIGNs. Now, since both ASSIGN and SELECT are option-driven, their parameters can be obtained from a file (being read by a Reader) or a table (using a table look-up component) and sent to their OPT ports. The possibilities are endless! The important decisions are not "how do I get this working?", but "what solution will give me the best balance between performance and maintainability?" When I was teaching FBP concepts, I used to tell my students that the machine will accept almost anything you throw at it—the real challenge in programming is to make your program comprehensible by humans (whether they are other people looking at your code years later or your own self one week later!). This is far more of a challenge than simply getting the code working.

There is yet another way to look at this example: What we are really doing (in the last diagram) is converting one code to another under control of a table. One of the generalized component types that we found most useful was a group of table look-up components. The table could be held as a load module (in MVS), in which case it would have to be maintained by the programming department, but a better technique is to hold it on a file. The table look-up component will then look like that in figure 6-12.

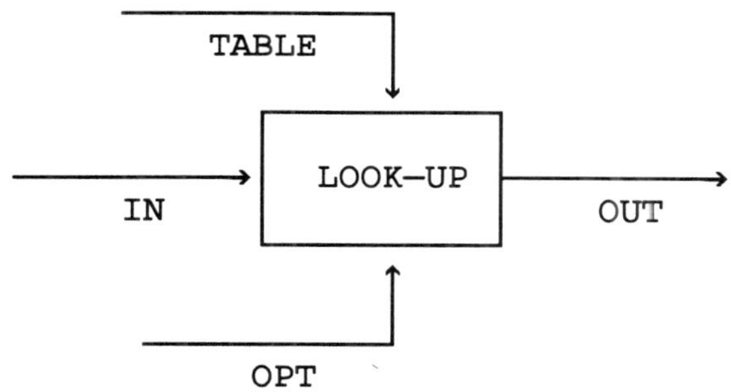

Figure 6-12.

What will happen here is that at start-up time the component will read all the IPs from the port named TABLE and build a table in storage. It then starts a process of receiving IPs from IN, looking up a specified field in the table, inserting the found value into the IPs, and then sending them to OUT. Of course, this needs to be parametrized—probably you will need to specify the offset and length of the search field in the incoming IPs, as well as the offset and length of the field that is to be inserted. We will need a Reader to bring in the table IPs from a file, so the resultant network will look like figure 6-13.

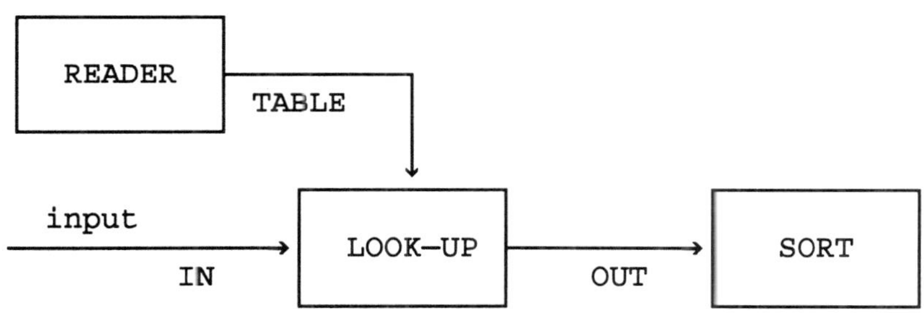

Figure 6-13.

Table look-up components have been found to be very useful in the various dialects of FBP. In DFDM, the system was distributed with two "off-the-shelf" table look-up components. One of them was much like the one just described. However, the other one gives you some idea of what can be provided in the form of reusable code, with a little more imagination. It's pretty complex, but it is a "black box" piece of reusable code, and I am showing it just to indicate what can be done with a single component. Of course, it violates some of the rules given earlier, so maybe this should sound some warning bells! However, it is still a "stream" process rather than just a complex algorithm. Basically, it does table look-ups on a table that is being refreshed from some kind of backing store—it doesn't care what kind, so long as the other process conforms to a certain protocol. It therefore acts as both a table look-up component and as a buffering device. See figure 6-14.

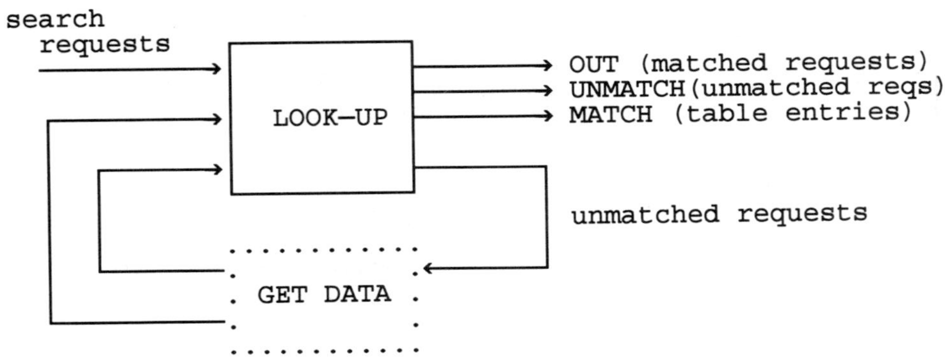

Figure 6-14.

This look-up component always works with another process (shown in dotted lines) that is used to access a direct access file or database. These two components work together as follows:

- The top component builds the table, which starts out empty.
- As each search request comes in, it is checked against the table; if a match is found, the search request goes out of OUT and the table entry goes out of MATCH.
- If a match is not found, the search request is sent to the other process, which will either find it or not; if it finds it, the search request and the found table entry are sent back to the top component, to be respectively sent to OUT and added to the table.
- If it does not find it, a zero-length IP is sent to the top component, together with the search request; the zero-length IP tells it not to add an entry to the table, and the search request is sent to UNMATCH.

This may seem complicated, but once set up, it is very easy to use, and any process can occupy the "bottom" position, provided that it behaves as described. This DFDM component (the "top" component) only needed four parameters, of which one was the (optional) maximum number of entries in the table. If this limit was specified and was reached, entries would start to be dropped off the table in FIFO sequence. Another possibility could have been to use an LRU (least recently used) sequence.

This chapter has tried to give some idea of what can be done using only reusable components. Of course, the number of these is going to grow steadily, and, especially if you have made some of the organizational changes suggested in an earlier chapter, you may wind up with a sizable number of useful, reusable tools. We don't know what this number is, but my guess is that it will taper off in the low hundreds. The amount that these are used will follow a curve with the general shape of the curve in figure 6-15. In this curve the less frequently used components may be used only in a few applications. Given this kind of distribution, you may wonder whether it is worth maintaining the low-frequency components in a support department or whether they should be made the property of the using departments. The answer will depend on whether specialized knowledge is encapsulated in them, whether you are trying to sell them outside the company, and so on.

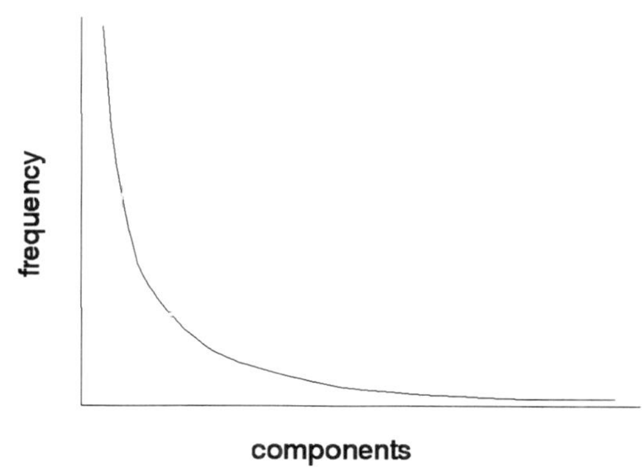

Figure 6-15.

This kind of rarely used component has similarities with what we have called "custom" components. Until all code is "off the shelf" (if that ever happens), there will be a need for customers to write their own components. This is not as easy as just hooking reusable components together, but it is also pretty straightforward. In the next chapter, I will talk about the idea of composite components and then in the following chapter start to discuss some concepts for building systems by combining "off the shelf" and "custom" components.

7

Composite Components

In chapter 3, I talked about hierarchic structures of substreams. There is obviously another type of hierarchic structure in FBP, which has been alluded to earlier: the hierarchical relationship between components. Although the processes in an FBP application are all little mainlines, cooperating at the same level to perform a job of work, it is easier to *build* the total structure hierarchically, with a "top" structure comprising two or more processes, most of which will be implemented using composite components. Each composite component in turn "explodes" into two or more processes, and so on, until you reach a level where you can take advantage of existing components or you decide that you are going to write your own elementary components, rather than continuing the explosion process. Apart from the emphasis on using preexisting components, this is essentially the stepwise decomposition methodology of Structured Analysis.

The application of this approach to FBP is largely due to Wayne Stevens, arising from his work on structured programming and application development methodologies in general. From a hierarchy point of view, a running program built using AMPS (the first FBP dialect) was "flat"—it had no hierarchic structure at all. People drew application networks on *big* sheets of drawing paper and stuck them up on their cubicle walls. These drawings would then gradually accumulate an overlay of comments and remarks as the developers added descriptions of data streams, parametrization, DDnames, and so on. When the time came to implement the networks, the developer simply converted the drawing into a list of macro calls.

Wayne realized that a better way to develop these networks was to use the decomposition techniques of Structured Analysis, but that, unlike conventional programming, *there was no change in viewpoint as you moved from design to implementation*. In conventional program development, there is a "gap" between the data flow approach used during design and the control flow viewpoint required during programming, which is extraordinarily difficult to get across. Therefore, when building DFDM, we provided a way for developers to grow their systems by stepwise decomposition, but at structure build time the hierarchy got "flattened" into the conventional AMPS-type network. This approach turned out to be very successful. (I alluded earlier to a colleague who built a 200-node network without once drawing a picture of a network!)

So DFDM networks can be built up hierarchically, but are flat at run-time. This approach lets developers build up their applications layer by layer. As we have shown in some of the examples, you could also take a simple component and replace it by a subnet—this gives an additional dimension of expandability. In DFDM subnets can be stored on reusable libraries for later use. However, they must be stored in interpretable form, so their internal structure is visible (although they are built out of black boxes). It would be even better for someone marketing an application to be able to store the proprietary parts of an application as "black box" subnets, so that the customer cannot see inside the subnets Remember that DFDM has the ability to take an interpretable network and convert it into a directly executable load module. Later we were able to do this with a subnet as well, so that a *part* of an application could be held as a black box as well. The original motivation for doing this, however, was performance of interactive systems.

Consider an application comprising 200 processes. When you link all the code together into a single module, the result is a pretty big load module. The particular application mentioned above ran under IMS/DC, and the network was executed once for each transaction. However, when we started measuring performance, we found that, on each pass through the network, even though IMS loads in the whole network for most transactions, only about one-third of the processes actually got executed for a given transaction. We wondered if we could just build a framework for an interactive application and load in the required chunks of logic dynamically. This would have the advantage of taking less time to load in the application on each transaction, because the individual load modules would be smaller, thus improving response time. Also, on each transaction you would only need the framework and the particular dynamic chunk involved, so the framework could actually be made resident, improving response time even more. It should also make it easier to expand the application and even change it on the fly. The problem was how to run a network that modifies itself dynamically without losing track of the data.

For a long time, I resisted this idea, as I had a vision of a complex subway system like the London underground, but with the added complexity that stations would be appearing and disappearing at random. How would it feel to be a passenger in such a system?

I had experimented with loading in individual components dynamically under AMPS. I was able to read in or load a piece of code, treating it as pure data, and let it travel through a network, until it arrived at a "blank" process (one that was connected to other processes, but had no code assigned to it—a sort of "tabula rasa" process), at which point it would get executed, so I felt that dynamic process modification could work under controlled circumstances. Wayne Stevens had also proposed a particular case of dynamic network modification, which is simpler than what we eventually landed up with, but we never got around to trying it out: His image was of engineers repairing a dam. The water has to keep flowing, so the engineers divert the water through a secondary channel. After the dam has been repaired, the water flow can be restored to its original channel. This seems like it would be a good way to do maintenance on an FBP system that has to keep running 24 hours a day, like a banking system.

I myself came up with a different and somewhat more complicated approach, which, however, was also safe and manageable and also solved the problem of load module size described earlier. The trick was to have a "mother" process load a subnet (in compiled and linkedited form), start up the processes in the subnet, and then go to sleep until all of her "daughter" processes had terminated. At subnet start time, the daughters are counted, so the subnet is finished when the count of active daughters has gone down to zero. While the mother is sleeping, some of the daughter processes can be given control of their mother's input and output ports. There will be no conflict over who has control of the ports, as the mother and the daughters are never awake at the same time.

We called these subnets in DFDM *dynamic subnets.* The "mother" was a generalized component called the Subnet Manager, which continuously iterated through the following logic:

- Receive the name of a subnet in an IP.
- Load the subnet load module.
- "Stitch" it into the main network.
- Start it up and go to sleep.
- Wake up when all the daughter processes have terminated.
- Dispose of the subnet load module and repeat these steps.

In addition to the Subnet Manager, we added special precoded components (Subnet In and Subnet Out) that were used for input and output handling by the subnet. Figure 7-1 shows a picture of a very simple dynamic subnet (with one input data port and one output port).

When 'X' is given control, it behaves just like a mini-application. Technically SUBIN has no input ports, so it gets initiated. The other two processes have input ports, so they will not be initiated until data arrives. SUBIN and SUBOUT have the ability to use their mother's input and output ports respectively. They have to be separate processes, as they have to be independently suspendable. Thus, if mother had two input data ports, the subnet would have to have two SUBIN processes to handle them.

Now we noticed a strange thing. Normally, once a process terminates, it can never be started again. We saw that the Subnet Manager had to have the unique ability of being able to restart terminated processes. This was the only function in DFDM that had this ability, and it was in a very special off-the-shelf component.

In the work that followed DFDM (referred to earlier under the name FPE), we realized that these characteristics of dynamic subnets could be extended to static

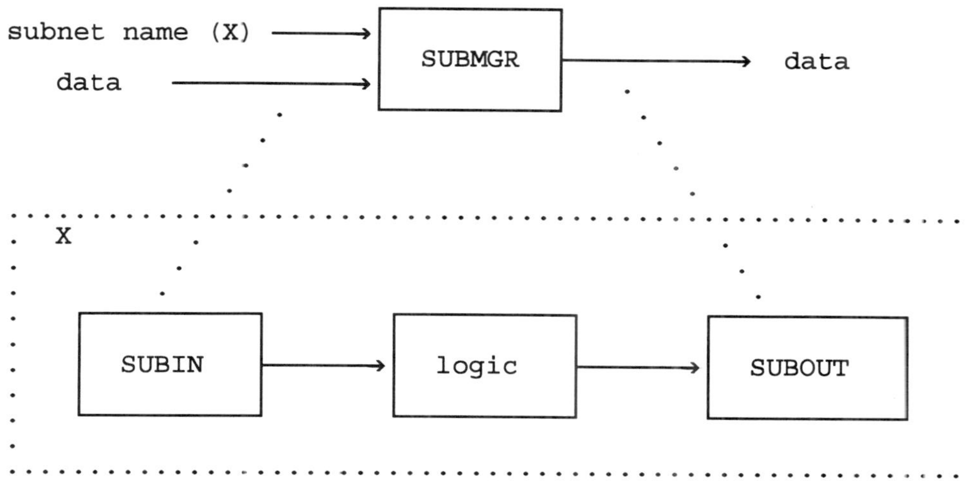

Figure 7-1.

networks as well. We moved this ability into the infrastructure (removing the subnet names port), so that all subnets had a built-in "mother" process. This approach naturally coordinated the hierarchy of processes with the stream hierarchy. In addition, since the "mother" process's other job is to stitch the composite into the main network, we could now have "black box" composite components. This facility would allow subnets to be packaged as separate load modules for distribution, which could later be linked with other components by a developer to form the full application network. This seems very attractive, as a software manufacturer will be able to sell a composite component without having to reveal its internals (as would be required by DFDM). You will also see later (in chapter 20) that these concepts give an intuitively straightforward way of implementing fairly complex situations, such as checkpointing long-running applications.

I mentioned earlier how, in dynamic subnets, there is a "mother" process that monitors the execution of its daughter processes and can "revive" them after they have all closed down. However, since the subnet cannot close down until all IPs have been received at all input ports, what would be the point of ever waking up the subnet again? Well, if that was all that could be done, it would just be a performance improvement. However, we came up with an idea that we thought dovetailed in pretty neatly. Why not put markers in the data stream, such that the internal subnet thinks it is seeing end of data and will terminate, but in fact there is more data to come, so it will be revived? We did this by adding an option to composite components called *delimiter sensitivity*. This was implemented in DFDM for dynamic subnets and in FPE as an option on all composite components. Delimiter-sensitive composites essentially keep track of the bracket nesting levels at each of their input ports, and whenever this level drops to zero for a given port, the port involved is closed *on the inside,* resulting in an "end of data" indication the next time the daughter process does a receive from that port. Essentially, they make substreams on the outside look like streams on the inside. Since you can nest subnets within subnets, each level of nesting strips off one level of bracketing (call it "the application onion").

Start with one input data port only. Suppose you have a "delimiter-sensitive" composite B, which contains C and D, as shown in figure 7-2.

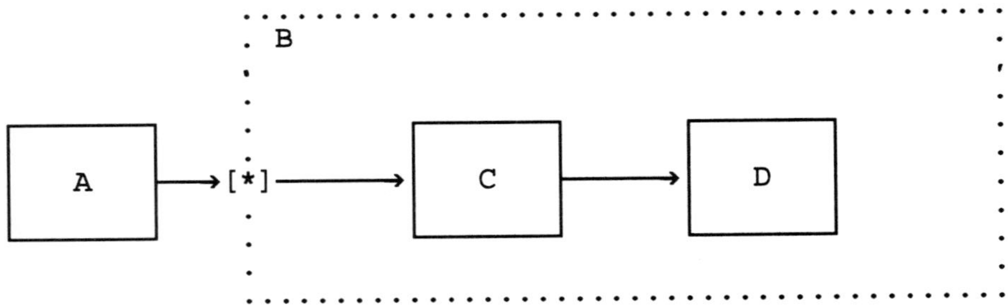

Figure 7-2.

The point shown as [*] is a delimiter-sensitive port on B. Suppose that A generates a stream as follows:

```
(a b c d e f)  (g h i)  (j k l m)...
```

reading from left to right. Then C is going to see IPs `a`, `b`, `c`, `d`, `e`, and `f` and then end of data. At end of data it terminates, as it has no upstream processes at the same level *within its enclosing composite,* enabling D to terminate also. If D was a Writer, it would then close the file it was writing to. However, you know (although the subnet doesn't) that C and D are not permanently "dead"—when the next open bracket arrives at B's input port, they will both be revived. As far as C and D are concerned, IPs `a` through `f` constitute a complete "application," but, as far as B is concerned, each substream, (e.g., `a` through `f`) results in a single activation of the internal subnet.

What happened to the brackets? Well, you could add a process to remove the enclosing brackets of a substream, but it seemed a good idea to give delimiter-sensitive ports the ability to drop the brackets if the designer wants. However, you may not always want this. For instance, if D was outputting IPs to B's output port, you might want to be able to put the brackets back on again.

In this example, you can see the insides of a composite working like a complete application within each activation of a composite. The power of this concept is that you can match levels of composite component to levels of nesting of substreams. So, *substream* structure can be related to *subnet* structure. This very powerful and elegant idea came from Herman van Goolen, of IBM Netherlands. It should now be clear why we use brackets both to delimit substreams and as the delimiters that (delimiter-sensitive) composites respond to.

If there is more than one input port on a delimiter-sensitive composite component, as described earlier, the composite will process one substream from each input port successively until all the input ports are exhausted. Processing these input streams will therefore be synchronized at the substream level. Other kinds of synchronization are also possible, of course, but we have found this type to be generally the most useful. It also ties in nicely with the requirements of check-pointing (see chapter 20).

8

Building Components and Some More Simple Applications

I am now going to describe some simple applications mixing reusable components and custom ones. We start with a fairly simple text processing application to make a few points about the design of applications in FBP. This is a classical programming problem, originally described by Peter Naur, commonly known as the "telegram problem." This consists of a simple task, namely to write a program that accepts lines of text and generates output lines of a different length, without splitting any of the words in the text (assuming that no word is longer than the size of the output lines). This turns out to be surprisingly hard to do in conventional programming and therefore is often used as an example in courses on conventional programming. Unless the student realizes that neither the input nor the output logic should be the main line, but that the main line has to be a separate piece of code whose main job is to process a word at a time, the student finds him or herself getting snarled in a lot of confused logic. In FBP, it is much more obvious how to approach the problem, for the following reasons:

1. Words are mentioned explicitly in the description of the problem.
2. Since we have to design the data streams between each pair of processes, it is reasonable for the designer to treat words as IPs *somewhere* in the implementation of the problem. It would actually be counter-intuitive to deliberately avoid turning words into IPs, given the problem description.
3. There is no main line, so the student is not tempted to turn one of the other functions into the main line.

Now let us step through the coding of this problem. There should be IPs representing words somewhere in the application. You will have realized also that there should be a Read Sequential on the left of the network, reading input records from a file, and a Write Sequential writing the new records onto an output file. A partial network is shown in figure 8-1.

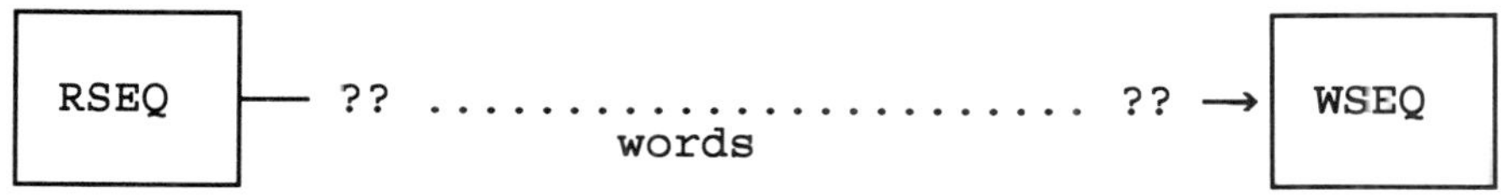

Figure 8-1.

Now the *output* of Read Sequential and the *input* of Write Sequential both consist of streams of IPs containing words and blank space, so it seems reasonable that what is needed, at minimum, is a component to decompose records into words and a matching one to recompose words back into records. Given the problem as defined, I do not see a need for any more components, but I want to stress at this point that there is no single right answer. Remember ROI? What you select as your basic black boxes depends on how much they are going to be used versus how much it costs to create them.

Figure 8-2 shows the two new components added into the picture.

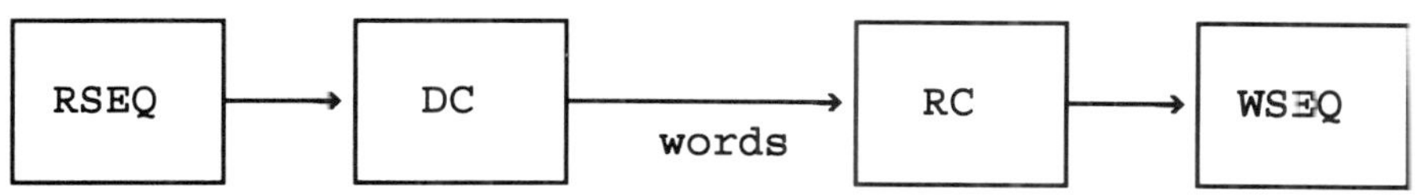

Figure 8-2.

Now we have another matched pair of components. In the figure they are labeled DC (for DeCompose) and RC (for ReCompose). Components can always find out the actual size of any IP, so we do not have to provide the size of the incoming IPs to DC as a parameter. However, RC cannot know what size of IPs you want it to create, so this size must be passed as a parameter to its OPTIONS port (I didn't have to call it that, but it is good a name as any). Figure 8-3 shows an options IIP on RC. RSEQ and WSEQ will also need to know the identifiers of the files they are working with.

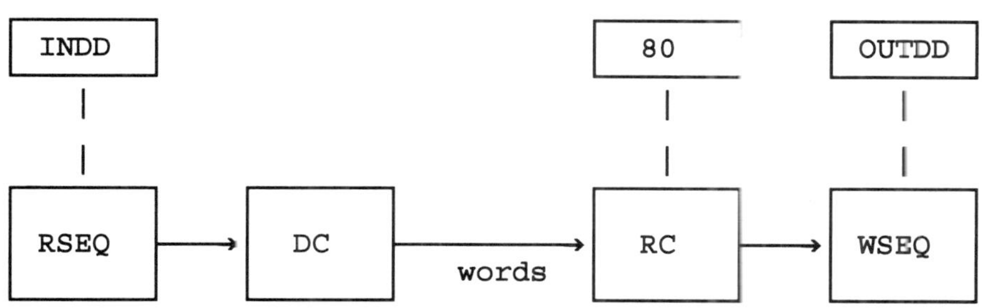

Figure 8-3.

For completeness, I will give some possible pseudocode for DC and RC. Remember that, once you have written and tested DC and RC, you have them forever. So it is worth the effort to get them "perfect" (or as close to perfect as software ever gets). Or you can do a rough and ready version first, and refine it later. One of the great advantages of FBP is that you can simply insert a Display process on any connection (e.g., between DC and RC) to see if the IPs passing across that connection are correct. So testing is very easy.

In the coding that follows, I have assumed (but have not shown) that the input port of both components is called IN and the output port is called OUT.

```
DC (Decompose into Words):

     define switch "in word" - initially off
     receive from IN using a
     do while receive has not reached end of data
          start at beginning of input IP
          do while not yet end of input IP
               if "in word" off and current char blank OR
                  "in word" on and current char non-blank
                    do nothing
               else
                    invert state of "in word"
                    if "in word" now on
                         save pointer
                    else
                         create word IP of same length as
                           word we have just scanned off
                         copy word to new IP
                         send created IP to OUT
                    endif
               endif
               step pointer to access next character
          enddo
          if "in word" on
               create word IP of same length as
                 word we have just scanned off
               copy word to new IP
               send created IP to OUT
          endif
          drop a
          receive from IN using a
     enddo

RC (Recompose Words into Records):

     receive word IP from IN using a
     do while receive has not reached end of data
          create output IP and set it to all blanks
          start at beginning of output IP
```

```
        do while output IP not yet full
             if received word will not fit into record IP
                  leave innermost loop
             endif
             move contents of word IP into output IP
             if there is room for 1 more character
                  move in single blank
             endif
             drop a
             receive word IP from IN using a
             if receive reached end of data,
                  leave innermost loop
             endif
        enddo
        send record to OUT
   enddo
```

Maybe this logic can be simplified, but a component does not have to be simple *on the inside*. It should be simple *on the outside*, and above all it must work reliably. This point really illustrates a fundamental difference between conventional programming and FBP: I have just shown some pseudocode, and you may be feeling that we are back to conventional programming. However, another way of putting what I am trying to say is that, because we *can* program, it does not mean that we *should*. Most conventional programming and even some of the new object-oriented approaches still stress the production of *new* code. Many reuse approaches are based on finding what source code is available and reusing it. Because code is such a malleable medium and does not have an inherent component structure, we are always creating new stuff and we forget that the results of our work may live long after us and that there is a cost to maintaining, documenting, and managing them. How many times have you heard, "It's less trouble to write my own than to find out what's out there"? In FBP, the orientation is the exact reverse—use what's out there, and only build new if you can justify the effort in terms of ROI. This is where experience becomes valuable. After you have done the same job many times, you *know* whether other people will find components like DC and RC useful. If you know they won't, find another way to do the job!

Now you have a matched pair of useful components, but, of course, you don't have to use them together all the time. Suppose you simply want to count the number of words in a piece of text. The Count component was mentioned in chapter 3—it simply counts all its incoming IPs and generates a count IP at the end. It has an option that is substream-sensitive (it generates one count IP for each incoming substream), but for now we will just use it in its most basic form. In this form, it simply sends the count it has just calculated out via one output port, while the original incoming IPs are sent out of another one *if it is connected* (this is an example of an *optional* port). This type of component is sometimes called a "reference" component, meaning that the original input IPs are passed through unchanged, while some derived information is sent out of another output port. So the resulting structure will look something like figure 8-4 (don't bother to connect up Count's optional output).

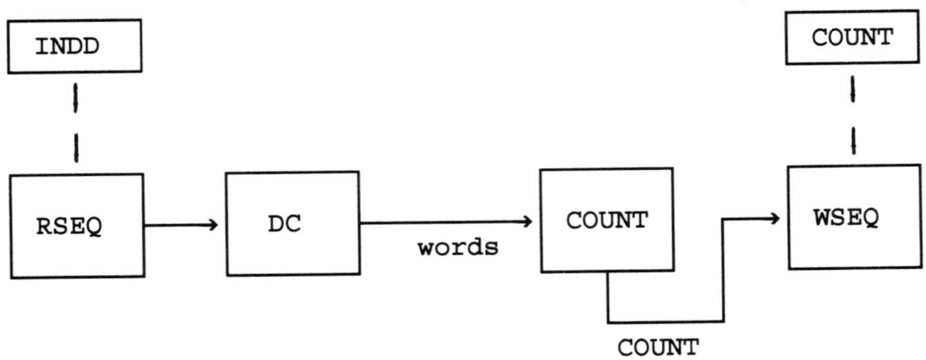

Figure 8-4.

You can keep on adding or changing processes indefinitely! These changes may result from changing or new requirements, or simply the realization that you can use a component that was developed for one application on another. I talked in chapter 4 about some of the principles behind designing components for reuse.

As another more elaborate example, instead of counting the words, you could sort them, alphabetically or by length. Once the words are sorted alphabetically, it might be nice to be able to insert fancy heading letters between groups of words starting with the same letters, like some dictionaries. Of course, once they are sorted, you should eliminate duplicates. The resulting diagram would then look like figure 8-5. In the figure, RDUP means "Remove Duplicates" and IHDRS means "Insert Header Letters."

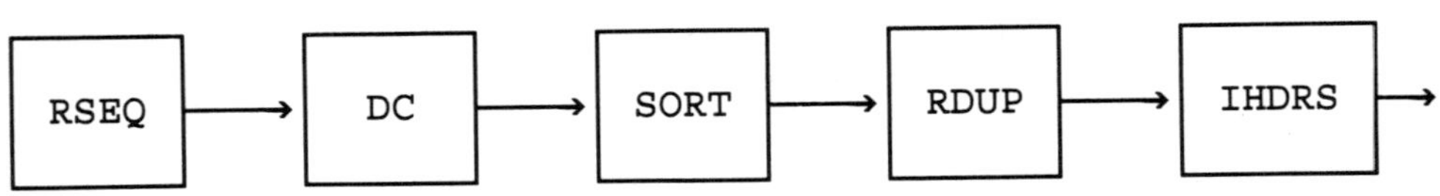

Figure 8-5.

It will come as no surprise that text processing applications have been very productive of generalized components. This is also the application area where the UNIX system has proven very productive. The UNIX pipe mechanism is very similar to FBP's data streams, except that UNIX communication is based on using streams of characters, whereas FBP's communication is by means of structured IPs.

An excellent example of this kind of text-processing application is P.R. Ewing's publication a few years ago of a Concordance to the Ukrainian Bible (1988). This was programmed using DFDM, which Philip found to be very well suited to this type of work. He has recently completed a Biblical Concordance for Xhosa (one of the languages of South Africa), using the PC-based THREADS software. He reports that, after spending between 100 and 150 hours trying to develop this Concordance using conventional (non-FBP) software, he eventually had to abandon it unfinished. With THREADS he was able to produce a completed Concordance with about 40 hours of work (not including the time needed to input the Bible text). He told me that, as far as he was concerned, the big advantage of FBP is the fact that it *simplifies* the complexity of an application, and 40 hours vs. more than 100 hours certainly seems to bear this out.

The Sort function has been used as a component a number of times in the foregoing examples. In conventional programming, Sort is usually packaged as a stand-alone utility, although various exits are provided to allow its behavior to be modified. What are the advantages of packaging it as an FBP component? People very often have the reaction that Sort cannot be a good FBP component because it is too "synchronous"—all the input has to be read in before any of it can be sorted; then the Sort proper takes place; then all the sorted records are output by a final merge phase. However, a stream-to-stream Sort is a very effective FBP component for the following reasons:

- Performance: A Sort that is run as a separate job step has to use files for its input and output, and the control fields have to be in the same place in every input record. If a Sort is provided as a stream-to-stream component, then data IPs that are to be sorted no longer have to be written to a file first (and do not have to be retrieved from a file afterwards), but can simply be sent across a connection to the Sort, which in turn sends them on to the next process when it is finished, resulting in a considerable savings in I/O overhead. Actually, the "central" Sort phase is the only part of the Sort that cannot be overlapped with other processes.
- Flexibility of positioning control fields: If the control fields are not in a standard place for all the input IPs, you can simply insert a transform process upstream of the Sort to make the key fields line up.
- Eliminating unnecessary sorting: Sometimes, some of the IPs are known to be already sorted, in which case they can bypass the Sort and be recombined with the sorted IPs later. This is often not practical when the Sort is a separate job step.
- Improved sorting techniques: If you know something about the characteristics of your keys, you may be able to build more complex networks that perform better than a straight Sort. For instance, if you are sorting on a name field, it *might* make sense to split the data 26 ways, sort each stream independently, and then merge them back together. I don't say it *will* definitely, but you can try it out. The Sort process can thus be implemented with other components or subnets for purposes of experimentation.

Although some Sorts are faster, a good rule of thumb is that the running time of most Sorts is proportional to $n.\log n$, where n is the number of records. Since this is a nonlinear relationship, it may be more efficient to split your Sort into several separate ones.

Figure 8-6 is a picture of a Sort with some IPs going around it and with Sort tags being generated on the fly by an upstream process (GTAG).

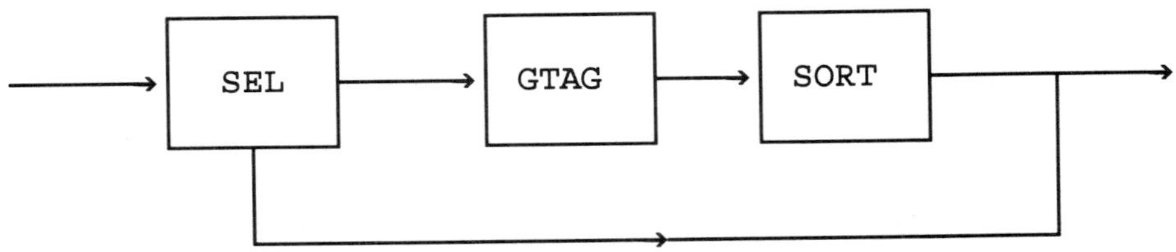

Figure 8-6.

Actually, Sort is an example of something I discovered quite early in the work on FBP: FBP enables you to tie together things that didn't expect to be tied together! If you can persuade something to accept and generate data packets, it can talk to other things that talk in terms of data. For instance, once you have converted Sort to a stream-to-stream component, it can talk to other utilities, HLLs, DB2, etc. They don't necessarily have to be callable—they just have to be able to accept and generate data once they are given control. I have written networks that contained Assembler, COBOL, and PL/I programs, all in the same network. I also built an application that used a screen manager written in Assembler, REXX for all of its calculation logic, reusable components for screen management, and GDDM/PGF for drawing charts when requested by the user. Another network spanned two CMS virtual machines, communicating by means of VMCF. This is a point we'll come back to later—you can design a big network, and then split it across different machines, processors, software systems, and so on.

Incidentally, there is a flip side to this ability to tie things together "without their knowledge": the fact that components have to be reentrant if they are going to multithread with each other. Strange things happen if you try to multithread processes that are not reentrant! After we had turned Sort into a stream-to-stream process, it seemed reasonable to want to run more than one Sort process in a single network. As long as one had fully completed before the other one started, we had no problems. When we tried to overlap two Sorts in time, strange things happened. We suspected that reentrancy was being violated, but it did not consistently cause problems. Some people reported that everything ran fine, others that their programs always crashed. After we ruled out the possibility that it was programmer-induced, we eventually figured out that some of the sort techniques used by Sort were reentrant (probably the more recent ones), and some not, so some file formats or volumes caused problems (because they triggered different sort techniques), while others did not. We decided that the safest thing to do was to interlock the Sorts so that one couldn't start until the other had finished (this is not a great solution, as it requires deciding which Sort should run first, which you will probably have realized by now runs counter to the philosophy of FBP).

This anecdote reminds me of a pitfall when using Writers to write to PDSs under IBM's MVS (even if you are not an MVS user, other operating systems support similar structures, so it may still be instructive). PDSs are data sets that contain a series of subfiles (members), with a directory at the front. A number of programmers used multiple instances of the Writer component in DFDM to try to write more than one member at the same time. What these programmers saw was that the resulting members seemed to have a mixture of each other's data. In MVS, programmers are so accustomed to treating PDS members as if they were ordinary files that it is not immediately obvious why writing two or more at the same time should cause problems. Of course, the moment it is pointed out, it becomes obvious: PDSs only "grow" at the end. If a PDS already has a member "A" and you decide to write to member "A," what actually happens is that you write the new data at the *end* of the PDS, and afterwards, when the new member is complete, the directory is updated to point at the new member (leaving what is often referred to as "gas" in the middle). If you try writing to two members concurrently, the two writer processes will see the same "end of PDS" and will both start writing at the same spot. The two processes then write blocks alternately, after which both directory entries are updated to point to the old end of the PDS! See figure 8-7.

```
 ______________________________|................
                              /    data written by process A
                             /
   previous end of PDS          ........................
                                   data written by process B
```

Figure 8-7.

Before continuing with FBP, we will describe how the "telegram problem" would be coded using conventional (control-flow) programming.

From the previous discussion, it is clear that *words* are the key concept needed to make this problem tractable. Once you realize this, you can go ahead and code it up, using something like the call hierarchy shown in figure 8-8.

As we said earlier, at first it is not at all obvious in conventional programming that this is the right way to tackle this job. Most people who tackle this problem start off by making GETWORD or PUTWORD the "boss" program and promptly get into trouble. So we now realize that we have to "bring in a boss from outside" (call it MAIN), instead of "promoting" GETWORD or PUTWORD to boss. Now MAIN can call GETWORD and PUTWORD to retrieve and store a single word at a time, respectively. To do this, GETWORD must in turn call GETREC and PUTWORD must call PUTREC, to look after the I/O. Now note that all four of these subroutines have to "keep their place" in streams of data (streams of words or streams of records). In the old days we did this by writing them all as non-reentrant code, so the placeholder information essentially became global

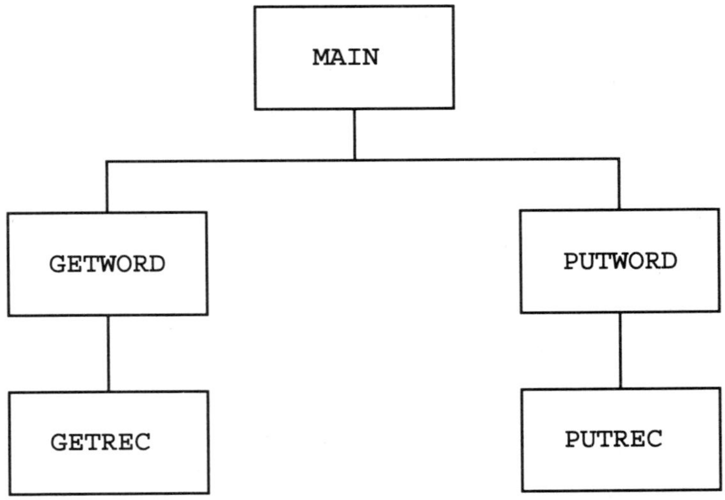

Figure 8-8.

information. This is quite correctly frowned upon as poor programming practice, since it has a number of significant disadvantages, so today this kind of placeholding logic is normally handled using the concept of "handles." The general idea (for those of you who haven't had to struggle with this kind of logic) is for MAIN to pass a null handle (in many systems this will be a pointer that is initially set to zero) to GETWORD. When GETWORD sees the null handle, it allocates a block of storage and puts its address into the handle. Thereafter, it uses this block of storage indirectly via the handle, and at the end of the run frees it up again. Although this block of storage is allocated and freed by GETWORD, it is considered to be owned by MAIN. This same logic is also used between MAIN and PUTWORD, between GETWORD and GETREC, and between PUTWORD and PUTREC. At the basic level, the problem is that subroutines cannot maintain internal information that lasts longer than one invocation. Actually, COBOL does support this, but at the cost of much greater complexity internally. In contrast, FBP components are long-running objects that maintain their own internal information. They do not have to be continually reinvoked—you just start them up and they run until their input streams are exhausted. Thus, FBP components can do the same things subroutines do, but in a way that is more robust and, something of considerable interest for future needs, that is also more distributable. It is important to note that FBP does not prevent you from using subroutines, but they are most appropriate for such tasks as mathematical calculations on a few variables, doing look-ups in tables, accessing databases, and so on—in other words tasks that match more closely the mathematical idea of a function. Such subroutines are said to be "side-effect free," and experience has shown that side effects are one of the most common causes of programming bugs. Hence, subroutines that rely on side effects for their proper functioning are a pretty poor basis on which to build sophisticated software!

Now compare this with the FBP solution shown in figure 8-3. At this point, to get back in the data flow mood, let's go back to the text-processing example mentioned earlier, where you take some text, split it into individual words, sort them, remove duplicates, insert fancy letters on every letter change, and print out the result. Oh, and print it out in two columns. Using FBP, this is quite simple—actually, I have just described the FBP network structure. I will leave this as an exercise for the reader. It also illustrates a point Wayne Stevens has made frequently—namely, that you very often want to string a whole bunch of functions together in a serial manner. You say "do A and B and C and . . .," which is basically the same as "take the output of A and feed it to B; now take the output of B and feed it to C, and so on . . ." This is exactly the same as the pipelines of the UNIX system or DOS. This is a very natural and important function, and it is essential to be able to express this kind of linkage with a minimum number of keystrokes. In the DFDM and THREADS interpretable notation, we use two keystrokes (->) to represent this relationship.

So far, our examples have been quite simple structures that string together "filters" in what is sometimes called a "string of pearls" pattern or in which one data stream generates more than one ("divergent" patterns). There is a point to be made about divergent flows: Once two streams diverge, they will no longer be synchronized. Some software systems go to a lot of trouble to keep them synchronized, but our experience is that, most of the time, it is not necessary or desirable. There are ways to resynchronize them if you really have to, but you may find it's not worth the trouble. For one thing, in the chapter on deadlocks, you will learn that resynchronization is a potential cause of deadlocks.

People very often split data streams so that different parts of their networks can handle different IP types. This works best if you do not need to retain any timing relationships between the different types. If you do, there is a variant of the "string of pearls" technique that may be useful: Have each "pearl" look after one IP type and pass all the other ones through. Its (partial) pseudocode would then look like the following:

```
receive from port IN using a
if type is XXX
     process type XXX
endif
send a to port OUT
```

You can then string as many of these together as you want, and each pearl will look after its own data type and ignore all the others.

Now it's time to talk about various types of Merge functions. There is a basic merge built right into FBP—the first-come, first-served merge. This is done very simply by connecting two or more output ports to one input port, as in figure 8-9. Ports OUT of A and OUT of B feed into port IN of C. IPs being sent out along this connection to the IN port of C will arrive interleaved. The IPs sent out by a single process will still arrive in the correct sequence, but their sequencing relative to the output of the other process will be unpredictable. When would you use this structure? Surprisingly often! C might be a Sort, so the sequence of its incoming

IPs is going to be changed anyway. The IPs from the two output streams may be easily distinguishable, so you can always separate them out later. C may be interested in receiving its input data as fast as possible—any additional sequencing may cause delays and in fact may even cause deadlocks.

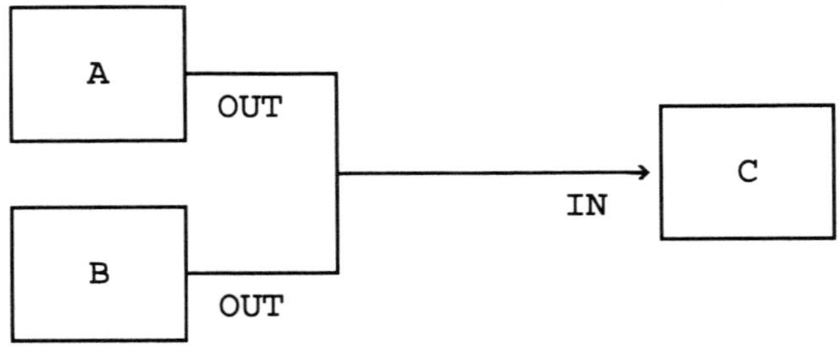

Figure 8-9.

Now perhaps the first-come, first-served merge may not be adequate, in which case you will need a process at the junction of the two streams. This may be a custom-coded merge component, or you may be able to use one of those supplied with the FBP software—for instance Collate or Concatenate. Both of these use one or more port elements of a single array port to handle their input streams, so we will use this convention. The reason for this is that this way they can handle any number of input streams up to the implementation maximum. Of course, custom components *could* call one input port JOE and the other one JIM—it's up to the developer (of course, assuming the component's users will put up with it!).

The diagram now looks like that in figure 8-10.

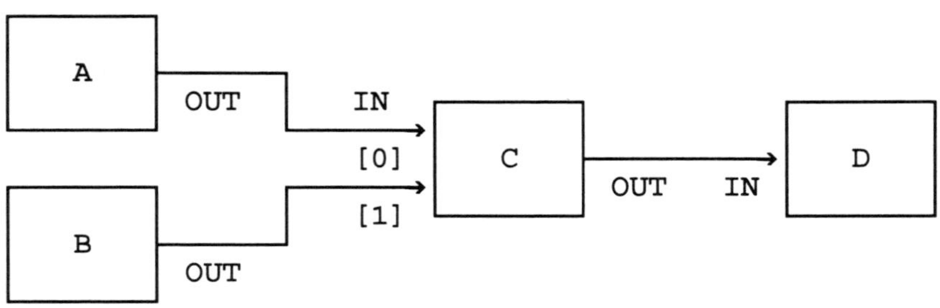

Figure 8-10.

Now you have:

- OUT of A connected to IN[0] of C.
- OUT of B connected to IN[1] of C.
- OUT of C connected to IN of D.

If C is a Collate, then the output of A will be merged with the output of B according to key values. Usually the key fields are specified to Collate by means of option

IPs. Alternatively, the Collate may use one or more named fields that will be related to the IPs by means of descriptors (see chapter 11). One might also visualize Collates that are substream-sensitive, allowing you to merge substreams based on a particular field in the first IP of each substream.

Now, if you were to use Concatenate instead of Collate, then what you are saying is that you want C to send all of A's output on to D before it accepts any of B's output. As said earlier, there are some situations where this can be useful, too. Collate, however, is a very powerful component and, in conjunction with the ideas described in the next chapter, significantly simplifies application programs that are extremely complex when using conventional programming techniques.

9

Substreams and Control IPs

This chapter will expand on the use of the Collate component mentioned in the previous chapter. It will also show how Collate, substreams, and control IPs can be combined to address one of the most difficult types of conventional business batch application. The main function of Collate, just as it was for the Collator Unit Record machine from which it gets its name, is to merge the IPs in its incoming data streams based on values in key fields (the definition of these key fields is normally specified in an options IP). In most applications there is more than one key field, which are used to specify different *levels* of grouping. As an example, consider a file of bank accounts within branches. In this particular bank, say that account numbers are not guaranteed to be unique across branches, so branch and account numbers must be combined to uniquely identify an account. Suppose there is an application where a stream of banking transactions must be run against a stream of account records. First sort both streams by account number within branch number. Now, in conventional programming, you would have to write an "update" program. I once figured that something like a quarter of all business programs running today are updates! Whether or not that is the right figure, update programs are hard to code and harder to modify, and yet the only assistance programmers have ever received is a piece of paper, handed down from father to son, showing the basic logic for updates, which is a pattern of moves and compares usually called the "Balance Line" technique. This logic then has to be modified by hand to suit the particular situation you are faced with. However, it is still only a description of an approach—to adapt it to a particular application you have to massively modify it. I once had the dubious pleasure of having to modify an update program whose author had written the client an explanation of why his request could not be satisfied, which started: "Owing to the limitations of data processing . . ." My clear recollection, after almost 25 years, is that modifying that program (and, for a conventional program, it was really quite well written) was *not quite* impossible!

Now imagine what you could do if you had a prewritten, pretested component for collating data streams. Imagine that there is a stream of transactions and a stream of accounts, both sorted by account number within branch. Now collate them into a single stream, specifying branch number and account number as major and minor control fields, respectively. When Collate finds two equal records from two different port elements, it outputs the one from the lowest-numbered element first. The resulting output stream will contain the sort of pattern shown in figure 9-1.

```
IP type      branch    acct #      date        amount    DEP/WD

account        1         1
trans          1         1      1992/3/12      12.82      DEP
trans          1         1      1992/3/12     101.99      WD
trans          1         1      1992/3/12      43.56      WD
trans          1         1      1992/3/26      54.77      WD
trans          1         1      1992/3/26      12.26      WD

account        1         2
trans          1         2      1992/3/03      34.88      DEP
trans          1         2      1992/3/03      10.00      WD
   .
   .
   .

account        2         1
trans          2         1      1992/2/29      25.99      DEP
trans          2         1      1992/3/25      87.56      DEP

account        2         3
trans          2         3      1992/3/01      34.88      WD
trans          2         3      1992/3/17      88.22      DEP
   .
   .
```

Figure 9-1.

Notice that the effect of Collate operating on sorted input streams is to give a nicely sequenced and grouped data stream, consisting of two kinds of data IP. The job of the process downstream of Collate is therefore much simpler than the conventional Balance Line, which has to do this grouping as well as implement the required business logic. A conventional update also has to worry about what happens if one file is exhausted before the other. Instead, in our FBP solution, the actual business logic (as compared with all the logic of synchronizing the two data files) sees one IP at a time, determines its type, and decides what to do with it. In what follows, I will call this process UPDATE_ACCTS. One rule of thumb in conventional programming is that the complexity of a program is roughly proportional to the square of the number of input files. Just one reusable component, Collate, therefore, can reduce the complexity of UPDATE_ACCTS significantly.

So far I have talked about the branch and account levels. Now assume that you want to group transactions by date—bank statements often show only one subtotal per day. This then gives three grouping levels, most of which are only recognized by changes in control fields. A change of account number is recognizable by the arrival of a new Account IP, but this cannot tell you when you have started a new branch. So a lot of the logic in a conventional update is keyed to *changes in value* of control fields. Now Collate has to look at all the control field values anyway, so it would be nice if Collate could figure out the groupings and pass that information to downstream processes, which would therefore be relieved of all this comparing to see when a given group starts or finishes. How does Collate pass this grouping information downstream? You guessed it! We use the "bracket" IPs mentioned in chapter 3.

Bracket IPs have a recognizable type that follows a special convention so that they can never conflict with user-defined types. Brackets come in two flavors: open and close brackets. They may also contain real data (if their IP length is nonzero), which by convention is used for the name of the group they delimit. Let's get Collate to insert some brackets into its output data stream, resulting in the collated data stream, shown in figure 9-2. As before, I am using bracket symbols to represent open and close bracket IPs, but this time the names of the groups they refer to are shown in the data part of the bracket IPs ("date" means a group comprising all the deposits and withdrawals for a given date). To make things a bit clearer, I will show a "level number" (L) in front of each IP—open brackets increase the number, close brackets decrease it. Figure 9-2 shows just the first few IPs of the collated stream.

L	IP type	branch	acct #	date	amount	DEP/WD
0	(	branch				
1	(	account				
2	account	1	1			
2	(	date				
3	trans	1	1	1992/3/12	12.82	DEP
3	trans	1	1	1992/3/12	101.99	WD
3	trans	1	1	1992/3/12	43.56	WD
3	)	date				
2	(	date				
3	trans	1	1	1992/3/26	54.77	WD
3	trans	1	1	1992/3/26	12.26	WD
3	)	date				
2	)	account				
1	(	account				
2	account	1	2			
2	(	date				
3	trans	1	2	1992/3/03	34.88	DEP
3	trans	1	2	1992/3/03	10.00	WD
2	)	date				

Figure 9-2.

Generally, the logic of UPDATE_ACCTS will consist of a "case" statement based on the type of the incoming IP. An open bracket will cause counters and totals for the correct level to be initialized to zero; a close bracket will cause an IP containing the counters and totals for that level to be sent to an output port. You won't even have to reinitialize the counters and totals at this point because another open bracket will be coming along shortly (or end of data). You can either update the counters and totals at every level for every incoming data IP or just roll the values into the next level up at close bracket time—it seems simpler to choose the latter. There is some redundancy in this particular data structure, as an account IP is always immediately preceded by an account open bracket, but this is much better than not having enough data. Since you will be needing information from the account IP, just ignore the account open bracket or do a cross-check that they are both present (belt and braces programming—that's suspenders for American readers!).

So far the main piece of logic for UPDATE_ACCTS (the process downstream of the Collate) looks roughly like this:

```
receive incoming IP
begin cases based on IP type
    case: open bracket for branch
       initialize counters and totals for branch

    case: open bracket for account
       initialize counters and totals for account

    case: open bracket for date
       initialize counters and totals for date

    case: account
       pick up account info

    case: transaction
       increment counter for debit or credit
       add amount to debit or credit total

    case: close bracket for date
       output IP containing counters and totals for
         date
       roll these values to account level

    case: close bracket for account
       output IP containing counters and totals for
         account
       roll these values to branch level

    case: close bracket for branch
       output IP containing counters and totals for
         branch
end cases
```

Notice that these groupings are perfectly "nested," and at any point of time we are only looking at one level or at most two adjacent ones. This suggests that this kind of logic can be handled very elegantly using a push-down or "last in, first out" (LIFO) stack. Remember that this is a storage structure that is added to and removed from at one end only. We also have to decide what kind of data structure to use to hold all these counters and totals in. One possibility would be an array, but for each level you have to eventually output an IP containing the values for that level, so why not hold the values in IPs all the time? This kind of IP is called a *control IP,* and it can be described as an IP whose lifetime corresponds exactly to the lifetime of a substream, which it can be said to "represent."

Now you can put all these techniques together and deduce that you will be working with a *stack containing control IPs* (actually their handles). So the above logic becomes much simpler. It now reads something like this:

```
receive incoming IP
begin cases based on IP type
    case: open bracket
       create IP for this level
       initialize counters and totals for this level
       push IP onto stack

    case: account
       pick up account info, insert into account IP

    case: transaction
       increment counter for debit or credit in IP
         currently at head of stack
       add amount to debit or credit total in IP
         currently at head of stack

    case: close bracket
       pop IP off stack
       roll counters and totals in this IP into IP
         currently at top of stack, if there is one
       output IP which was just popped off stack
end cases
```

What `create IP` in the above logic means is that you may simply use the incoming IP if there is a characteristic type at the beginning of the group. Bear in mind, however, that the IP must have data fields in it for the totals. The most obvious technique is to create a control IP, copy fields such as identifiers across from the incoming IP (frequently the one after the open bracket) into the control IP, stack the control IP, and throw away the original incoming IP. However, a faster technique that can sometimes be used is to arrange for the incoming data to be put into a bigger IP at the time it is read in by the application. It can then be stacked immediately, without the tedious "create new, copy, destroy old" sequence.

Now that you have your control IPs, what do you use as a stack? AMPS had a stack mechanism specifically for this kind of logic, which was actually a kind of connection (one that was only attached at one end, like a cul de sac street in a city). The later versions of DFDM did not provide stack mechanisms, but, since programmers were only dealing with one component, it was easy enough to set up an array of IP handles in the process's working storage and "push" and "pop" (the basic stack operations) by incrementing or decrementing an index over the array. However, I happen to like stacks, and you will see in a later chapter that there are striking similarities between the way components parse their input streams and the way compilers parse their input. In both cases stacks are the natural mechanism for keeping track of nested structures. We have accordingly provided a stack mechanism in THREADS.

You may have noticed that the last two sets of pseudocode did not have the familiar `do while receive has not reached end of data`. This is because they are written in a style that assumes that they end execution after processing each IP. In FBP an inactive process will be invoked the next time an IP arrives at any of its input ports, so this kind of component will be invoked once for each incoming IP. A result of this is that it cannot maintain continuity across multiple IPs, but this is where the stack comes in. Since the stack is outside the process's local storage, continuity can be maintained across the invocations using the stack. This style of component is called a "non-looper," as opposed to components written in the `do while receive has not reached end of data` style, which are referred to as "loopers." This is not an externally detectable attribute of a component, but just depends on when and how often the component decides to end processing—as long as there is data to be processed, it will continue being reinvoked.

You may be wondering what the advantages of non-loopers are, if any. Well, for one thing, non-loopers end execution more frequently, so IPs that have not been disposed of are detected sooner, making such errors easier to find. Also, non-loopers' local storage is only used within one invocation, so there is less opportunity for one IP's logic to interfere with another's. Finally, you will see in chapter 20, "Synchronization and Checkpoints," that there is an advantage to having processes yield control as often as possible. As always, there are pros and cons.

Obviously, there is still some application logic left to be written for UPDATE_ACCTS, but I have tried to show that the approach of holding control IPs in a stack (together with a generalized Collate) does significantly simplify the remaining piece of logic you do have to write. One of the things that also makes this logic simpler is the fact that every action is associated with the arrival of a distinct type of IP (this is even more obvious in the case of non-loopers) rather than a *change* in value. This is what allows one to cleave the logic of such a component into distinct self-contained cases. When talking about such logic, it is often useful to refer to "open bracket time," or "detail time." An incoming IP triggers an action, which starts up and then finishes, readying the process for the arrival of the next IP (or end of data). In a later chapter, I will try to show that the code still to be written has such a simple structure that you can begin to think about generating it semi-automatically from some kind of specification other than an HLL program.

By the way, as you work through this kind of logic, you may notice a characteristic flavor of FBP coding. Very little of the data you will be dealing with actually resides in a process's working storage. The vast majority of it will be in IPs, very often control IPs like the ones just discussed. When you think about it, this should not be that strange. In a real-life office, most of the data is in files, in memos, or on the computer. How much data do you have to hold in your personal short-term memory? I don't know about you, but I try to hold onto as little data as possible for as short a time as possible (after which it gets destroyed, passed along, or filed—just like IPs).

10

Some More Components and Simple Applications

This chapter will cover a more complex example, the Sales Statistics application found in Burt Leavenworth's paper, "Non-Procedural Data Processing" (1977). In the paper, Leavenworth describes an application in which a sorted detail file of product sales is run against a product master file, producing an updated master file and two reports: a summary by product and a summary by district and salesman. Figure 10-1, which originally appeared in my paper in the *IBM Systems Journal* (1978), shows the FBP process network for this application.

In the conventional approach to building this application, the programmer would first split off the district/salesman summary into a separate job step preceded by a Sort. This leaves a function that accepts two input files and generates three outputs (updated master, product summary, and Sort input, also referred to as extended details). This function must pass details against masters, take care of the fact that one of the files will usually terminate before the other, handle control breaks, detect out-of-sequence conditions, and so on. As I said in the previous chapter, the Collate component is the key to simplifying this kind of application.

The output of the Collate component consists of sequences of groups, called "substreams," each consisting of an open bracket, a master, zero or more details, and a close bracket.

This is shown schematically in figure 10-2.

J-D. Warnier (1974) uses a vertical form of the diagram in figure 10-2 to define the input and output files of an application and uses this to determine the structure of the code that will process them. Unfortunately, control flow programming requires that one of the files has to become the driver in terms of the overall program structure, so that, if there are any significant differences between the structures of the different files, the program structure becomes less and less easy

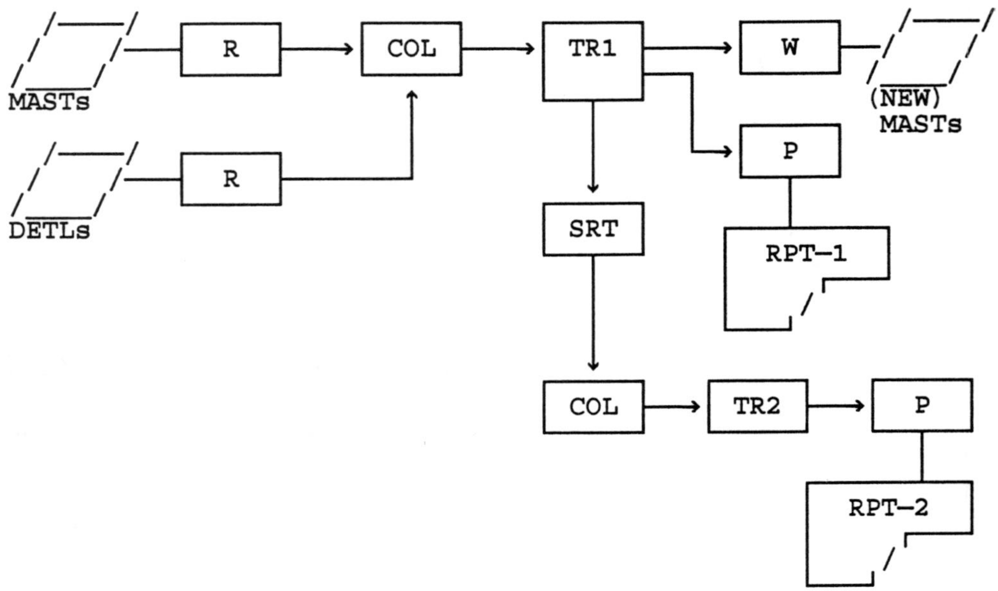

where

R is a Read component.

W is a Write component.

COL is a generalized Collate that merges two or more streams on the basis of specified control fields and inserts bracket IPs between IPs with different control field values. (If used with only one stream, it simply inserts bracket IPs – this is the case in the second occurrence of COL.)

P is a Print component.

TR1 and TR2 correspond to Tran1 and Tran2, respectively, in B. Leavenworth's paper

SRT is a generalized "Sort" component that Sorts the Extended Details coming out of Tran1, by Salesman within District.

Figure 10-1.

```
( M1 D11 D12    ...    D1m ) ... ( Mn  Dn1 Dn2 ... Dnm )
 Substream 1                      Substream n
                     STREAM
```

Figure 10-2.

to derive and understand and hence to maintain. In FBP, this structure tells us important things about just those components that receive or send this particular stream structure, so it remains an extremely useful device for understanding the logic of the application.

The input stream for TR1 is shown in figure 10-3 as it might be expressed using an extension of Warnier's notation. Of course, in Warnier's book, this type of diagram is used to describe actual files rather than FBP streams, but it generalizes quite nicely to IPs, substreams, and streams. The last column, of course, is fields within IPs.

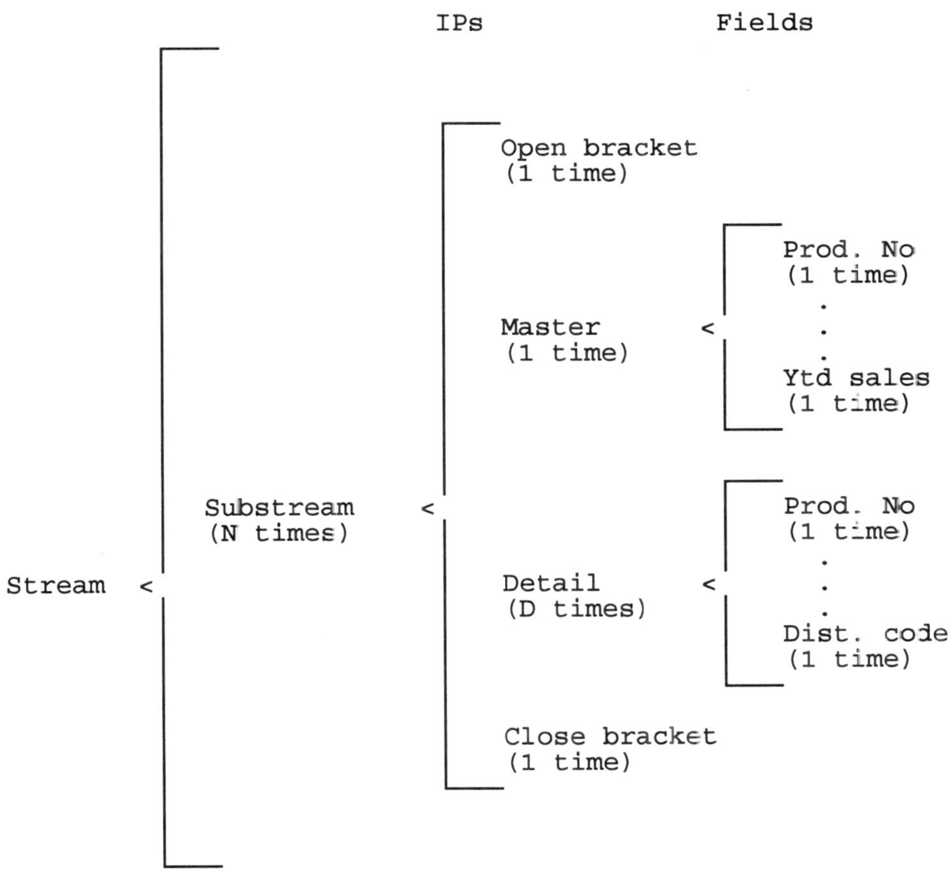

Figure 10-3.

Another methodology with close affinities to Warnier's is the Jackson methodology, already alluded to. He uses a horizontal version of this notation, using asterisks to indicate repeating items. Using his notation, this diagram might look like the one in figure 10-4.

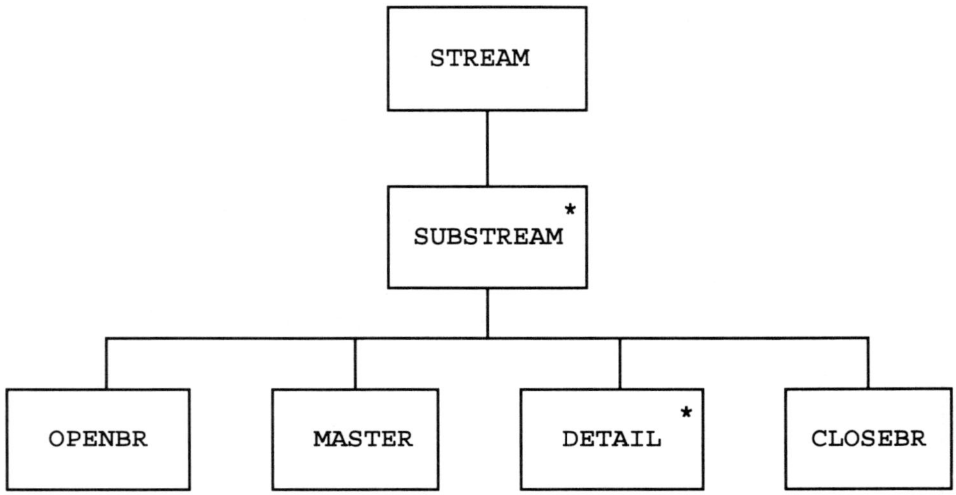

Figure 10-4.

Now, going back to the example, TR1 generates three output streams—one consisting of updated master records, one of summary records, which are similar to masters but have a different format (they are intended for a report-printing component), and one of "extended" details (detail records with an "extended price" field [quantity times unit price] added).

The following computations must be performed:

```
extended price (in detail):=
     quantity from detail * unit price from corresponding
         master record

product total (in summary):=
     sum of extended prices over the details relating
        to one product master

year-to-date sales (in summary and updated master):=

     year-to-date sales from incoming master record +
        product total
```

I have talked above about using non-loopers with stacks to handle nested streams and substreams. Adding a stack to the TR1 component gives the "blown up" picture of TR1 shown in figure 10-5 (the stack is not shown in a network definition—I just show it because it is "external" to the process).

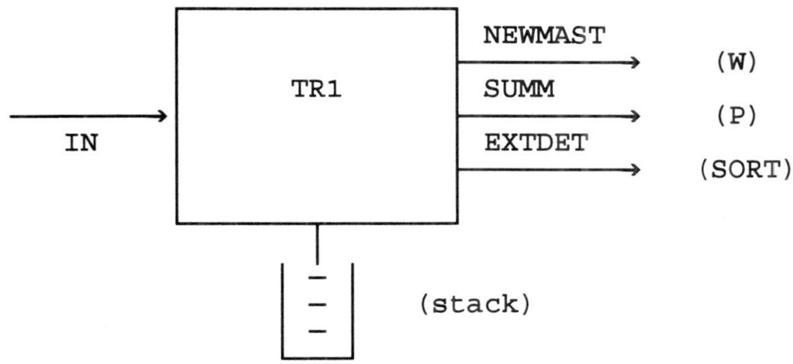

Figure 10-5.

Here is the logic that needs to be performed for each incoming IP (it is very similar to the logic shown in the previous chapter).

- At "open bracket time":
  - Create a control IP.
  - Clear the total quantity field in this new IP.
  - Store the IP in the stack.
- At "master time":
  - Obtain the control IP from the stack.
  - Copy the information from the incoming master into the control IP, such as unit price, year-to-date sales, and so on.
  - Discard the master IP.
  - Replace the control IP in the stack.
- At "detail time":
  - Obtain the control IP from the stack.
  - Update the total quantity by the quantity in the detail IP.
  - Calculate an extended price for the detail.
  - Put out the extended detail to its own output port.
  - Return the control IP to the stack.
- At "close bracket time":
  - Obtain the control IP from the stack.
  - Create a summary IP.
  - Calculate the product total (dollars).
  - Format the summary IP and put out to the summary port.
  - Create a master IP with the information from the control IP and put to the "updated master" output port.
  - Discard the control IP
  - The stack is now empty, so that when the next open bracket arrives,

a new control IP can be "pushed" onto the stack, preserving the stack depth

- At end of data, the process closes down, resulting in its output ports being closed, which in turn allows its downstream processes to start their own close-down procedures.

Note that summary and updated master IPs are not output until "close bracket time," as all the details for a given master have to be processed first.

FBP is chiefly concerned with dynamic IPs rather than with variables. Although it might at first glance seem that this would result in undisciplined use and modification of data, in fact there is better control of data because each IP is individually tracked from the moment of creation to the time it is finally destroyed, and it cannot simply disappear or be duplicated without some component issuing a specific command to do this. During an IP's transit through the system, it can only be owned by one process at a time, so there is no possibility of two processes modifying one IP at the same time. We in fact monitor this at execution time by marking an IP with the ID of its owning process. The act of getting addressability to an IP, if successful, confers "ownership" of that IP on the process doing it.

In fact, in this example almost all modifiable data is in IPs, and there is no global data at all. DFDM did not require a global facility during its earlier years, and, although it has been added to some dialects of DFDM, it is still only used very occasionally.

Figure 10-1 also illustrates how easy it is to modify this kind of network, whether it is to satisfy business requirements, improve performance, or for whatever reason. Here is what I said in my article (Morrison 1978) about how this diagram might be modified (this article uses the term DSLM for the cluster of concepts we now call FBP):

> A valid objection can be raised that sorting is just one way of arranging information into a desired sequence, and that the decision as to the exact technique should not be made too early. The point is that DSLM allows the designer to concentrate on the flow of data and in fact makes the available options more visible and more controllable. For instance, in the above example the designer may decide that, for various reasons, he prefers to construct a table of district and salesman codes and totals, which will be updated randomly as the extended details come out of TR1.

I apologize for the use of "he" and "salesman," but this was 15 years ago! I then went on to suggest that the subnet demarcated by the dots in the diagram in figure 10-6 could be replaced by a network that updates totals at random and then signals a scan and report function to display the resulting totals.

This is shown in figure 10-7, where RAND is a component that updates totals in a table at random, while SCAN goes through all the totals at end of job, generating report lines.

How does SCAN get triggered, and, once triggered, how does it get access to the table which has been built by RAND? Well, since in FBP all that moves through connections are the handles for IPs, why not have RAND just "send" the whole table? This ensures that SCAN doesn't start until RAND has finished, plus it takes

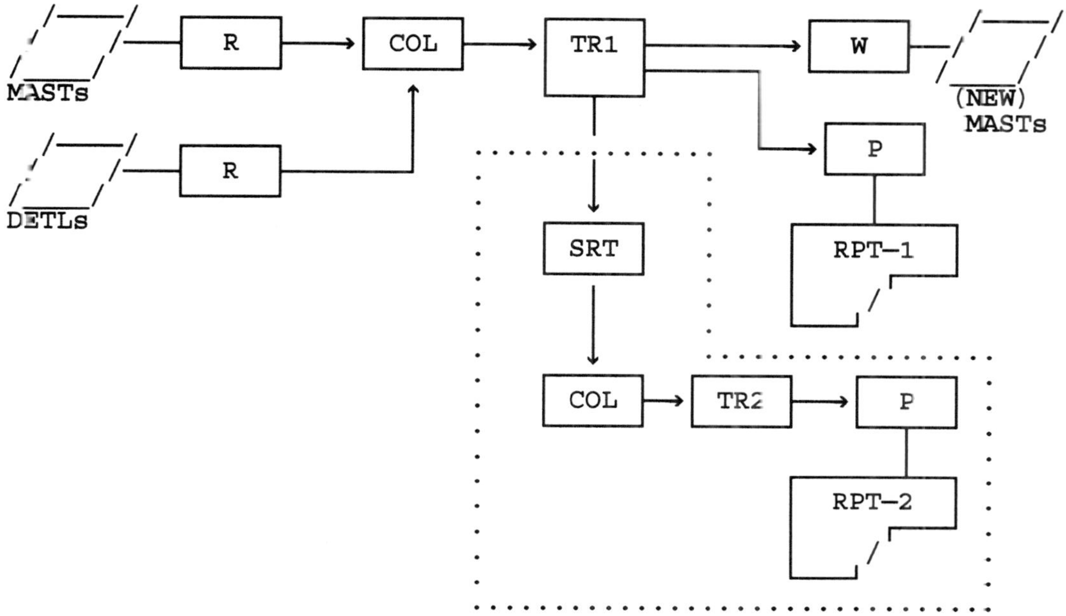

Figure 10-6.

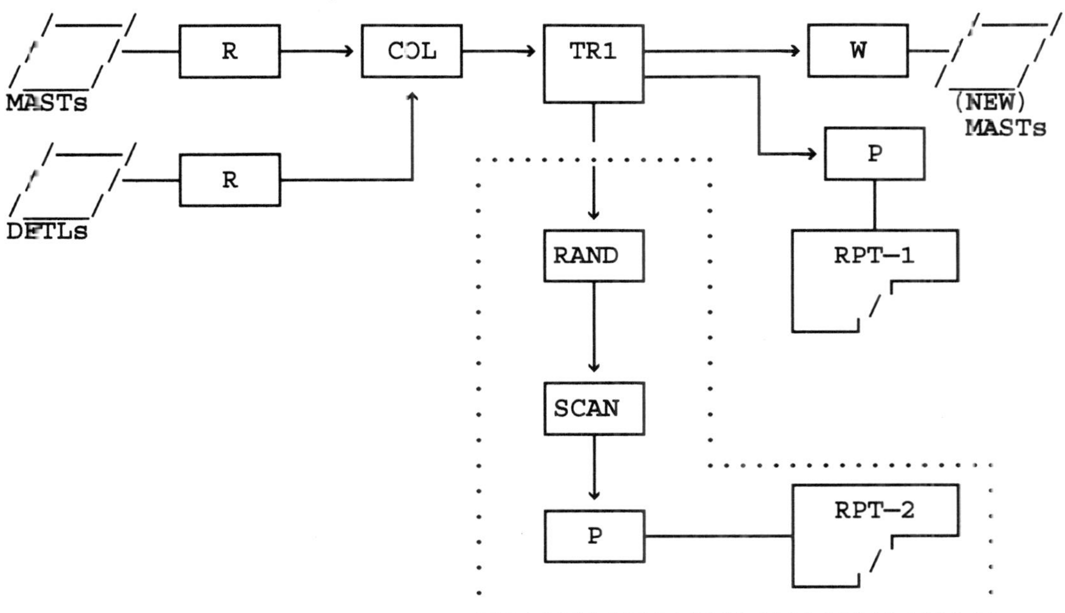

Figure 10-7.

care of SCAN getting addressability to the table—*at the right time!* In conventional programming, tables don't move around, and, in fact, in FBP they don't either, but it is very convenient to make them appear to.

I mentioned a "report generation" component earlier. You will find this essential for your batch business applications, and it illustrates the power of FBP and also FBP's ability to help you divide function into manageable components. For almost all business applications, we found that we needed a component that would accept formatted lines and combine them into report pages. An upstream process can have the job of generating the formatted lines, and this type of function should be kept separate from page formatting. FBP is a "black box" reuse tool, and in fact your Report Generator component can be used as a black box by your applications. As such, it can implement the standards for reports in your installation, and it can make it easier for programmers to conform to your standards by making it less work (definitely the best way to encourage adherence to standards). So far, so good. However, every shop has a different report standard, so you will have to build your own black box to embody your own standards. Luckily, it is easy to build new components using the FBP API calls. If you decide that you want to distribute this kind of component more widely, it seems to call for a different distribution technique: either in source format or implemented as a pure black box, but with installation-provided exits, or as a black box supporting a mini-language. Perhaps this should be called "gray box."

Here is a list of the facilities provided in the Report Generator that we used with DFDM in our shop:

- Accept two lines of permanent title information as run-time options and combine these with date information in an installation-standard format.
- Accept two dates for the run: the actual date and the effective date ("as of" date) from a specific input port.
- Accept additional title information from an additional IP stream that could be changed dynamically (on receipt of a "change title" signal).
- Generate page numbers.
- Accept a signal to reset the page number.
- Generate an "end of report" box at the end of the report (this lets the human receiving the report know it is complete)
- Generate a "report aborted" box on the report on demand.
- Support all of the above features in English, French, or bilingual English *and* French (under control of an option).

This may seem like a long list, but it basically embodied a preexisting set of shop standards, some that were supported by subroutines and some that weren't. Now, instead of having to mandate a standard that people would see as extra work, we had a component that did it "automatically." It is much easier to enforce a standard that saves people work. If they use your component, their reports will follow shop standards, and your systems will also be more reliable and cheaper to build and maintain. You can tell your developers, "We don't mind if you don't follow standards, but it'll cost you, and, if you miss your deadlines, we'll be asking for an explanation!" The same philosophy was followed in the early days of hardware development. Designers were perfectly free to create new components, but they had to carry the whole cost of development, testing, and so on, themselves. Today, it is no coincidence that the vast majority of personal computers are built around a very small number of different CPU chips. This is a variant of a point I can't stress too strongly—only by changing the *economics* of application development will you get the kind of behavior you are trying to encourage.

One last point may appear obvious at first: This Report Generator assumes that its input IPs are fully formatted report lines. Formatting of these report lines may logically be split off into separate components. Now, programmers rooted in conventional programming may feel that such rigid separation is not possible, but they have not had the experience of using a separate component that makes such separation attractive economically as well as logically. Once such a thing exists, people find that they can make intelligent decisions balancing esthetic considerations against economic ones. Without such a component, you don't even have a choice!

A component like the Report Generator can be added to your application incrementally—that is, you first get your application working with a simple line-by-line printer component and then replace that with the report generation component to produce a good-looking report. Although you are introducing more function into your application, you can predict very accurately how much time it is going to take to do this. In conventional programming, many writers have commented on the exponential relationship between size of application and resources needed to develop it. This graph typically has the shape seen in figure 10-8.

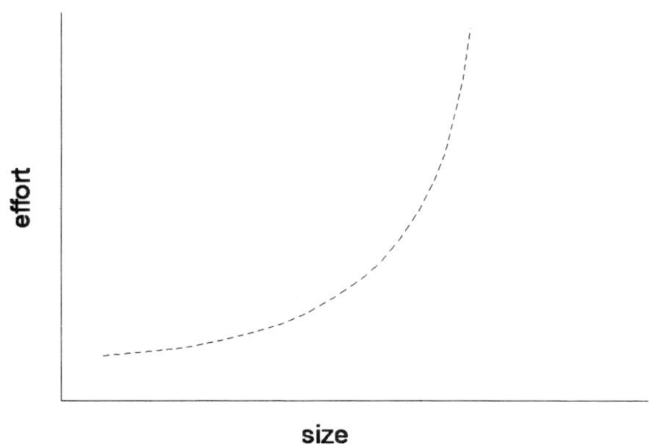

Figure 10-8.

Development using FBP shows an essentially linear relationship, as seen in figure 10-9.

Superimposing the two graphs (even allowing for the possibility that start-up costs may be slightly higher—in FBP you tend to do more design work up front) produces the picture seen in figure 10-10.

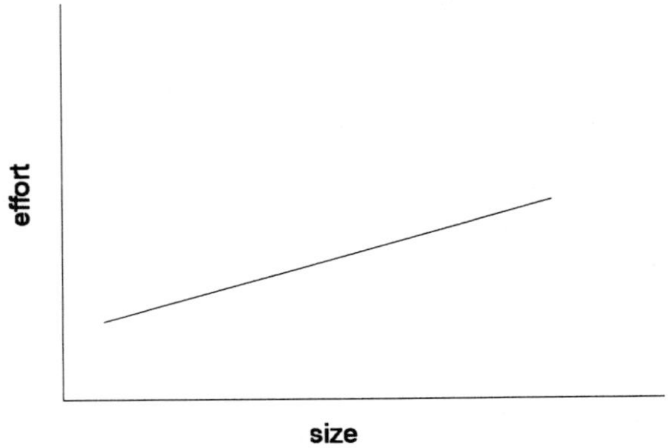

Figure 10-9.

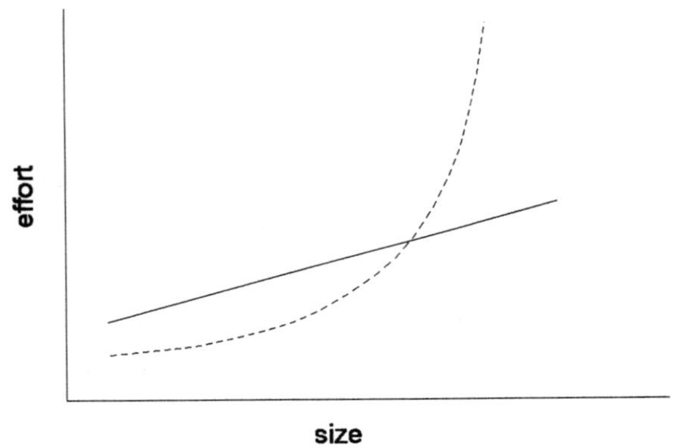

Figure 10-10.

Clearly, at some point (and this can occur even with surprisingly small applications), FBP's productivity starts to overtake that of control flow and in fact gets better the larger the application. *FBP scales up!* My colleague Chuck (he of the 200-process application) didn't have to worry that his application was going to become harder and harder to debug as it got bigger. He just built it methodically, step by step, and it has since had one of the lowest error rates of any application in the shop. Finally, in case you think that this only worked because he was a single individual who could hold it all in his head, ask yourselves what the requirements are for successfully managing a big project. Surely, some of the more important ones are exactly what FBP provides so well: a consistent view, clean interfaces, and components with well-defined functions.

11

Data Descriptions and Descriptors

Up to now, you have probably noticed that we have been assuming that all components "know" the layouts of the IPs they handle. The layouts of all IP types that a component can handle and the IP types that it can generate become part of the specification of that component, just as much as the overall function is. If you feed something raw material it can't digest, you are bound to have problems, just as in the real world!

In conventional programs, you usually use the same layout for a structure or file record in all the subroutines of a program; in FBP only each pair of neighboring processes has to agree on the layout. This means that a process can receive data in one format and send it on in a different format. If two neighboring processes (perhaps written by different suppliers) are using different layouts, all you have to do is add a transform process in between.

Now suppose you at first wanted to have two neighboring processes communicate by means of 20-element arrays. You then decide that this is too restrictive, so you stay with the arrays, but allow them to communicate the size of the arrays at run-time. This is a type of "metadata," data about data, and can be as much or as little as the two processes involved want. For instance, their agreement might specify that the array size is to be positioned as a separate field (or it could be a separate IP) ahead of the array.

Now most higher-level languages don't support metadata very well, so you are dependent on having the data formats embedded in a program. Also, it is easy for old data to get out of step with the programs that describe them. There is a perhaps apocryphal story that somebody discovered a few decades ago that the majority of the tapes in the U.S. Navy's tape library were illegible. It wasn't that the tapes had I/O errors—they were in perfect shape physically—but the problem was that the layouts of the tape records were hard-coded within code, and nobody knew which programs or copy code described which tapes! I sometimes wonder how they solved it!

In DFDM we extended the idea of metadata by providing run-time descriptions that could be attached to IPs passing across a connection. DFDM allowed the creator of an IP to attach a separately compiled *descriptor* to the IP, which was used by special DFDM services that allowed fields to be accessed by name. Whenever an IP was created, the "allocate" function could optionally specify a descriptor that was to be permanently associated with that IP. Since this is read-only data, all the IPs of the same type would share the same descriptor.

In DFDM the access services were called GETV and SETV ("get value" and "set value"). They had the advantage that, if you ever wanted to move a field (call it AMOUNT) from one place to another in the structure containing it, you didn't have to recompile all the programs referring to it. Another advantage was that, with a single call, a component could access a field that might be at different offsets in different types of incoming IP. For example, the field called AMOUNT could be at different locations in different IP types, and the component would still be able to access it or modify it, as long as the IPs had descriptors. The DFDM GETV and SETV services (and their descendants) were designed to be called from S/370 Assembler or from the HLLs we supported. They also provided limited conversion facilities between similar field formats (e.g., between 2-byte and 4-byte binary fields, between different lengths and scales of packed decimal, or between varying and non-varying character strings). Thus you could specify that you wanted to see a binary field as 4 bytes in working storage, even though it was only 2 bytes in the IP. As of the time of writing, these services have not been implemented for THREADS.

Without such a facility, the layout of incoming IPs has to be part of the specification of all components. This points up another advantage of GETV and SETV: If a component is only interested in three fields, only those specific field names have to be mentioned in the specification for the component, rather than the whole layout of the IPs in question.

When you add this facility to the idea of option IPs, you get a powerful way of building more user-friendly black boxes. For instance, you could write a Collator that specified two field names for its major and minor keys, respectively. It would then use GETV to locate these fields in the correct place in all incoming IPs. "Collate on Salesman Number within Branch" seems much more natural than "Collate on cols 1–6 and 7–9 for IP type A, cols 4–9 and 1– 3 for IP type B," and so on. Thus it is much better to parametrize generalized components using symbolic field names rather than lengths and offsets. The disadvantage, of course, is performance: The component has to access the fields involved using the appropriate API calls rather than compiled-in offsets. However, the additional CPU time is usually a negligible cost factor compared with the cost of the human time required for massive recompiles when something changes or, still worse, the cost of finding and correcting errors introduced while making the changes.

When we looked at the problems of passing data descriptions between components, we rapidly got into the problem of what the data "means": in the case of the older higher-level languages, the emphasis has always been on generating the desired machine instruction. For instance, on the IBM S/370, currency is usually held as a packed decimal field—two digits per byte (except the last byte, which has one digit and a sign), and usually amounts are held with two decimal places. Since the instructions on the machine don't care about scale (number of decimal places), the compiler has to keep track of scale information and make sure it is handled correctly for all operations. (You could conceivably use floating point notation, but this has other characteristics that make it less suitable for business calculations). Now suppose a component receives an IP and tries to access a currency field in it based on its compiled-in knowledge of the IP's layout. If the compiled code has been told that the field has two places of decimals, that's what the component will "see." So you can now do arithmetic with the number, display it in the right format (if you know what national currency you are dealing with), and so forth. But note that the layout of the IP is only defined in the code—the code cannot tell where the fields *really* start and stop. So there is a mutual dependency: The only definition of the data is in the code, and the code is tied tightly to the format of the data. If you want to decouple the two, you have to have a separate description of the data that various routines can interrogate, which can be attached to the data, independent of what routines are going to work with that data. You may decide to restrict the formats you allow, but then you have to consider what to do about "legacy" data—it may be simpler to do once-off conversions using conventional code.

Apart from format information, you also have to identify what *type* of data a field contains. For instance, the hexadecimal value

```
019920131F
```

might be a balance in a savings account ($199,201.31), but it could also be a date (31st January, 1992). Depending on which it is, you will want to perform very different operations on it. Conversely, a function like "display," which applies to both data types, will result in very different results:

```
$199,201.31
```

versus

```
31st January, 1992
```

Traditional HLLs will see both data types as FIXED DECIMAL (or COMPUTATIONAL-3). Again, only the program knows which kind of data is in the field (by using the right operations). There is also the issue of which *representation* is being used. Everyone has run into the problem of not knowing whether 01021992 is January 2 (American convention) or February 1 (British convention). So you have to record somewhere which digits represent the day, which the month, and which the year. Thus, a complete description of a data field has what might be called a "base type" (signed packed decimal), length (and perhaps scale), domain, and representation. Some systems use a standard representation for "internal" data or at least a format that is less variable than "external" formats, but the "data about data" (metadata) items that I have just described are pretty basic. (Base type could be treated logically as part of the more general domain information, but it turns out to be useful for designing such functions as "dumb" print processes.) In some systems, domain is referred to as "logical type" and representation as "physical type."

Here is another example of the pitfalls of programs not knowing what kind of data they are working with. Suppose you have coded the following PL/I statement in a program by mistake:

```
NET_PAY = GROSS_PAY * TAX_AMOUNT;
```

The compiler isn't going to hesitate for a microsecond. It will blithely multiply two decimal values together to give another decimal value (assuming this is how these fields are defined), even though the result is perfectly meaningless. Remember: Computers do what you tell them, not what you mean! A human, on the other hand, would spot the error immediately (we hope), because *we* know that you can't multiply currency figures together. The compiler knows that the result of multiplying two numbers, each with two decimal places, is a number with four decimal places, so it will carefully trim off the two extra decimal places from the result (maybe even rounding the result to the nearest cent). What it can't do is tell us whether the whole operation makes any sense in the first place!

One other (real-world) problem with currency figures is that inflation will make them steadily larger without increasing their real value. If 11 digits seemed quite enough in 1970, the same sort of information may need 13 or 15 digits in 1992. It is disconcerting to have your program report that you mislaid exactly a billion dollars (even though it is usually a good hint about what's wrong)! It would be nice if programmers could avoid building this kind of information into the *logic* of their applications. If there were an external description of a file, you could either use this dynamically at run-time or convert the data into some kind of standard internal format—with lots of room for inflation, of course! The other place where this affects systems is in screen and report layouts. These are also areas where it makes a lot of sense to hold descriptions separately and interpret them at run-time. What you don't want to do is have to recompile your business systems every time some currency amount gets too big for the fields that hold it.

This is another legacy of the mathematical origins of today's computers: everything is viewed as a mathematical construct (integers, real numbers, vectors, matrices). In real life, almost everything has a *dimension* and a *unit* (e.g., weight, in pounds or kilograms, or distance, in miles or kilometers). If you multiply two distances together, you should get area (acres or hectares); three distances give volume, in cubic centimeters, bushels, or liters. Currency amounts can never be multiplied together, although they can be added and subtracted. You could also theoretically convert currency from dollars to pounds or from francs to marks, but this is a little different, as it would need access to up-to-date conversion rate tables, and banks usually like to charge for converting from one currency to another, so it's not just a simple matter of multiplying a currency amount by a conversion factor. Dates can't even be added, although you can subtract one date from another. There is a temptation with dates to just convert them into a canonical form (number of days from a reference date—for instance, Jan. 1, 1800) and then assume that you can do anything with them. In fact, they remain dates, just represented differently, and *still* can't be added. On the other hand, you *can* do things like ask what day of the week a date falls on, what the date of the following Monday is, how many business days there are between June 30 and August 10, and so on.

The term "representation" has been used quite a lot so far. Some of the above complexities come from confusing *what the data is* with *how it is represented.* The data is really a *value,* drawn from a *domain* (defined as a set of possible values). It really doesn't matter how the data is represented internally—representation only matters when data is being handled by humans, or when a file comes from a system that does not use the same descriptor mechanism. However, it also makes a difference every time you interface with current higher-level languages. The requirements for interfacing with humans involve even more interesting considerations, such as national languages and national conventions for writing numbers and dates, which should as far as possible be encapsulated within off-the-shelf subroutines.

Multilingual support is an increasingly important area. Some Asian languages involve double-byte coding, which differs from machine to machine as well as from language to language. Computer users no longer feel that they should have to learn English to use an application, although most programmers are still willing to do so! This attitude on the part of programmers still sometimes laps over into what they build for their customers, but the more sophisticated ones know that they are living in a global market and that computers have to adapt to people, rather than the other way around. In many ways, Canada has been at the forefront of these changes, as it is officially a bilingual country, and French Canadians have historically been very insistent, and rightly so, that their language be written correctly.

If we separate the representation from the content of the data, we can look at the variety of possible representations for any given chunk of data, and consider how best to support conversion from one to another. I once counted 18 different representations of dates in use in our shop! These are all inter-convertible, provided you are not missing information (like the century). I imagine a lot of retired programmers are going to be called back into harness around the year 2000, converting programs with 6-digit dates to make them able to cope with the 21st century!

As I said earlier, the representation of data inside the machine is of less concern than the external uses of that data (being read or input by humans, being written to or read from databases, or being processed by HLLs). In some ways, this resembles the object-oriented view. However, when displaying data (e.g., numeric fields), we found that we needed "global" information to control how the data should be presented, such as:

- Currency symbol (whether required and, if so, which).
- Whether currency symbol is floating or fixed.
- Separators between groups of three digits (whether required and, if so, what symbol).
- Separators between integer part and fractional part (what symbol).
- Whether negative values should be indicated and, if so, how (DR, preceding minus, following minus, etc.)

In addition, these options usually come in "layers." There may be an international standard, a national standard, and a company standard, and a particular report may even use one or more such representations for the same domain (e.g., amounts with and without separators). Today it is not enough just to provide one conversion facility in each direction. Representations occur at the boundaries between responsibilities and, I believe, require sophisticated multilevel parametrization.

Given that you have to work with existing HLLs, probably the best thing to do is to describe fields and use smart subroutines as much as possible for all the conversion and interfacing logic. This will let you implement all known useful functions, *but it cannot prevent illegal ones.* Object-oriented and some of the newer high-level languages with strong typing are moving in this direction, but the older HLLs do not provide any protection. I suspect we will have to go further, though, as some form of dimensional analysis will probably be necessary eventually. Hardware designs may emerge that take into account the needs of business users, and when this happens, there will not be these drastic conversions back and forth between such different paradigms.

So far I have only talked about static descriptions of data. DFDM also had another type of data description that proved very useful, which we called "dynamic attributes." Dynamic attributes were also a form of metadata, but were attached to IPs, as well as to their descriptions. The first example of this that we came up with was the "null" attribute. We took this term from IBM's DB2, in which a column in a table may have the attribute of "may be null." This means that individual fields in this column will have an additional bit of information, indicating whether or not the particular *value* is null or not, meaning either "don't know" or "does not apply." Some writers feel that these two cases are different, and in fact the latter may be avoided by judicious choice of entity classes, but the former is certainly very useful. In DFDM interactive applications, we often used "nullness" to indicate fields that had not been filled in on a panel by the end user.

The "null" attribute also works well with another dynamic attribute that we also found useful: the "modified" attribute. Suppose that an application panel has a number of fields on it, some of which do not have values known to the program. It is reasonable to display "null" fields as blank or maybe as question marks. If the user fills one or more fields in, their attributes are changed to "modified" and "non-null." This information can then be used by the application code to provide user-responsive logic. We found that this kind of logic often occurred in the type of application that is called "decision assist": here you often see screens with a large number of fields, and it becomes important to know which ones have been modified by the user.

Many applications encode null as a "default" value (e.g., binary zeros), but there are a number of formats that do not have an unused value (e.g., binary), so how do you tell whether you have zero eggs or an unknown number? Does a blank street name and number in an address mean that we don't know the house-owner's full address or that he or she lives in a rural community, where the mailman knows everyone by name? Also, we saw no advantage to combining the idea of null and default—what is an appropriate default number of eggs?

Where DB2 has specific handling for the "nullness" attribute only, DFDM generalized this idea to allow you to attach any kind of dynamic attribute data to any field of any IP (e.g., "null" and "modified," but also "color," "error number," etc.). Since we felt we couldn't predict what kinds of dynamic attribute data we might want to attach to the fields of an IP, we built a very general mechanism, driven by its own descriptor (called, naturally, a Dynamic Attribute Descriptor or DAD). It allowed any number of attributes to be attached to each field and also to the IP as a whole. Thus, we had a "modified" attribute on each field, but, for performance reasons, we had a "modified" attribute on the IP as a whole, which was set on if any fields were modified.

"Null" and "modified" are of course Boolean, but we allowed binary or even character dynamic attributes. One character-type dynamic attribute that we found very useful for interactive applications was "error code." Suppose an editing routine discovered that a numeric field had been entered by the user incorrectly. It would tag that field with the error code indicating "invalid numeric value." Any number of fields could be tagged in this way. When the IP containing the screen data was redisplayed, the display component would automatically change all the erroneous fields to some distinctive color (in our case yellow), position the cursor under the first one, and put the corresponding error message in the message field of the screen. Without leaving the component, the user could then cycle through all the error fields, with the correct error message being displayed each time. This was really one of the friendliest applications I have ever used, and it was all managed by one reusable component that invoked ISPF services (under IBM's IMS you can do the same thing, but it would probably take a set of components working together).

Some writers have objected to the "null" attribute on the grounds that it introduces three-valued logic: yes, no, and don't know. Our experience was that, in practice, it never caused any confusion and in fact significantly reduced the complexity of the design of our end user interfaces.

A last point has been suggested by our study of object-oriented programming: IP types are often related in a superclass-subclass relationship. This comes up frequently in file handling. One may know that one is dealing with, say, cars, but not know until a record is read what kind of car it is. It would be very nice to be able to attach a "car" descriptor to each record as it is read in and then "move down" the class hierarchy for a given record, based on some indicator in the record. This is in turn related to the question of compatibility of descriptors: what changes are allowed between descriptors? It seems reasonable to be able to change a generic car into a Volkswagen as one gains more information about it, but not a car into, say, a beetle. In the later versions of DFDM, we decided that IP lengths should be completely specified by IP type—that is, if you created an IP with a given type, the length would be obtained from the type descriptor and couldn't be changed. The question then arises: If you change a car into a Pontiac (move from superclass to subclass), does the IP become longer, or does an "unstructured" portion of the IP become structured? Let's leave this as an exercise for the reader!

12

Tree Structures

Up to this point, I have been talking about single IPs traveling through networks, like cars and buses in a system of highways. I have also discussed how streams of IPs can be treated as higher-level entities and how these can in turn be given more complex structures by the use of "bracket" IPs. I hope I have shown that, using these concepts, quite complex applications can be handled in a straightforward manner.

However, what if you want to build more complex structures and move them through the network as single units? Streams take *time* to cross a connection, and you may want a whole data structure to be sent or received at a single moment in time. Since, as I said before, only the handles travel through the net, it is just as easy for an IP containing one bit of data to be transferred from process to process as one containing a megabyte, so why not allow complex structures to move as a unit? It turned out that there was a natural analogue to this idea in real life (which always tends to reassure us that we are on the right track!). I mentioned before the idea that IPs are like memos. You can dispose of a memo in one of three ways: forward it (send), discard it (drop), or keep it (using the various methods of holding onto IPs [e.g., stacking, saving on disk]). Of course, there is a fourth thing you can do with a memo (no, not wad it up and throw it at a neighbor): clip it to another piece of paper, and then do one of the previous three things with the resulting composite memo. Make that *four* things, actually, since you could clip the composite memo to another piece of paper, or to another composite memo, and so on.

Just as the composite memo can be sent or received as a unit, so the structure of linked IPs, called a *tree,* can be sent or received as a single object. Once a process has received the tree, it can either "walk" it (move from IP to IP across the connecting links), completely or partially disassemble it, or destroy it. For instance, the receiver might walk the tree looking for a particular kind of IP, and, for each one it finds, it could unlink it and dispose of it in one of the standard ways. Figure 12-1 shows two processes, one assembling trees and one disassembling them again.

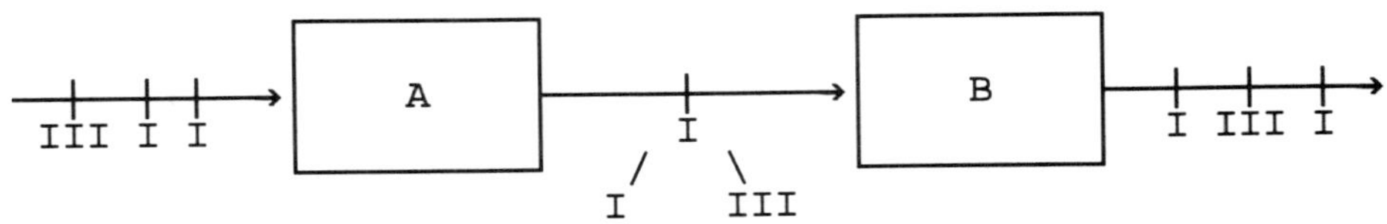

Figure 12-1.

A converts a series of three IPs of different types and sizes into a tree of IPs, and *B* disassembles the trees and outputs the component IPs (in a different order).

In all implementations of this concept so far, no IP could be attached to more than one "parent" IP, and we did not allow any loops—much like a real live tree. I do not believe we lost much expressive power by doing so. The main reason for doing this is to allow FBP's ownership and disposal rules for IPs to work.

No special software support is needed as long as the tree is assembled and disassembled within one activation of one process (activation is described in detail in the chapter 13, "Scheduling Rules"). For example, you could read in a set of IPs and build an array of pointers for sorting, all within a single process—this is in fact how a number of components work. It is only when a tree has to be passed from one activation to another or from one process to another that the IP disposition rules have to be taken into account. Thus, in figure 12-1, process *A* receives three IPs, assembles them into a single tree of three IPs, and sends it out. In this case *A* starts with an "owned IP count" of 3 and reduces it to 0 by attaching 2 IPs to the root (count is now 1) and then sending the tree as a whole out (count of 1 goes to 0). *B* receives one IP (count goes from 0 to 1) and detaches the attached IPs (count goes from 1 to 3). These detached IPs must then of course be disposed of by the normal rules. If any violations of the above rules about tree shape were allowed, it wouldn't be so straightforward to map between trees and streams.

In one application we encountered a striking example of how useful trees can be in the FBP environment. In a batch banking application, bank accounts were represented by complex sequential structures on tape. Each account record consisted of an account header, followed by a variable number of different trailer records belonging to a large number of different types (e.g., stops, holds, back items). The problem was that most of the time one could just process these sequentially, but sometimes processing later in the stream resulted in changes that should be reflected earlier in the stream. For example, an interest calculation, triggered by a particular type of trailer record, might require the account balance in the header record to be updated. You could always hold on to the header and put it out later, but then it would have to be collated back into its correct position.

Anyway, there was quite a lot of this "direct" access going on, as well as adds and deletes of trailer records. Using conventional programming, this application became fiendishly complex because all the logic had to be coordinated from a timing point of view, and there were timing conflicts between when things were required and when they became available! (We know this because originally it was coded using conventional logic, and it *was* very complex!) There were also large volumes of data involved—we had to be able to process about 5,000,000 every night. When we did this application using FBP, we realized that we could implement this application very simply and naturally by converting each account into a tree structure. Once the tree had been built, "direct access"–type processing could jump from one IP type to another within the tree structure, add or delete IPs, and so on, and then the whole thing could be converted back to linear form when we were finished. This solution turned out to be simple to understand, easy to code, and easy to maintain.

A simple tree of four IPs is shown in figure 12-2.

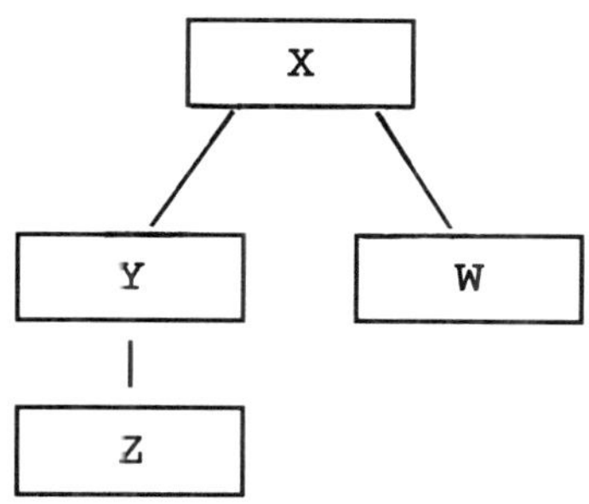

Figure 12-2.

The top box represents the "root" IP, and all the other IPs are descended from it directly or indirectly. In figure 12-2 (mixing our metaphors a bit):

- *X* is the root.
- *Y* and *W* are the daughters of *X*.
- *Z* is the daughter of *Y*.
- *Z* and *W* are leaves (terminal IPs).
- *Y* is a nonterminal IP.

AMPS and the earlier versions of DFDM took the approach that an attached IP required a pointer field to be specified as part of the mother's data. This meant that a tree structure could only be traversed using languages that supported pointers (e.g., PL/I, C), but it did have the advantage that, using these languages, we did not have to have any explicit tree traversal services. In fact, we only needed an "attach" service and a "detach" service. The more fundamental problem was that the layout of a given IP had to allow for the maximum number of children that it might have. Thus, in figure 12-2, *X* would have to provide (at least) two pointers, and *Y* one. This situation is shown schematically in figure 12-3 (with the pointers shown as *x*s).

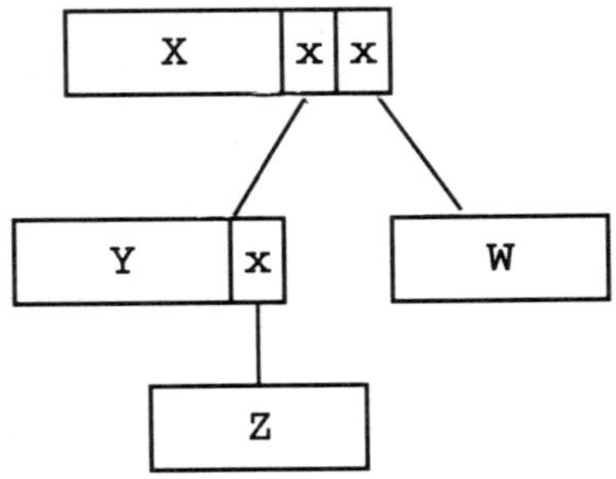

Figure 12-3.

However, if *Y* and *W* could be conceptualized as a single list (rather than two different kinds of relationships), say an employee's children, you could build "glue" IPs and use them to look after the linkage. The diagram in figure 12-3 would then look like the one in figure 12-4.

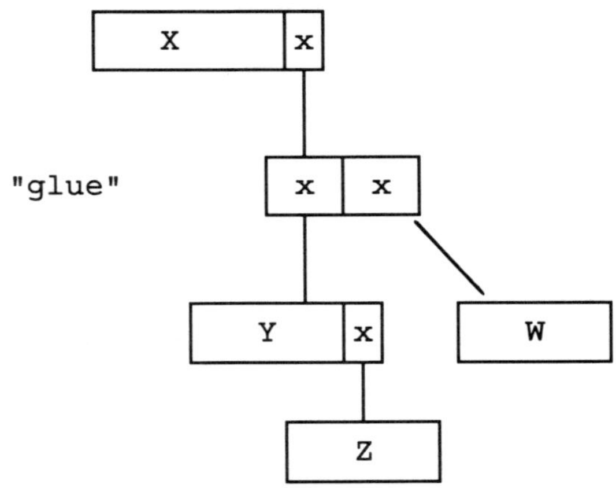

Figure 12-4.

Along these lines, the mechanism of providing space for pointers in the IP's data lets you build a wide variety of structures by creating special IP types that contain various arrangements of pointers. For example, you could build a chain by just adding a "successor" pointer field to each IP in the chain. You could build LISP-like lists by having "car" and "cdr" pointers on each IP or even only on certain reserved IP types ("glue"). My colleague Charles Douglas came up with the neat analogy that, when you use a paper clip to attach two memos together, the paper clip takes up some room on the paper!

For the Japanese DFDM product, our group felt that you should not have to preplan all the list structures that an IP might have attached to it or be part of. For instance, an employee might have lists attached to him or her, showing children, courses attended, departments worked for, salary history, and so on, and it would be very nice if this information could be added incrementally, without having to change the descriptions of participating IPs. We therefore introduced the idea of named *chains,* any number of which could be added to an IP, without that IP requiring any changes to its description. An employee IP could, for instance, have the following chains attached to it: CHILDREN, SALARY_HIST, COURSES, and so on. We then of course needed to provide traversal services and in fact built some fairly powerful services (e.g., add an IP to a named chain [it is created if it does not yet exist], get next chain [so you could walk the chains without knowing their names], get the first IP of a named chain, get next IP in a chain, detach an IP from a chain, and so forth). You could attach a chain to an IP or an IP to a chain, but not a chain to a chain or an IP to an IP. These trees thus had a less uniform structure (chains alternating with data IPs), but we felt that this still provided a powerful paradigm, and a less "programmer-dependent" approach to tree manipulation and traversal. An employee with one child, Linda, and who has taken two courses could be represented as shown in figure 12-5.

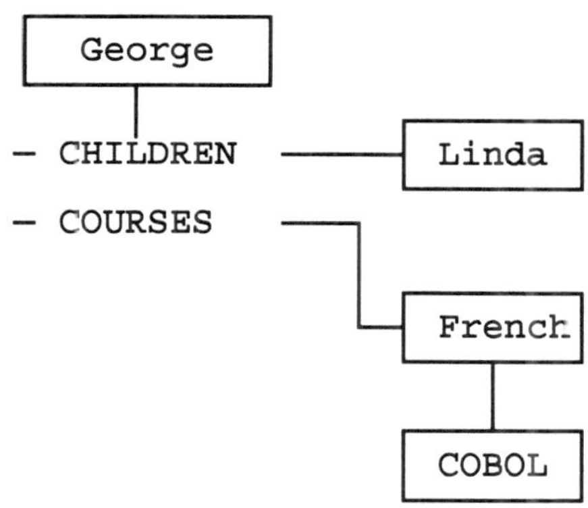

Figure 12-5.

Along the same lines as having to dispose of IPs explicitly, we had to put certain constraints on how trees could be disassembled. This is related to the above-mentioned ideas of "direct" and "indirect" descent. The root is owned *directly* by whichever process has just received it. IPs that are chained to that root are therefore owned *indirectly* by the same process (they are not owned directly by anyone, except possibly the root IP). You can only send or drop an IP you own directly—you have to detach a chained IP first, *then* send it or drop it. A process can, however, chain another IP (which it must own directly) onto an IP that it only owns *in*directly, but that's the only service it can reference it with, apart from looking at it. We also added logic to check that a process did not try to chain a root

IP onto one of its own descendants. That would have been allowed by the other rules, but would result in a closed loop!

If the above sounds complicated, try this analogy. Suppose you have just cut down a tree, and you want to dispose of it. It seems reasonable that, before you burn a branch, you should cut it off first. We could arrange that burning a branch without cutting it off first would "cauterize" the point of attachment, but this would add unnecessary complexity. Conversely, we will allow you to add leaves and branches to the tree, but only if they are not connected to another one. Also, you are not allowed to attach things to a tree in such a way that part of the tree becomes a closed loop.

One other point about trees is that hierarchic tree structures, no matter how they are implemented, can easily be converted into nested substreams like the ones described in chapter 11. For instance, the tree shown in figure 12-2 could be "linearized" as follows:

```
(X (Y Z) W)
```

where the convention is that the IP immediately following an open bracket is at the same "level" as the IP preceding the bracket, and is the "mother" of the other IPs at the same level of bracket nesting. This kind of transformation will be familiar to LISP users. In fact, I have just shown a LISP "list of lists."

In the "chain" implementation described earlier, chain identifiers have to be captured, so chain information can just be added to the left brackets, as we did in chapter 9. Thus, the tree shown in figure 12-5 might look as follows after linearization (as in earlier chapters, the "group name" is shown as the data part of open and close bracket IPs):

```
IP type     Data

(           employees
employee    George

(           children
child       Linda
)           children

(           courses
course      French
course      COBOL
)           courses

)           employees
```

This can then be easily converted back into tree format if desired. It also corresponds quite well to various database approaches: `children` and `courses` could be different segment types in an IBM DL/I database. In IBM's DB2, `employee`, `children`, and `courses` can be different tables, where `employee` is the primary key of the `employee` table and a foreign key of the other two.

One last point: Although I have stated several times my belief that IPs should be disposed of explicitly, it turns out to be very useful to be able to discard a whole tree at a time. The tree therefore has to have enough internal “scaffolding” to allow the “drop” service to find all the chains and attached IPs and discard them. The later versions of DFDM needed this anyway, so that they could provide services like “locate next chain,” but this ability to drop a whole tree turned out to be important even when there were no traversal services. Although at first it seemed that applications would always know enough about the tree structure to do the job themselves, we developed more and more generic components that understood about trees generally, but not about specific tree structures. This facility perhaps most closely resembles the “garbage collection” facility of object-oriented and list-oriented languages.

13

Scheduling Rules

So far, I have talked about processes running asynchronously, but have not discussed how FBP software manages this feat. This is a key concept in FBP, and you need to understand it thoroughly if you are to design reliable structures and debug them once they have been built. Although this subject may appear somewhat forbidding, you will need to grasp it thoroughly to understand how this kind of software works. After a bit it will recede into the background, and you will only need to work through it consciously when you are doing something complex or something unexpected happens. Of course, you are at liberty to skip this chapter, but, if you do, you will probably find some of the later chapters a little obscure.

Let us start by looking at the following component pseudocode (from a previous chapter):

```
receive from IN using a
do while receive has not reached end of data
     if c is true
          send a to OUT
     else
          drop a
     endif
     receive from IN using a
enddo
```

The job of this component is to receive a stream of IPs and either send them on or destroy them, depending on some criterion. As said earlier, this code must be run as a separate process in our application. I will use the term "component" when talking about the code and "process" when talking about a particular *use* of that code.

Before, we were looking at processes and components strictly from a functional point of view. Now instead let's look at a component as a piece of code. Clearly it is well-structured: it has a single entry point and a single exit (after the "enddo"). Once it gains control, it performs logic and calls subroutines until its input stream is exhausted ("end of data" on IN). It is therefore a well-formed subroutine. Subroutines have to be called by another routine (or by the environment) at a particular point in time. So, *what* calls our Selector component and *when?* The *what* is easy: the Selector component is called by the software that implements FBP, usually referred to as the "Driver." The *when* is somewhat more complicated: the answer is that a component is called as soon as possible after a data IP arrives at one of its input ports or as soon as possible after the start of the program if there are no input ports.

"As soon as possible" means that we do not guarantee that a process will start as soon as there is data for it to work on—the CPU may be busy doing other things. Normally this isn't a problem—you want to be sure that your process has data to work on, not the reverse! If responsiveness became a real issue, we would probably have to add some kind of priority scheme to the software. So far, the only implementation of the FBP concepts that I am aware of that implemented such a priority scheme was a system written in Japan to control railway electric substations (Suzuki et al. 1985). This software built on the concepts described in my *Systems Journal* article and extended it to provide shared high-performance facilities. None of the implementations that I have been involved with have needed this kind of facility.

The other possible start condition is what one would expect if the process has no input connections. In this case, one expects the process to be "self-starting." Another way of looking at this is that a process with at least one input connection is delayed until the first data IP arrives. If there are no input connections, the process is not delayed. Again, the process will start some time after program start time when the CPU is available.

Note that THREADS IIPs do not count as input connections for the purposes of process scheduling—when a process starts is determined by the presence or absence of connections with upstream processes. IIPs are purely passive and are only "noticed" by a process when it does a receive on an IIP port element.

Now we have started the process—this is called "activation"—and the process is said to be "active." When it gives up control, by dropping out of its logic, or by explicitly doing a RETURN, GOBACK, or the equivalent, it "deactivates" and its state becomes "inactive."

Now remember that the component kept control by looping until end of data. Now suppose the component doesn't retain control, but yields control after each IP has been processed. We therefore remove the "do while," resulting in the following pseudocode:

```
receive from IN using a
if c is true
     send a to OUT
else
     drop a
endif
```

I talked about this kind of component in chapter 9, where we called it a "non-looper," because it doesn't loop back to get more input, but just deactivates. When the next IP arrives, it is reactivated, and this will keep happening until the input data stream is exhausted. Typically, the process is activated as many times as there are input IPs. Since a process's working storage only exists from activation to deactivation, the storage of this kind of component cannot carry ongoing data values across multiple IPs. However, as we saw in chapter 9, the stack (which is outside the process's working storage) can be used for this purpose instead.

Now, unlike activation, the decision as to when to deactivate is made within the logic of the component. It is thus quite possible to have a "partial looper" that decides to deactivate itself after every five IPs, for example, or on recognizing a particular type of IP. This "looping" characteristic of a component is referred to as its "periodicity." While periodicity is determined by internal logic, it will determine whether an automatic port (see below) will generate signals or not, so it is something that should be included in the external specification of the component. For this reason, periodicity should be specifiable in terms of externally observable events. For instance, valid periodicity descriptions might be:

> "Deactivates on every incoming IP" (non-looper)
> "Only deactivates at termination time" (looper)
> "Deactivates after every high-level substream"

Consider an inactive (or not yet initiated) process with two input ports. Data arrives at one of the ports, so the process is activated. The process in question had better do a receive of the activating IP before deactivating; otherwise, it will just be reactivated. As long as it does not consume the IP, this will keep happening! If, during testing, your program just hangs, this may be what is going on. Of course, it's easy enough to detect once you switch tracing on, as you will see something like this:

```
Process_A Activated
  .
  .
Process_A Deactivated with retcode ...
Process_A Activated
  .
  .
Process_A Deactivated with retcode ...
Process_A Activated
  .
  .
```

```
Process_A Deactivated with retcode ...
Process_A Activated
  .
```

and so on indefinitely!

Our group discussed the possibility of putting checks into the scheduling logic to detect this kind of thing, but we never reached a consensus on what to do about it, because there are situations where this may be desirable behavior, as long as the activating IP does get consumed eventually. We did, however, coin a really horrible piece of jargon: such a component might be called a "pathological non-depleter" (you figure it out!). And besides, it's really not that hard to debug.

Returning to IIPs, I said that in THREADS processes read in IIPs by doing a receive on their port. If they do a receive again from the same port within the lifetime of the process, they get an "end of data" indication. This means that a component can receive an IIP exactly once during the lifetime of the process (from invocation to termination). If a component needs to hold onto the IIP across multiple activations, it can use the stack (described in chapter 9) to hold the IIP, either in the original form in which it was received or in a processed form.

So far, two basic process states have been introduced: "active" and "inactive." There are also terms for the very first activation and the very last deactivation of a process. These are called "initiation" and "termination," respectively. Before initiation, the process doesn't really exist yet for the FBP software, so initiation is important, as the driver has to perform various kinds of initialization logic. Termination is important because the driver must know enough not to activate the process again. Termination of a process also affects all of its downstream processes, as this determines whether *they* in turn are terminated (a process only terminates when all of its upstream processes have terminated).

A process may thus be thought of as a simple machine that can be in one of a small number of different "run states." The four main run states are the ones that have just been described:

- Not yet initiated
- Terminated
- Active
- Inactive

"Not yet initiated" is self-explanatory—it means that the process has never received control. All processes start off in this state at the beginning of a job step or transaction.

"Terminated" means that the process will never receive control again. This can only happen if all of a process's upstream connections have been closed. Each of the input connections of a process can be closed explicitly by that process, or an input connection will be closed automatically if all of the processes feeding it have terminated.

The underlying idea here is that a process becomes terminated if it can never be activated again. It can never be activated again if there is nowhere for more data IPs to come from. Note that, while a component's logic decides when to deactivate, termination is controlled by factors outside of the process. There is one exception to this, however—a component can decide not to be reactivated again (e.g., as a result of some error condition). It does this in both DFDM and THREADS by returning a particular return code value (or higher) to the driver. Earlier versions of FBP allowed one component to bring down the whole network, but in recent years we felt that this was not conceptually sound (parts of the network could be on different computers), so now a process can only terminate itself—no process can terminate another. There is a different way that a component can decide to terminate itself, and that is by closing its input ports. Some processes don't have input ports, but, for those that do, this has the same effect as terminating with a high return code. Of course, if a process terminates itself, this will affect its neighbors, who will in turn affect *their* neighbors, and so on.

A simple example will show why this function is needed. Suppose you have a Reader process that is reading a file of a million records, and a downstream process crashes. Under normal FBP rules, the Reader keeps reading all the records and sending them to its output port. As each send finds the output port closed, the Reader has to drop the undeliverable IP. Instead of making it read all the records, requiring a million each of "create," "send," and "drop," it is much better to bring the Reader down as quickly as possible, so it can stop tying up time and resources. Readers are therefore normally coded so that the first time they find their output port closed, they just deactivate with a high return code. This takes care of any necessary housekeeping, and eventually the whole network can close down. By the way, this practice makes sense for all components, not just long-running ones. It is good programming style for components always to test for unsuccessful sends. If this condition is detected, they must decide whether to continue executing or whether to just close down—this usually depends on whether the output port is related to the main function of the component or whether it is an optional port.

When all the processes in a network have terminated, the network itself terminates. Now, it is possible for one process to block another process so that the network as a whole cannot come down gracefully. This is called a "deadlock" in FBP and is described in some detail in a later chapter. This is however a design problem and can always be prevented by proper design. If the network is properly designed, it will terminate normally when all of its processes have terminated, and all resources will then be freed up.

Chapter 7 talked about various kinds of *composite components*. DFDM's dynamic subnets and the composite components of FPE had the ability to revive terminated processes. That chapter explained why this ability is necessary, and it will come up again in chapter 20, when I talk about checkpointing. Revived processes essentially go from the "terminated" state back to the "not yet initiated" state.

If there were a separate CPU for each process, the above-mentioned four states would be enough. However, in all FBP implementations so far, processes have to share a single CPU, so only one can be active at a time. All other processes that would, in this situation, be "logically" active have to be "suspended." This means that their internal states are saved in storage, so they can be resumed when resources become available. The inactive state must also be suspended, to avoid tying up the CPU while waiting for another IP to arrive. So, to allow an application to run on a machine with a single CPU, the active state is split into "normal" and "suspended." There are now five states:

- Not yet initiated
- Terminated
- Active normal
- Active suspended
- Inactive

At this point I would like to stress the point that a given process can only be in one of these states at a time, and, when suspended, a process can only be waiting for a single event. While you will occasionally feel that this too much of a restriction, we deliberately made this decision in order to make an FBP system easier to visualize and work with. At various times in the development of FBP systems, we were tempted to allow a process to wait on more than one event at a time, but we always found a way around it and never needed to add this ability to our model. Suppose you want to have a process, P, that will be triggered by a clock tick or by an IP arriving at an input port, whichever comes first. The rule about processes having a single state suggests that you should have two processes, one waiting on each event type. One possible solution, therefore, is to have one process send out an IP on each timer clock tick, and then merge its output stream with the IPs arriving from another source, resulting in a single stream, which is then fed to P. The overhead of the extra processes is outweighed in our experience by the reduction in complexity of the mental model and the consequent reduction in software complexity and improved performance. Figure 13-1 is a picture of the resulting network.

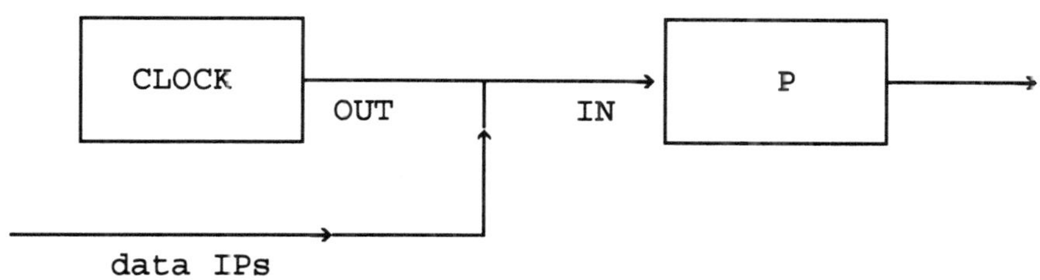

Figure 13-1.

Up to now, it has been assumed that all ports are *named.* Not all ports need to be known to the components they are attached to: sometimes it is desirable to be able to specify connections in the network that *the processes themselves don't know about.* These are especially useful for introducing timing constraints into an application without having to add logic to the components involved. In DFDM we used port 0 for various functions of this kind, but this idea has been generalized into what are called *automatic ports,* to reflect the idea that their functioning is not under the component's control.

Consider two processes, one writing a file and one reading it. You, the network designer, want to interlock the Writer and Reader so that the Reader cannot start until the Writer finishes. To do this, you figure that, if you connect an input port to the Reader, the Reader will be prevented from starting until an IP arrives on that port (by the above scheduling rules). On the other hand, Readers don't usually have input ports, and, if you add one, the Reader will have to have some additional code to dispose of incoming IPs, looking something like this:

```
receive from DELAY port
if connected
then
    if end of data
    then
        do nothing
    else
        discard received IP
    endif
endif
```

This logic works because the receive is not delayed if it is not connected, and, if it is not connected, there will be no IP to dispose of. On the other hand, if it is connected, it will be suspended until an IP or end of data arrives, and, if an IP arrives, it will have to be disposed of. Similarly, you will also have to add code to the Writer at termination time to send an "I'm finished" IP to an appropriate output port.

Now, to avoid having to add seldom used code (to put out and receive these special signals) to every component in the entire system, it is useful to have the driver provide two optional ports for each process that the implementing component doesn't know about: an automatic receive port and an automatic send port. If the automatic send port is connected, a zero-length IP (often referred to as a *trigger*) is sent through it every time (except the last time) the upstream process deactivates. This port is closed at termination time.

The automatic receive works like this: if there is an automatic receive port connected, process activation is delayed until an IP is received on that port, *whether or not there is data available at another input port.*

Figure 13-2 shows a picture of the Writer/Reader situation. The solid line indicates a connection between *W*'s automatic send port and *R*'s automatic receive port. The *O*'s at each end of the line don't touch *W* and *R*, indicating that they are automatic. Since *W* only deactivates (and terminates) when it has written the entire file, the automatic send signal (end of data in this case) can be used for the desired purpose. Of course, this behavior on the part of *W* must become part of its specification (but periodicity is part of a component's specification anyway). An automatic port need not only be connected to another automatic port—it can always be connected to a regular port or vice versa. Any IP that has been received (by the driver) at an automatic receive port is automatically discarded (better not use any *important* data for this job, unless you have taken a copy!).

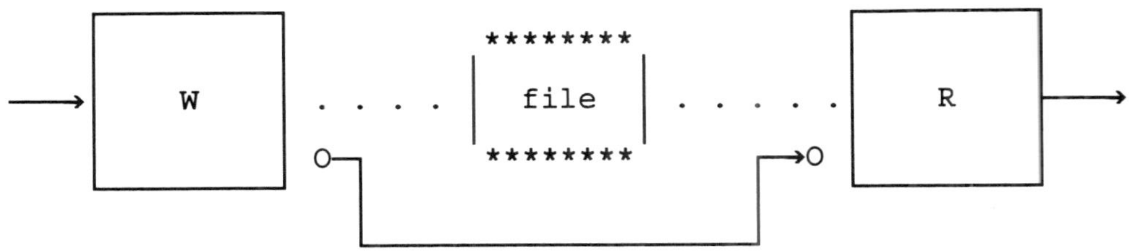

Figure 13-2.

Figure 13-3 shows a network where the automatic send signal gates an IP from another process. Assuming that *C* receives from *I1* before it receives from *I2,* then *C* will not process the input at *I2* until *A* has deactivated. If we made *I1* automatic, we would have essentially the same effect, except that *C* would not have to do a receive, but, conversely, it would not have the option of processing the input at *I2* first.

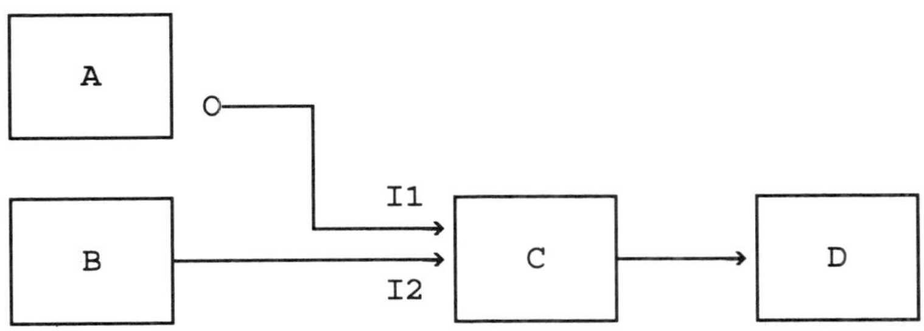

Figure 13-3.

If a connection feeding an automatic input port is closed, the downstream process terminates immediately after having processed the last automatic IP received, as it can never be reinvoked.

There is another situation that is similar to the automatic send port: All output ports of a component, *whether the component "knows" about them or not,* will present end of data when that component terminates. This can also be used to defer events until one or more processes have terminated (see chapter 20).

One last topic that should be mentioned is the problem of the "null" stream. In DFDM a component receiving a null stream (a stream with no data IPs) was invoked anyway. This logic, while perhaps consistent with the regular scheduling rules, tended to increase run-time costs. In one interactive application, we found that ⅔ of all the processes were error handlers and so should really never get fired up if no errors occurred. If they were fired up, as in the normal DFDM case, the added overhead became quite expensive, especially since most of the processes were written in HLLs, so the run-time environment of every process had to be initialized separately.

We therefore introduced the ability for the designer to change this behavior for a whole network. But then we had the problem of Writers and Counters. Consider a Writer component writing a disk file. When it receives a null stream, you want the Writer to at least open and close its output file, resulting in an empty data set. If it doesn't do this, nothing gets changed on the disk, and another job reading that file would see the data from the previous run. Counter components that generate a count IP at end of data have a similar problem: how can they generate a count of zero for an empty stream if they are never invoked? So then we had to add the concept of components that are "end of stream sensitive" (components that behave differently in these two modes—most do not need to), which could in turn be overridden by a "suppress end of stream processing" indication in the network (in case you really didn't want this special logic for a particular run). Old systems that have been in use for a number of years tend to develop layers upon layers of incrustations, rather like barnacles on a boat.

THREADS defaults the other way from DFDM, but for the cases where a process receiving a null stream needs to be activated, THREADS uses the concept of "must run at least once." This is an attribute of the component, not of the process, and means simply that the component must be activated at least once during each run of the network. So Writer and Counter components can do their thing, even when receiving a null data stream.

14

Loop-Type Networks

All of the network shapes encountered so far have been "batch" programs, and have generally had a left-to-right flow, with IPs being created on the left-hand side and disposed of on the right of the network. Sometimes, however, a different kind of topology, called a loop-type network, needs to be used. Several of the later chapters contain examples of this topology, so it is worthwhile spending some time talking about this type of network at a general level. Many networks will in fact be a mixture of the two types, but, once you understand the underlying principles, they won't present any problems.

Figure 14-1 shows a very simple example of a loop-type network.

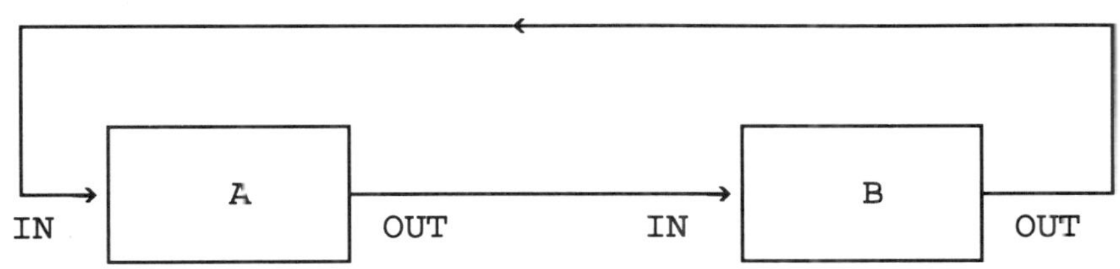

Figure 14-1.

You will see that it is incomplete, as we need to answer the question: how does it get started? You may remember that the only processes that get started automatically are those with no input connections (IIPs don't count). If you look at figure 14-1, you will see that there are *no* processes that have no input connections.

B has an input connection coming from *A*, but *A* has an input connection coming from *B*. Although on occasion we have been tempted to relax the restriction about which processes can start, the simplest thing to do is just to add an extra process that has no input connections and then use it to start *A* or *B*. So the picture now looks like that in figure 14-2. *K* is the starter ("kicker") process. *K* can be connected to either *A* or *B* as the logic demands and can use named or automatic ports, depending on what the downstream process expects.

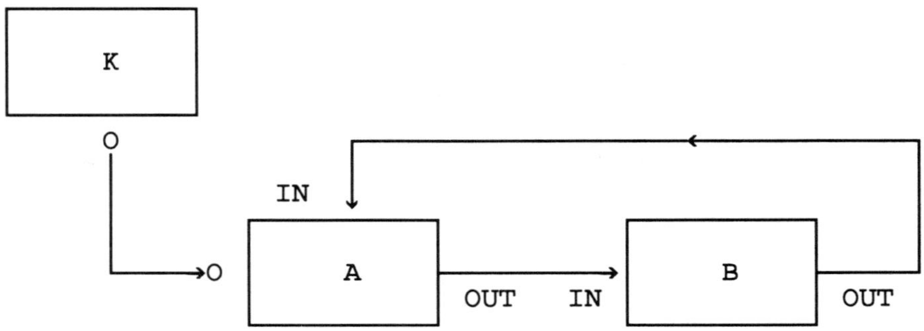

Figure 14-2.

Now that we have started our loop-type networks, not surprisingly, there is another problem: how do they close down? The problem here is in the definition of closing down a process. A process closes down on the next deactivation after all of its *upstream* processes have closed down. In figure 14-2, since *A* is upstream of *B*, but *B* is also upstream of *A*, there is a "catch-22" situation: *A* cannot close down because *B* cannot close down until *A* closes down, and so on. The solution is to provide a special service to components that makes a process look to its neighbors as if it has closed down. One of the processes involved must then *decide* to close down and will use this service to notify the other processes. In the batch situation, closedown of the network as a whole was typically initiated by readers closing down (because they had finished reading their files or had run into problems). In loop-type networks, one of the processes—usually one that is interacting with a user—has to decide that no more data is going to arrive and so close down.

The service that a process uses to tell its neighbors that it has closed down is one that we have mentioned in passing before: *close port*. FBP lets a component close an input port or close an output port. The function of this service is to close ports before they would automatically be closed. (This would normally happen at process close-down time, but there are cases, like this one, where you just can't wait that long). A process closing an output port has the same effect on its downstream processes as if the process had terminated. A process closing an input port has the same effect on its upstream processes; also, if all of its input ports are now closed, it automatically terminates.

So, to close down the network, *A* or *B* in figure 14-2 simply closes its input or output port—it doesn't matter which one. Suppose *B* closes its input port and ends execution: it will now terminate. *B* is in fact *A*'s upstream process, so *A* will also be able to close down, thus bringing down the whole network (the "kicker" process presumably will have closed down long ago).

Now that you know how to make loop-type networks start and stop, why would you want to use them? This usually has to do with synchronization, which will also be discussed in a later chapter. In a regular left-to-right network, the left side of the network will be processing the last IPs, while earlier IPs are being processed further to the right in the network. This asynchronism gives this technique a lot of its power, but there are situations where you have to coordinate some processing with a specific external event or make sure that two functions cannot overlap in time. One such example is that of an interactive application supporting one user. Here, *A* in figure 14-2 might be an interactive I/O component and *B* might be a component to handle the input and generate the appropriate output, such as in figure 14-3, where INTER controls a screen. In this figure, INTER receives some data from PROC, displays it on the screen, waits for some action on the part of the end user, and then sends information back to PROC. If the software infrastructure allows it, waiting for input need only suspend INTER, and other processes could be working on their input while INTER is suspended.

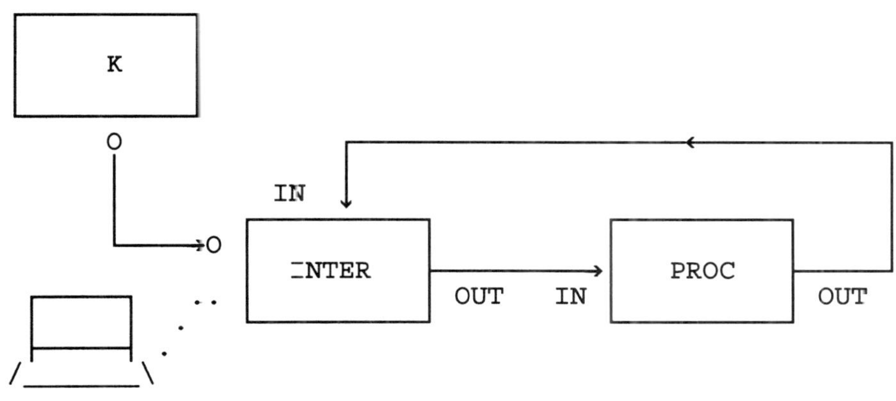

Figure 14-3.

If, on the other hand, this were a left-to-right flow and PROC were preceded by an input process and followed by an output process (without the "back flow"), input and output to and from the same screen would no longer be synchronized. You therefore have to synchronize at least one component to the pace of the user, so that he or she can act on the data presented on a screen before getting the next screen.

Since the IPs from which a screen is built must fit into the queues of the loop or/and the working storage of the processes, there must be enough capacity in these queues. One way to make sure we don't have to worry is to use the tree structures described in an earlier chapter. A tree of IPs can be used to represent the screen data and can be sent around the loop as a unit. Alternatively, the screen data can be represented as one or more substreams, and then you just have to make sure that the total queue capacity is set high enough.

As will be shown in chapter 19, where on-line applications using IBM's IMS are described, you also get a loop structure there, but with a different purpose. IMS is a queue-driven on-line environment, and its message-processing programs (MPPs) keep obtaining transactions from the IMS message queue until there are no more for that MPP, or until certain other conditions are met which cause the MPP to close down. Each time a transaction is obtained from the queue, IMS takes a syncpoint, so any positioning information from the previous transaction is lost, databases are updated, and so on. Therefore, in FBP, MPPs are built as loops where the next transaction is not read from the message queue until the previous one has been fully processed. The diagram would be the same as the previous one, except that INTER is replaced by a "transaction getter," as is shown in figure 14-4.

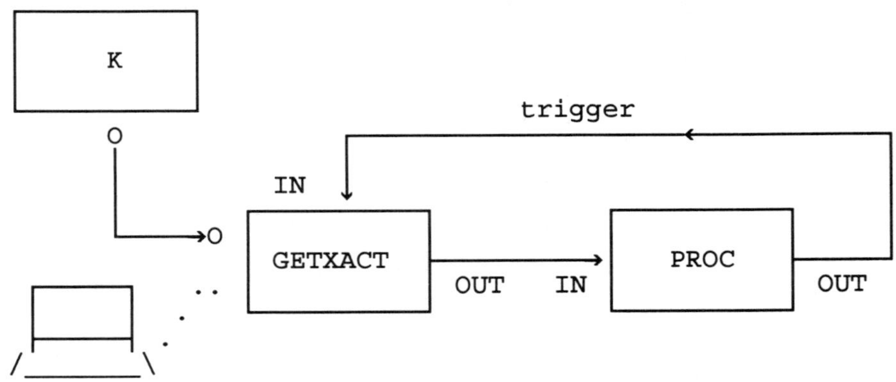

Figure 14-4.

In IMS, each time around this loop the program will normally be dealing with different users, so, unlike the previous example, you cannot use the working storage of the processes to save information relating to one user.

Obviously, in both of the previous cases, PROC is shorthand for a group of processes that collectively process one screenful or transaction. This group of processes will accept data from the screen and send out some kind of signal when they have finished with it. In both cases, it doesn't really matter whether the screen output data is routed back to INTER or GETXACT or is put out by a different process, as long as no more *input* is accepted until the *output* has been presented to the user. Chapter 7, "Composite Components," described two mechanisms that handle this quite neatly: dynamic subnets in DFDM or the composite components that developed from them in FPE. These can be used to ensure that all the processing and output processes have terminated before the dynamic subnet/composite is reactivated with more input data. Figure 14-5 is a diagram of such a composite and its connections. This kind of pattern will be seen again in later chapters.

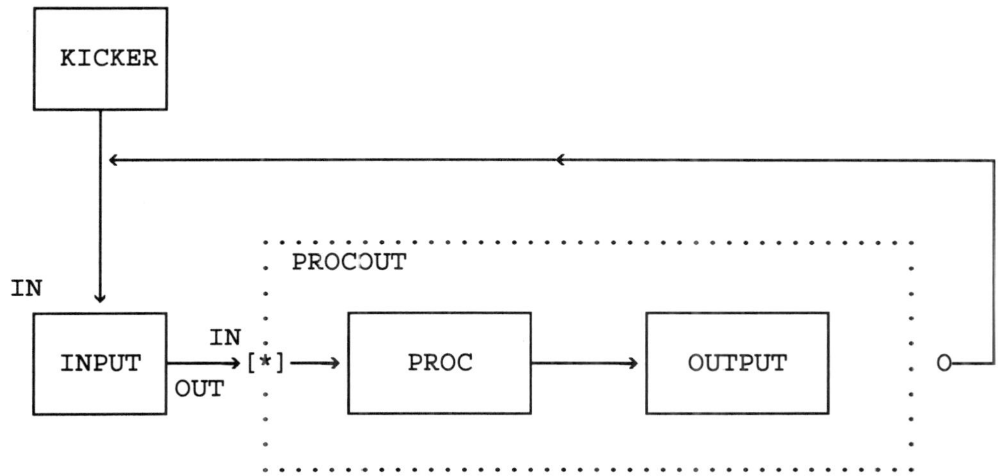

Figure 14-5.

Although this diagram seems simple, it has quite a few ideas combined in it. First you will notice that OUTPUT has no output connection—that makes sense, since it outputs to a device, not to another process. PROC and OUTPUT together also act as a "mini-batch" program, starting up and closing down as each group of IPs is passed to them. To make PROC "see" end of data, the delimiter-sensitive input port (shown as [*]) turns brackets into end of data, so INPUT has to surround each screenful of data with brackets.

Finally, an "automatic" signal (described in chapter 13, "Scheduling Rules") is sent from the composite component back around to signal to INPUT that it can display data and then wait for the user to enter another screenful. The automatic signal will be generated every time PROCOUT deactivates (composites deactivate when their internal processes have all terminated). The automatic port has been connected to the IN port of INPUT, to allow INPUT to be written as a looper that reads from the screen and sends this data to its OUT every time it is pulsed by IN.

Another use for loop networks is for "explosion" applications, of which the classic example is the Bill of Materials explosion, where components of some complex assembly will be "exploded" into subcomponents progressively until they reach ones that cannot be broken down any further. If you know that the largest possible explosion would not fill up storage, you could use a loop of two or more processes with very high capacity queues connecting them (it is dangerous to use a loop with only one process as you could end up getting deadlocked). Of course, the IPs for composite parts must be removed from the data stream when their subcomponents are added to it or when they are found not to be further reducible (like nuts and screws), so eventually the looping data stream will go empty.

This type of logic can also be useful when parsing other kinds of recursive structures (e.g., lists of lists or expressions in a language). A colleague, Charles Douglas, used it very effectively in a text processing application, where the user needed to be able to name lists of databases and in turn use those names in other lists. He implemented this very similarly to a Bill of Materials explosion. His application went through all the lists, progressively exploding them until it got down to the actual database level. Thus, suppose you have the following lists:

```
A:  B, C, D, E

B:  D, E, G

D:  E, F
```

Then, if you feed in A, the successive stages of explosion are as follows:

```
A

B, C, D, E

D, E, G, C, E, F, E

E, F, E, G, C, E, F, E
```

If the goal is to figure out how many of each atomic object you have, the totals are:

```
1 C, 4 E, 2 F, 1 G
```

If you simply want to list the different unique atomic objects involved, then you get:

```
C, E, F, G
```

Either way, the simplest technique is to follow the explosion with a Sort and then either count items or eliminate duplicates.

15

Implementation, Network Splitting, and Client-Server

> A complex system which works is invariably found to have evolved from a simple system which works.
>
> Systems run better when designed to run downhill. Corollary: Systems aligned with human motivational vectors will sometimes work. Systems opposing such vectors work poorly or not at all.
>
> Loose systems last longer and work better. (John Gall, 1978)

A colleague of mine, Dave Olson, has been studying the application development process in particular and large organizations in general and has realized that the budding science of chaos has a lot to tell us about what is going on in this kind of complex process and what can be done about it. In the study of chaos, one frequently runs into feedback loops, and, in the computer business, just as one example, everyone has experienced what happens when a project starts to run late. Fred Brooks described this kind of thing in his celebrated book, *The Mythical Man-Month* (1975). Dave's recent book describes many of these scenarios and also describes how the concepts of chaos can be applied to explain and handle many of the problems we run into in our business (Olson 1993). In a section on techniques for reducing disorder, he talks about DFDM and its relationship to the Jackson Inversion methodology (mentioned elsewhere in this book). He later gives more detail on DFDM and describes how you would approach designing an application with it, as follows:

> To use DFDM, you first define the data requirements of the application, defining how the data flows and is transformed during the application process. Then you create transform

> modules for the places in the flow where data must be merged, split, transformed or reported. The full application definition consists of the data definitions and data flows, defined to DFDM, and the transform modules that are invoked by the platform.

In a personal communication to me, he expands this into the following set of recommendations:

> View the application in terms of the information that needs to move from place to place.
> Create transform modules for the places where data must be merged, split, transformed, or reported.
> Separate data definitions from transform code so that transforms can be reusable code. Transforms thus care more about what has to be done, not so much about how individual pieces of information are represented.
> Provide certain building block transforms that will be needed by most applications, including file storage, file retrieval, file copy, printing, user interaction, etc.
> Build a systems framework so that an application can be defined in terms of its data flows and transforms; the framework handles scheduling, concurrency, and data transfers between transforms.

Doesn't sound much like conventional programming, does it? However, viewing an application in terms of data and the transforms that apply to it underlies many design methodologies. The problem has always been how to get from such a design to a working program. This is the "gap" I referred to earlier. With FBP, you can move down from the highest level design all the way to running code, without having to change your viewpoint.

The first stage of designing an application is to lay out our processes and the flows between them. This is pretty standard Structured Analysis and has been written about extensively by Wayne Stevens and others. Of course, the scope of your application is sometimes not obvious—you can draw a network of processes as large or as small as you want. A system is whatever you draw a dotted line around. By this I mean that the boundary of any system is determined by an arbitrary decision that, for practical purposes, part of the world is going to be considered and part is going to be ignored. In the astronomy of the solar system, influences from outside it can be treated as being effectively negligible, and this works fine most of the time, even though theoretically every object in the universe affects every other. You may think that your skin separates a well-defined "you" from the rest of the universe, but biochemistry teaches us that all sorts of molecules are constantly passing in and out through this apparent barrier. Indeed, all the molecules in our bodies are totally replaced over a period of a few years. This is rather a Zen idea—taken to the extreme it says that objects don't have an objective existence (pun intended), but are just the way we "chunk" the universe. You should also be aware of the way the words you use affect the way you view the universe. As a linguist, I find a number of B.L. Whorf's examples quite striking: in one example (Whorf 1956), he gives a word in one of the Amerindian languages that describes people traveling in a canoe, in which there is no identifiable root meaning "canoe." The canoe is so much an assumed part of their experience that it doesn't have to be named explicitly.

Thus, to design systems, you have to delineate the system you are going to design. This first decision is critical and may not be all that obvious. So consider the context of the system you are designing. Have well-defined (and not too many) interfaces with the systems outside your chosen system.

You can now lay out the processes and flows of your system. Explode the processes progressively until you get down to the level where you start to make use of preexisting components. In FBP, you will find these starting to affect your design as you get closer to them. This is one of the points where FBP design differs from conventional programming, but it should not really be surprising, as bridges or houses are not designed purely top-down or purely bottom-up. As I said before, how can you "decompose" the design for a house so that it results in the invention of drywall? But, conversely, you have to know where you're going in order to be able to determine whether you're getting closer to it.

On the way to your goal, like any hiker, you have to be willing and able to change your plans as you go. The nice thing about programming is that you can move between a "real" program and its simulation very easily, so you can try something and modify it until you're happy with it. In fact, with FBP it is possible to realize an old programming dream of being able to grow an application from its simulation. You can replace processes by components that just use up x seconds of time, and vice versa.

In programming I believe there should be no strong distinction between a prototype and a real program until the real program actually goes into production. If something in the environment or in your understanding changes so that an old assumption is no longer true, you have to be able to change your design. While I am very aware that the cost of change goes up the further back you go in the development process, you have to know when to cut your losses and go back and do some redesign. If it helps, consider how much harder it is for, say, a surgeon to do this!

If you combine FBP with iterative development, you have a very powerful and responsive application development technology. You can try different approaches, it's cheap to make changes, and, when it's time to dot the i's and cross the t's, it is essentially a linear process. By way of comparison, I believe that the chief failing of the "waterfall" methodology was that it was so awkward to go back that development teams would press forward phase after phase, getting deeper and deeper into the swamp as they went, or they would redesign and pretend they were doing development (or even testing!). Here is Dave Olson again: "Programmers know that highly detailed linear development processes don't match the way real programming is done, but plans and schedules are laid out using the idea, anyway." He goes on to stress that, while there are some projects for which the "waterfall" process will work fine, you cannot and should not shoehorn every project into it.

Apart from the iterative explosion process for networks that was just described (vertical), in FBP there is another process that is orthogonal to it. This is the process of cutting up networks horizontally, to decide how and where they are going to run. In this process, parts of a network are assigned to different "engines" or environments. Since FBP systems are designed in terms of communicating processes, these processes can run on all sorts of different machines or platforms—in fact, anywhere that has a communication facility.

When you think about the ways a flow can be chopped up, remember that you can use anything that communicates by means of data, which in data processing means practically any piece of hardware or software. I call this process "cleaving." Networks can be cleft (or cloven) in any of the following ways (in no particular order and not at all mutually exclusive):

- Multiple computers (hosts, mid-range, PCs, or mixture)
- Multiple processors within one computer
- Multiple tasks
- Different geographical sites
- Multiple job steps within a job
- Secondary transactions
- Client/server
- Multiple virtual machines
- Others we haven't thought of . . .

All of these have their particular design considerations, but that's just like the real world, where there are many different processes and they all communicate in different ways. Today I can call up a friend by phone, mail him or her a handwritten letter, fax it, communicate by E-mail, send a telegram, or stick a note in a bottle and throw it into the Atlantic. Each one of these has areas where it is stronger or weaker.

Take as a starting point one of the most common network cleaving techniques: multiple job steps in a job. Suppose you have decided that your network is going to run as a batch job under MVS. Figure 15-1 shows a simple network.

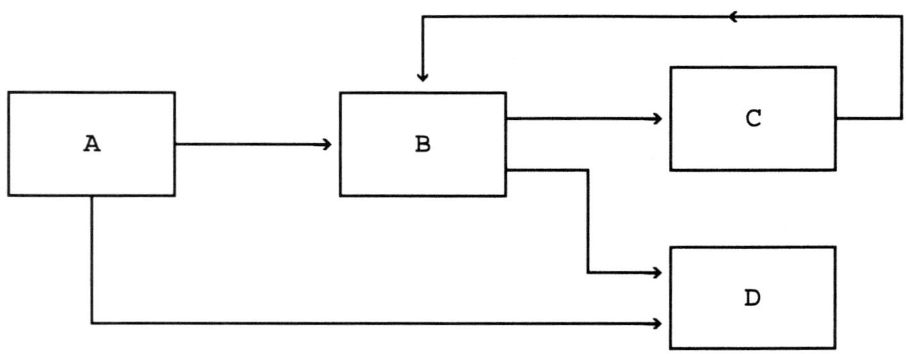

Figure 15-1.

Suppose that, for whatever reason, you want to run this as multiple job steps of a single batch job. Now you know that job steps can only run sequentially. While they can be skipped, they cannot be repeated. This means that *B* and *C* must be in the same job step. However, *A* and *D* can be split off into different job steps if desired. Suppose you decide to make both *A* and *D* separate job steps—this will result in three job steps, in total.

Job steps communicate by means of data files (yet another kind of data flow). In FBP you are free to replace any connection with a sequential file, so you can change the connections leading out of *A* and those leading into *D* to files. Once you separate two processes into different job steps, of course, *all* connections between them must be replaced by files. Each one of these will in turn require a Writer and a Reader. Using dotted lines to show step boundaries and [X]'s to indicate files, the diagram now looks like that in figure 15-2.

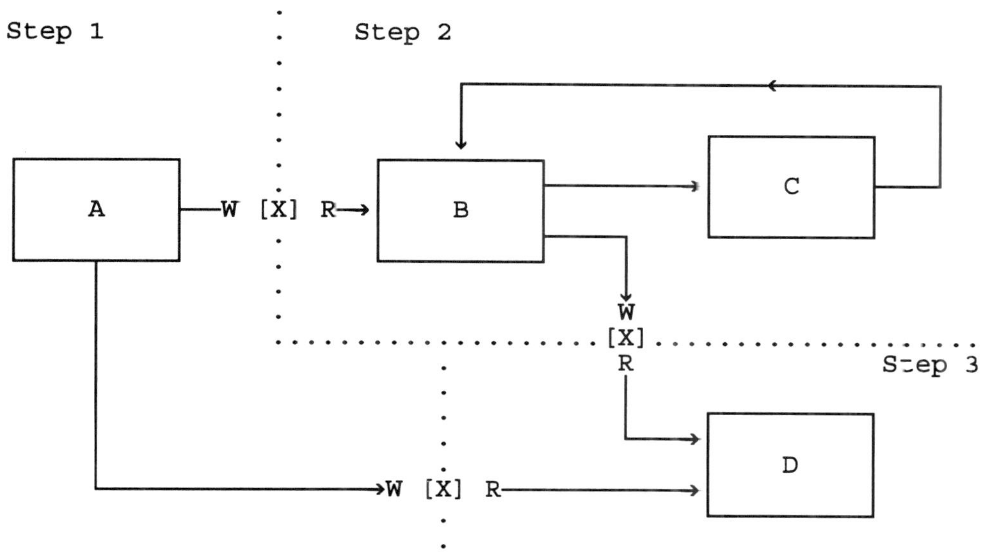

Figure 15-2.

I have shown the Writers and Readers around the files as *W*'s and *R*'s to keep the similarity between figures 15-1 and 15-2. These are proper processes, even though they are not shown as boxes. Steps 1 and 3 thus have three processes each; step 2 has four.

Showing figure 15-2 at the job step level, we get figure 15-3. From this we see that we could have designed the application this way earlier in the design process and then exploded it to get figure 15-2.

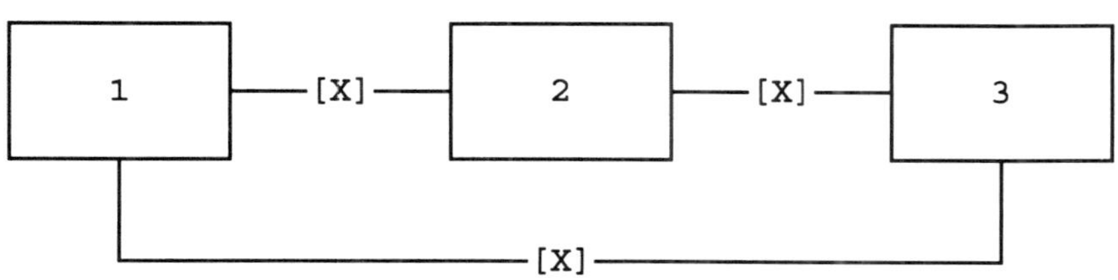

Figure 15-3.

However, our experience is that it is much better to design a complete application and then cleave it later, as other considerations may affect decisions on how the network should be split up. (For instance, the problem I mentioned in an earlier chapter of not being able to overlap Sorts forced many of them into separate job steps.) In fact, since it is so easy to move processes from one job step to another, there is no particular point in splitting up the network early—you can just as well leave it to the last minute. In conventional programming, moving logic from one job step to another is very difficult, due to the drastic change of viewpoint when you move from data flow design to control flow implementation, so the decision about what are going to be the job steps has to be made very early and tends to affect the whole implementation process from that point on.

I'd like to make another point about this rather simple example. In figure 15-2, you notice that communication between process *A* and process *B* is managed by two processes and a file. In FBP, this is a common pattern whenever any two processes communicate other than via FBP connections. Thus, a communication line might be "managed" by a VTAM Send process at one end and a VTAM Receive process at the other. I will give a few examples later in this chapter of other kinds of communication between networks, and you will see this pattern in all of them.

A more subtle point is that the transition from figure 15-1 to figure 15-2 was made entirely by manipulating the network, without having to add any complexity to the underlying software. This point is related to the principle of open architectures I talked about in an earlier chapter. Our experience is that it is much better to implement subsystems like file handling and communications as visible processes under the developer's control than to bury them in the software infrastructure. Consider the advantages: in this example, Write-file-Read becomes just one mechanism supporting a particular way of cleaving networks—we could have used many others, and in fact could change from one to another during project development.

To try to show what happens if you go the other way, consider what would have happened if we decided to support two kinds of connections: an intra-step connection and an inter-step connection. Take figure 15-1 and assign each connection to one of these two categories, depending on whether it crosses a step boundary or not (assume that you do this at the same time you divide the network up into job steps). The result will be as shown in figure 15-4.

Now, we have made both the implementation and the mental model more complex, without providing any more function to the developer. Not only will the added complexity make the system harder to visualize and therefore harder to troubleshoot, but we may have made some useful operating system features inaccessible or only accessible through still more complexity in the interface. Also, if a programmer wants to replace the inter-step connections with, say, a DB2 database, he or she is going to have to add extra processes anyway and change the inter-step connections back to intra-step connections.

Another way of presenting this discussion is that it is very important, when designing software, to decide on its *scope.* The scope of a given software system obviously depends on the particular environment it is running in, but it is sometimes not obvious which of the various constructs of that environment should

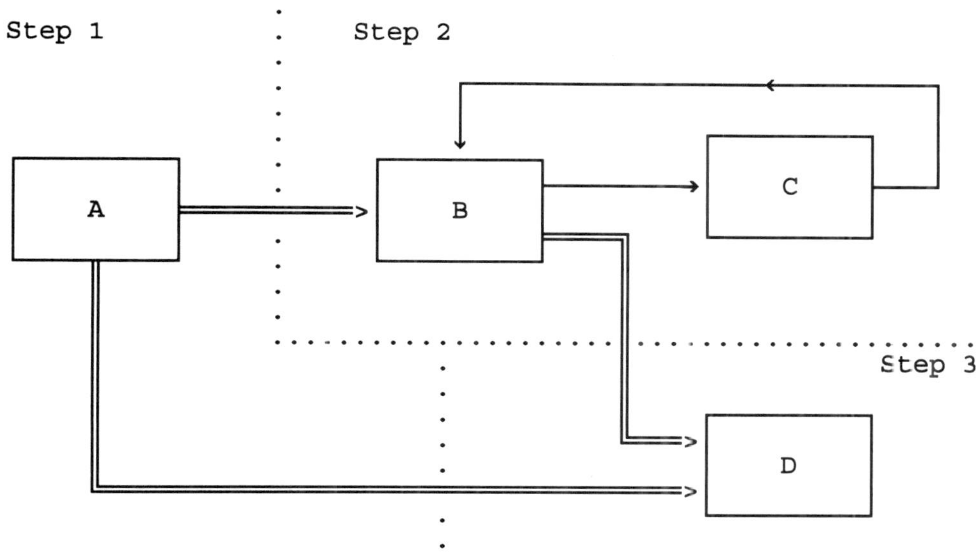

Figure 15-4.

be the basic "unit" of your software. In the case of DFDM, it will probably be obvious from all the foregoing descriptions and examples that a DFDM network corresponds to one of the following:

- An MVS job step
- An IMS transaction
- An IMS BMP
- An IMS batch job
- A CMS "program"

However, in the early stages of DFDM, it was not at all obvious that this was the right decision. Even the CMS statement above is somewhat vague because the word "program" is one of the most confusing in the whole science of "programming"! Consider figure 15-4. If we had implemented DFDM that way, the scope of a DFDM application would have been an MVS job, not a job step. There is no counterpart of this in IMS (except perhaps a "conversation") or in CMS, so it would have been harder for programmers to move from one of these environments to another. I have always considered our choice of the scope of a network as being one of the keys to the usability of DFDM. In THREADS, a network is implemented as an .EXE file, which I think is also usually referred to as a "program."

So a system should have components of well-defined scope, with visible, controllable interfaces between them—in fact, very much like FBP itself! Such systems (and, I believe, *only* such systems) can then be combined easily in open architectures.

Take another look at figure 15-2. You could draw a box around each of the patterns shown as

```
———W [X] R———
```

to make it a process in its own right. This process can run perfectly well within a job step, and in fact this pattern was shown in chapter 13, "Scheduling Rules," where it was drawn as shown in figure 15-5.

Figure 15-5.

As you will recollect, automatic ports were used to ensure that the Reader did not start until the writer had finished writing the file. Taken as a whole, this process is rather like a Sort without the sorting function! It writes a whole data stream out to disk and then reads it back and sends it on. We can also state this a bit differently. This process keeps accepting IPs and storing them in arrival sequence, until it detects end of data. It then retrieves them and sends them on. This suggests the other name for this structure. It will come up again in chapter 16, "Deadlocks—Their Causes and Prevention," where it is called, somewhat fancifully, an "infinite queue." You will find that it is one of the most useful techniques for preventing deadlocks.

Why did we call it an "infinite queue"?

1. In the old days "connections" were called "queues."
2. Using a file for this type of structure gives an effectively infinite capacity because, while a connection has whatever capacity the developer specified (or the default if none was specified), the pattern shown in figure 15-5 can keep on soaking up IPs until it hits the maximum number of records allowed by the operating system or storage device. Actually, we could increase its capacity still further by using smart code inside a special-purpose component.

Given that processes are connected by queues, how can a particular type of process also be called a "queue"? It was suggested at the beginning of the chapter that processes can be as large or small as you like. For pragmatic purposes, we have chosen to pick a certain "grain" of process as the one we will implement, and connect them with a different mechanism, the connection. There are higher-level processes, which we call subnets, and the highest subnets are job steps. Above this are still higher processes called jobs, applications, and so on. Different levels of this hierarchy will tend to be implemented by different mechanisms, but, if we need to, we can always move processes up or down the hierarchy. Treating a connection as a special type of process is like using a magnifying glass to zoom in on a part of a network. Any time you want a connection to behave differently from normal connections, simply replace it by a process (plus the required connections on either end). You could also use this technique if you wanted to have another type of connection between processes, say a connection supporting "priority mail." However, this will require additional port names. A number of writers have described processes implementing FBP's connections (also known as "bounded buffers"), but we have found it more convenient to put them in the infrastructure.

As I read the ever-growing body of literature on parallel processes, I have been struck by the variation in granularity across the various implementations, from fine-grained to very coarse-grained. In fact, FBP processes vary from very simple to quite complex. However, they do seem to agree on a certain "grain size." In chapter 22, "Performance Considerations," I will talk about how granularity affects performance and how this fact can be used to obtain trade-offs between maintainability and performance.

In addition, I do not claim that the level of granularity described in this book is the best or the final one for all purposes, only that it is a level that we have found to provide a good balance between performance and expressive power. It is productive of useful components, and developers seem to be able to become comfortable with it. Figure 15-6 shows a network that implements what used to be called a "half adder," using IPs to represent bits and FBP processes to model Boolean operations. While this worked fine as a simulation, I do not suggest that you could build a real machine on it (although you might be able to build a *slow* simulation of a machine). In the figure, RPL means Replicate, AND is the Boolean AND operator, and XOR is the Boolean exclusive OR.

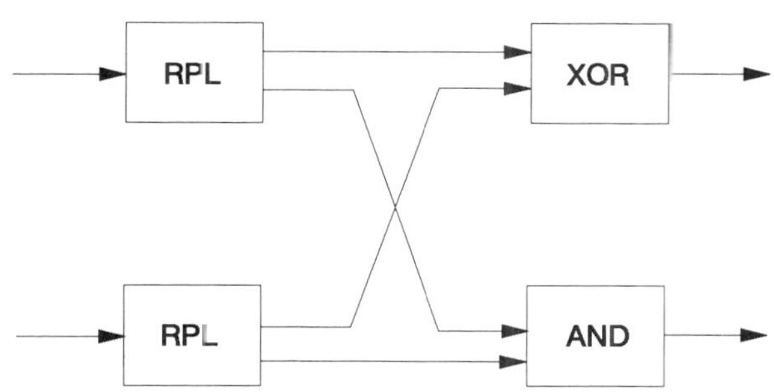

Half-adder

Figure 15-6.

Earlier I alluded to "managing" a communication line by means of matching VTAM processes. Here a network of processes can be distributed between multiple computers, which may or may not be in the same room, building, city, or country.

This is "distributed" processing, which is gaining more and more attention. Instead of each computer laboring away by itself in splendid isolation, people today are accustomed to having computers be able to talk to each other around the world, using a wide variety of different communication techniques. The Net (Cyberspace) of today was foreshadowed within the IBM Corporation by the internal network called VNET, which is an incredibly powerful medium for sharing information and ideas. I once impressed the heck out of a visitor by showing him how, from a terminal in Toronto, by using a one-line command, one could display the VNET file traffic between Australia and Japan!

While I am not an expert in distributed systems, it seems logical to me that, if we have two computers, each with multiple processes running on it, communicating asynchronously, then the two computers should be able to exchange data by simply using two dedicated processes at each end of the link. This is shown schematically in figure 15-7. This diagram shows two systems, each with a Sender and a Receiver process. The Sender of one system sends to the Receiver of the other, and vice versa. At the far left and far right of the diagram, there will be more processes, which are implementing the applications on each computer. You could view this whole structure as a single loop-type network that has been distributed over two systems.

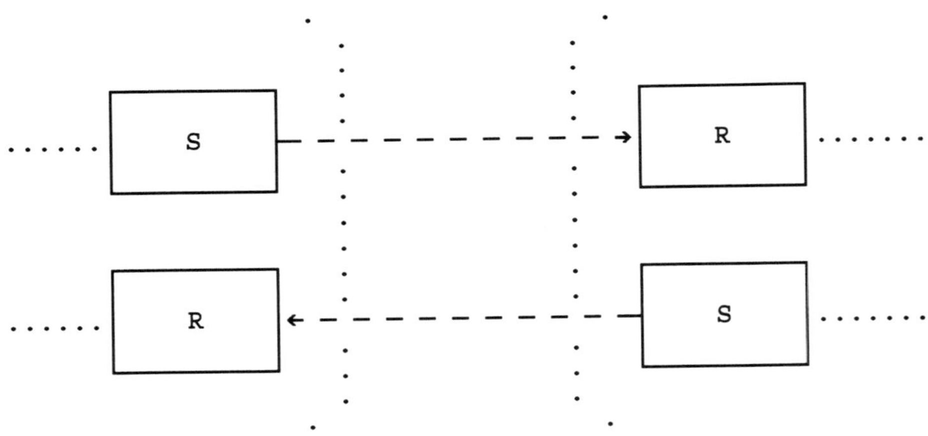

Figure 15-7.

Clearly, in this example, the two systems have been coupled together, so that the speeds of the two systems are effectively matched. However, if the traffic between the systems is low enough, this may not be a bad design for some scenarios. For example, suppose a bank decides to spread its processing over two or more machines in different regions, linked by communication lines. Banking transactions are usually characterized by high "locality." The largest proportion of banking transactions will be on the customer's branch, a smaller number will be between branches on the same regional computer (assuming the bank splits up its branches that way), and only what's left over will actually need to travel between different regional machines, and most of the time this traffic should be balanced in the two directions. So each machine can be visualized as a "cloud" of processes, and every so often a transaction gets sent across to the other machine. If response time is adequate and/or the traffic is low enough, the requesting process can actually wait until a response comes back. If this is not adequate, the requesting process must have some way of suspending the logic that needs the data and then resuming it later when the data arrives. This is exactly the problem of suspending and resuming FBP processes, but at a higher level. Also, there is the possibility that the link has gone down (when there is a physical medium like wire, it can be cut or struck by lightning), so some thought has to go into what kind of degraded performance the application should provide if one of the systems cannot communicate with another.

One topic that comes up a lot with distributed systems is the vexed question of how to synchronize events across multiple systems. If all of the FBP processes in an IMS application are running in the same IMS region, then issuing one Rollback command will undo all database changes since the last checkpoint, so it is easy enough to undo some database updates if it turns out that the larger action they are part of has failed. Now, however, imagine that you want to transfer funds between two different hardware nodes. You have to withdraw funds from an account on one node and deposit them into an account on the other one. Either of these operations can go wrong, so you need some handshaking to either delay both until you know it's safe or be prepared to undo an earlier operation if a later one goes awry. The latter approach seems more natural, even if less general. In this case, you do the withdrawal first; if that works, you send an IP representing a sum of money to the other node, specifying both source and destination accounts. If the receiving end for some reason cannot accept the transfer, it gets sent back to be redeposited. You might call this the "optimistic" strategy, while committing only when you know that both parts have worked properly is the "pessimistic" strategy. The point is that qualitative changes occur when a network is split between systems, but the arguments for distributing systems are so compelling that the new problems that it raises will definitely be solved. After all, systems of communicating humans have been working this way since time immemorial!

There is a lot of interest these days in what are called client-server relationships. In FBP, every process is a server to its upstream processes. In the banking example, where there are two or more systems involved, every system is potentially a server to all the others. So the client-server paradigm is a very general one, from the level of FBP processes as high up as you care to go. However, it is important to stress also that FBP processes are peers, and peer-to-peer communication, which is more general than client-server, is a very natural match with the FBP approach. The FBP model is cooperative rather than hierarchical.

One major addition we need to make to the above schema is to allow for the possibility of asynchronous flows from multiple sources. If the Toronto machine can have data flowing in from Montréal and/or Edmonton, it has to be able to accept data on a first-come, first-served basis (subject, perhaps, to a priority scheme if there is a need to handle express messages). You have already seen in FBP a mechanism that provides this—namely, multiple output ports feeding one input port. If you have this situation, you must have some way of routing the response back to the right source, so the data must be tagged in some way. In FBP, one way is to arrange for the incoming data to contain a "source index," which can be used as an output port element number. With just two clients, this is shown schematically in figure 15-8. In this configuration, "S.0" sends an IP to the server and then waits for the response to arrive back, after which it can send another request. Meanwhile, "S.1" is going through the same cycle. You can see from the figure that IPs from "S.0" and "S.1" will arrive at the server in first-come, first-served sequence. Of course, the server can only handle one request at a time, so it has to be able to process requests as fast as possible, relative to the arrival rate. Otherwise, a queue builds up that will in turn slow down *all* the processes requesting service. As in the previous discussion of "cleaving" networks, any line in figure 15-8 can be replaced by other forms of communication, including the above-mentioned "Send-line-Receive" pattern, resulting in various kinds of distributed network. The "n to one" connection in the middle of figure 15-8 would be implemented very naturally as multiple Senders sending to a single Receiver process. In FBP, the reverse situation, a "one to n" connection, is not implemented directly in network notation, but can be implemented simply by a Replicate process. In a distributed network, this would correspond naturally to a "broadcast" communication function, where one process sends the same message to multiple receivers. This is the kind of arrangement used by many taxi dispatching systems, where the dispatcher sends in broadcast mode, but individual taxis reply on their own wavelength.

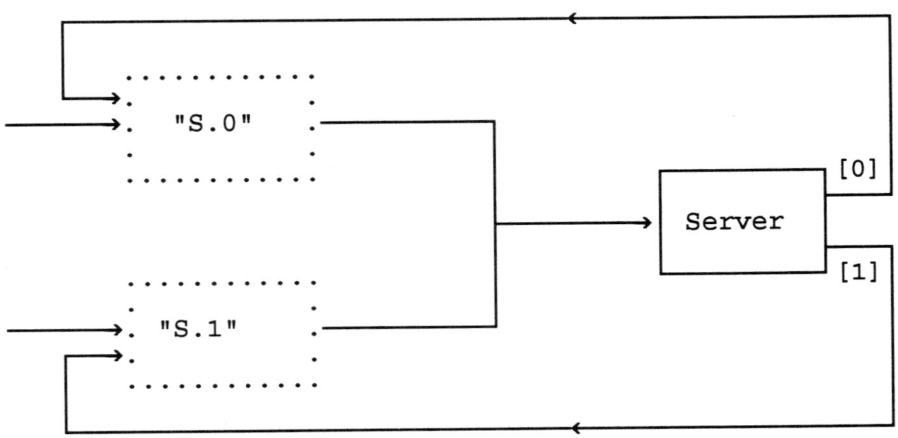

Figure 15-8.

I mentioned that the server in figure 15-8 can only handle one request at a time. This would be the simplest way of implementing its logic. Another wrinkle might be to add an "express" port, like the express lane at some banks. However, unless the express port has its own server, this scheme can still be degraded by a low-priority request that is tying up the server. So it might be better to have two processes running concurrently, one handling express requests and the other low-priority requests. Of course, this adds logical complexity, especially if the two servers are competing for resources. One possible solution is to implement an enqueue/dequeue mechanism to resolve such conflicts. This actually fits quite well with FBP and was implemented experimentally in DFDM. The previously mentioned article (Suzuki et al. 1985) also describes a similar feature that its authors developed as an alternative communication mechanism between processes.

Generalizing still further, we may multiplex the server by having multiple instances of the same component. For instance, suppose the server is doing I/O, which may be overlapped with processing. You could have many instances of the same component serving the client queue. This is like many bank branches today, where several tellers are servicing a single queue of customers. To allow them to overlap I/O, you have to be able to suspend only a single process on an event, without hanging the whole application. DFDM supported this for the MVS "basic" access methods (BSAM, BPAM, BDAM), VSAM, and EXCP. THREADS does not support this. Of course, this is subject to the same resource contention I talked about earlier.

If you are going to multiplex your server processes, you will probably need a "load balancing" process to ensure that queues don't build up more in front of some servers than others. The resulting diagram might therefore look like that in figure 15-9. In this figure, requests are assumed to be coming in at the left side, tagged with an indication as to their source. They merge into LB, which performs load balancing, sending the incoming requests to whichever server has the shortest input queue (number of IPs in its input connection). From the servers, the IPs then travel to RF, which is a redistribution facility. From there they eventually travel back to their original requesting processes. You will find a description in chapter 22 of how this technique was used very effectively to reduce the run-time for a disk scanning program from 2 hours down to 20 minutes.

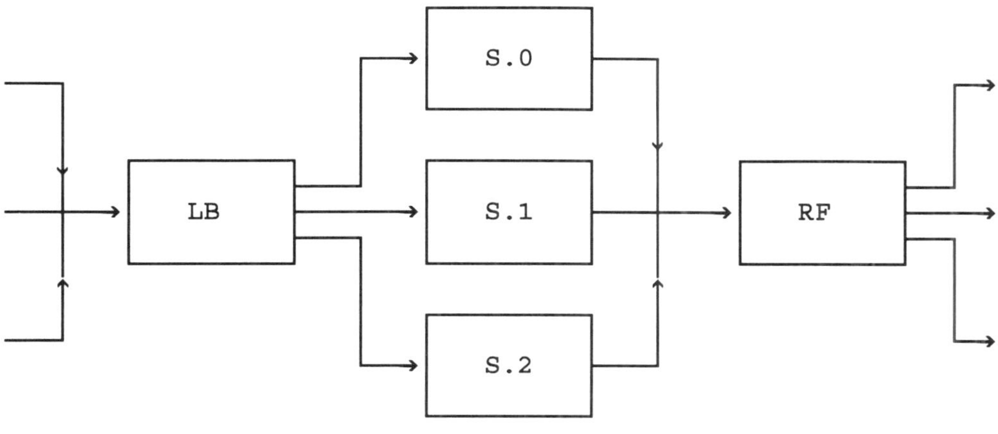

Figure 15-9.

One topic that has been getting a lot of attention recently is that of *portability* of code. This is certainly one of the appeals of HLLs, but my personal feeling is that their disadvantages seem to outweigh their advantages. But clearly you cannot port Assembler language from one type of hardware to another using a different instruction set. The solution is to port *at the function level.* A Collator can be defined to do the same job on two or more input streams, independent of what language it was coded in or what hardware it is running on. So we can move Collators from one machine to another and expect that our function works identically. Not only does this approach take advantage of the strength of the black box concept, but it removes the necessity for code to be white boxes written in a portable language (which usually results in lowest-common-denominator languages or frustrating and time-consuming negotiation about standards).

You have now seen how to decompose designs vertically, cleave them horizontally, and some other concepts, such as client-server relationships. But in what order *should* you develop your application? I don't think there is a fixed sequence, but I have found two sequences particularly productive. Along the lines of bottom-up and top-down, I call them "output-backwards" and "center-out." "Output-backwards" means that you start with the outputs intended for human consumption and work backwards deciding how this data is going to be generated. If it's an interactive application, output is the screen and you will eventually work back to the screen input, which closes the loop. "Center-out" means that you start with the core processes, usually the ones that do business logic, together with any required Collators and Splitters, and get them working using the simplest Reader and Display components. Fancy output formatting, input editing, and so on, can then be added incrementally, working out from the center. This approach is really a kind of prototyping, as you can develop the main logic and check it out first, before investing effort in making the output pretty, making the application more robust, and so forth. At selected points along the way, you can demonstrate the system to potential customers, prospective users, your manager, or whomever.

Last but not least, during this whole process of development, you will want to test your developing product. You can test any component by just feeding it what it needs for input and watching what comes out as output. You generate its input using Readers and its output using some kind of display component. In the early stages, the simpler these scaffolding components are, the better. The trick, as in prototyping, is to only introduce one unknown at a time. The more you can use precoded components, and the simpler they are, the less unknowns you will be dealing with. Any time you want to see the data that is traveling across a connection, just insert a Display process, like a probe in an electrical circuit. So testing is very simple.

As I have tried to emphasize in what went before, I feel that, while FBP is great for developing applications, it is perhaps even more effective in improving maintainability. After all, all attempts to make programs more maintainable after the fact have failed, so maintainability has to be designed in from the start. As some of the previous anecdotes attest, FBP seems to have it designed into its very fabric. Given that your program will change constantly over the years, you will also need a simple way to verify that the logic that you didn't change still works. Testing that a system still behaves the way it used to is called "regression testing." Wayne Stevens came up with an FBP-based technique for doing this. You take the original output of the system to be tested and store it in a file; you then embed your system in a network as shown in figure 15-10.

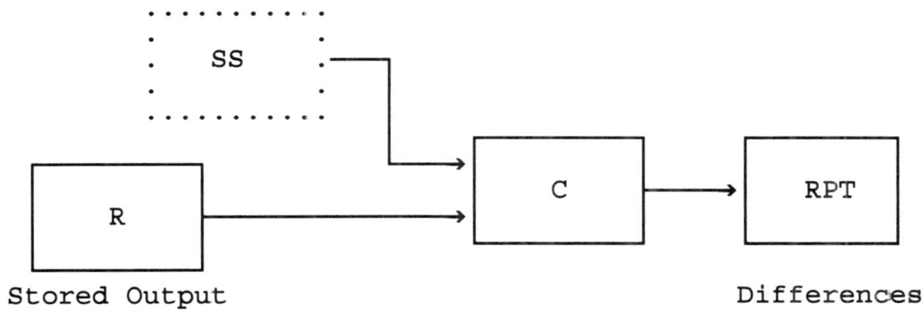


```
where
     SS represents the subject system
     R is a Reader for the previously stored output
     C compares the stored output against current output
     RPT generates a report on the differences
```

Figure 15-10.

This network is clear while also being generic. For instance, you might need to insert filters on *C*'s two input streams to blank out things that will vary between the two runs (e.g., dates and times). You might want to display the differences in different orders, so you can insert a suitable Sort between *C* and RPT.

A related (FBP-specific) problem comes up if *C*'s input streams are not in a predictable sequence, say because they are the result of a first-come, first-served merge or if overlapped I/O has been occurring, so some IPs may have overtaken others. The simplest solution is probably to sort them before *C* sees them, but a better one, if it is feasible, is to mark the IPs at a point where they still have a fixed sequence, so that they can be split apart again before doing the compare. Of course, any processing you do to the differences (after the compare) will be cheaper than processing you do before the compare process (assuming that most of the data has compared equal).

I have given you a very high speed description of some methodology and implementation techniques that are characteristic of FBP. No doubt you will come up with your own procedures, guidelines, and "rules of thumb," and I hope that eventually there will be a community of users of FBP all exchanging ideas and experience (and experiences) . . . and more books!

16

Deadlocks—Their Causes and Prevention

Deadlocks are one of the few examples in FBP of problems that cannot involve only one process, but that arise from the interactions between processes. They occur when two or more processes interfere with each other in such a way that the network as a whole eventually cannot proceed. I know some programmers feel that they have traded the known difficulties of conventional programming for a new and exotic problem that seems very daunting, and they wonder if we have not just moved the complexity around! Although deadlocks may seem frightening at first, you will gain experience at recognizing network shapes that are deadlock-prone and will learn reliable ways to prevent deadlocks from occurring. I know of *no* case where a properly designed network resulted in a deadlock during production.

First, however, I think we should look a little more deeply at the question I mentioned earlier: if FBP is as good as I claim, why does it give rise to a new and exotic class of problem that the programmer would not encounter in normal programming? Well, actually, it's not new—it's just that a conventional program has only one process, so you don't have to worry about deadlocks. In FBP there are multiple processes, and multiple processes have always given rise to deadlocks of various kinds. If I have convinced you in the foregoing pages that the FBP approach is worthwhile, then you will be relieved to know that there is quite a large literature on multiprocess deadlocks. Anyone who has designed on-line or distributed systems has had to struggle with this concept. For instance, suppose two people try to access the same account at a bank through different automatic teller machines (ATMs). In itself this doesn't cause a problem; one just has to wait until the other one is finished. Now suppose that they both decide to transfer money between the same two accounts, *but in different directions*. Normally, this would be programmed by having both transactions get both accounts in update mode (Get Hold in IMS DL/I terms). Now consider the following sequence of events involving two transactions, A and B (call the accounts X and Y):

1. A: get X with hold
2. B: get Y with hold
3. B: try to get X with hold
4. A: try to get Y with hold

At point 3, transaction B gets suspended because it wants X, which is held by A. At point 4, transaction A gets suspended because it wants Y, which is held by B. Now neither one can release the resource the other one wants. If A had not needed Y, it would have eventually finished what it was doing and released X, so that B could have proceeded. However, now that it has tried to grab Y, the result is an unbreakable deadlock. This is often referred to as a "deadly embrace," and in fact it has similarities to one kind of FBP deadlock. Usually, on-line systems have some kind of time-out that will cancel one or both of the transactions involved.

Normally, the chance of this kind of thing happening is infinitesimal, so a lot of systems simply don't worry about it. It can be prevented *completely* by always getting accounts in a fixed sequence, but this may not be possible in all situations, so it is probably true to say that some proportion (even if a tiny one) of transactions will deadlock in an on-line system, so you have to be able to take remedial action.

In FBP, we can also get deadlocks between the processes of a network. Of course, in an FBP on-line system, each transaction would be a network, so you can get deadly embraces *between* separate networks requesting the same resources, but we will assume that these are handled in the normal way for the underlying resource management software. However, because a network has multiple processes, deadlocks can occur *within* a network. In all these intra-network cases, we have discovered that it is always a design issue.

This type of deadlock can always be detected at design time, and there are tried and true techniques for preventing them, which will be covered in this chapter. Wayne Stevens also has a very complete analysis of deadlocks and how to avoid them in Appendix B of his *Software Design: Concepts and Methods* (Stevens 1991).

The general term for deadlocks like the deadly embrace is a "resource deadlock." There is a classical example of this in the literature called the "dining philosophers problem," which has been addressed by many of the writers on multiple processes. Imagine there is a table in a room, on which are five chopsticks, spaced equally around the table, and a bowl of rice in the center. Five philosophers use this room for eating. When a philosopher gets hungry, he or she enters the room, picks up the two chopsticks on each side of his or her place, eats until satisfied and then leaves, replacing the chopsticks on the table (after cleaning them off, I hope). If all the philosophers go in at the same time and each happens to pick up the chopstick to his or her right (or left), you get a deadlock, as nobody can eat and therefore nobody can free up a chopstick and therefore nobody can eat! Notice that the dining philosophers exhibit the same loop topology that I have been warning you about in earlier chapters. The dining philosophers can also suffer from the reverse syndrome, "livelock," where, even though there is no deadlock, paradoxically one of the philosophers is in danger of starving to death because there is no guarantee that he or she will ever get the use of two adjacent chopsticks. Kuse et al. (1986) proved that, although a network with fixed capacity connections (like the ones in FBP) can suffer from deadlock, it can never suffer from livelock.

I will use figure 14-2 from chapter 14, "Loop-Type Networks," to introduce an FBP version of a resource deadlock. Figure 16-1 shows it again here for ease of reference.

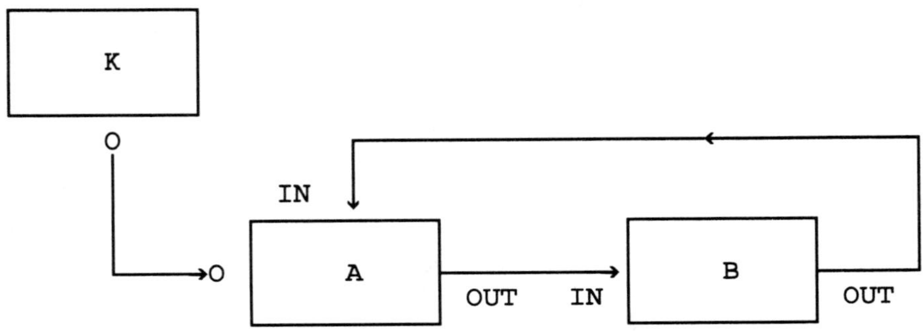

Figure 16-1.

Suppose that *A*'s logic looks like this:

```
/* Copy IPs from IN to OUT */

     receive from IN using a
     do while receive has not reached end of data
          send a to OUT
          receive from IN using a
     enddo
```

In other words, it is a simple filter. While B has similar logic, under some circumstances it fails to send the IP it has just received to its OUT port, so that its logic is effectively the following:

```
/* Copy c-type IPs from IN to OUT */

     receive from IN using a
     do while receive has not reached end of data
          if condition c is true
               send a to OUT
          endif
          receive from IN using a
     enddo
```

We'll begin by starting *A*. *A* sends an IP out of its OUT port. It next does a receive on IN, but there is nothing there, so it suspends. The connection between *A* and *B* now has something in it, so *B* starts up. Say condition c is false, so *B* receives the IP, but fails to send it out. *B* then goes on to its receive and suspends. *A* is currently suspended on a receive, but it is going to wait indefinitely as *B* hasn't sent the IP that *A* is waiting on. *B* is also suspended indefinitely, since *A* in turn cannot send what *B* is waiting on. This is very like the deadly embrace: two processes, each suspended waiting for the other to do something. Since *A* and *B* are suspended on receive, there is nothing active in our network (*K* has terminated). So no process can proceed. The program as a whole has certainly not finished normally, but nothing is happening! This is in fact how the driver recognizes that a deadlock has occurred.

AMPS and DFDM add a wrinkle to this: It is possible to have one or more processes suspended waiting for an external event (such as I/O completion) to occur. In this case, the network as a whole goes into a "system wait," waiting for one or more external events. When one of these events happens, the driver regains control and gives it to the process in question. If it weren't for the fact that a process is waiting on an external event, this would look just like a deadlock. Instead, the event will eventually happen, allowing the process to continue and thus allowing all the other interlocked processes to start up as needed. This feature is one of the important performance advantages of FBP. Unlike conventional programming, if a process needs to wait for an event to occur, it is usually not necessary with FBP to put the whole network into wait state (underlying software permitting).

In figure 16-2, the diagram is redrawn, with the states of each process shown in the top left corner of the process. This pattern of states is quite common and quite characteristic of a certain kind of deadlock. The drivers of all FBP implementations always list the process states as part of their diagnostic output in the event of a deadlock.

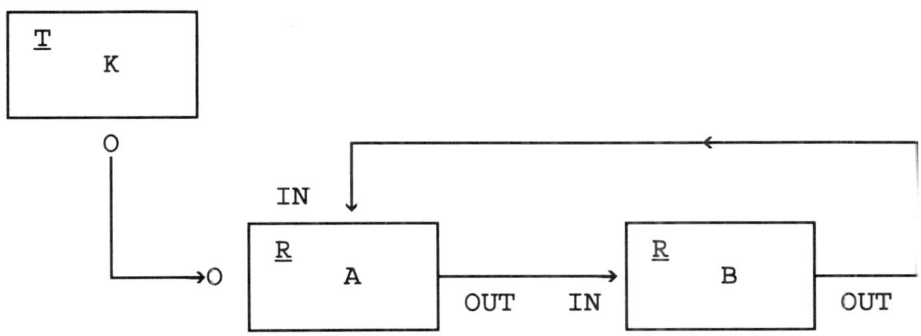

where T means terminated,
and R means suspended on receive

Figure 16-2.

Clearly, this kind of deadlock will occur any time a process outputs fewer IPs than the downstream process requires. Since the only kind of resource "native" to

FBP is the IP, the only problem can be non-arrival of IPs. So thorough testing will detect it. We could also have "infrastructure" or "hybrid" (FBP plus infrastructure) deadlocks, where, say, one process is waiting on an external event that never happens and another on an IP that the former is to send out. There is nothing to prevent a DFDM process from issuing an MVS ENQ, thus allowing two processes to interlock each other by both issuing two ENQs for the same resource, but in different orders. Old-style deadlock considerations apply here, but, as I've said, this is a well-understood area of computing.

The other class of deadlock familiar to systems programmers is the "storage deadlock." This kind of deadlock occurs because one process does not have enough storage to store information that is going to be needed later. This type of deadlock, unlike the resource deadlock, can usually be resolved by providing more storage (not always, because some variants of this continually demand more storage).

Here is an example of a storage deadlock. Suppose you are counting a stream of IPs and you want to print out all the IPs, followed by the count. The components for doing this should be quite familiar by now—the IPs to be counted go into the COUNT process at the IN port and emerge via the OUT port, while the count IP is generated and sent out via the COUNT port at close-down time. So all you have to do is concatenate the count IP after the ones coming from OUT. This is certainly very straightforward. The network is shown in figure 16-3.

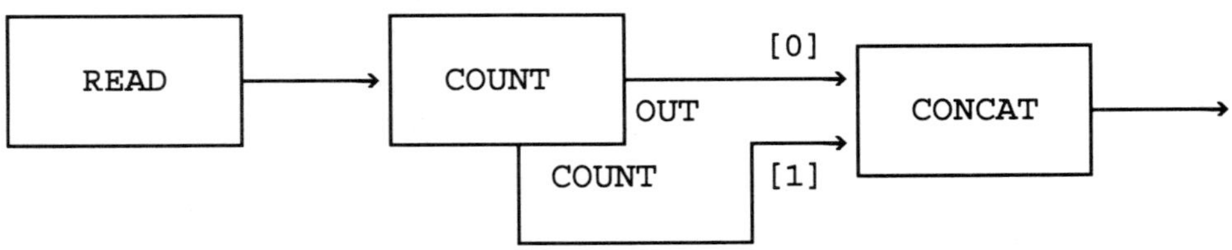

Figure 16-3.

You can code this up in THREADS, using the general purpose components available in THREADS. I will describe the THREADS syntax more fully in chapter 23, "Network Specification Notations," so the full network definition will not be shown here, but the essential point is that the OUT port of Count is connected to IN[0] of Concatenate and the COUNT port of Count to IN[1] of Concatenate, as follows:

```
....  Count OUT -> IN [0] Concatenate OUT -> ......
 Count COUNT -> IN[1] Concatenate......
```

Running this network gives the following result:

```
RUNNING NETWORK deadlk
......
Scan finished
```

```
Length: 3, Type: A, Data: 111
Length: 3, Type: A, Data: 123
Length: 3, Type: A, Data: 133
Length: 3, Type: A, Data: 134
Length: 3, Type: A, Data: 201
Length: 3, Type: A, Data: 211
Length: 3, Type: A, Data: 222
Length: 3, Type: A, Data: 234
Length: 3, Type: A, Data: 300
Length: 3, Type: A, Data: 450
Length: 3, Type: A, Data: 700
Length: 3, Type: A, Data: 999
Length: 10, Type: COUNT, Data: 12******70
Done
```

In this example, the extra asterisks and 70 in the count IP are due to the fact that this particular Count component (THCOUNT) allocates a ten-character IP, but uses the C function "ltoa" to display the count, in this case resulting in two characters followed by an ASCII zero byte. The rest of the IP is unchanged, so it contains "garbage" (official programming term).

But now suppose that, for some perverse reason, you want to see the count IP *ahead of* the ones being counted. Since you're using a Concatenate function, you might think that all you have to do is concatenate the count ahead of the IPs coming out of OUT. So you change the picture as shown in figure 16-4.

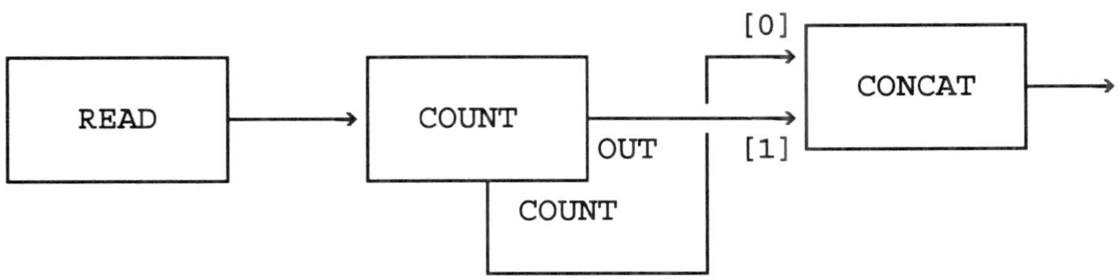

Figure 16-4.

Change the previous THREADS definition as follows:

```
  ....  Count OUT -> IN [1] Concatenate OUT -> ......
 Count COUNT -> IN[0] Concatenate.....,
```

To our surprise, the result of this is a little different:

```
RUNNING NETWORK deadlk
......
Scan finished
Deadlock detected
 Process Print Not Initiated
```

```
Process Concatenate Suspended on Receive
Process Count Suspended on Send
Process Read Suspended on Send
```

This is definitely not the result we wanted! Now, the message said `Deadlock`, so, as before, let's try taking the process states and inserting them back into the diagram, as shown in figure 16-5.

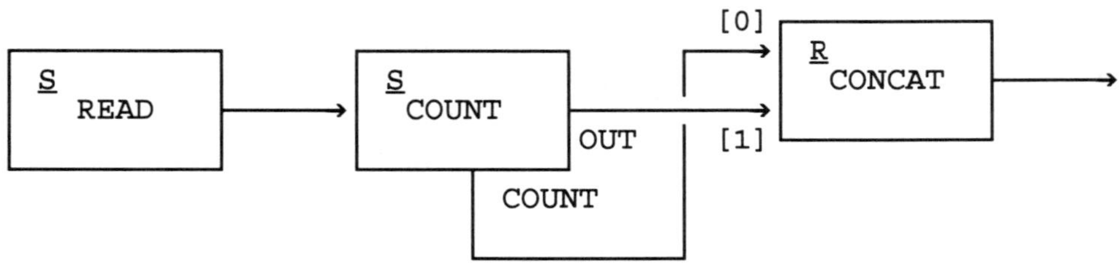


```
where S means suspended on send,
and   R means suspended on receive
```

Figure 16-5.

You will find that in this kind of deadlock there is always a "bottleneck," or point in the network where the upstream processes tend to be suspended on send and the downstream processes are suspended on receive. As we saw before, some processes may have terminated—these can be excluded from this discussion. Processes that are inactive or not yet initiated can be treated as if they are suspended on receive.

If COUNT is suspended on send and CONCAT is suspended on receive, but they are adjacent processes, then clearly COUNT is sending data to a connection *different from the one CONCAT is waiting on.* Although there is data on the connection labeled OUT, CONCAT insists on waiting on a connection where there is no data, and, at this rate, there never will be. The problem is that the COUNT IP is not generated until all of the input IPs have been processed, and the connection labeled OUT has a limited capacity, so there is nowhere to store the IPs after they have been counted.

Although this kind of deadlock resembles a resource deadlock (because each process is waiting on the other to do something it can't do), it can be resolved by giving one or more connections more storage, so it is of the class of storage deadlocks. You will remember that we don't make all our queues "infinite" because then you can't guarantee that everything will get processed in a timely manner (or ever, if you want to allow 24-hour systems). But, if you visualize the OUT connection bulging like a balloon as IPs are pumped into it, you can see that, eventually, COUNT is going to have processed all its input and will generate the count IP, and the balloon can start to deflate back to normal.

What's the best way of doing this? Unfortunately, the question depends on how many IPs are being counted. If you knew for sure the number of IPs, you could just make the capacity of the connection big enough. You can do this in THREADS by adding a capacity number in brackets after the arrow. Since the test data we are using has only 12 IPs, make the capacity 20:

```
    ....  Count OUT -> (20) IN [1] Concatenate OUT -> ......
   Count COUNT -> IN[0] Concatenate.....,
```

The result is as follows:

```
RUNNING NETWORK deadlk
......
Scan finished
Length: 10, Type: COUNT, Data: 12********
Length: 3, Type: A, Data: 111
Length: 3, Type: A, Data: 123
Length: 3, Type: A, Data: 133
Length: 3, Type: A, Data: 134
Length: 3, Type: A, Data: 201
Length: 3, Type: A, Data: 211
Length: 3, Type: A, Data: 222
Length: 3, Type: A, Data: 234
Length: 3, Type: A, Data: 300
Length: 3, Type: A, Data: 450
Length: 3, Type: A, Data: 700
Length: 3, Type: A, Data: 999
Done
```

Worked like a charm!

Hold on, though. How do you know the file will never exceed 20 IPs? Remember the provinces of Canada—the process has already started that should eventually lead to the creation of a new one (or several). It's a fair bet that there will always be 7 days in a week or 365¼ days in a year, but most other "constants" are subject to change, not to mention really variable numbers like the number of departments in a company.

Now follow the balloon analogy a bit further. What you could do is allow connections to bulge only if you would otherwise get a deadlock (i.e., no process can proceed) and let them bulge until you run out of storage. This initially seems attractive, but it makes error determination more complex. Remember that storage for IPs is allocated when they are created, not when they are put into a connection, so you will eventually run out of storage somewhere, and you won't know who the culprit is. And anyway, it's not a good idea to let the FBP driver grab *all* of storage, because then the storage some other subsystem needs to let it come down gracefully may not be available.

This whole area is tricky. If you know there will never be more than 50 provinces in Canada and that you will never need more than 1000 bytes per province, you could hold them all in storage for a total of 50,000 bytes, which is pretty small peas these days. But what if each province is a tree and you really don't know how many IPs are hung off each province or how big they are?

So far, the best general solution we have come up with is to use a sequential file. You will remember from chapter 15 that any connection can be replaced with a file. Let's change the network as shown in figure 16-6, using the notation used in chapter 15. In that chapter ——W [X] R—— was used to indicate a "sandwich," with the file being the meat and a Writer and a Reader being the bread on each side. In chapter 15, automatic ports were used to ensure that the Reader does not start until the Writer is finished.

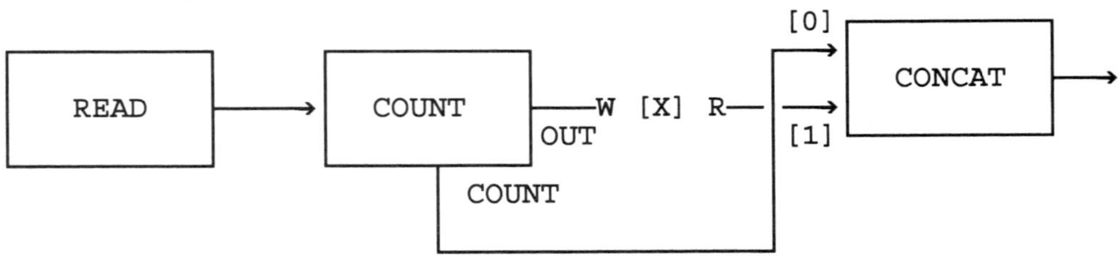

Figure 16-6.

Now, if you step this through in your head or try it out on the machine, you will find that the file soaks up IPs until it gets end of data. Meanwhile, CONCAT is waiting for data to arrive at IN[0]. The "meat" file's Reader can start at some point after this, but will only run until its output connection is full. At this point, the only thing that can happen is for CONCAT to receive the count IP, then end of data, and then switch to receiving from IN[1]. From this point on, the data IPs will just flow through IN[1] into (and through) CONCAT.

You have seen that capacities can be set on all connections. What would happen if all connections were given a standard capacity of ten? Then examples like the above would work fine as long as there were only ten Canadian provinces. Add another province one day, and your nice production program goes boom! Since amounts of test data tend to be smaller than production amounts, programmers would never be sure that programs that worked fine in test would not blow up in production. We therefore recommend the strategy of making connection capacities as small as possible during testing to prevent this kind of thing from happening. Zero-capacity connections would be very nice, but they are qualitatively different from non–zero-capacity connections (there are some situations where they really don't behave in the same way), so we use one-capacity connections. Once you go into production, however, you can safely increase connection capacities to reduce context-switching overhead. This strategy has been followed in both DFDM and THREADS and has been very successful in helping to reduce the occurrence of deadlocks. Apropos, my son, Joseph Morrison, an experienced programmer, has suggested the following aphorism: "During testing, better to crash than to crawl; in production, better to crawl than crash!" The second half of this doesn't mean, of course, that you should put poorly performing systems into production. It just means that in production, when problems arise, it is better to try to keep going, even if in a degraded mode, but make sure someone knows what's going on! There is a story about one of the early computers (either SAGE or STRETCH) that did such a good job of correcting storage errors that for some time nobody noticed that it was running slower and slower!

In chapter 15, I talked about how the Writer/Reader sandwich is sometimes referred to as an "infinite queue." This is a general solution for storage deadlocks, and the only slightly tricky thing about such deadlocks is figuring out which connection has to be expanded. If you bear in mind that it must be a connection that is full (i.e., its upstream process is suspended on send) while its downstream process is suspended trying to receive from a different port, you'll find it pretty easily.

This dependency on number of IPs occurs in conventional programming, and you are probably familiar with the problem of having to make design decisions based on number of items. Michael Jackson gives an example in his *Principles of Program Design* (1975) of a file that consists of two types of groups of records (we would call them substreams), where the substream type is determined by the type of the *last* record rather than the *first*. He gives as an example a file consisting of batches, each with a control record: if the control record agrees, you have a "good" batch; if it doesn't, it is a "bad" batch. The problem of course is whether the batch will fit in storage. If it will fit safely, there's no problem. If not, you either use a file or provide some form of backtracking (going ahead with your logic, but being prepared to undo some of it if it turns out to be a bad batch). In the foregoing I have tried to stress that it's not good enough if the batch fits into storage *now*—you have got to be sure it will fit in the future!

There is one final type of deadlock that again involves a loop-type network, but where most of the processes are suspended on send. This is more like a resource deadlock than a storage deadlock and usually arises because one or more processes are consistently generating more IPs than they receive. In this kind of deadlock, giving them more storage usually doesn't help—the network just takes longer to crash. However, in the case of a loop structure like a Bill of Materials explosion, some processes are consistently generating more IPs until you reach the elementary items, so you have got to think pretty carefully about how many IPs may be in storage at the same time. When in doubt, use a file!

If all this seems a trifle worrying, in most cases you will find that you can recognize deadlock-prone network topologies just by their shape. In fact, the very shapes of the previously mentioned networks constitute a clear warning sign: any loop shape in your network diagram, whether circular, as in figure 16-7, or divergent-convergent, as in figure 16-8, should be treated with caution, as they are possible sources of deadlocks.

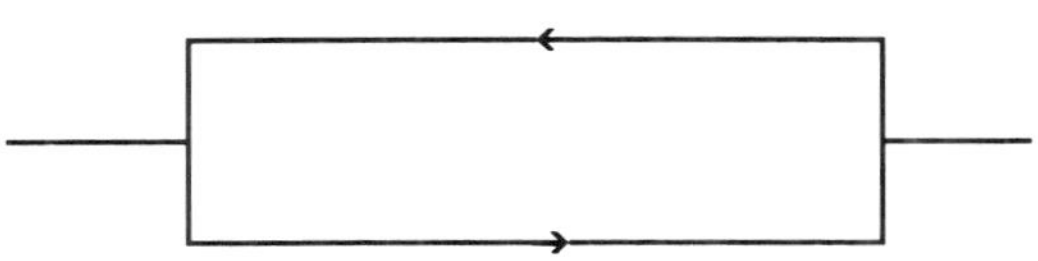

Figure 16-7.

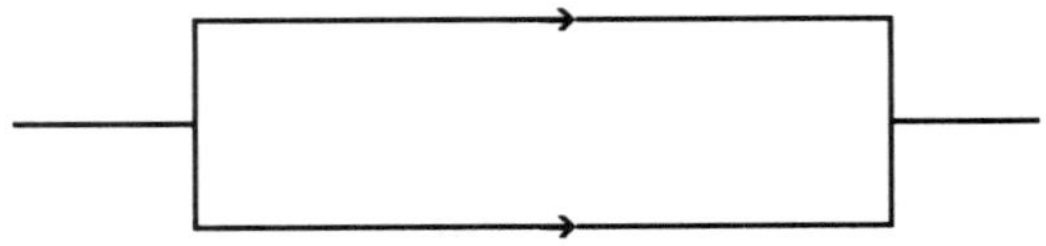

Figure 16-8.

In chapter 8, I talked about how, after you have split a stream into multiple streams, the output streams will be "decoupled" in time. If you decide you want to recombine them, you will usually land up with a variant of figure 16-8. Unless you are willing to use the first-come, first-served type of merge (by connecting multiple output ports to one input port), you will create a very fertile environment for deadlocks. Generally speaking, the split and merge functions have to be complementary, but that may not be enough. Here's an example. Suppose you want to spread a stream of IPs across three servers and then combine them afterwards. One approach might be to use a "cycling" splitter, which sends its incoming IPs to its output port elements 0 to $n-1$ in rotation. You will also need a merge that takes one IP from each port element in rotation and outputs them to a single output port. Setting n to 3, the resulting picture looks like figure 16-9.

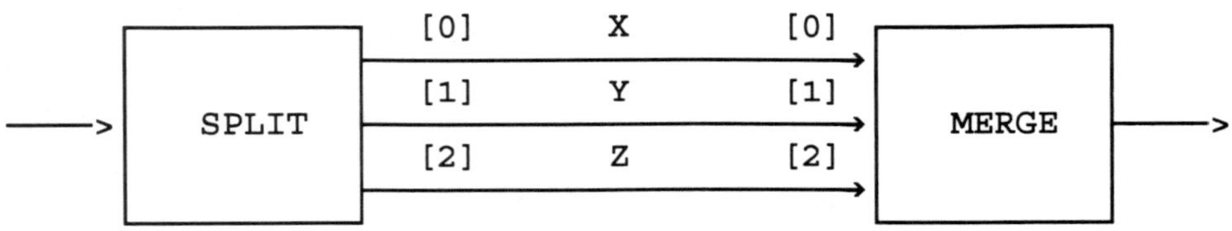

Figure 16-9.

Now you can add any processing you like at the spots marked *X, Y,* and *Z*. Well, not quite, as a number of people have discovered. For one thing, MERGE must see 0's, 1's, and 2's in strict rotation. If you want to drop an IP, you had better make sure there is a "placeholder" IP in its place, unless you can arrange to drop one or more entire sets of 0, 1, and 2. If you don't do this, the least that will happen is that your IPs will be out of order, and you may eventually get a deadlock (actually that might be better from a debugging point of view!). The same thing applies if you want to add extra IPs, except that the place-holders will have to be in the *other* streams. This impulse to split up streams into multiple ones is common among FBP programmers, and it can certainly simplify your programs. This example is just a warning of some of the pitfalls that await you when you try to recombine them. In fact, *it may not even be necessary.* You may find that the assumption that data has to be kept in strict sequence is just a hold-over from the old synchronous style of thinking.

I am going to show one more deadlock example, because it illustrates the use of the "close port" service, which has been required by all FBP dialects. Consider figure 16-10.

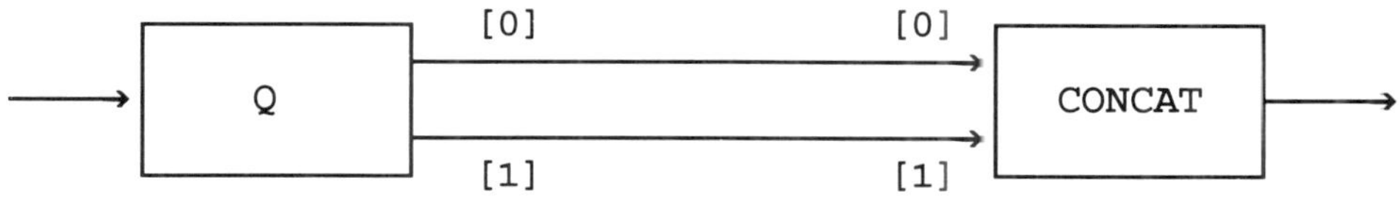

Figure 16-10.

You know by now that CONCAT receives all IPs from [0] until end of data and then starts receiving from [1], and so on. What can you deduce about the upstream process *Q*? Well, it should somehow be able to generate two output streams that overlap as little as possible in time. We also notice that this (partial) network has a divergent-convergent topology, which suggests that it is deadlock-prone. What might cause it to deadlock? One possibility is if *Q* starts to send IPs to [1] while CONCAT is still expecting data at element [0]. What causes CONCAT to switch from [0] to [1]? CONCAT switches every time it detects end of data on an input port element. But end of data is normally caused by the upstream process terminating, and *Q* has not terminated. So *Q* has to have some way to signal end of data on [0] to CONCAT, so that CONCAT can start processing the data arriving at [1]; otherwise, CONCAT will still be waiting on [0] while data builds up on [1]. What *Q* has to do is close each of its output ports before it switches to the next one. This will send a signal downstream enabling CONCAT to switch to its next input port.

The example shown in figure 16-10 is interesting, as it illustrates a useful technique for subdividing a problem. What *Q* is really doing is subdividing its input stream into "time domains," which CONCAT can then safely recombine into a single stream. A lot of sequential files in the business world have this "time domain" kind of structure (e.g., a file might have a header portion, perhaps a list of cities followed by a list of sales staff, followed by a trailer portion containing the actual sales information). This kind of structure can be handled nicely by splitting processing into separate "time domains."

17

Problem-Oriented Mini-Languages

> One of the greatest advantages of little languages is that one processor's input can be another processor's output. (Jon Bentley 1988)

> Another lesson we should have learned from the recent past is that the development of "richer" or "more powerful" programming languages was a mistake in the sense that these baroque monstrosities, these conglomerations of idiosyncrasies, are really unmanageable, both mechanically and mentally. I see a great future for very systematic and very modest programming languages. (E.W. Dijkstra 1972)

Problem-oriented mini-languages can be thought of as essentially an extension of the types of parametrization discussed in chapter 5. Bentley, like many other writers, has pointed out the importance of finding the right language for a programmer to express his or her requirements. This language should match as closely as possible the language used in the problem domain. If you view the programmer's job as being a process of mapping the user's language to a language understood by the machine, then clearly this job becomes easier the closer the two languages are to each other.

You may have gathered, correctly, that I am not overly excited about the HLLs (higher-level languages) of today. They appear to me to occupy an uncomfortable middle ground between more elegant options at each end of the spectrum. At the low end is Assembler language; at the high end are reusable "black box" modules. Some jobs can really only be done in Assembler (although C is moving in on its turf)—the problem is portability. Black box modules solve the portability problem much more effectively than HLLs—you just port at the function level, rather than at the code level. Historically, HLLs evolved out of "small" languages like FORTRAN by the gradual accretion of features as people tried to extend the languages to new application areas. Most of them are on the firmest ground when dealing with arithmetic, because here they had traditional notations and experience to build on.

There are three major problem areas common to almost all HLLs:

- The data types of variables.
- Constants.
- The basically synchronous nature of these languages.

I have already talked about variables in the context of the usual computer concept of storage. Data types were discussed in chapter 11, "Data Descriptions and Descriptors." Now let's talk about constants.

Constants are usually not (constant, that is!). Constants are vastly overused, mostly because it is so easy to hard-code a constant into a program. To take an extreme position, I would like to see constants used only when they represent the structure of the universe, such as Planck's constant or π, or conversion rates between, say, kilometers and miles—they're not likely to change. I also vote for zero and one—they're too useful (for things like clearing and incrementing counters) to give up! Also, to one and zero let's add their Boolean cousins, "true" and "false." But that's all!

An ex-colleague of mine *claims* that he knew someone who wrote a program for a company that had exactly 365 employees. You guessed it—an employee left the company, and all the date calculations were off! While this story is probably apocryphal, there is an interesting point here: the only way it could have happened is if the program used the *same* constant for both numbers. Many shops ban literals, in an attempt to reduce this kind of thing, whereas, of course, it only helps if people are also encouraged to use meaningful symbol names. If, as many programmers do, the constant in question was labeled F365, it would actually make this kind of error *more* likely.

Literals would actually have prevented this kind of thing from happening, whereas calling a constant F365 works the other way. One of the constants should have been NUMBER_OF_DAYS_IN_YEAR (that's non-leap, of course), and the other one shouldn't have been a constant at all! Remember, *most constants aren't.*

So far I have mostly talked about numeric values. There is another class of constants that one runs into quite often in programs: strings that identify entities or objects. Consider a test like the following:

```
IF PROVINCE = 'ONT'.....
```

There are two reasons why this shouldn't be used. The first point is that in HLLs we are forced to compare two *character strings,* whereas what we would like to ask is (in English):

```
If this province is Ontario,....
```

This may not look very different, but the first case deals with how affiliation with Ontario is encoded in a *particular* field; in the second, you are asking if the *entity* being referenced is the entity Ontario (with all its connotations). Smalltalk is better in this regard: `province` would be an attribute of one object that contains the handle of another object (`ontario`) belonging to the class `Province`, and you can ask if two objects are the same object (==). Using conventional HLLs, another programmer or even a different field of the same object that needs to reference Ontario might specify it using the value 2, so you would spend all sorts of machine resources converting back and forth between 2 and `'ONT'`. Nan Shu has identified conversions between codes as one of the most common functions performed by business application code (Shu 1985).

The second point is more subtle: even if you can refer to unique objects as a whole, rather than by an indirect encoding, should you? Consider the following sort of code, which is often found in business applications:

```
IF PROVINCE = 'NB' OR PROVINCE = 'PEI' OR PROVINCE = 'NS'...
```

If Canada adds a new province, how do you find *all* the lists like the above, and how do you decide if the new province should be added or not? What is the concept that makes *this* set of provinces different from all the others? This is an example of a very common problem with code that is probably responsible for significant maintenance costs in shops around the world. At this point you will probably realize that we haven't done anything yet in FBP to prevent people from doing this. And as long as we are stuck with today's computers as the underlying engine, we probably can't, unless we ban constants entirely! What we *can* do is provide tools to help with this kind of situation (i.e., support the logic that people are trying to implement) and raise the consciousness of programmers by means of walk-throughs, inspections, apprenticeships, buddy systems, or whatever.

The general concept that I would like to see known and used more widely is what IBM's Bucky Pope calls "class codes." He suggests that you first ask what the underlying concept is behind the list; then build a table or database and implement the concept as an attribute of the entities (in this case, provinces). So the above test becomes something like this:

```
FIND PROVINCE IN PROVINCE_TABLE

IF MARITIME, .....
```

The overhead goes up a bit, but maintenance costs go down drastically, and since it is now generally accepted that human time is a lot more expensive than machine time (Kendall 1977), it seems shortsighted to keep on perpetuating this type of code and incurring the resultant costs. By the way, this principle applies equally if only one province happens to be mentioned in a particular list. How do you know that a new province won't show up that shares attributes with the one you've picked?

If you are going to (almost) ban constants from code and put entity attributes and what have been called "variable constants" on disk, why not put logic on disk as well? This gets into the domain of rules-driven systems. Remember that FBP gets rid of a lot of the nonbusiness logic, so most of the remaining logic in code should be either general purpose (e.g., the logic to collate two data streams) or business related, (e.g., IF INCOME >$50,000, CALCULATE SURTAX USING FORMULA . . .). Now, both the criterion and the formula are certainly going to change and on a regular basis, so why put them in code that requires programmers to change it, after which the changed programs have to be recompiled, approved, and promoted, the old ones archived, and so on? It seems much better to put the whole thing somewhere where it can be maintained more easily, perhaps even by nonprogrammers. I believe that much business logic, perhaps almost all, can be put on disk and interpreted using simple interpreters.

One important question remains: whether to put our attribute tables, rules, and so on, in load modules (created with a compiler and linkage editor) or in data files. The former is really a halfway house, as you still need programmers to maintain them, but at least the information is separate from code, so it can be shared and is much easier to manage and control than when it is buried in many different code modules. However, I believe that putting this kind of information into databases is an even better solution, as it can be updated by nonprogrammers (e.g., clerical staff) and it can have separate and specific authorization.

In rules-driven systems, straight sequential logic may not be the best way to express the rules. PROLOG and its derivatives provide a very interesting approach to expressing logic. It should be stressed that logic programming is not incompatible with FBP. I once wrote an experimental FBP component that drove a PROLOG set of rules to perform some logic tests on incoming IPs. The effect was like having a friendly database, because you could ask questions like "list all the mothers older than 50" even when you had not stored the attribute "mother" explicitly in the database (just tell PROLOG that a "mother" is anyone who is female and has offspring). The logic programming people have independently explored the possibilities of combining logic programming with parallelism (e.g., such languages as PARLOG).

Now, if business rules can be put out on disk, avoiding such perilous traps as variables and constants, and program code restricted to nonbusiness-related logic, then it seems that there really isn't much of a role for today's HLLs.

So far, I have talked about the basics of most programming languages as being arithmetic and logic, but there exist languages today that address quite different domains. Over the years, there have been a number of other kinds of specialized languages, such as SNOBOL (pattern-matching) or IPL V (list processing), that have appeared and sometimes disappeared. Since in conventional programming it is hard to make languages talk to each other, it is generally the richer ones that have survived. FBP, on the other hand, makes it much easier for languages to communicate, which suggests that we may see a larger number of more specialized languages communicating by means of data streams. Based on our experience with human languages, it would be very nice if they could all share the same *syntax,* but work with different classes of objects (*semantics*). It has been found that humans have a lot of difficulty switching from one syntax to another, whereas they can hold many different vocabularies independently without getting them confused. This is supported by recent work with bi- and multi-lingual communities—people tend to use one syntax for both languages, or a hybrid, but they can keep the vocabularies quite well separated.

Dave Olson's book (mentioned earlier) points out that if you consider the total application space as chaotic, then you will get areas of order and areas of disorder (Olson 1993). Each mini-language can handle its own area of order, and can communicate using standard interfaces (IPs) with other areas of order. Each mini-language defines its own paradigm—while no paradigm should be expected to do the whole job, a judicious combination of many paradigms is often highly effective.

I would argue that, any time a set of parameters reaches a certain level of complexity, you are approaching a mini-language. The parameters to the IBM Sort utility almost constitute a language about sorting, and in fact IBM has added a free-form, HLL-like syntax to the older-style pointer list. Since decoding the Sort parameters is relatively fast compared with the Sort itself, it is reasonable to make the Sort parameters as human-convenient as possible. The semantics of a set of Sort control statements are quite simple, just referring to objects of interest to the Sort (and its user).

Earlier in this book I mentioned a prototyping system that I built, in which you could describe screen layouts in WYSIWYG form. For fun I added a graphics subsystem, for specifying simple pictures. The problem was: What mental model would its users find convenient? I decided to use the idea of color-filled polygons, which had been used successfully by the Canadian videotext system, Telidon. I later added the capacity to have curved edges, as well as straight ones, plus various fill patterns, such as cross-hatching. While this choice of mental model may seem fairly obvious, I could have used bit maps, straight lines, or some other primitive, but I found the polygon idea an especially good bridge between the artist and the computer. Not only was it a good match with the software I was using (GDDM), but also I was pleased to discover how fast I could develop a drawing or modify an existing one. The artist I was working with found that he was able to adapt to this medium, and I was impressed with the quality of what we turned out, working together. I use this perhaps rather simple example to make the point that it is the *mental model* that is important and makes the most difference in how usable people find a tool. Humans are visualizing creatures and, if they have trouble developing a mental model of your tool or system, it will never become *real* to them, and they will have endless trouble with it.

If you have spent the last few decades laboring with a conventional HLL, by now you may be wondering how one can do *anything* without using variables or constants. Well, quite a bit, as it turns out. In chapter 25 ("Streams and Recursive Function Definitions"), we will talk about a style of programming that is called generically *applicative* or *functional*. When you combine the idea of functions with recursive definition, it turns out that you can express quite complex computations without ever using a variable (Burge 1975). As for constants, as long as we put most of them on disk, I'll be quite happy! Of course, I am not suggesting that tax specialists learn recursive programming in order to be able to describe tax calculations to the computer, but, based on various experiences, I have a strong intuition that, by judiciously combining a number of the ideas described so far in this book and some that are about to be described, we could develop user-friendly languages that would be decades ahead of the user-hostile tools we are forced to use today.

In the next chapter I am going to describe an approach to a mini-language for describing business processes running in an FBP environment that takes advantage of the fact that there are other precoded FBP components (such as Collate) to do a lot of the hard work. It is applicative, in that it doesn't use variables but defines its outputs purely in terms of operations on its inputs. This is not supposed to be a definition of a complete language, but more of a sketch of how a language might look that breaks with many time-honored but rather shopworn traditional solutions.

18

A Business-Oriented Very High Level Language

The following is a sketch for a different kind of language—one that specifies business logic descriptively rather than procedurally. I was reading an article by M. Hammer et al. (1977), describing a system that they called the Business Definition Language and I started thinking that some of BDL's basic ideas were really complementary to FBP. FBP doesn't have a native way to express business logic, but does provide simple solutions to some of the awkwardnesses that I spotted in BDL. BDL might be described as a tabular/functional approach to expressing business applications that embodies a number of desirable program attributes listed by B. Leavenworth in his 1977 paper:

- Elimination of arbitrary sequencing (sequencing not dictated by the data dependencies of the application).
- Pattern-directed structures (non-procedural specification).
- Aggregate operations.
- Associative referencing.

Of course, these are embodied in BDL, which the following language is modeled on, but it seems to me that FBP can make BDL even more friendly, so these attributes should carry over to the resulting language.

I want to expand on these four points a bit. The following are my interpretations, but I hope that I don't depart too far from the spirit in which he intended them.

Leavenworth sees the first point, "arbitrary sequencing," as one of the serious problems with procedural languages, and of course it has come up frequently in various forms in this book. As I said before, the von Neumann machine forces you to fix the sequence of every statement, *whether it matters to the logic or not.* Consider the following two statements:

```
MOVE A TO B

MOVE C TO D
```

Clearly it makes no difference to the logic what order they are executed in, but change the first statement to refer to *C* or *D,* and you reverse them at your peril. Thus,

```
MOVE A TO C

MOVE C TO D
```

is *totally* different from

```
MOVE C TO D

MOVE A TO C
```

It is also worth noting that much of the optimizing logic in compilers involves trying to determine which statements can be moved and which ones cannot.

It should also be clear in light of what has gone before why "pattern-directed structures" are desirable. Humans are much better at working with descriptions (especially visual ones) than lists of instructions.

"Aggregate operations" is closely related with trying to avoid procedural solutions. The higher the level of the constructs that the language deals with, the more powerful it is, and the less of a barrier there is between the programmer's concept and its expression in the language. Of course, higher-level constructs require higher-level operations.

An example I have always found interesting is the APL language. It is highly expressive, and a lot of its power derives from the foundation work that Ken Iverson did while investigating the basic theory of matrices. While most of us were taught to treat matrix multiplication as an atomic operation, Iverson found a simple yet powerful way to make visible the fact that it is really a particular relationship between two binary operators, which he represented using the "dot" symbol. This is a second-order operator, as it works with other operators rather than variables. Not only did this allow other binary operators to be combined in the same way (like "or" and "and," or "min" and "max"), but it freed up the simple "multiply" operator so that it could be generalized smoothly from scalars to vectors to matrices.

As an example of aggregate operations, let's compare the way PL/I and APL handle matrices. In PL/I you can write the following statement:

```
A = A + A(2,3);
```

This is implemented in a very procedural manner. PL/I executes this statement one element at a time and does it in such a way that the rightmost dimension is the one that cycles most rapidly. So the sequence will be A(1,1), A(1,2), . . ., A(1,n), A(2,1), . . ., A(2,n), and so on. When these additions hit A(2,3), all "later" elements (those following A(2,3)) will have the new (doubled) value added to them, rather than the original one. In APL, on the other hand, matrices are treated as "aggregates," which are conceptually handled all at the same moment of time. Thus, you can write

A ← *A* + *A*[2;3]

and it behaves much like the PL/I example, *but* A[2;3] does not change halfway through execution. This of course means that APL has to be able to manage matrices as more or less opaque objects, while in the PL/I model a matrix is just another part of the machine's memory, with a particular structure superimposed on it. In FBP, although for performance reasons you have to process a stream one IP at a time, you very often can *think* of it as a single object. If you really have to process a whole stream as a single object, you can turn it into a tree and then turn it back later. Chapter 25, "Streams and Recursive Function Definitions," will show how one can use recursive function definitions to effectively treat a whole stream as a single aggregate object.

"Associative referencing" means the ability to locate an object by content rather than by location. On most modern machines, this is done with a look-up of some sort, although there have been machines designed that did it by hardware. A few years ago there was a lot of interest in associative or "content-addressable" memory. While it is certainly nice to be able to find things that have moved, my feeling is that "handles" are fine, provided you have a way to find new things that you have never searched for before. Once they are found, they shouldn't have to move again, and their handles can be passed from process to process. An additional wrinkle is to leave a trail in the rare event that things do move (of course, in both cases we are talking about a single shared memory). It is interesting that the main difference between Carriero and Gelernter's Linda (1989) and FBP is that the former is associative, while FBP uses connections and handles. Linda will be covered in more detail in a later chapter, but it seems that Linda's design should increase its overhead considerably over FBP, without a corresponding advantage in expressiveness. An example in one of the articles about Linda describes how to simulate an FBP connection, and it would be trivial to write matching FBP components that store and retrieve Linda tuples. Of Leavenworth's four points, this last seems to me the least exciting, but it should certainly be borne in mind as a design technique.

To give you a flavor of BDL, table 18-1 shows a sample definition for the "extended details" file (or stream) in Leavenworth's paper. This is the same TR1 that was used in chapter 10. In the table, "'s" is the BDL notation denoting a collection or group.

I have labeled the columns as shown to give an indication of their purpose and interrelationships (BDL proper does not do this). The first two columns express the hierarchical structure of the file in question and the derivations of each of the entries, while the last two columns give definitions of all names appearing in the second column and of any new names introduced in these definitions. The fourth column uses some reserved words to describe relationships between words in the first column and their sources. Thus, the derivation of "Ext price" is shown in the second column, and uses "Unit price" and "Quantity," whose definitions are in turn shown in the third and fourth columns. The whole approach is based on *definitions,* rather than *procedures,* which I found very appealing.

The structure shown in the first column is considered to repeat indefinitely through the "Ext detail's" file.

If a job step produces more than one output file, a BDL "program" similar to that shown in table 18-1 must be given for each one separately. Clearly, since each one is "driven" by the same input file, there is unnecessary duplication of logic here. In fact, in an attempt to avoid uncontrolled "global" definitions, the BDL language is considerably more redundant than one would like—every duplication increases the risk of one or more of the copies getting out of step.

TABLE 18-1. Sample BDL Program

Specification		Glossary	
Name	**Derivation**	**Name**	**Definition**
1 Ext Detail's	ONE PER Detail	Detail's	INPUT
2 Ext Price	Unit price x Quantity	Unit price	IN Product Master
		Product Master	Master WITH Master Product number = Detail Product number
		Master product number	IN Master
		Detail product number	IN Detail
		Detail	CAUSE OF Ext detail
		Master's	INPUT
		Quantity	IN Detail
2 Salesman	Old Salesman	Old Salesman	IN Detail
		Detail	CAUSE OF Ext detail
3 District	Old District	Old District	IN Detail
		Detail	CAUSE OF Ext detail

A more subtle problem arises from the lack of an explicit stream concept. In column three of table 18-1, "Product Master" is defined as that Master record (hopefully unique) whose "Master Product number" field is equal to the "Detail Product number" in the Detail record. WITH is an example of what Leavenworth calls "associative referencing"—it describes an implicit matching process. However, there is no indication of *how* the appropriate master record is located. While this is to some extent deliberate, when you actually come to build an application, you will eventually have to choose between various techniques for relating details and their corresponding masters (e.g., direct access, sort and merge, and perhaps others), which will have a profound effect on the basic structure of our design. It is true that the software could be allowed to select the technique automatically, but I feel that it is better to leave developers free to choose whichever technique seems most appropriate. Remember there will be prewritten, "black-box" code available to support whatever approach they select.

In what follows, I will assume that sorted streams of data have been merged using Collate, so the master records will precede their associated details. I will now give a sketch of a mini-language that holds to the spirit of BDL, but takes advantage of the fact that only a single FBP process is being described.

Three types of non-procedural information together describe what you want this kind of process to do:

- A description of the input and output streams, down to the IP level, and the creation and output criteria for the output IPs (let's call it an IP Relationship Diagram).
- Descriptions of the various IPs involved (IP Descriptions).
- Description of the calculation basis for "derived" fields—fields not present in the input IPs or whose values are changed by the component (Derivation Descriptions).

Together these will comprise a Component Description. A free-form notation is used in the accompanying figures, using English-like names for fields and uppercase strings for "reserved words."

In what follows, square brackets will indicate that a clause seems slightly redundant and could easily be eliminated by adding a new rule to the set of evaluation rules. These are usually reasonable defaults, which can still be overridden if the developer needs to.

I will now show the three portions of a Component Description, listed above, using the component TR1 from chapter 10.

The following shows the IP Relationship Diagram (IRD) for TR1:

```
INPUT STREAM

1. Merged Input
 2. Product Substream: REPEATING
  3. Product Master
  3. Sales Detail: REPEATING
```

```
OUTPUT STREAMS

1. New Masters
 2. Product Master: ONE PER Product Substream

1. Sort Input
 2. Sales Detail: [ONE PER Sales Detail]

1. Report1
 2. Product Summary: ONE PER Product Substream [,NEW]
```

This table describes relationships among IPs, so the lowest-level items at any point always describe IPs—all higher-level items are substreams, while all level 1 items are streams. Only one input stream may be specified in the IRD, but there may be any number of output streams. All streams consist of repeating patterns of IPs, and a COBOL-like "level" notation is used to show how they are nested to form a complete data stream.

The repeating pattern may be trivial (e.g., the stream may consist of only one IP), or it may be as complex as desired, consisting of a variable number of substreams, each of which consists of a variable number of substreams, and so on. In what follows, unless explicitly stated otherwise, the word "substream" will be taken to allow a single IP. This way I don't have to keep on saying "IP or substream." Similarly, "substream" can also refer to the whole stream, except where explicitly stated otherwise.

A substream in an IRD always has a "quantifier," which may, for an input stream, be one of the phrases REPEATING, OPTIONAL, or ONE OR MORE, or be absent; for an output stream, it may be either ONE PER or be absent. These quantifiers describe the number of occurrences of the substream in question *within the next higher level substream.* If no quantifier is specified, then there is exactly one such substream in the next higher level substream. REPEATING, OPTIONAL, and ONE OR MORE, mean respectively, zero or more, zero or one, and at least one occurrence. ONE PER x indicates that the substream in question is to be generated once for each occurrence of substream x (let's follow BDL in calling x the "cause" of the substream being described).

Examining the IRD for TR1, we note that the input stream consists of zero or more Product Substreams, each of which consists of *one* Product Master, followed by zero or more Details. You will remember that substreams are delimited by bracket IPs, so a Product Substream is additionally marked by the presence of a Product Master. This kind of redundancy appeared before, but it doesn't hurt, and, if the Product Master had been OPTIONAL, the brackets would be the only way to separate Product Substreams.

In the output streams, two of the IP types (Product Masters and Sales Details) actually came from the input stream, and are referred to as OLD, while the Product Summary IPs are created by TR1 and are called NEW.

The PER clause on Sales Detail is shown in square brackets because a reasonable additional evaluation rule might be: if the PER clause is omitted on an OLD IP, the IP is its own "cause."

Now you will need some kind of description of the IPs. This was discussed at length in chapter 11, so I will not go into much detail here. The designers of BDL also saw the need to allow a more varied set of field types than conventional HLLs. A Sales Detail IP could also be described using COBOL-style level numbers to show relationships between fields, but the positioning of the fields is only important when importing or exporting files. The other main function of level numbers—to show groupings—either goes away when one has more powerful field types or can be handled in other ways. Therefore, the fields of Sales Detail IP might be shown as a simple list, as follows:

```
Sales Detail:
{
  Product Number: IDENT,
  Salesman Number: IDENT,
  District Number: IDENT,
  Quantity: QUANTITY,
  Unit Price: $CDN,
  Extended Price $CDN;
}
```

The last thing to specify is the derivations of any derived fields. Table 18-2 shows the algorithms for those fields that are changed or created by the action of the component in question. Fields that are unchanged from the values they had on entering the component are not shown. Indentation might be used to relate fields to the IPs they are part of.

When a field in a "new" IP is not mentioned, it is assumed to have the same value as the field with the same name in the "cause" IP.

The function SUM of A OVER B sums all occurrences of field A within substream B (which is called the "range" of the OVER). Thus, Product Total is defined as the sum of Extended Price OVER Product Substream. The OVER clause is shown in

TABLE 18-2. Field Derivations

Name	Derivation
Product Master	
Year-to-date Sales	Year-to-date Sales [IN Product Master] + Product Total
Sales Detail	
Extended Price	Unit Price * Quantity
Product Summary	
Product Total	SUM of Extended Price [OVER Product Substream]
Year-to-date Sales	SAME as IN Product Master

square brackets in this example, as it becomes redundant if the following rule is added: if OVER is omitted, the "range" is taken to be the "cause" for the field being computed. Although this may seem arbitrary, in fact it covers all the SUMs so far encountered in sample problems.

The IN in Year-to-date Sales is similar to qualification in COBOL or PL/I. It can be omitted if it is understood that it is the field of the same name in the "cause" that is meant.

"SAME as" is self-explanatory.

The Product Summary report poses a different kind of problem, as it has to do with printing a human-readable report. Of course, screens are also human-readable, so many of the same solutions should apply to both. There are many possible approaches to parametrizing a report, and, under FBP, there is no need to decide on a single unique solution, as many printer components can all coexist in your library of components, just as a carpenter can have many different kinds of glue for different jobs. However, it is not hard to imagine that a useful component would be a "report interpreter" similar to the interpreter that interprets the derivation rules. I am not going to show how reports could or should be defined, but am rather going to mention a few ideas that might be considered in designing such general components.

Chapter 10 covered what a useful report generator component might look like, so we will concentrate on the components that generate the report lines upstream of it. This of course brings in the question of "representations" talked about in chapter 11 ("Data Descriptions and Descriptors"). There I talked about how representation standards normally come in layers: in a given application you may have an international standard, a national standard, and a company standard, and a particular report may even use two or more such representations for the same domain (e.g., amounts with and without separators). Since reports and screens have to be human-readable, you also have the problem of multilingual support, and two very noticeable differences between languages are that:

1. Phrases in different languages are frequently of different lengths.
2. Values may have to be embedded in text in different orders.

The previously mentioned problems have been solved quite well in the area of message-handling. A common solution is to simply provide "skeletons" that contain the fixed information and have "insertion points" for variable information. This assumes that most of the variable information is not language-dependent, but it covers most common reporting requirements. So a report or a screen would probably be like a set of messages with fixed columns (and maybe rows) added.

Reports (and screens that reflect reports) also will have subtotals and total lines, which can be driven by special IPs generated upstream at close bracket time. There are a number of report generation tools, of which RPG is one of the oldest and best known, that can act as mental models. The report design files or screens should resemble the final document in layout (WYSIWYG), but with the addition of IP type information (e.g., heading, detail, total for such and such level) and codes for common variable information, such as date, time, and page number. Such a design can then be encapsulated in a component or maybe more than one—remember, you are not restricted to only one report generator. Similar specifications are showing up in popular PC applications—for instance, the Report Generator function of the Database subsystem of Microsoft's Works.

The foregoing is just a sketch for a mini-language that might do some of what people use HLLs for today. Because FBP allows you to mix languages freely, no one language has to be able to do everything, so you can design languages to specialize in different subject areas. By the same token, the same mental model is not valid for all possible uses—if you want to do some logic by pattern-matching, you do not have to do it *all* by pattern-matching. Similarly, while mathematics is a great foundation for some types of programming, that does not mean that all programmers must become mathematicians. Lastly, a language can be expressive and still be rigorous. If the mental model is one that people find easy to grasp, it should enhance productivity, rather than just becoming an extra burden on the developer. It is absolutely crucial that we shift some of the responsibility for developing applications onto people who are not necessarily professional programmers, both to reduce the DP bottleneck and to take advantage of their expertise.

The various diagrams and lists shown here provide the advantages of applicative programming notation without the complexity of nested functions, which are normally required in such a notation. FBP does this by making explicit the timing relationships of the different processing events and the derivational relationships of the IPs involved in that processing. The right-hand side of a derivation specification is in fact a functional expression of any desired complexity (it can even include conditional parts analogous to the *cond* function of applicative programming), and such a specification conforms to the "single assignment" characteristic of applicative programs.

Because of the open-endedness of the FBP architecture, a component of this type does not have to cover all possible applications and can be part of a total application comprising both custom and off-the-shelf components. One can easily visualize a whole range of such components relevant to different application areas, essentially acting as repositories of specialized knowledge about these areas. If one component is more powerful than another one or covers a wider application area, a sort of evolutionary "survival of the fittest" would be expected and is in fact desirable. The problem is that some dinosaurs have survived far beyond their "natural" span because of the enormous inertia of our environment rather than because of any intrinsic superiority!

19

On-line Application Design

An increasing number of computer applications are interactive—that is, they have to communicate with an end user, with the result that some (but not necessarily all) application processes must be geared to the user's pace. An end user will enter commands and data on a screen, select among options, and so on, and the results will be displayed on the screen. Usually, these events alternate, but some displays occur unexpectedly, and the user must also be able to interrupt processes or switch to other activities. Hardware and software environments vary. The screens may range from "dumb" terminals to graphics terminals to programmable workstations with powerful logic capabilities; terminals may be connected in various ways to the host; and, finally, the host may be running different software platforms (e.g., IBM's CP/CMS, TSO, IMS, or CICS) or 4GLs based on them. While it is hard to generalize between all these variations, it is a safe bet that there will always be a need for a program to be able to present text, numeric, and alphameric information to a screen and for the user to be able to send commands and data to the computer. There is also a need to format a screen, including specification of fixed or user-specifiable information on one or more screen and window layouts. The user and program must further be able to select among different such layouts.

In chapter 14, I talked about "loop"-type networks supporting one interactive user (as in the IBM TSO and CMS environments and on PCs) and how this changes when you move to multiuser environments, such as IBM's IMS/DC (of course, TSO and CMS support multiple users, but in their case a whole program is dedicated to a single user, while an IMS/DC program supports a series of different users one at a time). In what follows, I will go into more detail on IMS/DC and also concentrate on one type of screen, the 3270 (without graphics capability). I believe these concepts generalize well to other environments, even to the new GUI-style interfaces with drag 'n' drop interaction (by assigning a different process to each window), but this chapter would get much too long if I tried to cover even just the IBM host environments.

First I want to describe at a high level how TSO (or CMS), CICS, and IMS/DC differ. By the way, IMS/DC is now IMS TM, but I will continue to use the older term. The basic problem that they all address in different ways is how to trigger program activity as a result of a user action on a screen or keyboard. In TSO (or CMS), the user has a whole program dedicated to his or her use, which multithreads with other such programs. During his or her "think-time," the program has to wait, but the other parallel programs (either supporting other users or running batch) can use the available CPU time.

CICS and IMS/DC are both very popular for IBM hosts, and they are both delivering very respectable transaction rates. Traditionally, CICS has had lower overhead but has provided less protection between users. These distinctions may be breaking down as these systems evolve. CICS runs a number of parallel tasks. When one of these tasks is triggered by a user's action, it executes the appropriate logic. After output has been generated, the task can be suspended ("conversational" processing) or can terminate after user-oriented information has been saved ("non-conversational"). If all code were conversational, a CICS program could only support as many users as there are tasks, so this mode is not recommended, especially since human think-times are long compared with the CPU time required by the machine. CICS, like all FBP implementations so far, can suspend a task at any API call. In fact, allowing tasks to be suspended elsewhere than at an API call would make FBP (and CICS) programming much harder, so it is unlikely that this will change. I have always felt that the internal logic of CICS is so similar to that of FBP that a hybrid system combining ideas from both might be extremely interesting.

IMS/DC also uses a number of parallel programs, but, unlike TSO, each program services multiple users, one after the other. Each user "occupies" a program from the time a screen or keyboard action takes place until the response has been sent back to the screen, at which point the program is free to service a different user. In fact, an IMS program never waits for the user to finish thinking—if there is no work waiting to be done, it just terminates. So IMS/DC cannot use CICS's "conversational" approach; while it also uses the term "conversational," it is actually very similar to CICS's "non-conversational." Also, IMS programs run in separate regions, so they can interrupt each other preemptively, whereas CICS tasks can only lose control at an API call.

IMS transactions are driven from a "message queue." Each message was added to the queue as a result of a user taking some action, such as hitting ENTER, a Program Attention key, or a Program Function key at his or her terminal or they may arrive from other sources, such as other programs running on IMS. IBM 327x terminals are "buffered," meaning that information is accumulated on the screen until one of the above keys is hit, at which time all modified data is sent to the host, together with an indication of what action was taken by the user and where on the screen the cursor was. All this information is collected and put into an "input message," which is then placed on the message queue. In addition, each message contains an 8-character code indicating which processing is to be applied to this data. Very often it is used to identify the screen that was being displayed when the interrupt occurred, allowing the program to select the processing. This code is called the "transaction ID."

The transaction ID is used by IMS to select, based on rules the installation has specified, which of a set of programs, called "message-processing programs" (MPPs), is to service this transaction. The MPP may already be running; if not, it will be started in an available "message-processing region" (MPR).

When the program logic decides that a new screen is to be displayed on the terminal, it puts an "output message" on the message queue containing the data to be displayed and the position at which the cursor is to be positioned. The program usually specifies which screen layout is to be used for this.

An MPP processes serially the transactions it is supposed to handle. It continues picking its transactions off the message queue and putting output messages onto the queue until one of the following occurs:

- There are no more transactions waiting.
- A higher priority transaction needs the region.
- It reaches a predefined limit called the "program limit count" (PLC).

When one of these occurs, the MPP's attempt to get the next transaction fails with a specific return code ('QC').

Now note that the MPP serially processes transactions from *different* users, rather than being dedicated to one user. Also, a given user's interaction with the host (mainframe computer) will jump about from one screen to another and therefore from one MPP to another and therefore from one message-processing *region* (MPR) to another. This means that any information that has to be carried from one screen of such a "conversation" to another has to be held on disk or in a storage area that is reserved for that one user (IMS provides such an area, which is called the "Scratch-Pad Area," or SPA). Some applications also use the message itself for this kind of information, as not all the information in the message actually has to be displayed on the screen.

While there are a number of other types of IMS/DC application, such as WFI and pseudo-WFI, the above sketch will suffice to give a background for building on-line applications using FBP.

Note that the term "transaction" in IMS is quite ambiguous. I will try to avoid using it, since the terms "MPP" and "input message" cover most of its meanings. One other usage of the term "transaction" means the processing within an MPP that runs from the reading of an input message to the writing out of the corresponding output message. This processing is dedicated to a single user, and hence it is important that no data belonging to another user be picked up inadvertently, even though a given MPP may service a number of users before it terminates.

An interactive application differs from a batch application primarily in that some (not necessarily all) of its logic is synchronized to the speed of the user. If you visualize an interactive application as an alternation of screens and processes, the screens can themselves be treated as processes whose job is to convert between internal and external data formats.

Figure 19-1 is an example of a *very* simple application, showing the flow between three screens.

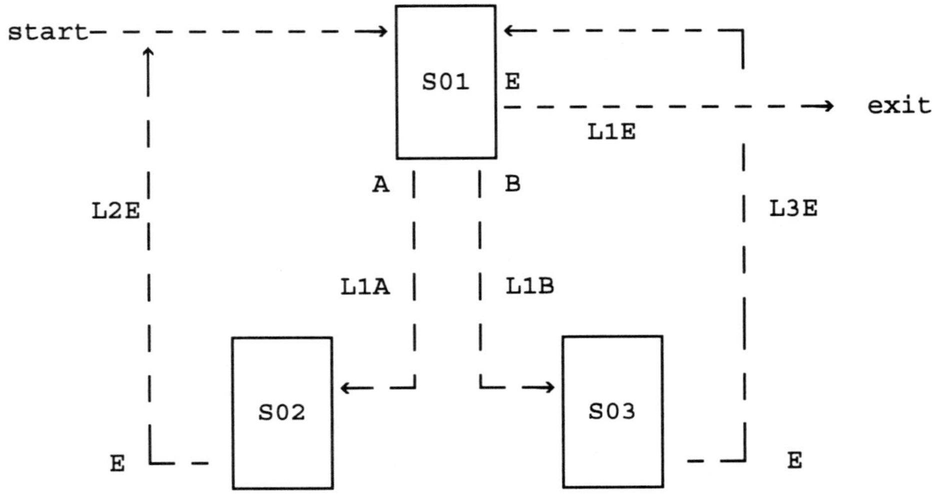


```
where S01, S02, and S03 are screens
      A, B, and E represent user actions
      L1A, L1B, L1E, L2E, and L3E represent logic

(user actions are commonly either function keys being pressed
or commands being entered)
```

Figure 19-1.

The first step is to convert all the screen blocks to processes and add in the logic processes (plus one to start the network). This gives the diagram in figure 19-2. In this figure, the screen processes must output the IP streams that the logic processes expect, and the logic processes must output the streams that the screen processes expect. In designing the application, the designer must coordinate the screen designs, IP streams, and logic processes.

There is another consideration: A typical application may have quite a few different screens, and expert users increasingly want to be able to jump from any screen to any other, without being required to go up and down through menus. In other words, the network becomes more and more thoroughly interconnected. Through all of this, the designer must make sure that each screen process gets the data it expects.

Now, if the network structure reflects the possible paths between the screens, it is clear that it will become more and more complicated as the connectedness between screens increases. You could eventually get a network where every process is con-

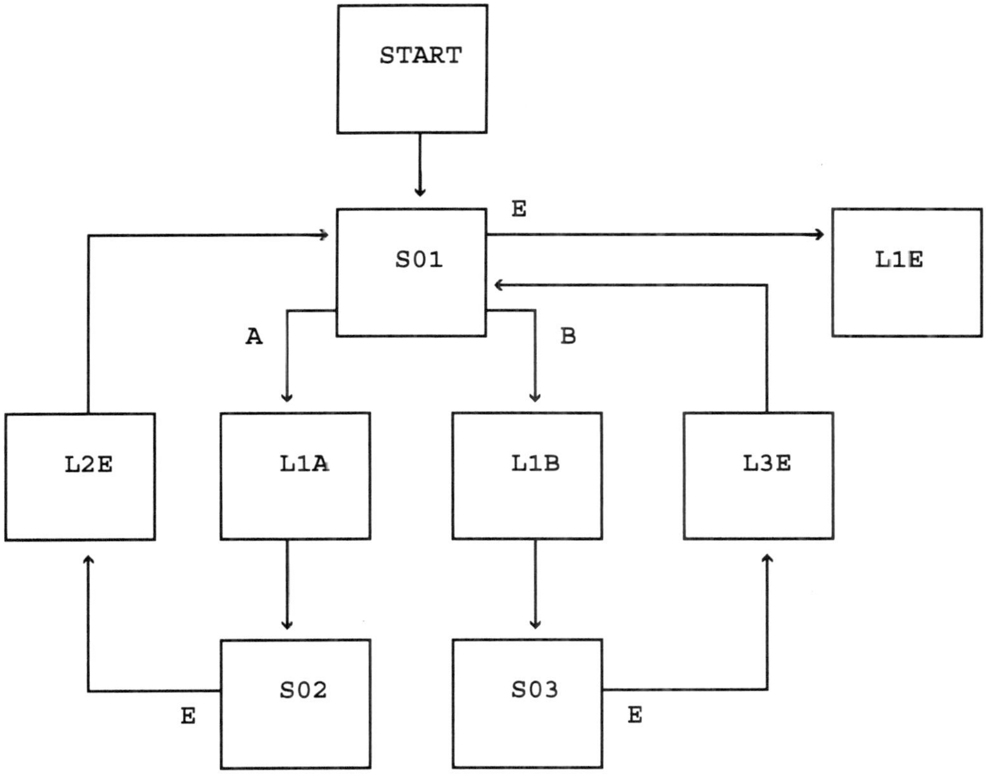

where S01, S02, and S03 are screen processes
A, B, and E represent user actions,
L1A, L1B, L1E, L2E, and L3E represent logic processes

Figure 19-2.

nected to every other process, so that the network no longer provides any assistance to the developer in understanding what is going on. Instead of using the network to define the flow between screens and logic, it is much better to do this with a table. This table specifies the screens and processes resulting from each possible combination of screen displayed and user action taken. This will allow the application to be "grown" in a natural way, without a corresponding increase in network complexity. The network shape arising from this approach actually becomes simpler, as much of the complexity will have been moved into a table. The network topology will now usually be a simple loop, comprising processes to display a screen, analyze the user action, trigger any processes, select another screen, and so on.

In conventional batch programming using data flow, the flow of data, and therefore the sequence of data transformations, is predominantly in one direction across the network. This kind of topology arises from the fact that there is no real-time interaction with human beings. As described earlier, interactive application networks usually have some kind of loop structure. These were covered in chapter 14, so you are already familiar with how these work.

Figure 19-3 shows a diagram of such a network.

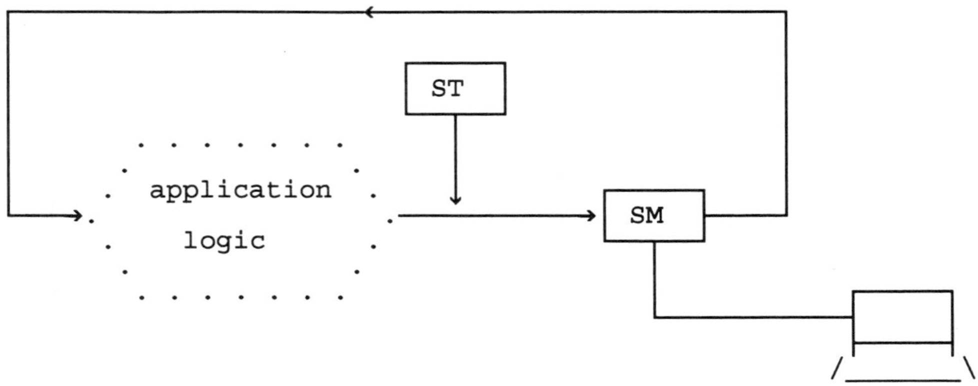


```
where SM  is a Screen Manager
      ST  starts the network as a whole
      the dotted line represents logic processes
```

Figure 19-3.

In this network, there is one process, the Screen Manager, that controls the user's screen. An IP (or group of IPs), sort of like the token in a token-ring type of LAN, travels around the network, triggering processes to execute. The bracket IPs provide a convenient way of grouping IPs for this kind of function. Typically, the first IP of each substream is used for such information as screen name, name of key struck, position of cursor, and so on, and the remaining IPs, if any, for the data. When the substream arrives at the Screen Manager process, it triggers the display of data on the screen, waits at that process until the user responds, and then proceeds to the next process in the loop. The data IPs, if any, will hold the data to be displayed on the screen and will receive any data that the user enters on the screen. The first IP, referred to as the "request IP," can also contain an indication of which key was pressed, after the user has responded (e.g., function key, enter), and where the cursor is.

The next process in the network will usually be a process that analyzes the response and takes appropriate actions, perhaps routing the request IP (with its accompanying data IPs) to a process that will do the appropriate application processing.

Eventually, the application logic will request that another screen (or the same one again) be displayed, and the request IP will be sent back to the Screen Manager to achieve this. This then is a very standard topology that you will often run into when building interactive applications in one-user environments.

This type of logic now has to be converted into IMS transactions. You will see that IMS transactions are also loops, but the function of the loop is slightly different.

You saw earlier how a data IP can be associated with a request IP and then act as a carrier for the screen's variable data. If you temporarily ignore the request IP and simply picture the data IP triggering a screen display, you see that this is very much the way an IMS transaction asks for a screen to be displayed. An IMS "output message" containing the data to be displayed is generated by the program and is sent to the message queue. This signals IMS/DC to display a screen. When the user responds, IMS/DC places an "input message" on the message queue. Soon afterwards, a transaction is triggered, and the transaction program code, the MPP, gets the message from the message queue and processes it.

Take as an example the screen flow used in figure 19-2. Each screen in this diagram, plus its downstream logic, becomes a separate transaction. We convert the above screen diagram into IMS transactions by "cleaving" each box representing a screen into two pieces: an "output" piece and an "input" piece. This results in a number of "batch-like" networks, with a screen input process on the left and one or more screen output processes on the right. It is IMS/DC that provides the linkage between them. These screen handling processes appear to the transactions just the way File I/O appears to a batch program.

Figure 19-4 shows a single "screen process" being split into separate output and input processes. If you look at the "loop," you see that it is topologically a straight line, starting with SI and ending with SO. Each of these "opened up" loops becomes a separate message processing transaction.

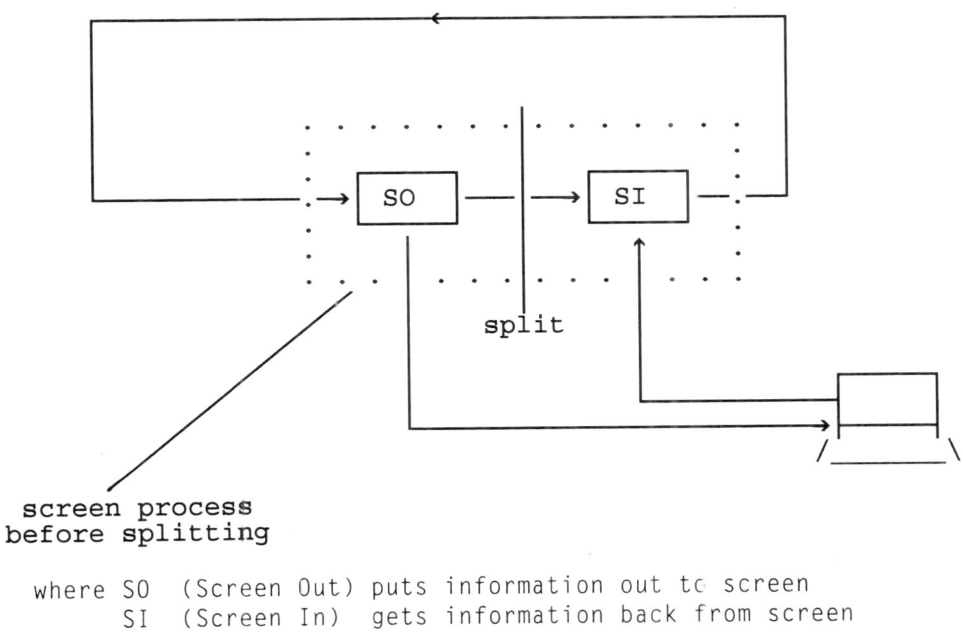

Figure 19-4.

Figure 19-5 is a diagram of a number of IMS transactions resulting from cutting up the screen flow shown in figure 19-2. In this diagram I converted the application logic into a network structure. Clearly, this would not result in a very maintainable application—as said earlier, it is much better to use a single network and encode this kind of information in tables. Just as, in chapters 6 and 16, I advised against encoding the number of Canadian provinces into the network structure, in the same way the screen flow should not be embedded into the network structure.

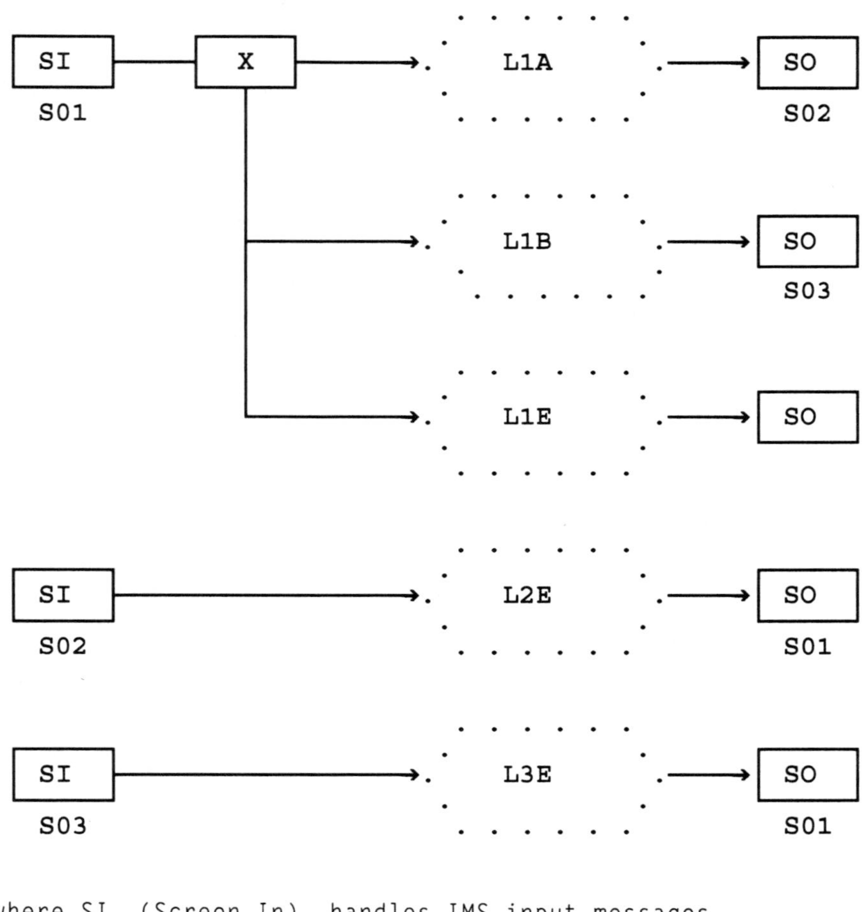


```
where SI  (Screen In)  handles IMS input messages
      SO  (Screen Out) handles IMS output messages
      X   is a Selector that decides whether L1A, L1B, or L1E
          is to be given control
      L1A, L1B, L1E, L2E, and L3E are instances of the logic
          "legs" in figure 19-2.
```

Figure 19-5.

To keep the structure flexible, we will need to hold the output screen name or transaction ID in the "request IP" and allow this to trigger the display function. This allows us to have a single instance of SO that is completely general and will dramatically simplify the transaction networks. In the IMS/DC environment, SO will use this information to select the next screen to be displayed. Of course, the data being presented to SO must match the specified screen, but this is easy to control because the screen name will be in the same substream as and followed by the data that relates to it.

As I said earlier, the loop topology turns up again, but with a slight twist, when we actually try to build an MPP using FBP. The reason for this is that MPPs are normally coded so that they check (using an IMS "get" call) if there are any more messages waiting to be processed before they close down, and it is this check that provides the "sync point" that causes the screen to be displayed and files to be updated. It is not essential for the MPP network to "loop back," but in this case various expensive types of overhead would have to be repeated for every single message. Accordingly, MPPs are usually written so that they loop back to check for more input. On the face of it, it would seem that a straight left-to-right topology would be adequate for an MPP, but this would result in a second message being read before the previous message has been displayed, and the above-mentioned function of the "get" as a sync point absolutely requires that inputting a message not be allowed to happen before any database records have been modified and the output message has been written—hence, the reemergence of the familiar loop-type topology.

The FBP network for an MPP now looks like figure 19-6. The real difference from the CMS or TSO case is that each iteration around the loop may involve a different user, so the discipline of reentrant coding is particularly important here.

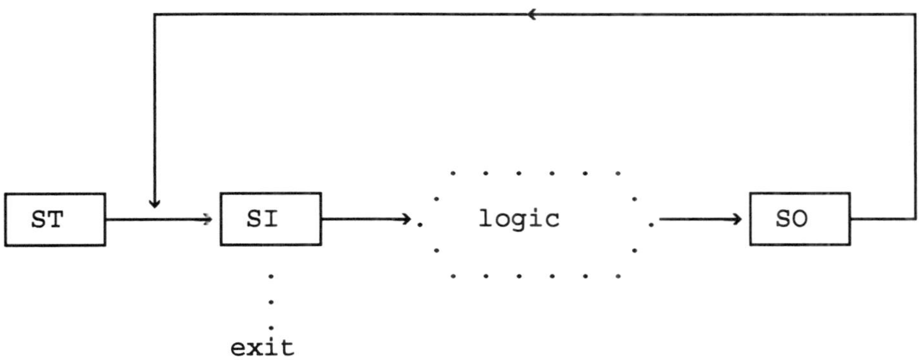


```
where SI    is a process which handles IMS input messages
      SO    is a process which handles IMS output messages
      ST    starts the network
     'logic' represents application logic
     'exit'  indicates that SI may bring down the whole
          network if there are no more messages waiting
          or the PLC has been reached
```

Figure 19-6.

In DFDM we developed components for the functions shown as ST, SI, and SO, although these were not part of the DFDM system as it was marketed. These provided an environment that allowed the intervening logic to be coded as though it were simply processing records from a file. In addition, SI and SO collaborated to support a single message format only for a given screen, instead of two separate ones (input and output), as presently required in IMS. While an IMS output format includes all variable fields that may be displayed on the corresponding screen, the input message format only contains the fields that the user may change. People often get around this by telling IMS that even the protected fields have been modified (the screen has an attribute that lets you force the "modified" flag on for a field), but this results in more data traffic between host and terminal than is necessary. Instead, SO can save the output message in the SPA or in a user database, and SI can then use that information both to create a "complete" message and to report on which fields have actually been modified. You now have a pair of collaborating components that make the job of handling IMS messages significantly easier.

Analogously to the paradigm shift seen in batch, FBP also forces a shift from concentrating on screen layouts to concentrating on IP layouts. For a given data entity in IMS, there will in general be three layouts: the "in-storage" format, the input message, and the output message. However, it is possible to combine these down to two or even one layout, by using the MFS MFLD macros to act as a "bridge." Designers of IMS applications don't generally realize that IMS MFS allows the sequence of fields on the screen to be quite different from the sequence of fields within the area in storage containing the data. This will also allow the same data IP to drive a number of different screen layouts, which is a useful characteristic in on-line systems. One might, for example, want to use a single data IP and show different parts of it, depending on the authorization level of the user.

One last topic that is relevant to the design of on-line applications in IMS/DC is that of storage of information within a "conversation" (the suite of transactions interacting with a single user to do a job of work). I mentioned above that we can use the message Scratch-Pad Area (SPA) or disk storage. The problem with the SPA, from a modularity point of view, is that information in it has to be accessed by offset (i.e., one declares a structure to describe the SPA, and all transactions participating in a conversation have to use the same layout). So you essentially have an entity, the "conversation" (not otherwise recognized by IMS), which is tied to the SPA layout. If you then want to share transactions between conversations, you constrain them all to share the same SPA layout. This is another form of the "global" problem. Since FBP forces modularity, you have to find a way around globals, and our group did this in one of our applications by storing data associatively in a storage area associated with the user—initially the SPA and later a special database—using data areas chained into a list and identified by 8-character names. We defined three components, which could be used in the application networks to manage the user's storage area. Let's call these components Input from Area, Output to Area, and Free Area. When we wanted to store a piece of data for use later in the conversation, we simply sent it with an identifying name to an occurrence of an Output to Area component, which either replaced the data in an existing area of the same name or created a new area. Input from Area was used to retrieve data, given an area name. The interesting thing was that (apart from Free Area) these behaved exactly like I/O components and allowed us to maintain the "mini-batch" metaphor in the logic processing within a transaction.

There is (was) also another breakdown of modularity in IMS—namely the layout of the PCB List. Originally, IMS and transaction code had to agree on the sequence of the PCBs in the list, and the only way code could reference a PCB was by its position, so every subroutine in a transaction had to "know" the same PCB List layout. Again, this made sharing subroutines between transactions very difficult. To solve this, DFDM provided a "locate PCB" function as a basic service, allowing PCBs to be located using the DBD name. IBM has since recognized this problem in IMS and now provides the AIBTDLI interface, which allows PCBs to be referenced by name (FBP ports went through a similar evolution from numbers to names).

One last topic I want to touch on is DB2, appropriate in a chapter on designing on-line systems. The relational paradigm is very powerful and is very compatible with FBP's concepts. In FBP it is very straightforward to specify an SQL request in a component and then have it turn the rows of the resulting table into a stream of IPs. You saw in chapter 11 how information about "nullness" can be attached to IPs—this is a natural match with the "null" concept of DB2. You can even use the DESCRIBE facility of DB2 to generate IP descriptors automatically.

While in many ways DB2 is a marvelous system, it also suffers from what I have called a breakdown of modularity. In hindsight, it would have been better if its interfaces had been designed to be used in black boxes. Unfortunately its designers did not foresee the need to use DB2 inside asynchronously executing black boxes, but we have found ways to live with this omission, so overall the two systems work pretty well together.

DB2 differs from most computation-oriented programming languages in that any components that contain SQL statements have to be precompiled as well as compiled, resulting in a separate type of output called a Data Base Request Module (DBRM). DBRMs are combined or "bound" (much as components are linkedited) into what is called a "plan," which is required at run-time. One of the nice things about using DB2 in an FBP environment is that the whole network only needs to be rebound when a component issuing SQL statements has to be recompiled (re-precompiled, actually). If you therefore write all your Static SQL components and compile and bind them into a "plan" early in the development cycle, you can add logic and other functions incrementally without ever having to rebind the application plan.

The major problem we ran into was that the DB2 "cursor" (the "pointer" that programs running under DB2 use to step through a table) is not a variable, so it cannot be moved around or passed to subroutines. So you can't do a SELECT in one component and the related UPDATE in another one. In FBP we can get around this problem by using a single component to do both actions, either by using two separate input ports or by using a single input port with two different types of request IP.

The other problem is that there is only one DBRM for a component per MVS task, so there is only one cursor, so a single component doing cursor-type SELECTs cannot be executed by two different processes at the same time in the same MVS task, unless you give it multiple cursors (we did that experimentally—if the component needs a cursor and finds the current one busy, it just grabs the next one). Alternatively, you could eventually develop means to automatically generate the code for this kind of component as required. Dynamic SQL does not suffer from this limitation, but it provides weaker security, so most installations prefer to use Static SQL. You could also use Dynamic SQL for prototyping, and migrate to Static later.

Last, but probably not least, when preparing a component to run under DB2, you have to specify at linkedit time whether the program is to run under TSO or IMS. This means that a component cannot be "ported" from TSO to IMS or vice versa in load module form unless it is relinked at its destination.

I'd like to close this chapter by addressing an argument that you may hear from time to time—namely that batch is dead and that everything can now be done on-line and therefore synchronously. As you have been reading the foregoing pages, you may have been wondering what the relevance of data streams and components like Split and Collate is to today's interactive applications. For a while I also believed that FBP was less relevant to interactive systems than to batch, but, as we built more and more on-line systems, we found that the benefits of reusability and configurability are just as relevant to on-line as they are to batch, if not more so. Also, by removing many of the old distinctions between on-line and batch, not only do programmers move more easily between these different environments, but code can be shared by batch and on-line programs, allowing large parts of the logic to be tested in whatever mode the developer finds most convenient. There have even been cases where data was validated in batch using the same edit routines that would eventually handle it in the on-line environment. Once you remove the rigid distinction between batch and on-line, you find that batch is just a way of managing the cost of certain overheads (the same reason we use batches in manufacturing), and therefore it makes a lot of sense to have systems that combine both batch and on-line. If you take into account distributed and client-server systems, you will see that there are significant advantages to having a single paradigm that provides a consistent view across all these different environments.

20

Synchronization and Checkpoints

This chapter starts with a discussion on how to synchronize events in an FBP application. After having stressed the advantages of asynchronism so heavily, it may seem strange to have to talk about strategies to control it, but there are times when you simply have to control the timing of events precisely, so it must be possible to do this. It is just that synchronization shouldn't be forced where it isn't required. You have already seen various kinds of synchronization, such as loop-type networks and composites, so let us look at synchronization a bit more generally.

Typically, something in a process may have to be synchronized to an event elsewhere in the processing logic, or to an event in the outside world. Only certain events in certain processes need this treatment. It would be against the philosophy of FBP to attempt to synchronize a whole network. That belongs to the old thinking. In fact, writers on distributed programming often show a certain nervousness about not knowing exactly when things will occur. It used to be considered necessary to synchronize commits on two different systems, but we are beginning to realize that it may not be possible to scale up this philosophy across an entire network in an enterprise or across multiple enterprises. In fact, IBM has recently announced a set of Messaging and Queuing products (MQ Series) that provide asynchronous bridging between all sorts of different hardware and software. A basic assumption of this software is that it is possible and desirable to coordinate processing asynchronously across multiple systems, without needing to lock everything until the whole process is finished.

The most basic kind of synchronization is synchronizing a point in the logic of a process to a point event in time. In IBM's MVS, this is implemented using POST/WAIT logic. This involves a thing called an "event," which may be in one of three states:

- Inactive
- Being waited on
- Completed

Only one process can wait on an event at a time, but any process that knows about it may "post" it, thereby changing it to completed. If a process issues a "wait" when the event is inactive, it is suspended on that event, and the event is marked appropriately; if the event has already completed, the process that needed to know about the event just carries on executing. MVS uses this concept for its "basic" I/O. A process starts an asynchronous read or write channel program going and then continues executing. When, some time later, it needs to know whether the request has completed, it issues a "wait" and either is suspended or continues execution, depending on whether the asynchronous I/O routine has posted the event complete or not. Once posted, the event shows complete until it is set back to one of the other states, presumably by the requesting process. All dialects of FBP, except THREADS, have implemented an event-type wait service to suspend a single process. A nice feature of the FBP environment from a performance point of view is that one or more processes can be suspended on events without suspending the whole application. The application as a whole is only suspended if *no* process can proceed and at least one process is waiting on an event (if there are no processes waiting on events, you've got a deadlock). We found that applications with many I/O processes often ran faster than if they were coded conventionally using buffered I/O because, in control flow coding, only one I/O is logically being executed at a time, so if it suspends, the whole application hangs.

Instead of a point event, you might instead have to synchronize an application to a time of day clock (e.g., "run this job at 5:00 P.M."). All you need is a process that sends out an IP at 5:00 P.M., every day (or you could arrange for it to send out IPs every hour on the hour, or every five minutes, or every 20 seconds). Such a process can act as a clock, just as the clock in a computer sends out pulses on a regular schedule. These IPs can then be used to start or delay other processes.

Like the "wait on event" service, DFDM also has the ability to suspend a process for a specified amount of time or until a particular time of day. This uses the facility provided by MVS to post an event at a particular time. In the case of DFDM, this function was only provided as an off-the-shelf component. It could either delay incoming IPs by a certain amount of time or generate a stream of IPs at given intervals. Where multiple time intervals are required, you can have as many of these processes as you like in a network (DFDM keeps track of which one is due to go off next).

Another kind of synchronization referred to already is the need to delay something until a process has completed. In DFDM, any unused output port would automatically present end of data to its downstream process when it closed down. In THREADS the same thing applies, or you can use automatic ports to automatically generate a signal IP when a process deactivates. Imagine that you want to delay a process until two others have completed. You have already run into Concatenate—this provides a simple way of doing this, as shown in figure 20-1. In this figure, say the network specifies a port called END on processes *A* and *B*, which they don't know about. In this case, end of data is going to be presented on these ports when *A* and *B* close down. CONCAT will not close down until both *A* and *B* have terminated, so either the end of data output by CONCAT (when *it* closes down) can be used to delay process *C*, or a third data stream could be fed into CONCAT, which would therefore not be passed through until after *A* and *B* had completed.

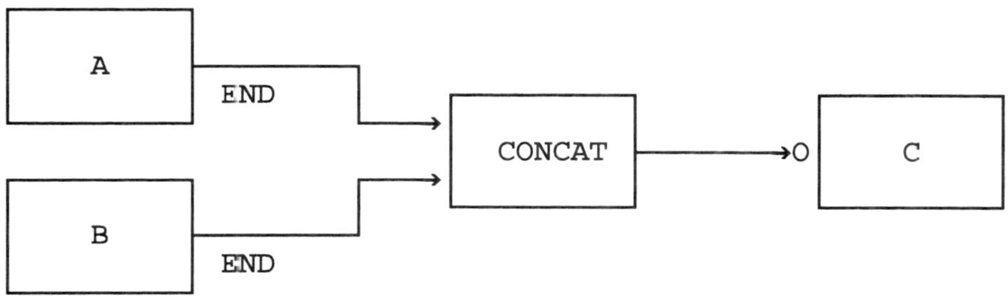

Figure 20-1.

Client-server relationships are a good way to solve a particular synchronization problem. Suppose you have a stream of transactions that all access the same database. If you allowed every transaction to run in parallel and your programs were managing their own data, you would have to provide some kind of enqueue/dequeue mechanism to ensure that different threads were blocked from executing at the same time when this might cause problems. A simpler technique is to make one process a server and only allow that process to access the database. This is in fact a common type of encapsulation because it allows the server to control what it will accept and when. This kind of approach was described in chapter 15. The disadvantage of this arrangement, of course, is that you are serializing the data handling part of the transactions, so this may become a bottleneck, but this is a trade-off that should be the decision of the application designer. It's even better if only a small proportion of the transactions need the server's services or if you have several databases, each with its own server (like the different stations in a cafeteria or the tellers in a bank). One other possibility is to use some kind of batch approach, especially in cases where the hit rate (transactions per data record) is fairly high. After all, batching is just a technique for lowering the per-item cost at the cost of increased start-up and close-down costs. Since a server "batches up" its incoming transactions, you may be able to preprocess them to improve performance.

Another kind of synchronization is built into the "dynamic subnet" mechanism of DFDM. We said before that a composite component monitors the processes within it. In particular, if the composite is substream-sensitive, it handles exactly one substream from every input port on each activation. These input ports are therefore also synchronized, so you can visualize the composite component advancing, one substream at a time, in parallel, across all of its input streams.

Of course, most often such substream-sensitive composite components only have one input port, in which case they process one substream per activation. These were described in some detail in chapter 13, "Scheduling Rules." Now you will get to use them on something that seems to give programmers a lot of trouble.

Interactive systems and systems that share databases have to wrestle with the problem of checkpointing. In the old days, checkpointing just meant saving everything about the state of a program, and restart meant loading it all back in and resuming execution. Well, for one thing, a program had to come back to the same location, and this might not be available. It became even harder as systems were distributed across multiple tasks or even multiple systems. In FBP, the states of the processes aren't in lock-step any more, so it becomes harder still. In general, as the environment becomes more complex, checkpointing needs more information to be provided by the programmer. However, it would be great to be able to write a general checkpoint component that could be used across a wide range of applications, and we feel it is possible with FBP. In the following paragraphs I will describe an approach that seems to fit the requirements. Rather than trying to create an enormously intelligent and complex module, the approach is to provide a series of points in time where as many processes as possible are quiesced, so that they do not require much data to be saved about them.

Consider the following three scenarios:

1. IMS MPPs take a checkpoint every time they go back to the input queue for another transaction. This "commits" the updates and unlocks the data records so that other users can access them. If the system crashes before the checkpoint, the updates have logically not been done, and IMS has to ensure that this is logically true (even if it has happened physically).
2. A long-running batch application should checkpoint about every half hour, so that the amount of the job that has to be rerun is never more than a half hour's worth (this applies both to programs updating databases and to batch jobs using ordinary sequential files).
3. An IMS BMP should checkpoint much more frequently—perhaps as often as every few seconds—as on-line users of the same data may become hung waiting for the BMP to release data that they need.

The common idea in all these cases is that the system saves the logical state of the system, so that it can be restored if required. The information needed to restore a process to an earlier state is often called its *state data*. On the other hand, the less data you can get away with saving, the less time checkpoint will take and the faster any restart can occur if it is needed.

FBP's approach to checkpointing is to quiesce as many of the processes in the application as possible and have as few IPs in flight between processes as possible. The more this can be done, the less state data you need to save. Here's an analogy. A number of people are swimming in a pool, and a member of the staff decides it's time to put chlorine into it. Since this chemical would be highly irritating to the swimmers, the first thing to do is to get them all out of the water. So the staff member blows the whistle. She now has to wait until everyone is out of the water, which might take a little while, as everyone has to finish what they are doing. Once they are all out, she puts the chlorine in, waits some amount of time, and then blows the whistle again to indicate that it is safe to go back in.

Let's reuse a diagram from chapter 7, showing it in figure 20-2. This shows a delimiter-sensitive composite *B,* containing two processes, *C* and *D.* You will remember that, provided the data coming from *A* is grouped into substreams using bracket IPs, the inside of *B* will behave like a little batch job, starting up and closing down for every incoming substream. The composite deactivates each time its inside processes close down, and it reinvokes them when the next IP arrives from outside. During the times when *C* and *D* have closed down, there will be no IPs in flight, and *C* and *D* will not even have any internal storage allocated. The composite itself will be inactive. This then provides a rather neat mechanism for "getting everyone out of the water," because, remember, processes cannot be closed down until they themselves decide to allow it. Not only that, but you can ensure that the next substream isn't admitted until the "chlorine has had time to dissolve." Just provide the composite with an automatic port, which will prevent it from inputting the next substream until a signal arrives. The diagram might now look something like figure 20-3.

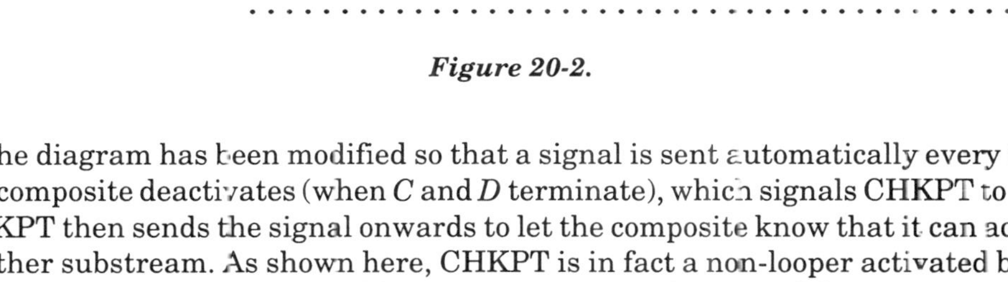

Figure 20-2.

The diagram has been modified so that a signal is sent automatically every time the composite deactivates (when *C* and *D* terminate), which signals CHKPT to run. CHKPT then sends the signal onwards to let the composite know that it can accept another substream. As shown here, CHKPT is in fact a non-looper activated by an automatic connection and enabling *B* again via another one. Of course, you could also make CHKPT a looper and/or have it use explicitly named ports.

There is another idea that is suggested by the swimming pool analogy: a swimmer who will not get out of the water will hold up the whole process. Remember the term "periodicity," referring to whether a component is a "looper" or a "non-looper." Non-loopers are quiesced between every invocation. The more often a component gives up control, the more flexible it will be from the point of view of fitting into the checkpoint process.

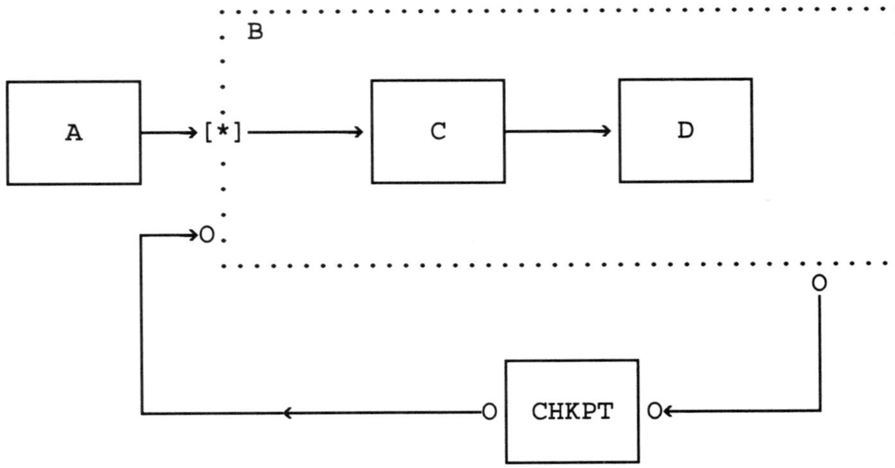

Figure 20-3.

Since *B*'s regular (nonautomatic) input port is delimiter-sensitive, you now have to get delimiters into its input stream to make this whole thing work. It may seem strange to use external markers to control what is going on inside the swimming pool, but this is really only a technique for dividing up the incoming stream into well-defined groups—and we want *all* the processes inside the composite to be able to close down. So what you must do is insert delimiters into the incoming stream of IPs at the points where you want checkpoints to occur.

Now, there are two main criteria for when to take checkpoints: amount of I/O and time. Since in IMS a checkpoint will unlock changed records, checkpoints should be taken more frequently if there has been more update activity. Conversely, if the activity is low, checkpoints should be taken occasionally anyway, to make sure that other programs are not hung for too long waiting for records to be unlocked. How can you drive checkpoints on both these criteria? Well, a close approximation to the amount of I/O is to count transactions and do a checkpoint after every *n* transactions, where *n* is specifiable from outside. In addition, we want to trigger a checkpoint if *t* seconds or minutes have elapsed without a checkpoint.

Let's do the transaction counting first. You can just have a Count process that inserts a close bracket/open bracket pair every time the count of input IPs reaches a number *n* (obtained from the option port). This Count process also has to send out an open bracket at the beginning and a close bracket at the end. This is shown schematically in figure 20-4.

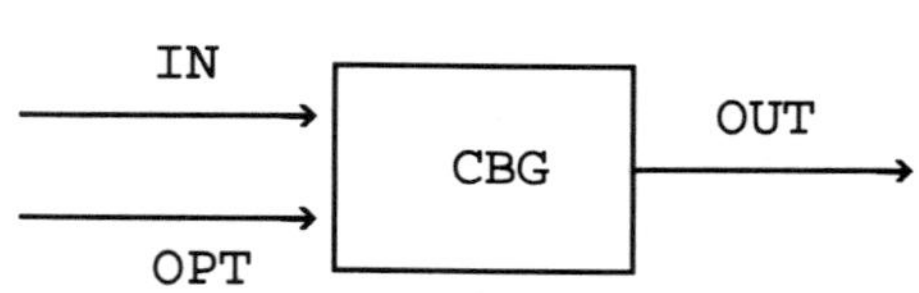

Figure 20-4.

Call this component CBG for Count-Based Grouping. OPT can specify *n;* OUT passes on the incoming IPs divided into substreams. So if the input to CBG is

```
a b c d e f g h i j k l ...
```

and *n* is set to 5, the output looks like this:

```
(a b c d e) (f g h i j) (k l ...
```

This also works if the input consists of substreams rather than just transactions. In general, the count should apply to the highest-level substreams (individual IPs can be treated as trivial substreams). If you were to interrupt a substream to take a checkpoint, you would have to save and restore more data to restart from where you left off.

But now suppose that, during the "quiet" times, you decide that you also want to insert a bracket pair if *t* seconds or minutes have elapsed without a checkpoint. Let's take a "clock" process referred to at the beginning of the chapter, which generates an IP on every clock tick (specifying the interval via an options port), and merge its output with the input of CBG, as shown in figure 20-5. If the original data stream consisted of substreams, you would of course need a more sophisticated merge process.

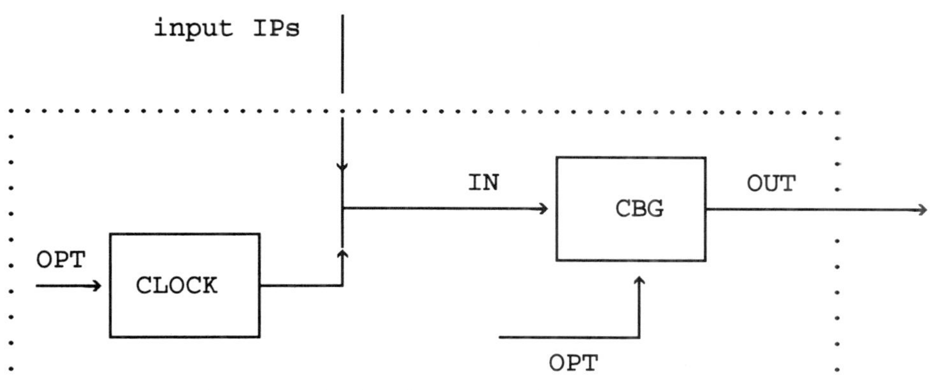

Figure 20-5.

The input stream to CBG now looks something like this:

a b c t_0 d e f g h i j t_1 t_2 k l t_3 m t_4 n o p q r t_5 s ...

Now, the present FBP implementations do not *guarantee* that these clock ticks will ever get into this data stream unless there are simply no data IPs coming in. This is because we have always concentrated on making sure *that* all data is processed, but not *when*. In fact, this is probably adequate in this case, since the clock ticks are important only when the frequency of incoming data IPs is low. To absolutely guarantee that the clock ticks are inserted "in the right place," we would need to implement something called "fair scheduling." I will not describe it here, as it is well covered in the related literature.

Clearly, when there are fewer data IPs between a pair of clock ticks (e.g., between t_1 and t_2), there is less activity; when there are more IPs, there is more activity. So a simple algorithm might be to drive a checkpoint (insert back-to-back brackets) on every incoming clock tick and also after n IPs following the last clock tick IP. You might want to fancy this up a bit, by preventing checkpoints if a previous one occurred within some minimum interval, but the simple algorithm should do fine for most purposes. A lot of applications use a time interval only, especially in batch applications, where the problem is to reduce the cost of reruns rather than releasing locked up records. Having identified the "bracket insertion" subnet (the dotted subnet in figure 20-5), you can now insert it between *A* and *B* in figure 20-2, as is shown in figure 20-6.

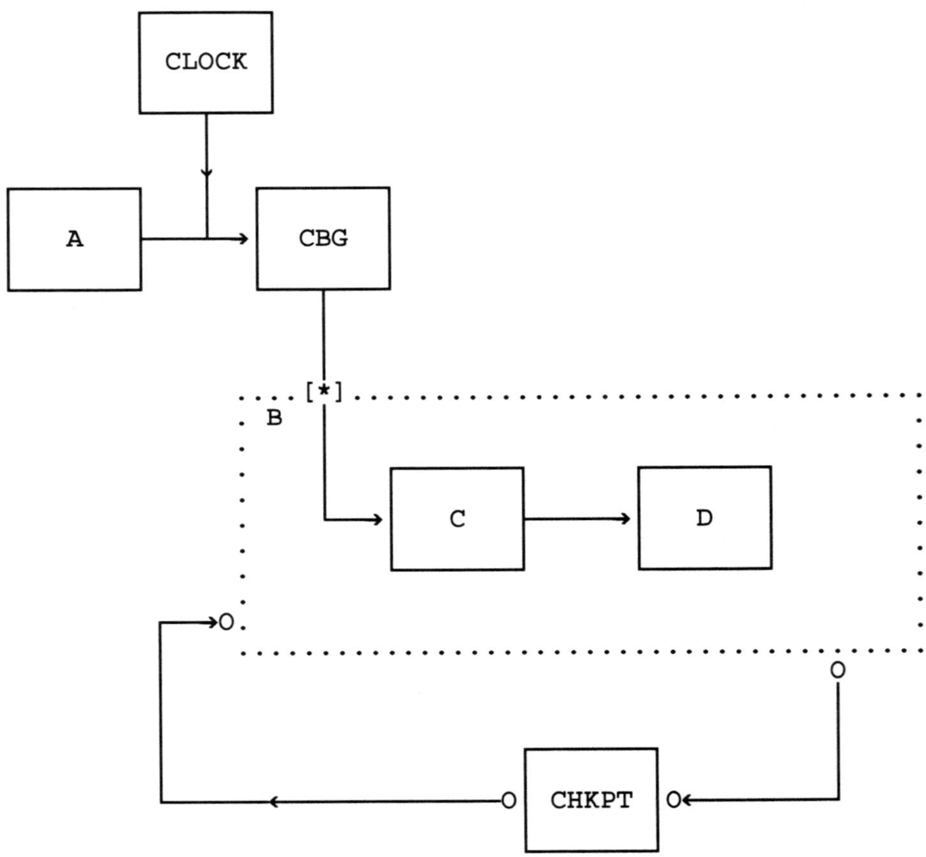

Figure 20-6.

I have talked about *when* to take checkpoints and now need to discuss *what* should be saved when taking a checkpoint. Not only does state data have to be saved in case a restart is needed, but in some systems when you *take* the checkpoint you lose your place—all your fingers get pulled out of the telephone book—so you have to be able to reposition them. Therefore it makes sense to have as few processes as possible active at checkpoint time. In the example shown in figure 20-3, process *A* is active at checkpoint time—since it has no input connection, it won't terminate until it has generated all its output IPs. Neither CLOCK, CBG, nor CHKPT have any internal state information that needs to be saved if a crash occurs. So this means that *A* is the only one that needs to be restartable, and there must be a way to make sure that it only generates IPs that have not been processed completely. If *A* saves state data on a database or file, the checkpoint mechanism itself will ensure that the state data gets saved when it should and rolled back when it should. The exception to this is that data IPs that have caused errors should probably not get reexecuted, so you may want to store information about them in a non-checkpointable store.

Apart from such oddball cases, we can generalize across the different environments and say that *A* and processes like it should save their state data on a checkpointable backing store and be able to be restarted using it and that this whole process should be as automatic as possible. Say that the state data has some recognizable empty state—the state information on the backing store should start off in that empty state, it should be updated for each incoming IP or substream, and the program as a whole should reset the state data to empty when it finishes. This way *A* can determine if a restart is required and, if so, at what point. Since it is always a good idea to separate logic from I /O, *A* can be split as shown in figure 20-7. In this diagram, *A* only needs its state data at start time, so RSD (Read State Data) can start at beginning of program and send the data to *A*. Every time *A* needs to store its state data, it sends it to WSD (Write State Data). *A* needs to be notified that WSD has stashed it away safely, so we must provide a return path for this information.

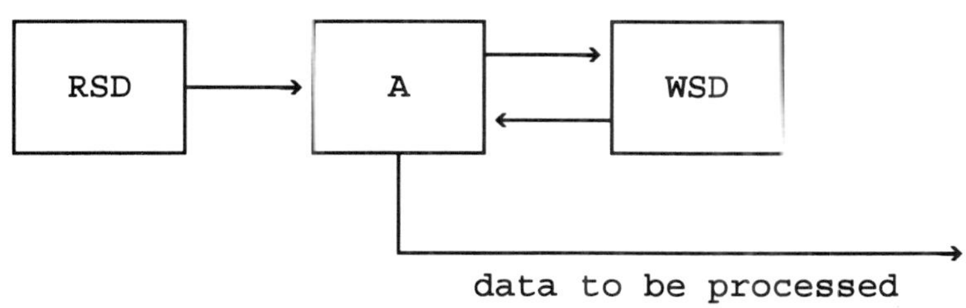

Figure 20-7.

Although *A* doesn't really need to save its state data until checkpoint time, it doesn't know when CBG is going to decide that a checkpoint is needed—this suggests that you might want to find a way to combine CBG or CHKPT with *A*'s writing to backing store. The other thing you might do is have a general repository of state data and let *A* request it, say, by providing its process name as a key. A solution that combines all these ideas is to use a process like the List Manager (to be described in chapter 21) to hold up-to-date state data in high-speed memory and then expand the function of CHKPT so that it writes out this information to disk before requesting the checkpoint. We therefore replace WSD by a State Data Repository (call it SDR). CHKPT has to request the state data from SDR, so there will be connections in both directions between these two processes. The final diagram might therefore look something like figure 20-8, where there are two connections between SDR and CHKPT, one in each direction. The connection from CHKPT to SDR is used to allow CHKPT to request its stored data; the reverse connection is for SDR to send the requested data.

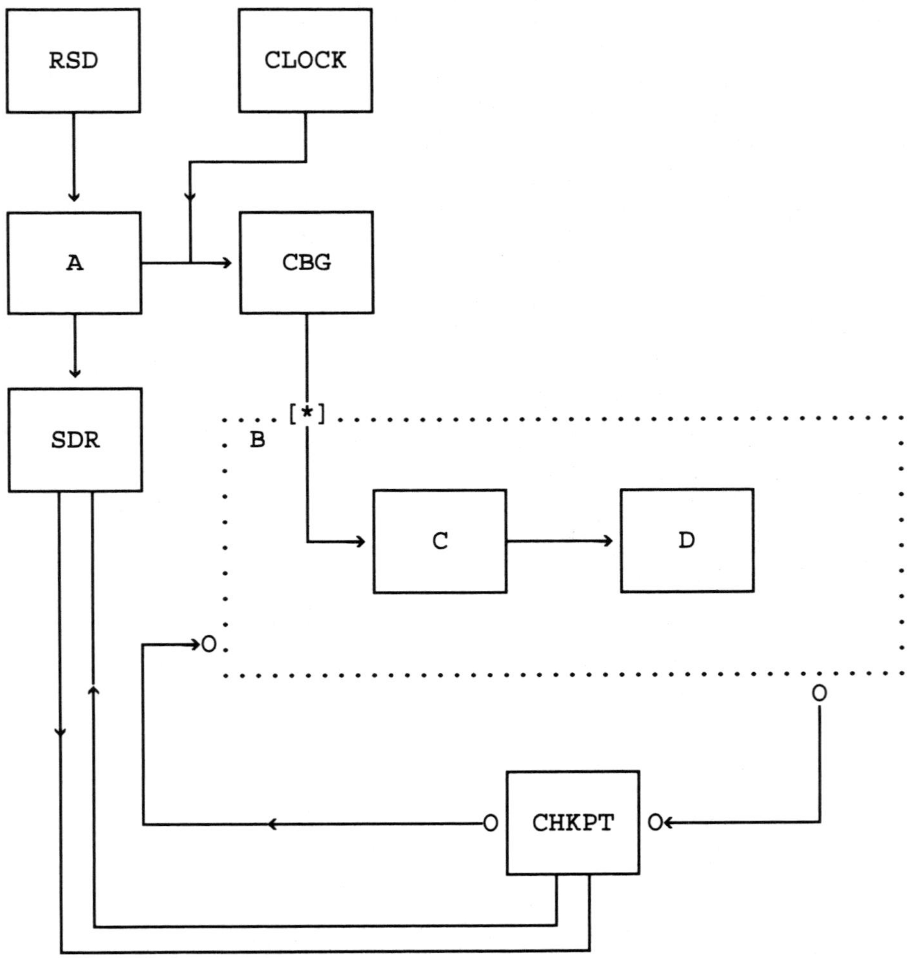

Figure 20-8.

You may have noticed that *A* is slightly ahead of CBG, CHKPT, etc. A way will have to be found to compensate for this.

This is just a sketch, and even at that it's starting to look a bit complicated, but most of the components can be off the shelf, so they won't have to be programmed from scratch for every application. At this point, I'm sure you can all come up with better solutions that draw on your own expertise. The point is to design generalized utility components that encapsulate expertise, but that still are easy for other, less expert programmers to use. When you consider the potential cost of reruns to your shop, you can see that some standard, easy-to-use checkpointing approaches and components will be well worth the effort that goes into developing them, and I have tried to show that FBP's powerful modularization capabilities will make that job much easier.

21

General Framework for Interactive Applications

In this chapter I am going to describe a general framework for interactive applications, showing a general structure and some component types that could help in the design of such applications. I touched on this in chapter 19, but now I will go into more detail.

I will start by reproducing figure 19-3, which shows an IP substream traveling from application logic to a Screen Manager process and back again, and will show how this can be fleshed out to produce a very general design for interactive applications. You will remember the diagram, now shown in figure 21-1 (I have omitted the kicker process, for simplicity).

You will remember that in IMS we had to split the process marked SM into SI and SO (Screen Input and Screen Output, respectively) and change the function of the "return connection." However, for now, we will work with the diagram in figure 21-1, bearing in mind that it is very easy to convert it into one that will run in the IMS/DC environment.

In what follows I will describe a system we built using a single generalized Screen Manager component (which I will refer to as ISM1—ISPF Screen Manager 1) that used ISPF both to write to and read from a terminal. However, the concepts are extremely general and can be applied to other screen management software.

Let us assume that every application starts by putting up a "What do you want to do?" type screen. So assume that ST causes the Screen Manager to output a menu screen. The Screen Manager will have to have a place where the user's answer can be stored, so let ST send out a substream consisting of at least three IPs: open bracket, "request" IP, one or more data IPs, and close bracket. The brackets are needed to allow a variable number of data IPs in the substream. The

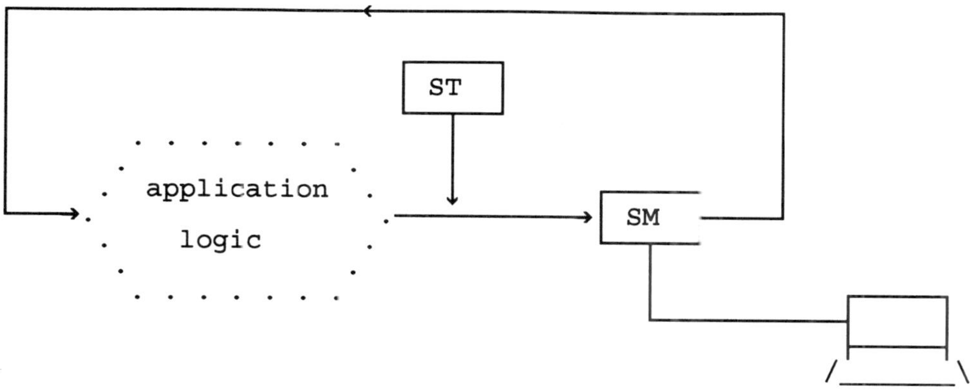


```
where SM  is a Screen Manager
      ST  starts the network as a whole
      the dotted line represents logic processes
```

Figure 21-1.

request IP will have, among other data, the name of the screen to be displayed. This substream then arrives at ISM1, which puts up a menu; the user enters a choice; the substream goes through the processing logic (which may change the contents of the IPs or even add or remove IPs from the substream); and eventually you get back to ISM1, which puts up a new menu.

Now let's look a bit more closely at ISM1. This component accepted an input substream, put any variable data into position on the screen using the data descriptors associated with the data, and waited for action on the part of the user. When that occurred, the modified data was placed back into the right places in the data IPs, and the substream was then sent on to the next process downstream. ISPF identifies fields on the screen by name, so ISM1 used the field names from the descriptor to determine where to put each variable field based on the ISPF field names.

In addition to this substream, referred to as the "fixed substream," ISM1 also accepted an additional, optional substream, called the "repeating substream." The mental image supported was that the screen has a fixed part, normally describing one or a small number of individual entities, and an optional *list* of entities. Thus you could show a person's family on the screen—his or her personal information, the spouse's information (a separate IP), these providing fairly complete information, and zero or more children, showing just name, age, and gender, say. If the user wanted more information on a child, he or she would select the child and get a full screen devoted to that child, which might have further lists (e.g., education). One of the neat things about being able to use IPs in this way is that both the list of children and the full screen describing a single child can be driven by the same IP. By the way, since each screen was built using two substreams, we bracketed them together so that

ISM1 would think of them as a unit—so ISM1 was using a substream of substreams.

Because field names are not unique in the repeating part of the screen, we could not use ISPF field names to control this part of the display, so we used a run-time table describing which fields from each IP went where in the repeating section. This had some interesting capabilities—ISM1 allowed you to specify more than one line per repeating IP, and the developer could also specify whether a "select" column (simulating the 1-byte column that ISPF provides for selecting one or more items from a list) was required or not.

ISM1 also used the dynamic attributes described in chapter 11 to keep track of which fields had been modified and which were null. As I mentioned in that chapter, ISM1 also provided a special display for fields that had been "tagged" with error codes and would let the user step through these errors using a reserved function key. ISM1 actually would not allow the user to go on to the next screen until all these "tags" had been removed one way or another. There has been lots of debate about whether this is a good idea or whether systems should be more forgiving! However, the important thing to remember is that I am talking about the design of a single component. This in no way affects or is affected by the basic architecture of FBP.

So far, ISM1's abilities might seem to be what you would need if you were "black boxing" a display function. However, it also provided another capability, which dramatically simplified the logic in the other components of the application: I discussed this in chapter 11 under the title of "representations." As I said in that chapter, representations mainly come into play when you need to present data to humans or port it across systems.

In a prototype of an interactive application using straight ISPF written in PL/I, I found that three PL/I fields had to be defined for every numeric field on the screen:

1. The field in a computational format.
2. A zoned decimal field (e.g., 000001234).
3. A character field for input in case the user wanted to modify the field.

When we converted this prototype to use ISM1, the number of fields we had to declare in the HLL portion of the application dropped to one per field. We also discovered a number of additional bonuses:

- You could send an IP with an attached descriptor to ISM1, and it would automatically be displayed in the desired format.
- The user could enter the data in free-form, but you could be sure that it wouldn't get into the system unless it was valid data.
- You could implement a standard input convention for your whole shop (e.g., require that the field be clear apart from the incoming data [some screen managers allow you to leave junk at the end of a field following the data just entered]).
- You could send an IP to ISM1 for interactive handling, or you could send it to a file writer without needing to make any changes to your

data IPs. The effect of this was enormously improved testing and regression testing, because you could test a lot of your logic in batch.

On one project in IBM Canada, this last technique was used very effectively by my colleague, Philip Ewing. Later in this chapter I will share with you what he has written about that project.

We have now sketched out a screen management component, which accepts one or two substreams as input and outputs them again after the user has responded. If you are working in the IMS/DC environment, it wouldn't be all that hard to split these functions and link them together using persistent storage.

Now let's look at figure 21-1. You need to fill in the logic between SM and the application logic. To do this, the first step is to interpret the user's action. Restricting ourselves for simplicity to ISPF and 327x-type terminals, the user may decide to:

- Modify any data field, including Select fields as a special case.
- Enter a command in the command area.
- Hit a function key.
- Hit a `Program Attention` key (this will lose modified data).
- Hit `Attention`.
- Position the screen cursor to a particular field.

These will of course often be combined (e.g., putting an *M* in the command line and hitting `PF8` causes a jump to the bottom of the data in ISPF).

All these actions have to be encoded so that downstream processes can decide what the appropriate response is. If you add in more modern devices and interfaces, obviously there are still more variations (e.g., monitoring keystrokes and mouse movements in real time), but it seems that there will still be the cycle (or maybe many concurrent ones) of display–user action–interpret user response–program action–display.

In the ISPF world and also IMS/DC, function keys are usually treated as commands, so one of the standard outputs of our Screen Manager will be a "command." These may be the very frequent ones like UP, DOWN, END, and HELP, which are almost universal, or more application-specific ones. It turns out that these commands are convenient bases for the decision about what to do next. Always remember that each of the components described here can be used independently of any other. Chapter 7 described DFDM's dynamic subnets—subnets that were linked as separate load modules and were loaded in dynamically and given control by a special component called the Subnet Manager. This provides a convenient way of subdividing and managing the application. The Subnet Manager is driven by IPs containing dynamic subnet names, so you need a component that will take the output of the Screen Manager and generate the subnet names for the Subnet Manager. Let's call this the User Response Analyzer (URA).

The URA component's job is to look up, in a table, patterns consisting of screen + action, screen only or action only, and decide what to do about them. Since it sits upstream of the Subnet Manager, its main job is to select subnet names to be sent to the Subnet Manager, but you might decide to have it bypass the Subnet

Manager, and send its input IPs directly to the Screen Manager. In this case, you could have it decide screen names. You could also have it do both.

You will notice that I haven't said where this table should be held: it could be compiled into a load module, stored as a flat file, or held in a database. Perhaps a file would be appropriate during development, and a load module in production. You will perhaps notice our predilection for tables—this is one of the most important ways of achieving portable code (remember Bucky Pope's class codes, alluded to in an earlier chapter).

The URA table might therefore look something like table 21-1.

Obviously, this table is very easy to modify. In fact, if you add a comment capability, it really becomes self-explanatory.

The last component I am going to describe is the List Manager, another general component. Its fundamental metaphor was sets of lists that persisted in storage, organized by "levels"—thus, employees might be on one level, while their children, departments worked in, and courses taken might be three different lists at the next level. It could accept commands to do various things with these lists and levels, such as "create a new level," "insert a list at the current level," "jump to the next lower level," "pop up one level," "output a list (nondestructively)," "delete a level," and so on. Although (because?) this component was very powerful, it took the most work to manage its input and output. It was very interesting for another reason also: the List Manager perhaps most closely resembled an OO "object," in that it had an internal state, being constantly modified by incoming commands (messages), with or without accompanying data. Its structure seemed to match our perception of what was going on in the prototypical interactive application (i.e., the user would display an employee, then ask to go down one level to find his or her children, pop back to the previous level, and so on). Because it was a single looper process, we could manage these lists just by working with IP pointers—we didn't have to pay the overhead of chaining or unchaining IPs. Also, it provided a focal point, in case we needed to store really big lists, where lists could overflow to disk. We also expected that, when we implemented this design on IMS, it would be very easy to dump all our lists to disk at the end of a transaction and retrieve them when they were needed again.

In hindsight, the problems we ran into with the List Manager should probably have been expected, but they came as somewhat of a surprise to us! I believe we

TABLE 21-1. User Response Analysis Table

Old Screen	User Action	Subnet	New Screen
A	CHOICE1	SUBNET1	B
B	END		A
A	HELP		HELP_FOR_A
HELP_FOR_A	END		A
.			
.			
.			
.			

were still thinking of interactive applications as sequential, so the command-driven single store made sense. However, it was so convenient to stash things away in the List Manager's storage that we had more and more processes sticking stuff in there and taking it out. The more complex our networks became, the harder it became to control the exact sequence in which the commands arrived at the List Manager. What we had done, of course, was to implement a somewhat more complex array of pigeonholes, and the nondestructive readout that seemed so attractive at first caused the same problems that FBP was trying to avoid! Strange sequencing problems started to show up—lists would get attached to the wrong level, lists would show up on two different levels, and so on. In turn, the sequence of the command IPs had to be controlled more tightly, introducing still more complexity. In hindsight, I believe we would have been better off using tree structures flowing *between* processes, rather than complex data structures *within* a process. Alternatively, a List Manager should only be fed by a single process, and this is the way I have shown it in figure 21-2. Lastly, I believe that the underlying metaphor may not have been quite correct. For instance, suppose the user is stepping through an employee's employment history and decides to start looking at his or her courses. Should this be made another level? Or are all these lists at the same level? A better metaphor might have been to be able to pop up new windows as new lists are requested. It's also useful to be able to open multiple windows on the same list (but you have to be careful about updates!).

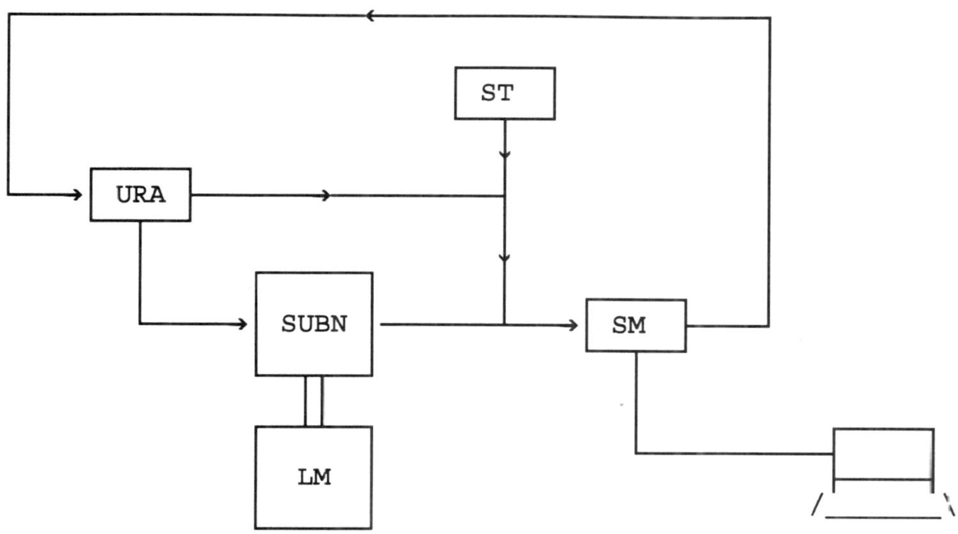


```
where SM   is a Screen Manager
      ST   starts the network as a whole
      URA  is the User Response Analyzer
      SUBN is the Subnet Manager
      LM   is the List Manager
```

Figure 21-2.

Remember that the network shown in figure 21-2 is only a skeleton—you can add additional processes to the diagram and extend it in other ways also. Also, the List Manager, although I have shown it in the diagram, is not the only way to manage storage of persistent data.

What I have described here is the structure we called the DOEM, pronounced "dome" (DFDM On-line Environment Manager), still fondly remembered by some of the people who worked on it! It was at the same time a skeleton structure, a set of components, and an approach to designing interactive applications. This is reuse at a higher level than the level I have been mostly talking about up until now and, from that point of view, a precursor of the way that interactive systems will be built in the future. While the DOEM was a very powerful set of concepts, some of its components were more satisfactory than others in terms of their encapsulation of useful function and the simplicity of the underlying mental image. In some ways, the DOEM fell into the pitfall I have warned about elsewhere in the book—we tried to make it very general, based on our ideas of what a DOEM should provide, without frequent consultations with real users. Or we may have been talking to the "wrong" users. We never did build it for the IMS/DC platform, although we basically knew how to go about it. As it turned out, we didn't need that implementation anyway, for the reasons I am about to relate. This story is salutary, so I am going to tell it in some detail, as a cautionary tale for those embarking on developing reusable code.

Most of the time we were working on the DOEM, we were supporting two projects—let's call them A and B. The intent was to provide team A with an IMS/DC version of the DOEM and team B with a CMS version. This seemed reasonable because a number of the components could be shared, and, although the CMS version was certainly simpler (single Screen Manager module, etc.), we understood pretty much how to build the DOEM on IMS/DC. However, the two teams' approaches to working with us were very different. The A team seemed to regard our group as an extension of their project, asking for specialized modifications of components or new facilities just for their own application, while B was more willing to work *with* us and to stay within the facilities that were already available or in plan. Both projects had the potential to be very important products, for different reasons, and both groups felt that they were getting benefit from DFDM, but both of them required quite a bit of our time, both to provide general support and to code and test the reusable components being supplied for the two environments.

Our development team was a small one and, under the circumstances, was getting stretched very thin trying to support both projects! Finally, management decided that we could only support one of these projects, and, after much soul-searching, they picked B. We started working intensively with B to make sure that the CMS DOEM worked well with their product, and as the two started to come together, we all realized that this had been a good decision. This product is now a successful product in its own right in the Latin American market.

The A team were told that they could continue to use DFDM, but not the DOEM, and that we could no longer afford to give them special support. We really expected them to decide to drop the use of DFDM altogether, and while this would have been disappointing, we felt that this would be a pragmatic decision on their part.

However, at this point, a very strange thing happened: faced with the possibility of losing the use of this productivity tool and having to redesign and rewrite a lot of their code, the A team turned right around and started to solve their own problems using basic DFDM! Instead of having us build complex generalized components, they found simpler ways of doing what they needed, and the result was a less complex, more maintainable system. Their product is also now a success and is saving the company considerable amounts of money.

Actually, an additional project using the DOEM appeared suddenly on the scene one day, rather to our surprise! It seemed that a bright young contractor had been given the job of building a small interactive system and had built it in a matter of a few weeks, using the DOEM, without telling any of the DOEM development team! We were very conscious that our documentation was nowhere near adequate at that time, but he said he had no trouble understanding and using it! Of course, he is very bright, but how often does something like that happen using conventional programming tools?

Since fairy tales usually have morals, let me propose the following: "Sometimes it is better to redesign a squeaky wheel than to just put more oil on it."

The Screen Manager, ISM1 (actually an earlier version of it), was also used by itself, before we even thought of the DOEM, on an earlier project within IBM Canada. This project became very successful, not least because Philip Ewing was excited by the concept of FBP (he still is!) and was discovering neat new uses for it all the time. As you may have gathered, ISM1 was a very powerful component and all by itself considerably simplified the development of interactive applications. Its development predated the rest of the DOEM by several years, so we had used it for several small projects. Here is what Philip has written about our experience on this project (called BLSB):

> DFDM was selected for use on the BLSB project because of the significant productivity improvements that were anticipated. The development team was not disappointed. Significant savings were realized in the following ways:
>
> 1) We were able to prototype more easily, beginning with a simple screen display, and adding functions one by one until the user was satisfied. The full function prototype could be modified to add a new edit or data-base lookup in a matter of hours, without disrupting the existing code.
> 2) Testing was made simpler because we were able to unplug the online screens and feed in test SCREEN REQUEST ENTITIES [abbreviated to SREs—these correspond to the "request IPs" referred to above] from files, and save the returned SREs into separate files based on type of error. In this way all of the application function in the online system could be tested in batch.
> 3) Building on the experience gained in the function testing, the legacy data was converted to the new database format by feeding in the old data in SRE format (simulating re-keying all of the previous 3 years of data through the new system). The errors were saved in separate files based on the ERROR CODE that the application put into the SRE before returning it to the screen. Each file was known to contain only one type of error. In three iterations through this process we were able to convert and load 64,000 history records with only 12 records needing to be re-keyed manually. In addition to not having to write a separate conversion program, we were also assured

that all of the data that was now in the database had passed all of the rigorous editing that had been built into the new application logic.

4) A great deal of effort in the design stage was saved because we could decompose functions to very granular levels before implementing. This meant that less thought needed to be put into the way different functions might affect each other, because different functions were now completely decoupled.
5) The "off the shelf" screen display function alone saved about 700 lines of application coding to handle ISPF panel displays. We did know ISPF before starting this project, but would not have needed to, since all of the ISPF specific code was in a DFDM-supplied function.

Less than 24% of the functions needed to be coded by the project, the rest came off the shelf. Furthermore, of the ones that we did have to code, the most complex was about 100 lines of code.

A comment made to me recently about the BLSB project: "We allowed three weeks for testing, but it worked the first time."

Another project that was very interesting was a system we built to do project resourcing, called PRORES, designed by A. Confalonieri and built by myself, using a Screen Manager similar to ISM1 and a User Response Analyzer, running on CMS. This Screen Manager was also driven by IPs with descriptors, but generated and accepted 3270 data streams (extended data stream) rather than using ISPF. It used a WYSIWYG representation of the screen and was the heart of the prototyping tool that I have mentioned elsewhere in this book.

The logic for PRORES was all written in REXX, and, considering that PRORES had to do a very large number of date calculations for each screen, its performance was surprisingly good. The basic idea was that, for each project that you were working on, you just entered a number of person-months and PRORES would generate all the dates and staffing requirements for the standard five phases of a project (Requirements, External Design, Internal Design, Development, Implementation), using formulae based on the standard "Volkswagen" shape or "snail curve" that most projects follow. You could also specify that a project should be "flat" instead of standard. If you constrained the end date to be earlier or later, you would get a more humped or flattened staffing curve. You could also request a graphical display of a department or division's projects, and it would use PGF (GDDM's Presentation Graphics Facility) to show all the projects in stacked bar format on a single chart across time. The stacked bar format meant that the project loadings were displayed cumulatively, so the top edge of the diagram showed the total staffing curve for the whole department or division. Management could then flatten and lower the overall curve by shifting projects around, stretching them out or compressing them, or moving projects between departments.

Suppose you had two projects, PROJ1 and PROJ2, both with the characteristic snail curve, as shown in figure 21-3. Now getting PGF to superimpose them gives the kind of picture seen in figure 21-4.

The outer "envelope" then shows the total cumulative loading for the two projects. With a relatively large number of projects, you can adjust things so that the top line is flat most of the time. "Flat" projects (projects that had a

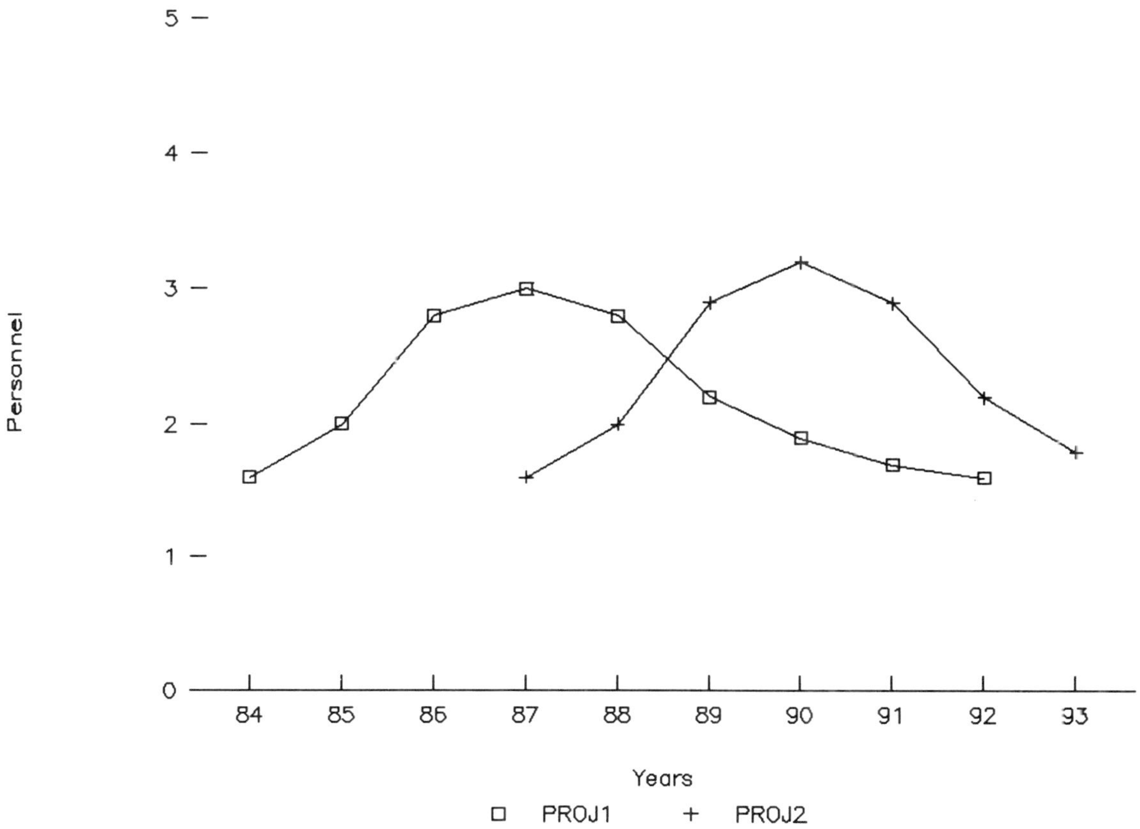

Figure 21-3.

constant loading over their whole lifetime) could be used to handle things like vacations, education, overhead, and so on. All dates were constrained to business days, and, once they were all calculated, individual project dates could be modified as desired.

Technically, this project was interesting because of the languages and software involved. It was also a decision assist–type application. You would get a screen just full of generated dates, and then, depending on which dates were changed, it would do intelligent things with them. This meant that it was very important for the Screen Manager to report on which fields had been modified. All the calculations were done in REXX. Date displays were handled by means of date input and output routines written in Assembler, driven by the Screen Manager using descriptors, so that REXX only saw dates in canonical form (number of days from a reference date). If you pick your reference date correctly, then day of the week is just "date modulo 7," and you can make Sunday 0, Monday 1, and so forth up to 6 (Saturday). This system was used intensively over a short period to help reorganize a portion of our division.

I am going to mention briefly another use I made of the Screen Manager because, although it was not a complete project, I found it very suggestive of

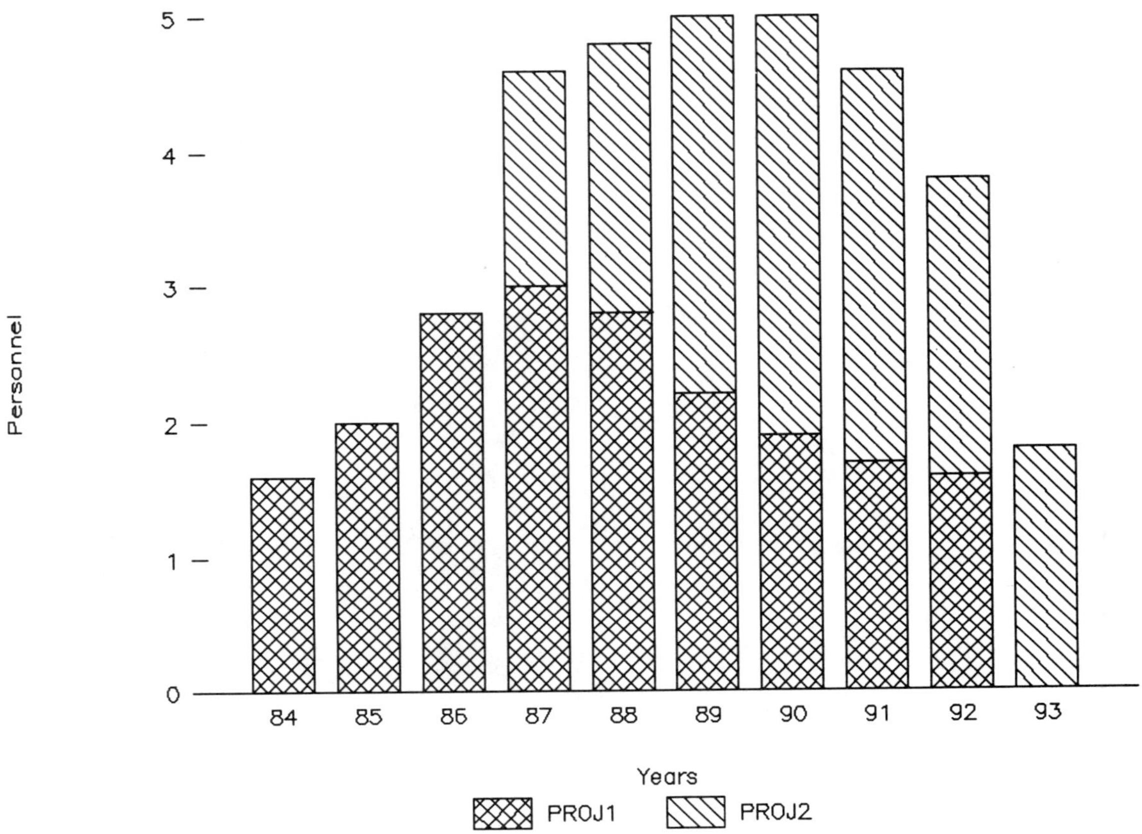

Figure 21-4.

the shape of user workbenches to come. Most of the application development on IBM hosts is done today (1994) using ISPF/PDF on TSO or CMS EXECs. Within this kind of workbench, developers use quite a wide range of "languages": HLLs, Assembler, JCL, DBDs, PSBs, MFS, FBP networks (hopefully!), 4GLs, and, of course, documentation in their own national language. All of these are held in different data sets and have different, although standard, processing applied to them. PDF follows the "action/object" paradigm: decide the action, then select the object. Having to choose the action first means that you always have to know what language the thing you are working on was written in. Also, in PDF you pick the same EDIT for everything, but then usually have to go to a completely different menu to process the text you have entered, and you *always* have to reenter the object's name, even if you were working on it just a few seconds ago! Native CMS is a little different, since it is command-oriented, but here you have to remember the command name to do the desired processing. Of course, both support lists with optional "wild cards," but it is still hard to move a single object through a series of phases (like edit, compile, run test, etc.).

I figured that it would be nice if everything a developer was working on could be treated as an object of a particular type, with a unique name. The developer could just select the object that he or she wanted to work on, and the system would know what language it was written in and display an action bar showing what actions could be applied to it. So the interface would prompt you for a component name (with optional "wild cards"), or you could ask for all components of a given type and just click on an entry in the action bar, without having to worry about choosing an inappropriate action for the object's type. Make the whole thing table-driven, and you have a very powerful, friendly system for application development—I know, because I built one for the CMS environment! All I had to do was select the object, and an appropriate action bar would come up, which would let me select from a list of CMS EXECs (e.g., EDIT, COMPILE, and the most important one of all: DESCRIBE). If the object types are user-modifiable, you can be more specific, i.e., "Assembler source" could be split into "programs" and "macros," or you could have types like "screen," which will generate MFS or BMS, plus declares for the message layouts. You could drive syntax-sensitive editors for different languages, or, for objects of type "diagram," you could make the EDIT option call a picture editor. I also felt that each action should go as far as possible (i.e., if you decide to COMPILE an Assembler source program, what you really want to do is translate it from human format to machine format—there is no particular point in making ASSEMBLE one action and then LINKEDIT another). The COMPILE action could also automatically update control tables for use by tools like symbolic debuggers or impact analysis tools.

The reason I said that this prototype was suggestive is that, if you can build this kind of development environment using FBP (and we know that FBP also lends itself to building compilers and text processing software), this conjures up the very appealing image of a totally user-modifiable development environment, built out of communicating standard components. This wouldn't be just a set of tools—this would let developers continuously expand and improve the workbench itself!

Last but not least, in this rather varied set of examples, there was a project, which might be called an electronic information booth, to provide a visitor to our building with such information as how to find people, facts about the building (layout, statistics, etc.), promotions during the month, a "trading post," and the cafeteria menu for the week. Everything was to be highly graphical and menu-driven. I prototyped this using the same screen manager I described above and a User Response Analyzer to implement the paths between the screens. As I mentioned above, this screen manager had a fairly complete graphical specification facility based on polygons, so it was well suited to developing a lot of pictures in a hurry! Since I already had the Screen Manager and User Response Analyzer, it was really just a matter of working with our very talented resident artist, Bob White, to develop the pictures. As it was around Thanksgiving, we decorated the Thanksgiving menu with a rather nice stylized corncob. During the Christmas season, we put the Christmas menu on its own screen with a little Christmas tree at the top! Later on, it was decided to implement this application using PCs, but our prototype certainly played a significant role in convincing management of the validity of the idea.

22

Performance Considerations

I cannot stress too strongly that FBP is intended for building *real* systems, and indeed the various dialects I have been describing in this book have been used successfully for this purpose many times! To achieve this, you *have* to keep performance in mind—not only must a system do what it is supposed to do, but it must do it in a "reasonable" amount of time. While admitting that this is a subjective measure, I submit that, at a given point in time, people generally have an image in their heads of what constitutes a reasonable amount of time for a particular function. While there will almost certainly be disagreements, say between users and developers, we see the use of SLAs (service level agreements) becoming more and more widespread, which requires the parties involved to reach some sort of compromise between what one wants and what the other will commit to. Response time is another area that is highly subjective, but studies have shown that there are observable differences in behavior as response time changes, which match the users' subjective impressions. Once people get used to subsecond response time, anything worse is highly frustrating. If it gets really bad, their whole style of interacting with the machine has to change.

Now, a system that has to deliver function to real-life users has to be reliable and also has to perform. A system may provide wonderful function, but if you cannot produce adequately performing systems, it will only be of academic interest. Suppose you decide that you are going to interpret English descriptions of function using a natural language parser—it may be a great research project, but, *given present-day (1994) technology,* you probably can't run a bank on it! Can you "run a bank" on an FBP implementation? Yes, it's been used for a large chunk of the batch processing of a bank's bread and butter transactions for the past 20 years!

Now, not only must the infrastructure be fairly fast, but it must be *tunable*. Key to this, I believe, is being able to form a mental model of what is going on and where a performance or logic problem may be occurring. If a developer or debugger cannot do this, the reaction may be to throw the baby out with the bathwater. Adequate performance is important even when a new system is in the evaluation stage. At this point, overall impressions can be very important. The system has to have knobs and levers that let the developers tune the system, and the system has to behave in a linear manner. Linearity means that systems must "scale up." As you add function, not only should you not get sudden breaks in continuity—crashes, unexpected results—but ideally the curve should be as close to linear as possible. In conventional programming environments, complexity (and therefore development time) goes up exponentially as program size. Humans tend to have difficulty grasping the implications of exponential curves.

While it is possible that software could do automatic balancing between variables in simple situations, performance is a multiple variable problem. In any given application, a programmer has to juggle resources, algorithms, and whole design approaches. Given this complexity, the software should be made as transparent as possible. In FBP, although there are many possible solutions to a problem, the developer can select a solution and then see the results and can in fact iterate quickly through a large number of possible solutions.

In my experience, the single most important factor affecting performance is the *design*. In general, shaving a few microseconds off a subroutine will not make much difference, unless it is being performed billions of times. But a different approach to a design can often save seconds, minutes, or even hours. Here is a simple example. About 20 years ago, a programmer on a project I was involved in needed to calculate the day of the week, given a date. He decided he would need a database running 3 years into the future and 3 years into the past. Of course, the database would have to be maintained by hand, so he planned for it to be updated once a year. Even without taking into account the manual labor and difficulty if he was presented with a date outside the database's range, I just figured that it might be a lot simpler to calculate it mathematically! Eventually, this huge effort turned into a macro of about 12 statements, guaranteed until the year 2099! I am sure you are saying that's a trivial example and that we were all ignorant, but I am sure there are examples in your code where a small change of viewpoint can yield a big dividend in performance or maintainability, or both!

However, to be able to take advantage of these changes of viewpoint, you have to have a modular system. With FBP, as we saw elsewhere in this book, you can replace a Sort by a table look-up or a file by a connection; you can move function from one job step to another, from one system to another, and so on. As the programmer I quoted earlier told me, "One of the things I like about AMPS is that there are so many more ways to do a job than with conventional programming." *There is never just one way to do a job.* Also, an FBP developer is continually making conscious trade-offs between different factors. For instance, he or she might decide to favor response time over throughput, so that might tilt the scales towards direct access instead of sorting. Or there is the old storage vs. CPU time debate. Or within a component, you can trade off state data against code: Boolean switches can either be held in a variable or can be implemented by choosing between two code paths (the state of the choice is specified by which part of the code is being executed). It is important to know what options are available to you, and the system must allow you to choose the one you want.

The fundamental trade-off in FBP is that we have decided to spend a certain amount of CPU time to get improved programmer productivity and program maintainability. Of course, the industry has been doing this since HLLs and operating systems were invented, so this is nothing new, but you always have to decide how much you are willing to pay. Also, the amount has to be controllable—a certain cost may be appropriate for one type of application, but wildly inappropriate for another.

In the case of FBP, the cost is closely related to the number of processes, which in turn is related to what is called "granularity." In general, the finer the granularity, the more CPU time gets used, so you can afford smaller "grains" in an infrequently used part of an application network. Conversely, 5,000,000 IPs going through a path of 12 processes will cost at least 120,000,000*t* units of CPU time, where *t* is the cost in CPU time of one API call (each process is going to cost at least 2*t* units per IP, for a receive and send). Depending on the speed of your machine and what *t* is, you may decide that 12 is too many. Reducing this number will probably entail some sacrifice in terms of reuse or modularity, as you will be combining smaller, more reusable functions into larger, more ad hoc components.

Periodically, people will write an FBP network and a PL/I program that do the same thing and then compare their performance. This is like comparing chalk and cheese! The maintainability of the two programs is totally different, as a PL/I program adds far more maintenance load to your DP department than does an FBP network. Furthermore, if a bug in a generalized component is fixed, everyone benefits, while if a PL/I program bug is fixed, usually there is no spill-over to other applications.

Susan came to us with a program that she felt was slow compared with a "reasonable" execution time. I noticed that she was using the Assign component to set a 1-byte field in every IP, and there were a *lot* of IPs. She had been told to make her program very modular, but also she probably felt that Assign was a neat function, and it meant that much less PL/I had to be written and maintained. I suggested that she add a single statement to each of a couple of her hand-coded PL/I components. There were other things we could do that together improved the running time significantly. Although we "improved" her program to the point where its performance was acceptable, we probably reduced its maintainability slightly. But this is another trade-off for which no general rules can be given—each situation has to be decided on its own merits. I mention this example mainly to stress that it's a complex decision whether to use a separate generalized component or add function to custom components, involving issues of maintainability, performance, predicted use, ROI, and so on. There is a strong element of the aesthetic here—nobody *should* make the decision for you, just as nobody can tell you which paintings to like. Maybe someone *will,* but that's life!

The bottom line is that we have to give application designers as many choices as possible and as much control as possible, and systems that won't or can't do this won't survive. Why has COBOL survived when so many more sophisticated products have fallen by the wayside? Because, even if you don't like it aesthetically, COBOL does provide this control, even if it takes years to write a system and, once written, is even harder to maintain. However, COBOL systems degenerate over time, as the developers lose knowledge of and control over what's going on under the covers; FBP systems don't.

Now let's talk about specific techniques for tuning the performance of FBP applications.

In chapter 20, I talked about the basic MVS synchronization technique of WAIT on ECB. We found that quite often, when the same program was written in, say, PL/I and in DFDM, the elapsed time of the DFDM run would be less than that of the PL/I run, but the CPU time would be somewhat greater. It becomes obvious why this should be so if you visualize an FBP network with six processes all doing I/O: provided the I/O is using different channels, drives, and so on, it can all be happening concurrently, while the scheduler will always be "trying" to find CPU work to do to fill available CPU time. FBP programs tend to be CPU gluttons, but that is also the designer's choice— if he or she is concerned about this, I/O processes can be prevented from overlapping by synchronization signals. Usually, however, programmers want to reduce elapsed time (e.g., to fit into a processing "window" [time-slot]). Today, windows are getting shorter and shorter, so there is pressure to reduce elapsed time, even at the cost of more CPU time.

As described earlier, using FBP connections in place of intermediate files definitely saves elapsed time, as all the records no longer have to be written out to disk and read back in again, but it will save CPU time as well, due to the reduction in the number of EXCPs (EXecute Channel Program). In MVS, although the EXCP count is maintained as a separate piece of statistical information, people tend to forget that EXCPs are quite expensive in terms of CPU time as well.

Here are some statistics recorded during an evaluation of DFDM against an existing PL/I application, done by an IBM I/S site in the United States:

I/O EXCP requests: 53.6% reduction.
CPU usage: 16.7% increase.
Elapsed execution time: 37.7% reduction.
External DASD requirements: 84% reduction.

Here is what the people at this site said about those figures:

> We attribute the above reductions in resource usage to the improved design of the application (as a result of using structured analysis which is promoted in conjunction with DFDM). The slight increase in CPU usage is a small trade-off when you take into consideration the improved design of the application which should significantly lower future maintenance.

Let's say that you have tuned your I/O as well as possible and that you are now trying to estimate how much CPU time your application will take. I have found that the main predictor for CPU time is the number of API calls. On the IBM Model 168 (this was about a 2 MIPS machine), each API call took approximately 10 microseconds. Of course, later machines are much faster, but later implementations of FBP are typically written in higher-level languages, have more features, and do more checking, so the time has probably stayed approximately constant. Just for comparison, I recently did some measurements on THREADS, running on a 33-MHz 80486DX, and the time per API call was approximately 50 microseconds (THREADS is written in C, so this figure could probably be improved by rewriting critical sections of the scheduler in Assembler).

In most networks, there is usually a "backbone": a path where most of the IPs travel. You could think of this backbone as being like a critical path in a critical path network. Now suppose that this path consists of 12 processes, each sending and receiving. Then, taking the figure of 10 microseconds, you get a cost of 240 microseconds per IP. If 5 million IPs travel this path, you get a total CPU time for API calls alone of 1200 seconds, or 20 minutes. You may therefore decide that you want to consolidate some of the processes in the application "backbone" into larger, less generalized ones. As said earlier, this will reduce maintainability, but you may well decide that it is worth the price. Of course, you don't have to consolidate all the processes in your network. Areas of the network which are visited less frequently, like error handling logic, may be left more granular.

It is common wisdom nowadays to concentrate on developing function first and then worry about performance afterwards. This is quite valid as long as you don't squander performance up front by poor design. And here of course is where aesthetics comes in. I started my programming career on an IBM 650, where instructions were stored on a spinning magnetic drum, and I believe that it became almost an instinct to make programs as lean in terms of time and storage as possible. But, even in those far-off days, there was wide variation in the performance of code by different programmers. I believe that the most successful ones never lose sight of the performance requirement, so that it is a constant undertone to their program designs. If you ignore performance and expect to add it back in later, you will generally be disappointed in the results!

Having said that, I must also warn against the other extreme. Wayne Stevens repeatedly stressed that you will generally not be able to predict the best place in your application to focus your tuning efforts on. You may spend lots of time trimming a few seconds off some code that turns out only to be used occasionally. It is much better to run a performance tool on your application, using representative data, and find out where you should really be putting tuning effort. You can actually use the time you have saved by using an improved methodology to tune the parts of your system that make a real difference. One of the satisfying things about FBP is that, once you have improved the performance of a component, all future users of that component will benefit.

Similarly, you may decide to create a variant of a component to exploit a trade-off, and again you have increased the range of choices for future users. An example of this is a coroutine I built 20 years ago to read disk files faster than the standard reader, but at the cost of more storage. We had a large BDAM data set that had to be read as fast as possible. The regular sequential reader worked fine, as this data set could just be treated as a sequential data set (in MVS, BDAM and BSAM files are held on disk in essentially the same format), but I also knew that all the records of a BDAM data set were the same length, which is not necessarily true for sequential files. Now the tracks of an IBM disk drive start at a point called the index point, so, to read a track, the access method has to wait until the index point comes around before starting to read the data (this is called "latency"). If you miss it, you have to wait a full revolution for it to come round again (and we could see this happening in our performance studies). I also knew that each record is physically labeled with a record number on the track, so I figured that it should be possible to start reading anywhere on the track and just determine the record sequence afterward. Since this technique would be embedded in an FBP component, it could still generate the records in the correct sequence. You do have to calculate the number of records per track first, but all the records are the same length, so there are standard formulae and tools for doing this. On the minus side is the fact that this approach takes up a track's worth of storage, and your code is somewhat tied to the device's characteristics; on the plus side, it's *fast!* In our case, this Read Track component was definitely worth it—it didn't get used widely, but, when we needed it, there was nothing like it! Remember also that in FBP there is never just one way to do a job, so nobody is forced to use your component. This component can just be added to the tools available for your programmers to use—they just have to understand its behavior, not how it works inside. By the way, training programmers to think like users is not that easy!

Another kind of trade-off can be made in FBP by varying the capacity of connections. FBP's connections provide a powerful way of trading off CPU time against storage. All FBP schedulers so far have followed the strategy of having a process continue running as long as possible, until it is suspended for some reason. Now the more IPs there are in a process's input connection(s), the longer that process can go on before a context switch has to take place (assuming there is room in its output connections to receive the output). So, in general, larger capacity connections reduce context switches and therefore CPU time. But, of course, larger capacities mean that more IPs can be in flight at any point in time, so your application will take up more storage. Another way of looking at this is that you are effectively loosening the coupling between processes, so larger capacity connections equals looser coupling, whereas smaller capacity connections equals tighter coupling. For instance, we discovered that sequential readers perform best if their output connections can hold at least a block's worth of records.

The Read Track coroutine described earlier was used in conjunction with some other techniques to reduce a disk file scanning job from 2 hours to 18 minutes. The original running time of 2 hours was a cause for concern, as we knew that the data we would eventually have to process was several times the amount we were using in the 2-hour run. It therefore became imperative to see what we could do to reduce the running time of the job. We achieved this significant reduction just by changing the shape of the network and adding one new component. This example used AMPS and is described in my *Systems Journal* article (Morrison 1978), but for those of you who may not have access to it I think it's worth repeating here, as it embodies some very important principles.

The application scanned chains of records running across many disk packs. One set of packs contained the "roots" of the chains, while another set of disk packs contained what we might call "chain records." Each root contained pointers to zero or more chain records, which in turn might contain pointers to other chain records, which could be spread over multiple packs. The problem was that our application's insert and delete code was occasionally breaking chains, so I was given the job of running through every chain looking for broken links, but obviously the scanning program could not use the same code that was causing the problem! So I had to write all new programs to do the scanning job. These programs understood our pointer structure, and there was enough internal evidence that I could always detect a broken chain.

My first approach looked like figure 22-1, where RS means Read Sequential. This was the standard reader—we just concatenated its input files together, so its disk packs were read one after another. CF is the Chain Follower, which follows chains from one record to the next and outputs diagnostic information only when it finds a broken chain. SRT sorts the output of CF to put it into a sequence that is useful for humans, and PRT prints the results of the Sort process.

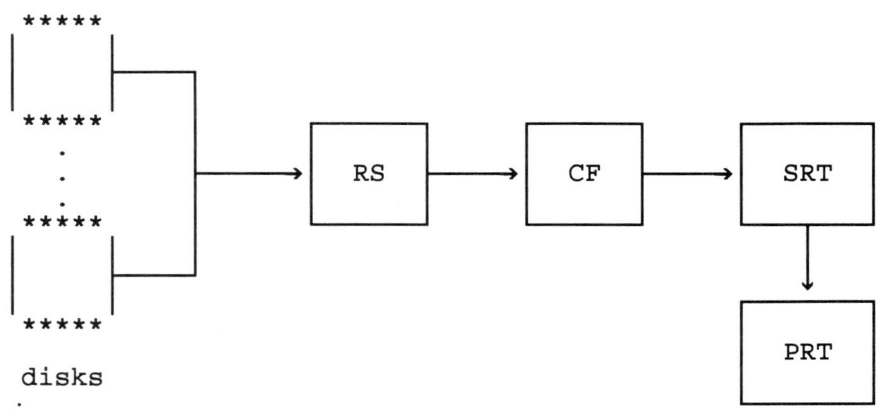

Figure 22-1.

The reason for the Sort is that the root records were scattered randomly on the root disks, whereas it was more useful to see the errors ordered by, say, account number within error type. Since the number of errors should gradually diminish to zero as program bugs in the access methods were fixed, the overhead of the Sort process would diminish over time also.

This program as shown in figure 22-1 took 2 hours to run, even though we were using a test database, so we absolutely had to speed it up!

My first realization was that the CF component was heavily I/O-bound, as it was spending most of its running time doing direct accesses to disk records, which usually included a seek, disk latency, and then a read of a record into storage. I figured that, if we could run a large number of these processes concurrently, the I/O times of the different processes would tend to overlap. However, if we had too many parallel processes, they would start contending for resources (i.e., channels and arms). I therefore decided rather arbitrarily to have 18 of them running concurrently.

I also thought that, since the roots were scattered across multiple packs, we might as well assign each pack its own reader and let them run in parallel also. Also, if I was going to do that, why not use the full track reader I described earlier in this chapter? Its output is data records, in the right order (although this wasn't even strictly necessary for this application), so the next process downstream wouldn't see any difference.

Lastly, I needed something to tie together these two kinds of process. I needed a process that would assign incoming root IPs to one of the CF processes, in a balanced manner. I could have just done this using a round-robin technique, but I wanted to try something a little "smarter": could I select the CF process that had the least work to do and thus keep the load across all the CF processes in balance? I reasoned that the most lightly loaded process should have the smallest build-up in its input connection, so if I always sent a root IP to the CF process with the fewest IPs in its input connection, this would have the desired effect. I therefore wrote a load-balancing component that checked its output connections looking for the one with the smallest number of IPs. I feel that this approach is quite general and could be used in many multi-server situations.

Figure 22-2 is a picture of the final structure, where RT is the full track reader, LB is the Load Balancing component, and the other processes are as before.

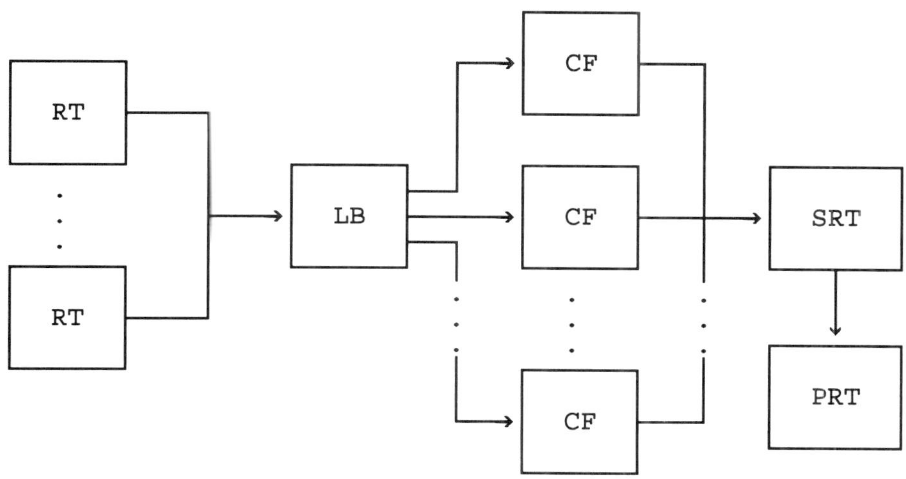

Figure 22-2

Final result: elapsed time down from 2 hours to 18 minutes.

Programming cost: one new generalized component (LB) and a change to the network. You might want to count RT, depending on whether you feel that this was written for this purpose or independently of it (it sort of happened along at the right time!). Furthermore, all these generalized components can be used in future applications.

You may have been wondering how a component can check how many IPs are in a downstream connection when I have never mentioned a service to do this. This is an area of technology that I'm afraid is not "pure," but that I suspect comes up often when a concept has to come down out of its ivory tower into the world of real applications. We never did build an encapsulated service to count the IPs in a downstream connection, and, if we had, it probably would have had to be a lot more complex. Instead, we allowed *one* special component to peer into the insides of the infrastructure, so it effectively became an extension of the scheduler. I understood that it would have to change any time the internal structure of the scheduler changed, but that seemed better than providing a new service for the benefit of just one user. In hindsight, it might have been even better to package the whole component as part of the scheduler, since then it would automatically participate in any changes made to the scheduler.

In DFDM, we had a very similar situation with the Subnet Manager, which also did strange things to the innards of the scheduler (you will remember that it can "revive" dead processes). DFDM's Time coroutine is a little bit like that too—this coroutine uses an existing, but unpublished, service to generate "clock tick" IPs and is the only coroutine that is allowed to use this service.

DFDM's NIP (Next Input Port) service is an example of something that we were enthusiastic about at first, but we later felt less excited about. In fact, we did not include it in the Japanese version of DFDM. It is also appropriate to mention it in a chapter on performance, as it was intended as a performance tool. The idea was to be able to monitor which input port data had arrived at and signal this fact to the component, which could then do a receive from that port. If no data was waiting at any input port, the component code could specify that NIP was to suspend until some data arrived or that you didn't want to suspend. The latter option provided a way of polling (which I think should be avoided anyway); the former option is much the same as tagging all incoming IPs to indicate their source and then merging them into a single input port on a first-come, first-served basis. So all NIP really saved us was the need to allocate a field in each IP to indicate the source number and the need to set it. Perhaps its main appeal was that it matched very closely one's mental model of how a server servicing requests from multiple sources should work, but, as I said earlier, this can be handled very nicely, just using FBP's many-to-one connection facility, so you really don't need to provide a separate service to do this.

I mention these situations to describe a type of problem that will certainly come up from time to time. Under the pressures of deadlines, performance requirements, or just because you get a neat idea, you will either be tempted to introduce small breaches in the bastions surrounding your system, or you will be persuaded to put in complex facilities for one or two users. Conversely, you may put your foot down and refuse to give in and lose some customers. Should you give in to those temptations, or should you stick to your guns because you know the possible pitfalls if you don't? I can't answer that for you. All I can recommend is that you try to make sure that you have thought through all the pros and cons before you make your decision! One hint: good code (no, make that any code) lasts a lot longer than you would ever expect, and, when some dialect of FBP (hopefully) becomes more widely used, it will last longer still. Will you still be proud of your code 20 years from now? I sincerely hope so, because there's a good chance you'll meet it again!

23

Network Specification Notations

FBP applications start off life as pictures or as hierarchies of pictures that have to be made "machinable" for execution. During most of our 20 years of experience with FBP, we have never had advanced picture-drawing tools, so we tended to draw networks using pencil and paper and then convert them by hand into executable networks. Although we have experimented with different notations over the years, the information that needs to be captured has remained fairly constant. It is certainly true that FBP lends itself to visual programming techniques, so what I am going to describe will become less important as time goes on, but, for now, you still have to have notations that allow networks to be input directly into the machine.

The diagrams typically used for Structured Analysis represent processes and their connections. To turn such a diagram into an FBP diagram, which can actually be executed, you only have to add the following data:

- Port names (or numbers)
- Parametrization
- Automatic ports

For ease of understanding, you could always add the following to Structured Analysis diagrams:

- Stream descriptions
- Component names (e.g. process "merge masters and details" uses COLLATE)
- Icons for external objects, users, etc.

The same is true for FBP diagrams. Since we mostly used pencil and paper, we never really worried too much about the exact diagramming conventions to be used.

In fact, if some Structured Analysis diagramming convention is in use in a given shop, it makes sense to just expand on whatever convention was used for analysis.

Clearly, there is a great opportunity for powerful picture-drawing tools to assist in the design and development process. It would be nice to be able to "explode" a process and see its structure at the next lower level or to look at a connection and see the data stream that passes over it. When building networks, it would be even nicer to be able to pick up an icon for, say, Collate and place it on the diagram, complete with "sticky" ports ready to be connected to its neighbors.

I have drawn a number of pictures in what has gone before in this book, but I have yet to talk about how we get these into the machine to be executed.

The very first FBP software, AMPS, was written in IBM S/370 Assembler language, and networks were also expressed using Assembler macros. Each process was specified using a single macro call, which also listed the named connections between that process and the other ones. In what follows, I will use a simple network and show how it was specified to the system in the various FBP dialects. Let's use figure 23-1 as a sample network. In AMPS and DFDM, ports are specified numerically, so I have marked the ports as numbers in this diagram. (In DFDM, input and output ports were numbered separately, while in AMPS one set of numbers covered both—the figure follows the AMPS convention.)

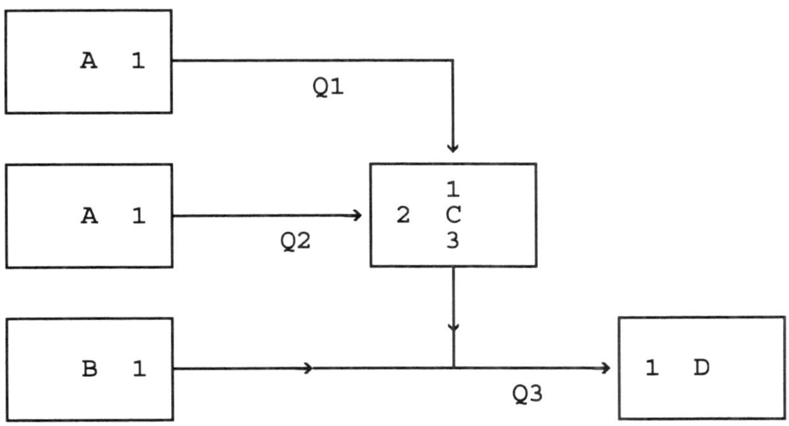

Figure 23-1.

In AMPS this would have been specified approximately as follows (I will use PROCESS rather than the actual macro name used, to show the analogies with present-day terminology):

```
PROCESS PROG=A,AQ=Q1
PROCESS PROG=A,AQ=Q2
PROCESS PROG=B,AQ=Q3
PROCESS PROG=C,Q=(Q1,Q2),AQ=Q3
PROCESS PROG=D,Q=Q3
```

where the PROCESS macro shows a process, `Q=` lists the queues inputting to the process (feeding the process), and `AQ=` lists the queues fed by the process. Communication between processes is thus set up by *naming the connections* (called "queues" in AMPS). Numbering is sequential, starting with `Q=` and then going on through `AQ=`. Parameters could also be specified in the network and were added using `PARM=` as an address-type parameter on the PROCESS macro, when required. As each macro describes a separate process, there is no need to distinguish between different uses of the same component (indicated by the `PROG=` parameter).

Notice a concept common to all the varieties of FBP: when more than one output port is connected to one input port, *it is treated as one connection* (queue). Connections can be many-to-one, but not one-to-many.

Parameters in AMPS were more general than DFDM's: an AMPS parameter could be a data structure of any form, while DFDM parameters were always variable length character strings; DFDM's were consistent with the format of parameters passed to a job step by the MVS operating system.

DFDM has two different notations: *interpreted,* which is used to build the network dynamically at run-time, and *compiled,* where the control blocks for the network are built as a single Assembler program, which when compiled and linkedited results in a ready-to-run network control block structure. The interpreted notation allows a program to be modified and tested many times during a session. Test components can also be added easily to monitor the contents of connections or to create test data. The compiled format does not have the interpretation overhead, but takes a little longer to generate and so is more appropriate when a network is put into production or you want to study a program's performance. Once you are ready to go from interpreted to compiled format, you use a utility program (called "Expand") to do the conversion. The other main difference is that, in the interpreted case, components are loaded dynamically at run-time, while in the compiled case all the components are linked together, along with the network, into a single load module.

Both of these DFDM notations are based on specifying a list of *connections* rather than processes. These connections specify the processes that they connect, but are themselves unnamed. Processes are named by component name, plus an optional qualifier (indicated by a period). The interpreted notation uses arrows (->) (originally also ampersands [&]) to indicate connections. Port numbers are shown *before and after* the connection mark (if not specified, the default is 1). Connections can be strung together in "paths," with a comma marking the end of a path. Earlier versions of DFDM did not mark the end of a network, but the Japanese version used a semi-colon. So the previous example in DFDM interpreted notation would read as follows (since in DFDM input and output ports are numbered separately, C has input ports 1 and 2 and output port 1):

```
A -> C -> D,
A.X -> 2 C,
B -> D;
```

where I have distinguished the second occurrence of A with the qualifier X (any character string would have done).

The corresponding compiled specification would then be:

```
MAIN  NETWORK
      CONNECT A,C
      CONNECT C,D
      CONNECT A.X,(2,C)
      CONNECT B,D
      NETEND
      END
```

As can be seen, both notations use the same qualifier notation.

One other major difference between the interpreted and compiled notations of DFDM is that the interpreted notation is hierarchical, whereas the compiled is "flat" (it is "flattened" when it is expanded, so that the whole network becomes a single module). In the interpreted notation, you can define a subnet, call it *G*, with sticky connections—for example:

```
G:  -> A -> 2 B ->, I -> B
```

would mean that *G* has one input port and one output port that will be connected when *G* is used. Arrows with an open end are the external interfaces of the subnet—in this example, the arrow feeding *A* and the arrow coming from *B*.

G's picture therefore looks like that in figure 23-2.

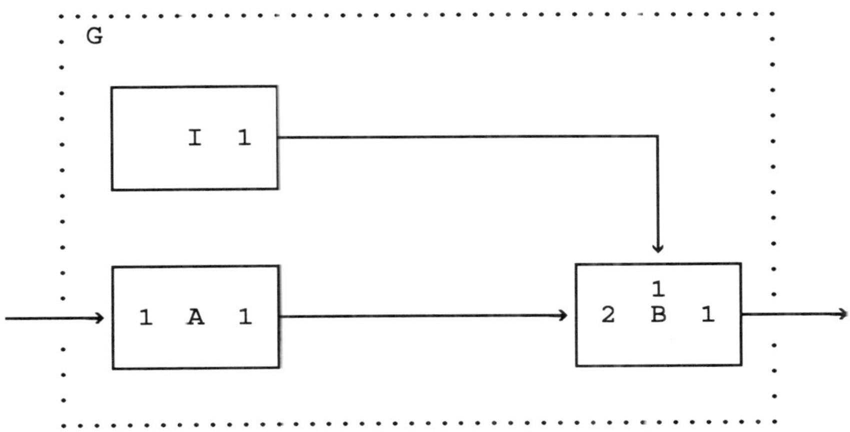

Figure 23-2.

G has two external ports: one input and one output. These are the arrows that cross the "boundary" of *G* (shown as a dotted line). *G* can therefore be used as an ordinary filter in a network and, like all components, can be used more than once in a network.

Figure 23-3 shows a network that uses *G*.

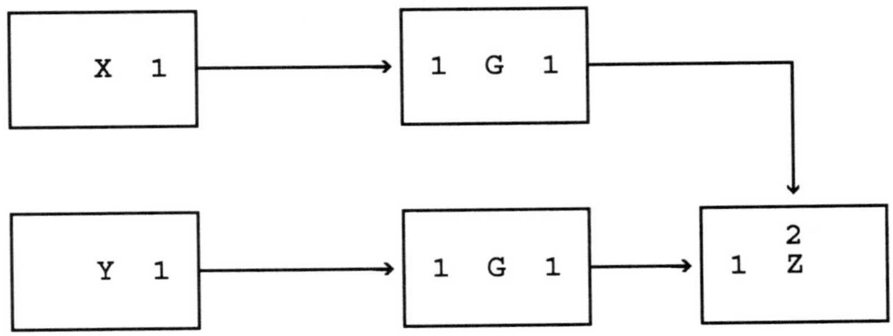

Figure 23-3.

This might be coded as follows in the interpreted notation:

```
X -> G.FIRST -> 2 Z,
Y -> G.SECOND -> Z
```

Note that composite components can be qualified just like elementary components. At this level, the network doesn't know that *G* even *is* a composite. If this network is then expanded to form a single flattened network, you will see two instances each of *I, A,* and *B,* as follows:

```
MAIN  NETWORK
      CONNECT X,A.1
      CONNECT I.1,B.1
      CONNECT A.1,(2,B.1)
      CONNECT B.1,(2,Z)
      CONNECT Y,A.2
      CONNECT I.2,B.2
      CONNECT A.2,(2,B.2)
      CONNECT B.2,Z
      NETEND
      END
```

The Expand function automatically assigns qualifiers to all the resulting processes. Composite components like *G* can be coded in the same file or file member as the network that references them or in a separate file or file member.

When the network using *G* is expanded, you see that *G* loses its identity and merely becomes a pattern within the total network. Since *I* has no inputs and *G* has lost its identity at run-time, all the *I*'s will start up at start of run.

One other thing to notice is that the expanded list is not very easy to grasp. People generally find that it is easier to work with the interpreted form for two reasons: you can see the effect of a modification immediately, and also an individual network or subnet is easier to understand when it has no more than about seven processes (human short-term memory seems to be able to handle up to seven plus or minus two objects), so you can build up quite complex applications, as long as they are built up out of layers none of which exceed more than about seven processes. Ideally, of course, this should be done using a graphic interface, but we did not have such tools available.

In the experimental THREADS system mentioned earlier, there is both an interpreted and a compiled network specification. Here is a rather trivial example of a THREADS network in the interpreted notation to illustrate some of its features:

```
'data.fil' ->
    OPT Reader(THFILERD) OUT ->
    IN Selector(THSPLIT) MATCH ->
    IN Replicate(THREPL) OUT[0] ->
    IN Display(THVIEW),
    Replicate OUT[1] -> IN Display,
   '11,2,0' -> OPT Selector;
```

This represents the network in figure 23-4.

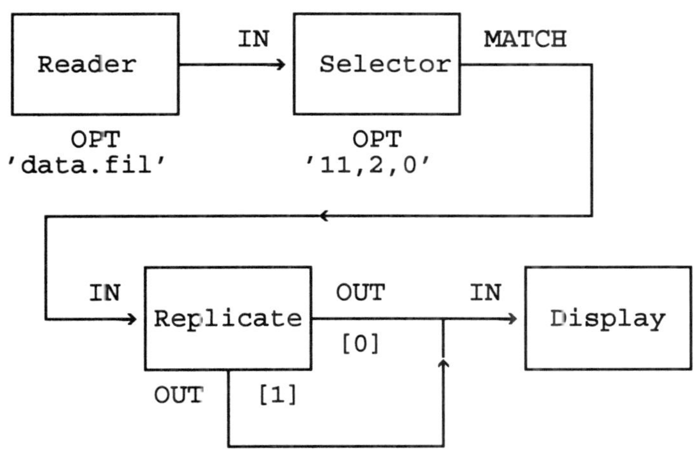

Figure 23-4.

The above notation follows DFDM in that you trace a path until you hit a dead end, insert a comma, and then start on the next path, and so on, until the whole network is specified.

Whereas DFDM named processes by giving a component name plus qualifier, THREADS names processes directly and attaches a component name in brackets to one of the occurrences of the process name. Ports are named, rather than numbered, so the notation for a connection is:

```
... process-name port-name -> port-name process-name ...
```

As befits the "C" basis of THREADS, elements of array-type ports are identified by:

```
port-name [ element-number ]
```

numbering up from zero.

The end of a network is marked with a semi-colon.

The other major way in which THREADS differs from AMPS and DFDM is its concept of initial information packets (IIPs). These are shown as quoted strings followed by arrows (indicating that these are really a special form of connection)—for example:

```
'data.fil' -> OPT Reader(PROCR) ....
```

This attaches the string `data.fil` to port OPT of Reader in such a way that when Reader does a "receive" from its OPT port, the string is turned into a "real" IP and becomes accessible to the Reader's code. After processing, the Reader has to dispose of it as usual. If Reader does a receive from that port again, it will receive an "end of data" indication.

Automatic ports can be specified by putting an asterisk in place of a port name.

You can also specify subnets following the main network in the same file or as separate files, which are started with a label (symbol followed by a colon) and terminated with a semi-colon. Here is an example of a THREADS network definition together with some subnets:

```
'data.fil' -> OPT reader(R1) OUT ->
  IN  thcount(THCOUNT) COUNT ->
  MIN display(C1),
  'H' -> MOPT display;

C1:
 MIN =>IN process_C(THVIEW),
 MOPT => OPT process_C OUT => MOUT;

R1:
OPT => OPT reader(THFILERD) OUT => OUT;
```

Process names only have to be unique within a given subnet, so the two uses of `reader` do not conflict. You will also notice that the port names on the subnets are identified with the corresponding internal ports by means of an arrow-like equals sign. This is to stress the fact that these are not really connections, but are more like equivalences. In both DFDM and THREADS, a subnet may specify ports that are not used in the network referencing it, but the reverse situation is not allowed (if a port is referenced at a higher level, it must be specified in the definition of the subnet).

THREADS also has a compiled format—it differs from DFDM in that it does not generate the run-time control blocks directly, but is still a list of the connections, in fixed format rather than in free form. The advantage of this is that we can change the implementation of the THREADS driver and the format of its control blocks, without the user having to recompile all of his or her applications.

I have gone into some detail on the various approaches to notations because, for many jobs, the network notation is all the code a programmer ever has to write! Whether you name the connections or the processes, all you are really doing is telling the machine about a list of connections. As such, sequence really doesn't matter, so, even if you feel this should be called a programming language, it is definitely a nonsequential one! It also has a natural relationship with pictures, so in the future I hope there will be graphical tools that will make entry of this information into the machine even easier. For debugging conventional languages, we are just starting to get packages that allow the developer to walk through a program interactively. A graphical aid to debugging FBP networks should allow you to monitor the data passing across a connection or track a single IP as it travels through the whole network and observe its transformations. As with any debugging tool, the real challenge is to provide ways for the developer to build mental models, both of the way the program should be working and also of how it is going wrong.

24

Related Compiler Theory Concepts

It has been noted by several writers that there seems to be a good match between compiler theory and the theory of sequential processes. FBP processes can be regarded as parsers of their input streams.

The component labeled TR1 in the example in chapter 10 can be considered as a "parser," while the structure of its input stream can be specified using a syntactic form called a regular expression. This allows a number of the concepts of modern compiler theory to be applied to it. Let us express the input stream of component TR1 in that application as a "regular expression," as follows:

```
{ ( m d* ) }*
```

which can be read as:

> Zero or more groups of:
> One open bracket,
> One master IP (m),
> Zero or more details (d),
> One close bracket.

(In what follows, I will use brackets to represent bracket *IPs,* and curly braces will have syntactic meaning.)

Each of TR1's output streams consists of repeating strings of identical IPs. Representing modified masters as `m'`, extended details as `d'`, and summaries as `s`, we get the following "regular expressions" for the three output streams:

```
m'*
d'*
s*
```

Each of these output streams has a well-defined relationship with the input stream, and it would be very nice if some notation could be developed to show this relationship clearly and concisely. In fact, this would constitute a complete description of what TR1 *does:* a component's function is completely described by its input and output streams and the relationships between them.

In their 1972 book, *The Theory of Parsing, Translation and Compiling,* Aho and Ullman show that a regular expression can be parsed by a deterministic one-way finite automaton with one tape, usually referred to simply as a "finite automaton." This tape contains "frames," usually containing characters, but in what follows we shall think of the frames as containing entire IPs. As each frame is scanned, the automaton may or may not change state and may or may not perform an "action," such as reading or writing a frame. Whether or not there is an action, the tape continues moving.

A convenient way to represent the various state changes is by means of a "transition graph," where each node represents a state, and each arc represents a transition from one state to another (or from a state to itself) and is marked with the name of the IP being scanned off, as shown in figure 24-1.

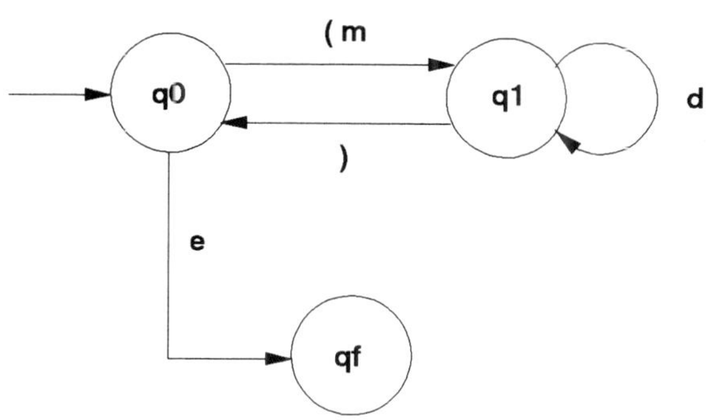

Figure 24-1.

In these diagrams, *e* is used to indicate the "end of data" condition; *m, d, (,* and *)* represent masters, details, open brackets, and close brackets, respectively. Since open bracket is always followed by a master in this example, I have shown them combined on a single arc.

An alternative to the transition graph is the "State Table." This uses a tabular format, which is often more convenient. Table 24-1 is equivalent to figure 24-1.

Aho and Ullman next show that any regular expression may be described by a "right linear grammar," expressed as a series of "productions," each of which describes a pattern in terms of the sub-patterns or final symbols that make it up.

Productions can be understood in a generative sense—that is, all legal streams

TABLE 24-1. State Table

State	Input	New State
q0	(m	q1
q0	e	qf
q1	d	q1
q1	)	q0
qf		Final State

can be generated by successively taking choices from the set of productions, starting with *S*. Alternatively, productions can be used to describe relationships between patterns being scanned off by a parser.

A grammar is called "right linear" if pattern symbols on the right-hand side may only occur *at the end* of a production. Here is a right linear grammar that is equivalent to the "regular expression" given earlier, using the notation of productions, but using lowercase letters to represent IP types, as in the State Table above. In this, we use Λ (meaning null stream) in place of e.

```
S -> Λ
S -> (mR
R -> )S
R -> dR
```

The two lines starting with *S* indicate two patterns that both constitute valid *S*'s, and similarly for the two lines starting with *R*.

Since lowercase letters in the productions represent objects that cannot be parsed further (i.e., IPs), uppercase letters may be thought of as representing expectations or hypotheses. Thus, *R* in the above productions represents "that part of a stream that can follow a master or detail." Thus, when a master is detected, the automaton's expectation of what may follow changes from what it was at the beginning of the stream, and, when a close bracket is detected, it changes back. This exactly mirrors the state changes of the finite automaton shown earlier.

While the right linear grammar shown earlier adequately represents the automaton traversing the stream one IP at a time, it cannot "see" patterns which consist of more than one IP and therefore cannot express one's intuitive feeling for the hierarchic structure of the IP stream. For this we must go to a more powerful class of grammar, called the "context-free grammars."

The set of context-free grammars (CFGs) is a superset of the set of right linear grammars, in that a pattern symbol is allowed to occur anywhere on the right-hand side of a production. Since CFGs are more general than right linear grammars, they require a more complex type of automaton to process them: the "pushdown automaton" (PDA), which has, in addition to its input tape, memory in the form of a "pushdown stack." This may be thought of as containing *subgoals* or *hypotheses* established during stream processing, to be verified or discarded.

The following set of productions of a context-free grammar is also equivalent to the regular expression given previously:

```
S -> Λ
S -> AS
A -> (mT
T -> )
T -> dT
```

where you will notice that pattern symbol *A* appears at the beginning of the right-hand side of the second production. The first two productions together can therefore be read as follows: a stream consists of zero or more *A* patterns (or substreams).

A pushdown automaton will have "stack states" in addition to "automaton states": in this example the automaton state is trivial, as there is really only a "normal" state (q0) and a "final" state (qf), to enable the automaton to stop.

In table 24-2, *Q* means "automaton state" and *S* is the "stack state" (— means empty, and *x* means that there is an *x* at the top of the stack). It will be noticed that "push" and "pop" change the "stack state" in the same pattern we saw in connection with the "automaton state" in the transition graph shown earlier. *Q'* and *S'* mean the new states of the automaton and the stack, respectively.

The actions denoted

```
push x
pop x
```

are to be read as "push IP x onto stack" and "pop IP x from stack," respectively. You will recognize that this use of the stack exactly parallels the use of a stack in FBP to hold IPs being worked on.

In FBP the use of the stack is restricted as follows: while an IP is in the stack, it is not available for use by the component's logic. It must therefore be "popped" off the stack to make it available for processing. At the end of processing, it must be explicitly disposed of before the automaton leaves that state, either by being returned to the stack or by being sent or dropped. This is the reason for the pop/push combination—when not using an FBP implementation, you could leave

TABLE 24-2. PDA State Table

Q	S	Input	Action	Q'	S'
q0	—	(m	push A	q0	A
q0	A	)	pop A	q0	—
q0	A	d	pop A/push A	q0	A
q0	—	e	—	qf	—
qf			Final State		

it out altogether, as it leaves the stack state unchanged, but in FBP it is required in order to make *A* available for processing.

It can be seen from the above that the only function of the state *Q* is to determine when the automaton has reached a final state—the rest of the time the automaton is in its normal state. The two states of the stack correspond one-to-one with the states q0 and q1 in the non-pushdown automaton, so that the stack has a dual function: that of storage for IPs being worked on and control. This exactly mirrors the way FBP uses a stack for holding control IPs. The process of stacking a subgoal that represents a substream corresponds to the FBP concept of stacking an IP to denote the entire substream.

Where do we go from here? There has been a lot of work done on describing applications using PDAs, but I am not aware of much work tying them together with data streams. (I would appreciate hearing about such work.) This seems to me a fruitful direction for more research and may yield new ways of looking at applications or even new hardware designs.

25

Streams and Recursive Function Definitions

It is easy to see that an FBP component can be regarded as a function transforming its input stream into its output stream. These functions can then be combined to make complex expressions, just as, say, addition, multiplication, and so on, can be combined in an algebraic expression. A number of languages have used this as a base for notations. Figure 25-1 shows a simple example.

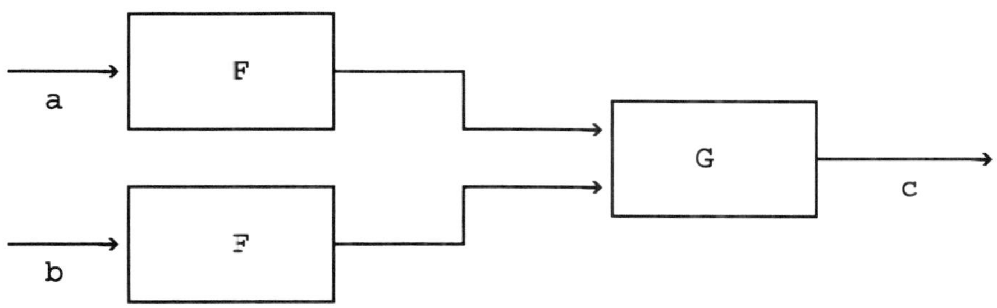

Figure 25-1.

If you label streams as shown with lowercase letters, then figure 25-1 can be represented succinctly as follows:

```
c = G(F(a),F(b))
```

I deliberately used F twice to underline the fact that the same function can be used many times in the same expression. Of course, this relies on the function *having no side effects*—this is one of the desirable characteristics of functional languages (and one of the qualities that are desirable when designing FBP components). I will return to this point later on.

Now you have seen that streams are made up of patterns of IPs, which in turn have fields or data items. Is it possible to carry functional notation to the point where you can actually build systems processing real data? I believe it is, but in a way that will not be as "mathematical" as most treatments of recursive programming. Also, the applicative language described in chapter 18 maps onto a functional notation without its using recursion at all. In the rest of this chapter, I will develop the concepts of recursive stream definitions. But first, for those of you whose math is a bit rusty, I will talk about what recursive definitions are exactly. The rest of you can skip ahead!

Recursive techniques are often taught using the formula for factorials as an example. A factorial is the product of all the integers greater than zero up to and including the number whose factorial you want to calculate. Factorials can be (and often are) calculated iteratively—that is:

```
factorial(x):
     a = 1
     do varying y from x to 1 by -1
          a = a * y
     enddo
     return a
```

Now, the classic expression for calculating factorials really does the same thing, but it does it *recursively,* as follows:

```
factorial(x):
     if x = 1
          return 1
     else
          return x * factorial (x - 1)
     endif
```

Here you can see that "factorial" is actually defined in terms of itself, but used on a "smaller" part of the problem. Since factorial is used on $x - 1$ and the first test is always to see if 1 has been reached, you are actually getting one step closer to your goal each time around the definition. If you want to visualize how this might execute, think of a stack holding the environment for each invocation of factorial. Each time you start a factorial calculation, you push the information you will need onto the stack, so the stack gets deeper and deeper. When you eventually get a true condition on the first test, you can calculate a factorial (1) without pushing a new environment onto the stack. Now you can finish all the factorial calculations (in reverse sequence), so that eventually you arrive back at the top of the stack and you're finished. Speakers of German will be familiar with a similar phenomenon that occurs in that language, where several "contexts" may be "stored" until the end of the sentence, at which time each context is terminated with the production of an infinitive or past participle.

The advantage of the recursive definition is that it has *no local storage variables.* We therefore suspect that this characteristic may have a bearing on some of the problems identified earlier in this book with the "pigeonhole" concept of storage. Recursive functions are also attractive to mathematicians because they have no side effects and therefore are easier to analyze and understand. In W.B. Ackerman's paper (1979), he states: "the language properties that a data flow computer requires are beneficial in their own right, and are very similar to some of the properties that are known to facilitate understandable and maintainable software . . . ." Some of these beneficial properties are as follows:

- Locality of effect
- Freedom from side effects
- "Call by value"

Ackerman defines an *applicative* language as one that does all of its processing by means of *operators* applied to *values.* The earliest known applicative language was LISP.

By now you should be familiar with the use of the term "stream" in FBP to describe the set of IPs passing across a particular connection. The stream does not all exist at the same time, but is continuously being generated at one end and consumed at the other. However, it has a "real" existence, and it can be manipulated in various ways. W.H. Burge (1975) showed how stream expressions can be developed using a recursive, applicative style of programming. D.P. Friedman and D.S. Wise contributed a number of papers relating applicative programming to streams by adding the concept of "lazy evaluation" (1976) to Burge's work. This style has the desired freedom from side effects and has another useful characteristic: the equals sign is *really* a definition statement and can be used for proving the validity of programs as well as for doing the actual data processing. Such a language is called "definitional."

Quoting W.B. Ackerman (1979) again: "Such languages are well suited to program verification because the assertions one makes in proving correctness are exactly the same as the definitions appearing in the program itself." One can put a restriction on assignment statements to the effect that the definition should not assign a value to a given symbol more than once in a single scope. Thus, a statement like

```
J:=J+1
```

is ruled out because J would have to be given an initial value within the scope, resulting in two assignments within that scope. Also, viewed as a definition, it is obviously a contradiction! A number of writers on programming have described their feelings of shock on their first encounter with this kind of statement, only to become so used to it over the years that they eventually don't notice anything strange about it!

I will now talk a little bit about the possibility of writing programs in a way that avoids the problem of rebinding variables within a scope, following Burge (1975) and Friedman and Wise (1976) in the area of stream functions.

Typically, like the definition of factorial shown earlier, the desired output is defined in terms of two functions:

- A function of the first item in the stream,
- A function relating this item to the rest of the stream,

and a termination rule specifying a value to be returned when the function bottoms out.

The following example resembles the definition of factorial shown previously, but moves closer to business applications. Even though it may not much resemble the type of business applications that you are accustomed to, you will have to admit that it is very compact! Suppose you want to count all the IPs in a stream. Then, analogously to the earlier factorial calculation, you could write a "counter" function F as follows:

```
F(S) = if   S is null,
       then  0,
       else  1 + F(rest(S))
```

where the result is specified directly by a value (e.g., `0`, or `1 + F(rest(S))`.

With respect to the rest of this notation, functions are expressed using the conventional bracket notation, and sublists will be specified by means of curly braces. For instance, {*w,x,y,z*} is a sublist consisting of *w, x, y,* and *z.null* tests for a stream with no IPs in it (i.e., { }); `first(S)` is the first IP of a stream (i.e., *w* in the above example) and `rest(S)` is a list comprising all the rest of the IPs in the stream (i.e., {*x,y,z*}) Notice that, while *rest* returns a list, *first* only returns a single IP. Each time you use *first,* it drops one pair of curly braces.

In this first example, *F* is called recursively to return a value based on processing a stream *S*. At each invocation of *F,* its environment (the part of the stream that it can see) is pushed down on a run-time stack. When an invocation of *F* finds itself looking at an empty stream, the null test returns true, *F* bottoms out, and the stacked environments are progressively popped up, until the original one is reached, at which point the process stops. Notice that there is a family resemblance between recursive definitions that only "recurse" at the right-hand end and right linear grammars. This kind of recursive definition can also have special processing applied to it that maintains the stack at a constant depth.

Now so far you haven't actually used the data in the stream IPs. Suppose, therefore, that you want to sum all the quantity fields in a stream of IPs. We will introduce the convention *a:x* to mean "field *a* of *x*." This notation and the "mini-constructor" notation described below are based on the Vienna Definition Language, developed some years ago by the IBM Laboratory in Vienna. The desired calculation can now be expressed recursively as follows:

```
F(S) = if    S is null,
       then  0,
       else  q:first(S) + F(rest(S))
```

where q is the quantity field of an IP.

So far, we have only generated a single quantity from processing the stream. To do anything more complicated, you will need to be able to generate IPs and string them into streams. To do the former, you need something that can build an IP given a set of values for its fields. We will use a special function for this, which I will call the "mini-constructor" (μ). This takes as its argument a list of selector symbols and values and returns as a result an IP with those values inserted into the fields designated by the selectors. A selector and its value are separated by commas, while selector/value pairs are separated by semi-colons. The mini-constructor is a concise way of specifying how new IPs are to be built.

To combine IPs into a stream, we use a variant of the well-known list-processing function *cons,* which was first used in functional languages to join two lists together. The following equivalence holds:

```
a = cons(first(a),rest(a))
```

Friedman and Wise (1976) have extended this concept by removing the requirement that both of the arguments of *cons* be available at the same instant of time. Their "lazy *cons*" function does not actually build a stream until both of its arguments are realized; before that it simply records a "promise" to do this. This allows us to imagine a stream being dynamically realized from the front, but with an unrealized back end. The end of the stream stays unrealized until the very end of the process, while the beginning is an ever-lengthening sequence of items.

Suppose you want to create a stream of extended details (where the quantity field has been extended by the unit price for the product): if the unit price were repeated in every IP, there would be no problem, as all the information that a particular call to the function requires is immediately available. Assigning selectors *p, s, d, q, u,* and *e* to product number, salesman number, district number, quantity, unit price, and extended price, respectively, you would then be able to define the extended details stream as follows:

```
F(S) = if S is null,
       then null
       else cons (E(first(S)), F(rest(S)))

E(x) = μ(p,p:x; s,s:x; d,d:x; u,u:x; e,q:x*u:x)
```

where E is a function that creates a single IP. The expression after the last semi-colon in the definition of E(x) would read in English: "set the extended price field of this IP to unit price multiplied by quantity." This would be fine except for the fact that unfortunately the unit price is *not* in the same IP as quantity.

In fact, in the case of the merged stream being processed by TR1, the unit price for a given product is held in only one IP per substream—namely the master IP for that product. We could define a function "PM" ("previous master"), but that would violate the rule that a function can only "see" an IP optionally followed by its successors. Instead, let's broaden the concept of *first* and *rest* to work with lists of lists (just as LISP and the other functional languages do).

This concept of lists of lists allows us in turn to take advantage of the fact that a stream can automatically be structured into substreams by a Collate type of component. Thus, suppose the output of a Collate run is as follows:

```
((m1,d11,d12),(m2,d21),(m3,d31,d32,d33))
```

where brackets represent bracket IPs. Then to convert this logically into a structure of lists and sublists, merely replace the open and close bracket IPs with curly braces—that is:

```
S:= {{m1,d11,d12},{m2,d21},{m3,d31,d32,d33}}
```

Now *first* and *rest* at the list level will return sublists—that is:

```
first(S):= {m1,d11,d12}
```

and

```
rest(S):= {{m2,d21},{m3,d31,d32,d33}}
```

Note that, analogously to what we saw with simple lists, *first* reduces the "nesting level" of a list by one level, while *rest* leaves it unchanged. The processing for extended details can now be shown succinctly, as follows:

```
F(S) = if S is null,
       then null
       else cons(G(first(S)), F(rest(S)))

G(x) = G'(first(x),rest(x))

G'(x,y) = if y is null,
          then null
          else cons (E(x,first(y)), G'(x,rest(y)))

E(x,y) = μ(p,p:y; s,s:y; d,d:y; e,q:y*u:x)
```

Here the one-argument function `G` is defined in terms of a two-argument function `G'`, whose first argument is always a master, and `E` now takes two arguments instead of only one.

In the above it can be seen that we will generate one output IP for each incoming detail (all IPs within a lowest level substream are details except the first one, which is the master). You can also see that `x` in `G'` acts as a placeholder for the master IP—it remains unchanged throughout the whole evaluation of function `G`.

I have alluded to the need to minimize the gap between the business requirement and the means of expressing it. What is the absolutely most concise way of expressing the requirement "build a stream of IPs containing extended quantities calculated as follows: . . ." to a machine? In a 1990 article, K. Kahn and V. Saraswat suggest that it may not even have to be text as we know it—they propose that it may be possible to express both definitions and execution using a visual notation with almost no text at all, except for strings and comments. They point out that a major use of names is to make connections, something they are not particularly well suited for! Perhaps someone will come up with a way to represent the previous example purely visually!

Part of my motivation in this chapter (and in this book as a whole) is to try to shake up some preconceptions about how programming has to be done! No one can predict where the next breakthrough will be made, so it is important to remain as open as possible to new ideas and new ways of doing things. The concepts presented in this chapter also suggest some desirable characteristics that these new ways should have, so we can measure whether we are moving in the right direction or away from it. As I shall suggest in the last chapter of this book, everyone should have their minds stretched regularly, and this kind of exercise is nowhere more important than in the computer business!

26

Relationship with Object-Oriented Approaches

Object-oriented programming (OOP) has captured the imagination of a sizable and influential segment of the computer world, and understandably so, since it promises solutions to many of the problems that confront our industry. Not only does it have proven successes in the area of user interfaces, but it offers the very inviting prospect of libraries of reusable programming components that can be bought and sold on the open market. On the other hand, its very success has resulted in its being broadened until the term OOP now covers a wide spectrum of different technologies with a few basic concepts in common. The literature on the subject is confusing to the uninitiated, and the more one reads about the subject, the more variations one encounters, all rallying behind the object-oriented banner. Given all the excitement, I have spent some time trying to understand what is being offered and what it can do for the world of application development. This chapter is the result of this work, and I hope that some readers will find it helpful. Naturally, one of the effects of the diversity of different views about what OOP is is that almost any comment I may make about it can be countered by someone who has a different view, but I base these observations mostly on the most widespread dialects of OOP, so I believe they have some validity. However, what follows is based on concepts presented earlier in this book, so I do not recommend the reader jumping right into this chapter without having read the earlier ones.

I believe that FBP shares many characteristics with OOP, but at this point in time I hesitate to call it object-oriented, as there are certain fundamental differences of approach. However, after reading this chapter, some readers may conclude that any differences are basically surface ones and that FBP is an object-oriented technology. Interestingly, Rob Strom, who developed NIL (Strom and Yemini 1983), described in the next chapter, which has strong similarities with FBP, tells me that initially his group thought it important to disassociate themselves from OOP, but they now feel that there are many similarities between NIL and OOP, and are now actively working with the OO community.

OOP is also another perfect example of the gap between business and academia that I talked about earlier. A lot of the interesting research work on OOP is hard to apply to business needs, while business badly needs technologies that can ease the burden of developing and maintaining application code. When academics start using payroll applications for their examples, rather than rotating squares and rectangles, we will know that we have turned a corner!

It is generally accepted that the first OOP system was Smalltalk, from Xerox PARC, although some writers identify SIMULA as the first OO language. It seems that many people today still consider Smalltalk the archetypal OOP language, although it is many ways a "small" implementation of the concepts, by which I mean that it is great for exploring a number of the OOP concepts, but it is not clear that its concepts scale up to large-scale business applications. I have used Digitalk's Smalltalk V/PM, so most of my examples will be drawn from that system. C++ is a different, and in some ways more pragmatic, approach to implementing object-oriented concepts, which is gaining increased acceptance, but, since it is a hybrid between OO concepts and a conventional HLL, its users have to contend with a more complex mental model. A different approach to hybridizing a HLL with OO concepts is Brad Cox's Objective-C (1987), which is not as well known as the other two, but also has a number of interesting concepts. All of these languages are basically control-flow oriented and therefore suffer from the problems described in previous chapters. A number of workers in the OO field are starting to recognize this, and I will be describing some of their work later in the chapter.

Before I talk about differences and similarities between FBP and OOP, I need to talk about a few of the basic concepts of OOP for those not familiar with its concepts. The basis of Smalltalk and all OOP systems is the "object," which can be described as a semi-autonomous unit comprising both information and behavior. OOP objects are usually selected to reflect objects in the real world, and this relationship is a major source of the appeal of OOP to application developers (as I mentioned earlier, it is also a characteristic of simulation languages and of IPs in FBP). Of course, since real-world objects vary widely in size and complexity, it becomes far from trivial to decide what the objects in your universe of discourse are going to be. Just as it is in conventional programming, it is extremely important to do a good job of modeling your data before you start an OO design. The approach of object-oriented analysis is somewhat different from that of conventional data modeling, but many workers in the field claim that proper modeling is even more important with OO as an error at this stage can adversely affect your whole design. This is also true of course for FBP.

One very powerful but nonobvious similarity between FBP and Smalltalk is that they both use "handles" to refer to objects (except in the case of Smalltalk integers). When you request a new instance of a class in Smalltalk, you get a set of instance variables "out there" and a handle to let you refer to it, just as you have seen happens when you create a new IP in FBP. You can then do things with this object handle (e.g., send messages to it or use it as a parameter in a message to another object). Smalltalk also looks after "garbage collection" of the object if its handle is no longer in use—this function could easily be added to FBP, but as I said earlier we're not sure whether it's desirable.

These object handles are the mechanism that allows objects to talk to each other. Once you have selected classes of objects that will represent the real-world objects of interest to your application, the next requirement is that these objects be able to communicate—in short, that their behavior be cooperative. For this function, Smalltalk uses the expressive metaphor of "message sending": Smalltalk objects are said to send messages to each other, resulting in activity on the part of the receiver, which may in turn send messages on to other objects. This also is a good fit with how we think of the real world. Unfortunately, this Smalltalk terminology is misleading if it suggests any kind of asynchronous message flow, as Smalltalk's "message sending" is purely synchronous: the sender has to wait until the receiver comes back with a reply. In today's terminology of parallel processes, the sender is "blocked" until the reply is received. This mechanism is essentially equivalent to a subroutine call, which is in fact how it is implemented (with a subtle difference that we will discuss in the next paragraph). Smalltalk does support asynchronism by means of its fork and semaphore facilities, but the basic paradigm is synchronous, and, as we have seen, this restricts the developer in certain fundamental ways. In C++ (and also sometimes in Smalltalk) this is referred to as "method invocation," which is a more accurate description of what is really going on.

Method invocation is essentially an indirect subroutine call. The caller specifies an operation, and it is the class to which the receiver belongs that determines the actual piece of code that is executed. In both Smalltalk and C++, each such piece of code (called a "method") is part of a class, and its address is not directly known to its caller. The caller specifies the function desired by naming an object (or the class itself) and the desired function (e.g., it might tell an object of class "rectangle" "rotate 90 degrees"). The underlying software then uses the class information of the object to locate the actual code to be executed.

Although this seems very straightforward in the classical OO examples, in practice I found myself really frustrated as a user, because it is inherently asymmetrical. Many of these requests involve more than one object, so you have to pick one as a receiver and pass the others (or their handles) as parameters. This means that I, the user, was never quite sure which object should be the receiver, and sometimes a series of similar functions would flip back and forth bewilderingly. For example, when displaying a series of data objects, I had to use several different messages, some of which were sent to the medium object with the data object as parameter and some of which were the other way around. Similarly, Smalltalk has problems with such simple commutative operations as + and *. Smalltalk V/PM has actually implemented a facility where, if an operation fails, the system reverses it and tries again. This function is only available to primitive operations and is not even used there consistently. Although some OO dialects, like CLOS, select the method based on the classes of more than one participating object, I would expect that allowing method selection to be based on the classes of all the parameters, although symmetrical, would result in even larger numbers of methods, and therefore in significant management problems.

The indirect call characteristic of OOP systems does provide a degree of configurability, since it is true that the caller does not have to know the name of the subroutine that will actually be executed. In addition, since different classes can support the same function identifier (sometimes called the "selector") in different ways, you get an additional useful characteristic sometimes called "genericity," which some writers consider the basic characteristic of OOP systems (many others don't, though). However, the requester of a function does have to be able to locate the object that it wants to send the message to and also has to specify the name of the desired function (e.g., "print" or "rotate"), so there is still a configurability problem, once removed, unless the process of identifying the recipient object can be completely externalized from the requester's code. Remember, to achieve full configurability, you need to be able to hook together components into different patterns *without modifying them in any way,* which also means having an independent specification of how things are connected. This can only be done today in OOP by having "high-level" methods that specify how things are hooked together. I find it interesting that, in most of the literature, the orientation of Smalltalk is very much towards building new classes rather than towards reuse. Applications are developed mainly by cloning old methods, with its attendant problems, rather than by using black box code. The very idea of allowing a developer to modify the behavior of an existing class, even if only for his or her own purposes, runs counter to the reuse concepts described in this book.

Two last comments about genericity: my (limited) experience is that application developers don't use it very much, and its main triumphs seem to be in the GUI area. When asked to give examples of genericity, writers on OO always seem to pick "display" and "destroy." It may be that, in business, you don't often use the same messages for different classes. For instance, at the numeric value level, subtracting a number of days from a date is quite different from subtracting a date from another date, or a date from days (you can't), so the user has to be very aware of the types of the operands. To me this means that it doesn't buy you much to be able to call them all "-". In fact, in Smalltalk you often see message names like "subtractDaysFromDate," to tell the user what types the message expects (there is no type checking at compile time, so this is particularly important). Now, if you don't make much use of genericity, all you have left is the indirect call mechanism, which should be part of any programmer's toolkit anyway!

The following three attributes seem to be present in all OOP systems to a greater or lesser extent, but they are given different weights by different writers: genericity, encapsulation, and inheritance. We have already talked about genericity in OOP. Genericity is also implicit in FBP as the same IP can be sent to different processes to achieve different results (and usually is), or components can be designed to accept a narrower or wider range of possible input formats as determined by reuse considerations. For instance, a Collate could accept only two input streams or n input streams. It could accept either just one input IP format or many, determined by descriptors as described earlier or by some other mechanism.

Inheritance is claimed by some to be the major characteristic of OOP, and it is certainly an important concept, but my personal view and that of other people I have talked to is that its use should not be pushed to extremes. As long as inheritance is used to reflect the fact that things in real life can usually be grouped into classes that are subsets and supersets of other classes, it works quite well and would in fact fit in quite well with the IP type concept that is implemented by descriptors in FBP. For instance, a file might contain records representing vehicles, which you would then "specialize" into Volkswagens, Pontiacs, and so on, based on a code within the common part of the records. Some processing would then be valid for all vehicles, other processing just for Pontiacs. If a message cannot be answered by a Pontiac, it is passed up to the "vehicle" level. Generally, as you move down the class hierarchy, you add more attributes—so you start off with the set of attributes common to all vehicles. When you discover that a file record represents a Pontiac, you now know how to read the remaining attributes. This concept could in fact be added quite naturally to the descriptor mechanism of FBP.

The major difficulty with classification, however, is that, as soon as you try to become more analytical about what a class really is, things start to get more confusing. What seems clean and intuitive when applied to oak and fir trees becomes less clear when you look at it more closely. In fact, the OO concept of "class" seems to involve several different concepts that are combined in different combinations in different OO implementations. For those interested in this topic, there is an interesting recent article by W. Lalonde and J. Pugh (1991) that attempts to separate out the different ideas underlying the idea of "class." To give you some flavor of this debate, consider the difference between a square and a rectangle from an OO point of view. There was a recent and interesting exchange of letters on this topic in *Communications of the ACM,* triggered by a letter from J. Winkler in the August 1992 issue: in a hierarchy of geometrical shapes, a square is usually defined as a rectangle with all four sides equal. From one point of view, it is therefore a subclass of rectangle. However, subclasses usually have more instance variables (attributes) than their superclasses, while a square can be completely specified using only one measurement instead of two. As if that weren't bad enough, OO rectangles can accept messages asking them to change individual dimensions (e.g., "set height to:"). If you change a rectangle's height to be the same as its width, does it change to being a square, or must you create a new intermediate class—that of "square rectangles"? The point is that this is an example of specialization by the addition of constraints. There needs to be some general mechanism to specify constraints on objects, and you also have to decide whether to *use* the constraint (e.g., by allowing one dimension to change the other) or just use it to detect errors on the part of the client (e.g., "violates constraint—please check dimensions"). The heading on Winkler's letter is "Objectivism: 'Class' Considered Harmful" (Winkler 1992)!

While human beings naturally try to classify the world to make it easier to grasp, the real world may resist being so classified. Not being a zoologist I had imagined that all mammals had been neatly categorized long ago, so I was amused recently to run into this description of the difficulty zoologists encounter in trying to classify the hyrax (Krishtalka 1989): "They resemble a cross between a rhinoceros and a rodent. . . . the hind limbs have three toes (rhinos), one of which ends in a long claw (rodents), the other two in hooflike nails (rhinos). . . ." The list goes on for a bit, then Krishtalka writes: "Such a smorgasbord of physical traits earned a dyspeptic taxonomy. . . . Recent opinion is divided between a horse-rhino-hyrax evolutionary connection and a sea cow-elephant-hyrax linkage." While this kind of confusion can actually be amusing, our tendency to make snap classifications and then act as if they were the whole truth may actually be harmful, either to ourselves or to others. While everyone today with a reasonable education knows that whales are mammals, not fish, the old mental association may be what allows officials to refer to "harvesting" whales; presumably based on the idea of "harvesting" herring. If you are interested in this area of linguistics, you should take a look at the work of the linguist B.L. Whorf (1956), alluded to elsewhere in this book, on how the words we use affect our actions.

As you move into the world of business programming, you run into situations where class hierarchies may seem very natural at first sight, but in fact are really not appropriate. For instance, it might seem natural to assign a bank account object to one of a set of account type classes: SAVING, CHECKING, or COMMERCIAL. This way, a deposit could be sent to an account and automatically cause the right piece of code to be invoked as a method. While this seems quite attractive at first, at best it would result in a number of very similar methods that would have to be separately managed and maintained. At worst, it could make it very difficult to develop new, hybrid offerings, such as a checking account that offers daily interest. Banks have found that it is better to make this kind of processing "feature-oriented"—one should decide what are the atomic features of an account (e.g., interest-bearing or not, bankbook vs. statement, checks to be returned or not) and then implement them under switch control to produce the various types of account processing. Hendler gives a somewhat similar example (1986), using professions. He points out that, while professions are often used as examples of classes, they may not be mutually exclusive—a person might be both a professor and a doctor—so a person may carry attributes that relate to both of these professions. Mixed classes provide a possible solution, but this technique has problems as well. In FBP, the "tree" technique seems a natural way to implement this kind of thing (see chapter 12, "Tree Structures"), as the data associated with each profession can be held in separate IPs attached to the IP for the person, or the data for a given feature can be hung off the account root.

In spite of what I said previously, I do believe that one of the most important contributions OO has made towards changing the way application design is done is that it has moved data to the foreground. Programmers coming to FBP from conventional programming have to undergo precisely the same paradigm shift: from concentrating on process to concentrating on data. Typically, in FBP, as you have seen in the foregoing chapters, you should design the IPs and IP streams first and then decide what processes are needed to convert between the different data streams. In OO, you have to decide on the object classes and then decide what messages each class should be able to respond to.

For many OO enthusiasts it is the concept of "encapsulation" that is the central concept of OO. In fact, this is not a new concept at all (one of Dijkstra's famous remarks was that programs should be "like pearls"), and Parnas wrote one of the seminal articles on encapsulation in the early 1970s (Parnas 1972). Encapsulation simply means the idea of having the vulnerable insides of something protected by a protective outer coating, sort of like a soft-centered candy (or a turtle). This is obviously a good design principle, and the reader will notice that FBP components in fact have this characteristic, as they are free to decide what IPs they will accept into themselves and can perform more or less validation of their input data, depending on how reliable their designers judge their data to be. Encapsulation can also be implemented at the network level, by having outer processes protect inner ones or by inserting transformer processes into the network. This is a better solution than building the validation into every component, as the processing component can just provide the basic function and the designer can request more or less validation by adding or removing editing processes. In OO, an object is encapsulated together with all of its methods, which involves predicting all the services that an object may ever be requested to perform. This, however, is very hard to do and may result in a never-ending stream of requests for enhancements as new requirements come up. How can one predict all the functions that, say, steel might be used for? Remember Wayne Stevens' story about an airline attendant using a hearing set to tie back a curtain!

In FBP, we *always* encapsulate processes and can also encapsulate IPs if desired. The former occurs automatically as nobody has access to the internals of a component except the supplier: users can only know its inputs, outputs, parametrization, and *some* behavioral aspects, such as what it does when it sees a closed output port. As far as protecting IPs is concerned, a number of techniques are available, as required by the designer, and it is quite possible to have IPs whose structure is never seen by application code. However, FBP does not insist that you predict all the processes that will ever handle a particular IP type. Rather, the emphasis is on deciding which IP types a given process will accept or generate. Instead of having to predict all the uses that steel might be put to, you only have to decide which materials you can build a bridge out of. The latter seems a much more manageable problem!

Because Smalltalk's "message sending" terminology sounds like data flow, it is often thought that OO should be relevant to distributed systems design, but, in fact, as Gelernter and Carriero point out in an article analyzing the differences between their Linda (described in the next chapter) and OO (Carriero and Gelernter 1989), it is actually irrelevant to it. In fact, as they say, a truly distributed message passing system has to be built on top of an OO system, just as it does on top of a conventional subroutine-based approach. Here is a quote from a paper by another of the gurus of this area, Barbara Liskov, and her coworkers: "We conclude that the combination of synchronous communication with static process structure imposes complex and indirect solutions, and therefore that it is poorly suited for applications such as distributed programs in which concurrency is important" (Liskov et al. 1986). It is interesting that "basic" FBP occupies the "asynchronous, static" quadrant of figure 2-1 of this article, while the addition of dynamic subnets moves FBP into the "asynchronous, dynamic" quadrant, which the authors of this article say is unoccupied to the best of their knowledge. Interestingly, they go on to say, "Although such languages may exist, this combination appears to provide an embarassment of riches not needed for expressive power." Our experience, on the contrary, is that adding a dynamic capability to asynchronous communication can be extremely productive!

Most OO implementations are synchronous, so the basic primitive is the indirect call through the class. As I said elsewhere in this book, our experience with FBP tells us that the subroutine call is *not* the best foundation on which to build business applications. A "call" can in fact be simulated very nicely by issuing an FBP "send" followed by a "receive." This will have the effect of suspending the requester on the "receive" until the downstream process returns an answer, just as a "call" suspends the caller. Gelernter and Carriero make the same point and go still further in the above-mentioned article:

> In our experience, processes in a parallel program usually don't care what happens to their data, and when they don't, it is more efficient and *conceptually more apt* to use an asynchronous operation like Linda's "out" than a synchronous procedure call. . . . It's trivial, in Linda, [or FBP] to implement a synchronous remote-procedure-call-like operation in terms of "out" and "in" [FBP "send" and "receive"]. There is no reason we know of, however, to base an entire parallel language on this one easily programmed but not crucially important special case. [Italics added.]

A call that spans multiple machines is sometimes called Remote Procedure Call (RPC), and a number of the people working on distributed systems have pointed out the inappropriateness (as well as poor performance) of this algorithm when building complex distributed systems. K. Kahn and M. Miller (1988) point out the problems of basing a design for distributed systems on RPC. They also stress the desirability of having a single paradigm that scales up from tightly coordinated processes within a single processor to largely independent cooperating processes, perhaps on different machines.

FBP and Linda (I will talk about Linda in more detail in the next chapter) are fundamentally asynchronous, whereas Smalltalk-style OO is synchronous. The real difference here is that, although the methods of an object are the only routines that can have access to the object's internal data, *when* these methods are to be executed is determined by other objects, whose methods in turn are driven by other objects, and so on. While such synchronous objects show autonomy of data and behavior, they do not have autonomy of control. As such, I feel that synchronous OO objects are more similar to FBP IPs than they are to FBP processes. In a Smalltalk (not counting "fork") or C++ application, there is actually only one process. This can lead to counter-intuitive solutions. For example, in a recent book about C++ (Swan 1991), in an example involving a simulation of people using elevators, the class Building (which is really running the whole simulation) apparently has to be treated as a subclass of the class Action. The problem, of course, is that there is only one process, external to all the objects, which is basically "Run the simulation."

If you cast your mind back to the "telegram problem" described in chapter 8, you will remember that the conventional programming solution required several of the routines to be invoked repeatedly using handles to maintain continuity. This solution maps very nicely onto an OO "collaboration diagram," which changes subroutine calls into "message sends" and "replies" between objects (remember the caveat about what "message sending" actually means). Figure 26-1 is basically figure 8-8, recast into OO terms (I have created four "stream" objects: two word streams and two I/O streams).

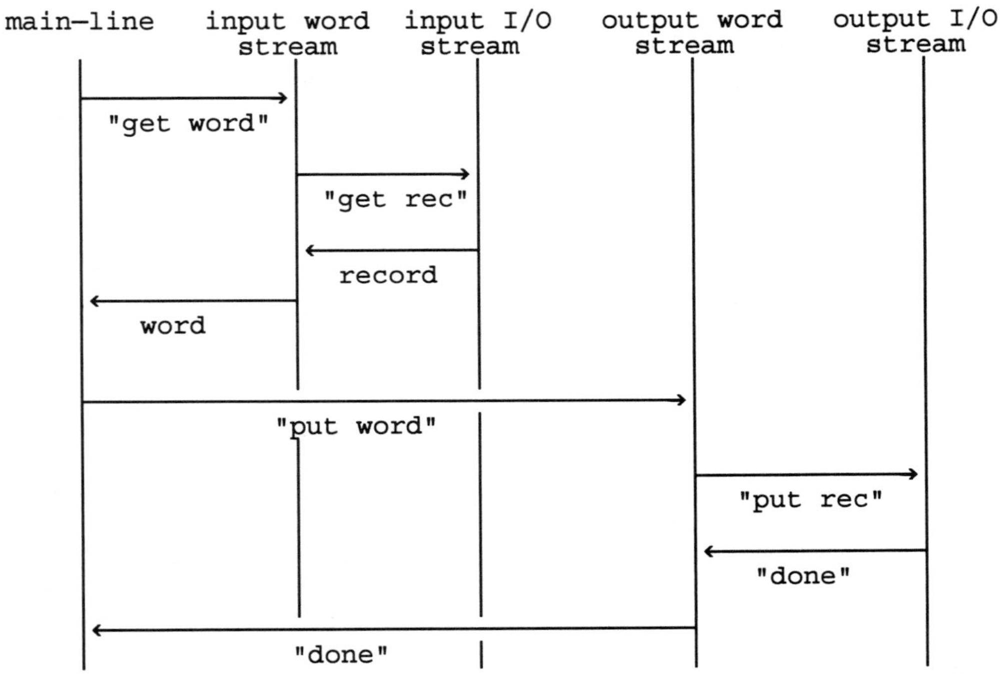

Figure 26-1.

While this solves the problem of subroutines that have to maintain continuity between successive invocations (the infrastructure maintains the continuity), this is still a purely synchronous solution. Figure 26-2 shows an FBP solution to this problem (from figure 8-2).

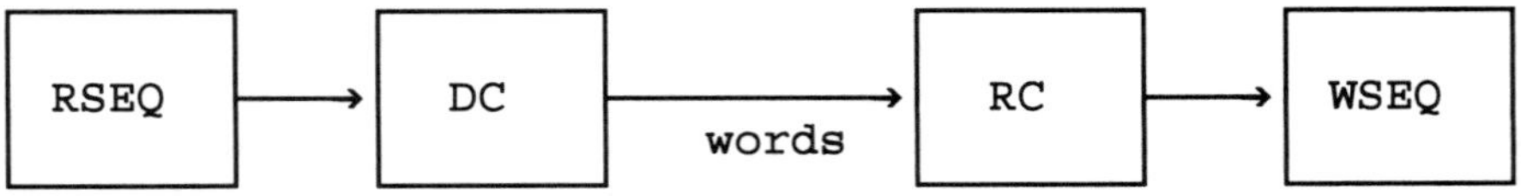

Figure 26-2.

Not only is this much easier to grasp intuitively, but it also uses reusable components, plus it is very obvious how the function can be extended if the designer ever needs to.

I have tried to show in the earlier chapters that asynchronism is liberating, and I hope I have managed to convey some feeling for its power. In fact, many of the leading thinkers in OO also realize the need to add asynchronism to OO to relax the tight constraints imposed by the von Neumann machine. In fact, many of today's advanced machine designs require these asynchronous design concepts (for a survey, see a recent [1990] article by Gul Agha). Agha uses the term "Concurrent OOP" (COOP) to describe his approach, which combines the concept of "actors" with OO. Another term you may run into is "active objects," which act, as opposed to "passive objects," which are acted on. In modern user interfaces there already are functions that behave much like active objects, such as printers (for printing objects), shredders (for destroying objects), and so on. You just drag and drop the icon (small graphical symbol) of an object (e.g., a file) onto a shredder icon—this is like pressing the start button on a trash compactor. Before it starts, however, the shredder politely asks you if you really want to do this. This is another characteristic of this kind of object: they can independently gather information for themselves. Once the shredder or printer has started, the user is then free to attend to other things.

Another researcher who feels that basic OO has to be broadened by the addition of asynchronism is de Champeaux at Hewlett-Packard. He is looking at the use of a trigger-based model for inter-object communication. Here is a quote from an article about OO research directions in the *Communications of the ACM:* "This model [where the sender is suspended until the receiver sends the result back] is not rich enough to describe all the causal connections between objects an analyst needs to model." (Wirfs-Brock and Johnson 1990) Interestingly, de Champeaux's work suggests that a richer interaction model than (data-less) triggers is necessary. One of the forms he is looking at is "send-no-wait" (where data and the trigger are simultaneously transmitted). One of the chapters in a recent book (Kim and Lochovsky 1989) is called "Concurrent Object-Oriented Programming Languages," written by C. Tomlinson and M. Scheevel, and provides an excellent survey of this new thinking about ways to combine OO with concurrency. Again, Brad Cox, who is the inventor of Objective-C and one of the acknowledged gurus of OO, has come to feel that OO alone is not adequate for building large systems. He came to the conclusion that FBP concepts should be implemented on top of Objective-C and then could be used as building blocks for applications. Using a hardware analogy, he refers to Objective-C as "gate-level" and FBP as "chip-level." He had in fact already started experimenting with processes and data flows independently when he found out about our work and contacted me. He has advanced the idea that the time is ripe for a "Software Industrial Revolution," much like the previous Industrial Revolution, which has so totally transformed the world we live in over the past couple of centuries. Like Brad, I believe that many of the tools for this revolution are already in place, but many writers have remarked on the enormous inertia of the software industry. This has always struck me as ironic, given the incredible rate of change in the rest of the computer industry.

Here I will try to show with an example some other differences between synchronous OO and FBP. It is quite hard to find an example that lets one compare the two technologies fairly, as the synchronous orientation of most OO work means that their examples tend to be synchronous as well. However, given that batch programs are not going to go away (in fact, there are good theoretical reasons why they never will), I will use as an example Brad Cox's example of calculating the total weight of a collection of objects in a container, say, pens and pencils in a pencil holder. While being totally procedural, it is an example of the "small batch" logic that is also handled very well by FBP.

The basic design mechanism in this kind of procedure is the collaboration diagram, of which I gave an example earlier. To diagram this example, we need to show three objects: a requester, a container, and an object within it. The interaction is shown in figure 26-3. I can still remember my feeling of dismay at seeing the right-to-left, returning flows in the diagram—these mark this diagram as being call logic, rather than flow logic. Every pair of lines represents a client-server relationship. OO people call this "delegation," but it is not delegation as humans practice it. Rather, it is like standing over someone and saying, "Now type this line; now type this line." In fact, client-server relationships make much more sense when the relationship is asynchronous, allowing the client to go about his or her business while the server is doing its thing. Human beings don't see any point in delegating work to others unless it frees them up to do something else. This kind of interaction is also not "cooperative" as FBP understands the word. In FBP all the processes are at the same level—there is no boss. In figure 26-3, while there may well be situations where either object can drive the other, one of the objects still has to be the driver (as long as one stays with passive objects only). There is very definitely a boss, and it is the object at the far left.

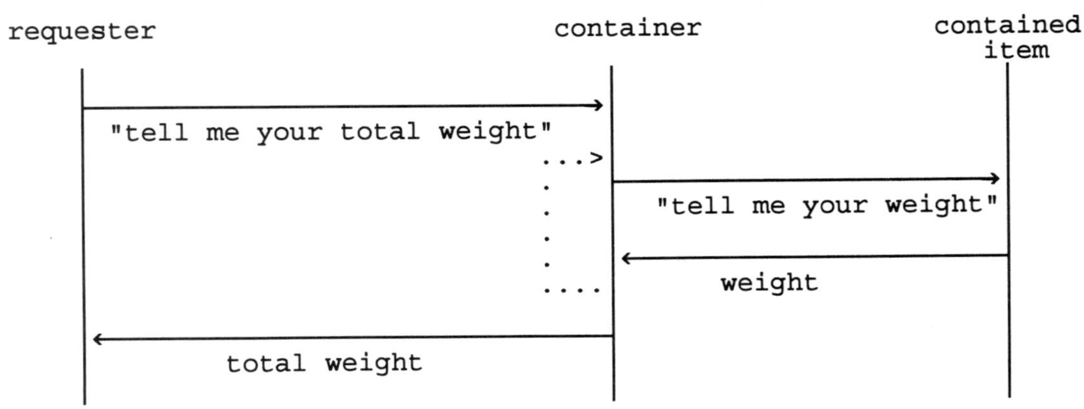

Figure 26-3.

The logic for the "compute total weight" method of the Container object is a loop that steps through its contained items. It could be described by the following pseudocode:

```
set total weight to tare weight of self
get first item 'a' in (attached to) self
do as long as get is successful
   send message to 'a' to get its weight
   add result to total weight
   get next item 'a' in (attached to) self
enddo
return total weight
```

(where "self" refers to the object whose method this is, and "tare weight" means empty weight).

This method needs functions to "get first" item and "get next" item within the container. These functions would return an item's handle, plus an indication of whether the request was successful. Once an object has been located, the container can send messages to it.

Although the same general logic can step through a variety of different collection structures (you basically need different method subroutines for each collection type), there is a basic assumption in the above logic, namely that all the items in the collection are available at the same time. As we have seen in previous chapters, this is not really necessary (since only one item is handled at a time) and may not even be possible. In addition, our experience with FBP tells us that this function should really be designed as a reusable component that is usable as is, in object code form, without needing any modification or recompiling. Most programming systems tend to present their ideas from the standpoint of someone writing new code, whereas FBP experience tells us that people don't want to write new code if they can get something off the shelf that does the desired job. Key to this (and also to being able to distribute such systems, now or later) is the requirement to avoid calls. As I pointed out earlier, the subroutine call mechanism forces tight coupling, whereas the data being generated by a procedure should go onwards, not back. The only way I know of to achieve all these goals is to design the function as a stand-alone function that uses ports to communicate with its neighbors. This results in a component with the shape seen in figure 26-4 (you will recognize this as a "reference" type of component).

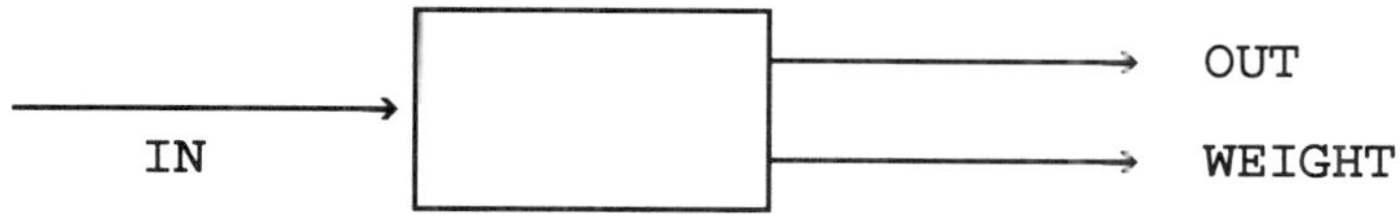

Figure 26-4.

This component accepts a stream or multiple substreams of IPs and generates one IP containing the total weight (or one per substream). Since the container has weight (its tare weight), let's provide it as the first IP of the (sub)stream. This diagram is really a fragment of an enhanced collaboration diagram connecting multiple processes with one-way flows instead of a single process talking to itself with two-way flows!

The logic of the above process can be represented by the following pseudocode (which should be familiar from earlier chapters):

```
create IP to contain total weight
receive from port IN using handle 'a'
set total weight to (tare) weight of 'a'
send a to port OUT if connected,
     else drop a

receive from port IN using handle 'a'
do as long as receive is successful
   add a's weight to total weight
   send a to port OUT if connected,
     else drop a
   receive from port IN using handle 'a'
enddo
send weight IP to WEIGHT port
```

Not surprisingly, it has the same general structure as the method pseudocode shown earlier, but there are certain key differences. The FBP component logic shown here can process any data stream for which "a's weight" is defined for each IP in the stream. Incoming IPs are passed on to OUT (if it is connected), and the weight goes in an IP of its own to the port called WEIGHT. Remember Gelernter and Carriero's remark that "processes in a parallel program usually don't care what happens to their data." Since "receive" and "send" can be suspended until data or queue slots, respectively, are available, this routine works even though not all IPs are in storage at the same time. You now have a portable component that can compute the total weight of any stream of IPs for which "weight" is defined.

In addition, in OO, this function has to be a method contained in any collection class for which you might need to perform this function (or their superclass), whereas in FBP, once this function has been built, you can use it (just by referencing it in a network) on any data stream that conforms to certain conventions, without having to modify the definitions of any of the classes involved. As I said earlier, "*a*'s weight" has to be defined for each IP in the stream. However, you can even parametrize the attribute name, so you can use the same object code to get a "total x" from all data streams for which x is defined. Instead of having a myriad of small, special-purpose methods for different classes in the system, you arrive at robust, flexible functions that are highly portable. In fact, you could even generalize this function still more: you could parametrize the function shown as "add" in this logic to get, say, the maximum or minimum weight of all the contained items.

As I talked to people about OO, however, I came to realize that there is one area that OO (Smalltalk anyway) does address that is absolutely unique to it and in fact takes care of a problem that has been worrying me for several years and that I alluded to in chapter 11: the need to be able to prevent illegal operations on data fields (e.g., to stop currency values from being multiplied together or dates from being added). However, this ability can only be taken advantage of if one does everything in OO, rather than combining it with existing HLL facilities. As said before, the vast majority of HLLs are based on mathematical ideas of data and treat numeric fields as being dimensionless. Thus, they cannot provide intelligent handling of most of the numeric values one runs into in business applications—these are either dimensioned numeric quantities (like money or weight) or aren't even in the domain of integers or real numbers (e.g., dates). In HLLs, all of these types of data are typically compressed into a single numeric data type. In Smalltalk, all accesses to data values are via methods, so you are not forced to throw away your knowledge about what fields *really* represent. A "multiply" operation can be resolved to one or more methods that know how (or whether) to do the appropriate operation on the fields involved. Hybrid approaches lack this power, and any attempt to combine OO with conventional HLLs in the same process vitiates this checking ability. Some of the newer HLLs provide similar forms of checking (e.g., Ada), so a possible solution is to restrict the "business logic" parts of an application to using an OO language or one of these newer compilers. Ironically, it will be very hard for most business applications to take advantage of this useful capability.

If some of the foregoing seems unduly negative, it is mainly that I feel it is important to put OO into a proper perspective. OO is a simple technique, whose main value is that it has started a sea-change in the way programmers think. It is definitely a step on the way, but my 20 years of experience with FBP tell me that, if we stop at this point, eventually frustration on the part of programmers is going to win out over the initial excitement. While I recognize that learning and using OO is an important learning experience, it is a hard way to learn and, in its present form, an expensive way as well, since without configurable modularity the result will only be marginally more maintainable code. Configurable modularity *can* be added to OO, as can multithreading, just as they can be to conventional programming, and it is exactly the combination of these that starts to open up interesting possibilities.

In an FBP environment, it is possible and, I believe, highly desirable to mix processes running different languages, some OO and some non-OO. For instance, one process might be running a pure OO language, another one COBOL, another Assembler, and so on. Such a mixture would require that IP layouts become a public interface between processes. We now have a natural role for IP descriptors: to allow us to retain the IP attributes' domain information, which could be exploited by OO, across processes that do not use this information (e.g., ones written in existing HLLs). OO processes could in fact be protected by interface processes that turn IPs into some format acceptable to the OO language chosen. We could even hang methods off FBP descriptors, providing some very interesting capabilities.

Wayne Stevens suggested a few years ago that objects might split very naturally into "process-like" and "data-like" objects, where, essentially, process-like objects would correspond to FBP processes and data-like objects to IPs. In the phrasing I used earlier, data-like objects are passive, while process-like objects are active.

Process-like (active) objects are able to act without necessarily always having to be triggered by an event external to them. In traditional OO systems, all objects are passive, and the whole assemblage is triggered by one (non-object) trigger that starts the whole thing running. This approach is obviously going to suffer from the same difficulties as traditional hierarchic non-FBP programs. If, instead, some of the set of objects can be active, we can start to capitalize on our experience with FBP. You will also notice that FBP processes have their own internal working storage, which looks very much like an OO object's "instance variables." Having process (active) objects and data (passive) objects looks like a very good way to combine the strengths of these two complementary technologies. In fact, with the appropriate infrastructure, different objects can be coded in different languages. Since, as I have shown, one of the basic reuse mechanisms in FBP is the external definition of connections, you could also add a "driver" or "network" object. This would be an active object using the network definition as reference data.

My belief in the potential for combining the strengths of these two approaches is bolstered by the fact that, in FBP, we actually built processes that behaved much like objects and also by the observation that traditional OO applications often have objects that should really be separate processes. An example of the former is the List Manager, described in chapter 21. This component managed multiple lists arranged in levels. An example of the converse is a Database Manager object, which accepts requests to get, insert or delete data. As shown in earlier chapters, this is better implemented as an asynchronous process, rather than being driven synchronously by other objects. The List Manager suffered from the problem that it was very sensitive to the exact sequence of requests, which made it hard to use in a highly asynchronous environment. It would have been better implemented by externalizing the lists as FBP trees, so that one or more processes could work on these trees asynchronously. In other words, objects with overly complex internal data will be hard to use when you start to have more processes running in parallel. I expect this will apply even more noticeably as you start to distribute logic across multiple processors.

A number of writers in the OO field have started to explore the possibilities of active objects. In chapter 1 of a collection of essays compiled by Kim and Lochovsky (1989), O. Nierstrasz makes the point that systems that mix active and passive objects would not be uniform, and this seems a valid point. However, one possible solution is offered by a system called Emerald (Black et al. 1986), which was designed for implementing highly distributed systems and which maintains uniformity across all its objects by allowing every object to have a single process in addition to methods. Not all objects may activate their processes, but the potential exists for them to do so. This suggests a very workable generic structure for all the objects in a combined FBP/OO hybrid.

OO research and development seems to have entered a stage of accelerated growth, and it is very exciting to me that some of the newer work bears an uncanny resemblance to FBP. A dichotomy seems to be developing between the synchronous and asynchronous OO approaches, just like the one we have seen in non-OO. A number of OO researchers believe it is the asynchronous approaches that will turn out to have the most to contribute to the programming art in the long run. More people are discovering the power of active processes to broaden OO and make it better match the real world. Tsichritzis et al. (1987) have used the concept of active objects in knowledge processing—they call their objects KNOs (KNowledge Objects). KNOs can also have a complex structure, analogously to FBP composite components.

More recently, Nierstrasz, Gibbs, and Tsichritzis have collaborated on another paper, "Component-Oriented Software Development" (1992), that approaches FBP even more closely, but is still based solidly on traditional OO concepts. While their terminology is different from that of FBP, many close correspondences between the two can be established. They use the term *script* to mean "a set of software components with compatible input and output ports connected." While scripts can be data flow or object-oriented, the data flow version corresponds closely with FBP networks. *Scripting* means the construction of scripts, so the term *visual scripting* is defined as "the interactive construction of applications from prepackaged, plug-compatible software components by direct manipulation and graphical editing." In their article they talk about reusable components, ports, SACs (scripts as components) and visual scripting—all ideas that have direct counterparts in FBP. The same article goes on to describe an application of these concepts to multimedia called the "visual museum." "Media objects" (which are active objects, i.e. processes) work on "media values," which are ". . . temporal sequences. . . . Media objects produce, consume and transform media values. . . . Media objects, in turn, are grouped into multimedia objects by specifying the flow of values from one object to another—we call this flow composition . . . . flow composition actually produces applications. . . ." Another interesting remark in the same paper is, "One benefit of flow-based composition is that new functionality can be added, or removed, by simple modifications to the script." In the conclusion of their article they stress a number of the points I have made elsewhere in this book: the difficulty of generalizing to create good reusable components, and the economic and project planning impediments to producing such components. This equation of objects = processes seems to be gaining acceptance: the article describing A'UM (Yoshida and Chikayama 1988) matter-of-factly describes the system as consisting of streams and objects (for more on this interesting paper, see the next chapter). They then go on to say that, of course, streams can be objects also—which seems very close to the FBP concept ot the duality of processes and streams.

From an FBP point of view, the concept that I feel is missing from traditional OO (not from the work on active objects) is the concept of "transformer" processes (many of the media objects described in the above-mentioned paper are explicit transformers). As Nan Shu (1985) has pointed out, much of business programming has to do with transforming data from one format to another. The paradigm of passing a stream of data packets through a transforming process seems to fit very naturally with this image, but this does not seem to fit well with traditional OO. Since the traditional OO paradigm specifies that only the methods of a class should know an object's internal state, this would seem to imply that transformations are only of interest at the boundaries of an application (when one is bringing in or outputting "foreign" files, reports or screen data). In practice, as businesses build bridges between more and more of their applications, a lot of time will be spent converting data between different formats. Some of these applications will be vendor-provided, so users will have even less control over their data formats. If these applications are OO, how will their classes be merged with the corresponding classes of the users? Data conversions will also be required for many of the common data transportation techniques, which will become more and more important as we move towards distributed systems. Thus, you might decide to convert binary data into character format to simplify transportation between PCs and hosts. Descriptor-driven transformers in an FBP environment will provide a simpler paradigm and will help to make all this run smoothly. Interestingly, in the paper I was talking about above (Nierstrasz, Gibbs, and Tsichritzis 1992), the authors also feel that multi-media applications will require a wide range of transformations of media values into different forms, depending on the various uses they need to be put to.

Significantly, many of the media objects in this same paper have names that are verbs, rather than nouns, e.g., *render, interpret, provide* (in FBP, processes are usually verbs, while IPs are nouns, e.g., *customer, account, department*). Traditional OO essentially works with nouns, with the verbs relegated to the methods—for instance, the fact that a student has taken a course is recorded by having the student send messages to the course, or the course to the student. From an FBP viewpoint, it seems more natural to handle this with a process that transforms the student in well-defined ways. So, an OO approach perhaps closer to FBP's way of thinking would be to send both student and course to a separate "attacher" object, which has the ability to associate students and courses. This object would be an active version of the general category of object called "dictionary" in Smalltalk. These are two different, not necessarily incompatible, viewpoints.

It seems quite probable that powerful hybrid FBP/OO systems will be built within the next few years. Such a combination may well have some interesting and unexpected capabilities. Unfortunately, one problem the OO part is almost certain to have (until the new highly parallel hardwares appear on the market) is that of performance. For every field in every information packet accessed by an OO method, you need a call, plus logic to locate the method. In FBP, you can totally hide the layout of your IPs, and you can control your performance—accessing a field may be as little as one instruction, or it may be a complex function: it is your choice. Incidentally, the performance issue makes it especially important to be able to select which part of an application is to be written in an OO language, and which in a conventional language.

The performance problem and the many arguments in favor of the asynchronous-process approach to applications design lead me to believe that, if OO starts to be used for business-production programming, it will be the concept of active objects (process objects) that will turn out to be more productive for OO than the original indirect call mechanism. To me active objects seem to be a natural evolution of OO in a direction that will eventually converge with FBP. If one can say that conventional OO (static) objects provide autonomy of data and autonomy of logic, then active objects also provide autonomy of control. Without the last, I believe it is not possible to build the systems we need in the future.

After I wrote the above, I came across the following comment by C. Ellis and S. Gibbs in Kim and Lochovsky (1989): "In the future, as we move beyond object-oriented programming, it is likely that one of the useful enduring concepts is that of 'active objects'." I agree absolutely! Over the next few years I believe we will see more and more OO proponents talking about the advantages of active objects. This will expose FBP to a wider audience, but it may leave the programming public with the erroneous impression that FBP is a complex extension of the basic OO set of concepts. In reality, as I have shown in the foregoing pages, FBP can in fact be implemented with quite simple software and yet yield great gains in productivity, while OO can only do this if it incorporates advanced concepts which seem to be converging with FBP. To quote Ellis and Gibbs again on this matter: "Although we foresee that object-oriented programming, as we know it today, is close to its deathbed, *we foresee tremendous possibilities in the future of active object systems* [my italics]. . . . Vive l'objet actif." The celebration may perhaps be premature, but, if you have read this far, you will have some idea why so many of us feel so excited about these concepts.

Before leaving this topic, I would like to make a last point that I consider vitally important: Any evaluation of a programming technology must be done in the context of building and *maintaining* real business applications. There are only three reasons I am aware of for adopting a new technology: performance, productivity, and maintainability. Even if a new technology allows us to get applications working faster or sooner, if it does not result in significant gains in maintainability, it may not be worth the effort. As I said earlier, we have to try out potential tools on the day-to-day concerns of business programmers, rather than on artificial, theoretical puzzles, no matter how intellectually stimulating they may be! When we have an OO application that processes every one of over 5,000,000 accounts, five days a week at a bank, is *easy to maintain,* and does not use prohibitive amounts of resources, we will truly be able to say that OO has come of age.

27

Related Concepts and Systems

This chapter provides an overview of some of the work going on in universities and business that has concepts in common with FBP. My main problem with trying to give a good overview is that new software is appearing faster than I can keep pace with it! Every time I open a magazine I see work that has resonances with FBP, which I therefore resolve to read. Then I have to follow up on their bibliography, which results in more to read, and so on! This is a roundabout way of apologizing to all those researchers and developers out there: if I have omitted your favorite piece of software or research effort from what follows, please accept this apology and send me information about it for my ever-growing files!

In a similar vein, I will summarize what I perceive as the salient features of each item, and I may have misunderstood their thrust. In most cases I have had no contact with the authors, and I will inevitably tend to look at their work through FBP-colored glasses. Again, please contact me to exchange ideas or to throw brickbats!

For the above reasons, what follows is probably only a fraction of what is out there—I just hope I have included enough to pique your interest.

FBP seems to me to stand on three main "legs":

1. Asynchronous processes
2. Data packets with a lifetime of their own
3. External definition of connections

You will find one or two of these in many systems, but it is the combination of all three that makes FBP unique. Even when all three of these items are present

- -

PACKING SLIP:
Amazon Marketplace Item: Flow-Based Programming: A New Approach to Application Development by Morrison
Listing ID: 0310W698084
SKU:
Quantity: 1

Purchased on: 17-Mar-2006
Shipped by: daveotlc@aol.com
Shipping address:

Ship to: Stephen Brewell
Address Line 1: 1 St Martins Close
Address Line 2: Stubton
City: Newark
State/Province/Region: Notts
Zip/Postal Code: NG23 5BT
Country: United Kingdom

Buyer Name: Stephen Brewell

- -

in a system, you will find that they have been used to address a particular area or problem, such as distributed systems. I believe that many of their developers have not yet understood the potential of this combination for improving *all* application development.

The first system listed is not even an application development system, but a simulation system. In a preceding chapter I pointed out that FBP allows simulations to be "grown" into full-scale applications, which the developers of GPSS also saw as a desirable goal.

GPSS (General Purpose Simulation System)

This is a simulation system developed by Geoffrey Gordon and his team at IBM in the early 1960s. I am including it because it shares all three of the characteristics mentioned (the data packets were called "transactions"), and it was a very successful system for simulations. It was also (or could be) a highly visual system and it profoundly influenced my thinking about how to do application development. Gordon had hopes of extending it to run as an operating system control program and did quite a bit of work in this area. Many other people have also imagined that it should eventually be possible to "grow" an application from its simulation, and in fact this was tried out in 1963 (30 years ago!) using GPSS and was quite successful. Using FBP, this process is now very straightforward.

MASCOT (A Modular Approach to Software Construction, Operation, and Test) (K. Jackson and H. Simpson 1975)

This system, built by Ken Jackson and his team at the Royal Radar Establishment in England, also shares all three of the characteristics. Jackson's motivations for developing MASCOT were similar to ours, plus a desire to make interrupt-driven software resemble the remainder of the computer load, as a lot of their signals work involves handling asynchronous interrupts. In MASCOT an IP is called a "message," as in much of the work listed below, and a connection a "channel. " The basic MASCOT unit of software is a subnet, called a "subsystem," and is drawn graphically and then converted into a textual representation. MASCOT's services are of a somewhat lower level than FBP's, but its channel management is very similar overall. Here's a quote on how well the developers feel they met their objectives:

> . . . the overall philosophy of MASCOT operation . . . is to process data when it is available, to explicitly wait when no data is available and to pass on a stimulus to adjacent data users when data of interest is passed on. . . . Further, the use of the control queue within the interrupt handling software enables the expression of interrupt handling software to be unusually straightforward. The elimination of polling and searching within the kernel is complete . . . .
>
> *CONCLUSION*
>
> MASCOT provides a very basic yet sound machine independent kernel to produce a suitable environment for real-time programming . . . . Finally MASCOT looks to be a

promising base upon which to build the high integrity systems which are the subject of current research.

CHIEF

CHIEF seems to be a classic case of parallel development, as this work must have been going on at about the same time as ours was going on in Canada, but was totally independent of it. J. Boukens and F. Deckers, working for the Shell Company in Holland, came up with a system that shows a number of really remarkable similarities to FBP. In fact, the main difference is that their diagrams are vertical, whereas FBP's are horizontal! Another difference is that they allow multiple consumers for a connection (causing the records to be automatically copied), while in FBP we do not allow this. On the other hand, FBP dialects usually have an off-the-shelf Replicate component, which has the same effect. CHIEF's ports are numbered, as in AMPS and DFDM. To convert one of their diagrams into machinable text, they list the connections (called "buffers"), naming their producers and consumers. A list of such specifications is called a "cooperation." To program individual processes, they developed their own interpretive language, whose execution was integrated with the multithreading driver. There is also a discussion of deadlocks in their paper.

Actually, speaking of parallel evolution, after I had been working on these concepts for a few years, I came across two papers dating back quite a while: one was written in 1967 (27 years ago!) by two people at the Rome Air Development Center, E. Morenoff and J.B. McLean, entitled "Inter-program Communications, Program String Structures and Buffer Files" (1967), describing a program interconnect structure based on the control of data flow via intermediate queues. For a single processor, queues could be maintained in main memory. For a distributed processor structure, queues could be held on disk.

A few years later (1971), R.B. Balzer published a paper on what he called PORTS, describing work done at RAND where modules could be shielded from other modules by utilizing such software commands as "connect," "disconnect," "send," and "receive." It is interesting that this paper is one of the most cited papers in the field, but, according to private communications with the author, little came of it.

STREMA

Another related system I came across in my reading was developed by Ian Clark of IBM UK (1976). It is described as a graphic conversational language for specifying and running application processes. STREMA uses a relational model and is intended to allow relational data to be treated in a uniform manner with flat files and *subroutines*. In STREMA, all these are made available to the programmer as "streams," which resemble most closely the processes of FBP. You can specify graphically how "streams" are connected and what happens to the fields in the records traveling through them. Clark uses the term "component" to describe what a field resides in as it is in transit through a given stream (not to be confused with FBP "components"). Streams drive each other, are described by a "relator," and may be subject to constraints on their components. Components (fields) have values, but they also have status: UNDEFINED, VALID, or INVALID (similar to DFDM's dynamic attributes). As a record enters a stream, what happens is determined by the stream's "relator," as well as the constraints on, and status of, the incoming components. Constraints may be such things as bounds on a value, type specifications, or forcing a value not to repeat or descend in a run. This concept can support processes as diverse as applying subroutines to streams, collating data streams, or getting data from or writing data to a relational table. Combining the concepts of relators and constraints simplifies a lot of the logic that conventional programs have to do validating fields and deciding what to do if things go wrong. While Clark's thrust was different from that of FBP, there are concepts here that could very well be combined with those of FBP to provide some useful capabilities.

LGDF

R.G. Babb II (1984) uses the term "large-grain data flow" (LGDF) to describe a level of granularity like FBP's, which he describes as a compromise between fine-grained data flow and traditional approaches. He points out that, under LGDF, the lowest-level programs can be written in almost any language (he uses FORTRAN). He also starts the design process by showing data flow dependencies in diagram form and then converting them to what he calls a "wirelist." Here's a quote: "We have come to some unexpected conclusions. . . . The most surprising is that sequential programs are often easier to design and implement reliably when based on a parallel (asynchronous) model of computation."

In case you start getting confused as you read this chapter: please take note that the term "message," used in MASCOT and other systems, is not the same as the Smalltalk "message," which is basically a linearized subroutine call, comprising a selector (which indirectly specifies the code to be executed) and the parameters to be passed to it. The more common use of "message" is similar to its meaning in everyday English: a short piece of text carrying instructions and/or information from one process to another.

NIL

NIL, developed by Rob Strom and his team (1983) at the IBM Research Center in Yorktown Heights, has some very strong similarities to FBP, except that it is a programming language rather than a coordination language. The original motivation for NIL seems to have been for programming communication software—you will perhaps have noticed that the multiple layers of communications software can be implemented as pairs of complementary processes. Strom and his team also wanted good inter-process protection, which, as you have seen, means minimizing side effects. Like FBP, NIL also allows applications to be built up out of communicating sequential processes; only one process can own a data object at a time; "send" is "destructive" (the sent object can no longer be accessed by the sender);

and so on. Strom makes the point that the ability to have processes on the same machine run in a single address space makes the cost of a message exchange very low, comparable to the cost of a subroutine call, and also makes it possible to have larger numbers of smaller-grained processes.

While it does not have an explicit coordination language, NIL is so powerful that this kind of language can easily be added—a parent process has enough facilities available that it could build a running program based on a file that specifies the connections between processes. NIL was deliberately designed to allow dynamic modification of networks, where processes can be created dynamically. Also, ports of the created process can be dynamically connected to ports of other processes, both at process creation time and during subsequent execution of the process. The way it does this is by making ports objects, so that the process of connecting ports happens at run-time, under control of what are called "capabilities."

Just as in FBP, the only way that processes can affect each other is via the communication channels. Strom and Yemini point out in their paper that this fact, plus an extension to strong typing in the NIL language called "typestate checking," provides a high degree of security. Since NIL has its own compiler, it can enforce typestate checking and thus eliminate the risk of moving data to an address defined by an uninitialized pointer. DFDM, on the other hand, was explicitly designed to interface with existing languages (S/370 Assembler, PL/I, and COBOL), and THREADS is C-based, so this risk is present with these implementations. However, it can be minimized by good programming techniques and inspections. DFDM and THREADS also adopt the strategy of invalidating a pointer to an IP after that IP has been disposed of—this ensures that an erroneous attempt to access that IP afterwards will cause an immediate crash. Like the NIL group, we also found that this kind of environment provides very good isolation between processes. I believe we ran into very few cases where one process damaged another one's code or data.

Strom's group has since developed a follow-on to NIL, called Hermes (Strom et al. 1991) because Hermes was the "process-server of the gods"! They are currently building a "global desktop," which will allow applications to be developed graphically. This is reminiscent of the work we did generating running programs from diagrams, alluded to in chapter 2, but the global desktop will also allow programs to be connected up and reconfigured while they are actually running. It is designed to be used by people who may or may not be knowledgeable about programming. Strom's team has also been doing interesting work on what they call "Optimistic Recovery"—recovery strategies based on the idea that failures are rarer than successes, so one should go ahead with logic on the assumption that things will work and only undo it if there is a failure. Their infrastructure keeps the required information so that programmers really don't have to think about recovery.

In chapter 26 I mentioned Rob Strom's remark about his team's decision to think of themselves as part of the OO world. In that chapter I also alluded to FBP-like work coming out of the OO fraternity, such as the media objects of Nierstrasz et al. (1992).

Parallel Logic Programming

There is an ever-growing series of parallel logic programming systems, such as Parlog, Vulcan, and a number of projects proceeding under the aegis of ICOT in Japan. One of the latter is A'UM by K. Yoshida and T. Chikayama (1988), which I find very interesting. Incidentally, this article has an excellent bibliography. The subtitle of this article is itself quite evocative: "A Stream-Based Concurrent Object-Oriented Language"—all the good words in a single title!

This same article started me thinking again about "streams." In A'UM and some of the other systems related to it, a distinction is made between "streams" and "channels." If I understand it right, in A'UM, a "stream" runs from one source to one destination, whereas a "channel" may contain more than one stream, coming from different sources: the items in each stream must stay in sequence relative to each other, but the streams in a channel are not constrained relative to each other. In A'UM, only one reader is allowed for a channel, while in Tribble's paper on channels (Tribble et al. 1987), he allows multiple readers for a channel. The authors of A'UM feel that not allowing multiple readers makes their semantics sounder and the implementation simpler. Our experience tends to support this view.

In FBP we define a stream as the set of data IPs passing across one connection, but we also allow multiple sources (but only one destination). It may well be that the distinction between stream and channel is more rigorous than the FBP concept, and I look forward to seeing how these concepts evolve. We also pragmatically allow a stream that is accepted by one process to be passed on to the next (e.g., a stream of detail records might flow from a Reader, through an Edit, and on to a Process component). Some writers might prefer to call these multiple streams that just happen to contain the same data. I admit in hindsight that our concept of streams is a little fuzzy at the edges, but I feel it has never caused confusion in practice and has been implemented in all of the FBP dialects. Multiple destinations, on the other hand, have never been implemented in any of our implementations, partly because it is not clear whether the data should be replicated or should be assigned randomly to the receivers, like Linda's piranhas (described later in this chapter)—in any case, both solutions can be realized very easily by means of generalized components.

Actors

Hewitt's Actors take the concept of processes down to the finest possible granularity. "Hewitt declared," to quote Robin Milner (1993), "that a value, an operator on values, and a process should all be the same kind of thing: an actor." This approach has considerable theoretical attractiveness, but in my view, to be practical, it basically has to be implemented as hardware rather than software. There are also, of course, a number of projects growing out of Hewitt's Actors, which also seem to be on a converging path with all the other work, albeit at the more granular end of the scale (e.g., Agha's COOP [1990]).

BSP

In chapter 1, I said I would describe L.G. Valiant's work (1990) in a little more detail, so this is as good a time as any! BSP stands for "bulk-synchronous parallel," and it is of considerable interest because the author proposes it as a new "bridging model," to replace the current, von Neumann bridging model. He stresses that he is proposing it neither as a hardware nor a programming model, but to "insulate software and hardware development from each other, and make possible both general purpose machines and transportable software." The BSP model is comprised of the following three attributes:

1. A number of components. . .
2. A *router* that delivers messages point to point between pairs of components,
3. Facilities for synchronizing all or a subset of components at regular intervals of L time units, where L is the *periodicity* parameter. A computation consists of a sequence of *supersteps*. . . . After each period of L time units, a global check is made to determine whether the superstep has been completed by all the components. If it has, the machine proceeds to the next superstep. Otherwise, the next period of L units is allocated to the unfinished superstep.

Now look back at chapter 20, and you can see that Valiant's third attribute is very similar to FBP's use of subnets in checkpointing, except that he checks for completion on a regular basis—in FBP implementations, we usually count the processes in the subnet and then wait until that number have terminated. Otherwise, it is very similar.

Valiant describes a variety of implementations, plus their appropriate performance measures, such as packet switching networks, a hypercube-connected computer, and optical crossbars. Here is an interesting comment in his conclusion: ". . . if the relative investment in communication hardware were suitably increased, machines with a new level of programmability would be obtained." Note the juxtaposition: not just improved performance, but improved programmability.

The UNIX system and its descendants

There is another group of related approaches, based on the very popular UNIX system. In these systems, the connectivity does not seem to be as rich, but the data passing between the processes is more like IPs or file records than messages. UNIX supports the concept of "pipelining," where the output of one process becomes the input of another, and so on repeatedly. This is definitely a form of configurable modularity, and I found a lot of their experience using this technique relates closely to things we discovered using FBP.

You will find the word "pipe" used quite often for what we call "connection" in FBP. In UNIX, the '|' operator represents what it calls a "pipe." Processes can be assembled into working systems by connecting them together using this operator. For instance, suppose a user enters:

```
ls | pr -2 | lpr
```

The effect is for `ls`, `pr`, and `lpr` to be assembled on the fly in such a way that the "standard output" of `ls` feeds the "standard input" of `pr`, and so on. So this command means "list the files in the current directory; format the result 2-up and send the results to a line printer." This is very similar to the interpreted mode of DFDM and THREADS. UNIX's equivalents to ports are the file descriptors 0 (standard input) and 1 (standard output), which are automatically open whenever a process gets control. What flows between the UNIX processes are streams of characters rather than structured IPs, so the metaphor is not as powerful as FBP's, nor does UNIX pipelining support complex networks. On the other hand, UNIX's character string orientation makes it very suitable for text manipulation, and a large number of the well-known UNIX components address this application area.

OS/2 Interprocess Communication

Orfali and Harkey (1991) list four techniques for interprocess communication in OS/2: anonymous pipes, named pipes, queues, and shared memory. Anonymous pipes can be accessed by means of a write handle and a read handle and are mostly used by parent processes to communicate with their descendants, while named pipes allow communication between unrelated processes. Named pipes are accessed using standard OS/2 file services, so code does not have to distinguish whether it is writing to a file or to a named pipe—this will be determined by the file name.

CMS Pipelines

This system was developed by John Hartmann of IBM Denmark for the CMS environment. It is also consciously modeled on UNIX, but since it is specialized for the CMS environment, it is record-oriented rather than byte-oriented. It supports more complex topologies than UNIX does by means of a notation for ending one pipeline and starting a new one attached to a previous "stage" in the pipeline definition (using a label notation). I therefore see it as a halfway house between UNIX and FBP (again, developed independently of FBP). A program may also dynamically redefine the pipeline topology by replacing itself or one of its neighbors with a newly defined pipeline.

Here is an example of a CMS Pipelines pipeline:

```
pipe < logged users | split , | take 5 | console
```

This is a CMS command to set up a pipeline that reads the file called LOGGED USERS, splits each record into multiple records, using the comma as the delimiter, selects the first five, and displays them at the console.

Pipelines components are written in REXX, using a SUBCOM environment for the "pipe" services.

CSP (Communicating Sequential Processes)

This seminal work by Tony Hoare (1978) has been the basis for a large amount of work by other writers. Here, the external specification indicates which processes are running concurrently (using the || operator to indicate parallel execution), not how they are connected. The actual connectivity is implied by the send and receive commands, which must explicitly name the process being communicated with. Connections are assumed to have zero capacity.

As an example of the CSP coordination notation, here is Hoare's notation, given in his article, for what I referred to earlier as the "telegram problem," as follows:

```
[west::DISASSEMBLE||X::COPY||east::ASSEMBLE]
```

Here `west`, `X`, and `east` are process names, while the capitalized names stand for program sections (analogous to FBP components).

The problem is that DISASSEMBLE has to know the name "X," COPY has to know the names "west" and "east," and so on. Hoare's orientation seems to be towards "write new," rather than reuse. He does mention port names as a possible solution to this problem, but doesn't stress the fundamental paradigm shift involved in changing from "write new" to reuse, nor the importance of finding a good notation for combining black box components.

Interestingly, he also makes the same point that Carriero and Gelernter made about a subroutine being a special case of a coroutine.

You will notice the frequent occurrence of processes, connections, and sometimes ports, with different names being used from system to system. Also, configurable modularity at any more complex level than that of UNIX usually requires some agreement of names (or numbers) between the outsides and insides of processes. NIL avoids this by making ports local to a process, but allowing a parent process to pass information about connections to the child process in the form of parameters.

Linda

Now let's move off in a different direction: Carriero and Gelernter, whom I mentioned previously, have developed and written extensively about a very interesting system called Linda (1989), which has stirred up a lot of interest in academic circles. Instead of IPs, Linda uses "tuples," ordered lists of values. "Tuples" are created in "tuple space," just as FBP IPs are created in space managed by FBP, not by the components. Unlike FBP's IPs, however, a tuple just floats in tuple space until retrieved by a process that knows its identification (or part of it). Professor Gelernter uses a neat analogy in a recent *Scientific American* article to explain his concept of a "tuple." Imagine two spacemen working in space building a space station: one of the workers has finished working with a wrench and wishes it to be available for other workers—he or she can put it "down" (so that it follows its own orbit in space), and the other worker can then pick it up whenever convenient. In the same way, tuples or FBP IPs have an independent existence and follow their own orbit from one worker (process) to another.

How does the spaceman actually pick up the wrench? Here is chiefly where Linda diverges from FBP: in Linda, access is done by pattern matching. A process may need a tuple with value *X* in field *Y*—it just has to request a tuple matching those specifications, and it will eventually receive an appropriate tuple. Receiving a tuple can be destructive or non-destructive ("consume" or "read"). If more than one tuple matches the specification, the system picks one at random. If there are none, the requesting process is suspended. Values are not communicated back from the receive to the tuple.

One other important feature of Linda is that of "active" tuples—these are tuples that execute code at the moment of creation and then turn into ordinary "passive" tuples. You can do distributed logic such as matrix operations this way, where each tuple does a calculation when it is created and then becomes a passive matrix element. Perhaps the nearest to this in FBP is something like the Subnet Manager, which takes a passive chunk of code and turns it into a process.

Another Linda image that is evocative is the "school of piranhas." Here a number of processes lie in wait for a tuple, and when it appears in the tuple space any one of them can grab it. This is an effective technique of load balancing. In chapter 22, I described a performance improvement technique where there were 18 occurrences of a process executing the same disk traversal logic. In this case, we had to provide connections from the client to the 18 servers, so we had to have a "load balancing" process in between—the piranha technique would do this without the need for the extra process.

To summarize the essential difference between Linda and FBP, Linda is a bus while FBP is a tram—Linda has more degrees of freedom, but I believe is more expensive in terms of resources. If one Linda process generates a series of tuples with an extra field containing numbers in ascending sequence, you could have another process request them in sequence. So Linda can simulate FBP. Conversely, FBP can just as easily simulate Linda's associative style of retrieval by having one or more processes manage an associative store. It seems to me that Linda and FBP are so closely related that systems of the future may combine both approaches. After all, there may be areas of an application where tracks are more appropriate and others where you want more degrees of freedom—sort of like containers moving from rail to ship and back to rail. Here is a final quote from Gelernter and Carriero (1992): "In general we see computation and programming languages as areas in which further progress will be slow, incremental and, in many cases, of marginal importance to working programmers. Coordination languages are a field of potentially great significance. A growing number of groups will play major roles in this work." I couldn't agree more!

RIG, Accent, Mach

These are a series of network operating systems (Rashid 1988), each one evolving out of the previous one. RIG (Rochester's Intelligent Gateway) was an interprocess communication facility allowing processes to communicate by means of information packets. RIG allowed any process to access any other's port using a pair of integers (process number.port number). While this allowed port numbers to be passed around as data, it meant that port-defined services could not be easily moved from one process to another. Also, if a process failed, this information could not be signaled back to processes depending on it. Processes therefore had to register their dependence on other processes with a special process that was notified of process death events (called the "grim reaper"). This makes me wonder if systems like Linda may not suffer from the same problem.

Accent evolved out of RIG, by defining ports to be capabilities as well as communication objects and adding an integrated virtual memory management system that allowed processes to transmit large objects (RIG could only transmit 2K bytes at a time). Here is a quote about Accent: "Experience with Accent showed that a message based network operating system, properly designed, can compete with more traditional operating system organizations. The advantages of the approach are system extensibility, protection and network transparency."

Mach then evolved out of Accent because of the need in their environment for complete UNIX compatibility, and "to better accommodate the kind of general purpose shared-memory multiprocessors which appear to be on their way to becoming the successors to traditional general purpose uniprocessor workstations and time-sharing systems." Among other things, Mach splits the Accent concept of "process" into "task" (basic unit of resource allocation) and "thread" (basic unit of CPU utilization).

Advanced Hardware Designs

Another characteristic of the three "legs" of FBP listed above is that they could actually describe a network of independent processors, all interacting to do a job of work. This approach to building super-powerful machines is getting a lot of attention lately, as it is generally recognized that the single processor is running out of steam. Although you can probably make individual processors smaller and faster (after all, a bit is simply a choice between two states—for instance two states of a molecule), you start to run into limitations, such as the speed of light or the potential damage that can be caused by a single cosmic ray! A lot of work is going on on linking multiple processors together to achieve enormous amounts of computing power without any one processor having to be incredibly fast. Suppose you put 1000 processors together, each running at 20 MIPS (millions of instructions per second). This would provide 20 billion (20,000,000,000) instructions per second. Since such a machine is normally thought of as being oriented towards scientific calculations, so that the instructions would tend to be floating-point operations, this machine would be a 20 gigaflop machine. Multiply either of these factors by 50 (or one by 5 and one by 10), and you are into the "teraflop" per second range or 1 trillion (1,000,000,000,000) floating-point operations per second.

The two main approaches here are multiprocessors and multicomputers. I am indebted to my son, Joseph Morrison, for some of the following comments. A number of writers seem to favor multiprocessors (with shared memory) because they do not require us to radically change our approach to programming. The programming technique I described in the foregoing pages seems to be a good match with this approach, as it can be mapped onto a multiprocessor in a straightforward manner: IPs are allocated from the shared memory, and FBP processes are spread across the available processors to obtain parallelism. All commercial multiprocessors provide concurrency control mechanisms such as semaphores; these can be used to manage the concurrent accesses to the IPs. Examples of this type of machine are the KSR 1, CEDAR, DASH, T*, Alewife—this list is from Bell's article (Bell 1992).

FBP networks also have a natural mapping to multicomputers. Here parallelism is obtained by having a network of connected processors, each with its own memory. The data must be transmitted from one processor to another, as required, so communication speed and bandwidth become important considerations. Examples of this type of machine are the Intel Paragon, CM5, Mercury, nCube 2, and Teradata/NCR/AT&T systems. A number of different network topologies have been investigated—examples are meshes, tree structures, hypercubes, and ring structures.

FBP could be mapped onto multicomputer systems by again evenly distributing the processes among the processors. An IP would be created in the local memory of the processor on which the creating process resides. If an IP had to be transferred to another processor, the entire IP could be copied over the communication network. Although this sounds inefficient, communication costs can be minimized by having "neighbor" processes reside in directly connected processors or even in some cases time-share the same processor, where the economics justify it. There is a considerable body of work on different strategies for handling communication between processors and for doing the routing when paths are tied up or damaged, and I was struck by how similar some of the problems they have to solve are to those we had to solve for FBP. I found the article by P. Gaughan and S. Yalamanchili (1993) a good survey, as well as providing some interesting solutions and simulation results. Of course, I am not a hardware person, but it does seem that some of the techniques described would support future FBP systems quite nicely.

Most of the academic work with multiprocessor configurations seems to be oriented towards determining what parallelism can be obtained from a COBOL or FORTRAN program. However, MIT has a dataflow computer called Monsoon, which "demonstrates scalability and implicit parallelism using a dataflow language" (Bell 1992), to be followed by one called T*, which will be "multithreaded to absorb network latency." Researchers at Berkeley are using a 64-node CM5 to explore various programming models and languages, including dataflow. The Novosibirsk Computing Center (Kotov 1991) initiated the MARS Project (Modular Asynchronous Reconfigurable System) to investigate this kind of architecture in conjunction with parallel programming languages, including one similar to CSP.

There is an enormous amount of research going on in the areas of multiprocessors and multicomputers. This is a whole area of specialization within computing research and one that I expect I will never get to know very much about! However, a lot of people who do have some understanding of this area see a good match with FBP. Applications designed using FBP should map very naturally onto a system of communicating processors. If you have more processors than processes, this mapping should be pretty easy; if less, then some processors are going to have to time-share, just as the present implementations of FBP do today. Here is a quote from an article (Cann 1992) comparing FORTRAN with functional languages for programming tomorrow's massively parallel machines (remember that I related FBP to functional languages in an earlier chapter):

> Tomorrow's parallel machines will not only provide massive parallelism, but will present programmers with a combinatorial explosion of concerns and details. The imperative programming model will continue to hinder the exploitation of parallelism.
>
> In summary, the functional paradigm yields several important benefits. First, programs are more concise and easier to write and maintain. Second, programs are conducive to analysis, being mathematically sound and free of side effects and aliasing. Third, programs exhibit implicit parallelism and favor automatic parallelization. Fourth, programs can run as fast as, if not faster than, conventional languages.

One last point about the data flowing between these computing engines: a lot of the mathematically oriented work with big computers (and most of this work is mathematically oriented) seems to assume that what should travel between the processors is either values, like integers or strings, or messages. I actually started out with values in my early work, in 1967, but became convinced over the years that you should send whole "things" (entities, records, or IPs), which stay together as they travel, rather than low-level data types (e.g., integers or strings), which are not in the application domain. Our experience is that, if you decompose a record into individual values, it may be so expensive to recombine them that it's not worth it. A greater danger is that the need to keep related data synchronized prevents the designer from taking advantage, in the first place, of the power of asynchronism.

FBP Without FBP

Maybe now is the time to talk about how to do FBP without FBP software. This could be a stepping stone to full FBP for a number of companies. Many of the basic concepts can be simulated with conventional languages without any special software. A friend of mine took our AMPS course, but then went to work on a COBOL application. In those days we had no FBP support for COBOL, but he told us that AMPS had helped him write better COBOL programs by suggesting better ways to structure his code.

Of course, you could even use JCL, using files for your connections, if you didn't care about overhead. Remember that the steps in a job must execute in a fixed order, so you would have to string out your network into almost a straight line—and forget about loop-type networks. Another similar approach is to use secondary transactions in IMS. This has actually been tried several times, but the overhead prevents the granularity from being made fine enough to be really productive.

A number of Data Flow COBOL products available in Japan generate pure COBOL from data flow specifications, which can then be compiled and linkedited like any other COBOL program. They support rather simple networks, but require no special run-time software.

An article (Kar 1989) written by a senior engineer with Intel shows how to do calculations using data flow, rather than synchronous code. He gives the actual C code to do this. He sees what he calls "data flow multitasking" as a way that we can use today to write programs that will not only be easy to port to the powerful multiprocessing machines coming on stream during the 1990s (and he should know!), but that will take advantage of these machines' capabilities. In the summary section, he says:

> Data-flow multitasking is a promising solution to the challenges software faces over the next decade. *It involves looking at a sequential program through new eyes.* . . . Data-flow multitasking is particularly relevant for real-time applications. [Italics added.]

Along somewhat similar lines, some of my early data flow research was done using a single APL program to simulate the scheduler. In this case, different processes were implemented as sections of a single APL program, and control was transferred between them by using a computed "goto." This would be very easy to do in any HLL. Another approach would be to use single data areas to represent connections, together with a switch to indicate whether a given area is occupied or not. The scheduler could then cycle, looking to see which process has data waiting to be processed. Wayne Stevens pointed out (1991) that non-looping FBP components are very similar to subroutines, and therefore networks consisting mostly of non-loopers should be easy to implement directly using an HLL.

At the beginning of this chapter, I mentioned the growing use of these concepts for programming distributed systems. IBM's recent announcement of their Messaging and Queuing set of products, already referred to in chapter 20, fits in here. Similar efforts by other companies are listed in a recent article (Moad 1993). IBM is bringing out a set of products that will allow asynchronous communication between a large set of IBM and non-IBM platforms. There is a standard interface based on the concept of queues, which will relieve programmers from the complexities of communication between different vendors' hardware and software. Instead of having to use one set of macros for VTAM, different commands for CICS, and still another set for IMS, all applications will use the same simple set of MQI (Messaging and Queueing Interface) calls. This concept seems to me to be completely compatible with the application structuring ideas presented in this book. In chapter 15, I talked about FBP's ability to "cleave" networks across systems—the combination of FBP and MQ Series or similar software should provide a very powerful way of splitting an application across multiple systems or locations or of moving functions from one node to another, as desired. As I said in that chapter, cleaving applications between different computers introduces new problems of synchronization, but it clearly doesn't make sense to try to pretend that a distributed system is one big synchronous application. If you request data from a remote location, you want to be able to do other things while the data is working its way through the system, especially when, as is happening increasingly, the other end is under the control of another department or even another company. Systems are getting just too big. Also, many of the systems that are being connected "speak different languages," so we are seeing the development of standards that will allow them to interpret each others' data formats. As business systems become increasingly interconnected, companies find that applications that used to be independent and "barely communicative" (Yeamans 1993) can be combined into one overall business unit of work, but without depending on one overall commit. However, if anything goes wrong, all the constituent processes can be rolled back in a coordinated way. Users of Messaging and Queuing are now starting to promote it to their own customers because it allows them to offer new and better services.

As you read this chapter, I hope you got some impression of how ideas spring up independently in different places and times, how they flower in unexpected places, how they cross-pollinate and give rise to interesting new hybrids. There are many other concepts and languages, other than the few I have mentioned here, that have points in common with FBP and that have certainly been influential in the field of computing, but there is not room in this book to do them justice. They have cross-fertilized each other, and in many cases only industry archivists know which led to which. Examples that spring to mind are SIMULA, MODULA-2 (and now MODULA-3), Concurrent Pascal, Ada, Lucid, and Occam.

It would be wonderful if any readers who are expert in these different languages could share their knowledge and insights with the rest of us. I have occasionally dreamed of collecting all the developers and theoreticians of concurrent, stream-oriented, modular systems together in a huge symposium and seeing if we can't get some synergy going. I have found that there is something about data-orientation that seems to allow practitioners of different disciplines to communicate (just as IPs do for different languages!). I sincerely hope that we won't waste our energy in internecine wars, as has happened in some disciplines, but that we will all be able to work together towards a shared goal. There are far more similarities than differences in our work, and if we can get a real dialogue going, who knows what we might achieve together!

28

Ruminations of an Elder Programmer

The following was sent to me by a colleague named Art Huber a few years ago. It is reprinted with his permission.

Subject: DFDM thoughts

Last night, when I couldn't sleep because of a cold, I thought about DFDM. Why not?

I thought about the analogies we use as an aid to understanding it. None will be completely satisfactory, but I have been working on one that I have not heard previously. I think it is most useful for old farts such as me. Less experienced programmers and analysts, whose synapses are not already connected hierarchically, don't need this one.

Once upon a time there were no computers. There were, however, unit record machines. There were collators, sorters, keypunches, printing accounting machines, calculating summary punches, etc.

I think a DFDM network is very similar to a job in a unit record shop.

Batches of records move from machine to machine.

Each machine performs a single operation on the data.

Each machine is a general purpose machine that is programmed to customize it for the required task. Note that by "general purpose," I do not mean that it can perform any task; I mean that it is not tied to a particular record format or job.

There are some significant differences, of course, between DFDM and a unit record shop.

The DFDM "machines" run at electronic speed rather than mechanical speed.

They are cheaper to build. If you need a new special function machine, you can create it in software.

Consequently, there is no economic advantage to creating multi-purpose machines as there would be with real unit record machines.

DFDM machines can be replicated as needed. The new copies don't cost anything to operate and don't take up floor space or use additional electricity.

DFDM machines are not restricted to 80 character records.

The records will not fall on the floor between steps.

Parameters that tailor DFDM machines can be much simpler than unit record plugboards. For example, in DFDM, a field can be defined by specifying its starting position and length. Unit record machines require a character by character definition.

Because setup is so much cheaper (since the DFDM machines are virtual), it is viable to process batches of one record with DFDM.

DFDM machines need not be limited in the number of accumulators they contain, since they are implemented in software.

Jobs do not have to be scheduled based on machine availability, since DFDM machines are virtual. Of course, they are implemented on real machines (computers) and are constrained by availability of computer resources.

Isn't this fun?

I offer this for your consideration. It does point out that the job of "programming" in DFDM is very different from what we think of traditionally. We may even have an opportunity for old unit record analysts.

AND EVERYTHING OLD IS NEW AGAIN!

29

Endings and Beginnings

> Herakleitos, in about 500 B.C., said "Panta rheei," usually translated as "Everything changes." What he actually said was: "Everything flows."

I did not want to call this chapter "Conclusion," as I hope it is more of a beginning than an ending. We have certainly traveled a long distance, and if you have stuck with me you are definitely to be congratulated! However, the journey in many ways is just beginning. We have come a long way, but these are only the first small steps.

Programming in the year 2010 is going to be very different from what we are used to today—it is going to *feel* very different, and it is going to be done by people different from the practitioners of today. Brad Cox wants to get his "Software Industrial Revolution" started, and I agree the concepts are there and the time is right. He points out that today we are still software craftsmen, making once-off items one piece at a time with very simple tools. If you want to read about how things were done before mass production, read *A Book of Country Things* (Needham 1965). The people described in the book were smart people who knew their materials, and many of their techniques were excellent. But you didn't go to the store to buy a standard part—you made whatever you needed yourself. Now, isn't it rather strange that so many programmers today would still rather build a new piece of code than (re)use one that already exists! Some of them certainly do it because they love it, and there is a role for these people to play, but modern business cannot afford to continue to have code built laboriously by hand. In the old days, people did this because they *had* to; today, we have had to divide up the work—some people do the designs, others make them. Machines make everyone more productive. Are people less happy today? I believe that only a Luddite would maintain that the old days were better—yes, some of those old tools were works of art, but we have magical things available at our fingertips that many of those old-timers would give their eye-teeth for. Cheaper doesn't have to mean nastier. If you believe that programmers don't reuse on account of their love of their craft, I think that's wrong. Most programmers don't reuse because it's just more trouble than building new. But, you see, our experience with FBP has been completely different. In one case I mentioned earlier, a programmer used an off-the-shelf component to do a function, even when she could have done the same thing by adding a single line to an adjacent PL/I component she was writing! So there are profound psychological differences between the two environments.

I believe that an important part of the change is that application developers who are trained in FBP are moving away from procedural thinking towards what you might call "visual" or "spatial" thinking. Procedural thinking is quite rare in ordinary life, so it's not surprising that people find it difficult and that its practitioners are (viewed as) different in some ways from ordinary mortals.

If you start to look for examples of procedural thinking in real life, you discover that there are in fact very few areas where we do pure procedural thinking, but there is one that we have been doing since we lived in caves—cooking. Some years ago at the IBM Research Center in Yorktown, Dr. Lance Miller started studying the differences between recipes and programs. He noticed that recipes often had implicit parallelism. For example, "add boiling water" implies that the water must have started boiling while some other step was going on, so that it would be available when needed. The term "preheated oven" is so common that you probably don't even notice that it also violates sequentiality. People say and write things like this all the time without thinking. It is only if you try to execute the instructions in a rigidly serial manner (i.e., play computer) that you may run into some surprises!

The other thing he noticed was that the individual steps of the process very often start with a verb and then add qualifiers (e.g., "boil until done," "beat egg whites until soft peaks form"), so you know very early in the sentence what kind of activity you will be doing. In programming, you usually bury the "verb" deep inside a nest of do-loops to get the same effect, for example:

```
do while a....
  if c is true
  then
     do until b...
        compute
     enddo
  endif
enddo
```

The effect of this is that you don't know what operation you are going to do until you are deep inside a nest of do-loops or conditional statements. This would be like telling a visitor to town, "Until you come to the fountain after the church across from the train station, keep going straight." The visitor would get a pretty strange impression of your town and its inhabitants!

The other main kind of procedural behavior in fact is just this one: following directions. Have you ever tried following someone's directions, only to find out that they forgot one item or that someone changed a street sign and you are now facing north instead of west (if you can even figure that out). If you want to make a grown man or woman cry, ask them to assemble a child's tricycle, whose instructions have been translated into English from another language by a speaker of a third language and which probably describe the wrong model anyway, if you could figure out what it meant. A lot like programming, isn't it? Maps are much easier because they let you visualize relationships between places synoptically, so you can handle unexpected changes, make corrections, and even figure out how to get to your destination from somewhere your informant never imagined you'd end up! On a recent trip to England, I found myself very impressed with the amount of information packed into the signs announcing "roundabouts": general shape of the roundabout, angles, destinations and relative sizes of roads entering the roundabout—and all specified *visually!*

This is something like the difference between conventional programming and FBP—FBP gets you away from procedural thinking and lets you think map-style.

It occurred to me recently that we finally have a unique opportunity, both to take advantage of the CPU power available on most programmers' desks today and to actually use this power to take advantage of natural human abilities. Just like other human abilities that people take for granted, visual processing is extremely difficult to program into a computer and requires a lot of computer horsepower. However, many programmers today have powerful machines sitting on their desks that are basically being used as "dumb" terminals. A few years ago, Bucky Pope of IBM did a study in which he concluded that "editing" text really doesn't exercise a machine much. Most of the time the programmer is just thinking. So entering a linear string of COBOL doesn't take advantage of the power on his or her desk. And what power! If you remember chapter 22, "Performance Considerations," I said that it took 10 microseconds to do an API call on an IBM 168 (on which we ran a bank—5,000,000 accounts) 20 years ago and 50 microseconds on the machine on my desk at home today. So that means I have the processing power to run 1/5 of a bank right here on my desk (yes, I know that's stretching it a bit!). What might be called "visual programming" could actually start to take advantage of the relatively enormous processing power available to each programmer today. And visual programming means much more than drawing pictures to represent logic—it means developing a synergy between human and machine that takes advantage of one of the human's strong suits, not his or her weakest. A recent article by K. Kahn and V. Saraswat (1990), alluded to earlier, which I found absolutely visionary, describes an approach to a totally visual style of programming, which would not only have a visual syntax, but would also show computation using visual transformations. Software supporting this would have to be able to perform and understand topological transforms, just as humans do without effort. Interestingly, my group at IBM built a visual animation showing the creation and movement of IPs through an FBP network and showed this at a CASE conference a few years ago—this proved a very effective way of conveying some of the basic concepts of FBP. We have also speculated that visual interaction with a picture of a network would be a very natural debugging environment. At this juncture, 6 years from the end of the century, I believe we have the computer horse-power to make such approaches economically feasible—now we just have to develop the technology.

Up to now, I have concentrated on technology, and I confess to being technologically oriented, so assume we have gotten these details out of the way. However, we also have to look at the sociological and psychological factors. What will be needed to get such a technology into use in the workplace? Well, for one thing it is going to need extensive cooperation between business and academia. As long as business and academia are two solitudes, staring at each other across a deep chasm of noncommunication, we as an industry are not going to be able to make the transition to a new way of thinking. Business has gotten the impression that it has to become a bunch of mathematical geniuses to do the new programming, because the academics are broadcasting that image. So it retreats into its corner and keeps trying to build and maintain systems using linear COBOL text. However, I don't believe that we all have to become mathematicians. Nothing in this book would give a bright 16-year-old any difficulty at all.

Instead, at this point in time, businesspeople are more willing to hire hundreds of COBOL programmers than to invest in new technologies. The problem is, if you were a CIO (maybe you are), which technology would you invest in? Well, currently it is not a very hard economic decision—it makes more sense to stay with the COBOL coders. At least you can do anything with COBOL (no, I am not refuting everything I have said in this book), but it takes ages to do it, and the result is almost unmaintainable. Now suppose you were running a cotton plantation a century or so ago, using all manual labor—not very productive, but at least output was predictable, if slow. Imagine, now, that some city slicker comes along with a cotton-picking machine, which he claims is going to improve productivity enormously. But you, the landowner, figure that you are going to need more highly trained people to run it, it may break down at awkward moments, it's going to need parts from halfway across the country, and so forth. You'll do the "smart" thing, right? It wasn't until the prevailing morality started to take into account the feelings and needs of *everybody* involved *and* the technology reached a certain level of maturity that the balance tilted in favor of using technology (I wish I could say that this has happened universally, but at least we've made a start). I date many of my feelings about technology to a visit I made to a match factory as a schoolboy (circa 1948)—that was the nearest I've ever come to seeing humans used as robots, and I never want to see anything like it again.

I often think that the attitude of business is best summed up by a cartoon I saw a few years ago—a scientist type is trying to sell a medieval king a machine-gun, and the caption says, "Don't bother me—I've got a war to fight"! Why should we change the way we do application development? Everyone's happy with the status quo, right? I don't think so. I think in fact that there is a general dissatisfaction with the way things are now—it's just that nobody has shown a clear way to solve it that will benefit *all* the stakeholders. Over the last few decades, there has been an unending series of snake-oil salesmen, each peddling their own panacea. Why do you think each new remedy gets adopted so enthusiastically? Because there is a real need out there. So far, they have all turned out to be inadequate in some way and usually get dropped. This is understandable, but it is very important to learn from each such experience, so that collectively we move forward, rather than just jigging in one place all the time.

But, to give all groups a chance to take potshots at me, I am afraid that academia is partly to blame as well. Some academics, I am afraid, are doing the modern equivalent of fiddling while Rome burns. A professor of computer science told me a few years ago that, at his university, a thesis on application development technology just wouldn't be accepted. I found this short-sightedness absolutely incredible, and he agreed! It would seem to be obvious that application development technology is fascinating stuff, and it's even useful! Hopefully, this attitude has changed in the years since, but I'm sure it has cost application development research a good decade or two. Even if theses on application development are now being written, how do we get these ideas into programming shops around the world?

I have a warning for any academics who may be reading this—there is so much stuff to read now in this area that it would be quite understandable if you ignored papers like the one that appeared in the *IBM Systems Journal* back in 1978, because they aren't full of Greek letters. However, we were using these concepts to run a real live bank, and building up real experience trying to make these concepts work. This experience is *priceless* and perfectly complements the interesting theoretical work that you people are doing all over the world.

Inflexible systems not only cost money, but they contribute to users' perceptions of computers as inhuman, inflexible, and oppressive. How many times have you been told, "It's the computer," when confronted with some particularly asinine bit of bureaucracy? We know it's not the hardware's fault, but too often it's the fault of some short-sighted or just over-burdened programmer. Does the public know this? If they do, they've probably been told, "Yes, we know it's awkward, but it would cost too much to change it." Why does it cost so much? If there is only one message I want to leave you with after reading this book, it's that *the root cause of the present state of programming is the von Neumann paradigm.* It's that simple and that difficult (you know that we humans prefer things to be complex but easy, like taking a pill, but life isn't like that).

I started this book talking about how people have to relax the tight procedural nature of most of today's programming, imposed not so much by the von Neumann machine as by the mistaken belief that programmers still have to code according to the von Neumann model. Internally, today's computers are no longer tightly synchronous, nor are the environments that they run in. This can now be seen as a special case of a much larger issue: the key to improving productivity and maintainability in application development and to making programming accessible to a wider public is to make the world inside the computer match more closely to the world outside it. The real world is full of many entities all doing things in parallel: you do not stop breathing when I draw a breath. It is therefore not surprising that we were specifically designed to be able to function in such a world, and we get frustrated when we are forced to only do one thing at a time.

In a similar development, but at a different scale, we are starting to distribute our systems across different machines and/or different geographical locations. Imagine a world of multiprocessor machines communicating over LANs, WANs, or satellite links across the whole world, and you get a vision of a highly asynchronous, massively parallel data processing network of worldwide scope. Since this is clearly the way our business is going, why should we have to be restricted to using the synchronous, nonparallel von Neumann model at the processing nodes?! So our applications would be networks, networking with other networks, extending eventually around the planet.

Fact is starting to catch up with fiction: John Brunner is thought to have originated the use of the word "worm" in his 1975 novel, *The Shockwave Rider,* to describe an autonomous program traveling the computer net. Hackers (using both the positive and negative connotations of that term) have developed computer viruses, whose behavior mirrors that of biological viruses. If you have had a system attacked by one of these critters, it may be hard for you to think kindly thoughts about what are usually perceived today as nuisances at best and at worst as something downright dangerous and destructive. However, a lot of recent work by responsible scientists has suggested that crossbreeding these two species may result in very powerful tools for making computers more user-friendly. Read what E. Rietman and M. Flynn (1993) have to say about worms and viruses in the future. They describe scenarios such as: worm programs assembling personalized newspapers for subscribers, using data extracted from databases all over the world; "vampire worms" taking advantage of available CPU time to do useful jobs (at night, mostly—hence the name); viruses automatically inserting hypertext buttons into text databases; viruses doing automatic database compression and expansion as time becomes available, scavenging dead data, monitoring for broken data chains, and on and on. In fact, there is already a precursor of this kind of facility roaming the net, called "Gopher" (Martin 1993), which lets you look at the weather in Australia from a terminal in Ohio and generally roam around "gopherspace" from any terminal connected to Internet or from a terminal talking to a remote computer that can access Internet. Gopher now seems to have been upstaged by the WorldWideWeb (WWW), which sounds truly marvelous (Cramer 1994)! As an interesting aside, Rietman and Flynn also point out that worms could be a useful method to "*program massively parallel computers*" [their italics].

Talking about fact catching up with fiction, some recent work coming out of Xerox PARC is even more incredible. Instead of creating make-believe environments, which people can move through using the computer (Virtual Reality), how about enhancing our real-world environment with a myriad of small computing devices that we can talk to, using voice or gestures, *and that talk to each other,* perhaps about us? How about an office that automatically adjusts the temperature and humidity to suit whoever is occupying it, and plays soothing music if you want it to? How about children's building blocks that can be assembled into working computerized structures, or a pipe that you can use to point at a virtual blackboard, has a small microphone and speaker inside it, and perhaps monitors its user's health as well?! A lecturer once asked us: "Where will computers be used?" and he answered: "Anywhere that it makes sense to put the word *intelligent.*" For example, not just intelligent cars or planes, but intelligent offices, desks, and blackboards, intelligent bookshelves—maybe even intelligent paper and pencils. This work goes under the general name of "ubiquitous computing" or "ubicomp," and you can read about it in Vol. 36, No. 7 of *Communications of the ACM* (Wellner et al. 1993). This enormously exciting work seems to me totally compatible with everything that has gone before in this book.

The IBM scientist Nat Rochester once described programmers as working more closely than any other profession with what he called pure "mind-stuff." If you imagine a worldwide network of "mind stuff," then this corner of the universe is starting to see a new type of intelligence or at least a new vehicle for intelligence. Baird Smith of IBM describes software as "explosive" and hardware as "implosive." While software, which is built out of mind-stuff, is becoming more and more powerful and complex, hardware is getting smaller and smaller (although more complex!) and cheaper and cheaper—as it should since, after all, its basic building material is sand! This is a perfect example of what Buckminster Fuller called "doing more with less."

I think we are starting to see a truly massive convergence of ideas. It is unfortunate that most of the science fiction that has been accepted by the main stream is dystopian, because most good science fiction is very optimistic and upbeat. It has always surprised me how few programmers, who live their professional lives on the cutting edge of change, actually read science fiction. Does this reflect a perception that what they do is not imaginative and exciting? Is this still another vicious cycle?

J.W. Campbell Jr., the editor of *Analog,* originally *Astounding,* was an inspiration to a generation of science fiction readers. He taught us the value of considering new ideas objectively, avoiding the extremes of either rejecting ideas out of hand because they are new and different or accepting them instantly without proper evaluation. It was from his editorials that I learned the idea of "rope logic," which I believe this book embodies: the ideas described in this book are not built up on a basis of Aristotelian syllogisms, but as a multitude of small threads. While *individually* none of the threads may be particularly strong, they complement each other, resulting in a rope of logic that, in its totality, is strong enough to move pyramid blocks around (and maybe even a whole industry)! By the same token, you, my readers, may be able to snap a few of these threads, but my conviction is that the rope as a whole will remain as strong as ever. Am I deluding myself? The only possible test is the systems built using these concepts, and they are some of the sturdiest systems the companies that use them have in their collection.

While it may be true that some science fiction is naive, some of the most exciting and forward-looking thinking going on today is described in the fiction and fact pages of today's science fiction magazines. Read them and stretch your minds! If we have the will, we can make pretty good lives for ourselves. In my experience it is the pessimists (have you noticed they usually call themselves realists?) who show a certain naiveté—the naiveté of believing that things will go on just the way they are, that there will *not* be technological, political, commercial, social, artistic, or spiritual breakthroughs. In fact, the pace of change in all areas is on an accelerating curve. If you doubt this, just look back 50 years and see how far we have come. We are only limited by our imaginations, and that's a resource that is never going to be used up! Even if you feel that solving the world's problems is too big a task, I see no reason why we can't at least tackle the smaller task of making programmers more productive and programming more fun—there is no law that says work has to be drudgery. In fact, when one masters a medium and the medium fits the hand, there is a feeling of being at one with one's tools that can border on the transcendent. That's what training is about—not to turn out a generation of button-pushers, but to produce "masters." Our goal in our profession is not to be able to push a button and turn out a payroll program, but to be more like those ancient Celtic artisans who made a drinking vessel a work of art. Were they having fun? You just bet they were! And so can you. So why not start right now?! And if this isn't sufficient justification by itself, wouldn't it be neat if the world's programmers could be happier and more productive, working for companies that are more responsive to their clients and saving everybody money as well (and therefore improving the quality of life for you and me). Utopian? Perhaps, but if we have a goal, we can start moving in that direction, and we can measure how much progress we have made towards getting there. If we have no goal, then we'll be just wasting energy running round in small circles. Programming is a part of life, so this really shouldn't surprise anybody!

So what's going to happen over the next couple of decades? I used to think that if you built a better mousetrap, everyone would beat a path to your door. I learned differently by personal experience, and then I read Kuhn (1970), who put it all in perspective for me. Did you know that the phlogiston theory didn't yield instantly to the oxygen theory the moment someone did the deciding experiment? Some people *never* really took to this weird oxygen idea! Here is a new paradigm that is clearly superior, but experience shows that it may take as much as a generation for it to catch on. But it could take a lot less than that! By the way, if you want to learn more about paradigms, how they affect how we think, and how they get adopted, Kuhn's ideas have been extended over the last few years in a series of thought-provoking books and videotapes by Joel Barker (e.g., Barker 1992). Absolutely necessary reading!

As I tried to show in chapter 26, some of the most advanced practitioners of OOP are discovering FBP or something very close to it. There will be people who will say that programming will never become simple or that the man or woman in the street will never see it as enjoyable. I personally believe that computers and people will always need go-betweens, just as people from different cultures do (sometimes so do members of the same family!). Programmers are skilled at interpreting between people and machines, and there will always be a need for their services. However, giving programmers inadequate tools and then blaming them if they aren't successful scares off the very people who would be best at this work. It is time to stop doing that! It's never too late to realize that we took a wrong tack a few decades ago and change direction.

One of the most exciting things about FBP for me is that it provides a bridge between ideas that are currently restricted to very technical papers and businesses that think they are stuck with COBOL assembly lines forever. We also have today the potential to create a new era of productivity, based on a marketplace of reusable components. Wayne Stevens, who is responsible for a number of the ideas in this book, was very optimistic about the potential of these concepts and was tireless in promoting it within the DP community, putting his not inconsiderable reputation behind them. Where I was the paradigm shifter, to use Joel Barker's phrase, he was the paradigm pioneer. He believed, as I do, that these concepts will have a big effect on our future as an industry, and I deeply regret that he was not able to see them become widely accepted in his lifetime. I have always liked the phrase, "Will those who say it can't be done please move aside and let the rest of us get on with doing it"—this was very much his approach to life! He was, and continues to be, an inspiration to us all.

My colleagues over the years and I have had a glimpse of the future of the DP industry, and I have tried to share this vision with my readers. I hope that you have enjoyed reading about it as much as I have enjoyed telling you about it!

Appendix

THREADS API and Network Specification

In chapter 23, I described the THREADS notation for linking components into networks—this will also be repeated here in summary form. However, perhaps even more important are the conventions for writing components, as these are what will allow independently developed components to be combined into a single network without the requirement that they be developed by the same person or even in the same location (apart from the normal requirements for consistency of IP and stream formats).

Here is a simple component written in C to copy IPs from IN to OUT. Let's call this rather unoriginally "copydata." I am using the "large" model and C calling convention.

A THREADS component is a regular C subroutine, so, as you might expect, the first few statements are the declares.

```
#include "compsvcs.h"
/* This header file also includes definitions of "anchor"
   and "port table" */

/* Prototype for component code */
int copydata(anchor proc_anchor)  {

/* Initialization of "port table" - the array dimension
   must equal the number of ports expected by the component */
port_ent port_tab[2];
```

```
  /* Declares for variables used in component body*/
  void *ptr;
  int value;
  long size;
  char *type;


  /* Component Body  */

    value = dfsdfpt(proc_anchor, 2, port_tab, "IN", "OUT");

    value = dfsrecv(proc_anchor, &ptr, &port_tab[0], 0,
         &size, &type);
    while (value == 0)
    {
     value = dfssend(proc_anchor, &ptr, &port_tab[1], 0);
     if (value != 0)
       value = dfsdrop(proc_anchor, &ptr);

      value = dfsrecv(proc_anchor, &ptr, &port_tab[0], 0,
           &size, &type);
    }
  return(0);
}
```

The first action is always to initialize the port table using a call to `dfsdfpt`—the second parameter of the call to `dfsdfpt` must match the dimension declared for the port table. This number must also match the number of port names specified in the parameters to `dfsdfpt`. Note: `dfsdfpt` modifies the port table, so this must not be defined as constant.

The `return` statement causes deactivation (but not necessarily termination, as described earlier). The return code value on the `return` statement determines whether the process is willing to be *re*activated: a value of 5 or greater forces termination even if data is available.

API CALLS

Here are the API calls available to components in THREADS:

```
Create a Packet:
  value = dfscrep(proc_anchor, &ptr, size, type);

Define ports:
  value = dfsdfpt(proc_anchor, port_count, port_tab,
                  port_name_1, port_name_2, ....);

Receive an IP:
  value = dfsrecv(proc_anchor, &ptr, &port_tab[port_no],
           elem_no, &size, &type);
```

```
Send an IP:
  value = dfssend(proc_anchor, &ptr, &port_tab[port_no],
          elem_no);

Drop an IP:
  value = dfsdrop(proc_anchor, &ptr);

Pop an IP off the stack:
  value = dfspop(proc_anchor, &ptr, &size, &type);

Push an IP onto the stack:
  value = dfspush(proc_anchor, &ptr);

Close a port element:
  value = dfsclos(proc_anchor, &port_tab[port_no],
          elem_no);
```

PARAMETERS

Note that the ptr, size, type, and port table element parameters all have &'s attached, except in the case of dfscrep, where only ptr has it. The &'s are required because these parameters may be modified, and C parameters are all passed by value (except for strings and arrays).

port_count and elem_no are all binary integer variables ("int"); size is binary long.

proc_anchor	A variable of type anchor (defined in thxanch.h).
ptr	A void pointer used to point at IPs.
size	A long variable containing the IP's size.
type	A null-terminated string of up to 32 chars.
port_count	Parameter to dfsdfpt—must match the dimension of the defined port_tab array for this component.
elem_no	This specifies the element of the appropriate port to be used in a *send, receive,* or *close*. Non-zero values are only allowed for array-type ports, where they number up from 0. For non-array ports, this parameter must be 0.
port_tab	This parameter is declared as an array of type port_ent (declared below), where each element corresponds to one of the ports known to the component; the whole structure is passed to dfsdfpt, while specific elements of port_tab are passed to *send, receive,* and *close* using &.
port_name_n	One of series of port names passed to dfsdfpt; the number of these must match the port_count parameter.

All pointers in the following declarations are "far" pointers.

Declare for `port_ent`:

```
struct _port_ent
  {
     char port_name[32];
     void *reserved;
     int elem_count;
     int ret_code;
  };

  typedef struct _port_ent port_ent;
```

After a call to `dfsdfpt`, `elem_count` in each `port_ent` instance will be set to the number of connected elements for that port, and `ret_code` will be set to 0 or 2, depending on whether that port was connected or not.

Declare for "anchor" (`thxanch.h`):

```
struct _anchor {
   int (* svc_addr) ();
   void *proc_ptr;
    } ;

typedef struct _anchor anchor;
```

SERVICE RETURN CODES

```
dfscrep:
     0    OK

dfsdfpt:
     0    OK  but some elements of port_tab may have their
          ret_code fields set to 2, meaning "port name not
          found"; a receive or send from or to such a
          port_tab element will result in a return code value
          of 2.

dfsrecv:
     0    OK
     1    port element closed (end of data)
     2    port element not defined or not connected
     3    receiving from output port or element number invalid

dfssend:
     0    OK
     1    port element closed
     2    port element not defined or not connected
     3    sending to input port or element number invalid

dfsdrop:
     0    OK
```

```
dfspop:
     0    OK
     2    stack empty

dfspush:
     0    OK

dfsclose:
     0    OK
     1    port element already closed
     2    port element not defined or not connected
```

LIMITATIONS

There is a limit of 4000 elements per array port.

Working storage for a component should not exceed a few thousand bytes (including the working storage of any subroutines it calls). If the component needs more than this, it should use one of C's dynamic allocation functions (e.g., *malloc* or *calloc*) to allocate the additional storage.

NETWORK NOTATION

Networks are defined initially using a free-form notation, described briefly in chapter 23. The general syntax for networks is quite simple and is shown in figure 1 (using a variant of the notation that has started to become popular for defining syntax).

I have labeled the ports above and below the connection indicator (arrow with optional capacity figure) "up-port" and "down-port" to indicate that they are upstream and downstream, respectively, of the connection.

The main network may be followed by one or more subnets, which have basically the same notation (each one starting with a label and finishing with a semi-colon). However, a subnet has to have additional notation describing how its external port names relate to its internal ones. Since this association is like an equivalence, use the symbol => to indicate this relationship. Thus,

```
, port-name-1 => port-name-2 process-A port-name-3 -
```

indicates that `port-name-1` is an external input port of the subnet, while `port-name-2` is the corresponding input port of `process-A`. Similarly,

```
- port-name-1 process-A port-name-2 => port-name-3,
```

indicates that `port-name-3` is an external output port of the subnet, while `port-name-2` is the corresponding output port of `process-A`. For an example, see the example of subnets given in chapter 23.

The result of adding this notation to figure 1 is shown in figure 2. `ext-in-port` and `ext-out-port` cannot have element numbers.

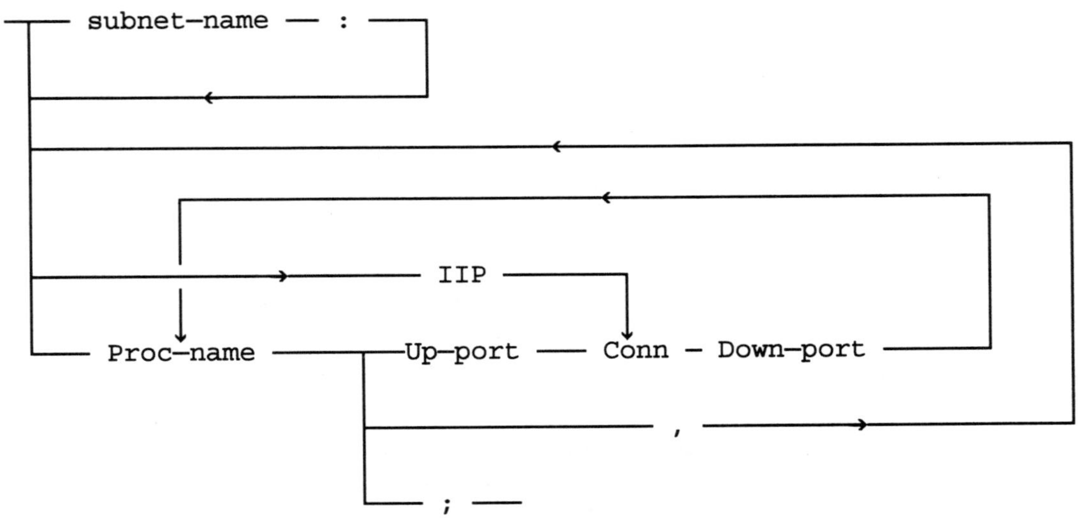

Figure 1.

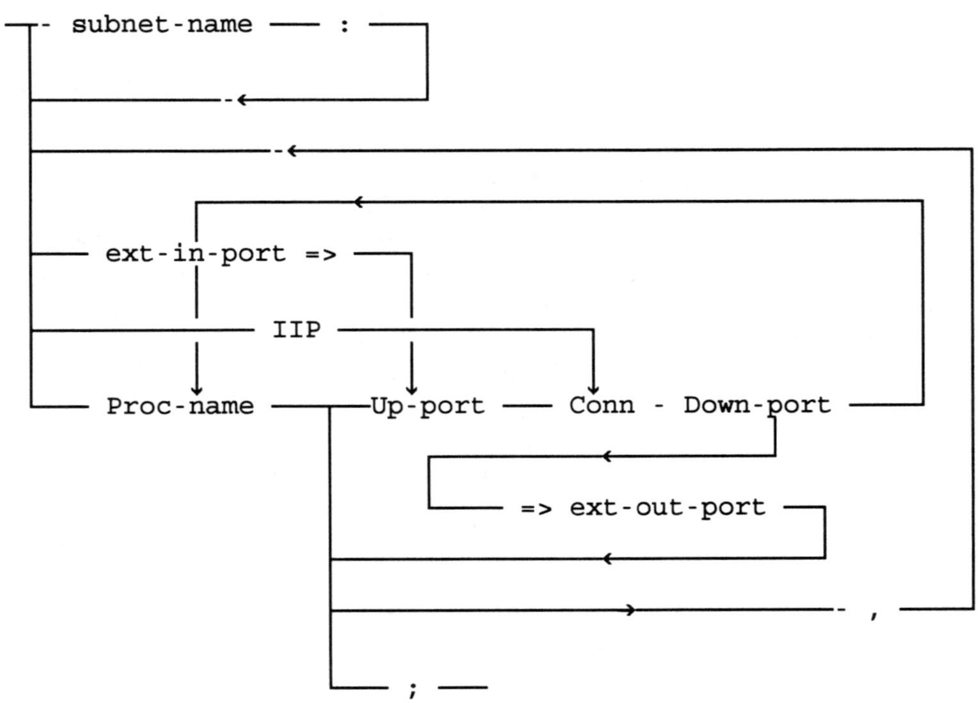

Figure 2.

IIP is shown in figure 3. Two consecutive quotes are taken to mean a single quote.

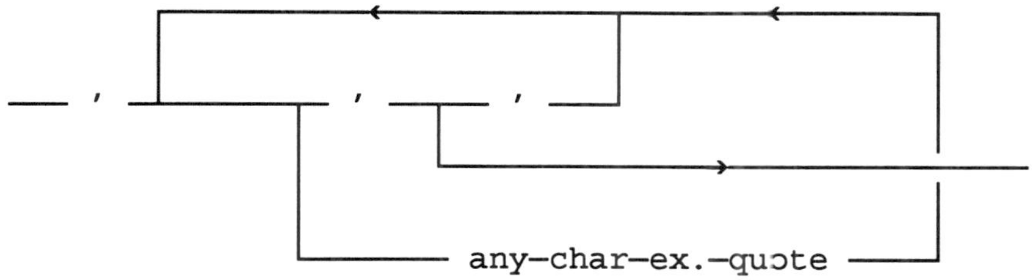

Figure 3.

Up-port and Down-port are shown in figure 4. Element-number does not apply to the external port names of subnets. The asterisk indicates an automatic port (see chapter 13).

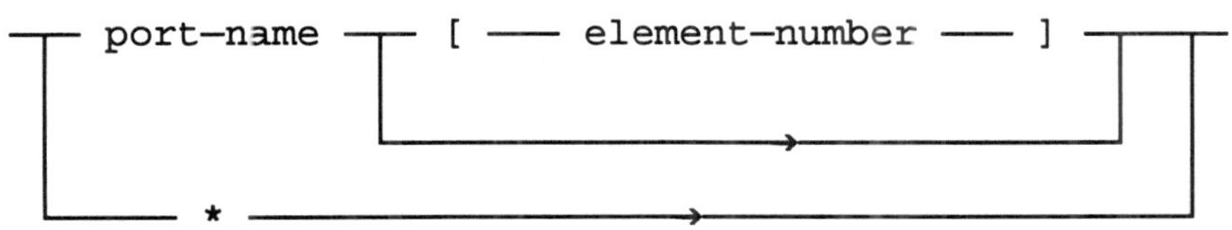

Figure 4.

Conn is shown in figure 5. Capacity does not apply to the external port names of subnets.

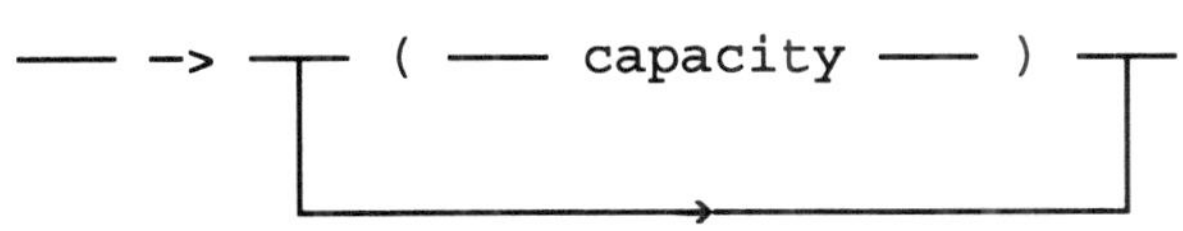

Figure 5.

Proc-name is shown in figure 6. The component name can be specified on any occurrence of the process name. The question mark indicates that tracing is desired.

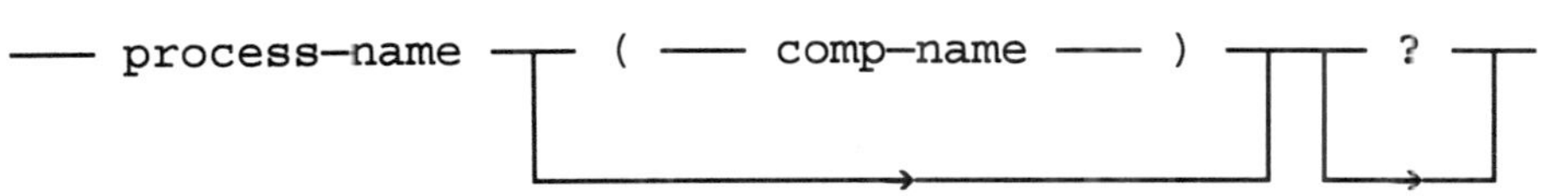

Figure 6.

In chapter 13 I alluded to the fact that you can specify that a process "must run at least once"—this is specified by means of an *attribute file* for the component, which has the name of the component and an extension of `atr`, (e.g., `thcount.atr`). These files must be provided by the supplier of a component and must have a specific format. So far, only the "must run" attribute has been defined—it is specified by coding one of the character strings `must_run`, `Must_run`, or `MUST_RUN`, with optional preceding blanks, in the attribute file for a given component. If no attribute file is found for a component, default values are assumed to apply (the default for the "must run" attribute is "need not run").

As mentioned in chapter 23, there is also a compiled (or compilable) format for specifying networks. While this is obviously not appropriate for hand-coding by human users, it is easy enough to generate by means of software. It is a data-only C program and specifies a network, together with all referenced subnets. Its importance is that this will be the source form for networks owned by customers, so THREADS must guarantee that any enhancements to it will be upwards compatible. These guarantees are essentially encoded in the C headers that it uses: `thxiip.h`, `thxanch.h`, and `thxscan.h`.

`thxanch.c` was given earlier. The other two are defined as follows:

thxiip.h

```
struct _IIP
   {
      int IIP_len;
      char datapart[1];
   };

typedef struct _IIP IIP;
```

thxscan.h

```
   struct _cnxt_ent {
     char upstream_name[32];       /* if 1st char is !,   */
     char upstream_port_name[32]; /*   gen points at IIP */
     int upstream_elem_no;
     char downstream_name[32];
     char downstream_port_name[32];
     int downstream_elem_no;
     union cnxt_union {IIP *IIPptr; void *connxn;} gen;
     int capacity;
     };

typedef struct _cnxt_ent cnxt_ent;

struct _label_ent {
     char label[32];
      char file[10];
     struct _cnxt_ent *cnxt_ptr;
```

```
     struct _proc_ent *proc_ptr;
      char ent_type;
     int proc_count;
     int cnxt_count;
     };

typedef struct _label_ent label_ent;

     struct _proc_ent {
       char proc_name[32];
       char comp_name[10];
       int (far *faddr)();
       void *proc_block;
       int label_count;
       int trace;
       int composite;
       int must_run;
       };

typedef struct _proc_ent proc_ent;
```

Note: The above structures are not the internal control blocks of THREADS—they are an encoding of the free-form network specification notation. This separation will allow THREADS to be extended in the future without requiring network definitions to be reprocessed.

Glossary

AMPS: Advanced Modular Processing System—first version of FBP used for production work (still in use at a major Canadian company).

Applicative: describes a language that does all of its processing by means of operators applied to values.

Asynchronous: independent in time, unsynchronized.

Automatic ports: unnamed input or output ports used to respectively delay a process or indicate deactivation of a process, without code needing to be added to the processes involved.

Brackets: IPs of a special type used to demarcate groupings of IPs within IP streams.

Capacity: the maximum number of IPs a connection can hold at one time.

Component: reusable piece of code or reusable subnet.

Composite component: component comprising more than one process (same as subnet).

Connection: path between two processes, over which a data stream passes; connections have finite capacities (the maximum number of IPs they can hold at one time).

Connection point: the point where a connection makes contact with a component.

Control IP: an IP whose lifetime corresponds exactly to the lifetime of a substream, which it can be said to "represent."

Coroutine: an earlier name for an FBP process.

Delimiter sensitivity: a characteristic of some ports of a composite component where brackets are treated as end of data.

Descriptor: read-only module that can be attached to all IPs of a given type, describing them to generalized components.

DFDM: Data Flow Development Manager, dialect of FBP.

Dynamic attributes: data attributes attached to individual IPs, or to their fields.

Elementary component: component that is not a composite component.

Higher-Level Language (HLL): a language intermediate in level between lower-level languages (e.g., Assembler) and 4th-Generation Languages (4GLs).

Information Packet (IP): an independent, structured piece of information with a well-defined lifetime (from creation to destruction).

Initial Information Packet (IIP): data specified in the network definition, usually used as a parameter for a reusable component; it is converted into a "real" IP by means of a "receive" service call; it is only supported by THREADS.

Looper: a component that does not exit after each IP has been handled, but "loops" back to get another one.

Non-looper: a component that exits after each IP has been handled.

Port: the point where a connection makes contact with a process.

Root IP: the root of a tree of IPs.

Process: asynchronously executing piece of logic.

Stack: in FBP, a LIFO list associated with each process for holding IPs across activations of the process.

Stream: sequence of IPs passing across a given connection.

THREADS: C-based FBP implementation, supported by HOMEDATA (Rochester) Inc. of Rochester, NY.

Tree: complex structure of linked IPs, able to be sent and received as a single unit.

Synchronous: coordinated in time (at the same time).

WYSIWYG: "What You See Is What You Get" (used to describe a tool where the image shown to the developer closely matches the final result in appearance).

Bibliography

W.B. Ackerman, 1979, "Data Flow Languages," Proceedings National Computer Conference, pp. 1087–95.

G. Agha, 1990, "Concurrent Object-Oriented Programming," *Communications of the ACM,* Vol. 33, No. 9, Sept. 1990.

A.V. Aho and J.D. Ullman, 1972, *The Theory of Parsing, Translation and Compiling,* Englewood Cliffs, NJ: Prentice-Hall.

R.G. Babb II, 1984, "Parallel Processing with Large-Grain Data Flow Techniques," *Computer,* July 1984.

J. Backus, 1978, "Can Programming be Liberated from the von Neumann Style? A Functional Style and its Algebra of Programs," *Communications of the ACM,* Vol. 21, No. 8, Aug. 1978.

R. M. Balzer, 1971, "PORTS—A Method for Dynamic Interprogram Communication and Job Control," The RAND Corporation, Spring Joint Computer Conference, 1971.

J.A. Barker, 1992, *Future Edge: Discovering the New Paradigms of Success,* New York: William Morrow and Company, Inc.

G. Bell, 1992, "Ultracomputers: A Teraflop before its Time," *Communications of the ACM,* Vol. 35, No. 8, Aug. 1992.

J. Bentley, 1988, "More Programming Pearls—Confessions of a Coder," AT&T Bell Laboratories.

A. Black, N. Hutchison, E. Jul, and H. Levy, 1986, "Object Structure in the Emerald System," OOPSLA '86 Proceedings, Sept. 1986.

J. Boukens and F. Deckers, 1974, "CHIEF, An Extensible Programming System," *Machine Oriented Higher Level Languages* (W.L. van der Poel and L.A. Maarsen, eds.), Amsterdam: North Holland Publishing Company.

B.V. Bowden, Ed., 1963, *Faster than Thought, A Symposium on Digital Computing Machines*, Sir Isaac Pitman and Sons, Ltd., London, England, 1st Edition 1953.

F.P. Brooks, 1975, *The Mythical Man-Month: Essays on Software Engineering,* Reading, MA: Addison-Wesley.

J. Brunner, 1975, *The Shockwave Rider*, New York: Ballantine Books.

W.H. Burge, 1975, *Recursive Programming Techniques*, Reading, MA: Addison-Wesley.

D. Cann, 1992, "Retire FORTRAN: A Debate Rekindled," *Communications of the ACM,* Vol. 35, No. 8, Aug. 1992.

N. Carriero and D. Gelernter, 1989, "Linda in Context," *Communications of the ACM,* Vol. 32, No. 4, April 1989.

I.A. Clark, 1976, "STREMA: A Graphic Language for Relational Applications," IBM UK, *Technical Report,* UKSC 0084, October 1976.

M.E. Conway, 1963, "Design of a separable transition-diagram compiler," *Communications of the ACM,* Vol. 6, No. 7, July 1963.

B.J. Cox, 1987, *Object Oriented Programming—An Evolutionary Approach,* Reading, MA: Addison-Wesley.

J.G. Cramer, 1994, "The Bandwidth Revolution: Internet and WorldWideWeb," *Analog, Science Fiction and Fact*, March 1994.

E.W. Dijkstra, 1972, "The humble programmer," *Communications of the ACM,* Vol. 15, No. 10, Oct. 1972.

N.P. Edwards, 1974, "The Effect of Certain Modular Design Principles on Testability," IBM Research Report, RC 5060 (#22344), T.J. Watson Research Center, Yorktown Heights, NY, 9/30/74.

N.P. Edwards, 1977, "On the Architectural Requirements of an Engineered System," IBM Research Report, RC 6688 (#28797), T.J. Watson Research Center, Yorktown Heights, NY, 8/18/77.

P.R. Ewing, 1988, "Bibliyna Simfoniya, 988-1988, Yuvileyne Vidannya," Prisvyachene Tisyacholittyu Khristiyanstva, GLINT Canada, Toronto.

D.P. Friedman and D.S. Wise, 1976, "CONS should not evaluate its arguments," *Automata, Languages and Programming*, Edinburgh University Press, Edinburgh.

J. Gall, 1978, *Systemantics: How systems work and especially how they fail,* New York: Pocket Books, Simon & Schuster.

G.R. Gao, 1991, *A Code Mapping Scheme for Dataflow Software Pipelining*, Boston/Dordrecht/London: Kluwer Academic Publishers.

P.T. Gaughan and S. Yalamanchili, 1993, "Adaptive Routing Protocols for Hypercube Interconnection Networks," *Computer,* 0018-9162/93/0500-0012, IEEE.

D. Gelernter and N. Carriero, 1992, "Coordination Languages and their Significance," *Communications of the ACM,* Vol. 35, No. 2, February 1992.

M. Hammer, W.G. Howe, V.J. Kruskal, and I. Wladawsky, 1977, "A very high level programming language for data processing applications," *Communications of the ACM,* Vol. 20, No. 11, November 1977.

J. Hendler, 1986, "Enhancement for Multiple-Inheritance," *SIGPLAN Notices V21,* #10, October 1986.

C.A.R. Hoare, 1978, "Communicating Sequential Processes," *Communications of the ACM,* Vol. 21, No. 8, August 1978.

IBM, "Messaging and Queueing Technical Reference," SC33-0850, IBM Corp.

IBM, "VM/System Product *CMS Pipelines,*" Program No. 5785-RAC.

IBM Japan, 1989, "Data Flow Programming Manager (DFDM)," Product Number 5799-DJB, Form No. N: GH18-0399-0.

K. Jackson and Gp. Capt. H.R. Simpson, 1975, "MASCOT—A Modular Approach to Software Construction, Operation and Test," *RRE Technical Note,* No. 778, Royal Radar Establishment, Ministry of Defence, Malvern, Worcs., UK, 1975.

M. Jackson, 1975, *Principles of Program Design,* London, New York, San Francisco: Academic Press.

R. Jones, "Legoland Software," *Computing* , 1988.

T. Capers Jones, 1992, "CASE's Missing Elements," *IEEE Spectrum,* June 1992.

K.M. Kahn and M.S. Miller, 1988, "Language Design and Open Systems," *The Ecology of Computation,* B.A. Huberman (ed.), North-Holland: Elsevier Science Publishers B.V.

K.M. Kahn, 1989, "Objects—A Fresh Look," Proceedings of the Third European Conference on Object Oriented Programming, Cambridge University Press, July 1989.

K.M. Kahn and V.A. Saraswat, 1990, "Complete Visualizations of Concurrent Programs and their Executions," TH0330-1/90/0000/0007, 1990 IEEE.

R.P. Kar, 1989, "Data-Flow Multitasking," *Dr. Dobb's Journal,* Nov. 1989.

R.C. Kendall, 1977, "Management Perspectives on Programs, Programming and Productivity," IBM Report 1977.

R. Kendall, 1988, "Manufactured Programming," *Computerworld Extra,* June 20, 1988.

W. Kim and F.H. Lochovsky, 1989, *Object-Oriented Concepts, Databases, and Applications,* ACM Press, Reading, MA: Addison-Wesley.

V.E. Kotov, "Concurrency + Modularity + Programmability = MARS," *Communications of the ACM,* Vol. 34, No. 6, June 1991.

L. Krishtalka, 1989, *Dinosaur Plots and other Intrigues in Natural History*, New York: Avon Books.

T.S. Kuhn, 1970, *The Structure of Scientific Revolutions*, Chicago: University of Chicago Press.

K. Kuse, M. Sassa, and I. Nakata, 1986, "Modelling and Analysis of Concurrent Processes Connected by Streams," *Journal of Information Processing,* Vol. 9, No. 3.

W. Lalonde and J. Pugh, 1991, "Subclassing ≠ subtyping ≠ Is-a," *Journal of Object-Oriented Programming*, January 1991.

B.M. Leavenworth, 1977, "Non-Procedural Data Processing," *The Computer Journal,* Vol. 20, No. 1, 6–9, February 1977.

B. Liskov, M. Herlihy, and L. Gilbert, 1986, "Limitations of Synchronous Communication with Static Process Structure in Languages for Distributed Computing," *Communications of the ACM,* 1986, pp. 150–159.

J.L. Martin, 1993, "Travels with Gopher," *Computer,* May 1993, pp. 84–87.

R. Milner, 1993, "Elements of Interaction," Turing Award Lecture, reprinted in *Communications of the ACM,* Vol. 36, No. 1, Jan. 1993.

J. Moad, 1993, "How to Break the Distributed Logjam," *Datamation,* May 15, 1993.

E. Morenoff and J.B. McLean, 1967, "Inter-program Communications, Program String Structures and Buffer Files," Rome Air Force Base, New York, Spring Joint Computer Conference, 1967.

J.P. Morrison, 1971, "Data Responsive Modular, Interleaved Task Programming System," *IBM Technical Disclosure Bulletin,* Vol. 13, No. 8, 2425–26, January 1971.

J.P. Morrison, 1978, "Data Stream Linkage Mechanism," *IBM Systems Journal,* Vol. 17, No. 4, 1978.

W. Needham, 1965, *A Book of Country Things,* Recorded by Barrows Mussey, Lexington, MA: The Steven Greene Press.

O. Nierstrasz, S. Gibbs, and D. Tsichritzis, 1992, "Component-Oriented Software Development," *Communications of the ACM,* Vol. 35, No. 9, Sept. 1992.

D. Olson, 1993, *Exploiting Chaos: Cashing in on the Realities of Software Development,* New York: Van Nostrand Reinhold.

R. Orfali and D. Harkey, 1991, *Client-Server Programming with OS/2 Extended Edition,* New York: Van Nostrand Reinhold.

D.L. Parnas, 1972, "On the criteria to be used in decomposing systems into modules," *Communications of the ACM,* Vol. 5, No. 12, Dec. 1972, pp. 1053–58.

J.E. Petersen, 1976, "Data State Design," Digest of Papers, Fall Compcon 76 (13th IEEE Computer Society International Conference, Washington), September 1976, 102–104.

R.F. Rashid, 1988 "From RIG to Accent to Mach: The Evolution of a Network Operating System," *The Ecology of Computation,* B.A. Huberman (ed.), North-Holland: Elsevier Science Publishers B.V.

E. Rietman and M.F. Flynn, 1993, "FAT-Eating Logic Bombs and the Vampire Worm," *Analog, Science Fiction and Fact,* Feb. 1993.

N. Shu, 1985, "FORMAL, A forms oriented visual directed application development system," *Computer,* Vol. 18, No. 8, Aug. 1985, 38–49.

W.P. Stevens, 1981, *Using Structured Design: How to make Programs Simple, Changeable, Flexible and Reusable,* New York: John Wiley and Sons.

W.P. Stevens, 1982, "How Data Flow can Improve Application Development Productivity," *IBM Systems Journal,* Vol. 21, No. 2, 1982.

W.P. Stevens, 1985, "Using Data Flow for Application Development," *Byte,* June 1985.

W.P. Stevens, 1991, *Software Design: Concepts and Methods,* Hemel Hempstead, Herts., UK: Prentice Hall International.

W.P. Stevens, 1991, "Structured Design, Structured Analysis & Structured Programming," *American Programmer,* Nov. 1991.

R.E. Strom and S. Yemini, 1983, "NIL: An Integrated Language and System for Distributed Computing," Proceedings of SIGPLAN '83 Symposium on Programming Language Issues in Software Systems, June 1983.

R.E. Strom, D.F. Bacon, A.P. Goldberg, A. Lowry, D.M. Yellin, and S.A. Yemini, 1991, *Hermes: A Language for Distributed Computing,* Englewood Cliffs, NJ: Prentice Hall.

Y. Suzuki, S. Miyamoto, and H. Matsumaru, 1985, "Data Flow Structure for Maintainable Software in Railway Electric Substation Control Systems," CH2207-9/85/0000-0219, IEEE.

T. Swan, 1991, *Learning C++,* Sams, Englewood Cliffs, New Jersey: Prentice Hall.

E.D. Tribble, M.S. Miller, K. Kahn, D. Bobrow, and C. Abbott, 1987, *Channels: A Generalization of Streams, Concurrent Prolog* Vol. 1, Cambridge, MA: MIT Press.

D. Tsichritzis, E. Fiume, S. Gibbs, and O. Nierstrasz, 1987, "KNOs: KNowledge Acquisition, Dissemination and Manipulation Objects," *ACM Transactions on Office Information Systems,* Vol. 5, No. 4, pp. 96–112.

L.G. Valiant, 1990, "A Bridging Model for Parallel Computation," *Communications of the ACM,* Vol. 33, No. 8, Aug. 1990.

J-D. Warnier, 1974, *Logical Construction of Programs,* 3rd edition, New York: Van Nostrand Reinhold.

G.M. Weinberg, 1975, *An Introduction to General Systems Thinking,* New York: John Wiley and Sons, Inc.

P. Wellner, W. Mackay, and R. Gold, "Computer-Augmented Environments: Back to the Real World," *Communications of the ACM,* Vol. 36, No. 7 , July 1993.

B.L. Whorf, 1956, *Language, Thought and Reality,* Cambridge, MA: Technology Press, MIT.

J. Winkler, 1992, "Objectivism: 'Class' Considered Harmful," Letter in Technical Correspondence, *Communications of the ACM,* Vol. 35, No. 8, Aug. 1992.

R.J. Wirfs-Brock and R.E. Johnson, 1990, "Surveying Current Research in Object-Oriented Design," *Communications of the ACM,* Sept. 1990, Vol. 33, No. 9.

L. Yeamans, "Transactional Messaging," OTM Spectrum Reports, Vol. 7, Report 4, Nov. 1993.

K. Yoshida and T. Chikayama, 1988, "A'UM, A Stream-Based Concurrent Object-Oriented Language," Proceedings of the International Conference on Fifth Generation Computer Systems, 1988, ed. ICOT.

Index